ALL · IN · ONE

GSEC
GIAC® Security Essentials
Certification

EXAM GUIDE

Second Edition

ABOUT THE AUTHOR

Ric Messier is an author, consultant, and educator who holds GCIH, GSEC, CEH, and CISSP certifications, and has published several books on information security and digital forensics. With decades of experience in information technology and information security, Ric has held the varied roles of programmer, system administrator, network engineer, security engineering manager, VoIP engineer, consultant, and professor. Ric is currently a Senior Information Security Consultant with FireEye Mandiant.

About the Technical Editor

Fred Wright, PhD, is recognized as an expert and researcher in cyber security. For the past two decades, he has focused on security issues and, in particular, the "innovation gap" between cyber threat capability and defensive technology. As a result, his research is focused on the most challenging problems in protecting enterprises. One example is critical data protection for large enterprises where robust, complex systems-engineering approaches are needed to address architecture, defensive solutions, security operations, and policy.

At Georgia Tech Research Institute (GTRI), Fred founded a cyber security incubator, which led to the formation of a major business unit, the Cybersecurity, Information Protection, and Hardware Evaluation Research (CIPHER) Lab. His research focused on novel security architectures, risk assessments, and cyber situation awareness. Fred also focused on diversifying GTRI's research business into the commercial sector, including Fortune 500 companies and startups.

Fred also serves as an adjunct professor in the Georgia Tech School of Computer Science. He led the development of Georgia Tech's Professional Education Cyber Security Certificate Program and is currently a lead instructor.

ALL · IN · ONE

GSEC
GIAC® Security Essentials Certification

EXAM GUIDE

Second Edition

Ric Messier

New York   Chicago   San Francisco
Athens   London   Madrid   Mexico City
Milan   New Delhi   Singapore   Sydney   Toronto

Cataloging-in-Publication Data is on file with the Library of Congress

McGraw-Hill Education books are available at special quantity discounts to use as premiums and sales promotions, or for use in corporate training programs. To contact a representative, please visit the Contact Us pages at www.mhprofessional.com.

GSEC GIAC® Security Essentials Certification All-in-One Exam Guide, Second Edition

1 2 3 4 5 6 7 8 9   QVS   23 22 21 20 19

ISBN   978-1-260-45320-1
MHID   1-260-45320-0

Sponsoring Editor Wendy Rinaldi	**Technical Editor** Fred Wright	**Production Supervisor** Pamela Pelton
Editorial Supervisor Janet Walden	**Copy Editor** William McManus	**Composition** Cenveo Publisher Services
Project Manager Harleen Chopra, Cenveo® Publisher Services	**Proofreader** Claire Splan	**Illustration** Cenveo Publisher Services
Acquisitions Coordinator Claire Yee	**Indexer** Karin Arrigoni	**Art Director, Cover** Jeff Weeks

CONTENTS AT A GLANCE

CONTENTS

ACKNOWLEDGMENTS

This feels suspiciously like some televised award ceremony where the winner trots out a long list of everyone they've ever known who contributed to their success. With a book, of course, there is no music to cue a more rapid wrap-up, but you are, of course, free to fast-forward to the next section if this is of no interest to you. I'd like to acknowledge, as always, my terrific agent, Carole Jelen, who continues to take good care of me. Also, thanks to Wendy Rinaldi and Claire Yee for continuing to guide the process over many, many months.

INTRODUCTION

The difficulty with security is the number of areas it touches. These days, all you have to do is turn on the news and you'll see at least one story indicating the importance of security. Whether it's a major company losing a lot of data that affects their customers, or a governmental agency losing sensitive information, security can have a significant impact on many people. The GIAC Security Essentials (GSEC) certification attempts to address that issue with a test that covers a number of technical areas that security impacts.

SANS offers training courses to prepare individuals for the GSEC exam, though you can take the certification exam without attending a training course. In terms of the financials, the difference is that without taking the training, you will pay more to take the exam itself. For instance, you'll pay a few hundred dollars more for the exam without the training, but well over a thousand dollars more with the training, and that doesn't include travel to the training location. It really comes down to how best you can learn the subject matter, and how much money you want to pay. In the end, the exam is still the exam, and you'll have to know the same material either way. If you are motivated to do the work you need to do to absorb the lessons, you should be able to pass the exam without needing to take a week of training. If you need to be pushed and guided, you may do better doing the training before taking the exam.

Either way, this book will be a valuable asset to you. It is designed to provide you with the information you need to pass the test. Beyond the information needed to pass the test, I've added in some interesting and helpful text to explain concepts better and give the subjects some additional context. Sometimes, these supplemental texts will be a bit of history, to help you put things into perspective.

Registration

Once you have decided whether you want to take the SANS training course or study on your own, you can register for the exam at the GIAC website. After registering and paying your fee, you will have four months in which to take the exam. Getting registered, though, will give you access to two practice tests that should give you a sense of how prepared you are, and also provide an example of the material presented on the exam. These two timed tests are similar in tone and content to the actual exam. They are timed, just like the real test, and consist of 180 multiple choice questions (again, just as in the real test). The one difference is that when you get a question wrong on the practice tests, it provides you with the correct answer, as well as an explanation about the right answer. You can also flag questions for comment.

Taking the Test

As mentioned earlier, the certification test consists of 180 multiple choice questions. You will have five hours to complete it. Following every 20 questions, there will be a checkpoint indicating your current percentage correct. You will also be able to flag questions for follow-up. This does not mean you can go back and change your answers, but it does let you make comments about the question or answers. These comments are limited to providing feedback about typographical errors, technical inaccuracies, questions that seem to have multiple correct answers, and spelling and grammatical errors. You will not get credit for making comments, but you will be notified that your comments have been received.

Since you can't change your answers to earlier questions, you need to spend whatever time you can trying to get the answer right on your first pass. You can bring a backpack or briefcase of books and papers into the exam to help you find the right answers. You cannot, however, bring any computers or computing devices like phones, calculators, or tablets into the room where you will take the test. Having the ability to bring books and notes may change your strategy on how you study since you won't have to memorize everything for the exam. You should, however, carefully choose the materials you take to the exam since your resources are limited.

Proctoring

The exam is proctored, and you will take it at a Pearson VUE facility. If you can't find a Pearson VUE facility within a reasonable driving distance of home—say, one to two hours away—SANS will try to make arrangements to find something closer for you. You will have to check in when you get to the exam room and ensure you have left everything other than your books outside. You will also need to provide two forms of identification. On questions where you need to perform calculations, you will be given an onscreen calculator. There will also be an erasable noteboard and pen provided in case you need to draw, make notes, or perform hand calculations.

You can cancel and reschedule exams within one business day (24 hours) of your exam without penalty. If you need to cancel with less than 24 hours' notice, you will give up your seat at the exam and also be charged a $150 cancellation fee. You can cancel and reschedule your exam through the web portal on the GIAC site, using the username and password you created when you first registered.

Post-Test

A passing score is 73 percent. Anything below that fails, and so you would need to schedule and pay for another test if you still want to pursue certification. You will be charged to take a second test if you fail the first one, but the fee will be less than for the first test. Check with the GIAC site to see the current pricing. You will also have to wait 30 days before taking the follow-up exam. This is intended to prevent you from rushing back to take the test and throwing money away when you aren't as prepared as you should be.

If you pass, you will know right away because you will be provided with your score. You will also get a summary sheet telling you how you did on each area of knowledge, just as you did on the practice tests. You will then receive your certificate in the mail. You can get your certificate framed (or not) through SANS.

Once you have the certification, you will need to maintain it with continuing professional education (CPE) credits. Every four years, you need to renew your certification and you will need to have obtained 36 CPEs in that time.

The Value of the Certification

Having the GSEC certification will prove to potential employers that you have demonstrated technical knowledge in the areas the exam covers. Many government agencies place a high value on the certifications from SANS because, unlike other certifications that cover material at a higher level, SANS ensures that the people who take the exam have a fairly deep level of technical knowledge. Once you have the certification, you can be a security analyst or a security engineer, go on to working on incident response teams, or use it as a starting point to pursue other more specific certifications. The GSEC certification is very broad, meaning you must have a solid understanding of a lot of security information. While studying for the GSEC, you may find you want to delve deeper into one particular area and pursue the knowledge needed for a certification to be an incident handler, penetration tester, or Windows security administrator. With the GSEC, you may have everything you need to pursue those jobs without additional certifications, depending on your potential employer and their requirements. You certainly have enough applied knowledge to be successful in a number of security-related jobs.

How to Use This Book

This book covers everything you need to know for the GSEC exam. Each chapter covers specific objectives and details for the exam, as defined by GIAC. I've done my best to arrange these objectives in a manner that makes sense to me. I hope you feel the same.

The chapters have several components designed to effectively communicate the information you'll need for the exam:

- Sidebars are designed to point out information, tips, and stories helpful in your day-to-day responsibilities. They're also downright fun sometimes. Please note, however, that although these entries provide real-world accounts of interesting pieces of information, they are sometimes used to reinforce testable material. Don't just discount them as simply "neat" stories—some of the circumstances and tools described in these sidebars may prove the difference between correctly answering an exam question and answering it incorrectly.

- Exam Tips are exactly what they sound like. These are included to point out a focus area you need to concentrate on for the exam. No, they are not explicit test answers, but they will help you focus your study.

- Specially called-out Notes are interesting tidbits of information that are relevant to the discussion and point out extra information. Just as with the sidebars, don't discount them.

- Some chapters have step-by-step exercises designed to give you hands-on experience and reinforce the chapter information. As your system and circumstances are no doubt different from mine, these may, from time to time, need a little adjustment on your end.

Exam Objective Map: GSEC Exam

The following table lists the exam certification objectives and where each is covered in the book.

Official Exam Objective	Chapter No.	All-in-One Coverage
Access Control & Password Management	4	Entire chapter
Active Defense	11	Entire chapter
Contingency Plans	9	"Contingency Plans" section
Critical Controls	9	Entire chapter
Cryptography	8	"Foundations" section
Cryptography Algorithms & Deployment	8	"Symmetric Encryption" and "Asymmetric Encryption" sections
Cryptography Application	8	Entire chapter
Defense in Depth	3	"Defense in Depth" section
Defensible Network Architecture	3 15	"Network Security Technologies" section Entire chapter
Endpoint Security	8	Entire chapter
Enforcing Windows Security Policy	8	"Foundations" section
Incident Handling & Response	13	Entire chapter
IT Risk Management	9	Entire chapter
Linux Security: Structure, Permissions, and Access	6	Entire chapter
Linux Services: Hardening and Securing	6	"Hardening Linux" section
Linux: Monitoring and Attack Detection	6	"Logging and Log Management" section
Linux: Security Utilities	6	"Security Tools" section
Log Management & SIEM	15	Entire chapter
Malicious Code & Exploit Mitigation	12	Entire chapter
Network Device Security	3	"Network Security Technologies" section
Network Security Devices	3	"Network Security Technologies" section
Networking & Protocols	2	Entire chapter
Securing Windows Network Services	7	"Securing Windows Networking" section
Security Policy	9	"Security Policies" section
Threat Hunting	13	Entire chapter

Official Exam Objective	Chapter No.	All-in-One Coverage
Virtualization and Cloud Security	5	Entire chapter
	10	Entire chapter
Vulnerability Scanning and Penetration Testing	11	Entire chapter
Web Communication Security	8	"SSL/TLS" section
	11	"Web Application Security" section
Windows Access Controls	7	"Resource Management" section
Windows as a Service	7	"Windows as a Service" section
Windows Automation, Auditing, and Forensics	7	"Windows Management" section
Windows Security Infrastructure	7	"Windows Security" section
Wireless Network Security	14	Entire chapter

Information Security and the GIAC Security Essentials Certification

In this chapter, you will learn:

- The evolution and importance of information security
- The general types of security threats
- About the SANS organization and its GSEC certification

For several years now, the news in the tech sector has been "this is the year of cybersecurity." As more and more people become aware of the threats that exist in the world, organizations have been forced to increase their spending on information security. You've also likely read about the so-called cybersecurity skills gap. This translates simply to not having enough people to fill the expected number of information security jobs available. A related issue is that among the limited number of people who "speak" information security to fill jobs, not enough of them are highly skilled and speak it well. Companies want to hire highly skilled and knowledgeable staff for these critical roles, not just bodies to fill positions.

This is where a certification like the GIAC Security Essentials Certification (GSEC) becomes valuable. The GSEC certification provides a way for professionals to demonstrate to potential employers (and others) their knowledge and expertise in the area of information security. It is a broad-ranging certification, so if you, like many tech professionals, have specialized experience and knowledge, you can expect to have to study a lot to fill in gaps in your general knowledge of information security.

It doesn't take much more than following a few news cycles to understand the importance of information security, but in this chapter we're going to take a tour through the current landscape so that you can get a sense of the common threats that businesses are experiencing … and what information security professionals are having to deal with. This includes an overview of the different types of security threats, since there are many, and some old ones have become even more predominant since the last edition of this book came out a few years ago. You'll get a sense of where the field of information security stands, the threats that exist and relevant protections against those threats.

You will also find it useful to understand a little about the SANS organization and why it exists, as well as GIAC, its relationship to SANS, and the certifications it offers. This includes how GIAC and its certifications are, in turn, accredited.

The Evolution and Importance of Security

Computer security issues have been a problem since almost the beginning of computing, especially when considering security issues in the context of the Confidentiality-Availability-Integrity (CIA) triad. The apocryphal story of the origin of the term computer bug presents an early example of a security issue, since it attributes a physical issue with a computer (an insect in the hardware) as the cause of system failures. It caused failures of integrity and availability. This is a story that dates from the very earliest days of computing. Computers at that time were never considered highly secure, with the primary security being physical, meaning that if you could get to the computer, you had complete access to the system to do what you wanted, including potentially rewriting the system software.

As computers started gaining the potential to have multiple users connected at the same time, all sharing computing resources and what limited storage that was available, security became more of a concern. This meant that physical security was no longer adequate. Instead, users had to be protected from other users. If two users were working on the same mainframe and one user caused a catastrophic failure in a program that in turn caused a failure in the kernel, the other user was impacted by that failure. This meant that the kernel in early operating systems needed better protection. It also meant that each user's process space needed to be protected from other users' process spaces so that users couldn't do bad things to each other's running programs.

As a result, the operating system Multics was developed as a way of implementing security in the operating system while also allowing multiple users to be connected and working simultaneously. You might think of it as prehistoric cloud computing—users connecting to a resource that was located somewhere else in order to accomplish computing tasks. At the time, computers were enormous devices, often taking up a large room to house a single device. Users were usually in at least a different room if not a completely different building. A user may not ever have seen the computer they were actually working with. There was no need. All they needed was some form of input/output like a screen and keyboard or even paper tape drives.

Today, practically everyone has their own computer. Even multiple computers. As I sit here writing this, I am working on a laptop with a tablet sitting next to me and a smartphone not too far away. Today, each one of these devices has several orders of magnitude more computing power than the room-sized devices that Multics was created for. This is more than a cliché, though. The point is that with so much computing power in the hands of people who know very little about computers and how to secure them, security is more important than it's ever been. We all have enormous computing capacity and a world of information storage at our disposal, nearly all the time.

We haven't even talked about networking capacity. The very first wide area network (WAN) link from one system to another had a bandwidth capacity of 50 kilobits per second (Kbps). That's 50,000 bits per second, or 6250 characters per second.

Today, I am connected to the Internet with a 1 gigabit per second (Gbps) connection. That means 1 billion bits per second, or 125,000,000 characters per second. Just to give you a sense, this chapter has roughly 4000 words in it. With an average word length of 5 characters, which is about average for English, my connection has the capacity to transmit 25,000,000 words per second. That's more than 5 million copies of this chapter. In a single second.

In the 1980s, there were some well-publicized security incidents, though not nearly as many as what you will find in the news today. One of them occurred when members of the Chaos Computer Club in Germany infiltrated systems at labs in the United States, hoping to obtain military secrets for the USSR. This was when the systems were still mainframes or, often, minicomputers, which were slightly smaller than mainframes but still considerably larger than a personal computer. The network speed used to connect to these systems was still measured in kilobits per second. These hackers stole whatever data they could find on systems belonging to universities and research labs, pulling the data back across very low-bandwidth connections.

The reach and capacity of the Internet has provided not only easy access to information but also easy access to systems. This access can be used to learn about the systems, including how to attack or defend them. It can also be used for malicious purposes, such as actually attacking them. The information available through the Internet has also changed. In terms of proportions, the amount of information about things like the Star Wars missile defense system is dwarfed by the amount of personal information. Because of that, the threat landscape has changed. Not only are governments and corporations at risk, but, more and more, individual users are at risk, and not just for their credentials, which may provide access to intellectual property or confidential information.

Prior to ubiquitous Internet access, to learn about attacking systems, you typically had to have access to them. You also had to have access to some documentation to learn about them. Perhaps you had access to something called Usenet, which was a collection of what were essentially mailing lists (for those who aren't familiar with the idea of news groups). While attacks were happening on these large systems, it wasn't that common for the attacks to be reported in the mainstream news. You had to be aware of the greater network and events at other sites to even know an incident was going on. The number of people who had that awareness wasn't very large. According to the National Science Foundation, the number of computers connected to its backbone, the NSFnet, was 2000 in 1985. This meant the number of users who had access to the NSFnet was also measured in the thousands. The NSFnet was the backbone that all the existing wide area networks connected to, eventually allowing commercial entities to connect, creating what we now call the Internet. In 1993, the number of computers connected had risen to 2 million. That still meant the number of users was measured in the millions. As of the end of 2017, it's estimated by internetworldstats.com that more than 4 billion users have access to the Internet. Other sources have similar statistics.

In spite of the dramatic increase in the number of attacks, the number of users, and also in the ease and breadth of those attacks, we as a society are pushing more and more into the network. Online banking, managing our credit card and utility accounts, purchasing goods and services, and even getting access to our library accounts are all being done online. Life is increasingly moving online. Social networking sites are more popular than ever, and people share a lot of their life, including their personal information, online. Companies who regularly store customer information are targets of attackers. Data brokers are constant targets, which means that it's not just businesses who are under attack. It's people and their information, even if the pathway to their information isn't through the people directly.

Types of Security Threats

Computer incidents have increased dramatically since 1988, when the incident leading to the creation of the United States Computer Emergency Readiness Team (US-CERT). Figure 1-1 shows a graph of the number of incidents reported to the (US-CERT) over a decade. This graph appears in a report by the U.S. Government Accountability Office (GAO), based on data from the Office of Management and Budget (OMB). A computer security incident is an event that results in unauthorized access to systems or data. The decrease in 2016 isn't a downturn in incidents but a change in the reporting requirements, which may vary from state to state or vary based on federal regulations and guidance from law enforcement. These incidents are not all the same. They result from different threats that exist, which have evolved over time. The threats described in this section are just some of the reasons to gain a better understanding of what security is and how you can better prepare yourself and your organization. And these categories are just a partial list of the full catalog of the various risks that threaten your personal information and the well-being of your employer and its information, intellectual property, and resources.

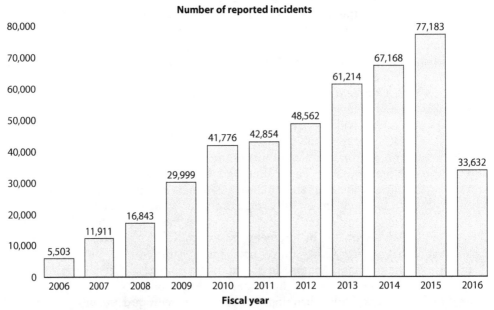

Number of reported incidents

Source: GAO analysis of United States Computer Emergency Readiness Team and Office of Management and Budget data for fiscal years 2006–2016.

Figure 1-1   Year-by-year number of incidents reported to US-CERT

Social Engineering

A primary attack vector is social engineering. In fact, some of the other attack vectors described in the following sections are sometimes teamed with a social engineering attack. Social engineering has been an aspect of computer security for decades. In fact, a notorious computer criminal from the 1980s, Kevin Mitnick, made extensive use of social engineering to gain access to facilities and systems. With the ever-increasing number of unsophisticated computer users, social engineering is an attack that has a high probability of yielding results.

Social engineering is any attack in which an attacker takes advantage of human nature and psychology to get one or more persons to do something they shouldn't do. This may include directly providing credentials to an attacker. It may involve getting a user to visit a website that has malicious software installed on it, or enticing a user to open an e-mail that has malicious software attached. It could be tricking a user into visiting a website that appears to be one thing when in fact it's another, enabling the attacker to obtain credentials or other information because the user believes they are providing data to a legitimate site.

Malware

As an information technology or security professional, your job is to worry about the latest threats and how you can protect yourself and your organization against these threats. It's no surprise, of course, that the number of threats in the cyber landscape continues to increase. Figure 1-2 shows the roughly exponential growth in the amount of malware just in the 2009–2018 period. This is the total number of different types or strains of malware that have been detected. We are rapidly closing in on 100,000,000 different strains of malware in the world. This is a pretty staggering number.

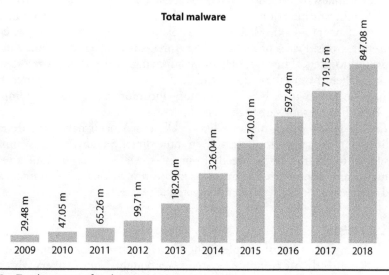

Figure 1-2 Total amount of malware

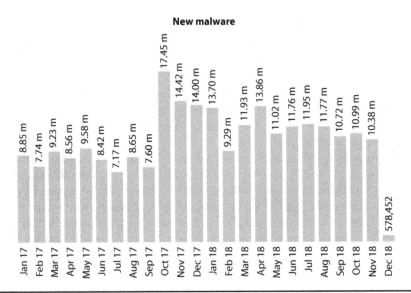

New malware

Jan 17	8.85 m
Feb 17	7.74 m
Mar 17	9.23 m
Apr 17	8.56 m
May 17	9.58 m
Jun 17	8.42 m
Jul 17	7.17 m
Aug 17	8.65 m
Sep 17	7.60 m
Oct 17	17.45 m
Nov 17	14.42 m
Dec 17	14.00 m
Jan 18	13.70 m
Feb 18	9.29 m
Mar 18	11.93 m
Apr 18	13.86 m
May 18	11.02 m
Jun 18	11.76 m
Jul 18	11.95 m
Aug 18	11.77 m
Sep 18	10.72 m
Oct 18	10.99 m
Nov 18	10.38 m
Dec 18	578,452

Figure 1-3 New malware detected by month

Not surprisingly, of course, the rapid rise of the total amount of malware in the world is accompanied by a similarly rapid increase in the number of new types of malware detected. Figure 1-3 shows the number of pieces of new malware that have been detected over the last two years, month by month. You'll see that over the last two years, the number of new pieces of malware detected each month has not dropped below 7 million. Despite these startling numbers, nothing that we, as security professionals, have done to date has slowed down that growth.

Talking about malware infections can often seem a bit dry and clinical. After all, some of the most significant infections over the last decade or so wouldn't have impacted the vast majority of people. Code Red and SQL Slammer, for instance, impacted servers but not user desktops. Pieces of malware like Anna Kournikova were annoying but not strictly harmful to users. They were far more annoying to the administrators who were trying to keep them from taking down the mail servers that were being used to spread them. This is no longer true, however, as more and more users are being impacted by malware. Types like ransomware make the impact far more direct.

Over the last several years, malware like ZeUS and Azorult have been developed to steal credit card information from users. Even more directly, malware like WannaCry has been developed to extort money directly from users. Malware has become a very lucrative income stream for organized crime. This means professional programmers are being employed to develop more effective and targeted malware.

Identity Theft

Identity theft impacts a lot of people. Whether it's information being stolen by way of phone calls, directly off computer systems, or bought from brokers who purchase stolen information, millions of people have been impacted by identity theft. The U.S. Federal Trade Commission has been tracking identity theft for years. Figure 1-4 shows

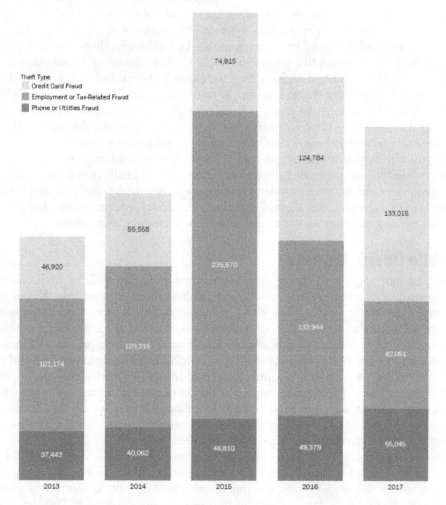

Consumer Sentinel Network Data Book 2017: Top Three Identity Theft Reports by Year

Figure 1-4 Identity theft complaints to the FTC by year

years 2013–2017 (the last year a full set of data was available when this was written) with the top types of identity theft reported each year. Keep in mind that this data reflects only the reported identity thefts in the United States.

Identity theft comes in many forms, and while the targets are certainly individuals, the means by which these thieves get to the individuals and their identities often is through businesses. The Ponemon Institute found in 2012 that each record stolen costs a business $194. As of 2018, according to IBM, that figure has dropped to $148. The cost of the Experian breach, reported in 2017, is expected to be hundreds of millions, perhaps up to $600 million, according to the chairman of the Ponemon Institute.

Organizations bear a significant part of the cost of identity theft, primarily because it is their responsibility to be trustworthy keepers of the information of their customers, patients, and subscribers. Those costs do get passed along, in turn, to the same customers, patients, and subscribers, so it is important for consumers to vote with their feet to ensure that organizations get the message that information security is important and that it is something they need to pay attention to. Unfortunately, there may be opposing lessons taught by instances like the one from 2011, where the group LulzSec acquired a large amount of subscriber data from the PlayStation Network and then published that information on a public website. The idea, of course, was to embarrass Sony into doing a better job with its information security, but if enough consumers didn't leave Sony, then the only damage was to the consumers when malicious people used that information to get into other accounts at other sites from username and password reuse.

As you are likely aware, there are laws in place that require companies to have processes and procedures protecting things like healthcare and credit card data. Laws aren't enough in cases like this because you can't protect against mistakes and you can't legislate against future vulnerabilities. Complex systems are much harder to protect because the number of components where a problem can occur increases exponentially.

Mobile Device Threats

More and more organizations are exposing themselves to new risks with the increase in the number of smartphones, tablets, and other portable networkable devices used by employees. Many organizations allow the use of mobile devices on their networks. Others allow users to access data like mail from their personal mobile devices. Not all organizations have policies to protect the organization from this uncontrolled access. Organizations want their employees to be able to work as efficiently as possible, and providing them with regular and continuous access to things like work e-mail may provide higher productivity, or at least a more regular flow of business activities and information. Knowledge workers want the freedom and flexibility to be able to do their work anywhere they happen to be, including at home, in an airport, or in a hotel. It's helpful for an organization to facilitate access to certain resources remotely.

The risk of allowing employees to access the network remotely is that mobile devices are easier to steal or lose and information related to the business can be stored on those devices, which not only exposes the individual who owns the device but also their employer, who may have data currently in the open without knowing it. This shared risk creates a challenge.

One of the vectors by which a mobile device can become a threat is through malware that has been injected into a software repository, such as an application marketplace. Think the Apple App Store or the Google Play Store. While Apple and Google both vet software that comes through their respective sites, malware still makes it through. Even without malware, though, mobile devices can get stolen and data can be accessed. This data may include personal information or it may provide a way to gain access to business data. Since employees often have business e-mail on their phones, attackers may be able to get access to details there.

Denial of Service

In the latter half of 2012, several banks came under cyber attack, including Wells Fargo and JP Morgan Chase. These persistent denial-of-service (DoS) attacks originated from outside the country and lasted for months, with the businesses having to survive up to 100 Gbps of traffic to their sites. The method by which the banks were attacked, using distributed systems in a coordinated way, and the length of time the attacks were sustained, was the first time something like this had been seen. In early 2018, the GitHub website (https://github.com) sustained up to 1.5 terabits per second. That's 1.5 trillion bits per second. For a sense of scale, that's more than a thousand times more data per second than the 1 Gbps mentioned earlier in the discussion of networking capacity.

The purpose of a DoS attack can vary, depending on who the attacker is. Sometimes the goal is business disruption. Sometimes extortion is associated with DoS attacks, where a business gets a threat of a pending DoS attack unless the business pays the attacker. Sometimes a DoS attack is a form of protest. This appears to have been, at least in part, the motivation for the attacks against the banks in 2012.

The challenge with attacks of this nature is that they require coordination with external entities and not simply good plans and strategies inside the organization. A large enough DoS attack can simply overwhelm the amount of bandwidth available to the organization. The only way to mitigate that is upstream, which means involving the service provider. If there were a single road leading to your house and that road suddenly became full of cars, as though there had been an advertisement offering free bundles of $100,000 to anyone who stopped by, putting a sign at the driveway saying it isn't true wouldn't change the fact that your friends still wouldn't be able to visit you because the road is overflowing with cars from all the people looking for a handout.

Denial-of-service attacks and malware have been significant risks for over 20 years. The cost of the various threats can be challenging to compute. While there are physical costs—the labor it takes to respond to them, mitigate the threat, and clean up after them—there are also less tangible costs involved. Downtime can incur costs, but in many cases estimating these costs can be difficult to put a real dollar value on. Additionally, while the physical costs can be calculated, there are subtleties about these costs that aren't often discussed. The labor costs it takes to respond to these threats are labor costs that the business is already paying for in most cases because the salaried system and network administrators are who handle the incident. These are people who should be doing other work, and responding to a DoS attack or malware pulls them off those tasks, but it may be slightly misleading to calculate their full rate in the cost statistics. However you slice it though, security incidents are pricey. Valuations of the cost of breaches differ depending on what gets factored into the total, the size of the company and the number of records lost but it's generally in the millions according to multiple sources, such as IBM.

It's these sorts of costs and getting them under control that is driving the need for more skilled security professionals and is a reason why the GSEC certification is very important in serving as a benchmark of the level of understanding professionals require in the IT industry.

Insider Threats

For years, it's been well known that insiders cause the most loss and/or damage to a company's infrastructure and information assets. The CERT Division of the Software Engineering Institute (SEI) at Carnegie Mellon University has a database of several hundred reports of insider threats. CERT has a repository of information about how to handle insider threats as well. While the threats listed previously are far more sensational, the insider threat may well be the most insidious, simply because it can be difficult to protect against. Such losses and damage aren't always even malicious in motivation. Often, the threat can simply arise from mistakes, though malicious activity certainly exists as well. It's often hard to get specific data about insider threats because most of the time the incidents are handled internally and aren't reported in the news.

About SANS

SANS is an organization that specializes in security training. It was founded in 1989 and provides training, conferences, certifications, and degrees. SANS offers regular trainings and conferences as part of its mission to help educate professionals about security in the IT industry. SANS offers not only in-class training at its conferences but also self-paced training over the Internet and mentored trainings around the world.

In addition to the training and certifications that SANS provides, it also does research and offers that research to anyone who asks. SANS is responsible for the Internet Storm Center (https://isc.sans.edu), which is like an emergency alert system for the Internet. At the ISC, you can find information about threats and vulnerabilities currently happening around the Internet. SANS also provides original research papers, which, as of this writing, number over 2800.

SANS offers news aggregation and analysis in the form of Twitter feeds, as well as regular e-mail newsletters. There is also a weekly news digest and a weekly vulnerability digest available to anyone who subscribes.

In 1999, SANS created the Global Information Assurance Certification (GIAC) program. The goal was to ensure that a set of criteria exits that information security professionals could be measured against. Several certifications currently are available, and as of the end of 2017, SANS had issued well over 115,000 GIAC certifications to professionals around the world. The GIAC certifying arm of SANS is responsible for managing and maintaining all the certifications.

About the GSEC Certification

The purpose of the GSEC certification is to certify examinees' understanding of security fundamentals. It is a technical certification, which contrasts it with a certification like the CISSP, which is well known as a certification with a strong security management focus. The GSEC is focused on more hands-on, technical material for security and IT practitioners. A broad range of topics is covered in the certification. The following are the documented GSEC exam objectives (https://www.giac.org/certification/security-essentials-gsec):

- Access Control & Password Management
- Active Defense

- Contingency Plans
- Critical Controls
- Cryptography
- Cryptography Algorithms & Deployment
- Cryptography Application
- Defense in Depth
- Defensible Network Architecture
- Endpoint Security
- Enforcing Windows Security Policy
- Incident Handling & Response
- IT Risk Management
- Linux Security: Structure, Permissions, and Access
- Linux Services: Hardening and Securing
- Linux: Monitoring and Attack Detection
- Linux: Security Utilities
- Log Management & SIEM
- Malicious Code & Exploit Mitigation
- Network Device Security
- Network Security Devices
- Networking & Protocols
- Securing Windows Network Services
- Security Policy
- Threat Hunting
- Virtualization and Cloud Security
- Vulnerability Scanning and Penetration Testing
- Web Communication Security
- Windows Access Controls
- Windows as a Service
- Windows Automation, Auditing, and Forensics
- Windows Security Infrastructure
- Wireless Network Security

Accreditations

The GSEC certification and several other GIAC certifications are accredited under ANSI/ISO/IEC 17024. This is a standard that has criteria for operating a Personnel Certification Body. The GIAC has to adhere to requirements for developing and maintaining a certification.

The Department of Defense Directive (DDoD) 8140 approves certifications that demonstrate a baseline set of knowledge for information assurance. Along with a number of other certifications, DoDD 8140 approves the GSEC. DoDD 8140 relates to full- and part-time personnel who have privileged access to DoD information systems.

Who the Exam Is For

The exam is targeted at IT professionals who have some responsibility for security. This might include system administrators, network administrators, security analysts, security engineers, network engineers, system engineers, and a number of other related professions. Additionally, it may benefit IT technical management to pursue this certification to have a better understanding of security and the broad range of topic areas that security both touches and encompasses.

About the Exam

The GSEC exam is proctored, which means there is someone to watch over you while you take the exam. The exam is proctored by SANS's partner, Pearson VUE. Pearson VUE has more than 3500 facilities around the world. You can register to take an exam at the GIAC website (www.giac.org). You will be required to answer several questions about your experience in order to qualify to be able to take the exam. Approval to take the exam can take a few days.

Once you receive your approval, you get access to two practice exams. The practice exams provide feedback to help understand the material better. You will have four months after registering to complete your attempt to pass the exam. Once you feel you are prepared, you can take your exam at the most convenient Pearson VUE testing center.

The exam is open book. You are allowed to take an armload of books and notes into the exam but no electronic devices. While it's open book, it is not open Internet. The exam is highly technical and you should be prepared to understand the material at a deep level.

If you have taken the SEC401 course that SANS offers, you can then take the exam for an additional fee. You can also take a Challenge Exam for a higher price without taking the boot camp–style training that SANS offers. The following are the basic parameters of the exam:

- 180 multiple choice questions
- Five hours given for completion
- Passing score: 73 percent

You will not be allowed to review any of the answers after the exam is over. This might impair the integrity of the exam and the certification because it would provide too much information about the exam. You will be given the opportunity to flag questions for comment once your exam is completed. These comments won't help your score, but they will be used to help improve the test for future test takers.

The Purpose of This Book

The primary purpose of this book is to prepare you for the GSEC exam. While the topics discussed here will help you pass the GSEC exam, there is also a great amount of information regarding security and networking that lies outside what is needed simply to pass the exam. Thus, once you have your certification, you can continue to use this book as a reference.

Test Tips

One difference between the GIAC exams and exams from other certification bodies like (ISC)[2] and ISACA is that GIAC exams are open book. Don't expect to rely on your reference materials, though. Getting through 180 questions if you have to look up every answer can take more than the 5 hours. This means you should internalize as much information as possible before you attempt the exam. You will get practice exams when you register for the test. Spend time taking those tests and working through the questions and answers so you understand the nature and type of the questions you will be asked. The practice exams may not have exactly the same questions you will find but they will certainly be similar in tone, focus, and style.

Much of this book will be focused on demonstrating the concepts with practical examples using readily available tools. You should spend some time working with the tools to get hands-on understanding and experience. This certification is focused on working professionals who have a practical understanding of the material, which is one reason there is a work requirement. Working hands-on will give you more of a depth of understanding for the material, which should help you do better on the exam.

Take notes. Even as you are reading through this book and other preparation materials, take notes. Taking notes will help with retention and understanding. It will also provide you more targeted reference material when you are in the exam. Even organizing your notes so they can be referenced faster will help you with retention and understanding.

Relax. Everything you've been learning takes time to synthesize. Cramming up until the last minute is just going to clutter everything. The night before your exam, take some time to enjoy yourself. Get a good night's sleep. Everything will settle and come together and you'll be better prepared for the exam.

Networking Fundamentals

In this chapter, you will learn:
- Network protocols and the OSI communication model
- TCP/IP design and functionality
- Network addressing
- Name resolution

Before we go anywhere, we need to talk about networking fundamentals. Too much of what comes ahead relies on a solid understanding of networking protocols. It can help to think about networking conceptually by breaking the functionality into chunks. When you have a clear understanding of a protocol's role and where it fits in the collection of protocols, sometimes called a network stack, you will have an easier time putting everything together. There are a lot of moving pieces in any given network communication. You'll need to understand how it's all put together.

 EXAM TIP   You will need to know details about what the packets look like at the byte level and how they operate in the context of the architectural models that define their use and functionality.

In order to get there, we're going to start with how the Transmission Control Protocol/Internet Protocol (TCP/IP) suite was developed. The TCP/IP architecture is presented as a layered stack, but how it came about is dramatically different from the other layered stack used to describe network communications—the Open Systems Interconnection (OSI) model. Once you have a grasp of the TCP/IP and OSI models, we can start filling in the layers with actual protocols—the ones you will need to have an understanding of not only for the exam but to better understand what we'll be talking about in the coming chapters. As an example, understanding how firewalls function is significantly easier when you know how TCP/IP works. So, we start with the different models and then move to the fundamental protocols in the TCP/IP network stack.

History of TCP/IP

The history of TCP/IP can't be discussed without briefly discussing the history of the Internet since their development has really been tied together inextricably. We have to set the Wayback Machine to the mid-1960s when the Advanced Research Projects Agency

Figure 2-1
The first two
nodes in the
ARPANET

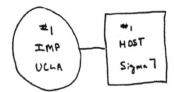

(ARPA) was developing plans for a computer network. While the money for it came out of the budget of the Defense Department, the goal of those involved in its origination was to be able to easily connect researchers across the country. In 1968, the plan for the creation of this computer network, later called the ARPANET, was approved by ARPA, and Bolt, Baranek, and Newman (BBN) was chosen as the company responsible for building this fledgling network. In fact, computer scientists at BBN originally proposed the idea of a network allowing for communication between computer users in different locations in the early 1960s, which inspired those at ARPA to build it.

In late 1969, the first link was up. Figure 2-1 shows a diagram of the connection between the very first Interface Message Processor (IMP) and the host it was intended to connect to on the network. An IMP was a ruggedized Honeywell minicomputer with custom-built components that was designed to act as a gateway to the network. Today, we typically call these devices "routers," and they pass messages from one network to another.

Initially, the interface software was called the Network Control Program (NCP). This interface software performed the functions that are now handled by the various protocols in the TCP/IP stack. In 1973–74, a specification for the Transmission Control Protocol (TCP) was written by Vint Cerf and Bob Kahn and proposed as a new protocol for host-to-host communications across networks. It wasn't until version 3 in 1977 that the Internet Protocol (IP) was added to the protocol specification, splitting the routing off into a separate protocol and leaving packetizing, error control, and reassembly to TCP. Work on version 4, the version most computers around the world currently use today, was begun in 1977 and published as a Request For Comments (RFC) document in 1980.

January 1, 1983 was known as Flag Day. It was the day that TCP/IP officially supplanted NCP as the only approved protocol on the ARPANET. While this was when TCP/IP took over on the ARPANET, there were still several other global research networks in use and it took several more years for all those networks to be merged and TCP/IP to be migrated onto all of them. While IPv4 continues to be in widespread use to this day, IPv6, the next-generation protocol, was proposed in 1995. One of the motivations for the move to IPv6 has long been the coming exhaustion of the IPv4 address space. A number of mechanisms have allowed for the IPv4 addresses available to last far longer than originally expected. At the time of this writing, in early 2013, there is still no clear plan to migrate to IPv6 and we are not yet officially out of available IPv4 addresses, though certainly we are very near to the end without opening up address spaces previously marked as experimental.

Figure 2-2 provides some insight into the speed at which the Internet has grown. It took decades to get to a significant number of users, which happened in the 1990s. Since then, it's really been an exponential growth curve, especially as less technologically

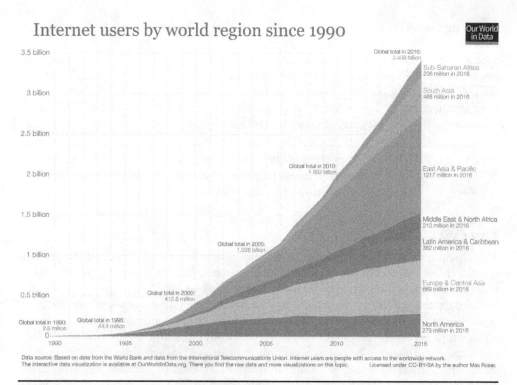

Internet users by world region since 1990

Our World in Data

Figure 2-2 The timeline of the ARPANET/Internet

advanced countries get online. On top of the exponential growth, the technology has been moving very quickly as more applications and protocols have been added to what the Internet is being used for. It took many years for TCP/IP to become the standard protocol on the ARPANET, and yet when you look at the number of technologies that have come into being in just the last few years, you can see the power of having ubiquitous Internet access.

Networking Stacks

Before talking about the different protocols, you'll get some reference points by going through different models. Models are common in the communications world. As an example, when it comes to mobile communications, they talk about the IP Multimedia Subsystem, or IMS. Once you understand that model, you can talk about where the device you are selling or buying, for example, fits into the IMS architecture. This discussion of the models provides a clear set of demarcation points between the different protocols—each serves a specific function. There are architectural models we use to provide a shorthand language in order to easily discuss specific functionality without getting hung up in vendor specifics or additional technical descriptions. As it turns out, when it comes to TCP/IP, we have two models we can use to discuss functionality.

The first model is the seven-layer OSI model that is the product of the International Organization for Standardization (ISO). It is an abstract model that was originally developed as part of a need for a model for a distributed database solution. The second model was developed by creating a set of networking protocols for the creation of the ARPA-NET and is less of a model because it's not abstract. The RFC that defines it refers to it as an architecture, so that's what we will be calling it going forward. The TCP/IP architecture was effectively developed over 20 years before it was documented in RFC 1122.

 EXAM TIP It's important to know the order of the different layers in the two models. There may be questions that ask you to put them in the correct order based on receiving or sending packets.

The OSI Model

The Open Systems Interconnection (OSI) model was developed, interestingly enough, to assist in the creation of a large-scale database system. Initially, it sprang out of work at Honeywell Information Systems because they needed an architecture to support a distributed database system with access from multiple places. The seven-layer design came as a result of studying work at ARPA on the creation of protocols, as well as on network architecture at IBM called SNA (System Network Architecture). In the late 1970s, ISO requested the American National Standards Institute (ANSI) to develop some proposals for an architecture to support communications for data processing. The work from Honeywell was the only proposal that was presented to ISO, and as a result, it was the one that was approved.

The OSI model is a generic, protocol-agnostic architectural model that any set of protocols can be slotted into. It's meant to describe a set of functionality in a clear and modular way, and as such is more about describing the ways in which protocols communicate and function together than it is about specifying or describing any particular protocol.

The Seven Layers

There are seven layers in the OSI model and each layer gets a set of tasks. Figure 2-3 shows the seven layers of the OSI model and the order they are typically presented in. Some people like to use mnemonics to be able to remember the order. One of my favorites comes from a student I had several years ago who suggested the mnemonic Please Do Not Touch Steve's Pet Alligator. This presents the different layers from bottom to top, so we'll go in that order.

1. Physical Layer   At the bottom, the Physical layer is everything about the physical connection, from wires and jacks to electricity and light. The physical layer also takes into consideration different types of networking infrastructure like the connectors used, whether it's an RJ45 connector and jack or an ST or SC connector for fiber. These physical manifestations may suggest some particular things about the next layer, but there are the physical attributes as well, which is all this layer is concerned with. The physical layer provides a place to talk about the hardware. When we are discussing network interfaces, cabling, switches, or anything else hardware-related, we are talking about the physical layer.

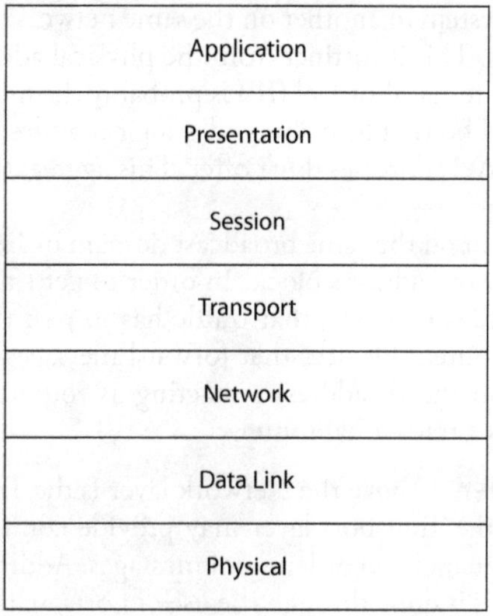

Figure 2-3
The OSI model

| Application |
| Presentation |
| Session |
| Transport |
| Network |
| Data Link |
| Physical |

There are physical layer protocols that may be familiar to you. There are aspects of Ethernet, for example, that exist at the physical layer. The distinction between different network speeds like 100BASE-T and 1000BASE-T is at the physical layer. There are elements of IEEE 802.11, the Wi-Fi networking protocol, that are at the physical layer as well.

2. Data Link Layer   Above the Physical layer is the Data Link layer, which describes how all of the data that has been flowing down from the top of the stack gets translated onto the physical transmission medium. This layer also handles things like error detection and correction should things like collisions occur on the physical medium. The Data Link layer also contains a set of addresses to ensure that systems can communicate with each other. While many protocols fall into the Data Link layer, the one most commonly used by people is the Ethernet. The Ethernet employs a Media Access Control (MAC) address. Any communication in layer 2 happens using a layer 2 address like the MAC address.

If you are talking about communication on the local network, you are talking about layer 2. Sometimes the collection of systems that communicates using layer 2 is called a broadcast domain or a collision domain. If you send a message to the broadcast MAC address and a system receives it, that system is in the same broadcast or collision domain as your system. Protocols you may be familiar with at layer 2 are Ethernet, 802.11, Frame Relay, Cisco Discovery Protocol (CDP), and Virtual Local Area Network (VLAN). Traffic that exists on the same local area network can be switched, meaning decisions about what port to send the traffic to happen using the MAC address, and switches know what MAC addresses can be found through which switch port.

3. Network Layer   The third layer is the Network layer, which manages the network communication. Primarily this has to do with addressing traffic and ensuring it gets to where it is intended to go. As a result, routing takes place at this layer. Layer 3 gets traffic from one network to another, which is in contrast to layer 2, which is about getting traffic from one system to another on the same network. The addressing done at layer 3 is logical addressing. This is distinct from the physical addressing that happens at the Data Link layer. The Internet Protocol (IP) is probably the most common layer 3 protocol that you'll recognize. The IP address provides logical addressing and the ability to aggregate addresses that MAC addresses don't offer. This aggregation enables routing that happens at layer 3.

If a system is not on the same broadcast domain or LAN as your system, it will exist in a separate IP network address block. In order to get traffic between systems on separate IP networks (different LANs), that traffic has to pass through a layer 3 gateway, which means that it is routed. Devices that forward messages from one interface to a separate interface based on the IP address are acting as routers, even if they are not what you might think of as a traditional router.

4. Transport Layer   Above the Network layer is the Transport layer. Depending on the protocol in use, the Transport layer may provide connection services as well as reliable delivery and the guaranteed ordering of messages. Additionally, the Transport layer offers multiplexing. This is done through the use of ports, which are the means of addressing at layer 4. Each system has 65,536 ports for both User Datagram Protocol (UDP) and TCP. This allows your system to be able to have multiple communication sessions open at any given time because, rather than just connecting to a logical address, like an IP address, an application can connect to an address and port combination, allowing multiple applications to communicate simultaneously.

The Transport layer is also responsible for end-to-end communication. This has several implications. The first is that the ports systems communicate to and from are in the Transport layer. Additionally, the Transport layer is responsible for any reliability that may be required. If messages need to be tracked to ensure delivery, that's the job of the Transport layer. In most cases, the order that messages arrive in matters. If you were sending a Word document or an e-mail to someone, you wouldn't want all the words to be out of order. It would mean that what you had written would become completely unintelligible.

5. Session Layer   Above the Transport layer is the Session layer. The Session layer, not surprisingly, handles sessions. A session is like a conversation. It's not just about sending a couple of messages back and forth, but instead a steady and coherent stream designed to accomplish a particular task. The Session layer offers authentication and authorization as well. It makes sure you are who you say you are but also ensures that you have the right permissions to access a particular resource. One of the protocols that falls into this layer is NetBIOS, which provides service-sharing services on Windows systems. NetBIOS establishes identity and permissions and also makes sure the session stays open until it is no longer needed. In the case of copying a file, for instance, the session needs to remain up until the file has been transferred. If something happens at the lower layer like a wire falling out if the clip on the RJ45 cable has come loose, NetBIOS will ensure the session gets reestablished, assuming the connection is reestablished within a short period of time.

6. Presentation Layer   The Presentation layer is responsible for the representation of data. As a result, the XML and JPEG formats are at this layer. This is where the data gets converted from a structured representation to strictly a series of bits and bytes.

Encrypting and decrypting data are examples of functions that would take place at the Presentation layer. There is a certain amount of translation services performed at this layer because it frees the application up from having to be concerned with how data gets represented at the lower layers of the stack. Again, this demonstrates a lot of modularity in the architectural model because this layer can have multiple implementations in any particular application, allowing these modules to be swapped in and out depending on the needs of the application. This modularity provides flexibility to the application.

7. Application Layer   The Application layer is where the functions closest to the user exist. The Application layer is responsible for generating and handling the data that goes to or comes from the lower layers. There are, of course, a large number of protocols that would fall into this layer of the model. Simple Mail Transfer Protocol (SMTP), Internet Message Access Protocol (IMAP), and Post Office Protocol (POP) are all Application layer protocols responsible for allowing users to send and receive e-mail. The protocols specify how to direct the application on what to do with particular chunks of data. When you send e-mail, for example, the protocol implementation specifies a set of directives telling the server where to send the message, who it is being sent to, and when the message itself is being sent, as opposed to the directives being what is sent. These are all behaviors that relate to the application and not about how the message gets there.

Layer-to-Layer Communication

The OSI model is layered and modular. This means that protocols are stacked up and functionality within the different protocols is consistent with the layer they live at. This also means that, for the most part, you don't have protocols that have functions that exist in three separate layers. You may have a protocol like Ethernet that appears to straddle two different layers, but in reality, something like Ethernet is actually composed of multiple protocols that work together to accomplish a larger goal. When we talk about "modular," it means that any protocol can be swapped out and replaced with another one. As an example, you may replace TCP with UDP at the Transport layer.

There is one important concept that may seem obvious based on these layers but should be called out specifically anyway. Every layer adds a bit of information that it tacks onto the existing data, much like adding Lego blocks. Every layer adds another Lego block to the ones that are there until we get to the very last layer. When the packet gets to the other end, the blocks are removed in order and examined before having the next block removed. Another way to look at it is a factory that makes packets.

Imagine a factory where we are assembling packets that need to be shipped out as quickly as possible. Initially, a box gets delivered to the factory floor. That box needs to be wrapped up before it can be shipped. The factory is organized into different groups and each group is responsible for wrapping the box up in a different paper that has a different label on it. If you look at Figure 2-4, you can see the box that gets delivered is the Application Data. After the box of Application Data has been delivered, the Presentation group wraps the box in orange paper with a label on it. After that, the Session group wraps it in blue with a different label on it. Each group wraps it up in their color wrapper with a label attached, indicating what to do with it.

Figure 2-4
Layer-to-layer
communication

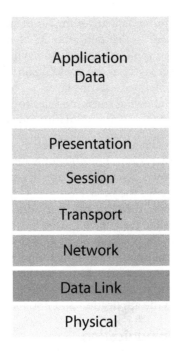

The thing about this factory, though, is that it's unionized, so when the box gets sent off and delivered, only members from the group that put each layer of packaging on are allowed to remove it. This is, in part, because only the members of each of the union groups know how to read the information that comes off. Any attempt by other union members to do the work is a violation and isn't allowed.

As each package gets delivered, it may also make stops at delivery depots (routers) along the way. Each of these depots has members of the Data Link group to remove that packaging layer and then put a new layer of packaging on before sending the package off to the next depot on its way to the final destination. These depots are along the lines of the waypoints you will see if you track a package being delivered by FedEx or UPS.

This layered approach to packaging is how packets are handled in the network. The layer of packaging has to be removed by the right "group" within the operating system so they can decipher the label on that layer of packaging and determine where the packet needs to go next. After the Network "group" is done removing the IP information, it needs to determine whether it's going to go off to the TCP, UDP, or some other group for packaging removal and handling. If the right component of the operating system doesn't handle the appropriate layer, the packet handling and delivery will fail, which is why we have the modular, layered approach so each section can be handled correctly and efficiently. Without this approach, you would end up with one large group (program function) handling all data, which would mean a lot of inefficient data handling. This, in turn, may lead to delays in delivery of the data.

TCP/IP Architecture

The TCP/IP architecture, also called the DoD (Department of Defense) model, is defined in an RFC dated from 1989, well after TCP/IP had been in widespread use. It specifies the layers required for communication between Internet hosts. RFC 1122, as it was named, specifies four required layers. Any host on the Internet must implement all four layers, which means having at least one protocol in each layer. There is a difference between the TCP/IP architecture and the OSI model, which is one reason I'm referring to it as the TCP/IP architecture rather than the TCP/IP model. The way the TCP/IP suite of protocols is put together is not conceptual. The description of the protocols and how they work are essentially as-built rather than concepts, meaning the implementation was done either before the documentation or at the same time. Because the documentation of the fundamental protocols describes what was implemented rather than what should be implemented when it is built, the description of the entire suite is really an architecture rather than a model. This is very different from the OSI model, which takes a conceptual idea of network communications and abstracts out different functions, allowing protocols to be mapped to the different layers well after the fact.

 NOTE RFC 1122 specifies that no matter which layer it is, protocols should follow one general rule called the *Robustness Principle*, which states "Be liberal in what you accept and conservative in what you send." The idea behind this principle is to ensure interoperability. With a large number of vendors expected to implement the protocols, there will certainly be different interpretations of how the software that uses these protocols should operate. If you gracefully accept different communications than what you might send yourself, you will remain functional and also continue to communicate with the sender. This reliability and robustness are very important and are big reasons why TCP/IP became the de facto networking protocol implementation around the world.

Four Layers

Instead of the seven layers of the OSI model, the TCP/IP architecture is only four layers. When you look at it, though, and compare the functionality sets between TCP/IP and OSI, you'll find that the bottom layer of the TCP/IP architecture includes the functionality of the bottom two layers of the OSI model. Similarly, the top layer in TCP/IP really comprises all of the functionality of the top three layers of the OSI model. Figure 2-5 depicts the four layers and the order they are presented in, from the bottom up.

Figure 2-5
The TCP/IP model

| Application |
| Transport |
| Internet |
| Link |

Link Layer The Link layer corresponds to the bottom two layers in the OSI model. The Physical layer and the Data Link layer are both represented in the functionality of the Link layer from the TCP/IP model.

Each layer has a protocol data unit (PDU) as a way of talking about the data in each layer separately from the other layers. Once a chunk of data makes it through the Link layer, it is called a frame. The Link layer is responsible for formatting a frame and getting it out onto the wire. There are a handful of requirements for the Link layer according to RFC 1122. The big ones are related to supporting IP encapsulated in Ethernet and related protocols. The Link layer also handles the Address Resolution Protocol (ARP), which translates higher layer addresses to a Link layer address. The Link layer is also responsible for preventing ARP floods and ensuring that the cache is kept up to date by flushing it as necessary. As noted in the RFC, which makes specific reference to it in order to ensure that TCP/IP will interoperate with another emerging standard, Ethernet falls clearly into the Link layer.

Internet Layer Not surprisingly, the Internet layer is where the Internet Protocol (IP) resides. RFC 1122 says that the Internet layer has two primary functions. The first one is choosing the next hop gateway, which means that it's responsible for handling routing functions. The second one is reassembling fragmented IP datagrams. Additionally, the Internet layer might also deliberately fragment datagrams and it should provide error and diagnostic functionality. Internet Control Messaging Protocol (ICMP) is at this layer to provide the error and diagnostic functionality.

The Internet layer in the TCP/IP model corresponds to the Network layer in the OSI model. The functionality is the same, though the specification of the TCP/IP model is very clear about the specific protocols that fill the functions for this layer. The PDU in the Internet layer is called a packet. You may hear any discrete set of network transmission as a packet. Technically, this is incorrect if it includes the Link layer header. If we are only talking about Internet headers and above, we're talking about a packet.

Transport Layer The Transport layer handles end-to-end communication for systems. While IP does bear some of the burden of that end-to-end communication, IP is really a best-effort delivery system and doesn't pay attention to whether datagrams arrive or not. This is the responsibility of the Transport layer. The Transport layer makes sure, if it is necessary, that datagrams arrive intact and in order. Sometimes it's not necessary to keep track of whether datagrams arrive or not, and we just want them sent. If they are received, great, if not, we aren't going to spend any time worrying about retransmitting. This sounds similar to the functionality of the Internet layer, but we need the additional functionality so we add on additional protocols. RFC 1122 is very clear that UDP and TCP are the protocols for this layer. UDP simply provides a datagram service. There is no reliability and no connection establishment. The datagrams are transmitted with absolutely no guarantee of their delivery or sequence when they arrive. TCP, on the other hand, provides both of those things. When you use TCP, you are guaranteed, within reason that datagrams will arrive at the other end and will arrive in the correct order.

The PDU for this layer depends on the protocol being used. If we are using UDP, the PDU is called a datagram. The datagram is very simple and, as noted previously, carries no agreement about whether the datagram will get to its endpoint. The PDU for TCP is a segment. In either case, whether we're talking about a datagram or a segment, we're talking about the Transport layer headers and the data from the Application layer.

Application Layer   In the TCP/IP model, there are two types of application protocols. The first is protocols that provide services to users directly. This would be a protocol like Telnet, for example. Telnet provides remote login services to users. The other type of application protocol would be a support protocol like the Simple Network Management Protocol (SNMP) or the Domain Name System (DNS) protocol. There are no requirements mentioned in RFC 1122 for the Application layer. In reality, the top three layers of the OSI model are accommodated in this top layer of the TCP/IP model. The Application layer here handles all of the functions of the Session, Presentation, and Application layers. This is primarily because this model is more focused on the network components and less on the aspects that deal more closely with the users. As a result, there aren't really any requirements or guidelines mentioned in RFC 1122.

 EXAM TIP   You will be expected to know the core protocols at a very low level. You will also need to be able to determine specific pieces of data when only shown a packet dump in hexadecimal, which means knowing how many bits each piece of header data consumes.

Protocols

At this point, you may be wondering about all of these protocols we've been discussing. Before going into the individual protocols that make up the core TCP/IP suite, it may help to define what a protocol actually is. In computing, we use protocols a lot, but we don't need to go to computing to find a functional definition of protocols. We make use of protocols every day, whether we realize it or not. When you greet a friend on the street and say hello to them, they likely respond with a similar greeting, whether it's "Hi" or "Hello" or "How's it going?" They probably make eye contact, however fleeting it may be. When you send e-mail to someone, you likely begin by saying something like "Dear Recipient" or "Hello" or some other greeting. These are examples of protocols and they are really just the rules we follow to assist in understanding the communication that is happening. They are markers of the way we communicate so you know when a conversation is beginning or ending. There may be specific protocols around the way you communicate with special people, whether it's the Queen of England, the President of the United States, or the parent of someone you are taking out for the first time. We probably are a bit more deferential to those people than we may be to someone we see every day. This is a protocol that we use to confer a measure of respect on those people, or maybe it's just a way of making them feel special.

When we are talking about computer-based protocols, it's really very similar. A protocol is a set of rules that we define that helps make communication faster, more efficient, and easy to understand. If one computer was to send a HELLO command while the other was expecting a LOGIN command, for example, that would lead to some communication challenges and they would be stuck waiting for the right command or response.

As a result, we put down a set of very clear definitions of these communications. These are defined, from an Internet-based protocol perspective, in Request For Comments (RFCs) that are managed by the Internet Engineering Task Force (IETF). Any time you want to know specifically how a protocol is expected to act, you should read the RFC for that particular protocol. You can easily locate RFCs by using the search features at the IETF RFC Editor website (www.rfc-editor.org).

Internet Protocol

The Internet Protocol handles a couple of really important functions. The first function is that of providing a logical address by which systems can be accessed. This logical address also allows us to group systems together, which a physical address doesn't allow us to do. As a result, we have the ability to route messages quickly and easily between systems on disparate networks. There are also other functional components of the Internet Protocol that require different header fields. Currently, we primarily use version 4 of the protocol, though usage of version 6 is increasing, primarily due to limitations of version 4, which is now approaching 40 years old. There are two basic functions that IP is meant to implement: addressing and fragmentation. The headers implement fields to assist with those functions.

IP Version 4 Headers

The IP header is defined as 24 bytes of data, though commonly you'll see 20 bytes since the other 4 bytes are options and padding. Table 2-1 has all of the fields in the IP header as well as their length and purpose.

Listing 2-1 demonstrates how a packet is broken up.

Listing 2-1   Sample IP Header

```
45 00 03 3D 1E EB 40 00 40 06 5D E8 C0 A8 01 16 AD C2 4B 6
IP Version: 4
Header Length: 20
ToS: 0
Total Length: 829
ID: 0x1eeb
Flags: 0x02
TTL: 64
Protocol: 6 (TCP)
Checksum: 0x5de8
Source: 192.168.1.22
Destination: 173.194.75.103
```

The hexadecimal in the top line is the raw packet. The hexadecimal is grouped into two digits because it takes two digits to make a byte—each hexadecimal digit uses four bits. The first byte, 45, includes the IP version (4) and the header length in 32-bit words. There are five 32-bit words in the header, which translates to 20 bytes since there are four bytes in a 32-bit word. The next byte (00) is the DiffServ Code Point and the Explicit Congestion Notification, which converts to a 0 for both values. The total length of the

Field	Length	Purpose
Version	4 bits (½ byte)	This is currently 0100 or 4.
Internet Header Length	4 bits (½ byte)	This is the length of the IP header in 32-bit words. The minimum value is 5, which would be 20 bytes.
DiffServ Code Point (DSCP)	6 bits (¾ byte)	This is used to help differentiate datagrams, typically for priority. This was originally the Type of Service field.
Explicit Congestion Notification (ECN)	2 bits (¼ byte)	This field helps provide congestion notification without packet loss.
Total Length	16 bits (2 bytes)	This is the total length of the datagram in octets (bytes). Considering the length of the field, this could have a value of 65,535, which means that systems could see datagrams that are 64K bytes.
Identification	16 bits (2 bytes)	This is used to identify an IP datagram and put fragmented datagrams back together.
Flags	3 bits	While there are 3 bits in the flag field, only two of them are in use. Bit 2 is the Don't Fragment bit, while bit 3 is More Fragments.
Fragment Offset	13 bits	This field is used to place a fragment into the right place in a reconstructed datagram.
Time To Live (TTL)	8 bits (1 byte)	While the protocol specification indicates this is a time-related field, measured in seconds, in practice this is used as a hop count. Each time a datagram passes through a router, the TTL field will be decremented by one. When the TTL reaches 0, the datagram should be discarded.
Protocol	8 bits (1 byte)	This field indicates what protocol is in the next set of headers. This is required to determine what set of processing the datagram will go through next.
Header Checksum	16 bits (2 bytes)	This is computed each time a datagram is processed to ensure that the datagram hasn't been manipulated or corrupted in transit. Each time the datagram is altered, the checksum must be recomputed. Every time a datagram goes through a router and the TTL is altered, as an example, the checksum would have to be recalculated.
Source Address	32 bits (4 bytes)	This is the IP address that the datagram originated from.
Destination Address	32 bits (4 bytes)	This is the IP address that the datagram is destined for.
Options	Variable length	There are a number of optional header values that can be inserted into the datagram here.

Table 2-1   IP Headers

datagram as seen in byte locations 3 and 4 is 03 3D, which is 829 bytes in decimal. The IP ID field has 1E EB for the hexadecimal values. The ID field is two bytes long. There is no particular need to convert the ID field to decimal, so we'll leave it alone at 1EEB. Flags take up the next three bits, and bit 2 is set there. It's worth taking a moment to demonstrate how to determine what bits are set from the hexadecimal.

In order to figure out the values from a set of bytes where there is a split, you need to change it over to binary and find where the bits are set. When we convert 40 00 to binary, we get 0100 0000 0000 0000. You can see that, of the first three bits, in these two sets of bytes there is only one bit set. In this case, that's the Don't Fragment bit, which is bit 2. This means we are not going to fragment the datagram. TTL is the next byte (40) and that converts to a 64, so the packet can go through 64 intermediate devices prior to the packet expiring and needing to be dropped.

The protocol field is one byte with a value of 06. Fortunately, this isn't difficult to convert. Since the first digit is a 0, 6 in hexadecimal is still 6 in decimal. The checksum is two bytes, and while we could go through the process of converting it to binary, we will just leave it at 5DE8. Those two bytes were 11 and 12, which brings us to byte 13. The last eight bytes are the source and destination IP address. In this case, we need to convert the hexadecimal back to decimal so it makes more sense to us. C0 converts to decimal by multiplying 12 × 16 and getting 192. A8 converts to binary by multiplying 10 × 16 and adding 8, leaving us 168. Continuing the conversion in the same way leaves us with a source address of 192.168.1.22 and a destination address of 172.194.75.103.

 EXAM TIP You will need to know how to convert hexadecimal to decimal. Although you are given a calculator, it's a basic calculator. You will be presented with bytes in hexadecimal form so the leftmost digit (corrected to decimal as necessary) is multiplied by 16 and then you add the rightmost digit to get the final decimal value.

Exercise 2-1: Hexadecimal Conversion
a. Convert 0xCD from hexadecimal to decimal.
b. Convert 132 from decimal to hexadecimal.

In looking at the sample header in Listing 2-1, there are several fields that are geared toward ensuring the validity of the data as sent. There is a header length, which not only ensures that the data can be checked, but also tells the parser where to begin looking for the next section of data: beyond the header. There is a field for total length, which can be checked to ensure the entire packet is intact, and finally, there is the checksum, which should guarantee that the data that's received is the same as what was sent and that it wasn't corrupted along the way. This shouldn't suggest it wasn't altered along the way, because any alteration would come with a new checksum, which is easy to calculate and insert.

IP is also a best-effort delivery protocol. This doesn't mean that it's half-hearted in its attempts to get messages from one endpoint to another endpoint. What it says is that it does the very best job that it can do to get a message out to the recipient but that there are things that can happen in the network and at intermediate systems that it can't control. Since IP has no capability to retransmit or even track messages through the network, the best it can do is say that it will get a message out onto the network and hope that the network does the right thing in getting the message to the recipient. This is why it's called best-effort. If an application needs something better than that, either it can use an upper layer protocol like TCP to ensure messages get delivered in the right order or it can implement mechanisms in the Application layer protocols to accomplish the tasks that need to be accomplished.

Addressing

As I mentioned, one of the primary purposes of the Internet Protocol is to provide a logical address for systems to communicate with. IP version 4 has a 32-bit address separated into four octets. In Listing 2-1, the final eight bytes are the two IP addresses: the source and the destination. An IP address is composed of two sections: the network address and the host address. You can determine which part of the address is the network and which part is the host based on the subnet mask that goes hand in hand with the address itself. In order to determine which part is the network and which is the host, you perform a bitwise AND between the IP address and the subnet mask. The result of the AND will give you the network portion. The remainder will be the host portion.

 EXAM TIP You need to be able to pull apart a subnet mask and convert the values into the number of bits. This will allow you to recognize how much of an IP address is the network and how much is the host.

Exercise 2-2: Subnetting

Given the subnet mask 255.255.255.128, how many bits are used for the network and how many bits are used for the host?

A subnet mask is created from the most significant bit to the least significant bit. Ordering our most significant bit on the left side, the first subnet mask you can have is 10000000 00000000 00000000 00000000. The bit in that first position gives you a value of 2^7 or 128. The reason it's 2^7 and not 2^8 in spite of it being in the eighth position is that in order to get a value of 1, we have to start counting positions at 0 because 2^0 is 1. The resulting subnet mask is 128.0.0.0. The next possible value is 192, because in order for the mask to work, it has to be filled in from the left side or else there is the possibility of gaps, and then we don't get a coherent result when we perform the AND with the IP address in order to get the network address. The first position is 128 and the next position has a value of 64, so adding the two together, we get 192. Table 2-2 shows the bit values and the resulting mask value.

The subnet mask will also tell you how many hosts can be on a particular network. A network with a subnet mask of 255.255.255.0 leaves eight bits for host values because the last octet is clear. Eight bits will give us 256 values (0–255), but two of those values are already spoken for. Every network has both a network address and a broadcast address, which takes two addresses away from the number of hosts we can have.

	Bit Pattern	Value
Table 2-2	10000000	128 (128)
Subnet Values by	11000000	192 (128+64)
Bit Pattern	11100000	224 (128+64+32)
	11110000	240 (128+64+32+16)
	11111000	248 (128+64+32+16+8)
	11111100	252 (128+64+32+16+8+4)
	11111110	254 (128+64+32+16+8+4+2)
	11111111	255 (128+64+32+16+8+4+2+1)

The network address is always the lowest address in the network range; the broadcast address is always the highest. In the case presented here, .0 would be the network address and .255 would be the broadcast address.

Every bit of subnet mask added divides the number of total addresses by two. Taking a bit of subnet away doubles the number of total addresses. While this may seem a trivial thing to say since we are talking about powers of two, remembering it makes calculating values a lot easier by just doing the math from a known starting point. For example, a typical subnet mask of 255.255.255.0 has 24 bits of subnet mask and 256 possible values. If we add another bit of subnet mask, we end up with 255.255.255.128 and we halve the possible address values to 128. From there, we subtract off the network and broadcast, of course, and we have 254 possible addresses that can be used. If we take away a bit of subnet, we have 255.255.254.0 and 512 possible values in the host portion of the IP address.

Classful Addressing

Initially, IP addresses were allocated in classes. These classes are based on the value in the first octet of the IP address. There are five classes that were defined, which actually leaves a significant number of addresses unused. The classes are defined in Table 2-3.

The bit pattern shown in Table 2-3 indicates the most significant bits in the first octet of the address. For example, a Class A address will always have a 0 in the most significant

Class	Bit Pattern	Start Address	End Address	Subnet Mask
A	0	0.0.0.0	127.255.255.255	255.0.0.0
B	10	128.0.0.0	191.255.255.255	255.255.0.0
C	110	192.0.0.0	223.255.255.255	255.255.255.0
D (multicast)	1110	224.0.0.0	239.255.255.255	undefined
E (reserved)	1111	240.0.0.0	255.255.255.255	undefined

Table 2-3 Classful Address Definitions

bit of the first octet, which means that the maximum value you can ever achieve in that octet is 127 since the 128 bit is never set. Similarly, with a Class B address, a 0 in the second most significant bit means that the 64 bit will never be set, so the most you can ever get is 191 because you need the 64 bit to be set to get to 192.

There are some special addresses that should be noted. The addresses 127.0.0.0–127.255.255.255 are allocated for loopback addressing. Any address in that range could be used to refer to the local system, although commonly, the address 127.0.0.1 is used for this purpose. The addresses 169.254.0.0–169.254.255.255 are reserved for self-configuration in cases where a server can't be located to provide an IP configuration. This is a link-local address, which means that it can't be used anywhere other than the local network the system is attached to. Addresses are determined randomly in order to assure that a number of systems can come up on the same network without any additional configuration.

Finally, there are three blocks of addresses that are called private addresses. They are defined in RFC 1918, which specifies that by convention they will not be routed across the Internet. They are often called non-routable, though that's a little misleading. They can be routed—in fact, many organizations do use large blocks of these addresses and instead route them internally. Since they are private addresses and require no allocation from anyone, there will be significant overlap, which means that attempting to route them across something like the Internet would result in ambiguous behavior. These private address blocks are as follows:

10.0.0.0–10.255.255.255

172.16.0.0–172.31.255.255

192.168.0.0–192.168.255.255

With classful addressing, the subnet mask is assumed in certain situations. This means that in the case of a Class A address, without any further subnetting, you would have 2^{24} addresses (16,777,216) available in the network, which is a pretty unwieldy network. As a result of this limitation, there needed to be a way of carving up addresses into more manageable blocks while still being able to easily transmit the size of the network in a meaningful way.

Another block of addresses that is considered special is the range of addresses from 127.0.0.0–127.255.255.255. You will typically see the address 127.0.0.1 in use. It's called the loopback address or the localhost address. Any address within that range can serve that purpose. Similar to the private addresses, the loopback or localhost addresses are, by convention, not routable on the Internet. The last block of reserved addresses is the multicast addresses, which start at 224.0.0.0 and end at 239.255.255.255. Multicast addresses are used to send traffic to multiple recipients simultaneously.

EXAM TIP The private addresses and the loopback addresses are considered not routable on the Internet, though it's sometimes expressed in a short-hand as simply being not routable.

Classless Inter-Domain Routing

The problem with classful addressing was that it was limiting. If you were provided a Class A address space, for example, you had 4 million addresses and no ability to share those out in any useful way. There had to be a better way, and as it turns out, there was. We needed to be able to subnet, which meant using subnet masks indicating which portion of an address identified the network and which part was for hosts. With this, we could chunk up large address spaces and share them out with friends and family, as seemed fitting. However, it's unwieldy to send an entire subnet mask, so instead we send just the number of bits that belong to the network. This is done by appending a / onto the network address, followed by the number of bits: 192.168.1.0/24. Since we aren't using classes to indicate the number of subnet bits, this notation where the number of subnet bits is indicated is called Classless Inter-Domain Routing (CIDR). The example /24 would indicate a subnet mask of 255.255.255.0. A 255 in each octet indicates there are 8 bits in use for the network in those octets. We have three octets of 8 bits, which is 24 bits.

Fragmentation

With a modular design like TCP/IP, you get a lot of flexibility, but you also get circumstances where you have to make accommodations for cases where two layers may not match exactly. The higher layer protocols like TCP and UDP allow for large messages, both allowing for 65,535 bytes to be transmitted. Lower layer protocols like Ethernet, however, have much smaller allowable sizes. The maximum transmission unit (MTU) of Ethernet is 1500 bytes, which includes the headers. As a result, you end up with situations where messages need to be fragmented into smaller-sized packets so they can be transmitted. IP is responsible for taking care of this, and there are headers that make that possible. The first IP header that allows fragmented datagrams to be put back together is the IP identification header. All packets belonging to a fragmented message will have the same IP identification number.

Internet Protocol Version 6

In the 1990s, the Internet Engineering Task Force, the group responsible for managing protocols across the Internet and generally trying to improve operations, recognized that IPv4 had a limited life to it. One of the reasons for that was because in the 1990s there was an explosion in usage of the Internet, which meant that addresses were being consumed at a rapid rate. The IETF determined that they needed a way to accommodate many more addresses, and so the next version of IP had to achieve that goal. Additionally, a number of other defects had been identified in the existing version and those needed to be fixed. IPv6 needed to have a larger address space, be more efficient in processing capabilities as the messages were passing through routing devices, and also have some level of security built in.

IP Security, also known as IPSec, was developed as a core part of IPv6. It was spun out and adapted for IPv4, but the way it operates is part of how IPv6 was created. You can use Authenticated Headers (AH) to ensure that messages haven't been tampered with. You can also use Encapsulating Security Payload (ESP) to encrypt the message contents. These two mechanisms provide a range of security capabilities and can be configured to be used on a per-system basis, depending on the implementation of security policies on each system.

Addressing

As noted, there had to be a much larger address space available in IPv6. The existing address space was 2^32 addresses, or roughly 4 billion addresses. This may seem like a lot but good-sized chunks have been carved out for other purposes and the need to assign them in blocks means there will be some inefficiency and a number of addresses that go unused. With people having multiple devices that need addresses now, that 4 billion, even if it could be fully used, is inadequate. IPv6 has an address space that is 128 bits wide. This gives us 2^128 addresses, which is a number large enough that it simply makes more sense to write it as 2^128 rather than trying to write out all the digits. If it's easier to think of it another way, it could also be expressed as 3.4×10^{38}. That's a lot of addresses, and you can probably be confident that we won't be running out of these addresses any time soon.

An IP address still has the primary function of needing to identify both the host and the network portion, in spite of the version change. We still haven't changed the need to route packets from one system to another, and in order to route, we need network identifiers in the addresses. Because of that, we are using the CIDR notation to indicate the number of bits in the network portion.

An IP address is composed of eight 16-bit words. A word is just a group of bytes bound together. In the case of an IP address, it made some sense to bind two bytes together to create a 16-bit word. All addresses in IPv6 are written in hexadecimal because it's more convenient. Two hexadecimal digits can represent one byte, so each word of an IP address is expressed in four hexadecimal digits. 8890:7764:f0ca:445d:9097:123a:cd b0:de41/64 is an example of an IP address. While it's quite a mouthful, it is the easiest way to express an IPv6 address.

There are shortcuts, however. You may find a situation where there are long sections of 0s, for example. In that case, you can abbreviate the address by just leaving the sections blank. You might have an address that was written fe80::1234:78fa as an example. The :: section indicates that there are 0s that fill all of those places.

Headers

The IP header has been simplified, but because of the address size, the total header length is still larger. Table 2-4 describes all of the fields in the IPv6 header, as well as their length and purpose. Table 2-5 shows the layout of the IPv6 headers, organized in 32-bit word blocks.

Field	Length	Purpose
Version	4 bits (½ byte)	This is the version of the protocol. The version here is 6.
Traffic Class	8 bits (1 byte)	This replaces the Type of Service (TOS) field from the IPv4 header and is used to provide quality of service capabilities.
Flow Label	20 bits (2½ bytes)	This field is to provide additional quality of service and real-time datagram delivery services.
Payload Length	16 bits (2 bytes)	This field is to provide additional quality of service and real-time datagram delivery services.
Next Header	8 bits (1 byte)	This provides identification of the type of the next header, which is similar to the protocol field but provides support for extensions as well.
Hop Limit	8 bits (1 byte)	This is a replacement for the Time To Live (TTL) field and indicates how long a packet should live in the network before being discarded.
Source Address	128 bits (16 bytes)	The source IP address.
Destination Address	128 bits (16 bytes)	The destination IP address.

Table 2-4 IPv6 Headers

Offsets	Octet	0								1								2								3							
Octet	Bit	0	1	2	3	4	5	6	7	8	9	10	11	12	13	14	15	16	17	18	19	20	21	22	23	24	25	26	27	28	29	30	31
0	0	Version				Traffic Class								Flow Label																			
4	32	Payload Length																Next Header								Hop Limit							
8	64	Source Address																															
12	96																																
16	128																																
20	160																																
24	192	Destination Address																															
28	224																																
32	256																																
36	288																																

Table 2-5 Layout of IPv6 Headers

Internet Control Message Protocol (ICMP)

ICMP is a support protocol for the other protocols in the TCP/IP suite. It is designed to provide error and diagnostic messages to assist in the delivery of messages. When packets run into problems on the network, ICMP messages are sent back. As an example, if you are trying to send a message to a system that is offline, an intermediate device ahead of that system, like a router or firewall, may send back an ICMP message indicating that the system is unreachable. You may also get a response back when a port is unreachable. There are two utilities that get used regularly as part of network diagnostics that make use of ICMP. The first one is ping. ICMP has two messages that ping makes use of. The first is an echo request, and the second is an echo reply. You would send an ICMP echo request to a system to verify its reachability, and if it is up and functional, it would send back an ICMP echo reply.

The second utility that makes use of ICMP is the traceroute utility. There are different implementations of traceroute that operate slightly differently, but they all rely on ICMP in the same way. Traceroute operates by way of a system sending a message out with the destination of the target, but the TTL is set at 1 to begin with. When it reaches the first router on the path, the TTL is decremented and becomes 0, which means it needs to be discarded. When it's discarded, the router sends back an ICMP error message indicating that the TTL expired. The TTL then gets set to 1 and keeps getting incremented, while the system that replies with the ICMP error message is noted, until finally the ICMP message changes to a destination unreachable message. Either the system itself is unreachable or the port is unreachable. Either way, traceroute knows that the trace is complete once it receives this error message.

 NOTE In Windows, because of the historical restriction on the length of filenames, the utility is called tracert but the functionality is the same as traceroute, and it relies on ICMP error messages in the same way.

ICMP uses a header to convey the information. The header is composed of eight bytes. The first byte is the type indicating the type of message that is being conveyed. Each type may have several different codes to specify a different condition. For example, the port unreachable message and the host unreachable message are both different codes inside a Type 3 message, indicating that the destination is unreachable.

The type and code both take up one byte. Table 2-6 is a listing of all the relevant types and codes. There are two additional bytes used for a checksum. The checksum is used

Type	Code	Description
0 – Echo Reply	0	Echo reply (used to ping)
1 and 2		*Reserved*
	0	Destination network unreachable
	1	Destination host unreachable
	2	Destination protocol unreachable
	3	Destination port unreachable
	4	Fragmentation required, and DF flag set
	5	Source route failed
	6	Destination network unknown
3 – Destination Unreachable	7	Destination host unknown
	8	Source host isolated
	9	Network administratively prohibited
	10	Host administratively prohibited
	11	Network unreachable for TOS
	12	Host unreachable for TOS
	13	Communication administratively prohibited
	14	Host precedence violation
	15	Precedence cutoff in effect

Table 2-6 ICMP Types and Codes

Type	Code	Description
4 – Source Quench	0	Source quench (congestion control)
	0	Redirect datagram for the network
	1	Redirect datagram for the host
5 – Redirect Message	2	Redirect datagram for the TOS and network
	3	Redirect datagram for the TOS and host
6		Alternate host address
7		*Reserved*
8 – Echo Request	0	Echo request (used to ping)
9 – Router Advertisement	0	Router advertisement
10 – Router Solicitation	0	Router discovery/selection/solicitation
	0	TTL expired in transit
11 – Time Exceeded	1	Fragment reassembly time exceeded
	0	Pointer indicates the error
12 – Parameter Problem: Bad IP Header	1	Missing a required option
	2	Bad length
13 – Timestamp	0	Timestamp
14 – Timestamp Reply	0	Timestamp reply
15 – Information Request	0	Information request
16 – Information Reply	0	Information reply
17 – Address Mask Request	0	Address mask request
18 – Address Mask Reply	0	Address mask reply
19		*Reserved* for security
20 through 29		*Reserved* for robustness experiment
30 – Traceroute	0	Information request
31		Datagram conversion error
32		Mobile host redirect
33		Where-Are-You (originally meant for IPv6)
34		Here-I-Am (originally meant for IPv6)
35		Mobile registration request
36		Mobile registration reply
37		Domain name request
38		Domain name reply
39		SKIP algorithm discovery protocol, Simple Key-Management for Internet Protocol
40		Photuris, security failures
41		ICMP for experimental mobility protocols such as Seamoby [RFC 4065]
42 through 255		*Reserved*

Table 2-6 ICMP Types and Codes *(Continued)*

like the checksum in other protocols—to ensure that the message hasn't been corrupted in transit. The ICMP header has four additional bytes that get used to convey additional information, depending on the specific message.

Transmission Control Protocol (TCP)

TCP is a Transport layer protocol providing, among other things, multiplexing. If we were to try to communicate with another system without having the ability to multiplex, we'd only have the ability to have one communication at a time, which would be pretty limiting. Additionally, it provides a reliable transport, ensuring that each datagram gets to its destination with all the data in the correct order.

The multiplexing in TCP is accomplished by using port numbers. Since TCP uses two bytes to designate a port number, we can have ports 0–65,535 giving us a total of 65,536 ports to use. This provides a lot of communication potential. Since we expect to receive messages back from those we communicate with, we need both a source port and destination port. When we send a message, it gets delivered to the destination port, but when that system then needs to communicate back to us, it turns the port order around and the original source port becomes the destination port on the return trip. As a result, the source port is effectively bound to the original sending application. The IP stack then knows that when the return communication comes back, it goes back to the application that started the process.

 EXAM TIP Expect that the exam will have questions where you will need to be able to decipher portions of the TCP header from just a set of raw bytes expressed in hexadecimal. Knowing the order and size of each component of the header is going to be critical to doing well.

Table 2-7 describes all of the fields in the TCP header, as well as their length and purpose. Table 2-8 shows how the different fields are arranged by byte.

Field	Length	Purpose
Source Port	16 bits (2 bytes)	The port that the communication is sourced from. Return communications would come back to this port.
Destination Port	16 bits (2 bytes)	The port that the communication is destined to.
Sequence Number	32 bits (4 bytes)	The sequence number is part of the conversation between the sender and the receiver and helps ensure that data has been received and is in the correct order.
Acknowledgment Number	32 bits (4 bytes)	The acknowledgment number works in conjunction with the sequence number to ensure that data has been received and is in the right order.

Table 2-7 TCP Headers

Field	Length	Purpose
Data Offset	4 bits (½ byte)	This field is actually the size of the TCP header. It's called an offset because it's the number of 32-bit words that the payload is offset from at the start of the TCP segment. The smallest value here is five words, which would be 20 bytes. Because of the size of the field, the largest number that could be held here is 15 words, which would be 60 bytes.
Reserved	3 bits	This should always be 0, because it was originally reserved for future use and hasn't been used to date.

Flags	9 bits	• This is a series of nine one-bit flags that are used for a variety of purposes, depending on the flag:
		  • NS – Used for congestion notification.
		  • Congestion Window Reduced – This is related to a congestion control mechanism.
		  • ECE – Used for congestion notification.
		  • URG – Indicates that the urgent pointer field has a value that should be looked at and used.
		  • ACK – This is an acknowledgment flag and indicates that the acknowledgment number has data that should be looked at.
		  • PSH – This flag is used to send data immediately to the receiving application.
		  • RST – Reset the connection.
		  • SYN – This flag is the synchronize flag, used to initialize a connection. This indicates that sequence numbers should be synchronized so the resulting conversation can ensure data arrives and is in order.
		  • FIN – Completes the conversation.

Window Size	16 bits (2 bytes)	This is the number of bytes that can be sent without receiving an acknowledgment back. This allows for a variable number of bytes not needing a response, which lets the connection adapt to the conditions in the network.
Checksum	16 bits (2 bytes)	Used to verify the integrity of the segment.
Urgent Pointer	16 bits (2 bytes)	If the urgent flag is set, this field is used to indicate the location of urgent data within the segment.
Options	Variable	This allows for optional header fields. There could be from 0–320 bits in the optional headers, divisible by 32.
Padding	Variable	This field would be filled with 0s as necessary to ensure the TCP header ends on a 32-bit boundary, because values in the header are based on 32-bit words, and so processing of the header is done based on those 32-bit words.

Table 2-7 TCP Headers *(Continued)*

Offsets	Octet	0								1								2								3							
Octet	Bit	0	1	2	3	4	5	6	7	8	9	10	11	12	13	14	15	16	17	18	19	20	21	22	23	24	25	26	27	28	29	30	31
0	0	Source port															Destination port															
4	32	Sequence number																														
8	64	Acknowledgment number (if ACK set)																														
12	96	Data offset				Reserved 0 0 0			N S	C W R	E C E	U R G	A C K	P S H	R S T	S Y N	F I N	Window size															
16	128	Checksum															Urgent pointer (if URG set)															
20 ...	160 ...	Options. Zero padded as necessary.																														

Table 2-8 TCP Header Layout

Reliable Delivery

TCP achieves reliable delivery through two mechanisms. The first is the three-way handshake that is used to establish a connection. The three-way handshake achieves a couple of objectives. The first is that each side assures that the other side is there, is listening, and is able to respond. The second, a side effect of the first, ensures that the communication is not being forged with a fake address, also called spoofed. Since the three-way handshake requires that the originator of the communication respond in a coherent way, it generally rules out the possibility of spoofing. Figure 2-6 shows a communication stream

Figure 2-6
Ladder diagram
showing
communication

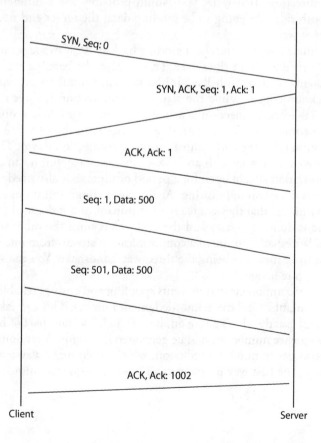

SYN, Seq: 0

SYN, ACK, Seq: 1, Ack: 1

ACK, Ack: 1

Seq: 1, Data: 500

Seq: 501, Data: 500

ACK, Ack: 1002

Client

Server

between a client and a server, presented as a ladder diagram so that it's easier to follow along with the explanation.

The three-way handshake is a pretty simple process, but it's critical to the way TCP/IP works. The first step of the three-way handshake is to send a SYN (synchronize) message. This is a TCP segment with the SYN flag set. This message is the same as someone welcoming an acquaintance in the street with a Hi! It says "I am looking to begin a conversation with you." Along with the SYN flag being set, the client initiating a connection to a server would send an initial sequence number. This sequence number establishes a baseline so that messages can be ordered correctly since we can't guarantee the messages won't get reordered by the network. This lets the receiving system put all the data back into the correct order. It also allows for a guaranteed delivery because the receiving system can send a verification back to the sending system that individual messages were received.

The second message is sent from the server back to the client. In this case, two flags are set. The first flag is an ACK, acknowledging that the initial SYN message was received. The second flag is a SYN flag so that the server can reply with its own initial sequence number. This does the same thing as the first sequence number. It establishes a baseline from the server to the client with a sequence number. The reason for doing this is because when you establish a connection with another system, the communication is going to be two-way for the most part. It's not typically a send-only connection in one direction. If it were, you would probably use a different protocol from TCP. Since both sides are going to be sending data, the server end needs an initial sequence number as well.

The final message is the client sending back an ACK message indicating that it received the SYN message from the server. This finishes the baseline establishment between the two systems so they both have initial sequence numbers set and those numbers have been acknowledged. While the setup of a connection is three messages, the teardown of an established connection is actually four messages. When one of the systems wants to tear a connection down, it sends a message with the FIN flag set. This says that it is done communicating and wants to tear the connection down. The system receiving the FIN message will reply with an ACK to that message, but it can also keep its side of the communication stream open for a period of time, so it also needs to send a FIN message when it is done communicating. Again, since communications are two-way, both sides need to indicate that they are ready to terminate, and it doesn't have to be mutual. When one side is done, it says so and then just waits until the other side is done. Figure 2-7 shows a Wireshark capture of a communication stream from one system to another with the first three messages being the three-way handshake. You can see the flags that are set in the capture image.

Another component that prevents spoofing and ensures reliability is the pairing of the sequence number and the acknowledgment number. This can take a little bit of looking to sort out exactly what's going on, but it's an important part of how TCP operates. The initial sequence number should be generated randomly. A random sequence number will prevent sequence number prediction, which could make a system vulnerable to session hijacking. The best way to understand how the sequence number and acknowledgment

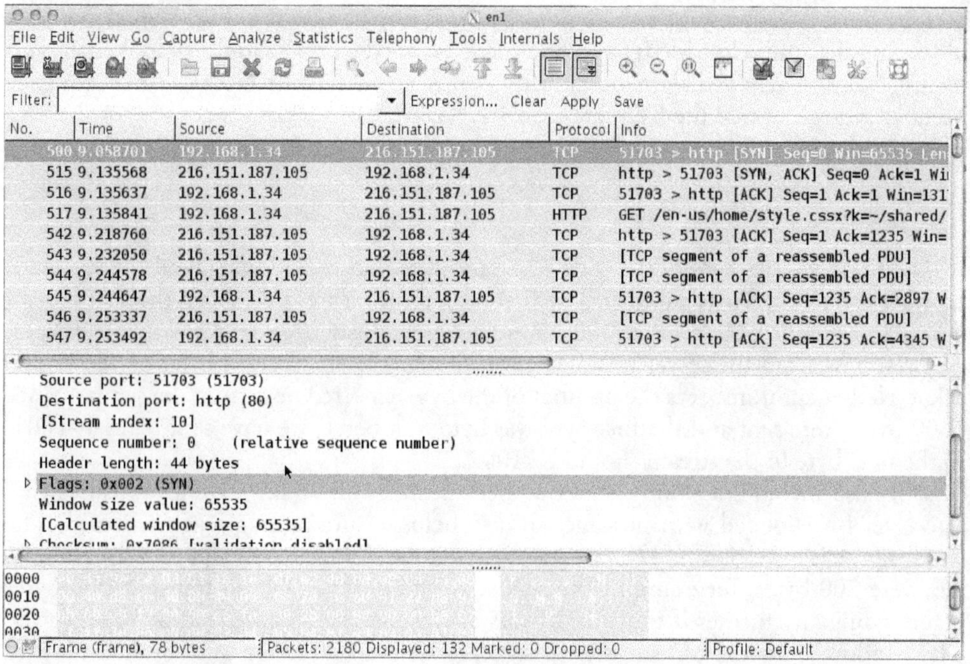

Figure 2-7 Wireshark capture of a three-way handshake

numbers work together is to see it in practice. So, as an example, let's say that client C is sending a message to server S, and for the sake of simplicity we will use small numbers for the sequence and acknowledgments. In practice, these numbers would be large and random but smaller numbers make it easier to do calculations so we can see what happens. The first message would be as follows:

```
C -> S Flags: SYN, Seq: 100
```

This is the first stage of the three-way handshake and the initial sequence number is set. Nothing else is set in this message.

```
S -> C Flags: SYN, ACK, Seq: 200, Ack: 101
```

This is the SYN/ACK message. In order to distinguish one side of the communication stream from another, I set the sequence number to 200. This is the initial sequence number from the server to the client. The acknowledgment indicates that the first message was received and indicates the next byte expected from the client. This is done by simply incrementing the sequence number that was sent by one because it was a SYN message.

```
C -> S Flags: ACK, Ack: 201
```

This is the ACK message completing the three-way handshake. The ACK flag is sent indicating that the acknowledgment flag carries some data that should be looked at, and in this case the acknowledgment number is just an increment of the initial sequence number indicating that the SYN message was received.

```
C -> S Flags: none, Seq: 1, Data: 500 bytes
C -> S Flags: none, Seq: 501, Data: 500 bytes
S -> C Flags: ACK, Ack: 1002
```

The first two messages in the code block indicate that there is data, and the sequence number is the initial byte number. The first message indicates that this is the first byte of data. The second indicates that 500 bytes have previously been sent in other messages. The response from the server to the client indicates that it received bytes 1–1001. The acknowledgment number is the number of the byte expected next from the sender. Since 1000 bytes were sent and the first byte was byte number 1, we have sent bytes 1–1001, so the next byte in the stream should be 1002.

TCP also includes a sliding window mechanism. This sliding window ensures that a receiver isn't flooded with messages. It also helps ensure messages get delivered. The window size is advertised in the messages and can be changed at any point. If a window size were 200 bytes, for example, the sender would only be able to transmit 200 bytes before going any further if those 200 bytes haven't been acknowledged by the receiver. The window locks the transmission into place. If the 200 bytes were broken up into segments A, B, C, and D, all 50 bytes long, the window would be locked at segment D. If A, C, and D are all received by the recipient, the window can't slide to the next set of bytes until B has been received. This ensures that no message has been lost and it makes it easier to reassemble.

In actuality, the sender in that case wouldn't even know that C and D had been received since it can't acknowledge those messages until the missing bytes are delivered. While it's possible to do selective acknowledgment, it's not common. Typically, bytes are acknowledged in order, meaning that you can acknowledge a number of segments simultaneously by simply acknowledging the last one received, which indicates that all the intermediate segments were also received.

In the preceding example, where we have segments A–D, if A and B are sent and received, the window can then slide along to C, D, E, and F, and that becomes the window until the first segments within the window are sent and acknowledged. As the window slides, we get orderly and controlled delivery.

A sender and a recipient may perform what is called a slow start if there is uncertainty about the other side's ability to send and receive. This is where the window size is set small and increased slowly as the messages pass back and forth and each side gets an idea of how quickly messages can be sent and acknowledged.

Keep in mind, though, that the window size being advertised is the number of bytes you are willing to receive at a time. You have no control over the number of bytes you will send because your send window is your recipient's receive window and they have control over their receive window. A sender must comply with the window size advertised by their recipient.

The Mitnick–Shimomura Attack

In the 1980s and 1990s, Kevin Mitnick was spending a lot of time breaking into systems. At some point in the 1990s, he broke into the system of a graduate student named Tsuturo Shimomura using a TCP sequence number prediction attack. Shimomura was able to follow this attack and capture messages to demonstrate how it worked. In the following, you will see the output from a packet capture. In the messages x-terminal.shell > Apollo.it.luc.edu.1000, notice the SYN/ACK message portion of a three-way handshake. These messages are all in bold face. When you compare the sequence numbers, which have been italicized, you will see that the sequence numbers go up by a predictable amount. Because the sequence numbers were predictable, Mitnick was able to spoof the connection between Shimomura's system and a server.

While the important part of this is the sequence number prediction, there is more to the attack than just sequence number prediction. Mitnick had to take the system he was pretending to be out of the equation so it wouldn't be able to reply. Once he had the three-way handshake completed from sequence number prediction, he was able to send shell commands to the system under attack, which would allow him to later on make a legitimate connection because he had opened up trust relationships

The Mitnick–Shimomura attack and the way it works is important because some of the implementations of TCP didn't adequately protect the systems by using random data. It wasn't until this attack became public that vendors realized that predictable data could be used to attack a system. This particular attack also highlights some of the vulnerabilities inherent in the design of TCP/IP, which led to some of the changes that went into the next version of IP.

```
14:18:25.906002 apollo.it.luc.edu.1000 > x-terminal.shell: S
1382726990:1382726990(0) win 4096
14:18:26.094731 x-terminal.shell > apollo.it.luc.edu.1000: S
2021824000:2021824000(0) ack 1382726991 win 4096
14:18:26.172394 apollo.it.luc.edu.1000 > x-terminal.shell: R
1382726991:1382726991(0) win 0
14:18:26.507560 apollo.it.luc.edu.999 > x-terminal.shell: S
1382726991:1382726991(0) win 4096
14:18:26.694691 x-terminal.shell > apollo.it.luc.edu.999: S
2021952000:2021952000(0) ack 1382726992 win 4096
14:18:26.775037 apollo.it.luc.edu.999 > x-terminal.shell: R
1382726992:1382726992(0) win 0
14:18:26.775395 apollo.it.luc.edu.999 > x-terminal.shell: R
1382726992:1382726992(0) win 0
14:18:27.014050 apollo.it.luc.edu.998 > x-terminal.shell: S
1382726992:1382726992(0) win 4096
14:18:27.174846 x-terminal.shell > apollo.it.luc.edu.998: S
2022080000:2022080000(0) ack 1382726993 win 4096
14:18:27.251840 apollo.it.luc.edu.998 > x-terminal.shell: R
1382726993:1382726993(0) win 0
14:18:27.544069 apollo.it.luc.edu.997 > x-terminal.shell: S
1382726993:1382726993(0) win 4096
14:18:27.714932 x-terminal.shell > apollo.it.luc.edu.997: S
2022208000:2022208000(0) ack 1382726994 win 4096
```

In this packet capture, we see that Mitnick, on the Apollo.it.luc.edu system, sent SYN messages to the target, x-terminal on the shell port, which would be port 23. He did this several times, sending an RST message after getting the SYN/ACK back so he could understand the pattern being used for the initial sequence number. Once he had gathered enough data from this set of messages, he was able to predict the sequence number. This was necessary to be able to send spoofed messages over TCP, because he needed to be able to respond with appropriate ACK messages, letting the target know that the messages had been received. This allowed him to carry on a conversation, knowing the data he was sending and the messages he expected to receive, along with the length of those responses.

 EXAM TIP The exam may have a question with a capture sample that looks like this. You should be looking at the sequence numbers to compare them. If you see a pattern (subtract one sequence number from the previous sequence number), the system is vulnerable to TCP sequence number prediction, which is the attack that Kevin Mitnick used.

He needed to be able to predict those, because when you are acknowledging received messages, the sequence number increments by the number of bytes that have been received. In order to know what that value is over time, you need to know what the initial sequence number is. This should be a random value, but older implementations of TCP/IP didn't implement random values, as they didn't anticipate the possibility of predicting the sequence number for a spoofing attack.

User Datagram Protocol (UDP)

UDP is considered an unreliable protocol. This does not mean that it fails a lot. What it means is that there are no mechanisms built into the protocol that would ensure that messages get delivered and that they are delivered in the correct order. Lacking those mechanisms, UDP provides no guarantees that messages won't get dropped or arrive out of order, so applications that require message fidelity should not rely on UDP.

Actually, there are several applications where UDP is more than useful—it's necessary. A typical application would be streaming media like voice or video. Voice over IP (VoIP) would use UDP to carry voice traffic. The reason for this is simply because when you are using something in real time, like a voice communication, your senses are capable of filling in the gaps where small amounts of data may be lost. Additionally, you don't want to spend the time waiting for messages to come in out of order and then have to reorder them. Since our senses can fill in spaces that aren't really there by automatically filling in what makes sense, we can drop messages that are out of order or not delivered and still be able to make some sense of what's going on. What we are really looking for is speed. We want messages to hit the wire as quickly as possible and get to the recipient fast. We also don't want to spend a lot of time processing the message, so the headers in UDP are minimal and easy to process quickly.

Similar to TCP, UDP offers multiplexing via port numbers. We have source and destination ports, which get reversed on the return communication. Unlike TCP, though, there is no way to ensure that messages get delivered. This is one reason why doing a port scan against UDP ports can be timely since we can't always guarantee what no response to

Field	Length	Purpose
Source Port	16 bits (2 bytes)	The port that messages are sourced from. This would be mapped to an application that response messages would get sent to.
Destination Port	16 bits (2 bytes)	The port that messages are being sent to on the recipient system.
Length	16 bits (2 bytes)	The length of the message. This is 2 bytes, which means UDP messages could be up to 65,535 bytes.
Checksum	16 bits (2 bytes)	This validates that a message wasn't corrupted or tampered with in transit.

Table 2-9 UDP Headers

Offsets	Octet	0								1								2								3							
Octet	Bit	0	1	2	3	4	5	6	7	8	9	10	11	12	13	14	15	16	17	18	19	20	21	22	23	24	25	26	27	28	29	30	31
0	0	Source port															Destination port															
4	32	Length															Checksum															

Table 2-10 UDP Header Structure

a UDP message means. If a message doesn't get a reply, we can't assume it's because there is no application listening. It could have been dropped in the network or potentially discarded by a firewall in front of the target system.

EXAM TIP Know the order of the headers for UDP. You may be expected to decode a set of raw bytes provided in hexadecimal in order to determine the source port or destination port, for example.

Table 2-9 describes all of the header fields contained in UDP as well as their length and purpose.

Table 2-10 displays the structure of the UDP header in a way that shows it in chunks of 32-bit words that other headers are organized in.

Domain Name System (DNS)

People typically have a hard time juggling a lot of numbers, and since that's the core of the addressing scheme for systems on the Internet, there needed to be a better way. Initially, it was done with a file that got shared around to all of the hosts on the Internet. This was acceptable because there were so few systems in the early days and everyone knew who was on. You could create a file that had a mapping of hostnames and IP addresses. Not surprisingly, this wasn't very flexible or scalable. If you needed to make a change because you had added or decommissioned a system, you needed to get that change to the person who updated the hosts file and it needed to be sent out to everyone. Fortunately, in an age where there were really large systems like mainframes and mini-computers, the number of changes was generally low. New sites were coming online on a regular basis, though. As a result, the Domain Name System (DNS) was created to have a way of looking up information about hostnames and IP addresses. It would give flexibility and scalability to the growing network.

DNS is a hierarchical system, and to best understand it you have to read it right to left. A system name that includes the domain name as well is called a fully qualified domain name (FQDN). On the right side of an FQDN, you have the top-level domain (TLD). Figure 2-8 is a visual representation of the hierarchical nature of DNS, and it may help to follow along using the figure. You may be most familiar with seeing .com or maybe .org here. Those are examples of top-level domains, and those TLDs have a map of the second-level domain. In the case of my own domain name, the second-level domain would be WasHere. My full domain name, including the TLD, is washere.com. If I were to have a system in my DNS tables, the FQDN would be something like opus.washere .com and that would map to an IP address, so rather than having to connect to the IP address, you would simply connect to the hostname.

In addition to the domain name, you may have subdomains. As an example, if my organization had a research and development lab, I may call the subdomain for that part of the organization labs.washere.com. The web server for that subdomain would be www.labs.washere.com.

Most often, you'll see these hostnames offering up service names rather than something more colorful. This makes it easier to remember. As a result, you get www.microsoft.com or mail.google.com or something along those lines. The reason for that is because, again, it makes it easier to remember. These service-based hostnames may actually be mapped to a different hostname altogether. They are used for convenience so everyone knows how to get to the web server for a particular domain.

DNS queries are recursive because the names are hierarchical. A series of root servers hold all of the authoritative name servers for each second-level domain. An authoritative name server is where the definitive responses for any given domain are. The administrators for each domain would be responsible for maintaining the tables of all the hostnames for that domain. The root servers would point to the DNS server maintained

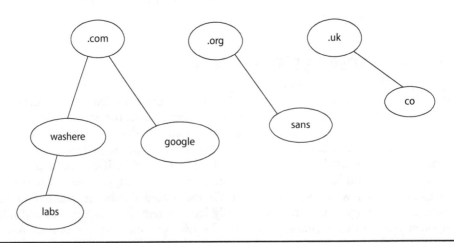

Figure 2-8   Visual representation of the DNS hierarchy

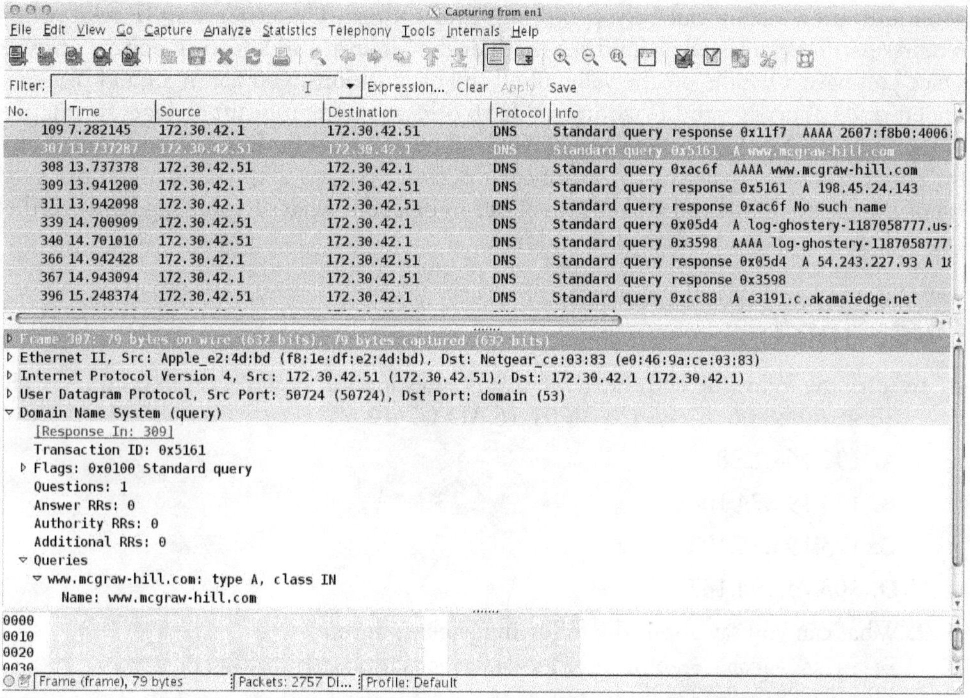

Figure 2-9   Sample DNS query

by each organization. Recursive means that the first response points to another server that would need to be queried. Again, by way of example, if you were looking for www .washere.com, you would go to the root server to get the authoritative name server for the domain washere.com. The root servers would reply with an IP address. Your system would then send the query off to the authoritative name server asking for the IP address for www.washere.com. If there were subdomains involved, there would be additional queries involved to get the authoritative name server for the subdomains.

You can see a Wireshark capture of a DNS query in Figure 2-9. Notice that the transport protocol is UDP and the request is for an Internet address for A (Address) record of www.mheducation.com. The query is followed later by a response. Much of the recursive nature of the DNS queries happens with the actual DNS server, not on the client side where this capture was taken.

Chapter Review

It can be challenging to keep straight all of the header fields for the core protocols of the TCP/IP suite—IP, TCP, and UDP—but it's one of the certification objectives. Plan to spend a fair bit of time here. It will be worthwhile exploring tcpdump or Wireshark and seeing how the protocols look in real life. Wireshark provides a graphical look, as well as extensive protocol decodes, so it may be more helpful to those who are new to packet captures and protocol interactions. Seeing the field values from an actual network communication stream can help put things into context. Understanding IP addressing requires getting your head around the math at the bit level and knowing powers of two. Once you have a handle on the value of all the bit positions, you are in a good place to understand subnetting and IP addresses. IPv6 offers some significant changes, primarily in the way that hosts are addressed. Having 16 bytes for addressing gives a lot of room for hosts, and making use of the number of network bits, as with CIDR notation, gets rid of the subnet mask and makes it easier to understand what's happening between the network and host component of the address.

Questions

1. With the following IP header, what is the destination IP address: 45 00 03 3D 1E EB 40 00 40 06 5D E8 C0 A8 01 16 AD C2 4B 67

   A. 192.168.1.38

   B. 173.195.74.108

   C. 173.194.75.103

   D. 103.75.194.137

2. What can you say about the following packet capture?

   ```
   14:18:25.906002 apollo.it.luc.edu.1000 > x-terminal.shell: S
   1382726990:1382726990(0) win 4096
   14:18:26.094731 x-terminal.shell > apollo.it.luc.edu.1000: S
   2021824000:2021824000(0) ack 1382726991 win 4096
   14:18:26.172394 apollo.it.luc.edu.1000 > x-terminal.shell: R
   1382726991:1382726991(0) win 0
   14:18:26.507560 apollo.it.luc.edu.999 > x-terminal.shell: S
   1382726991:1382726991(0) win 4096
   14:18:26.694691 x-terminal.shell > apollo.it.luc.edu.999: S
   2021952000:2021952000(0) ack 1382726992 win 4096
   14:18:26.775037 apollo.it.luc.edu.999 > x-terminal.shell: R
   1382726992:1382726992(0) win 0
   14:18:26.775395 apollo.it.luc.edu.999 > x-terminal.shell: R
   1382726992:1382726992(0) win 0
   14:18:27.174846 x-terminal.shell > apollo.it.luc.edu.998: S
   2022080000:2022080000(0) ack 1382726993 win 4096
   ```

   A. This is a sequence number prediction attack.

   B. This is a normal remote login sequence.

   C. This is a SYN flood.

   D. These are unexpected messages.

3. If you see the IP address fe80::0050:8790:4554:2300/16, the :: indicates what?

   A. There are 1s between the ::.

   B. There are 0s between the ::.

   C. This indicates empty space.

   D. This is a delimiter between addresses.

4. In the network 192.168.5.0/23, what would be the broadcast address?

    A. 192.168.255.255

    B. 192.168.4.0

    C. 192.168.1.0

    D. 192.168.5.255

5. In the address ab00:fc87:234a:0090:5120:ffab:bc8a:0098/23, what does the /23 indicate?

    A. The number of bits in the network portion of the address

    B. The address of the router

    C. The host address

    D. The position in the address where the messages should be sent

6. How many bits are in the NETWORK portion of the following address block:

```
Address: 10.1.0.0
Subnet:  255.255.255.224
```

    A. 24

    B. 32

    C. 27

    D. 29

7. What class is the address 170.19.82.45?

    A. A

    B. B

    C. C

    D. D

8. What is the order of messages in a three-way handshake?

    A. SYN, ACK, ACK

    B. ACK, SYN, ACK

    C. SYN/ACK, ACK, SYN

    D. SYN, SYN/ACK, ACK

9. Which of the following is a private address (RFC 1918)?

    A. 128.15.29.0

    B. 10.45.60.10

    C. 192.192.192.1

    D. 1.1.1.1

10. Which utility makes use of ICMP to function?

   A. icmpstat

   B. netstat

   C. whasup

   D. traceroute

11. Which TCP header field determines how much data can be transmitted before receiving an acknowledgment?

   A. IPID

   B. Sequence Number

   C. Window Size

   D. PSH Flag

12. Which protocol has only an eight-byte header?

   A. IP

   B. UDP

   C. TCP

   D. ARP

13. What is a significant change between IPv4 and IPv6?

   A. No UDP is needed IPv6.

   B. TCP doesn't use a three-way handshake in IPv6.

   C. Layer 2 is bypassed in IPv6.

   D. The address is longer in IPv6.

14. Which of the following is a new field in IPv6?

   A. Flow Label

   B. IPID

   C. IP Address

   D. Don't Fragment

15. Which of the following is not one of the layers in the OSI model?

   A. Application

   B. Transport

   C. Internet

   D. Presentation

Answers

1. **C.** The last four bytes of the header are the destination address. Converting the hexadecimal back to decimal gets the correct IP address. You would do this by converting each byte to decimal. You can do this by multiplying the value in the 16s place (what you would normally think of as the 10s place) by 16, and then adding the value in the 1s place. So, AD would be $10 \times 16 + 13 = 173$. If you start in the fourth octet and get the result, you may only need to calculate one value.

2. **A.** This is a sequence number prediction attack. If you look at the sequence number from the server, you'll see that it increments by a predictable amount each time. You would subtract 2021824000 from 2021952000 and see that it is 128000. Similarly, subtracting 2021952000 from 2022080000 will also give you 128000. That is a predictable value.

3. **B.** When you see :: in an IPv6 address, this indicates there are 0s that aren't being displayed.

4. **D.** 192.168.5.0/23 indicates that there are nine bits available for host addresses. The additional bit carries over into the third octet. In this case, you'd get two consecutive numbers in the third octet that were part of the same network. In this case, 0–1, 2–3, 4–5 are all in the same network. Since 5 is the top of the range and the broadcast is the last address in any network range, the correct broadcast address for this network is 192.168.5.255. The network address would be 192.168.4.0.

5. **A.** Just as with CIDR, in IPv6, the /23 would indicate the number of bits in the network portion of the address.

6. **C.** The first three octets are full, which means 24 bits are used for the network. Twenty-five bits would put a 128 in the last octet, 26 would be 192, and 27 would be 224, because we add on the next less power of two each time we add a bit. Thus, we have 128 + 64 + 32.

7. **B.** The first octet of the address is 170. A Class A address has 0–127 in the first octet, Class B is 128–191, and Class C is 192–223. 170 falls into the Class B range.

8. **D.** The three-way handshake in TCP begins with a SYN message to synchronize the initial sequence number. The response to that message acknowledges the SYN with an ACK and sends a SYN of its own, so the second message is a SYN/ACK. The final message is the sender responding with an ACK to the SYN.

9. **B.** The address 10.45.60.10 falls into the range 10.0.0.0–10.255.255.255, which is the Class A private address space.

10. **D.** The traceroute utility makes use of ICMP for a time exceeded in transit message and a destination unreachable message.

11. **C.** The window size is the amount of data that can be sent before getting an acknowledgment from the other end. This makes sure that the two sides are in sync and one side doesn't get too far ahead before an issue is identified. The IPID field is an IP header field used to identify all frames that belong to a single packet. The sequence number is used to keep messages in order. The PSH flag is used to push data to the application without buffering further.

12. **B.** The UDP header is just eight bytes. The IP header is 20 bytes long. The same is true as the basic headers for TCP, though TCP headers can be longer if there are options set. ARP is not a protocol that has headers. ARP makes use of layer 2 headers.

13. **D.** An IPv6 address is 128 bits while an IPv4 is only 32 bits. UDP has not been removed from IPv6. The layer 2 address can be part of the IPv6 address, but the layer 2 address is still necessary. TCP continues to use the three-way handshake in IPv6.

14. **A.** While the IPv4 headers have some quality of service capabilities, those capabilities are enhanced significantly in IPv6. Flow Label is one of the fields that helps to implement quality of service. All of the other fields exist in IPv4.

15. **C.** There are some similarities between the OSI model and the TCP/IP architecture. The Application layer and Transport layer are the same between them. The Presentation layer is a part of the OSI model. While the Network layer is part of the OSI model, the Internet layer is part of the TCP/IP architecture. The Internetwork layer doesn't exist.

Exercise Answers

Exercise 2-1

a. You convert the hexadecimal CD to decimal by multiplying C, or 12 in decimal, times 16. 12 × 16 = 192. Add D, or 13 in decimal, to the result and you have 192 + 13 = 205.

b. In order to convert 132 to hexadecimal, you may pass through binary first. This means you have to think in powers of 2. In a byte, 2^7 is 128 and the most significant bit in that byte. That means we know we have a 1 in the most significant bit position. 132 − 128 is 4. 2^2 is 4, so the third position from the right is a 1. If we break the byte up into nibbles, it looks like this: 1000 0100. This makes it easy to convert to hexadecimal, since a hexadecimal digit is represented as four bits in binary. What we end up with is 84. The most significant digit in that number is the leftmost position, which is $16^1 \times 8$, which is 128. The least significant digit is just the value in that position ($16^0 \times 4$).

Exercise 2-2   Twenty-five bits are used for the network, with three sets of eight bits, plus an additional bit in the last octet. There are a total of 32 bits available, so that leaves 7 bits for the host.

Network Design

In this chapter, you will learn:

- Network topologies, including network cables that may be used
- Fundamentals of switching
- Fundamentals of routing
- Security technologies as part of network design

Network design and architecture encompasses a lot of elements and every one of them has a potential impact on the overall security posture of a network. In order to design a network, though, and consider how to implement a network design, we are going to need to drop back to some layer 2 concepts. This means understanding cabling. Not every network is wireless. This is especially true in an enterprise network, even more so as you move closer to the core where essential systems and applications are. These systems are all going to be hard-wired, meaning they will be connected to the network with cables, rather than wireless. Depending on the network and the speed required, these systems may use different types of cabling, which will have different connectors and different needs when it comes to cabling and space.

There are a number of conceptual ways of putting the network together—meaning, how systems are logically connected. This is where topologies come in. In some cases, different cabling will lend itself more to one type of topology than another. You probably are familiar with some very common topologies and do not even realize it. As they are more conceptual than real, you will also find that you can put different topologies together to create hybrid models that work very well.

We're also going to revisit the differences between layers in this chapter. Getting traffic from one system to another will be different depending on where the systems are located. If they are located on the same network segment, the traffic will be transmitted using layer 2 addresses. This means, as far as moving through the network goes, the traffic is being switched. Decisions are being made at the layer 2 header. However, if two systems are on entirely different network segments—and this is especially true when you are communicating with a system on the Internet somewhere—you have to rely on your layer 3 headers to get from point A to point F. This means your traffic is being routed. It's very useful to understand the differentiation between switching and routing. This includes the different algorithms that are used to make routing decisions.

When it comes to designing a network, there is security technology to consider. Inside your network equipment, you may have some capabilities to filter traffic. That's one aspect of a complete set of security controls over network traffic. You may also find it necessary to have a firewall or an intrusion detection system. These days, intrusion prevention systems are also commonly found. These are essentially hybrids between firewalls and intrusion detection systems. There are also next-generation firewalls that combine multiple functions into a single device.

Cable Types

A number of different cable types are used in networking. They usually fall into two categories: copper and fiber. Copper tends to be either coaxial cable, along the lines of what you would see from a cable television or satellite television system, or twisted pair cables. In newer homes, you may see these twisted pair cables run through the house to provide networking and/or phone service. Older phone cables basically use the same wires, but the number of pairs and the twisting make them quite a bit different than networking cables.

Coaxial Cable

Coaxial, or coax, cable was first developed in the late 1800s and is constructed of a solid copper wire core that is surrounded by an insulator, then a metal shield, and finally an insulating jacket that can be made from a number of materials, including PVC. Coaxial cable tends to be thick and somewhat rigid, which can make it challenging to run since it often lacks the flexibility to be put easily into spaces where there are tight turns or changes of direction. Ethernet over coax cable was sometimes called thicknet because of the thickness of the cable. We will discuss the Ethernet protocol in more detail later in this chapter. A major advantage to coax cable, though, is that it insulates itself both from signal leakage out of the cabling and from interference into the cable from outside sources. This protects the integrity of the signal being carried.

Ethernet first used coax cable, and the standard was called 10BASE5 because it was capable of 10 Mbps using baseband signaling and was capable of transmitting a distance of 500 meters, which is where the 5 comes from. Coax cabling with Ethernet was used in a bus network topology, which is described later in this chapter. The 500-meter length of a single run is a significant advantage over other cable types, which is what made it ideal in bus networks where you needed one long run of cable to serve as the backbone or bus for the network.

Twisted Pair

Twisted pair cabling is a cable that has a number of pairs of thin wires twisted together. Typically, you would have four pairs of wires in a network cable, although only two pairs are in use. One pair is used to transmit and the other pair is used to receive. Standard twisted pair cabling for Ethernet is wired so the pins are connected to the same wires on each end. This is because when you connect to a network device like a hub or a switch, the device knows which pins are transmit and which are receive and it handles converting the transmit on the inbound to the receive on the outbound. You would use a crossover cable to connect two systems directly to one another. The crossover cable crosses the transmit over to the receive and vice versa; otherwise, you would be sending out on the transmit wires and having it come in on the transmit wires on the receiving end. As you might expect, this doesn't work too well. It's like whispering quietly into someone's mouth.

EXAM TIP   It's helpful to know how much bandwidth you can get from each cable type, so pay close attention to Table 3-1.

There are different categories of network cabling. Most of them are identified by Cat (short for category) followed by a number. Higher categories have better materials that allow for more bandwidth. The currently identified categories are shown in Table 3-1.

NOTE   The 100BASE-T4 indicates a standard that wasn't much used but got 100 Mbps by using all four pairs of wires in the cable rather than just the two pairs typically used.

You may well wonder why the pairs of wires are twisted. Alexander Graham Bell came up with twisted pair cabling in the late 1880s. If you just run wires together in the same sheath, you can end up with *crosstalk*, meaning the signals on each set of wires end up mixing with one another. You can mitigate this, though, by twisting the pairs of wires, because when you twist, each wire isn't close enough to one other wire long enough to actually exchange the signal. Twisted pair is typically unshielded, which means it's vulnerable to electromagnetic interference (EMI), something that can cause corruption of the signal going across the wire. This can be fixed by shielding the cable. This is usually done by wrapping the pairs in foil before putting the sheath on. When you wrap the bundle of pairs in foil, you get shielded twisted pair. You can also use a wire screen to wrap the wires and get screened twisted pair. This also protects the wires from EMI.

Some of the big advantages to twisted pair cabling have to do with how thin the cable is compared with the thickness of coax cabling. Additionally, it's very flexible, making it easy to run twisted pair cabling between walls, through cable ducts, and through ceilings.

Cable Type	Bandwidth	Use
Level 1	0.4 MHz	Phone lines
Level 2	4 MHz	Terminal lines
Cat 3	16 MHz (10 Mbps)	10BASE-T and 100BASE-T4
Cat 4	20 MHz (16 Mbps)	10BASE-T, 100BASE-T4, and 16-Mbps Token Ring
Cat 5	100 MHz (1 Gbps)	10BASE-T, 100BASE-TX, and 1000BASE-T
Cat 5e	100 MHz (1 Gbps)	100BASE-TX and 1000BASE-T
Cat 6	250 MHz (10 Gbps)	10GBASE-T

Table 3-1   Cable Types and Bandwidths

Figure 3-1
A network
interface with
coax adapter and
Cat 5 cabling

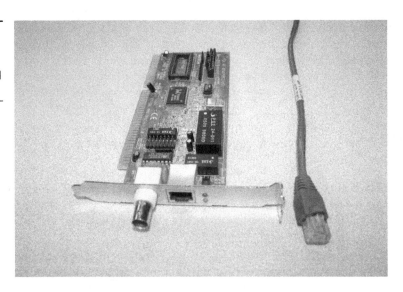

Twisted pair also minimizes crosstalk, although without shielding, it can be susceptible to EMI. In some areas, this can be a significant challenge.

Cat 5 cabling was the most common cable used for Ethernet networks, though Cat 5e or Cat 6 is superseding it primarily because Cat 5e has higher testing standards and Cat 6 supports higher bandwidths. All of those cable types have a maximum length of 100 meters (328 feet). Beyond this length, the signal begins to degrade to the point where it may become unusable. This is dependent, however, on how the cable has been manufactured. If you use homemade cables and the crimp at the terminator isn't strong, you may end up with significant attenuation well before the theoretical maximum length of the cable. Just because the cabling can support long runs doesn't mean that the environment or the rest of the equipment won't have an impact on the signal quality.

Figure 3-1 is a photograph of Cat 5 cabling alongside a network interface card (NIC) that has an adapter to take a coaxial cable with a BNC connector. The BNC connector takes up more exterior space with the NIC and, much like the RJ45 connector on the twisted pair cable, uses a quick connect/disconnect system. In the case of the BNC connector, there is a pin that goes into a groove on the cable portion that has a resting place, keeping the cabling on. The RJ45 connector is simply a female socket on the adapter. There is a clip on the terminator on the cable that will click into place in the adapter, keeping the cable from sliding out.

Fiber Optics

Fiber optic cabling, also called fiber, uses very thin strands of glass to transmit light signals. A fiber optic cable consists of the inner, glass core and the outer cladding. The cladding is selected for its reflective properties in order to keep the light within the glass core. A significant advantage of fiber optic cabling over other cable types is the speed at which the signal can be transmitted. This is different from the width of the signal, which gives you the amount of data you can send. The time it takes a signal to get from one end of a fiber cable to the other end is limited only by the speed of light. Copper cabling is significantly slower, sometimes having a velocity factor less than half of the speed of light. Not surprisingly, a faster delivery speed ends up providing better throughput on the line.

There are two types of fiber optic cable that can be used, and the equipment used to support each is different. The first type of cable is single-mode fiber. Single-mode fiber contains one ray of light per fiber, and the single-mode fiber is capable of carrying a signal thousands of kilometers. This distance is dependent on the amount of bandwidth being used. If you want to have more bandwidth, the signal won't go as far.

Multimode fiber contains a number of rays of light. The light source for multimode fiber is often a light-emitting diode (LED) and it won't carry nearly as far as single mode. While single-mode fiber can have spans in the thousands of miles, multimode fiber can only have runs in the hundreds of meters to about 2000 meters. As with single-mode fiber, the higher the bandwidth, the shorter you can run multimode fiber. While 100 Mbps can go 2000 meters, if you want 100 Gbps, you can only go as long as 150 meters.

A huge advantage of fiber is that it can carry data at much higher rates than other types of cabling. At this point, fiber has been shown to carry traffic at speeds over 100 Gbps, though commonly speeds are much lower than that. It's also very thin and lightweight, though it doesn't have quite the flexibility of other cabling like twisted pair. Wiretapping was previously more difficult to accomplish with fiber optic cabling since it had used a signal splitting technique where part of the optical signal was sent to one cable, while a smaller part was sent to another cable. There are other tapping techniques like using microbends that cause light to leak out of the bent cable, allowing it to be seen and collected. However, either of these types of techniques can potentially be discovered.

By comparison, coax cable can be tapped with a vampire tap that inserts spikes into the cable in order to extract the signal without significant degradation that may cause it to be noticed.

Figure 3-2 shows fiber optic cabling. You can see the cladding (orange) on the cable, which is pretty common. If you see big orange piping on the side of the road, it probably means they are running fiber and inserting it into that orange conduit.

Figure 3-2
Fiber optic
cabling

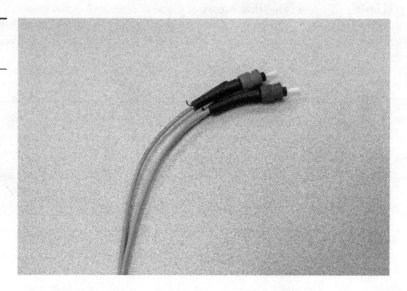

Network Topologies

Just as in looking at the geography of a particular area with hills and valleys, rivers and streams, networks have a topology to describe what they look like. A topology describes how systems are cabled to one another and to networking hardware. This is more of a logical notion to help explain how everything is put together, though there is enough of a physical connection to it that it is descriptive. There are a few different networking topologies, including star, bus, mesh, and full mesh, though you will sometimes see hybrids of those topologies.

The hybrids end up working well because you get the benefits of the component topologies and potentially minimize the downsides of each. As we get through the various topologies typically implemented, we will go over the ways that different topologies can be implemented in a hybrid manner and how those different topologies complement one another in a hybrid implementation.

Bus Topology

The bus topology is one of the early networking topologies. In this sense, it's not a conveyance like the large yellow vehicle you probably took to school every day. Instead, you can think of it as a way to get information from one place to another, similar to a system bus that moves data around inside of a computer system. The implementation of the bus here is one long cable that all of the systems attach to, as demonstrated in Figure 3-3. The bus topology has some advantages in that it's easy to implement and doesn't require any additional networking infrastructure outside of the cabling and the network interface cards needed for each system attached to the network. With a bus, you run one long cable passing by everywhere you want to have networking and then connect systems to it. This does require tapping into the cable that gets run. You also have an issue where an open cable doesn't actually transmit any electrical signal very well. Because of that, each end of the cable needs to be terminated to make sure the signal stays on the cable so all the data can be read when it's needed.

Having this one cable that everything else connects to helps save cable as compared to other topologies. You would be using roughly just the amount of cable you need to get everything wired up. Because of the way the network is cabled, having one system

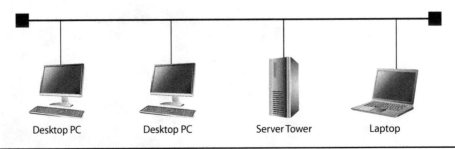

| Desktop PC | Desktop PC | Server Tower | Laptop |

Figure 3-3   Bus topology

go down won't affect the other systems on the network. There are also no networking components that could cause outages to the entire network, unlike other networking topologies. Since there is a single cable providing the backbone to the network, however, you need a way to connect other devices to the bus. This is done through the use of a T connector. The T connector is so-named because it resembles the letter. Imagine the backbone or bus cable providing the top line of the T while the system you are connecting goes out the single leg on the bottom. That's how a T connector works. You put a T in where you want to connect a system and then connect a separate cable to the T connector to run to the system.

In addition to T connectors being required to attach systems, a bus network using coaxial cable also requires a device on either end of the cable to ensure that signals don't get reflected back off the end of the cable. Too much signal being reflected back might cause all the systems on the bus to lose connectivity. This device is called a *terminator*, and it keeps the electrical signal from reflecting back by inserting a resistor onto the cable, since what's being transmitted is really just an electrical signal.

Other topologies may require more active participation by the nodes on the network. They may be required to send packets through to other network participants. This isn't true in a bus topology. With a bus topology, the participants are passive. They listen to the line to see when packets on the line are destined for them, at which point they pick up the message. When they send, they just drop the packets out on the wire. If there is a problem sending, they resend, but ultimately, there is nothing else required other than to just drop the message on the wire and let the wire deliver it to where it needs to go.

There are, however, some downsides, since any cabling has its physical limitations, beyond which the electrical signal passing through the cabling degrades to the point where it can't be measured well enough to do anything useful with it. The *gauge*, or thickness, of the cable determines how far the cable can run before it begins to lose the ability to effectively carry the signal. The thicker the cable is, the better the cable is able to maintain the signal over longer distances.

The biggest disadvantage to the bus topology is that it has a single point of failure. The main cable that forms the backbone of the bus is that one point of failure. If anything happens to that cable, all communications will fail. This could be a break in the line or another type of fault. Additionally, once you have the bus installed, it's difficult to make any changes without installing an entirely new bus.

If you're old enough to remember party lines on telephones, another downside of the bus topology may sound familiar to you. As the telephone system was being built out, the phone companies lacked the capacity to allow everyone to have a dedicated line in the switch at the central office where all the phone lines in a community ran into. The way they handled that was by offering party lines, which meant that several households would share a dedicated switch location. In a practical sense, this meant that when you picked up your phone to place a call, you might have been listening in on your neighbor's phone call, which would have prohibited you from making your call until the existing call completed. The same is essentially true on the bus topology. With the bus topology, you essentially get one big party line that everyone shares. When you send a packet, it may run into another packet on the line. This is called a *collision* and, just like when you picked up your phone to hear another conversation, it prevents you from completing your transmission. It may also disrupt the existing transmission, just as picking up your phone and making noise on the line may disrupt that existing conversation.

 CAUTION Collisions disrupt both the packet being sent and the packet already on the line. It will lead to retransmissions and, as a result, delays in eventual delivery.

In some ways, you may consider wireless networks to be examples of bus topologies since they are using a shared medium—the air. Just as you can run into collisions with a wired network, you can have problems with two stations transmitting on the same channel in a wireless network. When this happens, it's the same thing as when you are driving in your car listening to one radio station and you get just far enough away from the signal source that you cross into air space where another station starts to creep in. You get overlapping signals and maybe some static, which is what happens when two wireless devices try to communicate on the same frequency at the same time, because a wireless device is really just a radio transmitter using a different set of frequencies than those that radio stations use.

Star Topology

The star topology gets its name from the fact that there is a central networking device that systems connect to. That central networking device is a switch or a hub (described later in the chapter in the section "Hubs, Bridges, and Switches"). If you were to draw the topology logically, as in Figure 3-4, it does have a rough resemblance to a star with a center and arms reaching out from that center. You might also see it as a bit of an octopus

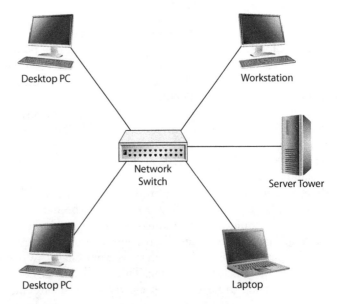

Figure 3-4
Star topology

if you were to draw out the way it really looks with cables on the floor and stretching in all sorts of wild directions.

There are advantages to using a star model. It's generally easy to implement and it's very flexible. Adding a node is easy because you just plug another device into your switch or hub. A star topology doesn't involve the same sharing of media that there is with a bus topology. This results in some additional performance since there isn't as much traffic running through each cable, particularly if you are using a switch that will further limit the amount of traffic by making intelligent decisions about where to send each packet as it passes through.

This centralized approach offers some other benefits. As noted, adding a network node is as simple as plugging another cable into the switch or hub, and centralizing can make that easier. Centralizing also provides the ability to monitor what's happening from one location. This includes not only network monitoring, along the lines of performing packet captures, but also physical monitoring. Since most switches or hubs have lights indicating various things like connection state or speed, you can get a quick sense of whether there is a problem with the network by checking the lights. If they are all off, you likely have a problem with the switch. Individual lights out can indicate a problem with either the cable or the system it's attached to. This saves running around the building checking individual systems. You may eventually need to do that anyway, but checking the lights is at least a starting point that can give you some indication as to where you may have problems.

You will also get the benefit of isolation with the star topology. In addition to the performance benefits you get from not having a single shared medium, the isolation gives you the ability to quickly remove a device from the network without impacting any other device. Also, if anything happens to any one particular device and it starts jabbering or sending out a lot of traffic, the impact to the network and other devices is minimized by using the star topology, particularly as compared with other topologies.

The primary disadvantage of the star topology is the fact that you have one central networking device and if anything happens to that device, your entire network goes out. This is a single point of failure and there is no way of protecting against it since you can't have redundancy here because of the physical restriction of having one cable running into this central networking device. You can have multiple power supplies and other capabilities in the switch that can keep it up and running, but ultimately you still have that single point of failure that can cause a network-wide outage.

 EXAM TIP A star topology uses a lot of cabling because it requires using home runs back to the switch or hub at the center of the network.

While a wireless network may look like a bus topology because of the shared medium of the airwaves the transmissions are happening over, it looks logically like a star topology because you have the central networking device, the wireless access point that all of the devices connect to. This isn't a hybrid topology. It just shares some characteristics of both networking topologies.

Star-Bus Hybrid

While bus topologies aren't as common any longer, the bus topology combined with the star topology is very common. The reason for this is that you often don't have a case where a single switch or hub can handle all of the connections within a network. As a result, you may have multiple switches in your network that all of your devices connect to. Without connecting those separate switches together, the only systems you would be able to communicate with are those that are also connected to the same switch as your system. You can fix this, though, by connecting all of the switches together. When you connect all of the switches together, what you have effectively created is a bus that connects all of the switches together, with a star radiating out from each switch. You can see this in Figure 3-5. The two network switches are connected together, and if you add more switches into your network, you would just extend the lines to any other switch in the network.

 NOTE   One consideration as you develop a star-bus hybrid network is the fact that you may have more traffic passing between switches than you would passing between each individual system and the central switch it's connected to. Because of that, you may want to ensure you have higher bandwidth connections between the switches to ensure you don't experience any bottlenecks.

Figure 3-5
Star-bus hybrid topology with two switches

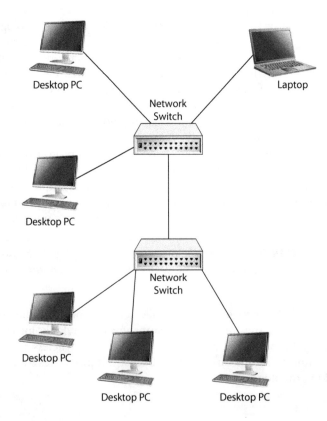

Mesh Topology

A mesh topology is not very common in a situation where you are connecting desktop systems, but it would be common in a situation where you are connecting multiple networks together. A mesh network is where each node not only has to send its own data but also move data from other nodes. This is actually common in a peer-to-peer network where messages may need to be forwarded from one system to another by way of intermediaries. This is because there isn't one central routing authority to refer to in most cases to determine how to get messages from one place to another, so the intelligence of the network is how messages get around. Figure 3-6 is an example of a simple mesh network. You can see that each node is connected directly to another node. There is no bus that they all connect to and there is no central networking device that they all connect to. However, every node doesn't have a direct, point-to-point connection to every other node on the network, and so this might commonly be called a partial mesh.

Skype was originally a peer-to-peer mesh network. The systems involved in the network had direct connections to one another. There was no central location where all the traffic went back to in order to be distributed out to the endpoints. Instead, the systems were responsible for getting the traffic off to the other locations on their own. Along the same lines, you might consider the Tor (The Onion Router) network to be a mesh network since all of the participants can act as both clients and the devices responsible for forwarding traffic through the network.

 NOTE Tor is a peer-to-peer network used to provide anonymity for its users by masking the original source IP address from the destination. In general, peer-to-peer networks are often mesh networks.

Similarly, the Internet as a whole is a mesh network. Different networks and locations are all connected together, and each node in the network is responsible for passing traffic

Figure 3-6
A mesh network

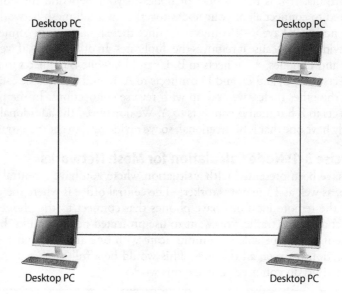

Desktop PC

Desktop PC

Desktop PC

Desktop PC

along so it can get from the source all the way to the destination. In the case of the Internet, each node in the mesh is actually a router, designed to be capable of forwarding packets coming in to another location altogether.

An advantage to mesh networks is that all the connections between nodes are dedicated, which can make troubleshooting much easier. If I can't get a message from A to B but I can get a message from C to A and C to B, the link between A and B is clearly at fault. Those dedicated links and having a network map make troubleshooting far more convenient than in a topology like a bus network.

 NOTE Mesh networks are special purpose and not commonly used in a situation like a desktop environment.

In a mesh network, every node either is a router, as in the Internet, or behaves like a router as in a peer-to-peer network. This can be a disadvantage in some cases. If you are in a peer-to-peer network, you may be expected to push traffic through your system, using up bandwidth and consuming other system resources. While this is known and expected in a group of networks like those that comprise the Internet, on a smaller scale the ramifications of participating in such a network may be less well understood.

Full Mesh Topology

A full mesh topology is related to a mesh topology, not surprisingly. The difference is that in a mesh topology you may have nodes that are connected minimally to the rest of the nodes in the network. You can end up with node isolation in that case. A full mesh network resolves that issue by having every node connected to every other node. This can, of course, result in a very complex network depending on the number of nodes. You can easily calculate the number of connections based on the number of nodes with a simple formula. If n is the number of nodes in your network, the number of connections required to connect all of your nodes together in a full mesh network is $(n \times (n - 1)) / 2$. Every node will have $n - 1$ connections since there is no point in connecting a node to itself. We divide by 2 because it removes the duplicates. In other words, if we have a network of A, B, C, and D nodes, A connects to B, C, and D, while B connects to A, C, and D, then C connects to A, B, and D, and D connects to A, B, and C. Because each node is connecting to all the other nodes, we end up with reverse connections. In the preceding example, A connects to B but then B connects to A. We don't need the additional connection since we already have one that is bidirectional, so we divide by 2 to get the extras out of the equation.

Exercise 3-1: Node Calculation for Mesh Networks

You have been presented with a situation where you have a central office and a satellite office, as well as 15 remote workers. The central office is where the phone system is, and all of the remote locations have phones that connect to the phone system. In order to protect all of the traffic, you want to use protected network links, but to allow all of the different sites to be able to communicate with one another, you need to set up a direct connection between all the sites. This would be a full mesh network. How many total connections do you need to make this work?

The downside to a full mesh topology, as noted, is complexity. The upside, as you may have guessed, is that you never end up with nodes that are isolated because another node has gone down. In a mesh network, you may end up relying on one node to get traffic from the rest of the network. In a full mesh, any node can send to your node, so there could be a number of routes for getting messages to your node. Not only does this lead to management and administrative complexity, it can also lead to routing complexity because every node now has a number of ways of getting to any other node. This can lead to a management challenge, too, if you are configuring the routing paths manually. Fortunately, there are better ways of handling that particular challenge.

Complexity not only causes administrative and management headaches, which can sometimes lead to unexpected outages, but it also leads to extensive costs. Having a direct connection between every single node on your network may provide good fault tolerance, but it can be very expensive, regardless of the connection type used between each individual node or location. Figure 3-7 demonstrates the complexity involved with having a full mesh topology.

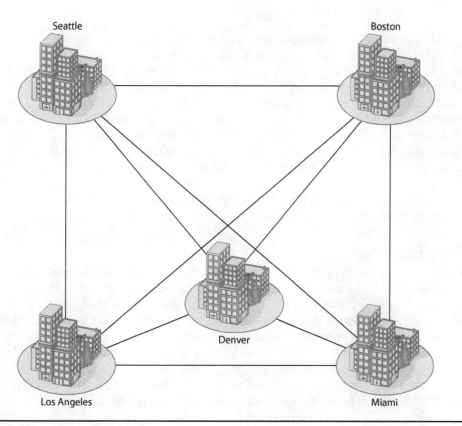

Figure 3-7 A full mesh network

You can see all of the connections required for even a simple network, as depicted in the five-node network in Figure 3-7. Using the preceding formula, we can see that there are $(5 \times 4) / 2 = 10$ connections required to have a full mesh network with five nodes. In this case, we get

1. Boston ↔ Miami
2. Boston ↔ Denver
3. Boston ↔ Los Angeles
4. Boston ↔ Seattle
5. Miami ↔ Denver
6. Miami ↔ Los Angeles
7. Miami ↔ Seattle
8. Denver ↔ Los Angeles
9. Denver ↔ Seattle
10. Los Angeles ↔ Seattle

You may use a full mesh topology when you are developing a wide area network (WAN) either using direct lines or virtual private network (VPN) connections. You may want to ensure that all of your office locations have connectivity to one another all the time without needing to rely on one location as a central hub that distributes messages around. In a mesh network, if a node goes offline, it may isolate other nodes, which could mean large sections of your organization don't have connectivity to one another. In the case of a full mesh network, you don't have that issue because you always have dedicated lines to all locations. If one of your sites goes offline, the only site affected is the offline site. Redundancy in your network connections is only one component of a fully redundant system. There are system-level components to take into consideration as well, but on the network side, a full mesh topology will provide the redundancy necessary to give connectivity to all of your locations.

Ring Topology

A ring topology or ring network is much like a bus network with the ends connected to one another. It also shares some characteristics with a mesh network in that the individual nodes on the network handle the messages and send them along. Because of this, a break in any line within the ring can mean that the entire network goes down. A ring network can perform better than a bus network under heavy load and also doesn't have the disadvantage of requiring a central networking device like a star topology does. However, the larger a ring network gets, the longer it takes communications to pass through the network. Any time a station is added or moved or removed can impact the network, unlike other topologies where similar changes would have no impact.

One implementation of a ring network that was very common for a while was developed by IBM. They created an implementation of a ring topology and called it Token Ring,

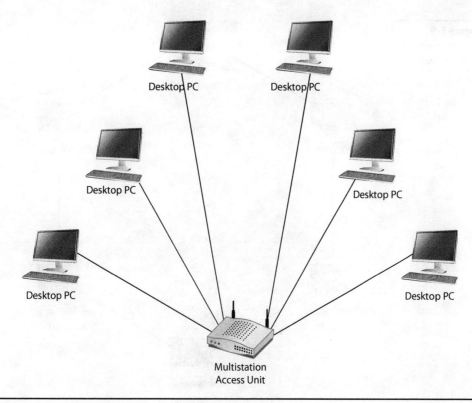

Figure 3-8   Physical layout of a ring network

but they did something a little different. A Token Ring network is implemented like a star at the physical layer with all of the stations being cabled to a central location. A Token Ring network uses a Multistation Access Unit (MAU) to make the network behave like a ring in spite of being cabled like a star. Figure 3-8 shows how a ring network is physically cabled between the workstations and the MAU. Figure 3-9 shows how the ring network is logically organized, making it seem as though the workstations are cabled directly to one another in a ring. The Token Ring implementation sought to solve the issue of collisions that can happen in other topologies by using an electronic implementation of a talking stick (used in a group discussion to limit who may speak—only the person holding the stick can speak). You can only communicate on the network if you have the token, which is passed continuously around the ring.

There are downsides to a Token Ring network, however, if the token gets lost, which could happen if a system that has the ring loses power or experiences some other type of outage. At that point, the token would need to be regenerated, and although there are specifications for how that happens, time is lost on the network because no station is able to transmit during the regeneration process. Similarly, as noted earlier, a break in the line can cause an entire ring network to go down. There are mechanisms to protect

Figure 3-9
Logical layout of
a ring network

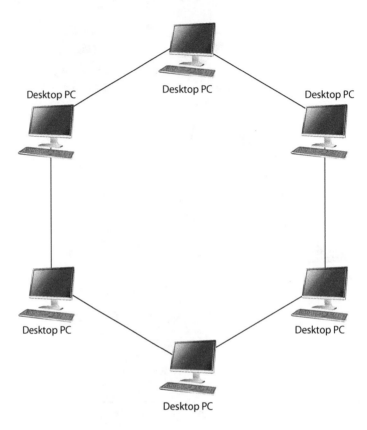

Desktop PC

Desktop PC

Desktop PC

Desktop PC

Desktop PC

Desktop PC

against that, but they are typically implemented only in high-end networks because they are expensive and typically require redundant paths around the ring.

Rings aren't only deployed in desktop environments. In fact, they are probably more commonly found in service provider or carrier networks where large rings of fiber using the Fiber Distributed Data Interface (FDDI) or Synchronous Optical Networking (SONET) protocols are used. SONET and FDDI are implemented as rings. These networks get around the issue of line outages causing the whole ring to go down by deploying redundant rings, thus ensuring that data can always be carried around the ring unless something catastrophic happens and takes down both rings simultaneously.

Switching

While some network topologies lend themselves to having the data make its way through the network with the assistance of each individual node, other topologies and network protocols need some assistance. In the case of the star topology, for example, since the cabling doesn't directly connect all of the nodes together, there is a need for a central device capable of pushing the signal around the network and making sure it gets to the right place.

Switching is how we move messages around at layer 2 of the OSI model. It relies on a physical address that is attached to the network interface of the recipient. The physical address is dependent on the protocol being used at layer 2. There are a number of layer 2 protocols, but there is one in particular that is commonly in use. That protocol is called Ethernet and we will use it as the model for our discussion about switching.

Ethernet

Robert Metcalfe developed Ethernet in the early 1970s at the Xerox Palo Alto Research Center (PARC). Metcalfe developed Ethernet as a result of studying ALOHAnet, a wireless network that began to be used in Hawaii in the late 1960s.

NOTE At the time, Xerox was doing a lot of work developing technologies that proved to be the foundation of desktop computing—development of the graphical user interface, use of the mouse, and development of a desktop networking protocol.

Ethernet specifies both physical (layer 1) and data link (layer 2) components. The cabling and NICs in use, of course, live at the Physical layer, while the means by which the cabling and interfaces are used are at the Data Link layer. Ethernet specifies a 48-bit address to identify each network interface. Since this address is attached to a physical device, the network interface, it is sometimes called a physical address, but it is also called a media access control (MAC) address. The MAC address is meant to be globally unique, meaning there will never be any two addresses that are the same anywhere on the planet.

Organizationally, the MAC address is broken up into two sections of three bytes. The first three bytes belong to the Organizationally Unique Identifier (OUI), which identifies the company that made the device. This is sometimes called the vendor ID. The second set of three bytes is the identifier of the interface card itself. A MAC address is typically written as a set of six hexadecimal numbers, usually separated by either a colon (:) or a hyphen (-). An example address is 34:15:9e:00:c0:64. The first three bytes are 34:15:9e, which are the hexadecimal numbers representing the vendor ID. The second three bytes are 00:c0:64, which is the interface ID.

NOTE Because the vendor ID is known, you can look up the vendor for any interface that you have a MAC address for. This can be very helpful in determining the system associated with it. As an example, if I were to scan my local network looking for the IP address for a Mac Mini because I'm too lazy to get up and go downstairs to look it up, I could check the scan results for a vendor ID of Apple in the MAC address. Tools like Nmap and Wireshark will translate the vendor ID for you and display it in human-readable form.

The MAC address is how systems on a local network communicate with one another. The MAC address doesn't work beyond the local network. In fact, as packets are transmitted from one network to another, the MAC address is removed along with the entire layer 2 header, and another layer 2 header is put on in its place. You may be wondering why we need two addresses on each interface—a MAC address and an IP address. Since a NIC may carry multiple higher-layer protocols aside from IP, it's easier for the network interface itself to be addressable. Also, IP addresses need to be aggregated in order to keep network maps down to a reasonable size to make routing more efficient. MAC addresses can't be easily aggregated, so they don't have much value outside of a reasonably sized local network.

Address Resolution Protocol (ARP)

This does bring up an issue, though, of needing to be able to translate an IP address to a MAC address. This is handled by using the Address Resolution Protocol. ARP is a two-stage protocol. The first stage is a request by a system that knows an IP address but doesn't know the MAC address to deliver to. The ARP request is sent as a broadcast to all of the devices on the network, indicating that it's a request and including the IP address. In the second stage, the system that has that IP address issues an ARP reply to that request and fills in the missing MAC address, sending it back out to the requestor. You can see an ARP exchange in the following text. The ARP request operation code (opcode) gets converted into the words who-has while the ARP response opcode gets converted into the words is-at. This is what the tcpdump utility and other packet capture tools use to make it clear what's happening.

```
09:53:05.956006 ARP, Request who-has oliver.westell.com tell dslrouter.westell.com, length 46
09:53:05.956084 ARP, Reply oliver.westell.com is-at f8:1e:df:e2:4d:bd (oui Unknown), length 28
```

There is a downside to ARP, however. You may have noticed that the simple two-step process of looking up addresses may be fast and efficient, but it's not exactly secure. There is no way to authenticate either the request or response. When you get a response to an ARP request, you trust it, assuming that the right system is replying. What happens, though, if someone wanted to see messages destined to a particular system? You might get ARP messages sent out suggesting that their IP address mapped to your MAC address. This would ensure that the messages were directed to you.

Taking it a step further, what happens if you simply send out an ARP response that wasn't attached to an ARP request? You simply send out a lot of messages indicating that IP addresses belong to your MAC address. The reason this works is because operating systems store information they receive in order to be more efficient. If they can skip a lookup, they can get messages out onto the wire a lot faster. Since ARP messages are sent out to everyone on the network, every system would see those ARP replies and they could populate their ARP caches based on that information. That way, a lot of ARP lookups can be avoided. However, ARP caches expire after a while, so these gratuitous ARP messages need to be sent out on a regular basis to ensure that all the system ARP caches stay up to date with the MAC address you want messages sent to. There are two problems with this scenario, however. The first is that when messages are sent to your system and not to the correct destination, the destination system will notice the missing traffic and the user will see what looks like their network connection no longer working. This can lead to detection. You can fix this by ensuring that messages get forwarded along to the correct destination after they have passed through your system.

The second problem is that all of these gratuitous ARP responses can be a lot of traffic and it's easy to see them. These two things can cause detection of what's happening, particularly in the case where a network intrusion detection system is in place and monitoring what's happening.

 EXAM TIP   ARP messages are limited to the local network only and would never be used to look up information outside of the local network.

This ARP spoofing will allow you to get messages sent to you in cases where messages may only be sent to you when the destination MAC address is your MAC address. This is true when you have a switch in your network. If your network just has a hub and not a switch, you wouldn't need to do any ARP spoofing because you would get all the traffic anyway.

Asynchronous Transfer Mode (ATM)

ATM is used primarily in large-scale networks to facilitate getting messages to their destination quickly. ATM uses a unit of transmission called a *cell* and the cells are fixed-length. Similar to Ethernet, ATM provides services at the Data Link layer. The question is, why use fixed-length cells when data is variable in nature? The reason is that when ATM was developed in the late 1980s and into the 1990s, there was a need for carriers to have both voice and data on the same shared, public networks. Having fixed-length cells meant that voice traffic would suffer fewer delays, while larger data messages were being carried across the network. Having the voice traffic maintain quality while still being able to carry data was an important factor. Initially, it was thought that ATM not only would work well in carrier networks but could also be extended to the desktop.

A 53-byte cell was a compromise between American and European desires where the Europeans wanted a smaller cell and the Americans, desiring to make the carriage of data more efficient, were looking for larger cells. Eventually, the different groups compromised on the 53-byte cell. This cell consists of 48 bytes of payload and 5 bytes of header. This puts the header at just under 10 percent of the total size of the cell, leaving 90 percent for data. Each cell has a Virtual Path Identifier (VPI) and a Virtual Circuit Identifier (VCI). These two fields together comprise the identity of the next stop a cell makes as it passes through an ATM network. Headers in an ATM cell vary based on whether it's a user-to-network interface (UNI) or a network-to-network interface (NNI). The difference is that with a UNI cell, a Generic Flow Control (GFC) header field is added and some bits are removed from the VPI. Figure 3-10 shows the ATM header fields of a UNI cell. The difference between a UNI cell and an NNI cell is that in an NNI cell, there is no GFC header and those four bits are taken up by an extension to the VPI header.

ATM uses virtual circuits as a way to emulate the circuit switching that the phone companies have been used to doing for decades. There are two kinds of virtual circuits: permanent virtual circuits (PVCs) and switched virtual circuits (SVCs). As you may

Figure 3-10
ATM UNI
headers

Generic Flow Control	Virtual Path Identifier	
Virtual Path Identifier	Virtual Circuit Identifier	
Virtual Circuit Identifier		
Virtual Circuit Identifier	Payload Type	Cell Loss Priority
Header Error Control		
Payload & Padding		

have guessed, a PVC is a dedicated circuit that gets nailed up by configuring it to be up permanently or at least until it is torn down by unconfiguring it. An SVC, on the other hand, is a dynamic circuit that gets tacked up as necessary and as requested by another switch in the network.

 EXAM TIP   Remember that PVCs are permanent and configured manually while SVCs are dynamic in nature and a device in the network would have to request one to be configured.

Hubs, Bridges, and Switches

Before we talk about switches, we need to talk briefly about two other networking devices. The first one is a hub. A hub is a very dumb networking device that is capable of taking an electrical signal in on one set of wires and sending it out across all the other electrical wires connected to it. It's very simply a repeater and nothing more than that. It provides network connectivity in a star network, but it's not very efficient. Everything that gets sent in goes out to all other systems attached. This means that if a system is pushing a lot of traffic through the network, it impacts all other systems on the network because a hub can't make any determinations about where traffic should be going. It is entirely indiscriminate, like an office gossip. We need to have a better way of getting information around local networks.

One way we can protect against a lot of traffic and limit the impact from broadcasts is by using a bridge. A bridge is a network device that connects two network segments, which doesn't sound like it's all that impressive. What a bridge does, though, is isolate the two networks from one another. Traffic that belongs on one side of the bridge stays on that side of the bridge. This means that the bridge keeps a table of all the MAC addresses that it has seen on each side of the bridge so it can filter one side from the other. This can help with network performance by limiting the amount of traffic on either side of the bridge. This doesn't mean there is no way to get packets from one side of the bridge to the other. The bridge operates at layer 2 and makes its decisions based on layer 2 addresses. In this case, it uses the Ethernet or MAC address to pass traffic from one side of the bridge to the other. Figure 3-11 shows a bridged network. If Desktop A is trying to communicate with Desktop E, the bridge will see that those two systems are in networks on opposite sides of the bridge and, as a result, the bridge will carry the frame across to the other network. This is switching.

Moving to switches, in essence, a switch is a multiport bridge. A switch carries a table of MAC addresses and knows which port the MAC address is associated with. This is just like a bridge. Switches use a form of memory called content-addressable memory (CAM) that makes the switch faster by allowing lookups based on a specific type of data. In the case of the switch, you could quickly perform a port lookup based on a MAC address. Rather than looking up a memory address and then accessing that memory address, the memory works by using the piece of data as the address. This saves steps in the lookup process, making the process of switching much faster.

A switch will help performance on a network as well as offer some limited amount of security. When you segment all of your network traffic so that traffic only goes to the specific destination, you get the performance benefit of limiting the number of packets going across each wire. This frees up bandwidth to be used for traffic specific to the system on the end of each wire. Think about it this way. When you want hot water, you turn on the hot water faucet and you get hot water. If you were to also turn on the cold water faucet, the pipe carrying the water would have to carry both cold and hot water, which means less room for the hot water and, as a result, water that is less hot. What you really want is the pipe being used for only hot water. Similarly, in a network, you really

Figure 3-11
A bridged
network

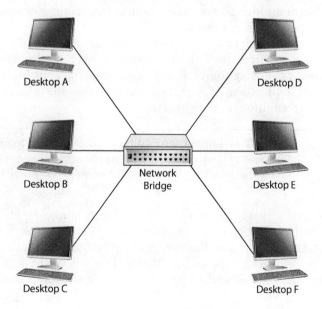

Desktop A Desktop D

Desktop B Network Bridge Desktop E

Desktop C Desktop F

want only traffic that is relevant to you to come to your system. A switch helps with this by ensuring that only traffic to your MAC address or broadcast traffic is sent to you.

 EXAM TIP Switches can make packet sniffing more challenging because you can't plug into a switch port and see all traffic passing through it as you can with a hub.

While you can use a hub instead of a switch in a star network because they behave identically when it comes to physically cabling to them in a network, a switch is far more common, particularly as the cost of switches has decreased dramatically in the last decade. Switches are currently the most common way to connect systems in a star topology.

Routing

Hopping into the Wayback Machine again, we find ourselves in 1969 when the ARPA-NET was being built. Those responsible at BBN for building the network realized they needed a way to get messages from one location to another if multiple nodes were going to be used on the network. They also needed a way to interface with the network to begin with. The traditional phone network was circuit switched, meaning the path to get a call from one place to another was determined and "nailed up" at the time the call was placed. So, you created a circuit from one phone to another phone and that circuit remained just as it was at the time the call originated until the time it was torn down. This was primarily because voice is an endless stream of an electrical signal, so it made sense to have a path for that signal to traverse. In the data world, however, there is no endless stream of an electrical signal because data is discrete and variable. You may have a large chunk of data to send at one point in time but then not need to send any more data for seconds, minutes, or maybe hours. As a result, you wouldn't nail up a circuit to communicate between two systems because you would never know when the circuit was going to be used, and keeping that circuit nailed up permanently could be a waste of expensive resources. Instead, data networks use a packet switching approach rather than a circuit switching approach. This means that data gets broken up into packets and each packet finds its way through the network at the time it needs to go. There is no one permanent path through the network.

 NOTE The company responsible for building and managing the ARPANET, BBN, wasn't even connected to the network for about six months after it was first turned on. They were the fifth node to be connected to the network.

BBN took a ruggedized Honeywell DDP-516 mini-computer and turned it into a device capable of taking packets and forwarding them along a network. They called this device an Interface Message Processor, or IMP. Imagine a device a bit larger than a typical refrigerator and then compare that to the tiny little box you have on your network that gets messages from your network to your network provider (cable modem, DSL, and so on).

The IMP performed essentially the same function as your small modem/router. The IMP was the first router. RFC 1 (http://tools.ietf.org/html/rfc1) describes the functions and operation of the IMP as well as the protocol for communicating between nodes.

NOTE   The first attempt at communication between two nodes in the ARPANET was a login attempt and the system crashed. Only two characters were transmitted before the crash.

Routing is the act of forwarding packets from one device to another using the IP address as the means of making decisions on where the messages should be going. Since we're using IP addresses to make decisions, routing is a layer 3 activity, unlike switching, which happens at layer 2. The reason that IP addresses get allocated in blocks rather than one at a time like driver's licenses is so that messages can be routed from one location to another. Being able to aggregate addresses makes routing significantly easier since you can send a packet to the network that the destination belongs to.

NOTE   Understanding the OSI model helps to make clear the distinction between activities like switching and routing, where switching occurs at layer 2 and makes use of the layer 2 addressing (e.g., MAC address), and where routing takes place at layer 3 and makes use of the layer 3 address (e.g., IP address).

Larger aggregate blocks make for smaller routing tables. A routing table is a way to look up where to next send a packet coming through your network. You would find the entry for the network that the IP address you want to get to belongs and then send the packet out the correct interface. It's a bit like tag, actually. The packet "tags" a router and it's up to the router to figure out whom to tag next to get the packet a little further along its way. This hop-by-hop approach, as distinct from the circuit switched approach, means you could send a dozen packets to a particular destination and each may take a different path to get there, for a number of reasons.

Assume that Marvin wants to talk to Zaphod using the network depicted in Figure 3-12. There are many paths that messages between the two could travel, but just the network diagram isn't really adequate to make the determination about which path to take. For example, it looks like the path A->C->G is the most direct, but there are considerations that may make that less ideal. If A->C were from Boston to Los Angeles and G was in New York, which is the router closest to Zaphod, that's a long way to travel, and the time it takes to get across that distance may be prohibitive, even if from a logical standpoint the path would work.

You may also run across an instance where A->C->G is all reasonably close, so the distance isn't prohibitive, but perhaps the speed of the connection going A->B->E->G is so much faster because of the individual link speeds that adding in the additional hop through the additional router still ends up making the trip time shorter. You could run into a situation where C is a heavily used router and the congestion causes queuing

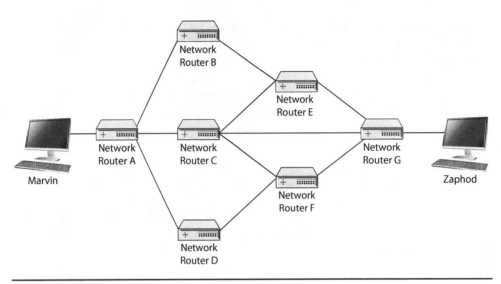

Figure 3-12 An example network

problems where packets get delayed in transit because the router has a hard time keeping up. This could also be a factor in deciding that another path is a better way to go.

Another consideration is cost. Everything comes at a cost, and bandwidth and circuits are no different. Router C has a choice of three routers to send messages to. It's possible that the circuit connecting C to F is very expensive on a per-bit basis and so that link is only used in emergency situations where other circuits are down and it has to be used. This could cause decisions to be made differently about how messages get passed through the network. Each link has a cost associated with it, whether it's measured in hop count or financial cost or just the cost of line speed. These costs are often taken into consideration in making routing decisions, which depends on the routing protocol being used.

How does the decision get made where a message ready for delivery needs to be routed as its next hop? Each system knows its own IP address and its subnet mask. This tells it which network it's on. If the destination IP isn't on the same network, the system knows it needs to send the message along to a device capable of getting it off of the local network. Each system has a routing table that will tell it where messages for particular networks are to be sent. Figure 3-13 shows a routing table on a Linux system, displayed using the system command netstat, which also works on other operating systems as well. The

Figure 3-13
The netstat
output

```
kilroy@bill: $ netstat -rn
Kernel IP routing table
Destination     Gateway         Genmask          Flags   MSS Window  irtt Iface
0.0.0.0         172.30.42.1     0.0.0.0          UG       0 0         0 br0
172.30.42.0     0.0.0.0         255.255.255.0    U        0 0         0 br0
192.168.122.0   0.0.0.0         255.255.255.0    U        0 0         0 virbr0
kilroy@bill: $
```

routing table shows the default route, indicated with a destination address of 0.0.0.0, and the address of the gateway to that network. The default route is used in cases where there isn't a specific route in the routing table. You can see two other routes indicated in this routing table, both of which are local networks. In the case of more complex networks, there may be multiple routers where some routers connect specific networks. If you had a message for one of those networks, you would forward your message to the IP address of the gateway for those networks. The gateway is actually just a router, but it's called a gateway because it's the device you pass through to get to the destination.

There is a need for dynamic routing, though, in cases where you have large networks and a lot of different destinations. There are two different major classes of routing protocols that get used on networks, and each type of protocol has several protocols that fall under that particular class. The first type of routing protocol is distance vector and the second type is link state.

Distance Vector Routing

A distance vector routing protocol takes two factors into consideration when making routing decisions. The name really gives it away. The first factor is the direction each message should be forwarded in. There isn't much point in forwarding a message that will take it further away from its destination. The second factor is the distance. The distance can be calculated in a few ways, but one simple way is just hop count—the number of intermediate devices or routers that a message has to pass through. RIPv1, RIPv2, and IGRP are all examples of distance vector routing protocols. While the Routing Information Protocol (RIP) simply uses hop count to calculate distance, the Interior Gateway Routing Protocol (IGRP) takes into account other factors like bandwidth and delay to make determinations of distance.

 NOTE Many factors could go into decisions about cost or distance, including the comparative cost per bit of transmission between two different paths that traffic can take.

In a distance vector routing protocol, each router is responsible for sending out periodic updates to neighbors about changes in topology within the network. The problem with that is that you can end up with routing loops. A routing loop is where a router forwards a packet on and then the new router forwards it back. This may happen if router A has a route to the destination that is the shortest path that passes through router B and vice versa. Routing loops can be prevented using a method called split horizon. A split horizon is where a router won't forward a route entry back to the router that it received it from to begin with. So if router A sends a route entry to router B for a particular network, router B won't send that route entry back to router A.

Distance vector protocols may also use route poisoning to ensure efficient delivery of packets across the network. Route poisoning is used when a route is no longer reachable. When a route that can't be reached is discovered, an update is immediately sent to all routers in the network indicating that that particular route is unreachable, effectively setting the hop count to infinity. Since everything along that particular route now seems further away than the restaurant at the end of the universe, no router will choose to send any traffic in that direction, preventing it from getting lost or discarded.

NOTE The routing protocol that runs between all the network providers on the Internet is the Border Gateway Protocol (BGP). BGP is a path vector protocol that is a variant of a distance vector.

Each router participating in a distance vector routing protocol sends either all or a portion of the routing table out to its neighbors periodically. The neighbors then update their routing tables accordingly, based on the information they have received, and then they send out their updated tables. Wash, rinse, repeat.

Link-State Routing

Where distance vector protocols work by having a router share the entire routing table with its neighbors, link-state routing protocols work by having routers tell everyone who their neighbors are. From that information, each router constructs a map of the entire network, from which it can build its routing table. Examples of link-state routing protocols are Open Shortest Path First (OSPF) and Intermediate System to Intermediate System (IS-IS).

In order for a link-state protocol to work, each router must first determine who its neighbors are. Rather than going door to door and introducing itself, each router sends a message using a reachability protocol. In the case of OSPF, a router sends a hello packet identifying itself to a neighbor. A neighbor in this case is any router directly connected to it through one of its ports. This connection could be a fiber line that ends up being several hundred miles away or more, but it's a point-to-point connection. Neighbors are anyone who is directly adjacent to you in this case, rather than someone who lives several doors down the street.

Once neighbors have been determined, a link-state advertisement (LSA) is constructed and sent out to neighbors. This advertisement includes the identity of the sending router as well as all of the routers that are directly connected to it. Additionally, a sequence number is used to ensure that all information is current and up to date. When an LSA is received, it can be compared against the most recent sequence number to ensure that the LSA received is more recent than the one currently in use. The LSAs are propagated throughout the network to ensure that all nodes in the network receive the announcement so everyone can have a complete, accurate, and up-to-date map of the network. When a router receives an LSA, it ensures that the LSA is more recent than the one in use, and if it is, it sends the LSA on to all of its neighbors. In this way, all of the routers get it in a way that doesn't involve broadcasts, which could allow for information leakage.

Once a map, in the form of a graph, has been created based on all of the information received in the LSAs, a router needs to be able to make a decision about how to forward messages along when it receives them. This is typically done using some variation on Dijkstra's algorithm, which is used for searching graphs. When you are in your car using your GPS device to find your way to your next meeting, you are relying on a device that is likely using Dijkstra's algorithm, because at the end of the day, the problem is the same

Figure 3-14
Graph of a
network

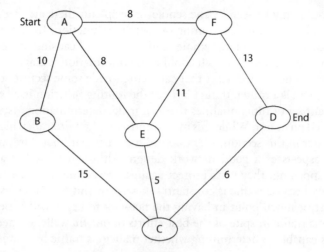

whether you are trying to find the quickest way through a set of crooked and alternating one-way streets to an office building downtown or you are trying to get a packet to its destination as quickly as possible. It comes down to a problem of graph theory and doing some calculations to determine the fastest way to get the message along its way. Where you see a map of streets or a diagram of routers and links, Dijkstra's algorithm simply sees a graph and a way to calculate the fastest way to a destination.

Figure 3-14 shows an example of a graph of a network, including the weights of each of the paths through the network. In the case where we want to get a message between nodes A and D, we could send it by way of A->F->D traversing two links along the way. The cost of those links, though, is 21. If instead, we go A->E->C->D, we add another link to the path but the total cost of all of those links is only 19, so while it may look faster to only take the two links through the network, the graph with all of the costs associated shows that adding another link into the path makes more sense to get the message from A to D.

Since a packet can't carry its route with it, a routing decision has to be made at each waypoint through the network. This is the reason why packets belonging to the same set of data may end up being sent in different directions. Based on the information available at any particular point in time, a packet may need to traverse a different path to get it there as quickly as possible. Since it can take time for all of the information in a network to get around to all of the other routers, it's possible that one packet can be sent in one direction just before an LSA is received, with information that would change the best path to get to the destination. This may end up meaning that subsequent packets actually get there ahead of the ones before them.

Network Security Technologies

When developing a network design, it's helpful to consider the sorts of security mechanisms that may be in place. So far, we have discussed routers and switches, but, while switches can help protect against sniffing traffic, a practice that can reveal information that should only be seen by the sender or recipient, there aren't a lot of security mechanisms built into either the routing or switching function. In fact, there are ways of causing switches to not work anymore, and also ways of causing routers to send messages to the wrong destinations, which could cause information leakage to unwanted places.

There are network devices that can help provide some security to a network, however. One of them is a router, though it's not the routing function itself that offers security but a different set of functionalities that can make determinations as to whether packets are forwarded on or not. While this may sound a bit like a firewall, which we'll discuss in more depth later in this section, it's more rudimentary than that. Firewalls are also considered critical aspects of a good network design. Although firewalls can prevent bad things from happening, they can't protect against everything bad that happens in a network, primarily because traffic is constantly flowing in and out of a network (otherwise, there wouldn't be much point in having the network to begin with). Because we may still get malicious traffic in spite of the best efforts of our firewalls, we need intrusion detection systems capable of determining whether malicious traffic has entered the network.

Routers

First, the routing design can offer security simply by providing better availability, which is one of the legs of the CIA triad popular among security professionals. Additionally, though, routers are generally capable of implementing access control lists (ACLs). Access control lists are simple mechanisms capable of preventing very specific traffic from either entering or exiting a network. This filtering would be done at a reasonably broad level, leaving the specific and targeted rules to the firewall to handle since the firewall is designed specifically for that task.

 NOTE The CIA triad is confidentiality, integrity, and availability, which are fundamental concepts in the world of security.

In a large network, you may have two different functional areas for your routers. A border router is one that is placed at the edge of your network and would typically perform a different function than core routers on the inside of your network. A border router is one that connects to an external entity, whether it's a service provider or a partner or maybe a vendor. Figure 3-15 shows a diagram of a network with core routers and a border router. The border router is tasked with passing messages into or out of the internal network. A core router, on the other hand, would be running a routing protocol that would be keeping all of your enterprise network locations communicating efficiently. A border router may only be running a routing protocol to get information from the core of the network and may not be exchanging any routing information with any external entities, instead acting as something of a default gateway where messages not destined for the inside of the network are sent.

Because of this, the border router is really the first or last stop on the path to or from your network. It's here where you probably want to do some sort of filtering as a way

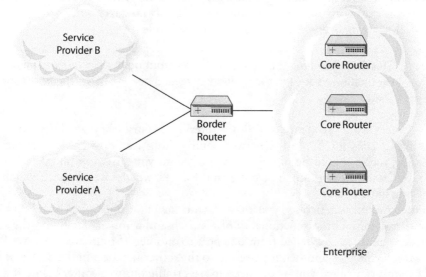

Figure 3-15   Border and core routers in a network

of blocking the easiest packets. The first thing you probably want to do at your border router is drop all packets with either a source or destination of a private IP address. If you are using the private address space inside your network, you don't want those messages leaving your network without being translated to something that could actually be routed outside of your internal network. Any message with a private address still being used as a source address may very well be malicious. Plus, there is no way a response would ever get back, so there is no point in even passing that message out of your network. You may as well drop it on the floor and forget about it.

EXAM TIP   The border router is often used to do a broad level of filtering of traffic that just shouldn't be hitting your network, like that sourced from private addresses.

Similarly, any message that hits your border router with either a source or destination address that is bogus in some way—private, loopback, experimental, and so on—should simply be discarded. Since there is no way any response to it is ever going to get back because those addresses aren't routed on public networks, by convention, there's no reason to allow them into your network. There is a good possibility that the traffic is malicious and intended for bad purposes to begin with, so filtering it out would be a good idea.

In addition to filtering, you may want your border router to do rate limiting, if it supports it. This would be used to protect your network against a flood. While you may want to allow ICMP messages into your network for diagnostic purposes, ICMP messages may be used in a flooding attack. Diagnostics don't require a large volume of traffic, so you may want to limit the number of ICMP messages you allow into your network to keep from overwhelming systems on the inside.

EXAM TIP Remember that a router makes routing decisions based on the destination address in the network or layer 3 header. This is the destination IP address.

Core routers wouldn't typically do any filtering because they are busy doing all the routing updates for inside the network and getting traffic where it needs to go. Additionally, traffic should be filtered before it gets to your network rather than once it's deep inside, so filtering should be done on the edges, which saves the core routers for their routing functionality.

In some enterprise networks, you may end up having a multilayer switch. This is a device that combines the functionality of a switch and a router. Traffic on the same network segment is just switched from one port to another. If traffic has to move from one network segment to another, it passes up to the router function in the device. If you didn't have this capability, you would need to pass traffic out to a router before it came back to either the same switch, if the VLAN needed was on that switch, or a different switch. Also, when it comes to protecting network segments, having the ability to place router ACLs onto these multilayer switches can help keep the network uncomplicated. If you need to filter traffic between one network segment and another, it can become complex to push all your traffic out to a firewall if the traffic has to pass between network segments.

Firewalls

Simple filtering with ACLs on the border isn't sufficient to protect your network against malicious traffic. Firewalls offer better protection because they give more control over the details that can be filtered. Figure 3-16 shows the placement of a firewall in a typical network design. This is the same diagram as Figure 3-15 but with a firewall added into the design.

While you may have several firewalls in your network, the first location for a firewall is as close to the edge of your network as possible. This would be between your router and the internals of your network. This placement provides the ability to filter both ingress and egress traffic. You may need to protect other parts of your network as well, but first, the entire network needs to have some level of firewalling to block malicious or simply unwanted traffic.

ACLs are typically static in nature, where you specify particular features of a packet—source, destination, ports, and so on—to filter on. Simple ACLs don't offer the ability to track whether each packet is part of a known and established connection. While TCP offers state as part of its core functionality because it's a connection-oriented protocol, UDP is more challenging. Knowing that a UDP message coming into a network belongs to a communication stream that was originated inside the network requires a device that will keep an internal state table by tracking all communication as it passes through.

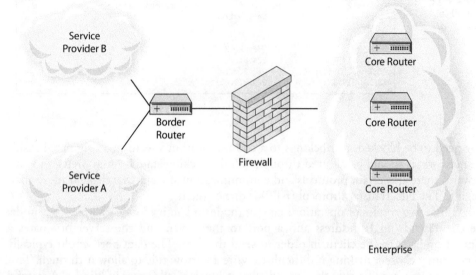

Figure 3-16 A network diagram with a firewall

A firewall that is capable of doing this sort of tracking is called a *stateful firewall*. Even this isn't enough, though. There are services that will be required to be allowed through, because there are e-mail servers or web servers on the inside of the network. It's possible to cause a denial of service (DoS) using malformed messages directed to those service ports. Ideally, there would be a device that understands what a malformed message looks like and could block those messages. Fortunately, such a device exists—the deep packet inspection firewall.

 EXAM TIP A first-match firewall will perform the action specified in the rule that is matched first. A best-match firewall rule set will find the best or most specific match in the rules and perform the action in that rule.

In addition to those two types of firewalls, there are application layer gateways. An ALG is a protocol-specific firewall like a proxy that can be used to filter based on specific content. A critical function of firewalls is network address translation, which switches out one IP address for another. This also requires connection tracking to function, similar to stateful firewalls.

Stateful Firewalls

A stateful firewall has to keep track of every message that passes through it, checking it against a table that is kept internally to determine if it belongs to a connection stream that has been seen previously. While traffic that has originated from outside the network

Figure 3-17
An iptables
state table

```
                          IPTState - IPTables State Top
Version: 2.2.3        Sort: SrcIP        b: change sorting    h: help
Source                    Destination            Prt  State       TTL
0.0.0.0                   224.0.0.1              igmp                0:09:08
127.0.0.1:53162           127.0.0.1:53162        udp                 0:02:43
172.30.42.51:58830        172.30.42.55:22        tcp  ESTABLISHED   119:59:59
172.30.42.55              224.0.0.251            igmp                0:08:39
172.30.42.55:47761        91.189.91.13:80        tcp  TIME_WAIT      0:01:08
192.168.122.1             224.0.0.251            igmp                0:09:10
```

may need to be blocked, if it belongs to a communication stream that originated inside the network, it should be allowed through. While tracking state is often pretty straightforward, there are certain protocols and communication streams that make it more challenging. The File Transfer Protocol (FTP) is one of them.

FTP has two modes of operation: passive mode and active mode. With active mode, the client sends an IP address and a port to the server, and the server originates a connection back to the client in order to send the data. The data port would typically be randomly chosen, making it difficult to write a narrow rule to allow it through. This would require a specific rule that would allow a block of addresses in blindly. A stateful firewall, though, can automatically allow the data connection through because it's related to the established connection. The data channel is a separate TCP stream, but since the source and destination are the same as the existing control channel, the firewall would allow it through. If the firewall had a level of protocol awareness, it could notice the port command as it comes through and proactively open the firewall to allow the data channel to come through.

Having a firewall that's stateful helps with situations like FTP. Otherwise, system administrators would need to make alterations to services to make them more firewall friendly, which could be a significant effort and in some cases just isn't possible. It's much easier if the firewall could be accommodating of these types of situations and allow communication through that should be allowed through. There are certainly ways of knowing when messages should be allowed based on the protocols/ports in use.

Most firewalls are stateful in nature. Many operating systems come with stateful firewalls built into them, so you can have host-based firewalls in addition to the network firewalls in an enterprise situation. Figure 3-17 shows the connection information from an iptables installation on a Linux system. In addition to the expected TCP connections and their state, you can see that there are also some UDP connections in the table.

Deep Packet Inspection

A firewall that has deep packet inspection (DPI) is protocol-aware. Having a firewall that's capable of DPI doesn't mean it can't be stateful as well. You can have a stateful firewall that is capable of doing all the things a stateful firewall does while also providing the functionality to open the packets and look inside them to analyze the protocol activity as well as the data being sent. Why would anyone want to do that? Because malformed messages cause DoS attacks. Sending protocol commands that aren't complete or are otherwise incorrect can cause problems for the application handling the protocol. When an application fails, this means that others can't use the service either. This situation should be guarded against if at all possible.

This requires that the firewall understands the protocols and what the interactions between a client and a server should look like. Figure 3-18 shows some attempts to send malformed data to an SMTP (Simple Mail Transfer Protocol) server in the process of sending e-mail. In this particular case, the server handles the bad data gracefully, but that's not always the case. Often, these sorts of attempts can crash a server. Having the firewall look into the packet to see this sort of exchange and block the message before it even gets to the server can help keep services up and running so everyone else can get access to them.

There are downsides to deep packet inspection, though. One downside is that the firewall will take time looking at the packet. While this is also true of a stateful firewall, the data that a stateful firewall looks at is always in the same place and it's very fast to parse that information quickly. A DPI firewall must be able to pull apart all sorts of packet types and find the right information in the right places. This can be time consuming. Even in the case of very fast hardware and finely tuned, well-written code, it simply takes time to parse through packets before making decisions about them. While it's generally not significant and no one will have time to go get a cup of coffee while the firewall does its work, it is something to take into consideration since there will be a delay.

You could also run into a situation where the firewall may actually drop legitimate traffic. Years ago, I was working with a client who had a firewall that was protocol-aware. After installing the firewall, the client stopped getting e-mail from certain sites. Upon investigating, we discovered that the mail servers that weren't able to get e-mail through were using ESMTP, an extended version of the protocol used to send e-mail. The firewall didn't recognize ESMTP, so when an ESMTP command was sent, the firewall would convert it to a NOP command, a no-operation in SMTP. Because of this NOP, a critical command wasn't getting through to the mail server, so all commands that came after didn't make any sense and the e-mail failed. In this case, using a more recent version

Figure 3-18
Malformed data
sent to an SMTP
server

```
oliver:~ kilroy$ telnet 172.30.42.55 25
Trying 172.30.42.55...
Connected to bill.westell.com.
Escape character is '^]'.
220 bill.westell.com ESMTP Postfix (Ubuntu)
HHLLOO AAAAAAAAAAAAAAAAAAAAAAAAAAAAAAAAAAAAAAAAAAAAAAAAAAAAAAAAAAAAAAA
502 5.5.2 Error: command not recognized
EHLO AAAAAAAAAAAAAAAAAAAAAAAAAAAAAAAAAAAAAAAAAAAAAAAAAAAAAAAAAAAAAAA
250-bill.westell.com
250-PIPELINING
250-SIZE 10240000
250-VRFY
250-ETRN
250-STARTTLS
250-ENHANCEDSTATUSCODES
250-8BITMIME
250 DSN
MLAI From" AAAAAAAAAAAAAAAAAAAAAAAAAAAAAA*AAAAAAAAAAAAAAAAA@AAAAAAAAAAA
502 5.5.2 Error: command not recognized
```

of the protocol than the firewall understood caused a DoS attack, and that can be a challenge with DPI firewalls if they aren't kept up to date, particularly in the case of some protocols that are constantly evolving. You could end up blocking legitimate traffic accidentally and not even be aware of it until customers or partners start calling to say they are getting messages bounced back.

Application Layer Gateway

While deep packet inspection firewalls are protocol-aware, meaning they are familiar with some application layer information, you can get a type of firewall, called an application layer gateway (ALG) that is specific to a particular type of protocol and application. One example that many people may be familiar with is a proxy server. A proxy server is used to perform requests on behalf of a client. This is most commonly seen with web proxies. A web proxy can have several benefits. The first is that you can speed up browsing and save bandwidth by using a web proxy. The proxy caches responses so that the next time a page (assuming it's a static page and not a dynamic one) is requested, the response is much faster because it's on the local network. When you aren't sending additional requests out to web servers off your local network, you are saving bandwidth.

A web proxy can also perform content filtering, which can protect your network from malware attacks hosted on websites. Many companies also use proxy servers to block access to particular websites. Sometimes this is an attempt to keep employees on task by blocking access to notorious time-wasting sites like Facebook and ESPN. Sites known to host malware can also be blocked to prevent users from inadvertently accessing them and getting infected. When you use a proxy to block access, it can cost a lot in maintenance and upkeep. There are always new sites that pop up that can be used to waste time or to host malware, so filter lists regularly need to be updated. You could subscribe to a service that can maintain lists, but it still takes someone to review the filters to ensure there aren't mistakes, or that sites that are legitimately needed for a particular business's needs aren't being blocked.

CAUTION   Application layer gateways that are expected to block traffic can be time-consuming to manage. As with many areas of security, it takes a knowledgeable professional to manage all the rules for blocking and ensure legitimate traffic isn't blocked.

When you implement a proxy server, you also need to consider controls to protect against someone bypassing the proxy and connecting directly to the Internet. Using a proxy is a setting in your browser and it's easy to remove that configuration to use the proxy in order to bypass it unless there are controls in place to prevent that direct access. The best way to ensure this is to install firewall rules to block external access over web ports. It takes some thought to ensure that security controls aren't circumvented, because if controls makes things more difficult, people will try to find ways around those controls. When you implement a solution like a proxy server, you need to backstop it with firewall rules to ensure that the proxy server is actually used, because otherwise you don't get the benefits from the proxy server installation.

Application layer gateways aren't only used with web requests. Other protocols can make use of ALGs as well. Voice over IP (VoIP) protocols like Session Initiation Protocol (SIP) can make use of ALGs as well. SIP has a number of issues that make it difficult to interoperate with traditional firewalls. However, a protocol-specific ALG like a session border controller (SBC) can help keep a network safe by only opening holes as necessary to allow voice traffic through. SBCs, like web proxies, can perform protocol inspection to ensure that only legitimate and legal requests make it through to the application server.

Where a web proxy would normally be installed on the client end of the transaction, an SBC is just as commonly installed on the server end since the server and associated infrastructure is primarily what needs protection. This is similar to using a web proxy in front of a web server. In that case, you would have a reverse proxy. The reverse proxy handles requests on behalf of the server that sits behind it. This way, the reverse proxy can do filtering and blocking as necessary based on the source or content of the request.

Network Address Translation

Firewalls often perform the function of network address translation (NAT). In fact, you probably have a device on your network now that is performing NAT. Devices sold to the home market that act as a router and firewall perform NAT by default. They do this primarily to help conserve IPv4 addresses. While you may have half a dozen systems on your network, they are using private addresses as specified in RFC 1918. Only one public address is used. When a request passes through the firewall, the source IP address is translated from the private address used on the inside of the network to a public address that can be routed over the Internet. The address used in this particular situation is the address of the external interface on the router/firewall. Figure 3-19 illustrates a typical home network with a router/firewall performing NAT functions. When one of the systems on the internal network wants to send a message to a system on the Internet, it forwards it off to 192.168.1.1 to be processed since that is the address of the default gateway on the network. When the message is subsequently forwarded out the Internet-facing interface, it is given a source address of 12.18.95.6.

Figure 3-19
A home NAT
scenario

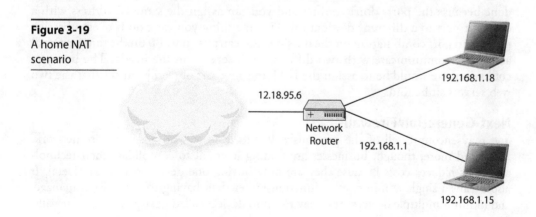

When the response to the message comes back, the firewall performs a lookup on the source and destination and determines the IP address of the sender in order to perform the translation back to get the response to the original sender. In a situation like the one in Figure 3-19 where there is a single public address and multiple internal systems, the translation that is being performed is not only on the IP address but also on the port. This is necessary to ensure that there are no overlaps based on multiple requests from multiple systems inside the network. The firewall maintains a map of all requests originating from inside the network and tracks source and destination ports and IP addresses in order to map the responses back to the original request.

There are multiple types of NAT. The one just described is a form of source NAT, where the source address is manipulated. Considering that there is one address involved on the public side, manipulating the ports is also a part of the NAT. In a larger organization, you may have a pool of addresses that are shared on a first-come, first-served basis. These addresses would get used for a period of time when a connection attempt goes out of the network. After a period of time, they would get released to the pool. These are both dynamic ways of performing the NAT function. You may want to assign one public IP address on a one-to-one basis to an internal client. This is a form of static NAT, where the NAT assignment never changes.

 EXAM TIP NAT can cause problems for some protocols. VoIP protocols like SIP can run into problems with NAT devices, as can FTP.

A more common purpose for statically assigning a NAT address is when you have a service on the inside of the network that you want external clients to be able to access and consume. You would need to perform a translation from a public address to a private, internal address. This would need to be configured on a firewall, configuring the translation. Just as in the source address translation, a destination NAT can be over-subscribed. You could assign the same public IP address to multiple servers on the inside hosting multiple services. As an example, you could use a single IP address to do a static destination NAT to a mail server, web server, and DNS server. This is done because the ports don't conflict and you can assign the same IP address with a different port to a different destination. The one thing you can't do is over-subscribe the IP and port combination on the outside. You can't use port 80 on the same external address to communicate with two different web servers on the inside. The best you could do there would be to assign the NAT to some sort of load balancer that the two web servers sit behind.

Next-Generation Firewalls

You may encounter all of the previously described devices on an enterprise network. More and more, though, businesses are finding it useful to consolidate their technology. This reduces costs because they are only buying one device instead of several. It also means a single administrative function rather than having to administer, manage, and monitor multiple devices. You may run into devices called next-generation firewalls.

These devices combine multiple functions into a single device, including functionality that isn't in more traditional firewalls. The reality is that the majority of attacks today aren't coming in as just IP addresses and ports that we can block and then forget about. The attackers are well aware of the existence of firewalls, so they take the path of least resistance and come in through ports that are open in the firewall. This means they aren't doing anything a traditional firewall could detect. They may not even do anything an application layer gateway could detect, even if there were one in place.

A next-generation firewall takes the capabilities of doing traditional network flow blocking by only allowing specified traffic into the network. Additionally, it may be capable of detecting attacks happening over the network, so dynamic rules could be created to block the traffic. If, for example, the next-generation firewall were to detect a port scan, it may create a rule blocking that IP address for a period of time—putting the system in the penalty box as it were. This is the function of an intrusion prevention system, discussed a bit later in the chapter. It would also, likely, generate an alert based on what it had done so there is some visibility into the changes on the device. This serves as an intrusion detection system, discussed next.

So much attack traffic happens through e-mail and web traffic today and often through the use of malware. As a result, a next-generation firewall will have the ability to scan network traffic for viruses. This, by necessity, brings in the capabilities of a deep packet inspection firewall. You can't look for malware, after all, by just looking at network headers. The firewall needs to understand the application protocols in order to look for network traffic that may contain malicious software.

Intrusion Detection Systems

Firewalls can't protect against everything. There will always be traffic entering the network from external sources, whether it's to connect to resources on the inside that are exposed purposefully or whether it's because a system inside the network has engaged in communication with a system on the outside. These are expected and allowed communications and, as a result, will not be blocked by the firewall. Because of that, it's useful to have a way to detect when bad things are happening. To be very clear here, an intrusion detection system (IDS) is simply that—it can detect when something is happening. It's like a fire or burglar alarm. It won't prevent the event from happening and it won't stop it once it's in progress. It will, however, notify someone who can do something about it.

 EXAM TIP An intrusion detection system only detects intrusions. There are host-based IDS (HIDS) and network-based IDS (NIDS) implementations, but an IDS can only detect potential intrusions. An IDS is *not* a replacement for a firewall.

That's the nature of an IDS. It serves as an alarm that something bad is happening. It's up to someone else to do something about the alert. As a result of this, it's beneficial to have an IDS that actually generates useful alerts so as to limit the number of alerts that are inaccurate. These inaccurate alerts are called *false positives*. Ideally, you want zero false positives, but that takes a lot of vigilance on the part of the person operating the system. Alerts fall into the following categories:

- **True positive**   A case where an alert happens for an intrusion that is real
- **True negative**   A case where an alert didn't get triggered because nothing happened
- **False positive**   A case where an alert happens that isn't real or accurate
- **False negative**   A case where an alert didn't happen but an intrusion did happen

EXAM TIP   Pay attention to the distinctions between the different categories that alerts can fall into.

We should investigate how these alerts are generated to begin with. Typically, there is a set of rules that defines what a specific event looks like. This is called a signature, and a signature-based IDS relies on these rules to generate quality alerts. The following listing demonstrates a set of rules used by Snort, an open-source IDS.

NOTE   IDSs cannot detect any malicious behavior on encrypted traffic without sitting in the middle of the encryption session.

```
alert ip $EXTERNAL_NET any -> $HOME_NET any (msg:"DOS Jolt attack";
dsize:408; fragbits:M; reference:cve,1999-0345; classtype:attempted-dos;
sid:268; rev:4;)
alert udp $EXTERNAL_NET any -> $HOME_NET any (msg:"DOS Teardrop attack";
fragbits:M; id:242; reference:bugtraq,124; reference:cve,1999-0015;
reference:nessus,10279; reference:url,www.cert.org/advisories/CA-1997-28.
html; classtype:attempted-dos; sid:270; rev:6;)
# alert udp any 19 <> any 7 (msg:"DOS UDP echo+chargen bomb";
reference:cve,1999-0103; reference:cve,1999-0635; classtype:attempted-dos;
sid:271; rev:5;)
alert ip $EXTERNAL_NET any -> $HOME_NET any (msg:"DOS IGMP dos attack";
fragbits:M+; ip_proto:2; reference:bugtraq,514; reference:cve,1999-0918;
reference:url,www.microsoft.com/technet/security/bulletin/MS99-034.mspx;
classtype:attempted-dos; sid:272; rev:10;)
```

This listing of rules is a small part of what Snort looks at when packets come through the system. If these rules are poorly written, they can generate false positives. You may, if you are conversant with such things, notice that the rules that are listed here refer to very old attacks. The Jolt attack in the first rule is a fragmented ICMP attack against Windows 95 or Windows NT. The Teardrop attack is another fragmentation attack where the fragments overlap. It also targets older versions of Windows and Linux that were susceptible to not being able to handle overlapping fragments well. What's the purpose of showing some rules against very old attacks? The purpose is to highlight that these rules have to be based on known vulnerabilities. Any rules-based approach to intrusion detection is going to require the knowledge of the attack in order to write the rule to alert against it. This means that a signature-based IDS can't alert on new attacks, so those attacks will continue to succeed because there is nothing to protect against them or even detect them—at least until the attacks have been successful long enough that someone looks into them and writes the necessary rules to protect the systems. This is the arms race of security. The bad guys come up with something new, so the good guys have to figure out what it is and try to prevent it from happening, and then the cycle continues all over again. Wash, rinse, repeat.

Anomaly Detection

There is a way out of the cycle just described, however. Instead of using a set of rules to determine when an attack is happening, meaning we are reliant on a very long list of rules that needs to be processed (or have the packet dropped on the floor if it's taking too long to process it in order to keep from developing a very large queue), perhaps a better approach would be to know what's good and allow that while blocking anything that's, by virtue of it being not good, bad. This is an anomaly-based approach and it takes a whitelist approach as opposed to the blacklist approach that signature-based programs take. A whitelist approach knows what's good, and anything that isn't on the whitelist is, by definition, bad. A blacklist approach takes the position that there is a list of all of the bad things, and anything that isn't on that list of bad things is probably good. Or at least we can't be sure one way or the other. The list of bad things continues to grow, meaning it's harder and harder to keep up with it. The list of good things should stay more or less constant, meaning it's easier to keep up with.

There are challenges here, however. The first is in knowing what's good. How consistent is the traffic on your network? Can you say that after a week of taking a baseline, you have a solid view of what is normal and acceptable traffic? What if there are payroll runs or other accounting activities that didn't happen during the course of that week but will happen down the road that weren't taken into consideration as part of the baseline. Will those activities be blocked? Additionally, while there is probably a pretty consistent set of "normal" activities, there are changes that happen in the course of doing business. Systems change, new processes are put into place, groups and employees move around and take on new responsibilities, meaning they may be engaging in new activities on the network. With all of this change, can we really say with a strong degree of conviction what's normal?

This is the challenge, of course. While the approach sounds far easier because the number of acceptable behaviors can't change nearly as often as the number of unacceptable behaviors, in reality it can be very challenging. Establishing a baseline for some organizations is far harder than for others. Once you have a baseline, it takes regular checking to ensure the baseline is still accurate and nothing has changed. Intrusion detection has to be built into the normal business operations and change controls so that any time something changes, a new baseline can be established. This can be very time consuming and challenging for some organizations, even if it can potentially make the life of a security analyst much easier.

The opposite of this approach, though, is the signature-based approach, as indicated earlier. Instead of embedding the process into business operations, the burden of keeping a signature-based IDS up to date falls entirely on the network or security operations team.

Signatures need to be updated on a regular basis because, as noted, there are new attacks coming out constantly. This requires downloading the new signatures, determining if they are appropriate for the network and business environment, and applying them if they are. This could be the work of one team or one individual, and it does nothing to enhance the security awareness of the rest of the organization.

A challenge that developers of anomaly-based systems have is keeping up with changes in protocols. They expect that protocol implementations follow the standards so they can accurately and reliably detect unexpected traffic. When a vendor implements a protocol in a nonstandard way, an anomaly-based IDS may trigger on that traffic because it may look as though it's malformed traffic. IDS vendors have to keep up with constant changes in protocols because of this.

 EXAM TIP Compression and encryption can cause problems for an IDS.

Intrusion Prevention Systems

Intrusion detection is limited to simply detecting something. A good IDS will also provide the ability to alert someone, and preferably in multiple ways, such as a popup window on a screen, an e-mail, text message, and so on. However, all it can do is alert someone. What if you could get a system that was capable of more than simply alerting—a system that could detect something was happening and act on it? That would be the function of an intrusion prevention system (IPS). While there are aspects of this that function on a host level, we will be focusing on the network aspect here. An IPS is capable of detecting that something is going wrong on the network and then performing an action to block that action. This may be a device that sits inline with the normal traffic flow at the edges of the network, or it may be a device that sits off to the side, monitoring traffic until it needs to act, at which point it interfaces with the firewall to generate a dynamic rule to block the traffic.

Using an IPS sounds like a terrific idea, of course, but there are downsides to it as well. One of the downsides is the same as using IDSs in general, in that you can't guarantee protection against all attacks because an IPS relies on signatures to determine when an attack is happening. Another downside is that an IPS can be used against the company that has implemented it. Since an IPS is capable of blocking traffic dynamically, without an intelligent oversight, it's possible to manufacture traffic to trigger a rule that blocks legitimate traffic from entering the network. This would create a denial-of-service attack against the company that has the IPS. This is a challenge, and as a result it's useful to ensure that only trustworthy and solid rules are used and that the system is monitored to protect against an accidental or even a malicious denial of service. The ability to automatically trigger blocks against traffic on a dynamic basis is very powerful, but also potentially very dangerous.

The biggest challenge, though, is to ensure that the IPS can keep up with the volume of traffic passing through it. If there is too much latency, the network starts to become unusable, and if the IPS can't keep up at all, we run the risk of dropping messages. The alternative is to allow potentially bad traffic through, which wouldn't be acceptable.

Chapter Review

A good network design takes a lot of consideration and thought. Understanding the difference between routing and switching is critical in order to size and distribute networks appropriately, keeping related systems and services together, since leaving them in the same subnet would ensure that traffic between them would be switched rather than routed. Alongside decisions about topology, cabling, routing, switching, and subnetting, you need to be considering how you will best secure the network. Where will you place firewalls, and will you use stateful or deep packet inspection firewalls? Will you use intrusion detection, and if so, how will you place sensors for the IDS since you need to be able to see relevant traffic to be able to alert on it? To determine where you will place IDS sensors, you must make some decisions about what resources you care about most so you can make intelligent decisions about the rules you will use.

Questions

1. You are implementing a star topology on your local network. What cabling are you most likely to use?

    A. Fiber optic

    B. Twisted pair

    C. Thicknet

    D. Coaxial

2. When you are deploying an intrusion prevention system on your network, what is the most important criterion?

    A. It is highly available.

    B. It has a ruggedized processor.

    C. It has encryption services.

    D. It has a low latency.

3. Your IDS sends an alert about an incident on your network. The alert indicates that there was a packet that had the same source and destination. This might normally indicate an attempt at a Land attack, which is a very old attack. After investigating, you see that the source address is 0.0.0.0 and the destination is 224.0.0.1. What would you consider this alert to be?

    A. A false negative

    B. A true negative

    C. A false positive

    D. A true positive

4. You have been asked to implement a security solution on your network to protect against employees browsing Facebook during the work day. What would you implement?

   A. A session border controller

   B. A proxy server

   C. A deep packet inspection firewall

   D. An intrusion detection service

5. You are seeing a lot of ARP responses with no corresponding ARP request. What are you most likely seeing?

   A. ARP cache flushes

   B. ARP spoofing

   C. ARP rewrites

   D. Gateway redirects

6. You would implement an intrusion detection system to perform which of the following?

   A. Test for vulnerabilities

   B. Detect vulnerabilities and exploits

   C. Prevent intrusions

   D. Detect intrusions

7. A border router would implement which of the following security controls?

   A. Access control lists to block broad categories of traffic

   B. Target rules to look at specific protocols

   C. Deep packet inspection

   D. Stateful firewall rules

8. Which type of routing protocol uses the same algorithm as the navigation system in your car?

   A. RIP

   B. Distance vector

   C. Link-state

   D. Border routing

9. Which of the following is a good example of a network using a mesh topology?

   A. The Internet

   B. A bus network

   C. A switched network

   D. A hybrid network

10. Which option represents big challenges for intrusion detection systems?

   A. Deep packet inspection

   B. Alerting

   C. Anomalies

   D. Compression and encryption

11. What will a next-generation firewall find that traditional firewalls won't?

   A. Malware

   B. Traffic from private IP addresses

   C. Multicast traffic

   D. Bogons

12. What topology are you most likely to see on the inside of an enterprise network?

   A. Ring

   B. Mesh

   C. Star

   D. Star-bus hybrid

13. Which OSI model layer does a switch operate at?

   A. 4

   B. 3

   C. 1

   D. 2

14. Which of the following devices is an example of an application layer gateway?

   A. Next-generation firewall

   B. Proxy server

   C. Multilayer switch

   D. Core router

15. Which of these network security controls are you most likely to find on a device that connects your home to your service provider's network?

   A. Malware detecting firewall

   B. Intrusion detection system

   C. Network address translation

   D. Deep packet inspection firewall

Answers

1. **B.** Twisted pair cabling is typically used in a star topology on a local network. Fiber optic would be highly unusual to run to the desktop. Thicknet is the same as coaxial, and coax is most often used in a bus network.

2. **D.** You really need an IPS that has very low latency, meaning it can keep up with high traffic rates without slowing the traffic down much, and thus not impact the user experience. Highly available may be nice to have, but it's not the most important criterion. A ruggedized processor is mostly a meaningless term. Encryption services aren't important in this context.

3. **C.** This is a false positive because the source and the destination are not the same, as the alert erroneously indicated. This is a false indication that something happened that didn't in fact happen.

4. **B.** A proxy server will block access to inappropriate sites. A session border controller is designed for Voice over IP systems. A deep packet inspection firewall won't provide the right functionality. We aren't looking at detecting an intrusion, so an IDS isn't the right solution.

5. **B.** A lot of gratuitous ARP messages is a likely indicator of ARP spoofing. Cache flushes wouldn't happen over the network, ARP rewrites aren't a thing, and if you were redirected to a different gateway, it wouldn't take place over ARP.

6. **D.** Intrusion detection systems are capable of detecting intrusions and nothing more than that. You would need an intrusion prevention system to prevent intrusions, and you would need a vulnerability scanner to detect or test for vulnerabilities.

7. **A.** A border router would be responsible for ACLs to block broad categories of traffic like private addresses and other non-routable traffic. Targeted rules for specific protocols would be the function of a firewall. A firewall would also be responsible for deep packet inspection and stateful firewall rules.

8. **B.** RIP is a distance vector routing protocol. Distance vector routing protocols don't use Dijkstra's algorithm. Border routing is meaningless. Link-state routing protocols use some variation of Dijkstra's algorithm to find the shortest path just like navigation systems do.

9. **A.** The Internet is a good example of a mesh network. The Internet has a lot of nodes that are connected to one another and are responsible for moving messages through to other nodes. The other answers are different types of topologies.

10. **D.** Compression and encryption are the biggest challenges to intrusion detection because either of these could prevent an IDS from seeing what is being carried inside the message. Anomalies and alerting could be challenges, but they are not the biggest challenges. Deep packet inspection is a type of firewall.

11. **A.** Next-generation firewalls often add in the capability of scanning network traffic for malware, in addition to the traditional capabilities of detecting traffic from IP addresses that shouldn't be sending traffic in, such as private addresses. Multicast traffic is generally allowed, but in cases where it isn't, a traditional firewall can make the decision since it's just an IP address that can be filtered on. Bogons are addresses that shouldn't be seen over the Internet, which includes the private address space.

12. **D.** A modern network of any size is likely to implement a star-bus hybrid because of the need for multiple switches to handle all of the connections. As soon as you have multiple switches, you need a bus to connect them together. While it's conceivable that you would run across a ring or star topology on the inside of an enterprise network, it would be on a much smaller and potentially a much older network implementation. You wouldn't likely see a mesh on the inside of an enterprise network, though you could very commonly see that within a service provider's network.

13. **D.** A switch operates at layer 2 of the OSI model—the Data Link layer. This is where the MAC address is located, and that's the address a switch uses to make decisions about where to send traffic. Layer 1 is the Physical layer. Layer 3 is the Network layer, where the IP address is. This is the layer a router functions at. Layer 4 is the Transport layer.

14. **B.** A proxy server is an example of an application layer gateway. It operates at the Application layer, making decisions about traffic passing through it based on an Application layer protocol. A next-generation firewall may potentially include the capabilities of an ALG but is not one in and of itself. A multilayer switch and a core router have entirely different functions that are not at the Application layer.

15. **C.** You are most likely to find the ability for your gateway device to perform network address translation (NAT). In fact, it's almost guaranteed that your gateway device is performing NAT for you, considering the limited amount of IPv4 address space. Network address translation obscures your internal address space from someone on the outside. Additionally, unless you have opened a connection through the NAT device, an attacker can't get in. This could be done by someone on the inside initiating a connection or by someone specifically configuring a mapping from the outside address to an address on the inside. While you very likely have a type of firewall, it probably doesn't do deep packet inspection or detect malware. It very likely also doesn't have intrusion detection capabilities.

Exercise 3-1 Answer

There are a total of 17 locations. This leads to a total of $17 \times (17 - 1) / 2 = 136$ connections ($17 \times 16 = 272$, and $272 / 2 = 136$). This allows for a single connection between all of the sites, with no duplicates. If you want duplicate connections, it would just be $17 \times 16 = 272$ connections. This many connections makes for a lot of configuration work.

Authentication and Access Control

In this chapter, you will learn:

- The difference between authentication and authorization
- Authentication types
- Authentication protocols
- Access control techniques

Authentication, authorization, and access control are layers of security controls to protect systems on your network, because at some point your users will want to make use of the systems and to do so, they need to verify they are legitimate users. All of these concepts are fundamental to providing your users with the ability to provide that verification so they can make use of the services that the systems offer. That's ultimately the name of the game. As information security professionals, we should not prevent users from being able to function or even make it harder for them to do their jobs. Providing strong authentication is important, but only if it doesn't drive users to find ways around that strong authentication by doing things like writing down passwords. As with everything in life, there needs to be a balance.

All of these concepts apply regardless of the type of system you are implementing and trying to protect. This can be a login to a desktop operating system or a remote login over Secure Shell (SSH) to a command-line environment. It can also be logging in to a virtual private network (VPN) or Gmail or Facebook. Web services all have authentication needs, and based on the frequent news reports about different accounts that have been cracked and broken into, there are still issues with fundamentally providing strong authentication that not only protects the systems but also protects the users and all of their data, including their credentials.

Beyond authentication is ensuring that each user gets access to the right resources and only those resources. This is what authorization is all about. Authentication is only the first step unless you intend for everyone to have the same rights and privileges all across the board, but that's not very realistic. In conjunction with that idea is the principle of least privilege, which should be followed to keep systems and resources better protected.

Certain protocols are responsible for authentication, access control, and ensuring that users get authorized to the right resources. Two such protocols are RADIUS and TACACS, which can be employed in a wide variety of situations, including being used for dialup users (perhaps for remote, out-of-band administrative access) and for providing access to network equipment and networks in general.

Authentication

Authentication is the act of proving you are who you say you are. You have credentials that you use to perform the act of authentication, and those credentials may come in various forms.

There are four potential factors of authentication:

- **Something you are**   This factor is inherent, meaning it's a part of who you are. This is commonly called biometrics.

- **Something you know**   This factor typically would be a password or personal identification number (PIN).

- **Something you have**   Commonly, your smartphone or cell phone might be the something you have. When you enable two-factor authentication on your banking website, for example, you may get a message sent to your phone. This message, which includes a value you provide back to the system you are trying to authenticate against, is sent to a preconfigured number, demonstrating that you are the authorized user.

- **Somewhere you are**   This factor is based on your location. You may have noticed that when you connect to your Google account or your Facebook account from a new location, you get an e-mail or a text message indicating that there was a connection attempt from a location that hadn't been noted before. This is because these sites know where you commonly connect from, via IP address or geolocation.

Imagine that you are crossing the border into Canada. You will be asked for your passport, which has your name and picture. Your name tells the border patrol agent who you are, and your picture assures them that you are who you say you are. This is reasonably straightforward. Passports are valid for ten years. However, consider how much you may change in ten years, and how difficult it would be to ensure that you really are who you say you are ten years after your picture was taken and you've aged ten years. During that time, you may have gained or lost significant amounts of weight, your hair may have turned gray, or you might have had cosmetic surgery to make alterations to your nose or lips. Such changes increase the challenge of performing authentication based on your passport. Beyond that, there is the question of the eyesight and facial recognition capabilities of the agent examining you and your passport. Also, the amount of light in your car and in the sky above the agent, which ensures a good look at both your face and your passport, comes into play. I'm reminded of a scene from the 1985 movie *Gotcha* where Anthony Edwards' character is crossing the East German border but doesn't want to be recognized, so the punk band he is traveling with paint him up with a lot of makeup.

Figure 4-1
An Auth log from
a Linux system

```
Mar 28 20:24:51 bill sudo:      kilroy : TTY=pts/5 ; PWD=/home/kilroy ; USER=root ;
 COMMAND=/usr/bin/lastlog
Mar 28 20:24:51 bill sudo: pam_unix(sudo:session): session opened for user root
by kilroy(uid=1000)
Mar 28 20:24:51 bill sudo: pam_unix(sudo:session): session closed for user root
Mar 28 20:24:56 bill sudo:      kilroy : TTY=pts/5 ; PWD=/home/kilroy ; USER=root ;
 COMMAND=/usr/bin/last
Mar 28 20:24:56 bill sudo: pam_unix(sudo:session): session opened for user root
by kilroy(uid=1000)
Mar 28 20:24:56 bill sudo: pam_unix(sudo:session): session closed for user root
Mar 28 20:25:01 bill CRON[24122]: pam_unix(cron:session): session opened for use
r root by (uid=0)
Mar 28 20:25:01 bill CRON[24122]: pam_unix(cron:session): session closed for use
r root
Mar 28 20:26:24 bill sudo:      kilroy : TTY=pts/5 ; PWD=/home/kilroy ; USER=root ;
 COMMAND=/usr/bin/tail /var/log/auth.log
Mar 28 20:26:24 bill sudo: pam_unix(sudo:session): session opened for user root
by kilroy(uid=1000)
```

EXAM TIP It's important to know the difference between authentication and authorization. Although they are related, they are very different concepts.

Given all of that, it's a wonder that travel happens at all with so many variables involved in the simple act of authentication. Fortunately, there are far fewer variables in computer-based authentication, but that doesn't make it any less challenging to find the right way to handle identity and proving you are who you say you are.

Figure 4-1 shows a partial log of users who have been authenticated on a Linux system on my network. Having this level of detail is a form of accounting, which is coming up later in more detail. This includes log information about cases where a user was authorized to perform a specific task. We will discuss authorization later in this chapter.

Credentials

Credentials are things you present in order to demonstrate that you are who you say you are. The credentials most commonly used in computing are a username and a password. These, however, are very weak credentials. Passwords can be easily guessed, particularly in this age of high-powered computers. Additional types of credentials are parts of your body in the case of biometrics, an access token, or a smart card. Combinations of these credentials can be used to perform authentication. When you use multiple methods of performing authentication, you are performing multifactor authentication. Not surprisingly, this is considered a best practice in implementing authentication. Single-factor authentication runs the risk of being compromised easily, particularly since single-factor authentication is typically a password.

Figure 4-2 shows a request from a Windows Server 2016 system for credentials. In this case, it's the login screen, and the figure shows an attempt to log in as the user Administrator on the system. Administrator is one half of the credentials being requested; the password is the other half. You'll see in the image that the user has filled in. Commonly, the user

Figure 4-2
The Windows
login screen

should have to enter the username rather than have it presented. An attacker, who could get access to this screen, including the possibility of a Remote Desktop Connection, would have half of the information they need. With the username already presented, the only piece that needs to be guessed is the password.

Passwords

A password is a secret word or phrase that is provided during the process of authentication. It is commonly paired with a username, although in some instances a password is all that is required to log in to some devices. There is a challenge with passwords, however. The best passwords are long and complex, with a variety of upper- and lowercase letters as well as numbers and symbols. The reason for this is mathematical. Let's take an eight-character password that just uses upper- or lowercase letters. There are 52 possible upper- or lowercase letters, so an eight-character password has $52 \times 52 \times 52 \times 52 \times 52 \times 52 \times 52 \times 52$ possible variations. This is simply because each position has 52 possibilities and there are eight positions, so you multiply the number of possibilities in position 1 by the number of possibilities in position 2, and so on. The total number of possible passwords in that situation is thus 53,459,728,531,456. While that may be a really large number, adding an additional position multiplies the potential outcomes by 52, and that's just if you only use letters. When you add in numbers, you get 62 potential values in each position, and thus 62^8 for an eight-character password. As you can see, adding additional positions and additional possible characters increases the number of possible outcomes.

Exercise 4-1: Password Values

How many potential passwords are there if you use a 16-character password/passphrase with all of the letters, both upper- and lowercase, as well as numbers and just the symbols that are above the numbers?

The problem is that humans just aren't typically capable of memorizing complex passwords with random letters, numbers, and symbols. This can lead to bad behaviors like writing down passwords on a piece of paper and leaving it someplace where it can be referred to when logging in. This really defeats the point of having complex passwords to begin with if they can be found written down. As a result, you dramatically reduce the number of potential passwords by limiting passwords to words or names that are more easily remembered. Thus, we move from potentially billions, trillions, or more passwords to something in the range of thousands. This makes guessing the password a lot easier. In some cases, you can convert letters to either numbers or symbols in order to increase the complexity of the password, but those conversions aren't typically challenging, and it ends up not really increasing the complexity. For example, using the word *password* for your password is, of course, a very bad idea. Changing the password to P455w0rd does a simple conversion from letters to numbers that look similar, but that strategy is pretty well known by attackers. If you change the letters to numbers or symbols that aren't reminiscent of the original letter, you run the risk of forgetting the conversions you did, which puts you back in the same boat with the long, random password—something that can't be remembered.

Often, people make it a lot easier to simply guess passwords by using ones that are easy to remember. Password123, the name of a significant other or child, and adding birthdates or anniversaries onto common words or names are all examples of typical strategies that people use in order to help them remember their password while still trying to ensure that it's complex enough to pass whatever rules an organization may have for a password policy.

Password policies also sometimes make remembering passwords too difficult. Requiring that passwords be highly complex can make it difficult for users to come up with a password, which may make them resort to using a dictionary word as a starting point and just adding enough numbers, symbols, and uppercase letters to pass the policy check. When you add in password rotation, particularly with fast cycles, you quickly run into a situation where average users may be forced to write down the passwords somewhere. There are challenges to cycling passwords every 60 or 90 days, too, especially when you don't allow for a reasonable level of reuse. Again, we run into the limitation where the human brain just doesn't really work that way. The brain is very associative by nature and strong passwords are non-associative and shouldn't be associative.

One tactic, in addition to a password policy, for ensuring the strength of users' passwords is to regularly run password-cracking checks against the password database. This is certainly something an attacker would likely do. Passwords are not commonly stored in plaintext anywhere since this would defeat trying to use strong passwords to begin with. If they were stored in plaintext, an attacker would only need to gain access to the system where the passwords are kept and read the file or files. As a result, there needs to be a way to protect the passwords in case the password files are actually discovered. One common way of doing that is to perform a cryptographic hash on each password. A cryptographic hash is a one-way function that generates a value that appears unrelated to the input. There is no way to run a cryptographic hash through an algorithm to reverse the process and get the plaintext password back, so this would seem to do a really good job of protecting the password.

NOTE One of the hash functions that has been very popular is based on the Data Encryption Standard (DES) algorithm. DES was specified as the encryption standard in the 1970s.

In addition to protecting password files by performing cryptographic functions like a hash on the password, the permissions on the file or files are typically set so that only the highest level of user can look at the results. You might think that hashing the passwords would be enough, given that the hash is one-way and can't be undone. The reason for this is that even with a one-way hash algorithm to protect the passwords themselves, there are ways of obtaining the password from the hash.

Password Cracking

Password cracking is the method by which passwords are taken from the place in which they are stored, typically having been hashed or otherwise encrypted, and obtaining the cleartext password. This is commonly done by simply performing the hash or encryption process against a list of possible passwords and comparing the output to the stored password. If the result matches, the password has been discovered. This can take time and computational power, particularly if there is a long list of potential passwords. Using a list of potential passwords and computing the hash or encrypted password from the plaintext is called a *dictionary attack*. Generating passwords using a specific set of criteria (e.g., a–z, A–Z, 0–9), computing the encrypted or hashed password, and then comparing the result to the stored password is called *brute-forcing*.

One way of limiting the processing time is to pre-compute all of the hashes ahead of time rather than when trying to crack the password. This means you are only computing the hashes of a dictionary or wordlist once and then comparing the stored password against the pre-computed hash value. This approach of using rainbow tables is a tradeoff of computing power versus storage space. Rainbow tables take up more disk space than just a wordlist because you are storing the pre-computed hash as well as the plaintext.

A number of password cracking utilities are available. One of the most popular is John the Ripper, an open-source utility that runs on Unix-based and Windows operating systems. John supports passwords that have been hashed using the Unix crypt function, which commonly uses DES as the algorithm to hash the password. John also supports passwords that have been stored in LAN Manager (LM) format, as well as passwords hashed with the Secure Hash Algorithm (SHA). This covers the majority of operating systems that are available. John can, and has been extended to, support even more password formats. This gives it a lot of flexibility.

Figure 4-3 shows the help feedback provided by John, indicating the number of options that are available in the course of a run. In addition to the command-line options, John also supports configuration files that can be used to provide information on how John should run.

NOTE In order to get the list of users and passwords from a Windows system, you can use the pwdump command. This will provide you with data that you can feed John to crack Windows passwords.

```
John the Ripper password cracker, version 1.7.8
Copyright (c) 1996-2011 by Solar Designer
Homepage: http://www.openwall.com/john/

Usage: john [OPTIONS] [PASSWORD-FILES]
--single                   "single crack" mode
--wordlist=FILE --stdin    wordlist mode, read words from FILE or stdin
--rules                    enable word mangling rules for wordlist mode
--incremental[=MODE]       "incremental" mode [using section MODE]
--external=MODE            external mode or word filter
--stdout[=LENGTH]          just output candidate passwords [cut at LENGTH]
--restore[=NAME]           restore an interrupted session [called NAME]
--session=NAME             give a new session the NAME
--status[=NAME]            print status of a session [called NAME]
--make-charset=FILE        make a charset, FILE will be overwritten
--show                     show cracked passwords
--test[=TIME]              run tests and benchmarks for TIME seconds each
--users=[-]LOGIN|UID[,..]  [do not] load this (these) user(s) only
--groups=[-]GID[,..]       load users [not] of this (these) group(s) only
--shells=[-]SHELL[,..]     load users with[out] this (these) shell(s) only
--salts=[-]COUNT           load salts with[out] at least COUNT passwords only
--format=NAME              force hash type NAME: DES/BSDI/MD5/BF/AFS/LM/crypt
--save-memory=LEVEL        enable memory saving, at LEVEL 1..3
```

Figure 4-3   John command-line options

Another password-cracking utility that has been very popular is L0phtCrack. L0phtCrack was written by Mudge, a member of the hacker group L0pht. It was designed to test password strength and also recover lost passwords. L0phtCrack uses a combination of strategies, much like John does. L0phtCrack uses dictionary, brute-force, and rainbow tables attacks against the Windows password database. Unlike John, however, L0phtCrack is commercial software and has been through a few owners, in part due to mergers and acquisitions.

Figure 4-4 shows the L0phtCrack wizard that starts up when you launch L0phtCrack. The wizard guides you through how you want to import passwords, how you want to try to crack them, and then how you want the results reported on. Of course, you can cancel out of the wizard and just use L0phtCrack without it. Figure 4-5 shows the main window of L0phtCrack, including the Statistics pane on the right-hand side that provides a status on the number of passwords cracked and how many passwords have been attempted. You can also see the passwords that are being attempted as they go by.

NOTE   Mudge (Peiter Zatko) formerly worked at BBN, the company responsible for building the ARPANET, and then went to DARPA, the defense analog of ARPA. Mudge once famously announced, with other members of L0pht, that they could shut down the Internet in 30 minutes.

LAN Manager Passwords

Windows originally took their password management from OS/2, which was the operating system developed by Microsoft in conjunction with IBM. OS/2 called their networking components LAN Manager, and the password storage was referred to as LAN

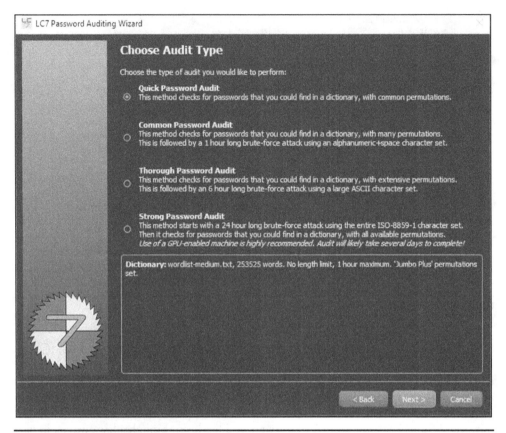

Figure 4-4 The L0phtCrack wizard

Manager (LM). There were a number of problems with the LAN Manager passwords, however. The first problem was that LM passwords were not case-sensitive. All passwords were converted to uppercase before the hash was generated. This immediately removed 26 characters from the possible characters in each position. You could always assume that any letter in the password was uppercase. Additionally, while the passwords had a maximum length of 14 characters, they were padded with NULL bytes (a value of 0) if the actual password was less than 14 characters. Finally, the password was broken into two seven-character chunks, a hash was computed on each chunk, and then the two hashes were put back together. If a password was only seven characters, the second half of the hash would always have the same value because it would be based on a hash of NULL bytes. A hash will always yield the same result through a hashing algorithm. If it didn't, it wouldn't be of much value to something like an authentication process since you wouldn't be able to compare a stored value against a computed value because the computed value would be different every time.

If you had a password that was less than eight characters, which is possible without a password policy, the value of the second part of your hash would be

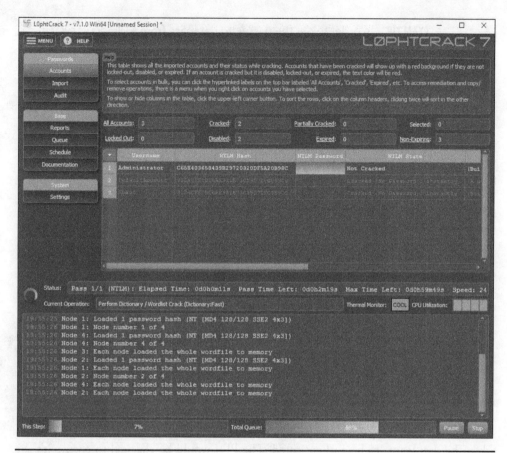

Figure 4-5 The L0phtCrack main window

0xAAD3B435B51404EE. When you saw this value in the second half of the hash, you could be assured you were looking for a short password, which significantly reduced the number of potential passwords on top of the already reduced number because all passwords would be uppercase after being converted.

All of these processing strategies led to very weak passwords. Microsoft called their implementation of LAN Manager NT LAN Manager (NTLM). Microsoft continued to use LM hashes for authentication until the release of NT4.0 Service Pack (SP) 4 in October of 1998. At that time, Microsoft released NTLM version 2 to remediate the flaws in the original NTLM implementation that led to easily cracked passwords.

Prior to the release of SP4, Microsoft attempted to protect their password database with Syskey. Syskey was introduced as an optional feature in NT 4.0 SP3. Syskey encrypted the password database in an attempt to protect against offline password cracking. Offline password cracking is where you take the static password database and run password crackers against all of the hashes, trying to determine what the plaintext password is.

EXAM TIP In order to get the password database from a Windows system using Syskey, you can use the pwdump utility. The results can then be fed into a password cracking utility like John.

Token-Based Authentication

Token-based authentication may make use of a physical token that provides an authentication value. The token is "something you have" and is typically used in conjunction with "something you know," like a personal identification number (PIN). It's possible to get software-based tokens that work like a hardware token. One of the great advantages to token-based authentication is that it commonly uses one-time passwords. The token generates a value that, employed in conjunction with the PIN, can be used to authenticate a user. Once the authentication value has been used, it can't be used again and the value provided by the token will refresh after a specific period of time.

Hardware tokens can come in several forms, and mobile devices such as cell phones can sometimes be used to perform the token function. Some tokens require being attached to the computer the user is trying to authenticate to. This could be done using a USB dongle that plugs into the computer using a well-known and widely used system interface. This is very similar to the dongle that has long been used by software vendors to ensure that the person using a piece of software is actually the owner. When you purchase some pieces of software, you get a hardware dongle. The software won't run without the dongle attached. The idea is that while you can make as many copies of the software as you like and distribute them, they won't be any good without the dongle, which is significantly harder to copy and distribute.

One method of implementing a token function is using a synchronized token and server. The token's values are synchronized with a server that is used to check the values when the user wants to be authenticated. The PIN would be checked to ensure it's the one provided by the user when the token was first initialized. Then the token value is checked to ensure that the user is in possession of the token.

Figure 4-6 is a picture of an RSA SecurID token. Notice that the display has a number in it. The number changes every 60 seconds and is synchronized with a server. The number, in combination with a PIN, is the one-time password that would be used to authenticate a user.

Figure 4-6
An RSA SecurID
token

Tokens can also be used for physical authentication to ensure that someone has the ability to access something, like entry to a building. A badge can be used in place of a key since keys can be lost or copied. A badge containing information about the holder is much harder to copy and can also be imprinted with the picture of the user, which provides additional authentication, ensuring that the holder of the badge is the right person. These types of tokens are also used in electronic payment solutions. You will sometimes see a place to wave your credit card instead of swiping it.

Tokens are not foolproof, however. If the PIN can be determined either by shoulder-surfing (looking over the shoulder of a user) or guessing, then the token can be used to authenticate as the user of the token. This form of two-factor authentication is still considered better than simply using usernames and passwords, because a password can be guessed, and while a PIN can also be guessed, you need to have physical access to the token in order to make use of it.

 NOTE Some financial institutions are using two-factor authentication that employs tokens to authenticate their customers to web-based portals.

RSA Security is one of the leading vendors when it comes to token-based authentication. Their SecurID product comes in a wide variety of forms and is often used for one-time password authentication in enterprises. RSA was breached in 2011 and one of the major concerns, in light of the fact that RSA admitted that information relating to their SecurID products had gotten out, was that information that would have allowed token codes to be predicted may have gotten out. This breach and the possible issues that may have resulted from it really highlight the challenges of strong authentication. It's very difficult to develop an invulnerable means of authentication.

Biometrics

One of the great things about biometrics is all of the movies that have made use of bio-metrics to one degree or another, typically demonstrating ways of bypassing biometric systems. Seen in everything from *Sneakers* (where they splice a tape together to get past a voice print recognizer) to *Demolition Man* (where Wesley Snipes uses an eyeball from a dead body to get past a retinal scanner), biometrics is the "something you are" part of authentication. Something you are can entail a number of aspects of your physical being, including your voice, your face, or portions of your hand or eye.

Biometrics work because we are generally physically unique in many ways, and these unique qualities can be used to identify us. Biometric systems are not infallible, however. There are a lot of different reasons why biometric systems can fail, which can sometimes make them weak authenticators. Some important metrics are associated with biometrics. The first is the false acceptance rate (FAR). Obviously, the FAR is a very important statistic because it means that sometimes biometric systems can be mistaken and thus allow someone access to a resource who shouldn't have access to it.

EXAM TIP Lowering the false acceptance rate (FAR) is a critical aspect of maintaining a biometric system.

Another important metric is the false rejection rate (FRR), which is the probability that someone who should have access is instead rejected by the biometric system. This is another statistic that takes careful monitoring to ensure that appropriate users get access to systems they should get access to. Tuning the biometric system and providing it with additional data points can reduce the FRR.

The Android phone software provides a way of authenticating users with facial recognition. When you hold your phone up to your face, as long as you have configured facial recognition as a means of authentication, your phone will recognize you and allow you access. Apple introduced Face ID in 2017, providing similar functionality to what Android already had. However, because of the FRR, there is a backup authentication mechanism on both types of devices because sometimes both Android's facial recognition and Apple's Face ID fail, which would lead to the user being unable to use their phone if it were the only means of identification/authentication. It's this sort of problem that can lead to challenges with the implementation of biometrics.

Biometric systems should have mechanisms to ensure that they can't be fooled by a photo of a fingerprint or an iris. This "liveness" characteristic could be a heat sensor or, in the case of eye recognition, some amount of movement to indicate that it's not a photo or other digital reproduction of the original.

Fingerprint Scanning

Fingerprint scanners are a very common type of biometric system. Such scanners have become so common, in fact, that many laptops have fingerprint scanners built into them as a way of authenticating users. The scanner looks at the pattern of whorls on your fingerprint because everyone has unique fingerprints. Fingerprints have long been used as a means of authenticating people. Children's fingerprints are taken at an early age so the child can be identified in case of a catastrophic event like a kidnapping. Criminals are also identified by their fingerprints. Because fingerprints can be so reliable as a means of identification, they make good biometric identifiers. Figure 4-7 shows the tip of a finger and its pattern of whorls and ridges that provides the foundation for the identification.

Figure 4-7
The whorls of a
fingertip

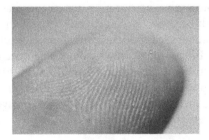

NOTE Fingerprints are left on surfaces that you touch as a result of the natural oils your body produces. These same oils can leave residue behind on a fingerprint scanner. Such oily residues may be used to lift fingerprints from a scanner, or they may cause problems with fingerprint identification.

There are challenges with fingerprint scanners, though. For example, with the built-in fingerprint scanner on a laptop, one finger is scanned. If you accidentally cut off that finger while woodworking, that fingerprint won't do you any good (unless you keep the finger for scanning, a morbid idea straight out of a crime novel or movie in which the finger is intentionally removed and used to bypass a biometric system). That's an extreme example of FRR, but there are other cases where your fingerprint may not be read accurately, leading to your fingerprint being rejected even though it really is your finger being scanned. Another challenge with fingerprint scanners is that some have been easily fooled by something as simple as a photocopy of a fingerprint.

A significant advantage of fingerprint scanners, though, is that your fingers are, assuming something catastrophic hasn't happened, something you always have with you. A token can easily be forgotten at home or at work. Also, you can't forget a finger like you can a password. Your finger remains static, so it's not something you need to change out on a regular basis like a password. This is convenient and pretty reliable as a unique form of identity.

Voiceprint Analysis

A voiceprint is pretty much what it suggests. You take the idea of a fingerprint, but apply the concept to your voice. You would typically speak a particular phrase to a voiceprint system so that the resulting waveform could be compared against a stored waveform of you speaking the same phrase at the time your authentication credentials were established. This always recalls to me the movie *Sneakers*, where a voice was taped and then the resulting tape was spliced to construct the passphrase necessary to allow access to a facility. This is one of the risks of voiceprint as a means of authentication. Additionally, your voice can change on a regular basis depending on how well you are, your level of hydration, your level of excitation, and many other factors. The voice isn't a constant. In addition to changes in pitch and inflection, there are changes in speed that can also factor into the difficulty of recognizing a voiceprint.

Even beyond the potential challenges in simply identifying the speaker accurately, there are the issues of ambient noise. Any noise within the environment, either at the time of initial identification or during the process of authentication, can potentially have an impact on the recognition of the sample since all noises will factor into a recorded waveform. These challenges are some of the reasons why voice recognition has a low adoption rate among biometric solutions.

NOTE It's hard to check for liveness with a voiceprint, which is easy to manipulate using an audio recorder and some audio editing software. You can easily interface with a voiceprint system at a distance, and devices like a cell phone have the capability of playing back audio that can be easily detected by the voice recognition system.

As with fingerprint analysis, however, voiceprint analysis has the advantage of being something you can't leave home without, except in the case of extreme illness, in which case you may well be better off staying home anyway. The one factor that may require memorization is the passphrase, unless it's something you are prompted for by the authentication mechanism.

Eye Scanning

Two components of your eye can be scanned because they are considered unique. One is the iris and the other is the retina. The iris is the colored part of your eye that controls the diameter of the pupil to allow either more or less light in so you can see in both dark and bright situations. The retina is on the inner surface of the eye and is the portion responsible for sensing the light coming in through the pupil. The iris has similar characteristics to a fingerprint. It has a high degree of variability, leading to something close to uniqueness, so it can be used to determine whether someone is who they say they are. Additionally, the iris is something determined before birth that is carried with you throughout your life. The static nature of the iris makes it a good prospect for an identification marker. Figure 4-8 is a photo of an eye, with the blue iris surrounding the black pupil in the center. If you look closely at the photo, you may be able to see the unique pattern of white and gray squiggly lines running from the outer portion of the iris to the inner portion. This is the pattern, along with the coloration, that makes the iris unique for the purposes of identification.

Iris scanners can fail because a dilated or constricted pupil, resulting from differences in the amount of light available in different circumstances, can deform the iris, making it difficult to match against the known signature. In Figure 4-8, notice that the pupil is actually dilated. When the pupil either dilates to let more light enter the eye or constricts to keep too much light out, it changes the size of the iris and the pattern of the lines in the iris. To accurately perform an iris scan, the eye must be in very close proximity to the scanner and the person cannot move while the scan is in progress; otherwise, they run the risk of causing a false rejection because the scan won't match. Without additional mechanisms to ensure the liveness of the subject, an iris scanner can be fooled by a very high-quality digital image of the subject's iris. This can expose an iris scanner to a very high false acceptance rate.

In the case of the retina, the complex patterns of capillaries form the basis of the biometric identification. The patterns are complex enough that they can be considered unique among individuals. The pattern is also so unique that there are very low error

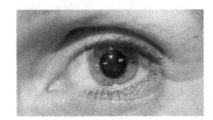

Figure 4-8
An iris

rates both on the false acceptance and false rejection side. The challenge, though, is that eye abnormalities like cataracts and astigmatism can cause problems with accurate identification.

> **NOTE** Retina scanning has been known for decades. In fact, *Batman: The Movie* from 1966 made reference to the complex pattern of capillaries in the retina and how they could be used to identify someone.

A challenge to both iris scanning and retinal scanning is the positioning of the sensor. If you position the sensor in such a way that tall people don't have to bend down too far to present their eye for scanning, you will make it too tall for shorter people to reach it. One way or another, unless you have a scanner that can be repositioned, or multiple scanners for different sets of heights, you are going to inconvenience users.

Hand Scanning

Hand scanners rely on the way your hand is shaped, using its geometry to determine whether it's a match. They make measurements of length, width, and other factors to help identify your hand. While hand scanners have been around for several decades and have been a very popular form of performing computerized biometrics for access purposes, they are not very accurate because hand geometry isn't very unique to any particular individual.

Hand scanning, or hand geometry scanners, can be used very effectively, however, with other forms of authentication like a card scanner. The presence of the card ("something you have") along with your hand ("something you are") can be a very effective two-factor authentication mechanism.

RADIUS

Remote Authentication Dial-In User Service (RADIUS) is a way of performing authentication across a network. This offers a centralized approach in a situation where you have a large number of network devices requiring the same user base as in a provider of dialup network access from back in the day when accessing networks and the Internet over analog modems was a common thing. RADIUS originated in 1991 as a way of providing authentication for access servers. In the time since then, RADIUS servers have been deployed to handle a wide variety of authentication needs. Since RADIUS is a standard protocol, it can be used as a front end or proxy for other authentication mechanisms, including other RADIUS servers.

> **NOTE** While RADIUS was developed in 1991 by the Livingston Corporation in response to a request for information (RFI) by Merit Network, maintenance and additional development of the protocol was taken over by the Internet Engineering Task Force, making it an Internet-wide standard.

RADIUS uses the User Datagram Protocol (UDP) for a transport protocol to send authentication requests and responses between the client and the server. A centralized server responsible for authentication is convenient and allows users to roam anywhere within the network and still make use of the same authentication credentials. In addition to authentication, RADIUS also offers authorization and accounting services. Both of these will be discussed later in this chapter.

Because of the generic nature of the protocol and architecture, RADIUS can be used to allow access to the Internet over a dialup modem or a DSL modem; it can be used to grant access to a wireless network; and it might be used to authenticate users in a virtual private network (VPN) solution. It has a wide variety of applications. Also, because it is a standard, it can be used as a glue protocol in between two different solutions. As noted earlier, a RADIUS server can behave as a proxy between a client and another authentication or authorization server. This may be a case where the network infrastructure makes use of a central RADIUS server that offloads requests for authentication to other servers based on the realm that the request references.

Clients belong to realms, which are ways of organizing users into specific groups. Each realm may have its own server. One example of this situation may be a case where one provider has the network infrastructure for a DSL network, but the customer-facing side is handled by resellers. Rather than allowing each reseller to make changes to a central database of users, which could be potentially problematic and may end up allowing poaching of users or accidental deletion, the network provider offers a RADIUS server where each DSL client authenticates, providing realm information as part of the request. This would allow the network provider's RADIUS server to offload the actual authentication and authorization to a reseller's RADIUS server. The network provider is proxying the authentication request on behalf of the reseller.

 EXAM TIP RADIUS uses UDP port 1812 for authentication and UDP port 1813 for accounting.

RADIUS does offer some security to the authentication process. While some authentication protocols transmit their credentials in cleartext, expecting that the connection to the authentication server will be either direct or at least private, RADIUS uses a shared secret in conjunction with a Message Digest 5 (MD5) hash to transmit the credentials. This prevents unauthorized users from performing packet sniffing on the connection and easily extracting user credentials. In this case, getting the user credentials is far more challenging than simply trying to brute force a password since almost nothing about the communication may be known in advance. Even without an encrypted link to transmit the RADIUS traffic over, this is a large hurdle to obtaining user credentials. However, if all you are looking for is access to the network, you may be able to transmit captured hashes in response to an authentication challenge and gain access.

While RADIUS is still in widespread use, a replacement protocol, Diameter, has been proposed. Diameter is widely used in the mobile space as well as in other voice-related networks like Voice over IP (VoIP). One of the hurdles to implementing Diameter is simply support for the protocol in the networking equipment that is currently making use of RADIUS.

NOTE You may have caught the fact that Diameter = 2 × RADIUS. Just another little joke among us Internet engineers.

TACACS/TACACS+

Terminal Access Controller Access-Control System (TACACS) is an authentication protocol that provides the ability for a remote access server (e.g., terminal server, dialup access server, and so on) to determine if a user can be authenticated based on the credentials provided. TACACS was developed in the early 1980s and has since mostly been replaced by the use of TACACS+ and RADIUS. TACACS, historically, used UDP for transport and operated on port 49. TACACS is a fairly simple and straightforward protocol, with a client sending a username and password to a TACACS server and getting either an accept or deny response back to the request. This request could be either a login or an authentication request. Cisco Systems eventually updated TACACS to a proprietary protocol they called XTACACS.

NOTE TACACS was developed by engineers at BBN Technologies, the company responsible for building the ARPANET, and BBN continued to work on developing and maintaining it over the years.

TACACS+ is considered an improvement on TACACS and XTACACS and was developed by Cisco Systems as a replacement protocol for the earlier two protocols. While the name is similar, it takes leaps forward because it is effectively its own protocol and is not backward compatible with the older protocols. A draft of the protocol was submitted to the IETF in 1997, though it never became an RFC or an IETF standard. In spite of that, TACACS+ is commonly used, particularly in networks with Cisco routers or switches in order to provide authentication services. Since Cisco has long been the predominant vendor for routing equipment to network service providers, TACACS+ has been implemented across the Internet in various degrees.

According to the TACACS+ draft, TACACS+ differs from TACACS by providing separate processes for authentication, authorization, and accounting, all of which can exist on separate servers. TACACS+ also uses TCP for reliable delivery, whereas the original TACACS protocol used UDP, as noted earlier. TACACS+ does listen to TCP port 49, which is the port previously assigned to TACACS in both the UDP and TCP protocols.

EXAM TIP TACACS is an older protocol, specified in RFC 927, while TACACS+ is the newer protocol, and includes authorization and access control in addition to the original authentication process. Both protocols use port 49, but TACACS is UDP, while TACACS+ is TCP.

TACACS+ messages may be encrypted, which is an upgrade in security over the older protocol. TACACS+ can carry authentication protocols such as the Password Authentication Protocol (PAP), the Challenge-Handshake Authentication Protocol (CHAP), and Microsoft's version of CHAP, MS-CHAP. PAP allows for the transmission of cleartext username and password while CHAP and MS-CHAP use an MD5 hash of the credentials and a challenge in place of the cleartext credentials. This protects the user's information during transmission of the authentication request.

Web-Based Authentication

So much of our lives takes place on the Web today. Whether it's social interaction via Facebook or Twitter or our financial life at our bank or broker, many people conduct a large portion of their lives online. The original technologies that made the Web possible didn't really have authentication in mind when they were developed. Because of this, we have had to implement authentication mechanisms into websites. This has provided some challenges, and these challenges have several potential solutions.

There are different authentication solutions for web applications, and some of them provide better security than others. The first is basic authentication, which allows the web server and client to negotiate the authentication. Digest authentication also has the server and client managing the authentication. Forms-based authentication is handled within the web application itself, relying on the logic of the web program to take care of authentication.

Basic Authentication

Basic authentication is handled within the context of the interaction between the web server and the client and is part of the Hypertext Transfer Protocol (HTTP). Authentication is handled within standard HTTP headers. When a client browses to a page requiring authentication, as specified by a mechanism on the server such as an access file within the server directory where the content is, the server generates a WWW-Authenticate header. The WWW-Authenticate header will be within the context of an error status like 401 Unauthorized, indicating that the client needs to be authenticated in order to gain access to the requested resource or page. The WWW-Authenticate header contains the realm that the user will authenticate against. The client then creates an authentication request by concatenating the user and password and inserting a colon (:) in between them. If the username were ric and the password were P4ssw0rd, for example, the authentication request would be ric:P4ssw0rd. Before transmitting this value to the server, however, the string is Base64 encoded. The following header would then be sent back to the server: *Authorization: Basic cmljOlA0c3N3MHJk==*, where *cmljOlA0c3N3MHJk* is the value of the username:password string after being Base64 encoded. Figure 4-9 provides an example of HTTP headers including the basic authentication request from a 401 Unauthorized message.

When the server receives the Authorization header, it decodes the username:password string and then compares the username and password against values stored on the server to determine if the user can be authenticated. The problem with this mechanism, of course, is that it's not any better than sending the credentials in plaintext since Base64 decoders are easy to come by and the Authentication header indicates very clearly that the authentication value has just been Base64 encoded and not otherwise

Response Header Name	Response Header Value
Status	Authorization Required - 401
Date	Fri, 29 Mar 2013 00:13:34 GMT
Server	Apache/2.2.22 (Ubuntu)
WWW-Authenticate	Basic realm="Password Required"
Vary	Accept-Encoding
Content-Encoding	gzip
Content-Length	344
Keep-Alive	timeout=5, max=100
Connection	Keep-Alive
Content-Type	text/html; charset=iso-8859-1

Figure 4-9 HTTP headers from a basic authentication request

encrypted or protected. Because of this limitation, the use of basic authentication is not recommended in any case other than very limited situations on private networks or where the data is otherwise forced to be encrypted.

Digest Authentication

Digest authentication also uses the HTTP protocol headers to pass the required information, but the information is better protected. In the case of a digest authentication, a server would reply with an error status like 401 Unauthorized, indicating that the user has to be authenticated in order to visit the page being requested. Additionally, the server provides a realm to authenticate against, just like in basic authentication. In the case of digest authentication, however, the server provides a nonce, which is just a random value generated by the server. This nonce is used to prevent replay attacks against the server, since every authentication request should include a different, random value for the nonce. When the client replies, it replies with a single hash value that has been generated from two separate hashes and the nonce. The first hash is generated from a concatenation of the username, the realm, and the password. The second hash is generated from the method (e.g., GET or POST) as well as the page requested, which is known as the request URI (Uniform Resource Identifier). Finally, the third hash is generated by concatenating the first hash, the nonce, and the second hash and then computing a cryptographic hash value from that string. Figure 4-10 shows headers from a 401 Unauthorized message, including the nonce.

Figure 4-11 shows a dialog box indicating that the user needs to be authorized before getting access to the requested page. Once the user enters values into the username and password fields, the request is sent to the server with an Authorization header. When the server receives the Authorization header, it will include the username, the realm, the nonce, the URI, and the response, which is the third hash value. The server will also generate a hash in the same manner as the client did and compare the value it gets to the response value sent in by the client. If the values match, the user is authenticated and the requested resource is presented to the user. Otherwise, the user is not authenticated and an error response is sent back to the user.

Response Header Name	Response Header Value
Status	Authorization Required – 401
Date	Fri, 29 Mar 2013 00:20:31 GMT
Server	Apache/2.2.22 (Ubuntu)
WWW-Authenticate	Digest realm="Password Required", nonce="DnEsPQXZBAA=717ea1e3d461d225...
Vary	Accept-Encoding
Content-Encoding	gzip
Content-Length	344
Keep-Alive	timeout=5, max=100
Connection	Keep-Alive
Content-Type	text/html; charset=iso-8859-1

Figure 4-10 HTTP headers from a digest authentication request

While the username is passed in the clear, the password is not. The username must be passed to the server in order for the server to know what user to look up and generate a hash value for. Without that data, the server would have to compute a value for all the users in the list of authorized users and that would just delay the response in addition to generating an unnecessary load on the server. Since the server generates a random nonce for each request, you can't have a list of pre-computed hashes sitting around to compare a response to. The response must be computed each time since it contains the randomly generated nonce.

Since the username is passed in the clear as part of the HTTP headers, this can provide an attacker with a list of usernames if the attacker can listen to the communication with the server over a long period of time. Because this is a potential risk, any time there are users being authenticated, it's a good idea to ensure the messages are being encrypted between the server and the client.

Forms-Based Authentication

Unlike basic and digest authentication, forms-based authentication doesn't make use of the HTTP headers to pass authentication information back and forth. This doesn't mean that HTTP headers aren't used at all, however. Since HTTP is a stateless protocol,

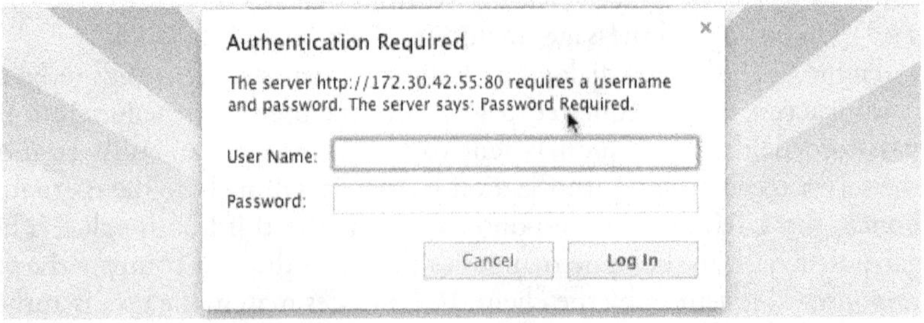

Figure 4-11
A dialog box requesting authentication

meaning every request to a server is considered standalone with no concept of connection state, most web applications need a way to ensure that users remain authenticated across multiple requests to the server rather than having to authenticate each request that gets made. Because of this state requirement, it was necessary to develop a way of tracking that state, and so cookies were created as a way of maintaining information across multiple requests or sessions between a client and a server. The cookies are maintained on the user's computer and managed by the browser.

The authentication itself, as well as the means of passing the authentication credentials to the server, is entirely up to the application. It is called *forms-based* authentication because, rather than having the browser itself handle it by popping up a login dialog box, the web page has a form embedded in it requesting a username and password or other forms of credentials. Once the credentials have been collected, it's up to the web page and the underlying application code to determine if credentials are sent in a GET or a POST request, if they are encrypted or hashed in any way, and if they are sent as part of a query string within the URL or are sent as parameters with the headers. Figure 4-12 shows an example of how a forms-based authentication page would be handled in PHP. You can see the script pulling the values out of the form and then rendering them into a SQL query. The results of the query and whether it's successful will determine whether the login succeeds. There is a potential issue with the statement checking whether the query resulted in a success since it never verifies that the username in the result matches the username in the query. This could potentially open the door to a SQL injection attack, which would allow unauthorized access.

```php
if( isset( $_POST[ 'Login' ] ) ) {

        $user = $_POST[ 'username' ];
        $user = stripslashes( $user );
        $user = mysql_real_escape_string( $user );

        $pass = $_POST[ 'password' ];
        $pass = stripslashes( $pass );
        $pass = mysql_real_escape_string( $pass );
        $pass = md5( $pass );

        $qry = "SELECT * FROM `users` WHERE user='$user' AND password='$pass';";

        $result = @mysql_query($qry) or die('<pre>' . mysql_error() . '</pre>' )
;

        if( $result && mysql_num_rows( $result ) == 1 ) {         // Login Success
ful...

                dvwaMessagePush( "You have logged in as '".$user."'" );
                dvwaLogin( $user );
                dvwaRedirect( 'index.php' );

        }
```

Figure 4-12 Forms-based login in PHP

NOTE Input validation is one of the biggest challenges for web developers in particular since a lack of input validation is often the cause of cross-site scripting (XSS), SQL injection, and command injection attacks.

Typically, forms-based authentication would make use of a database to store the authentication credentials, though that's certainly not a requirement. Using a database to store credentials, however, does lead to the risk of other attacks against the web infrastructure, such as SQL injections where the internals of the database may be used to gain unauthorized access or, perhaps worse, expose sensitive data from the database. Flaws in the program logic cause this vulnerability. This would be different from the other types of web-based authentication that don't rely on program logic and don't provide direct access to the data the application is storing.

Multifactor Authentication

Multifactor authentication is where multiple authentication mechanisms are used to grant access to a user. You may have seen this when interacting with your bank's website. Financial institutions, perhaps not surprisingly, have been some of the first to adopt stronger authentication mechanisms. In the case of your bank, you may have been asked to log in with a password and then asked a personal question that you would have established when you enrolled for access to the web interface. These are two instances of the "something you know" factor. Truly multifactor is when you are using two different factors, so you may be sent a message to your phone to take in the something you have factor. When you access your bank account through their automated-teller machine (ATM), you use two different factors—something you have (your bank card) and something you know (PIN).

Using a token and a PIN is two-factor—something you have and something you know. Adding biometrics to that using something like a fingerprint scanner will give you three-factor. In the case of the Android facial recognition backstopped by either a PIN or some other authentication mechanism, we are not talking about multifactor authentication. Multifactor is using multiple factors in the same authentication attempt. When one authentication attempt fails and you try another one, that's two different attempts at single-factor authentication and not multifactor.

Authorization

While authentication is proving that you are who you say you are, authorization is ensuring that you have the appropriate rights and permissions to access a particular resource. Authorization is tied inextricably with authentication, since in order to authorize someone to perform a particular action, you should first ensure they are who they say they are. Authorization is a process that commonly follows authentication. Once your credentials have been validated, the system can determine whether you have authorization to get access to the resource you have requested. Authorization can be very fine-grained. You may have perfectly acceptable credentials that you present to a login function, but you just don't have the rights to make use of a system in a particular way. As an example, you may be authenticated and authorized to log in to a system when you are sitting directly in front of it, but while your credentials are the same, you may not be authorized to log in remotely to the very same system. I may authorize you to read one file on my system but not authorize you to read another file. You may be able to write to one of those files but only read from another one without being able to write to it.

You may have noticed in the earlier discussion of the authentication protocols, such as RADIUS and TACACS+, that authorization was part of the discussion. Again, this is because we like to segment our infrastructure and our data. Just because you have valid credentials to log in to a system or network doesn't mean you get complete access to and control over all aspects of a system or a network.

Principle of Least Privilege

In information security, there is a principle of least privilege that states you should only be allowed to access exactly what you need in order to perform your job functions. You shouldn't get access to anything above what you need since that comes with the risk that you may make use of the excessive privilege in a way that may compromise resources in some way. Your credentials may also be used to gain access to those excess privileges in a malicious way, should someone else get your credentials. Least privilege is a good principle to live by to best protect systems and other resources.

 EXAM TIP   The Unix/Linux utility sudo is an example of the principle of least privilege because you have to be authenticated and authorized to perform higher-level functions using sudo than those granted to your user. sudo will determine what specific functions you are permitted to perform, but only when run through the sudo command.

While this principle has been used to varying degrees on Unix-like operating systems for years, it's a more recent development on Windows systems. It's easier for developers to simply expect to have system privileges in the services they may be developing than to specifically determine the privileges they need and have a user created with those specific privileges so the service can run in the restricted context of that user. Many system services operate with system privileges when they may not need to. Additionally, starting with Windows Vista, Microsoft implemented User Account Control (UAC), which required users to run in a context of least privilege. If additional privileges were required for a specific application, the screen would change and the user would be prompted about this elevation of privileges.

The challenge with this approach is that it could be turned off easily, meaning you would no longer be required to accept the risk that comes with elevated privileges. This is similar to simply logging on with full administrative privileges, which was the case previously with Windows operating systems, and is the case with Unix-like operating systems that allow someone to log in directly to root. In a Unix-like operating system like Linux, root is the administrative user. When someone logs in directly to the administrator account, no matter what the operating system, the principle of least privilege is violated and opens the door to potential damage to the system.

Accounting

Accounting is all the paperwork associated with system and user management. It keeps track of who has logged in, for how long, what they have accessed, and so on. This typically takes the form of logs on the system, from which you can derive a lot of information. Accounting provides the ability to determine who did what and when they did it. This is helpful in the case of attacks against a system or in the case of a misconfiguration of a resource. The logs will provide details about when the misconfiguration may have taken place and who may have done it. Obviously, the who depends on how authentication is done, since weak authentication can be broken and allow malicious users access to systems they shouldn't have access to because they have stolen the credentials of a legitimate user.

 TIP Phone systems, including VoIP systems and cell phone networks, use accounting to determine usage and billing. You may see this accounting detail on your billing statement. These are often called call detail records.

Accounting is also useful for providing details to enable billing for resources by tracking usage. You may also want to have details of system and resource utilization for trending and analysis. In addition, keeping track of capacity to determine when resources may need to be augmented, upgraded, or replaced is a good idea.

Figure 4-13 shows a list of the last users to log in to a Linux system. This list is generated from the wtmp log that is stored on Unix-like operating systems. This list of users helps narrow down who was logged in to a particular system at a particular time and from when. You can see in the third column where the user has logged in from. This is the hostname that the login originated from over the network.

Figure 4-13
The last users
to log in

```
kilroy@bill: $ sudo last
kilroy    pts/5    oliver.westell.c Thu Mar 28 20:24   still logged in
kilroy    pts/5    oliver.westell.c Thu Mar 28 18:43 - 20:23  (01:39)
kilroy    pts/5    oliver.westell.c Mon Mar 25 14:52 - 13:43 (2+22:50)
kilroy    pts/7    oliver.westell.c Thu Mar 21 20:52 - 22:58  (02:05)
kilroy    pts/5    oliver.westell.c Thu Mar 21 20:40 - 15:12  (18:31)
kilroy    pts/0    binkley.westell. Thu Mar 21 08:42   still logged in
kilroy    pts/0    oliver.westell.c Wed Mar 20 12:08 - 12:08  (00:00)
kilroy    pts/0    oliver.westell.c Wed Mar 20 11:54 - 12:08  (00:13)
kilroy    pts/0    oliver.westell.c Wed Mar 20 10:30 - 10:54  (00:23)
kilroy    pts/0    oliver.westell.c Mon Mar 18 20:56 - 10:17 (1+13:21)
kilroy    pts/5    yaz.westell.com  Mon Mar 18 15:03 - 17:15  (02:12)
kilroy    pts/0    oliver.westell.c Mon Mar 18 14:28 - 15:09  (00:40)
kilroy    pts/0    oliver.westell.c Mon Mar 18 13:51 - 13:57  (00:06)
kilroy    pts/0    oliver.westell.c Sat Mar 16 14:10 - 10:52  (20:42)
kilroy    pts/5    yaz.westell.com  Thu Mar 14 11:46 - 11:48  (00:01)
kilroy    pts/0    oliver.westell.c Wed Mar 13 16:04 - 13:36  (21:32)
kilroy    pts/0    oliver.westell.c Wed Mar 13 11:23 - 11:44  (00:20)
kilroy    pts/0    oliver.westell.c Wed Mar 13 11:00 - 11:02  (00:01)
kilroy    pts/0    oliver.westell.c Wed Mar 13 09:47 - 10:45  (00:58)
kilroy    pts/0    oliver.westell.c Tue Mar 12 14:59 - 15:01  (00:01)
kilroy    pts/0    oliver.westell.c Tue Mar 12 14:04 - 14:52  (00:47)
kilroy    pts/0    oliver.westell.c Mon Mar 11 17:58 - 18:26  (00:28)
kilroy    pts/0    oliver.westell.c Mon Mar 11 14:38 - 17:43  (03:04)
kilroy    pts/0    oliver.westell.c Sat Mar  9 21:28 - 13:39 (1+15:11)
kilroy    pts/0    yaz.westell.com  Thu Mar  7 14:05 - 14:05  (00:00)

wtmp begins Thu Mar  7 14:05:04 2013
```

EXAM TIP The utmp and wtmp files store the login information on Unix-like operating systems.

Access Control

Access control is tied up with all of the other concepts we've discussed so far—authentication, authorization, and accounting. Without knowing who is attempting to access a resource or what their permissions are, we can't make determinations about whether that access is allowed or not. Access control is about the whole process of determining what you have the rights and privileges to do on a system once you have been authenticated. Access control, in this sense, is very similar to authorization except that there are specific types of access control that different systems implement. Those different types of access control are Discretionary Access Control, Mandatory Access Control, Role-Based Access Control, and Attribute-Based Access Control.

Discretionary Access Control

Discretionary Access Control (DAC) allows the users to have the discretion to set access control rules on objects that they own. There is no overriding policy that sets the rules on what the controls on access should be. This is why it's called discretionary, because access controls can be set at the discretion of the user and not by the will of the security policies that govern the organization. This sounds good on the face of it. Surely the users should have the ability to determine who can get access to their files and data?

 EXAM TIP Windows Access Control Lists is an example of Discretionary Access Control, as is using the User, Group, and World permissions set in Unix-derived operating systems.

The biggest challenge with DAC is that typical users don't have the appropriate amount of knowledge about threats and risks to be able to make appropriate decisions about who has what level of access. Users may simply add Everyone as being able to read and write to simply not have to worry about either setting up a group and providing access to the group or adding each user individually. There are administrative challenges associated with putting access controls on every directory or file within the control of each user. This then relies on the defaults of the operating system in question to set appropriate levels of permissions. Having to set reasonable access controls on every directory or file because the defaults are unreasonable or lacking in sanity is too cumbersome to expect every user to perform those functions. This can leave the system and its data resources exposed to inappropriate or even unauthorized access.

In addition to being able to set permissions on files and folders, an owner may pass ownership permissions off to another user. Once that's done, the other user can set permissions and the original owner no longer has that ability unless the operating system supports having multiple owners.

Figure 4-14
List of permissions
on a directory

Figure 4-14 shows a list of permissions on a directory on a Windows 7 system. Note at the bottom of the window the different permissions that are available, from full control to read-only. This set of permissions provides very fine granularity on a Windows system, as you can see. In addition to read and write, there are also execute privileges, as well as the ability to list file contents. Directories may have slightly different needs for permissions than a file.

In a discretionary model, the users are responsible for maintaining the security of resources on the system. The entire overhead in this case rests on the user to set and maintain the correct permissions on documents they create. This is very different from Mandatory Access Control, discussed next, where the classification and security settings are far more centralized and controlled.

 EXAM TIP List-Based Access Control associates a list of users and their permissions with a particular object. For example, a file would have an access control list of all of the users and groups that have access to that file, as well as the level of access they have.

Mandatory Access Control

Mandatory Access Control (MAC) is a very strict way of controlling access to resources, and it's the type of access control typically implemented by governmental or military agencies. With MAC, access to a particular resource is determined by how that resource is categorized and classified. You would be allowed access if you had the same classification and the same category. This type of access control is based very strongly around security policy and data classification. Because it's based around policies, it requires a lot of work on the front end to establish the policies and rules that determine levels of access.

As an example, a document may be classified Secret and belong to the Operations group. If you have Secret clearance and also belong to the Operations group, you would be able to access that particular document. If you have Secret clearance but don't belong to the Operations group, you wouldn't get access. Both sets of criteria have to match in order to allow a particular user to access a particular resource. It's Mandatory Access Control because there is no way around it. The policies dictate access levels, and users have no ability to make changes, so from a user's perspective, the access control is mandatory and can't be altered to allow another user to access the file, even if the creator of the document would like a colleague to be able to see it.

There are challenges to Mandatory Access Control. The biggest one is the amount of overhead required to implement it. In addition to the work upfront that is required to establish rules for classification, there is the work to maintain the classification and labeling of documents. In this sort of model, you can't have documents that don't have labels and classifications. All documents must have labels and classifications in order to allow them to be accessed, based on the classification and categories a user falls into.

Role-Based Access Control

Role-Based Access Control (RBAC) may be the easiest access control model to figure out based solely on the name. In an RBAC deployment, users are assigned roles and rights, and permissions are assigned to those roles. You can think of these roles as groups, as they exist in both the Windows and the Unix worlds. Access privileges are not assigned to individual users in an RBAC deployment. All rights and permissions are assigned to the roles that users are then assigned to. This makes sense in an environment where users move around or leave on a regular basis. Where there is a lot of change, it can increase access creep, where users that no longer belong to a particular group may retain access if they haven't actually left the organization as a whole. Users who have been around a long time may retain rights and privileges from several previous positions, which may not be appropriate.

With Role-Based Access Control, you have to be assigned a role and then authorized for that role, which simply means that someone with the proper authority ensures that you correctly belong to that role.

When you assign access control based on role, you can add users to individual roles and then remove users from those roles when they have moved on. It makes management of access policies much easier because you are making changes to the role rather than to a lot of individual objects. Where you are assigning individual rights, it can be difficult to find all the documents and resources that a user has access to if they remain in the organization. Obviously, if they leave the organization, their user account should be deleted, at which point all the rights and permissions they have would be removed. It's because of the efficiency of granting and removing rights that the RBAC strategy is very often in use in larger organizations; managing rights based on the roles or groups that a user belongs to is far easier and has less overhead than doing it individually or on an ad hoc basis.

RBAC doesn't preclude the use of MAC or DAC. You may implement RBAC and still have DAC, giving the individual users the ability to control who has access to the resources they own. In the case of MAC, you can still use RBAC by assigning individuals to roles and then ensuring that the roles meet certain criteria before access is granted to a particular resource. You can think about it as a hierarchy where RBAC sits on top of either MAC or DAC to provide access to system or network resources.

RBAC also applies to specific applications. As an example, Microsoft SQL Server, Oracle's database management system, and PostgreSQL all provide the ability to assign rights to roles. In this case, you can provide granular access to individual tables or databases based on roles. You may have a large database where each table may have rights granted to different roles.

Attribute-Based Access Control

Attribute-Based Access Control (ABAC) requires that the user prove specific attributes. Rights are granted based on those specific attributes rather than on the identity and authentication of the user. An example of this would be allowing individuals to buy alcohol only after they have provided proof that they are at or above the legal drinking age. In the United States, individuals are required to prove that they possess the attribute of being at least 21 years old. Another example, more specific to a computer-based model, is proving that you are 18 years old in order to gain access to gambling or pornography websites. Once you have sufficiently proven that you have that specific attribute, or any other attribute required, you would be granted access to the resource in question. Another example is wanting to go on a particular ride at the fair or at an amusement park and needing to demonstrate that you are above a particular height.

 TIP Attribute-Based Access Control may have legal ramifications, as in the case of alcohol or access to gambling. It's worth knowing the legalities before implementing any ABAC system.

The challenge to this particular model is ensuring valid proof of the attribute in a timely fashion. As noted earlier, you may be required to prove that you are above a specific age before being granted access to a particular website. Often, this is done by having a user enter a birth date prior to being granted access. Facebook and Hotmail used this particular technique when they had a minimum age requirement. All you had to do was enter the right birth year and you were granted access regardless of your actual age. Really good mechanisms to prove specific attributes in a computerized, anonymous environment don't exist currently.

Single Sign-On

Single sign-on (SSO) is a way of managing a user's access to multiple systems and resources without requiring the user to log in for each individual system. There are several advantages to this approach. The first advantage is the obvious reduction in time spent typing in passwords. This can be a big time savings for users when they have to access a number of systems and resources during the course of the day. On top of that, different systems may have different password requirements, and those passwords may end up being different, which would require a user to have multiple passwords. When you expect a user to keep track of multiple passwords to multiple systems, each with potentially different password requirements, you again run the risk of the user needing to write those passwords down in order to be able to remember all of them.

A single sign-on solution requires a central authentication server to manage not only the authentication from a login but also the continued access based on additional authentication requests to further resources. Windows systems can use single sign-on using Active Directory and a Kerberos-based ticketing system (discussed in the next section). Any system within the Windows network would make use of the centralized authentication system to authenticate users, after which they could be authorized to access a particular resource. This might include file shares, printers, or SharePoint sites. Additionally, Internet Information Services (IIS) can make use of Windows Authentication, which is a simple way of referring to the various mechanisms that go into authenticating users on a Windows network.

A big risk that comes with single sign-on is that if an attacker can get access to a system using something like malware embedded in an e-mail message, they can gain access to all the resources on the network without ever having to authenticate again. Considering the number of applications that can and are willing to cache credentials, this particular risk may be a wash. If you have cached all of your credentials by asking the system to remember you when you gain access to a file share or a website, then any malicious user who had access to your system could still gain access to all of the systems you have access to. The only way to protect against this particular threat is to not use single sign-on and to never cache credentials. This seems unlikely to happen. The reason is people really don't like typing passwords over and over and they don't recognize the risk to other systems or infrastructure from caching their credentials so they don't have to type them again.

Kerberos

Kerberos came out of Project Athena at MIT. Athena was a project founded in 1983, designed to create a distributed computing environment. In addition to Kerberos, X Window System came out of the work done in Project Athena, and the project influenced the work of a lot of other protocols and applications. Kerberos is a way of performing network authentication. Kerberos will also help with a single sign-on solution because it has a central authentication server that all systems on the network can make use of to validate the credentials of any user attempting to access a resource. Figure 4-15 shows how systems interact with the Kerberos system.

Kerberos uses tickets to accomplish this. When a user logs in to a system on the network, the system contacts the Kerberos Authentication Server (AS). The AS gets a Ticket Granting Ticket (TGT) from the Key Distribution Center (KDC) and sends it back to the user's system. This TGT has been time-stamped and encrypted. The TGT is what a system uses to gain access to other systems. This only works, though, if the system the user is trying to gain access to uses the same Kerberos infrastructure. If a user wants to get access to a particular resource, the user's system will send its request and TGT to the Ticket Granting Service (TGS), which typically lives on the same system as the KDC.

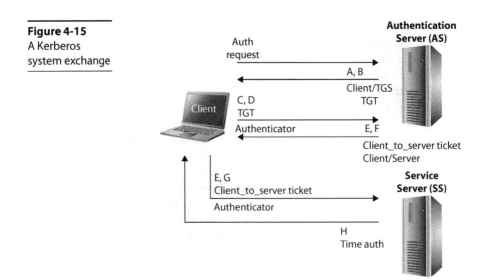

Figure 4-15
A Kerberos
system exchange

After the TGS has validated the TGT and ensured that the user has access rights to the resource in question, it will issue a ticket and session keys to the user's system, which then sends them off to the resource system along with a service request. Assuming the system hosting the resource is using all of the same Kerberos infrastructure, it should allow the resource request to proceed.

There are some downsides to using Kerberos, however. As with any centralized model, you create a single point of failure. If the Kerberos server goes down or is otherwise taken offline, no one can authenticate to anything and the network effectively becomes useless. As a result, the Kerberos server and infrastructure need to be highly available and reliable.

Also, because of the timestamps that Kerberos uses, all of the systems on the network need to use the same time source. If there is variation, users may have problems authenticating. This can be fixed by ensuring that systems sync their clocks to a Network Time Protocol (NTP) server. Assuming there isn't too much drift on the local system clocks, this should keep everyone well within the parameters that Kerberos requires.

Another issue is that gaining access to the Kerberos server could end up giving a malicious user access to any resource they want access to. It may also allow the malicious user to impersonate any user.

These risks may be considered acceptable in light of the upside of having centralized user management and reducing the need for users to have to keep track of multiple passwords, especially since those passwords may not all be subject to the same password requirements.

Chapter Review

Access control covers three areas that are highly significant: authentication, authorization, and accounting. All three are very important in protecting systems and resources. There are a number of ways to authenticate users, though requiring a username and password combination is the most common. Another popular method is the use of tokens, such as badges or swipe cards. In addition to that, there are biometric systems that authenticate based on physical characteristics by using voiceprint, iris and retina scans, or fingerprint scans. Adding additional authentication factors, called multifactor authentication, can improve reliability of authentication, although you should ensure that you are using mechanisms that are reliable, which can sometimes be challenging with biometric factors. The different factors that you would use fall into four categories: something you have, something you know, something you are, or somewhere you are.

Beyond authentication, users may then be authorized to access particular resources. Authorization has to follow authentication so you can know who you are authorizing. Authorization may be handled by using a single sign-on solution like Kerberos. Kerberos has been implemented into Windows Active Directory. Single sign-on does have benefits, including protecting against users writing down passwords. It also has downsides, including providing a malicious user access to an entire network once they have gained access to one system, although cached credentials can offer the same risk.

Questions

1. Microsoft Windows file security permissions are an example of what?

    A. MDAC

    B. RBAC

    C. DAC

    D. ABAC

2. RSA SecurID tokens provide what?

    A. Reusable passwords

    B. Security

    C. Usernames

    D. One-time passwords

3. Kerberos tickets allow users to do what?

    A. Not have to retype passwords

    B. Give other users permissions on the fly

    C. Get a time check

    D. Change passwords

4. What is the principle of least privilege implemented in?

    A. Windows Explorer

    B. Apache Web server

    C. The sudo utility

    D. RADIUS

5. Authentication is the process of doing what?

   A. Gaining access to critical resources

   B. Logging information about access

   C. Providing access to resources for users

   D. Proving you are who you say you are

6. Your bank is letting you know they are going to implement a token-based solution for authentication. You will be sent your token and you will need to establish a PIN. What type of authentication will the bank be implementing?

   A. Digest-based authentication

   B. Basic authentication

   C. Multifactor authentication

   D. SQL authentication

7. Network devices and dialup users may be authenticated using which of the following protocols?

   A. RADIUS

   B. Forms-based authentication

   C. Windows authentication

   D. Discretionary Access Control

8. Adding an additional alphanumeric character to the required length of a password will multiply the potential passwords by how many?

   A. 26

   B. 32

   C. 52

   D. 62

9. What can John the Ripper be used for?

   A. Authenticating against Windows networks

   B. Cracking Windows passwords

   C. Authenticating against Linux systems

   D. Encoding a Windows password before transmitting over a network

10. Which of the following can be used to authenticate someone?

   A. An iris pattern

   B. Weight and height

   C. A nose print

   D. Ear size

11. What is a significant problem with the use of basic authentication for web pages?

   A. It uses the MD5 hash.

   B. It uses Base64.

   C. It uses compression.

   D. It uses SHA-1.

12. What do you use the principle of least privilege for?

   A. Authentication

   B. Authorization

   C. Access control

   D. Biometrics

13. Why would you implement accounting?

   A. Verify access

   B. Verify usernames

   C. Verify Kerberos tickets

   D. Verify forms

14. What is the biggest problem with LANMAN passwords?

   A. Weak hash algorithm

   B. Inadequate access control

   C. Weak implementation of Kerberos

   D. Seven-byte hashes

Answers

1. C. While Windows does support RBAC, Windows uses Discretionary Access Control, where the user determines who has the rights to files and folders under their control.

2. D. A SecurID token, as with other token-based authentication mechanisms, rotates an access number on a regular basis. The username has to be provided by the user. Security is a very vague word. In this case, if a token is stolen and the PIN is known, anyone can get authorized as the user of the token.

3. A. Kerberos tickets allow users to not have to re-type passwords since Kerberos is often a component of a single sign-on solution. While time is an important component of Kerberos solutions, you wouldn't get a time check from a Kerberos token. Kerberos tickets are exchanged under the hood, so users certainly wouldn't use a ticket to provide another user permission for access. Finally, passwords are changed using another mechanism.

4. C. While Windows Explorer and the Apache Web server may have the principle of least privilege implemented in them somewhere, and RADIUS could help implement the principle of least privilege, it's the sudo utility that really implements it by expecting users to have to use sudo to gain additional privileges.

5. D. Authentication is about proving you are who you say you are. Authorization gives users access to resources once they have been authenticated, and accounting logs the access to resources.

6. C. Since the token is something you have and the PIN is something you know, this would be multifactor authentication. Basic authentication and digest authentication make use of the browser to request authentication credentials and then pass the credentials back either hashed or Base64 encoded. It's not SQL authentication because you are logging in to a website, not into a database.

7. A. RADIUS is the protocol that would be used to authenticate users on network devices as well as dialup users. Forms-based authentication is used with websites, and Windows authentication is how Windows users authenticate. Discretionary Access Control isn't an authentication protocol.

8. D. Lowercase and uppercase letters give you 52 potential characters (26 letters in both upper- and lowercase). Adding in 10 single-digit numbers gives you a total of 62 potential characters.

9. B. Among other things, John the Ripper can crack Windows passwords. It's not a tool for authentication. It's a tool for password cracking.

10. A. While weight and height can be used to help identify someone, an iris pattern is the only one in that list that can be used to uniquely identify and authenticate someone.

11. B. Base64 is easily decoded. There is no hashing or encryption involved.

12. C. The principle of least privilege is a way of implementing access control. By default, users are only provided access to the minimum amount of resources they need to do their jobs.

13. A. Accounting will give you details about who is doing what on your systems, and when they are doing it, enabling you to verify access in case something goes wrong.

14. D. LAN Manager broke longer passwords into seven-byte chunks. Rather than hashing the entire password, there are two hashes. If the password is not long enough to fill the entire 14 characters, the password is padded to fill out the entire 14 characters.

Exercise 4-1 Answer

There are 52 upper- and lowercase letters, and 20 numbers and symbols, so that's 72 potential characters. If we were to just do a 16-character password, it would be 72^16. That's 5.2 × 10^29 potential passwords.

Cloud Computing

In this chapter, you will learn:

- The various types of cloud computing services
- The security aspects of private and public clouds
- Cloud deployment strategies

To make a long story short (the "tl;dr" bit), cloud computing is just a new implementation of a means of obtaining computing resources that has been around for decades—outsourcing. IBM established the first service bureau for computing resources in the 1930s. IBM didn't have devices that we now think of as computers. Instead, they had devices that were called tabulating machines. They could take data from a company and shorten the time required to process that data considerably. Prior to that, the newly invented tabulating machines allowed U.S. census processing to be reduced from eight years for the 1880 census, which was processed by hand, to two and a half years using tabulating machines for the 1890 census. The company that started to sell these tabulating machines in 1911 would eventually be renamed International Business Machines (IBM) in 1924, after a couple of mergers.

Later, service bureaus such as IBM's were able to not only take data sources and organize them or tabulate them for clients, but also to offer time sharing of their computing resources. This meant companies were able to pay to use the service bureaus' computing resources for their own purposes. Because computers for decades were far beyond the reach, financially, of most companies, it made sense to rent out the power of these computing devices to make some jobs considerably faster and more cost efficient.

The idea of insourcing versus outsourcing has been around for years and it seems to swing back and forth a little, much like the idea of centralization versus decentralization. When we talk about cloud computing, we're talking about not only outsourcing, but also taking computing assets and associated data out of the direct control of an enterprise that is accustomed to having computing resources in a controlled data center (centralization) and entrusting those computing assets and data to third-party cloud providers (decentralization).

Cloud computing services have evolved and expanded quickly in the two decades since cloud computing first became a publicly known idea. You may be aware of storage as a service, software as a service, platform as a service, or infrastructure as a service (if you are not, all of them are introduced in this chapter). Modern platforms, or at least modern uses of these platforms, incorporate multiple of these different service elements to create a coherent service or application that can be consumed by a user or customer. So many companies are now using cloud providers for service delivery that the development of applications, as well as their deployment, has been impacted, which in turn has impacted the overall security of the applications and, by extension, the enterprises that use them. There are a number of ways that turning over control of the underlying systems can be beneficial to the overall security of the application.

There is some good news, of course. As companies start to make more use of cloud providers, a lot of vendors are making virtualized versions of security devices available. This makes it easier to develop a more robust design for a full multitier application. This does not mean, though, that you have to rely on traditional application design and architecture models. As the cloud computing providers mature, they are offering new services that can completely change the way applications may be developed.

Cloud Computing Services

On the consumer side, businesses consume cloud computing services in a manner that is very similar to the way they might consume virtual machines. In the end, what commonly underpins cloud computing services is just a very large-scale virtual machine infrastructure. On the provider side, this introduces a lot of security concerns that need to be addressed in order to ensure that one customer does not impact another customer. This is especially true if an application becomes compromised right down to the operating system. Cloud service providers must ensure that there is no way for an attacker to gain access to Customer B's data or systems by compromising Customer A's application.

 NOTE You can do many of the same things a cloud computing provider can with virtual machines using a Type 1 hypervisor, which runs on the bare hardware. A Type 2 hypervisor runs on top of an existing operating system. Cloud providers commonly run some form of hypervisor to support the virtual services they offer. Chapter 10 covers virtualization in depth.

One concept to understand is *multitenancy*. When you, as an enterprise, own your own systems, including the hardware and the physical space the hardware is housed in, you are the only *tenant*—the only user of those systems. Let's say, though, that as a cost-savings measure, your offices are in a building with several other companies and you put your systems into the same data center as the other businesses in that building. The building owner takes care of the facilities and operation of the physical data center, and also provides power and cooling. This is now a multitenant model, with all tenants sharing the cost of the data center. You need physical access to your systems, because hardware maintenance is necessary sometimes, but you should not be able to access the systems of the other companies who house their equipment in that data center, and vice versa. That would compromise integrity, confidentiality, and possibly availability (the CIA triad introduced in Chapter 1). The building owner must have some way to prevent any tenant from getting access to the physical systems of any other tenant, which means the owner cannot use traditional open computer racks in the data center.

The owner could divide the data center into individual rooms, one for each business who is leasing space, with an access-controlled door to each room. However, that would be inefficient and expensive and would defeat the purpose of a shared, multitenant model, because there no longer would be sharing of overhead. Your company would just be renting some additional space, with no ability to grow or shrink as you need to, adjusting your costs to exactly what you are using. A better way of doing it, perhaps, would be to have a single data center room and provide cabinets rather than racks. A cabinet offers the same manner of placing the hardware into a rack, but also has a locking door rather than being unenclosed. You can see an example of a cabinet in Figure 5-1.

This way, your company could rent as many cabinets as needed, and every other tenant could also have their own locked cabinets. The door to the data center would be locked to keep out everyone who is not renting space. Once you get inside the data center, though, you would still need to have some sort of keyed access to your own cabinet. A similar setup is to have separate cages that house several racks or cabinets, but either way, gaining access to the systems contained requires a key.

The multitenant model used by cloud providers has similar security concerns. A cloud provider does not have separate facilities for each of its customers. In the case of a cloud provider, *facilities* doesn't mean floor or rack space; it means system space—this might be storage space on hard drives or it might be virtual systems. It may also mean network utilization. All of these are resources that multiple cloud customers could be

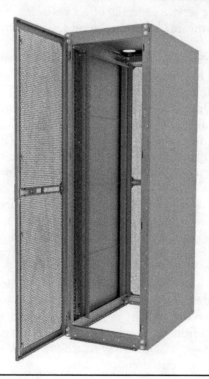

Figure 5-1   Telecommunications/server cabinet

using simultaneously. Every one of these resources needs to be logically separated to ensure one customer can't impact another customer. As more customers move more services to the cloud, this can become a big challenge.

Storage as a Service

Underpinning most other computing services is storage. However, this does not mean you can't separate out storage as its own entity, meaning the only thing you have is basically a disk drive you connect to over the Internet. This is a variation on something called network attached storage (NAS). A NAS device is often just a disk drive you plug into the wall without any traditional computer system connected to it. All access to the NAS is controlled through a management interface. This could be a command-line interface, but it's more often a web interface. You choose the methods of access, meaning the protocols you want to use to access the storage, such as the Common Internet File System (CIFS) or Network File System (NFS), as well as any authentication credentials necessary to gain access.

A NAS device presents as any other network file share, just as if it were a shared directory on a general-purpose computer system or a file server. It's an inexpensive way of providing a file server without the server part. Storage as a service is different. It doesn't present to you as if it were just a network file share on your network. You don't connect to storage as a service using the same protocols you use to connect to storage on your local network. Storage as a service generally offers a web interface to access and manage your stored data. In fact, you are likely using cloud storage even if you are not aware that you are using it.

Figure 5-2 shows an example of where you are probably using cloud storage where you may not be aware. This shows settings on an iPad indicating which applications should make use of Apple's iCloud storage and which should not. Similarly, Android devices can use Google Drive to store application data, files, and photos in the cloud. In the case of Apple, usually the cloud storage is managed through the application that is using the storage. This may be the Photos app or apps like Pages, for instance. When it comes to Google, the cloud storage is a little more wide open and less segregated by application. It's a different philosophy with respect to how users interact with the underlying components.

If you were to go to www.icloud.com and sign in with your Apple ID, you would see a list of applications. In order to get access to the storage, you would enter the application in the web interface. From there, you can see the individual files. This is different from Google Drive. Figure 5-3 shows an example of what it would look like in Google's web interface. Rather than a list of applications, you just see raw files and are expected to organize them yourself, in a way that makes sense to you. The same approach is true with other cloud storage providers like Dropbox and Box.com.

These cloud storage services are not only useful for remote storage. They are also useful for transferring files from one system to another. Let's say you want to make use of one file across multiple systems. One way to achieve this is to store it in, say, Google Drive and retrieve it as you need it, then replace it.

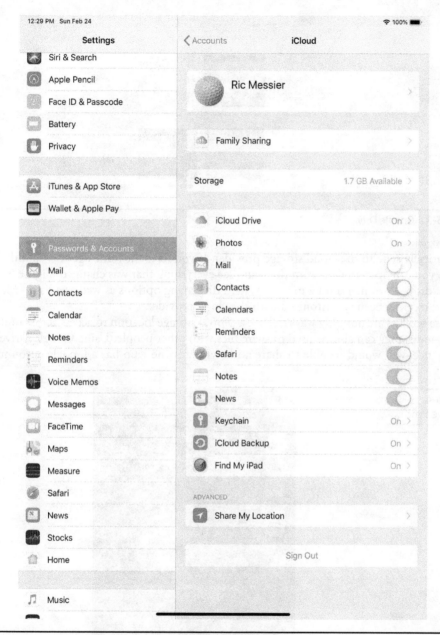

Figure 5-2   iCloud usage

There are, perhaps, easier ways to achieve this than using a web interface to retrieve and then re-store. For instance, you could use another storage provider, like Microsoft OneDrive, where you could install an agent onto your local system. This makes use of a local folder to sync files to. All you need to do is store a file out to that folder and it will

Figure 5-3   Google Drive

automatically sync to the cloud storage provider. If you have the same agent on another system, you can open the file from there and see everything that was changed. Figure 5-4 shows a drop-down menu on a macOS system displaying options as well as a list of files that had recently been synchronized with the cloud provider.

These services are not only ways to have a central storage location to access across multiple systems, they can also be used to share files with other people. Using Google Drive, for instance, you would be able to share a file with anyone who has a Google account.

Figure 5-4
OneDrive Sync

They would be notified by Google that you have shared the file and would get whatever level of access you provided. You could also, in some cases, allow access to anyone who had the URL without needing to provide specific access to individual users. This can be dangerous, since once a URL has been provided to anyone, that URL could be sent to anyone else or intercepted.

This sort of cloud storage means credentials are important. If someone's Microsoft or Google credentials are compromised, it's not only e-mail that would be in play. Anything that user stored in Google Drive or Microsoft OneDrive would be accessible by the attacker who had access to the credentials. This may be even more problematic when these same credentials can be used across multiple other services that may provide software access.

Software as a Service (SaaS)

While service bureaus, time share services, and application service providers are all variations on the concept of paying for the use of software or an application, software as a service is generally recognized as a different thing. Service bureaus and time share services, going back to the days of the mainframe, were companies who owned hardware and provided paid access to software or services. However, in general, this was access to commodity software and not individual licenses to software developed by the service bureau. The same is true for application service providers. You could get an application service provider (ASP) to provide an instance of content management software like WordPress to you. The ASP would handle the care and feeding of the operating system and all the relevant software, allowing you to focus on the content. However, that's not the same as an SaaS provider, which is a company that develops software and allows you to access that software, generally through a web interface, as part of their service delivery model.

In some cases, SaaS rides on top of storage provided by the same service provider. This is the case for services like Google Docs and Office Online (which may be referred to as Office 365, depending on the specific service purchased from Microsoft). With Google Docs, you can access files directly from Google Drive, and with Office Online, you can access files directly from Microsoft OneDrive. Additionally, you could use the online implementation of these office applications to directly edit or interact with the files. You don't have to make use of the web implementation, of course. You could also use the mobile versions of the applications to edit or view the files. In either case, you would be making adjustments to the files stored with the service provider.

Many applications have, to some extent, redefined the software category. One example is Salesforce. This is a piece of software that is, at its core, a customer relationship management (CRM) application. Unlike so many other CRM applications, though, Salesforce not only is available through a web interface, but also handles all storage of customer CRM data. Figure 5-5 shows one of the core features of Salesforce, the creation of a contact. This is not just about storing contacts, though. You can see there is a place for an account name. Ultimately, Salesforce is about managing sales leads and improving the sales process to not only make more effective use of your own people but also make sure you are being as efficient as you can with your customers.

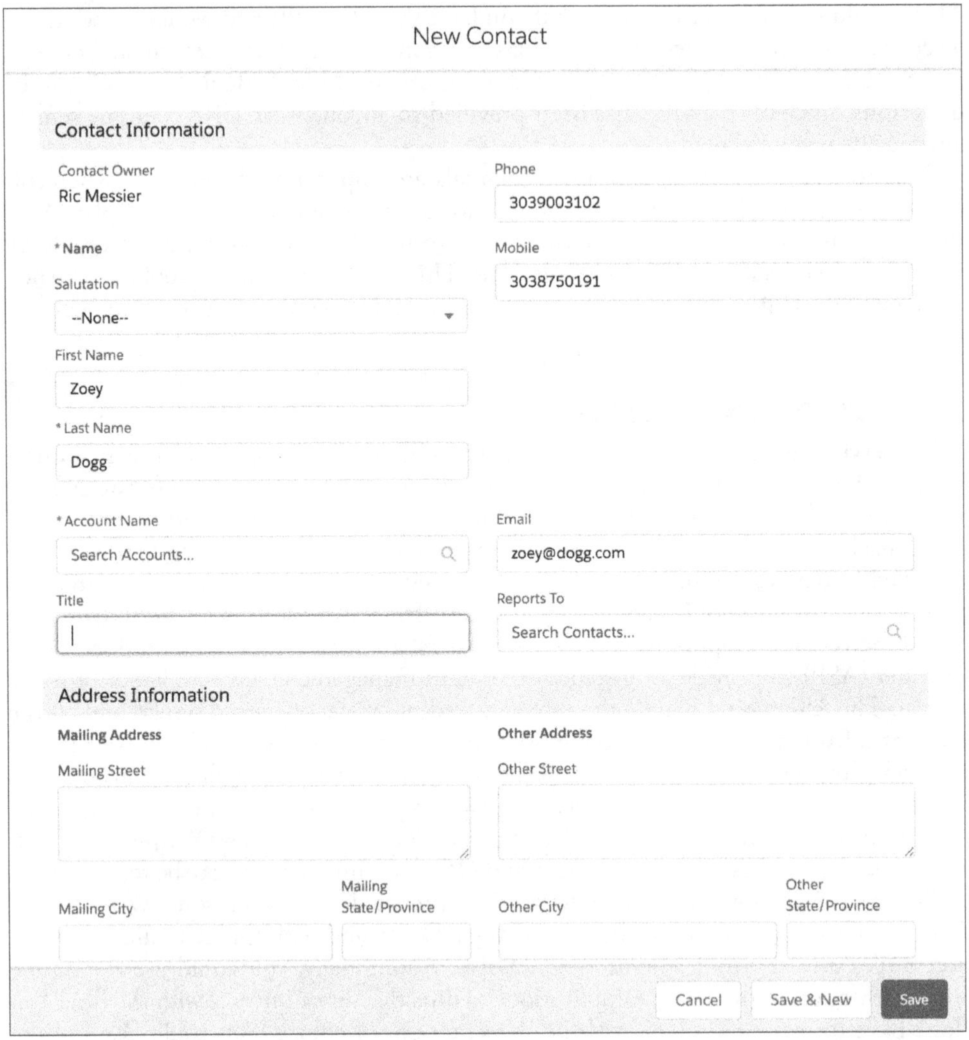

Figure 5-5   Salesforce.com New Contact form

Where Salesforce has significantly improved on other CRM solutions is that it provides the means for people and companies to create applications that make use of the Salesforce database. This includes automating workflows. This automation will significantly improve the productivity of a company's sales force. The company can automatically route leads to the right salespeople to ensure the customer isn't being bounced around from person to person to get to the right representative. These applications are made possible, in part, because data is stored with Salesforce, and that means you don't have to worry about obtaining the application and installing it on your premises. You can obtain the application and enable it, which requires no additional care and feeding on your part.

One significant advantage to SaaS, and one reason a lot of companies are making use of these services, is that the services can be very cost effective. For starters, you don't need hardware on premises to support the software, because you are accessing the application over the Internet through systems and interfaces provided by the vendor. As a side benefit, because you don't have to purchase or configure any hardware to support the software, the speed of deployment to the user who needs it increases dramatically.

Another cost savings occurs in scenarios where an organization needs particular software only for occasional use and that software is very expensive to acquire; SaaS has a very low cost of entry as a general rule. SaaS vendors often use a pay-per-month model that is on a per-seat basis. For example, if you have a small organization and need some project management software, but you need it for just a short period of time, you might look at the cost of purchasing the software and find it cost prohibitive. Without SaaS, you would have to resort to workaround software that is likely to be cumbersome and inefficient. Instead, you could use something like Smartsheet, which is a service that offers different types of sheet-based documents online, including project management. Using Smartsheet, you can collaborate with other users and share the access to the overall project plan. This means users can see the changes in real time rather than waiting for the project manager to export a Gantt chart to share…a chart that would be outdated pretty quickly, especially in an active project. So, with a service like this, you get a lot of utility that is also generally cost effective and cheaper than acquiring software that may require resources, support, and overall management. Figure 5-6 shows the start of a project plan using Smartsheet.

There are security considerations for SaaS, of course. In some cases, vendors may make use of authentication services provided by other vendors, like Google, Microsoft, or Facebook. If an attacker gains access to your Facebook account, for example, they will also be able to access all cloud-based services for which you are using that compromised account to authenticate. This is not to say you shouldn't use authentication services from a third-party provider. It does mean, though, that standard account hygiene becomes even more important when you are using that same account for access to multiple services. Strong passwords and multifactor authentication should always be used, but especially in cases where you have a service that is performing authentication functions for multiple services.

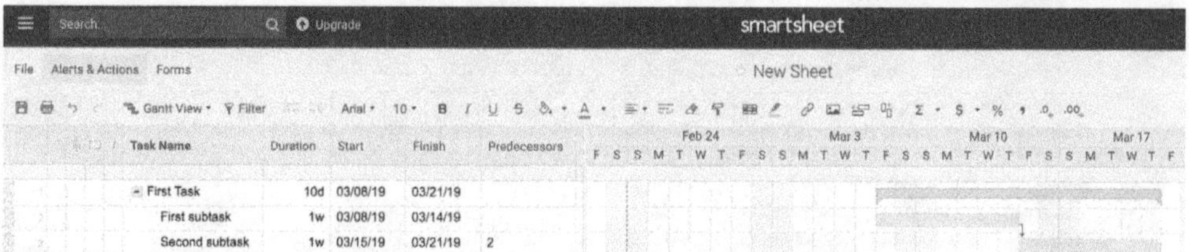

Figure 5-6   Smartsheet for Project Management

NOTE A cloud access security broker (CASB) is a way of providing management and monitoring of security policies between a user and a cloud application. A CASB solution would have to be in the direct flow between the user and the application in order to monitor and enforce policies.

One consideration when it comes to enterprise security is the ease of enrollment and usage for anyone. This means anyone could sign up for a service and store sensitive data with a cloud provider. Not all cloud providers are created equal, of course. Should an SaaS provider not be doing as much as they can to protect customer data and the user not have permission from information technology, the organization that owns the data won't have had the ability to have assessed the risk or the sensitivity of the data. The really short answer of this is the business has taken on risk they are not aware of because the data was exposed without the knowledge of anyone who could make informed decisions.

Infrastructure as a Service (IaaS)

If you build out your own setup with virtual machines, you are creating infrastructure. You have control over it and can connect it to anything you want to. You can use it for anything that you want, in any configuration you want. Infrastructure as a service enables you to do the same thing via a cloud provider. You can stand up virtual systems with essentially whatever CPU power and memory configuration you need. That virtual system can run any operating system, within reason, you need. Even better, you don't need to install the operating system or worry about licensing it. You just pick the options you need and everything else is taken care of for you. You select system configuration settings from your cloud provider and the system gets created. You can see a partial list of the operating systems that are available from Amazon Web Services (AWS) in Figure 5-7.

Figure 5-7 AWS operating systems offered as a service

Featured Software

Barracuda	JUNIPER NETWORKS	MATILLION	TREND MICRO
Barracuda CloudGen Firewall for AWS -...	vSRX Next Generation Firewall	Matillion ETL for Amazon Redshift	Trend Micro Deep Security
Rating ★★★★★	By Juniper Networks	Rating ★★★★★	Rating ★★★★★
By Barracuda Networks, Inc.	$0.55/hr or $2,280/yr (53% savings) for software	By Matillion	By Trend Micro
Starting from $0.60/hr or from $4,599/yr (12% savings) for software		Starting from $1.37/hr or from $9,950/yr (17% savings) for software	Starting from $0.01 per host/hr for software usage

Popular Software

f5	TLC	SoftNAS	f5
F5 BIG-IP Virtual Edition - BEST (PA...	CentOS 7.2 LAMP SELinux Enforcing	SoftNAS Cloud Enterprise - 20TB	F5 BIG-IP Virtual Edition - GOOD (PA...
By F5 Networks	By Technology Leadership	Rating ★★★★★	By F5 Networks
$2.50/hr or $13,797/yr (37% savings) for software	Corporation	By SoftNAS	$0.33/hr or $1,821/yr (37% savings) for software
	$0.01/hr or $79/yr (10% savings) for software	Starting from $1.509/hr or from $9,261/yr (30% savings) for software	

Figure 5-8   AWS networking devices offered as a service

There are many other vendors that offer similar infrastructure services. Google has Google Compute and Microsoft has Azure, just as a starting point. Those are the really big ones. Each of those providers has a lot of options for operating systems and computing resources. Of course, computers are not the only elements of infrastructure. You also need network devices and functionality—switches, routers, the ability to perform network address translation, and so on. You get all of these with the different IaaS providers. On top of all of the basic infrastructure, you get a lot of security elements. Typically, you would add firewalls and intrusion detection systems, just as a starting point. Many vendors have jumped on the cloud provider bandwagon and now offer virtualized editions of their popular devices. You can see a list of some of those devices in Figure 5-8. You can create a virtual Palo Alto Next Generation firewall, for instance.

With the larger IaaS vendors, you can also indicate where you want your devices installed. This means you select the region where you want your infrastructure hosted, and you will have systems stood up in the data center that resides in the region you are asking for. Using an approach like this, you can have infrastructure placed in a way that supports geographic redundancy, so that a natural disaster can't wipe out your operations. Again, this is at a much lower cost than you would spend leasing space in a third-party data center and standing up your own hardware there.

Utilizing these cloud providers, you could create an entire network infrastructure to support the needs of your organization. Figure 5-9 shows a sample network design to support a fairly classic web application architecture. In front is a load balancer.

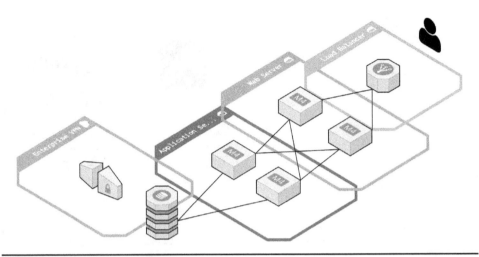

Figure 5-9 AWS network design

This takes in requests from the user and determines which web server is least busy to hand the request off to. Behind the web servers are application servers. Each web server could potentially send requests to either of the application servers. The application servers communicate with the database server that is the farthest away from the user. Along the side, there is a virtual private network (VPN), which some providers call a virtual private connection (VPC) that allows the enterprise access into the environment on the back end without needing to expose management ports out the front end.

Using AWS, you can define security groups. You can see these in the blocks where the servers live in Figure 5-9. The security group is a way of collecting a set of security requirements for access. This allows you to apply the same rules for open ports and allowed connections across all the devices within the security group. This use of security groups takes the complexity out of the overall design because you start with just defining the access requirements and then apply them where they are needed. You can have as many security groups as necessary for your overall design.

Developing a complete network infrastructure starting from the operating system is one way of accomplishing the needs of the business. It is not the only one, though. Cloud providers like Amazon and Microsoft also offer an even broader scope of management and implementation.

Platform as a Service (PaaS)

You can use IaaS to create an application design and implementation based on business needs, but it's not the only approach you could use. When you go shopping for services from AWS or Azure, you don't have to look for operating systems. Ultimately, your objective isn't to install operating systems. It's to install applications that provide functionality necessary to achieve what the business needs. This means selecting something like an application server. With platform as a service, you have a wide variety of options.

Figure 5-10 shows a list of some possible application servers that you could use in Microsoft Azure. From the Azure portal, you select Web App as the resource you want to deploy. From there, you can select which underlying operating system you want to use. On the right side of Figure 5-10, you can see this OS option, along with the App name field, Resource Group option, and the Runtime Stack field. When you click the Runtime Stack drop-down arrow, you see the list in the center of Figure 5-10.

You can see different versions of the .NET Framework as well as Java application servers and Node.js servers. You can also use a number of versions of PHP for your application runtime. When you select this, as well as the operating system, Azure creates an instance of a system running the operating system you selected as well as the application server. What is missing at this point is your own application code that uses the application server. You don't have to worry about installation of any of the elements up to your application.

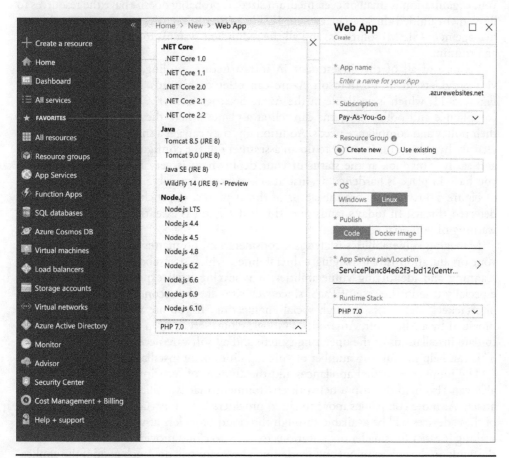

Figure 5-10   Selecting a runtime stack

Web application servers are not the only platforms that are available. As another example, web applications commonly use databases for long-term storage. Database servers can be complicated to install, configure, and maintain, especially when you start factoring in fault tolerance and redundancy. Cloud providers offer full installations of database servers, from the virtual machine to the operating system to the database install and configuration.

Security Considerations

Security can be expensive with so many technologies available via the cloud, and it can be hard to identify the right solution to address risks identified by the organization. Companies of all sizes and needs are using solutions like Microsoft Azure, Google Compute, and Amazon AWS. These providers can provide solutions some companies can't simply because of the cost and cloud providers can spread that cost out over a lot of customers. If your organization is small or even medium sized, it probably doesn't have the resources to implement unified threat management (UTM) systems, security information and event management (SIEM) solutions, and all the redundant systems to ensure systems stay up and running.

Because of all of this investment in infrastructure, tooling, and monitoring, service providers such as Microsoft Azure can offer dashboards like the one shown in Figure 5-11, which is available in the Azure Security Center. Organizations that have compliance and policy concerns can tell at a glance where they stand with respect to their policy and compliance needs. Additionally, they can get a snapshot look at resource security hygiene. This is a way to do an assessment of the configuration in place quickly and easily. This look at the status of your deployment is very helpful to ensure what you have in place is hardened against attack as best as possible. Finally, at the bottom of Figure 5-11, you can see the status of threat protection, including security alerts of detected threats. In today's landscape, threat detection is essential to give you advance warning of potential attackers.

Managing vulnerabilities is always a consideration, no matter what you are doing. If your organization isn't managing vulnerabilities, which goes above and beyond simply scanning and identifying vulnerabilities, it is leaving itself exposed to attack. This is especially true in the case of PaaS, since web sites are the second most common target of attackers, after users through social engineering. If you are using the latest images provided by a Microsoft, Amazon, or Google cloud service, you are using the most up-to-date installations of the operating system and all software necessary for the platform. This can help to limit the number of vulnerabilities in an installation.

The number of virtual appliances and the amount of security-related software available can also help develop a network environment that is resilient and protected from attack. As more companies move to cloud providers for infrastructure and service, more of these devices will be available through the cloud providers at very cost-effective rates, making it easier for smaller organizations to move to cloud providers. Of course, none of the work on the environment and hardening of systems will do much good if the application design isn't very good.

Figure 5-11　Microsoft Azure Security Center

Application Design

Web-based applications typically follow a multitier architecture approach. You may hear this referred to as an *n*-tier architecture. *Multitier* means that the different components of an application are separated. At a minimum, different elements of the overall application are in different services, if not different systems entirely. This approach allows tighter security controls at different levels of the application. The closer you get to the center, where the most sensitive data is, the tighter the controls can be. This approach isn't enough to keep a determined attacker out, especially if the application itself is not well designed and well written. Figure 5-12 shows a multitier application design diagram.

This design pattern is evolving. The compartmentalization has been taken a step further. It was initially called service-oriented architecture, but today, as virtualization has become far more efficient and cost effective, this model has become known as a

Figure 5-12
Multitier
application
design

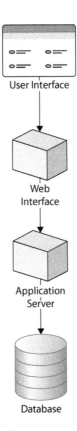

User Interface

Web
Interface

Application
Server

Database

microservice architecture. This means different components of the application are broken into very small components called microservices. The microservices can be split out across systems, and communication is handled through a form of interprocess communication. This may be something like remote method invocation (RMI), as in the case of Java programs. With Microsoft .NET, developers can use a method called .NET Remoting, which is a way to invoke functions or methods in another process when using the Microsoft languages VB.NET and C#.NET.

This application design uses the ideas of reusability and compartmentalization. When functions are compartmentalized like this, the only thing exposed is the interface. As long as the interface is replicated, all of the internals can be swapped out without impact to the overall application. When you break functionality into microservices, with clearly defined interfaces, you can end up making life easier in a number of ways. First, you end up with small services that can be tested in isolation because they are not as tightly coupled as when everything is entirely internal. Second, if one component ends up being inefficient, it can be replaced with another component without needing to overhaul the entire application. Small, isolated services have the potential to protect the overall application since there isn't a monolithic application with everything in the same place. A monolithic application design would lead to the problem of a broader range of access if the application is compromised by an attacker.

Secure Software Development Lifecycle (S-SDLC)

As security becomes more important to more organizations, and especially as more functionality moves to the open Internet where it is more exposed to attack, organizations are beginning to overhaul their old software development practices. One area of focus is making changes to the software development lifecycle (SDLC) to include security in more places within the cycle. A standard way of integrating security previously was to develop the software or service and toss it over the wall to a security team to perform some testing. Often, this testing was performed entirely separate from the development team and perhaps either concurrent with release or after release.

The landscape is changing. More organizations are recognizing the need to incorporate security into all phases of the SDLC to improve their reputation with their consumers and also reduce liability to the organization. This means introducing security earlier in the SDLC. This process is sometimes called "moving security left." A typical SDLC might look like Figure 5-13. On the left, you gather requirements. This may be based on what the product team wants, what marketing has identified, or even, in some cases, what users have requested. Once the requirements have been gathered, design can begin. This may be a structured, formal design or it may be looser than that. The design and requirements inform the development or coding effort. Following this is testing, and then deployment and release. The cycle may then begin again.

You can see why the expression is "moving security left." If you diagram a process from left to right, as we read in English, the beginning of the process is on the left. The idea is to get security as close to the start of the process as possible. Ideally, the security organization has input into the requirements gathering phase. That's not the only place, though. Security should be integrated into every step. This is certainly true when it comes to development or coding. All developers should be trained in secure coding practices that are specific to the language and development environment in use. Security, after all, is not only a function. It is an element of every position in an organization, especially in development and other IT roles.

Whereas testing traditionally happens after or in parallel with deployment, a fully integrated S-SDLC has security integrated into testing. This may mean that the normal software testers are trained in performing security testing. It may mean that the security team gets the application at the same time as the traditional quality assurance or test function. This may be especially true if there are specific security testing requirements that call for someone with experience and skill in security practices, risk assessment, and vulnerability testing.

One of the elements of testing that should be integrated into the S-SDLC is source code review. This may be automated, as part of a build of the software, or it may be manual, as may be the case for structured code reviews. Source code review is a good practice,

Figure 5-13
SDLC process

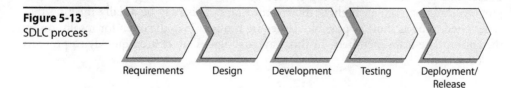

Requirements   Design   Development   Testing   Deployment/
Release

as it's helpful to have other sets of eyes take a look at work. Developers can become blind to issues in the code they write; they get so used to looking at it, they may overlook something. Having someone else review the code may turn up other ways of addressing a problem that may be more efficient and more secure. On top of that, programmers can learn from one another, since programming is not a static practice. There are usually multiple ways of approaching a problem, and hearing someone else's perspective can be beneficial in how problems are approached in the future.

Agile Methodology

As more applications move to web interfaces, the expectations and pressures on the development team tend to increase. Part of this is attributable to users having a more direct interface with the application and company, since the customer is interfacing directly with resources owned by the company rather than an application running natively on the user's computer. The company can then see how the user interacts with the application, and if there are any errors or failures, the company knows about them immediately. With this direct interaction and the information gained from it, the company has more of a sense of both urgency and connection with the user. How the company responds is where the Agile methodology becomes important. The goal of the folks who created the Agile methodology was to provide a more responsive methodology than the slower, linear waterfall methodology that separates all the elements. When following the waterfall methodology, each step of the SDLC is handled in isolation. Agile also introduced the idea of creating software that was directly applicable to the user. Requirements are built around user stories, indicating how a user is expected to or wants to make use of the software—what problem they want to solve.

Using the Agile methodology, the entire development team works as one. All user stories are collected and the work is broken up into time periods called sprints. These sprints are very short compared with the amount of time it typically takes a product to come to fruition using the waterfall method. You may commonly see sprints that are as short as two weeks. At the end of the sprint, development of a new feature will have gone through requirements, design, coding, and testing, resulting in a completely functional product. For this reason, the work in each sprint is kept small. Improvement in the product is incremental, one sprint, one feature at a time. In concept, the result of each sprint would be presented to the user for their feedback and another collection of user stories. This cycle continues until the user is fully satisfied with the product.

Part of the Agile methodology was inspired by the idea of peer programming. The belief of the group that developed Agile was that collaboration would result in better software. Agile continues this tradition through practices such as structured code walkthroughs and the preference for co-location of all team members. This increases face-to-face communication, improving collaboration and idea sharing. Additionally, Agile proposes holding regular, highly efficient meetings. This may be a daily meeting that is designed to be as short as possible. Issues are brought into the open for resolution by the appropriate team members. In this way, roadblocks are cleared quickly so progress can continue.

As development cycles become shorter, the number of deployments or releases increases. This means that testing, integration, and deployment must be tightly integrated with the development team. One way this can happen is through the use of as much automation as possible. Appropriate programming practices can help this. Unit tests, short programs that test functionality of methods and features, are developed alongside the code that is meant to be tested. These tests can be run automatically. Ideally, these unit tests should also include some amount of security testing, like boundary checking and input validation checking.

Cloud computing is starting to change the nature of application development. One way it does this is through the use of serverless functions. Applications may soon no longer need to have complete virtual machines installed to support some functionality. Instead, the function is developed using a feature like AWS's Lambda. This allows development of a function that is hosted in the AWS environment without the need for specific infrastructure or platforms to be deployed around it. The function gets instantiated and called when it is needed. This limits the surface area that an attacker can take advantage of. Microsoft Azure also has serverless functions that application developers can make use of. This sort of functionality can change the security posture of an application.

Deployment Considerations

Once software has been developed and is ready for deployment, there are several options. In the case of traditional software, software installers are created and pushed up to a download site, or maybe even installation CDs or DVDs are burned. In the case of web applications, the new software replaces the old software, which typically requires downtime as the new software is replaced and processes are restarted. Today, though, there are new possibilities, especially when it comes to cloud computing environments.

Earlier we talked about microservices. You may have imagined those small services needing entire virtual machines stood up to support the code. There is another type of virtualization that limits the resource footprint of applications, well below that needed by a virtual machine. Containers are a way of isolating application code in a way that is much more controlled than previous "jails" and other, similar protections. A container works through the use of processor namespaces. A processor partitions applications using namespaces, isolating one application from another by tagging the code in memory. The processor won't allow any interprocess communication from one namespace to another that doesn't pass outside of the memory space—meaning, it has to use a network connection to connect to another process rather than using in-memory connections.

Each container uses the same operating system (that is, kernel) as the host. This is very different from a virtual machine, which would have its own operating system. Additionally, memory and disk space are allocated to a virtual machine, both of which consume resources. A container needs the amount of space on the disk necessary to hold the application and all of its dependencies. The dependencies are necessary because of the isolation. The application can't rely on libraries that are in the host, because it can't get to them. The application resides in its own disk root from the standpoint of the host and the application itself. Fortunately, in most cases, the dependencies are not very big.

This limits the amount of disk space used. The memory utilization is the same as any other application, except that dependencies may be duplicated in the case of shared libraries. These shared libraries may reside in the host as well as the containers.

Containers provide a lot of flexibility. They can be spun up very quickly and also torn down very quickly. This helps with load management since containers with an instance of a service can be spun up very quickly in order to take up a flood of requests from users. Once the container is no longer necessary to support the load of user requests, it can be torn down. This approach creates not only flexibility but also a moving target for attackers. When they land in a container, that container could very easily go away. All memory that goes with the instance would disappear, as well as anything that had been stored to disk within the container instance. The attacker would completely lose their foothold and have to start all over again.

This approach also solves the deployment issue of needing to stop processes and replace code. The container template gets the new code, and the next time a container instance is called into being, it will be running the new code. If the application and its management is handled correctly, the containers are constantly being stopped and started, meaning all the old code would be swapped out in a short period of time. This is another advantage of the microservice model. Each microservice has its own code and container template. The entire application architecture could be deployed very quickly.

Since cloud computing is a pay-as-you go model, you don't pay for more than you use. This means you don't have to create a lot of expensive virtual machines and have them remain up and running, costing the business. Containers are only turned on as they are needed, so they only consume resources to support requests.

When it comes to deployment, there are also automation considerations. Containers and virtual machines can be deployed using a technique called *infrastructure as code*. Languages like Ansible, Chef, Puppet, and Terraform can be used to script out entire environments. This means systems and containers can be developed using programming practices, which can include testing as part of the development. What you end up with is something that is repeatable and consistent, avoiding misconfigurations and other mistakes. This automation is part of what allows the speed of deployment.

Private Clouds

One of the major advantages of cloud computing is that it offers flexibility and speed of development and deployment without a lot of investment on your part. However, there are plenty of reasons to not want your applications stored in a public space, regardless of the protections that are put into place around the systems there. If you still want flexibility and speed of development and deployment without the risk of public storage, you can implement a private cloud. Private clouds have the same capabilities that public clouds do—namely, elasticity (the ability to scale up or down), reporting, application programming interfaces, and the ability to support multitenancy. There are a number of vendors that provide software for private clouds, including IBM, Dell, and Red Hat. There is also an open source offering called OpenStack. Because it's free and easy to use, let's explore it in a bit more detail.

NOTE The expression "in the cloud" has come to mean somewhere unspecified in the Internet. In the case of a private cloud, the expression means replicating the functionality of providers like Azure, AWS, and Google Compute in a space within the enterprise network.

OpenStack is designed with multiple components, including Nova, which is the compute engine for managing virtual machines and containers, and Cinder, which is the storage engine, creating volumes for virtual machines to use. If you want to take a look at OpenStack, you don't need the multiple systems that would commonly be used in an OpenStack implementation. Instead, you could use a development configuration, such as the one called DevStack, which is intended to be installed on a single system. You don't get the power and capability of having multiple systems, and it's certainly not the sort of setup you would use in production, but it does provide you with the ability to see what OpenStack is all about.

In addition to all of the automation features that you'd expect, OpenStack also has a web interface, which you'd also expect. Figure 5-14 shows the compute dashboard, providing insight into the instance, volume, and network statistics. The web interface not only provides a reporting interface, such as what you see in Figure 5-14, but also provides an admin interface for creating resources within the OpenStack cloud. This includes creating a network topology. By default, you will have whatever network is in the OpenStack system configuration. Everything else becomes virtual. As an example,

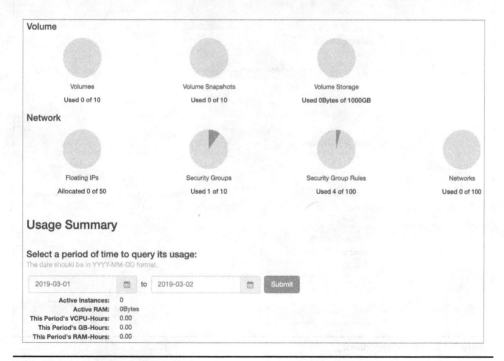

Figure 5-14 OpenStack Dashboard

you can add a router to connect to the public network interface on your system. Once you have a router in place, you can start adding additional networks that could be routed out to the external network. You can create subnets, networks, and routers to support the network topology you need.

Once you have networks in place, you can create complete configurations with as many operating systems as you have images for. The default image that is included with OpenStack is CirrOS Linux, which is a very small distribution designed for running in cloud environments. There are a number of images you can download from the Internet, including different Linux distributions and also Windows. OpenStack, just like the public cloud providers, supports multiple flavors. *Flavors* are really system configurations that are expressed in sizes. You can see the list of supported flavors in Figure 5-15. Smaller distributions like CirrOS can fit into the really small flavors. An instance of Windows 2012, such as the one that was selected for the instance being created in Figure 5-15, would require much more memory and disk space. This is where you would need to be aware of the system requirements for the operating system you are trying to create an instance of.

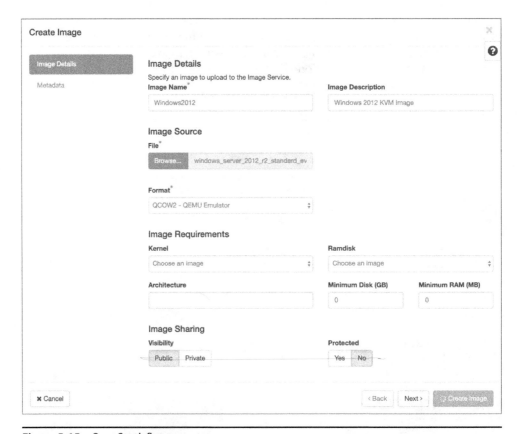

Figure 5-15   OpenStack flavors

You are not stuck with a web interface, though. You could use the command-line program openstack. To use this, you need a set of configuration variables that tell openstack how to authenticate. Once you have this file, available through the web interface, you can start using the openstack command-line program. You could issue commands all on a single line, or if you just run openstack, you are placed into a shell where you can issue one command after another to openstack. The following code shows the use of openstack to create a network. What you get as output is all of the settings used to create the network. Some have been provided. Others are the defaults.

```
(openstack) network create --project-domain admin labnet
+--------------------------+---------------------------------------------------------------+
| Field                    | Value                                                         |
+--------------------------+---------------------------------------------------------------+
| admin_state_up           | UP                                                            |
| availability_zone_hints  |                                                               |
| availability_zones       |                                                               |
| created_at               | 2019-03-02T02:02:57Z                                          |
| description              |                                                               |
| dns_domain               | None                                                          |
| id                       | 4fbf1160-0df1-4777-a6b6-ce43a47525b4                          |
| ipv4_address_scope       | None                                                          |
| ipv6_address_scope       | None                                                          |
| is_default               | False                                                         |
| is_vlan_transparent      | None                                                          |
| location                 | Munch({'project': Munch({'domain_id': 'default', 'id': u'
83a90f066ccc4d8cb5f7bf7ed46515d5', 'name': 'demo', 'domain_name': None}), 'cloud': '',
'region_name': 'RegionOne', 'zone': None}) |

| location                 | Munch({'project': Munch({'domain_id': 'default', 'id':
                           | u'83a90f066ccc4d8cb5f7bf7ed46515d5', 'name': 'demo',
                           | 'domain_name': None}), 'cloud': '', 'region_name':
                           | 'RegionOne', 'zone': None}) |
```

Of course, beyond the web interface and the command-line interface, there is always the infrastructure-as-code approach. You could use something like Ansible with its playbooks to automate the build of systems and networks.

Chapter Review

Cloud computing is an important concept to understand because it is starting to significantly change how applications are developed and deployed. There are a number of different types of cloud computing services, some of which have been in use for over a decade. Storage as a service, for example, has providers like Dropbox, Google, Microsoft, Apple, and others, providing storage space available through interfaces like websites or via clients that run on users' computers. These clients can synchronize the cloud storage across multiple systems, as needed. This means you could store data with a cloud provider and have it available on your phone or computer and any change made anywhere would be available across all other devices.

Applications can be delivered using web-based technologies, making them available anywhere they are needed. This is called software as a service (SaaS). In some cases, SaaS may use the storage in the cloud to store documents or application data. This is the case for SaaS solutions like Google Docs and Microsoft Office Online. However, that's not always the case. Vendors like Smartsheet and Salesforce provide applications without necessarily being tied to a specific storage vendor. Salesforce, for instance, provides its own storage for its service.

Cloud providers can also replace normal enterprise servers. This is called infrastructure as a service (IaaS). This means, essentially, that you get systems via the cloud and then you do what you want on them. Cloud providers will allow you to create your own OS images, within reason, and install them on virtual systems they provide. Operating systems that are too outdated and vulnerable may not be allowed. Of course, you can also start with the OS images provided by the cloud provider.

You can also take advantage of a complete platform for developing web applications, including a web server and application server. This is called platform as a service (PaaS). There are advantages for making use of a cloud provider when you have a platform you need to implement. For a start, cloud providers likely have more resources to be able to support fault tolerance and redundancy. Additionally, with so many vendors offering virtual implementations of their security devices, you may be able to get a complete set of security devices at low cost.

Many companies are migrating applications to web-based installations. This introduces the potential for vulnerabilities exposed to the outside world. Companies may need to think about shifting security considerations to the left in the software development lifecycle. This includes having security be part of the requirements phase and ensuring that software developers are trained in appropriate secure programming techniques. Web-based delivery of applications can increase the interaction with users, and that information may be used during the development. This is part of what drives Agile development—short development cycles focused on delivering user-requested or user-required functionality.

Deployment can be made easier through the use of infrastructure as code, which is a programmatic way of creating virtual machines and containers. This helps to ensure environments can be created in a repeatable way after having been tested thoroughly. Cloud platforms can also allow for elasticity, meaning systems can be created and torn down as needed to adjust for user demand.

This elasticity is one of the features of a private cloud. In addition to elasticity, private clouds would include the reporting, application programming interfaces, and multitenancy features that a public cloud does. A private cloud, though, would be implemented within the protected environment of an enterprise network rather than exposed through an Internet-facing network.

Questions

1. What does elasticity offer to an application?

   A. Faster deployment

   B. Faster performance

   C. Scalability

   D. Fewer vulnerabilities

2. If you need a complete application stack to develop applications against, which cloud service are you most likely to take advantage of?

   A. Storage as a service

   B. Platform as a service

   C. Infrastructure as a service

   D. Software as a service

3. What would Microsoft Word Online be an example of?

   A. Storage as a service

   B. Platform as a service

   C. Infrastructure as a service

   D. Software as a service

4. What is it referred to when security is introduced as early as possible into the software development lifecycle?

   A. Agile development

   B. Moving left

   C. Moving right

   D. Infrastructure as code

5. What is infrastructure as code used for?

   A. Automating system deployment

   B. Providing virtual machine interfaces

   C. Developing software applications

   D. Private clouds

6. If you wanted a virtual environment with limited overhead, what would you use?

   A. Type 1 hypervisor

   B. Type 2 hypervisor

   C. Container

   D. Virtual machine

7. What is one limitation of containers as compared with virtual machines?

   A. Uses the same operating system

   B. Requires more memory

   C. Uses more processor resources

   D. Only runs on a single operating system

8. Which of these is an important feature of cloud platforms that makes them cost effective?

   A. Reporting

   B. Multitenancy

   C. Application programming interface

   D. Agile methodology

9. What is the time period that software development in Agile is broken into called?

   A. Dashes

   B. Cycles

   C. Sprints

   D. Blocks

10. What is a security advantage of using elastic containers for application deployment?

    A. More up-to-date operating system

    B. Fewer resources

    C. More features

    D. Footholds disappear

Answers

1. **C.** Elasticity offers scalability to an application. It means that the deployment can grow or shrink as needed to support the demands of the application. Elasticity doesn't offer a faster deployment or faster performance. There also aren't fewer vulnerabilities.

2. **B.** Only platform as a service (PaaS) offers the full stack of the operating system, web server, and application server as needed to develop and deploy the application. Software as a service (SaaS) means accessing a software application through a web-based delivery system. Infrastructure as a service (IaaS) means having essentially bare virtual machines that you can do what you want with. Storage as a service offers storage space through an Internet-based service.

3. **D.** While Microsoft Word Online stores documents in OneDrive, which is storage as a service, Microsoft Word Online itself is an application, so it's software as a service. All infrastructure and whatever platform is used are handled by Microsoft and the user never sees it.

4. **B.** If you were to sketch the lifecycle the way English is read, you would start with the earliest phase on the left. Thus, moving to the left refers to introducing security as early as possible into the SDLC. Agile development is used to focus development efforts on a short, tight delivery. Moving to the right would mean the end of the development lifecycle, where introducing security becomes much more difficult. Infrastructure as code is a way of automating deployment of virtual machines.

5. A. Infrastructure as code is used to automate deployment of environments. It isn't used to develop applications. It can't be used for virtual machine interfaces, since that is the function of the hypervisor. While you might use infrastructure as code within a private cloud environment, it's not exclusively used there.

6. C. A container is a lightweight means of deploying virtual applications. A Type 1 hypervisor is its own operating system, meaning there is nothing between it and the bare metal. A Type 2 hypervisor installs on top of an existing operating system. Hypervisors enable the use of virtual machines.

7. A. Containers make use of the same operating system as the host. This means that you couldn't run a Windows container, for example, on a Linux host. Containers do not require more memory or processor resources. They also run on multiple operating systems like Linux, Windows, and macOS.

8. B. Multitenancy allows a cloud provider to support multiple customers at the same time and in the same environment, which is more cost effective. Reporting and application programming interface are features of cloud-based platforms but don't make them cost effective. Agile is an application development methodology.

9. C. When using Agile, programming is broken up into sprints. These sprints are commonly very short, measured in weeks. The time periods are not blocks, dashes, or cycles.

10. D. When using elastic containers, a container may appear and disappear within a short time period, so an attacker who has compromised a container loses that compromised "system" when the container is pulled down because it is no longer needed. While the cloud provider may keep operating systems completely up to date and while containers use fewer resources, these are not security advantages specific to containers. Containers don't necessarily offer more features.

Unix/Linux

In this chapter, you will learn:
- Linux security: structure, permissions, and access
- Linux security: hardening and security
- Linux monitoring and attack detection
- Linux security utilities

If you want to be technical about its parentage, the story of Linux goes all the way back to the 1960s. Most people, though, trace it to 1991 when Linus Torvalds first released Linux, a kernel based on the MINIX operating system, written by Andrew Tanenbaum, as a way to teach operating system design. Linux is one of many Unix-like operating systems, taking its operational concepts from the Unix operating system. However, we're getting a little ahead of ourselves here. We'll get into Unix's full history shortly, including the work of other groups that have contributed all of the bits that users primarily interact with, which is not generally considered Linux itself.

First, it's useful to discuss what an operating system actually is. An OS is often thought of as all the bits you get when you install something like Windows and you boot it up. Everything you see when you boot it up is often considered the operating system. In point of fact, what you are actually looking at is the shell, which, in the case of Windows, macOS, and other similar systems is graphical in nature. When we talk about the operating system, we are really talking about the piece of software that interacts with the hardware and that is responsible for things like process and memory management. In the Linux world, this is often called the *kernel*. Sun Microsystems, which developed Solaris, made a distinction between their operating system, which was called SunOS, and their shell or interface, which they called Solaris. The reason for making this distinction is that the shell or interface can be switched out and you can have multiple ways of interacting with the hardware as well as different ways to launch applications, while underneath this the operating system still makes everything possible.

When you get a system in your hands like Linux, you need to have an understanding of how it runs and where all the pieces can be found to manage it. Since Linux descends from Unix, and Unix was designed as a command-line system, much of how Linux operates is still based in text files and manipulating them in a non-graphical way, in spite of the fact that we have become a predominantly graphical world when it comes to computing. There are a lot of aspects to managing a Linux system, including configuring, updating and installing software, managing processes, and working with all the utilities that make its functioning possible.

Unix History

Unix, the precursor to Linux and several other operating systems, has its roots in a multi-organization project called Multics. Multics is something of an acronym, meaning Multiplexed Information and Computing Service. The project to create the operating system began in 1964. Multics was designed to be multiuser at a time when very expensive computers were primarily used as single-user devices simply because there was no operating system that allowed for the running of multiple programs simultaneously. Today this is something we take for granted, and while you may perceive your system as only running one application at a time because it's the one you are working on at any given moment (and you may not have any other applications open), in reality there are a large number of programs in some state of execution at any given time. These programs perform many functions, from ensuring you have a network address to sharing files or printers over the network, or perhaps they are waiting for you to plug a device into your system so they can perform some management functions on your device.

 NOTE Security was one of the design goals of Multics and it was the first operating system to be given the designation of a B2 level secure operating system using the Trusted Computer System Evaluation criteria. Multics is still available in open source.

Multics was originally projected to be a commercial project for both GE and Honeywell, though Honeywell is the only company that actually released a commercial version of Multics. In addition to GE and Honeywell, MIT and AT&T Bell Labs were both involved in the Multics project. After a few years of working on Multics, Bell Labs pulled out of the project, though some of the developers involved were left feeling like they should implement something on a much smaller scale than Multics. In 1969, the developers began work on an operating system that was originally expected to be a programmer's workbench and wasn't expected to be targeted at normal users. Early on, the project was called Unics, being a play on the name Multics.

Throughout the 1970s, Unix was developed by Bell Labs and distributed to educational and governmental institutions. It was designed to be multiuser and multiprocess as well as portable since it was originally running on whatever hardware could be found for the purpose. The programming language C was created as part of the development of the Unix operating system and much of Unix is written in C. C was ported to a number of architectures, thus helping in the portability of Unix. Because of the distribution of Unix to educational institutions, including the source code, it became popular as a way to teach operating system design. Eventually, AT&T UNIX had a competitor when a small group at the University of California at Berkeley rewrote all of Unix and also introduced some additional components. This was called the Berkeley System Distribution and was also available freely to educational institutions without some of the paperwork and red tape required by AT&T.

Over time, Unix came to be reimplemented by a number of companies and institutions. Sun Microsystems, Silicon Graphics, IBM, and Hewlett-Packard all had different implementations of Unix, spawned out of the move to high-powered workstations in the 1980s. Additionally, NeXT implemented a Unix-like operating system based on the Mach kernel, designed to be lightweight and fast, which eventually became Mac OS X. Even Microsoft had a version of Unix for a time, called XENIX.

 NOTE   You'll often see the term Unix-like. The reason for this is that Unix is a specific implementation of an operating system that was originally owned by AT&T, which was very good at looking out for its intellectual property. Currently, the trademark UNIX™ is owned by The Open Group, which is an industry standards consortium. Only systems that conform to a particular specification can be called Unix. All others are Unix-like.

It was really the use of Unix as a way to teach operating system design, though, that ultimately led to the creation of Linux. A number of books were written about the Unix design, with the rewritten code given a different name like XINU and MINIX. MINIX was a small implementation of Unix written by Andrew Tanenbaum for a book about operating system design. It was this implementation of a Unix-like operating system that Torvalds used as the genesis of his own implementation of a Unix-like operating system, Linux. What Torvalds wrote, though, is really just the operating system. He didn't write any of the components of the environment that users typically deal with. Once you have a kernel, you have something that can interface with hardware and schedule programs and manage memory, but you don't have any programs to load into memory. You still need an operating environment, complete with some form of user interface.

GNU

Unix was really designed as a programmer's operating system. All of the system utilities were created to be small, lightweight, and modular so they could be chained in order to achieve larger tasks. There weren't monolithic system administration tools. There wasn't one tool to do all of the system administration. There were a lot of very small tools that would primarily be single-purpose. The idea was to create a portable system that would be fast and extensible. After Torvalds created the kernel, he still needed all the system utilities that later came to define Unix. Fortunately, he didn't need to reinvent that wheel. It had been done for him a decade earlier.

In 1983, Richard Stallman was working in the Artificial Intelligence Lab at MIT. He had long been frustrated with the constraints of commercial software and the inability for programmers to take a piece of software and extend it in ways that made sense to them. Unix came with the constraints of the license that AT&T had, and while that license wasn't necessarily a motivating factor in driving his actions, the license would have prevented him from doing what he wanted to do. He decided to create an operating system developed with completely open-source software. He announced the creation of the GNU Project in the fall of 1983.

NOTE Programmers can have a quirky sense of humor. GNU is actually a recursive acronym that stands for *GNU's Not Unix*. My personal favorite of the little jokes like this is a replacement for the More paging program, designed to show a page at a time from a long file. The replacement is called Less. Because, of course, Less is More.

Stallman opted to make his operating system compatible with Unix because that was where the users were. If a user wanted to adopt GNU as their operating system, they were already familiar with how it worked. He also had a goal of portability and Unix was already portable. It seemed like a good fit. He started creating software for the GNU Project. Enormous volumes of software have since been generated under the GNU banner. Much of the software created was focused on developers, from the Emacs text editor (though text editor doesn't begin to describe what Emacs is or does) to compilers and parsers, debuggers, and automation tools. In addition, GNU rewrote the userland system utilities commonly associated with Unix and made them open source.

Torvalds actually used the GNU development tools to create his Linux kernel. At that time, the GNU Project had yet to create a kernel that would allow them to have a fully functional system. It seemed like a good marriage, putting a new kernel together with a set of well-known and well-supported user tools. Torvalds bundled software from the GNU Project together with his kernel to create what he called Linux. It's been a source of controversy that the various distributions that have followed have been called Linux. Supporters of GNU believe it should be called GNU/Linux because the kernel on its own is only a small part of what users get, and the kernel isn't useful without the software that is provided by the GNU Project. No matter what you call the full suite of software that you use, the bulk of what we will be talking about in this chapter is primarily from the GNU suite of tools, which are run inside the Linux operating system.

NOTE To date, the GNU Project has yet to release a stable version of their own operating system, which they call GNU Hurd—even though Hurd has been in active development since 1990.

The Kernel

As mentioned previously, Linux really refers to the piece of software called the kernel. The kernel is responsible for interfacing with the hardware, and as a result, it operates with the highest level of privilege with respect to the processor. CPUs often are designed with a ring protection scheme, with ring 0 having the highest level of privileges and ring 3 having the lowest. Applications live in ring 3 and the kernel lives in ring 0 where it has the highest level of access to the system hardware and processor.

Linux uses a monolithic kernel, meaning that everything related to the kernel runs in kernel mode, and, in fact, all of the kernel functions reside in a single large binary image. However, some of the functionality can be swapped in and out using loadable kernel modules (LKMs). In Figure 6-1, you can see the high-level menu where the Linux kernel is configured. As of 3.8, the Linux kernel had over 6000 settings that could be configured to enable or disable specific functionality, including hardware drivers.

Figure 6-1
The Linux Kernel
Configuration
menu

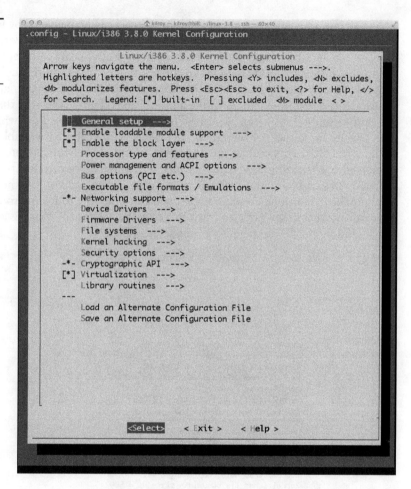

Exercise 6-1: The Kernel Version

To find the kernel version of your Linux system, open a terminal window, type **uname
–a**, and look for the version number in the output.

By comparison, a *microkernel* moves some of the functionality out of the kernel itself,
leaving only those functions that need it to live in ring 0. Functions like memory management and process scheduling, as well as basic interprocess communication, remain in the
kernel itself, while the device drivers function in higher-level rings where they have less
access and can do less damage should there be a problem. A microkernel may adopt a hardware abstraction layer to provide an application programming interface (API) that drivers
can access to control the hardware. This relieves the drivers from needing to implement
architecture-specific functions, leaving that to the kernel to manage.

At runtime, the configuration of the Linux kernel can be managed by interacting with a virtual filesystem created by the kernel when it boots. This virtual filesystem is a set of files laid out in a hierarchy that exists in memory but appears to be accessible through the normal filesystem. You could get to the system configuration through the /sys directory, which will allow you to look at all of the various settings that are active in the kernel at any given time. You can take a lot of time digging your way through all of the different settings. As you can see from Figure 6-2, running sysctl –a, which provides all of the values for kernel configuration, yields over 1000 different variables. You can also see how the different variables are displayed. Many of the variables are managed using true-or-false, 1/0 settings, so you either turn something on or turn it off—although there are plenty of variables that do take numeric settings. You can also use the sysctl utility to configure kernel settings. As an example, you could use the following to disable replying to broadcasts that might later lead to a successful smurf attack, which is an amplification attack sending ICMP messages to a broadcast address:

```
sysctl net.ipv4.icmp_echo_ignore_broadcasts = 1
```

Figure 6-2
A system
configuration
using sysctl

```
kilroy@bill: $ wc -l sysctl.out
1007 sysctl.out
kilroy@bill: $ sysctl -a
kernel.sched_child_runs_first = 0
kernel.sched_min_granularity_ns = 1500000
kernel.sched_latency_ns = 12000000
kernel.sched_wakeup_granularity_ns = 2000000
kernel.sched_tunable_scaling = 1
kernel.sched_migration_cost = 500000
kernel.sched_nr_migrate = 32
kernel.sched_time_avg = 1000
kernel.sched_shares_window = 10000000
kernel.timer_migration = 1
kernel.sched_rt_period_us = 1000000
kernel.sched_rt_runtime_us = 950000
kernel.sched_autogroup_enabled = 1
kernel.sched_cfs_bandwidth_slice_us = 5000
kernel.panic = 0
kernel.core_uses_pid = 0
kernel.core_pattern = |/usr/share/apport/apport %p %s %c
kernel.core_pipe_limit = 0
kernel.tainted = 4097
kernel.latencytop = 0
kernel.real-root-dev = 0
kernel.print-fatal-signals = 0
kernel.ctrl-alt-del = 0
kernel.ftrace_enabled = 1
kernel.stack_tracer_enabled = 0
kernel.ftrace_dump_on_oops = 0
kernel.modprobe = /sbin/modprobe
kernel.modules_disabled = 0
kernel.hotplug =
kernel.sg-big-buff = 32768
kernel.acct = 4 2        30
kernel.sysrq = 1
error: permission denied on key 'kernel.cad_pid'
kernel.threads-max = 31453
kernel.random.poolsize = 4096
kernel.random.entropy_avail = 182
kernel.random.read_wakeup_threshold = 64
```

NOTE While you can set the values using sysctl, they only remain at that setting until the system is rebooted. To keep the setting after the reboot, add an entry into /etc/sysctl.conf.

If you want to go to a particular setting in the virtual filesystem, use the dotted notation seen above as a guide. The setting to ignore ICMP broadcast messages would be located in /sys/net/ipv4/, and the "file" there would be named icmp_echo_ignore_broadcasts. If you were to look into that "file" after running the preceding sysctl command, you would only see the value 1. This is how the /sys tree works. The variables are stored in a manner that makes them look like files, and they are arranged in a typical hierarchical directory structure.

Filesystem Layout

Linux generally organizes its filesystem in the same way that most Unix-like operating systems do. The layout for Linux has been formalized into the Filesystem Hierarchy Standard (FHS), which more or less follows the standard BSD filesystem layout. Where Windows systems follow the convention of DOS and primarily use drive letters to indicate different physical devices or partitions, under Unix-like operating systems, everything appears within a single hierarchical filesystem, where / is the root and everything gets put somewhere underneath the root. This can avoid the problem of devices getting different drive letters on subsequent reboots since each device or partition is mounted into the Linux filesystem exactly where it is specified to be mounted.

One advantage to this approach is that it allows for upgrading storage in a more modular fashion. If you need more storage space in your home directories for your users, you can install a new hard drive and just mount it into the right place in the filesystem. Afterward, you will have more space for your users without impacting the rest of the system. The risk here is that if you don't partition correctly, you could run out of space in one part of the filesystem while swimming in extra storage in another part of the filesystem. You could certainly install new hard drives and copy files to make it all work with enough space, but this does incur downtime on the system, so it's best to try to get it as close to right as possible the first time around.

 NOTE The file where all of the mount points are kept so the system knows which devices to mount to which mount point in the filesystem is /etc/fstab.

As you can see in Table 6-1, binaries can be stored in a number of places. The way to direct the system in how to find them is by using a variable called PATH, which indicates to the system all of the places you want the system to search for executable programs so you don't have to specify the full path when you attempt to run the binary.

NOTE *Binary*, in the context discussed here, is another word for program or application, but is a bit more specific than that. Binary indicates that the program in question is a compiled program and exists in the filesystem in binary form. Not all binary files are programs, though. Programs written in a scripting language like Python or Ruby would be stored in ASCII form.

Figure 6-3 displays a directory listing on a Linux system showing a representation (on a live system) of the directories described in Table 6-1. You'll also see that while there are standard locations for things, a running system may have information in different places than where it is specified in the standard. As an example, you can see that the initial RAM disk and kernel image are in the root of the drive, whereas they would typically be in /boot instead.

Directory	Purpose
/bin	All binaries (programs) that would be needed in single-user mode. This is to allow for the potential troubleshooting and configuration changes necessary to repair a system that may be having problems in multiuser mode. This should be on the primary storage device rather than a mount point, in case there is a problem mounting it.
/boot	Files related to booting the system are stored here, including the kernel and any RAM disk files required for booting. Additionally, the boot configuration files may be stored here.
/dev	This is also a virtual filesystem, like /sys mentioned earlier. It is a collection of file representations of devices on the system.
/etc	This directory stores all of the configuration files for the system. There are a number of subdirectories here, including /etc/X11, which stores all of the configuration for the X Window system.
/home	This directory stores the home directories for any users on the system
/lib	Any libraries that are essential for the binaries (programs) in /bin. As with /bin, this exists in case /usr is a mount point rather than being physically located on the same partition as the root partition.
/media	This is a newer entry to the filesystem layout and exists to allow insertion of removable media like optical discs or USB sticks.
/mnt	A directory to put filesystems that are temporarily mounted.
/opt	This is where optional software packages from third-party vendors get installed.
/proc	A virtual filesystem where information about the different running processes is stored.
/root	The home directory for the root user. As with other directories in the layout, this is stored in the root directory rather than in the home directory, in case the home directory is a mounted directory that may not always be there.
/sbin	Similar to /bin, this is where essential *system* binaries are stored, as opposed to binaries that a user would be most likely to use.

Table 6-1 Filesystem Hierarchy

Directory	Purpose
/tmp	Temporary data. Anything in this directory may not persist across reboots.
/usr	The majority of read-only user data is kept here, including binaries, libraries, and utilities. There are a number of subdirectories here, including /usr/bin, /usr/lib, /usr/include, /usr/sbin, and /usr/src. Another set of directories exists in /usr/local, where there is a similar group of subdirectories as in /usr (i.e., /usr/local/bin, /usr/local/include, and so on). This is where locally installed and created data is stored. Binaries that have been created and installed locally would be in this directory.
/var	Variable data is stored here. This directory will most likely need space to grow, unlike some of the others that would stay reasonably static once they are created. Log data is stored here in /var/log. Information related to the state of an application like databases for MySQL would be stored in /var/lib. /var/spool is where temporary data is kept that is being prepared to be sent somewhere. Mail queues, as an example, would be stored in /var/spool prior to final delivery.

Table 6-1 Filesystem Hierarchy

Figure 6-3
Directory listing
of / on a Linux
system

```
kilroy@bill:/$ ls -la
total 525430
drwxr-xr-x  26 root root      4096 Nov 12 11:08 .
drwxr-xr-x  26 root root      4096 Nov 12 11:08 ..
drwxr-xr-x 399 root root     18432 Dec 31  1969 afs
drwxr-xr-x   2 root root      4096 Jan  7 09:10 bin
drwxr-xr-x   3 root root      4096 Jan  7 09:26 boot
drwxr-xr-x   3 root root      4096 Aug  3  2012 build
drwxr-xr-x  16 root root      4280 Jan 22 21:08 dev
drwxr-xr-x 209 root root     12288 Mar 13 11:33 etc
drwxr-xr-x   5 root root      4096 Jan 31 10:44 home
lrwxrwxrwx   1 root root        37 Jul 26  2012 initrd.img -> /boot/initrd.img-3
.2.0-27-generic-pae
lrwxrwxrwx   1 root root        36 Aug 19  2011 initrd.img.old -> boot/initrd.im
g-2.6.38-8-generic-pae
drwxr-xr-x  25 root root      4096 Jan  7 09:03 lib
drwxr-xr-x   2 root root      4096 Jan  7 09:02 lib64
drwxr-xr-x   2 root root      4096 Oct 24  2011 loop
drwx------   2 root root     16384 Aug 19  2011 lost+found
drwxr-xr-x   3 root root      4096 Jul 22  2012 media
drwxr-xr-x   5 root root      4096 Oct 12 12:54 mnt
drwxr-xr-x   4 root root      4096 Aug 18  2012 opt
dr-xr-xr-x 181 root root         0 Jan 10 06:42 proc
drwx------  12 root root      4096 Apr  3 20:49 root
drwxr-xr-x  33 root root      1260 Apr  3 20:17 run
drwxr-xr-x   2 root root     12288 Feb 19 19:14 sbin
drwxr-xr-x   2 root root      4096 Mar 21  2011 selinux
drwxr-xr-x   2 root root      4096 Aug 19  2011 srv
-rw-r--r--   1 root root 537894912 Nov  6 20:47 swapfile
drwxr-xr-x  13 root root         0 Jan 10 06:42 sys
drwxrwxrwt  12 root root     12288 Apr  4 08:35 tmp
drwxr-xr-x  11 root root      4096 Aug 25  2012 usr
drwxr-xr-x  16 root root      4096 Jan 31 07:06 var
lrwxrwxrwx   1 root root        33 Jul 26  2012 vmlinuz -> boot/vmlinuz-3.2.0-27
-generic-pae
lrwxrwxrwx   1 root root        33 Aug 19  2011 vmlinuz.old -> boot/vmlinuz-2.6.
38-8-generic-pae
kilroy@bill:/$
```

There are some virtual filesystems that are important to note. The first one is /proc, where information about running processes is stored. The kernel populates this directory as processes start and end. Devices on the system all have entries in the /dev directory, so you can directly access devices through simple file references. Finally, the /sys filesystem is where all of the running kernel configuration is stored.

NOTE The /dev filesystem includes character-generator devices like /dev/zero, which generates 0s, and /dev/random, which generates random characters. /dev/null is a sink where you can redirect any unwanted output and have it just disappear.

Using Linux

While all of the major Linux distributions include graphical desktops like Gnome, KDE, or Xfce, the underpinnings of Linux are still command-line oriented and there are a lot of useful things that can be done on the command line—and in many cases, better and faster than through a graphical interface. First, there are a couple of basic ideas worth mentioning here. Unix was meant to be modular with single-purpose utilities that were small and fast. In order to do this, there needed to be a way to chain the output of one command to the input of another command. You accomplish this through the use of a pipe, which is the | character. In order to send the output of one command into the input stream of another, you place the | character between them and thus the system knows you are piping the output of the first command into the input of the second command. This little tool is incredibly useful, and you will find yourself using it a lot once you have the hang of it. Beyond piping, you may want to simply redirect input or output. As an example, you may wish to send the output of a particular command into a file. You would do that by using the > character. So, you might type **foo > file.txt**, which would send the output of foo into the file file.txt. The > character overwrites the file. If you wanted to append to the file and start over, you would use >>.

There are three standard streams in Unix-like operating systems: stdin, stdout, and stderr. In the preceding example, we were making use of the stdout stream and redirecting it to a file. If you wanted to redirect stderr, which is where all of the error messages from any program are sent, you would use 2> because 2 is the numeric equivalent of the stderr stream, just as 1 is the equivalent of stdout and 0 is stdin. You may want to send output and errors to the same file, in which case you would use >&, which would send output and errors to wherever you specified.

Having gotten some of the basics out of the way, let's talk about some specific commands you may use under Linux in the terminal to accomplish specific tasks. Where possible, we will talk about how you might chain commands together.

General Utilities

The following are general utilities that are useful across the system, specifically in conjunction with other commands and utilities.

- **grep**   Short for global replace, it can be used to search for strings within a set of files or within the output from a chained command. grep –R will search recursively underneath the directory that grep is called from.

- **cut**   This will cut a specific field out of the text that is handed to it. This can be used to extract specific information from a set of data, specifically data that is ordered in a particular way with a delimiter like a space, tab, or colon (:).

File Management
The following commands are useful for performing file management tasks.

- **ls**   Lists files. There are a number of switches for ls that make the output more useful. As an example, ls –la shows the files in a list view with details about the file. It also shows all of the files in the directory, including the ones normally hidden because they start with a ".", called dot files.

- **mv**   Moves files from a source to a destination.

- **cp**   Copies files from a source to a destination.

- **rm**   Removes a file. Some distributions force this to be an alias for rm –i, which will prompt you for every file before actually deleting the file. Unlike graphical systems, when you use rm to delete a file, it is immediately deleted and not sent to a trash can or recycle bin where you can restore it at a later date.

- **rmdir**   Removes a directory. This will not remove a directory that has files in it. In order to use rmdir, you need to have an empty directory. To remove a directory that has files in it, you could use rm –Rf. Adding the –Rf will recursively go through all directories underneath the specified directory and remove all files and directories as it goes, finally removing the specified directory.

- **ln**   Creates a file link. This is similar to an alias or a shortcut used in other systems. A link will point back to a source file. In the case of a symbolic link, removing the link will not actually remove the file. Symbolic links are created using ln –s instead of simply ln, which creates a hard link.

- **pwd**   Prints the working directory. In other words, it will show you the directory you are in.

- **cd**   Changes the directory. This is used to move around the filesystem, changing directories you are working in.

- **cat**   Concatenates files into a single output stream. This output stream can then be redirected (>) into another file. If a single file is provided, cat sends the contents of the file to stdout, effectively displaying the file to the terminal.

- **less**   Presents a page of a particular file at a time, unlike cat, which sends the entire contents of the file to the terminal regardless of size. Less is a version of the file pager More (the joke is that Less is More).

Process Management

The following commands are useful for managing processes.

- **ps**   Shows processes currently running. Depending on the switches provided, the list may include all of the processes on the system or just the processes belonging to the user you are logged in as. ps works well with grep, if you are looking for a specific process. If I were looking for the Apache Web server, for example, I might issue the command ps auxww | grep httpd since httpd is the name of the process for the Apache Web server. grep in this case is being handed the output from the ps command and is looking for lines in that output that have the word httpd in it.

- **top**   Provides system information as well as a constantly updated list of all the processes running on the system, along with their usage information.

- **kill**   Can either terminate a process or simply send the process a specific signal. This requires the process ID (PID) of the process you want to send the signal to.

- **killall**   Is the same as kill in terms of functionality except it can take a process name instead of a process ID as an argument. If a process name is given, all processes with that name will get the signal that is being sent, if it's the interrupt signal, which is the default.

Networking

The following commands are useful in performing networking tasks for configuration as well as troubleshooting.

- **ifconfig**   Lists the configuration for all of the network interfaces on a particular system. It can also be used to configure a network interface.

- **netstat**   Shows network information and statistics like routing tables as well as a list of connections and listening services.

- **ping**   Issues ICMP echo requests to a specified host, expecting to get ICMP echo responses in return.

- **traceroute**   Used to trace the path through the network to a specific host.

- **route**   Can be used to add a network route to the routing table.

- **arp**   Shows the stored table of ARP entries that map MAC addresses to IP addresses.

Software Management

There are, as you may know, a number of different distributions of Linux. While the programs that get installed are primarily the same, there may be subtle distinctions between many of the distributions. This may have to do with the way the binaries are compiled, using different flags and settings, or it may have to do with graphics for the user interfaces. It may use different sets of binaries installed by default or it may have different management utilities. One of the differences between different distributions is how software is managed. When it comes to software management, there are three primary distributions to consider: Debian, Red Hat Enterprise Linux(RHEL)/CentOS, and Slackware. Numerous other distributions are available, but the majority of them are descendants in one way or another from one of these three primary distributions.

Debian

The first distribution to consider is Debian, in part because it's one of the oldest Linux distributions but also because a large number of Linux distributions follow the way Debian does things, from file layout to management utilities. Ubuntu and Linux Mint are two examples of Debian-based distributions. Debian uses apt (Advanced Packaging Tool) for package management. Various front-ends are available for the apt system, so you have a full range of options when it comes to interfacing with apt, depending on what you are most comfortable with. Using basic apt utilities like apt-get and apt-cache, you can install and update software packages. You could use aptitude, which is a utility that uses a user interface, though it's cursor/keyboard-oriented and not a keyboard/mouse graphical interface. Synaptic is a full graphical interface.

NOTE   The name Debian is a concatenation of the names Debra and Ian. Ian Murdock started the Debian distribution and Debra was his girlfriend in 1993 when Debian was first released.

Debian provides the ability to configure the location of where software packages come from, whether it's new software or updates to existing software. If you are inclined to manage the files yourself, you would look at the file /etc/apt/sources.list, which lists all the locations that software can be installed from. Configuration files for changing the behavior of apt, including having apt use a proxy server to get content from the Web, are in /etc/apt/apt.conf.d. There are a number of files in this directory, all of which cover specific configurations for different functional aspects of apt. All the configuration files get read in the order in which they show up in the directory, so each filename begins with a number to make the order in which the files are read immediately clear. If you prefer a graphical way of managing your sources list, including selecting the server that is best for you based on your location, you can use the Software Sources configuration utility, shown in Figure 6-4. This utility allows you to select the server you obtain your software from in a number of ways, including simply using the main software repository site, choosing geographically, selecting the best server based on responsiveness, or simply selecting a server you happen to like for your own reasons.

You can also manually install packages using the dpkg utility if you find Debian packages you'd like to install that either don't come from one of the online repositories or come from a specific repository that you don't want to add to your sources list. dpkg enables you to perform a number of actions, including install the package, unpack it, or get a status. With dpkg, you can manually work on the .deb files that the various apt utilities end up working with behind the scenes. Underneath the hood, .deb files are really a collection of compressed tape archives.

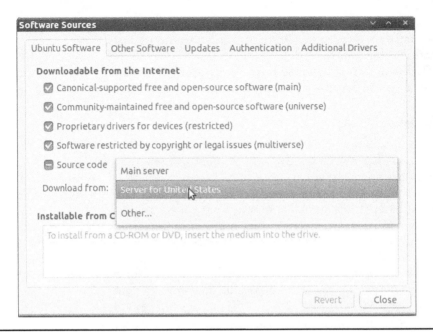

Figure 6-4 Configuring Ubuntu sources

In addition to the other capabilities, the various package management utilities will resolve dependencies for packages and get them installed to ensure the package you are trying to install will function correctly.

Red Hat Enterprise Linux/CentOS

RedHat has also been around for a very long time as a Linux distribution, starting in 1993 just as Debian did. Red Hat currently has two distributions that behave the same way: Red Hat Enterprise Linux (RHEL) and Fedora Core. Fedora tends to be more of a leading-edge distribution where eventually packages and features end up getting rolled into RHEL. CentOS is a fully open-source distribution that's completely binary-compatible with RHEL, but it uses different badging and graphics than RHEL because RHEL is commercial software. You can get all of the benefits and stability of RHEL without the RedHat support that goes with it by getting CentOS.

RedHat uses RedHat Package Manager (RPM) packages for software management. An RPM has four sections to it: the lead (identifies the file as an RPM); the signature (used to verify the file as complete and authentic); the header (contains the package name, the architecture, the version, and the file list); and the file archive (the meat of the package, which includes executables, libraries, configuration files, and documentation). The file archive is stored as a compressed cpio file. RPM is a very common package format and there are several front-ends available to manage these packages. One of those front-ends is the utility rpm, which can query an RPM file as well as install RPM packages. One thing rpm won't do is resolve and install dependencies for an RPM file.

One of the tools commonly used because it's available for RedHat, CentOS, and Fedora as well as other distributions is yum, which stands for Yellowdog Updater Modified. yum was created at Duke University as a full rewrite of Yellowdog Updater (YUP). Yellow Dog Linux was first released in 1999 for the PowerPC processor architecture and designed to run on Apple Macintosh PowerPC-based systems. yum is a command-line tool used to manage package installations under RedHat distributions. One of the advantages to yum is its ability to pull automatically from online repositories, which the tool rpm isn't able to do. In order to install a package, you could type **yum install packagename** and yum would go find the package named packagename and install it. In order to update all of the outdated packages on your system, you would use yum update. You could update just one package by using yum update packagename. yum will also resolve dependencies and install them.

 EXAM TIP While rpm can be used to install individual RPMs, yum uses a repository to check against for available updates and can be used to get all packages up to date automatically by running yum update.

One significant advantage to using yum is the ability to easily create a local repository of packages. This local repository may sync from a source online somewhere, but having the local repository allows you to keep multiple systems up to date using your local network without having to use bandwidth to the Internet. This provides you with better control, as well as faster updates, since you don't have to download packages for every system.

Slackware

Slackware has also been around since 1993 and also includes package management like the others discussed so far. Slackware uses a utility called pkgtool to manage its packages. pkgtool allows you to do the same sorts of things that the other package managers allow, but unlike utilities like yum or apt-get, pkgtool doesn't do dependency resolution. If a software package has dependencies, you have to install them manually. Slackware packages are also much simpler than the other packages. The structure of a Slackware package is simply a tape archive (tar) that has been compressed with gzip. The pkgtool utility keeps track of the package that has been installed, including its contents, so it can be upgraded or removed later. pkgtool is a menu-based system for managing packages. You can also use individual utilities to manage your packages like installpkg, removepkg, and upgradepkg.

Because of the popularity of the RPM package format, Slackware also offers utilities that will convert from an RPM format to a Slackware package. There are two utilities available to do the conversion: rpm2tgz and rpm2targz. The first creates a Slackware package with the .tgz extension and the second creates a Slackware package with the .tar.gz extension.

Boot Process

The beginnings of the boot process are the same as any other operating system since they start with powering the system on, where the BIOS takes initial control. Linux does have a well-defined boot process that includes some configuration settings and files that are worth going over. As expected, Linux takes the majority of the way it behaves from Unix. The issue with that is that there are, in effect, two different types of Unix: AT&T and BSD. Their boot processes are slightly different, but most Linux distributions seem to use the SysV (AT&T) style of managing their boot-time services, so that's what we'll be discussing here.

 NOTE SysV is short for System V or System 5, which is the last official major version of Unix from AT&T. The minor versions were called releases, so you could have SysV Release 4 or SVR4. Novell owned the rights to Unix for a period of time, before they were acquired by Santa Cruz Operation (SCO), which has become Tarantella.

The very first step is powering the system on, which triggers the system BIOS, getting the time and date and all the configuration settings for the hardware, followed by a Power-On Self-Test (POST). Once the hardware is ready, control gets transferred to the boot sector of the boot disk. The boot sector, or master boot record (MBR), is 512 bytes and contains the partition table as well as the first stage of the boot loader. Linux typically uses either of two boot loaders, GRUB (Grand Unified Boot Loader) or LILO (LInux LOader). The boot loader is responsible for locating the kernel, based on its configuration, reading it, loading it in memory, and starting it up. Once the kernel is fully up and running, the init process starts. Init is the first program that is run after the kernel is started and it's responsible for getting everything configured in order for the system to be ready for use.

 NOTE The MBR was first introduced in 1983 and many operating systems are moving away from it to a GUID Partition Table in order to support larger hard drives.

Init uses runlevels to distinguish which processes need to be started when the system loads. Init uses the file /etc/inittab to determine which programs need to be started. Different runlevels have different purposes, and you can set a default runlevel depending on what your needs are for a particular system. Setting the runlevel will allow you to do things like boot to a console mode, boot to a graphical interface, or boot to a single-user mode. Single-user mode is often used for troubleshooting and repairing problems with the system since some processes don't get started in single-user mode, so you end up reducing process clutter and interference. Table 6-2 shows the common runlevels for Linux, as well as their purpose.

 EXAM TIP You should know the format for an entry in /etc/inittab.

Table 6-2	Runlevel	Purpose
Runlevels in Linux	0	Halt
	1	Single-user mode
	2	Multiuser mode, without support for Network File System (NFS)
	3	Full multiuser mode (console mode)
	4	Unused
	5	X11 (graphical interface)
	6	Reboot (do not set the default runlevel to this)

The format for /etc/inittab is *id:runlevels:action:process*, where *id* is just a unique identifier for the entry, *runlevels* is a list of runlevels that the *action* will take place in, and *process* is the process that will be executed for that entry in the inittab. A sample inittab entry is 3:3:wait:/etc/rc.d/rc3, which says that in runlevel 3, execute the scripts in /etc/rc.d/rc3 and init should wait for its termination. Other actions are respawn, meaning that init will start the process over again should it fail, and once, meaning that the process will get executed once when the runlevel is entered.

The SysV style of init (AT&T) uses the /etc/rc*x*.d or /etc/rc.d/rc*x* directory structure to manage the different programs that run within different runlevels. The *x* in the preceding examples indicates the number of the runlevel. In each of these directories are scripts that start up the different services that need to be running for each runlevel. Typically, there would be a startup script and a script that stops the process. Startup scripts are prefaced with an S, while scripts intended to stop processes are prefaced with a K (for kill). They are run in order, so after the S, there is generally a number that indicates where they should be in the startup process. The lower the number, the higher priority a process it is.

Generally, the scripts to start up and kill a service that live in the individual runlevel directories are linked to the location where they are really stored, which is in /etc/init.d. Storing them in one location and linking to them in another location saves disk space and also ensures that when they need to be upgraded or changed, you don't have to do it in multiple locations. When you make changes, you change the single file, and the linked locations automatically pick up the changes since they are really just pointers to the real file.

 EXAM TIP Service management scripts are stored in the /etc/init.d/ directory, although there are links to those files stored in individual runlevel directories, allowing the services to be brought up by default in the appropriate runlevel.

Process Management

The very first process that starts is init, and as a result of being the first process, it receives process ID 1. All services that get started are started by init and become children of the init process. Each child may have children of its own, but all processes running on a Unix-like system such as Linux will trace their ancestry back to init. Init is responsible both for starting all of the services that are running and for starting the process that allows for login at the console. Typically, this process is called getty, which was once short for get teletype, since teletype machines were originally used for interactive access to computer systems. (Many long-since antiquated terms continue to exist in operating systems as old as Unix because descendants have simply picked up the terminology in order to preserve consistency and compatibility.)

If you were to diagram all of the processes running on a Linux system, you would start with init as the beginning. Everything would flow from that starting point. Figure 6-5 shows a diagram of the processes on a Linux system using a tool called pstree. The diagram might be called a process tree (thus the name pstree) because processes can be diagramed in a tree-like structure. The pstree utility shows the parentage for all the processes running, beginning with the super-parent, init, on the top-left side of the diagram. You'll also see the login session that pstree was run from, beginning with lightdm toward the bottom of the output. Lightdm is the display manager that handles all graphical sessions run using X11. If you look toward the right side of the output at the bottom, you can see that my login session through lightdm includes Firefox and a terminal window.

```
kilroy@yaz:~$ pstree
init─┬─.ruby.bin───13*[{.ruby.bin}]
     ├─NetworkManager─┬─dhclient
     │                ├─dnsmasq
     │                └─2*[{NetworkManager}]
     ├─accounts-daemon───{accounts-daemon}
     ├─acpid
     ├─apache2─┬─apache2
     │         └─2*[apache2───26*[{apache2}]]
     ├─at-spi-bus-laun─┬─dbus-daemon
     │                 └─3*[{at-spi-bus-laun}]
     ├─at-spi2-registr───{at-spi2-registr}
     ├─atd
     ├─avahi-daemon───avahi-daemon
     ├─bluetoothd
     ├─colord───2*[{colord}]
     ├─console-kit-dae───64*[{console-kit-dae}]
     ├─cron
     ├─cupsd
     ├─2*[dbus-daemon]
     ├─dbus-launch
     ├─dconf-service───2*[{dconf-service}]
     ├─gconfd-2
     ├─6*[getty]
     ├─gnome-keyring-d───5*[{gnome-keyring-d}]
     ├─gsd-printer───{gsd-printer}
     ├─gvfs-afc-volume───2*[{gvfs-afc-volume}]
     ├─gvfs-gphoto2-vo───{gvfs-gphoto2-vo}
     ├─gvfs-udisks2-vo───{gvfs-udisks2-vo}
     ├─gvfsd───{gvfsd}
     ├─gvfsd-burn───{gvfsd-burn}
     ├─gvfsd-fuse───4*[{gvfsd-fuse}]
     ├─gvfsd-metadata───{gvfsd-metadata}
     ├─gvfsd-trash───2*[{gvfsd-trash}]
     ├─lightdm─┬─Xorg───{Xorg}
     │         └─lightdm─┬─gnome-session─┬─cinnamon─┬─firefox───32*[{firefox}]
     │                                              └─gnome-terminal─┬─bash───p+
```

Figure 6-5 A process tree

The terminal window is running bash, which is the user shell. bash is the parent for pstree, the beginning of which you can see at the very bottom; however, pstree truncates at 80 characters since terminal windows typically open at 80 characters.

 NOTE Terminal windows, while software now, are designed to emulate what it was like to use a physical CRT display, which commonly were 80×24 characters. Some of this size irregularity has to do with the rectangularness of characters that may take up more vertical space than horizontal.

Processes and Threads

Conceptualizing a process may be difficult because we're used to dealing with applications and programs. Perhaps the best way to think about the concept is that a program is the collection of bits as they sit on the disk, and a process is how that program looks when it's in memory. One reason for making the distinction is that you can have multiple instances of a particular program running at any given time, and while they are the same program, they are different processes with different execution paths and different memory segments.

Processes can also create processes, as you might have guessed from the previous discussion about parents and so forth. The process of creating a child process is called *spawning*, or sometimes *forking*. Note that if the parent dies, all the children die along with it. As an example, let's say you have opened a terminal window and launched Firefox and Thunderbird, sending them to the background so you can get your terminal window back and they can continue to run. When you close your terminal window, Firefox and Thunderbird will also close. The terminal window, and specifically the bash shell running in it, is the parent of those graphical programs, even though they appear to be detached from it. When the parent dies or is killed, the children get killed.

Another thing to note is that processes are distinct from threads. A process can have multiple threads, but any threads created for multiprocessing purposes would belong to the context of the process. The threads would run in the same memory space as the parent process. They may follow different execution paths through the code, but the memory remains shared among all the threads within the process. The idea of multithreading is to get work done faster. The challenge is to break work up into tasks that can be performed simultaneously without impacting the other tasks or requiring that one task wait on another.

Under Linux, as with Unix, each process gets a process ID when it is created, which is how you would refer to the process if you needed to communicate with it. We'll go into how to communicate with processes and the sorts of communications you can engage in with processes shortly. The other thing that happens when a program is executed and a process is created is that an entry gets created in the /proc filesystem. Figure 6-6 shows a listing of the /proc directory. The subdirectories under /proc are created for each individual process, and inside each directory are a number of files carrying information and statistics about the process, including memory segments in use, as well as the list of recent functions called.

Figure 6-6
A /proc listing

```
kilroy@bill: $ ls /proc
1       1725    24      27532   3175    687     cgroups         misc
10      1746    2488    27533   3178    673     cmdline         modules
10035   1747    2489    28      3179    674     consoles        mounts
1066    1756    2514    2822    3180    677     cpuinfo         mtrr
10725   1764    2524    2823    3181    7       crypto          net
10726   1793    26      2824    3183    707     devices         pagetypeinfo
1094    18      2629    2837    3191    71      diskstats       partitions
11387   1873    2631    2849    3193    755     dma             sched_debug
1172    19      2641    2868    3194    765     dri             schedstat
12      1923    2647    2865    32      766     driver          scsi
1226    1948    2648    287     32158   796     execdomains     self
12659   2       2649    29      32162   8       fb              slabinfo
13      28      2658    3       32176   817     filesystems     softirqs
1387    282     2657    38      32667   847     fs              stat
1357    2852    2659    30113   3383    850     interrupts      swaps
1397    21      2665    30386   3337    853     iomem           sys
14      2154    2667    30428   3434    871     ioports         sysrq-trigger
15      22      2670    30423   3435    872     irq             sysvipc
1540    2256    2688    3043    40      883     kallsyms        timer_list
1567    2277    27      31      435     884     kcore           timer_stats
16      2278    271     3118    444     901     key-users       tty
1614    23      272     3112    454     983     kmsg            uptime
1618    2306    27521   3113    46      914     kpagecount      version
1642    23092   27525   3154    465     923     kpageflags      version_signature
1648    2310    27527   3163    47      924     latency_stats   vmallocinfo
1654    2313    27528   3164    471     acpi    loadavg         vmstat
1655    2320    27529   3165    48      asound  locks           zoneinfo
1658    2322    27530   3167    49      buddyinfo       mdstat
1724    2330    27531   3171    6       bus     meminfo
```

Process Tools

Now that we can figure out who our parents are and the lineage of Linux processes, we can move on to what to do with these processes once they are created. Perhaps the very first thing you want to do is to figure out what processes are running on a particular system. A couple of tools are available to do that. The first one is ps, a static tool that gives you a process list based on what's running at the moment the tool is executed. ps shows a process list and, depending on the arguments passed to ps, can provide that information in some different ways. ps can provide you with a list of processes that you own, and if you have root-level permissions, you can see all the processes running on the system. Additionally, with the right argument, you can see the process ID associated with each process. Figure 6-7 shows ps executed with different sets of arguments passed to it. The first run is without arguments and shows the processes owned by the user executing ps. The second run shows all processes with a terminal, which includes the bash process running in the terminal that ps is executing in, as well as ps itself. Finally, adding u shows the user who owns each process. ps reads the information displayed from the /proc filesystem.

ps is similar to other tools in the toolset of common Unix utilities in that arguments have historically varied between the way BSD implemented them and the way AT&T implemented them. As a result, some tools, like ps, have had to support different options, and potentially in different ways, depending on the other arguments that are passed. If you are familiar with one flavor or another of Unix, it's worth checking with the documentation under Linux to see which options do what.

Another way to look at processes is to use the top utility. Whereas ps shows a static list of processes, commonly just the ones belonging to the user issuing the command, top shows a dynamic list of all the processes running, updated every three seconds. top also provides additional details about the system, including the number of tasks currently running,

Figure 6-7
Some ps
variations

```
kilroy@bill: $ ps
  PID TTY          TIME CMD
  604 pts/0    00:00:00 ps
30423 pts/0    00:00:00 bash
kilroy@bill: $ ps a
  PID TTY      STAT   TIME COMMAND
  605 pts/0    R+     0:00 ps a
 1614 tty4     Ss+    0:00 /sbin/getty -8 38400 tty4
 1618 tty5     Ss+    0:00 /sbin/getty -8 38400 tty5
 1654 tty2     Ss+    0:00 /sbin/getty -8 38400 tty2
 1655 tty3     Ss+    0:00 /sbin/getty -8 38400 tty3
 1658 tty6     Ss+    0:00 /sbin/getty -8 38400 tty6
 1764 tty7     Ss+   82:59 /usr/bin/X :0 -auth /var/run/lightdm/root/:0 vt7 -nov
 3337 tty1     Ss+    0:00 /sbin/getty -8 38400 tty1
30423 pts/0    Ss     0:00 -bash
kilroy@bill: $ ps au
USER        PID %CPU %MEM    VSZ   RSS TTY      STAT START   TIME COMMAND
kilroy      606  0.0  0.0   4916  1060 pts/0    R+   10:48   0:00 ps au
root       1614  0.0  0.0   4632   344 tty4     Ss+  Jan10   0:00 /sbin/getty -8
root       1618  0.0  0.0   4632   344 tty5     Ss+  Jan10   0:00 /sbin/getty -8
root       1654  0.0  0.0   4632   344 tty2     Ss+  Jan10   0:00 /sbin/getty -8
root       1655  0.0  0.0   4632   344 tty3     Ss+  Jan10   0:00 /sbin/getty -8
root       1658  0.0  0.0   4632   344 tty6     Ss+  Jan10   0:00 /sbin/getty -8
root       1764  0.0  0.0  16432  1836 tty7     Ss+  Jan10  82:59 /usr/bin/X :0 -
root       3337  0.0  0.0   4632   344 tty1     Ss+  Jan10   0:00 /sbin/getty -8
kilroy    30423  0.0  0.4  12748  9072 pts/0    Ss   Apr10   0:00 -bash
```

CPU usage, memory usage, and the uptime of the system. Figure 6-8 shows an example of top with the list of processes currently running on the system. On the top of the screen, you can see the statistics for the system. While top updates every three seconds with new information, this is a point-in-time snapshot because it's a screen capture. At the particular moment in time that the screen capture was taken, asterisk was consuming 0.2% of

Figure 6-8
The top utility

```
top - 13:11:07 up 91 days,  5:29,  1 user,  load average: 0.13, 0.13, 0.14
Tasks: 168 total,   2 running, 166 sleeping,   0 stopped,   0 zombie
Cpu(s):  0.3%us,  1.3%sy,  0.0%ni, 94.7%id,  3.7%wa,  0.0%hi,  0.0%si,  0.0%st
Mem:   2029908k total,  1762284k used,   267624k free,    68928k buffers
Swap:  2065316k total,   198888k used,  1866428k free,   821004k cached

  PID USER      PR  NI  VIRT  RES  SHR S %CPU %MEM    TIME+  COMMAND
32667 root      20   0     0    0    0 R    2  0.0  1:32.92 kworker/0:1
  953 kilroy    20   0  2856 1188  888 R    1  0.1  0:00.07 top
  271 root      20   0     0    0    0 S    0  0.0  6:06.75 jbd2/sda2-8
 1397 ntp       20   0  5764  956  768 S    0  0.0  9:16.06 ntpd
 3112 asterisk -11   0 89544 3100  528 S    0  0.2 256:47.80 asterisk
    1 root      20   0  3660 1528  880 S    0  0.1  0:02.88 init
    2 root      20   0     0    0    0 S    0  0.0  0:04.68 kthreadd
    3 root      20   0     0    0    0 S    0  0.0 10:13.62 ksoftirqd/0
    6 root      RT   0     0    0    0 S    0  0.0  0:00.00 migration/0
    7 root      RT   0     0    0    0 S    0  0.0  8:05.72 watchdog/0
    8 root      RT   0     0    0    0 S    0  0.0  0:00.00 migration/1
   10 root      20   0     0    0    0 S    0  0.0 20:43.99 ksoftirqd/1
   12 root      RT   0     0    0    0 S    0  0.0  0:30.33 watchdog/1
   13 root       0 -20     0    0    0 S    0  0.0  0:00.00 cpuset
   14 root       0 -20     0    0    0 S    0  0.0  0:00.00 khelper
   15 root      20   0     0    0    0 S    0  0.0  0:00.01 kdevtmpfs
   16 root       0 -20     0    0    0 S    0  0.0  0:00.00 netns
   18 root      20   0     0    0    0 S    0  0.0  0:24.17 sync_supers
   19 root      20   0     0    0    0 S    0  0.0  0:00.64 bdi-default
   20 root       0 -20     0    0    0 S    0  0.0  0:00.00 kintegrityd
   21 root       0 -20     0    0    0 S    0  0.0  0:02.35 kblockd
   22 root       0 -20     0    0    0 S    0  0.0  0:00.00 ata_sff
   23 root      20   0     0    0    0 S    0  0.0  0:00.01 khubd
```

system memory. The kworker process was taking up the most CPU time, consuming 2%, which still isn't much. The downside to running top is that it will take up processor time.

 NOTE The kworker process handles kernel work queues.

You can control the behavior of processes, including forcing them to terminate, through the utility kill. A related utility is killall. With the kill utility, you have to know the process ID in order to send a message to the process, and by default the message is to terminate the process. killall makes it easier to work with processes by allowing you to communicate with the process by name rather than the process ID.

Signals

The kill utility not only sends a termination signal to the process, which should cause it to terminate, but also is capable of sending any other signal to the process. Programs can implement handlers for each signal or let the default behavior remain in place, with the exception of the SIGKILL and SIGSTOP signals. A list of common signals is shown in Table 6-3. In order to send a particular signal to a process, you would send kill –*SignalNumber process ID*. As an example, you could send kill –HUP 55.

Signal	Purpose
SIGHUP	Originally for when a line was disconnected (hung up)
SIGINT	Interrupt from keyboard (CTRL-C)
SIGQUIT	Quit from keyboard
SIGILL	Illegal instruction
SIGABRT	Abort signal generated by the abort() function call
SIGFPE	Floating-point exception
SIGKILL	Kill signal
SIGSEGV	Segment violation—trying to read from memory something that the process doesn't have access to
SIGALRM	Timer signal generated by the alarm() function call
SIGUSR1	User-defined signal
SIGUSR2	User-defined signal
SIGCHLD	Child stopped or terminated
SIGCONT	Continue if stopped
SIGSTOP	Stop process
SIGTSTP	Stop typed at terminal
SIGTTIN	Terminal input for background process
SIGTTOU	Terminal output for background process

Table 6-3 Linux Signals Defined by POSIX Standard

Figure 6-9

Duplicate

process names

```
kilroy@bill: $ ps eaf
  PID TTY      STAT    TIME COMMAND
 1900 pts/5    Ss     0:00 -bash USER=kilroy LOGNAME=kilroy HOME=/home/kilroy PA
 2015 pts/5    R+     0:00  \_ ps eaf GOHOSTARCH=386 rvm_gemsets_path=/usr/share
 1676 pts/0    Ss+    0:00 -bash USER=kilroy LOGNAME=kilroy HOME=/home/kilroy PA
 1764 tty7     Ss+   83:30 /usr/bin/X :0 -auth /var/run/lightdm/root/:0 vt7 -nov
 3337 tty1     Ss+    0:00 /sbin/getty -8 38400 tty1
 1658 tty6     Ss+    0:00 /sbin/getty -8 38400 tty6
 1655 tty3     Ss+    0:00 /sbin/getty -8 38400 tty3
 1654 tty2     Ss+    0:00 /sbin/getty -8 38400 tty2
 1618 tty5     Ss+    0:00 /sbin/getty -8 38400 tty5
 1614 tty4     Ss+    0:00 /sbin/getty -8 38400 tty4
```

Programs are free to implement handlers for nearly all of the signals, with the exception of the KILL and STOP signals. If a program were to receive the HUP signal, it could leave the signal alone, in which case the program would terminate. It might choose to catch the signal and ignore it, in which case the program would continue running as normal. It could also catch the signal and do something with it like go to a graceful shutdown. There have been programs that have restarted on receiving a HUP signal; basically, the program re-reads configuration files and starts over again. This may be helpful if you are making a lot of changes to configuration files, so that you don't have to actually shut down the service and restart it, which may take a little bit longer.

If you have a process that is being stubborn and won't close in spite of your best attempts to get it to, you can send a signal to the process. kill –9 or kill –KILL, which are the same thing since the KILL signal translates to number 9 in the definitions file where this information is kept, will send the KILL signal to the process. Since programs can't ignore a KILL signal, the process will terminate. As noted earlier, you need to know the process ID to send a signal to it. If you were to use killall, you could achieve the same functionality by sending whatever signal you want, but you'd be able to refer to the process by name rather than by number. The catch there is that if you have multiple processes running the same program, you may end up killing a process that you didn't mean to. As an example, if you have multiple bash (terminal) sessions open, as shown in Figure 6-9, and you issued a killall bash command, you may kill a login session you didn't mean to. In fact, you will probably kill the session you are logged into. At that point, you have a race condition. The moment the bash session that issued the killall command is killed, killall will be killed with it because it's a child process. Will it have killed the bash session you wanted to kill before it killed itself?

System Management

A number of tasks are necessary to maintain a well-run system, such as performing backups, patching systems, and applying updates. It's also helpful to be able to provide a schedule for these tasks to get the system to run them automatically without the administrator needing to kick them off manually. Unix has long had facilities that allow for backups, and the various Linux distributions offer ways of doing updates and keeping packages up to date. Unix has also provided facilities for scheduling tasks, and the task scheduler is probably running on your Linux system currently, even if you aren't aware of it.

Backups are a critical task for a system administrator, because at some point, either a user is going to lose a file they want back or, worse, you'll have a hard drive failure and lose all of the files on the disk. Assuming there is data you'd just as soon have back, you'll want a backup.

Backups

While there are certainly a large number of modern backup solutions, like Amanda and Bacula, there are also some tried-and-true standards that have been around for a while. The first utility you can use to perform backups is rsync. rsync allows you to copy files from one system to another, providing for a copy of the files on another system in case the original file is damaged or lost somehow. If you use rsync, you need a daemon (service) running on another system to run the rsync to. rsync is a fairly simple utility to run, as long as you have a system that's prepared to listen to rsync requests. An example use of rsync is as follows:

```
rsync -avz /home backup:mybackup/
```

This command would archive (a) all of the files in the /home directory. Archiving preserves links to other locations in the filesystem, as well as modification and user information. It would also compress the data (z) so it would take up less space on the storage medium. All of the files would be sent to the system named backup and be stored in a directory called mybackup. If you needed to restore, you would reverse the source and destination, pulling the files back. Of course, a lot of other options are available with rsync, letting you do things like select specific files to back up rather than backing up everything.

If you have an attached backup drive, you may want to use the tar command. tar originally meant tape archive, but it works just as well creating disk archives. tar allows you to create a single file containing all the files you specify. Since it's archiving the information, all the user and modification data is retained and not updated as it is stored out. tar historically didn't allow for compression of data, but the GNU version of tar, which is the one that runs on most Linux systems, does support compression. In fact, it supports two different types of compression. If you wanted to store all the files in your /home directory, you might issue the following command:

```
tar cvfz homebackup.tar.gz /home
```

In that example, you are asking tar to create an archive (c), provide verbose feedback (v) about what it's doing, store the result into a file (f), and compress it (z). The next argument is the file you are storing the archive in, and that's followed by a list of all the files and directories you want to archive. In this case, we are simply archiving the /home directory so it's the only thing listed. Once you have the compressed tar file, you could copy it to external storage or another system. In order to restore, you would issue the command **tar xvfz homebackup.tar.gz** and all of the home directory will extract into the directory you are in. You'll notice the command looks very similar to the archive creation. The only thing different is the method. In the creation process, we use a c, and to extract, we use an x.

There are also different strategies for backing up files. You could always do a complete backup, but you may want to reduce the amount of information you are transferring and storing, in which case you may want to implement something like a full backup once a week and then incremental backups on subsequent days. The incremental backup would only back up files that had changed since the full backup. An alternative to the incremental approach is the differential backup. A differential backup will back up all data that has changed since the last full backup. This means that if you do a full backup on Sunday and do differential backups the rest of the week, by Thursday you are backing up data that changed on Monday, Tuesday, Wednesday, *and* Thursday, in spite of the fact that Monday night you backed up data that changed on Monday, and Tuesday night you backed up data that changed on Tuesday, and so forth.

The advantage to this approach is that all you would need to do if you had to do a restore is restore the full backup and then the last differential backup. In the case of an incremental backup, you would need to restore the full backup, then each incremental backup performed between the full backup and the need for a restore. This provides a trade-off. Differential backups take more storage space but less time and effort to restore, while incremental backups take less storage space but more time and effort to restore.

Patch Management

Keeping systems up to date with the latest versions of software is a critical task in protecting your systems and network from intrusion. Older versions of software often contain vulnerabilities that may be exploited to gain unauthorized access by a malicious user. There are different ways of handling system updates, depending on the distribution of Linux you are using. If you are using a RedHat-based system, you would issue the command **yum update** as an administrator or root user and yum will go out to see what packages need to be updated, then update them after checking with you to see if you really want to do the update or not. You can also update individual packages using **yum update <packagename>**, replacing **<packagename>** with the package you want to update.

In the case of Debian-based systems like Ubuntu, you can use the apt utilities to update your system. **apt-get update** will update the list of packages that are available, as well as update the current version. In order to see whether you have packages that need to be updated, you would issue the command **apt-get upgrade**. Upgrading will install the latest versions of all the packages on your system. You may also have the ability to do a version upgrade in a manner similar to this.

If you are running a production system, be wary of just applying updates since it might impact the usability of your system. While the packages are generally tested, there may be specific version requirements for applications you are running, and updating a dependency may cause an outage. As an example, you may have a web application using a particular version of JBoss or Tomcat. Doing a blanket update may update one of these packages to a version that is incompatible with the application you have that is using these packages.

 EXAM TIP It's generally worth applying updates to a test system before rolling them into production, to ensure that they don't break things.

Job Scheduling

There are a number of system management tasks that are much easier when they are scheduled to occur on a predictable basis. One of these tasks is log rotation that compresses a log file and moves it to a backup location, including just renaming the file and leaving it in the same directory. This allows you to keep several days' or weeks' worth of log files without taking a lot of disk space, and it also keeps each log file to a manageable size, as well as a predictable set of dates.

You may also want to schedule your backups or even system updates, depending on the type of system you are using. One utility for doing that is cron. cron is a daemon that runs constantly on your system, waking up at set intervals to perform tasks. You can specify the tasks that occur in the /etc/crontab file, although if you want to run something hourly, daily, or weekly, your version of cron may already have jobs set up for those specific intervals. If that's the case, all you need to do is add a script into one of the directories where the jobs are stored. Hourly scripts are stored in /etc/cron.hourly, daily scripts are stored in /etc/cron.daily, and weekly scripts are stored in /etc/cron.weekly. The script is simply a list of commands that you want to perform, though you could also use shell scripting to perform tasks like checking for the existence of a file before executing a particular command.

User Management

Linux supports different ways of managing users and allowing them to log in to a system. It does this by using Pluggable Authentication Modules (PAM), which allow for swapping in and out of different types of authentication. Linux systems can employ a variety of authentication mechanisms using these modules, including RADIUS, LDAP, TACACS+, and others. These modules also provide the ability to ensure that passwords are sufficiently strong. One module you might install, for example, is the cracklib module that helps ensure passwords are strong and that when passwords are changed, there is enough variation between the old password and the new one. The following configuration line implements a password policy that allows a user three attempts to choose a strong password before the passwd utility, used to set or change passwords, quits:

```
password required pam_cracklib.so retry=3 minlen=6 difok=3
```

The minimum password length allowed with this module in place is six, and at least three of the characters in the new password have to be different from the old password. As a result, if you were to start with the password Abcd4321 and then try Bcde6789, the new password would fail because there wouldn't be enough letters different in the new one, compared with the old one.

EXAM TIP   Understand how PAM functions, particularly with respect to password strength, and how the pam_cracklib module works. Some Linux systems, like Ubuntu, use /etc/pam.d/common-auth for this, while others like RedHat use /etc/pam.d/system-auth.

```
# here are the per-package modules (the "Primary" block)
auth    [success=2 default=ignore]        pam_unix.so nullok_secure
auth    [success=1 default=ignore]        pam_winbind.so krb5_auth krb5_ccache_typ
e=FILE cached_login try_first_pass
# here's the fallback if no module succeeds
auth    requisite                         pam_deny.so
# prime the stack with a positive return value if there isn't one already;
# this avoids us returning an error just because nothing sets a success code
# since the modules above will each just jump around
auth    required                          pam_permit.so
# and here are more per-package modules (the "Additional" block)
auth    optional                          pam_smbpass.so migrate
auth    optional                          pam_cap.so
# end of pam-auth-update config
```

Figure 6-10   The /etc/pam.d/common-auth file

PAM has a series of files that dictate how it operates in different situations. In addition to the Linux login function, other applications can use PAM to handle authentication, like FTP servers, CUPS, Secure Shell (SSH), or e-mail servers. Figure 6-10 shows /etc/pam.d/common-auth, which has the common authentication settings, though this file is from an Ubuntu system. There are a few lines worth noting in Figure 6-10. The first is the first auth line. It is using the pam_unix module to perform a standard Unix authentication, checking the users and passwords in the shadow file. The nullok_secure option at the end of that line indicates that null passwords are okay, but only if the location they are logging in from is listed in the /etc/securetty file. The next auth line allows users to authenticate against a Windows domain, using Kerberos authentication and the Winbind daemon, if it's available. Further down, you will see a line that allows authentication using the Samba user database. That line references the pam_smbpass.so module. While Debian-based systems use /etc/pam.d/common-auth, under RedHat the file is /etc/pam.d/system-auth.

Users are typically stored in the /etc/passwd file, while passwords are stored in /etc/shadow. Figure 6-11 shows a sample of an /etc/passwd file with all of the fields. The passwd file includes a username; a password, though in most cases this will be an x indicating that the password is stored in the shadow file; a user ID; a group ID; a comment field, which may have a phone number, a user's full name, or some other extra information; the home directory; and the shell used. The shadow file stores the username along with the encrypted password. It also stores additional information about the password, including the last time it was changed, the minimum and maximum expiry age, and the warning period. If there is no password policy, these fields would be blank and the field delimiter would be a colon (:).

As an example, let's take the first line from the passwd file shown in Figure 6-11. The username is root, as indicated in the first field. After that is an x in the second field, indicating that the password is stored in the shadow file. The next field is the user ID, which is 0 for the root user. The group ID follows this in the next column, which is also 0 for the root user. The next field is a comment field, and in this case it indicates the user is named root. Anything could be put into this field since it is a comment field that, by convention, often has the real name of the user. After the comment field is the home

Figure 6-11
The /etc/passwd
file

```
root:x:0:0:root:/root:/bin/bash
daemon:x:1:1:daemon:/usr/sbin:/bin/sh
bin:x:2:2:bin:/bin:/bin/sh
sys:x:3:3:sys:/dev:/bin/sh
sync:x:4:65534:sync:/bin:/bin/sync
games:x:5:60:games:/usr/games:/bin/sh
man:x:6:12:man:/var/cache/man:/bin/sh
lp:x:7:7:lp:/var/spool/lpd:/bin/sh
mail:x:8:8:mail:/var/mail:/bin/sh
news:x:9:9:news:/var/spool/news:/bin/sh
uucp:x:10:10:uucp:/var/spool/uucp:/bin/sh
proxy:x:13:13:proxy:/bin:/bin/sh
www-data:x:33:33:www-data:/var/www:/bin/sh
backup:x:34:34:backup:/var/backups:/bin/sh
list:x:38:38:Mailing List Manager:/var/list:/bin/sh
irc:x:39:39:ircd:/var/run/ircd:/bin/sh
gnats:x:41:41:Gnats Bug-Reporting System (admin):/var/lib/gnats:/bin/sh
nobody:x:65534:65534:nobody:/nonexistent:/bin/sh
libuuid:x:100:101::/var/lib/libuuid:/bin/sh
syslog:x:101:103::/home/syslog:/bin/false
libvirt-qemu:x:102:105:Libvirt Qemu,,,:/var/lib/libvirt:/bin/false
sshd:x:103:65534::/var/run/sshd:/usr/sbin/nologin
landscape:x:104:112::/var/lib/landscape:/bin/false
tomcat6:x:105:113::/usr/share/tomcat6:/bin/false
kilroy:x:1000:1000:Ric Messier,,,:/home/kilroy:/bin/bash
postgres:x:1001:1001::/home/postgres:/bin/sh
ntp:x:106:116::/home/ntp:/bin/false
postfix:x:107:118::/var/spool/postfix:/bin/false
messagebus:x:108:120::/var/run/dbus:/bin/false
```

directory, and in this case the home directory is /root. Finally, the last column is the shell that the user uses, which is /bin/bash for this user.

Adding users is pretty simple, using the useradd utility. The useradd utility is a command-line utility. useradd takes a number of command-line parameters, allowing you to set the home directory, the shell, comments, and password expiration information. In order to make changes to any user, you can use the usermod utility to alter any of the parameters that go with user accounts. The shell is the command-line interface provided to the user in a terminal session. While Windows doesn't always require individual services to have user accounts to operate under (it sometimes uses a system account, which has a high level of privileges), Linux services typically run under a user account created specifically for that service. In Figure 6-11, you can see accounts like postgres, which is used to run the postgresql database server, as well as www-data for the Apache Web server. These user accounts don't have any advanced privileges and they would get access only to the portions of the filesystem that they need to access.

The challenge with any of these sorts of accounts is providing enough information to create the user, but not enough that the user could be used to exploit the system. Many service-based accounts don't specify a shell for the account, but instead specify something like /bin/false. This is done to ensure that the account can't be logged into directly. When a user logs in via a remote access service like SSH, the shell executable gets run and, presumably, then provides the user with an interactive experience. If the shell is specified to be /bin/false, /bin/false will get executed and not provide any way for the user to interact with the system at all. This provides another way to protect the system against attack.

Figure 6-12 Graphical user management

If you prefer graphical user managers, you can get those as well. Figure 6-12 shows a graphical user manager where you can see the users that were added after the system was installed. There is a significant difference between the list shown by the User Manager utility and those listed in the /etc/passwd file. The list shown in the graphical user manager only includes actual users and doesn't include all the service accounts. There are a couple of advantages to this, of course. First, it prevents an average user from making any changes to the service accounts. To make any changes to a service account, you'd have to know how to get to the files or use the utilities, as well as have administrative permissions.

Configuration

Most of the configuration settings for Linux systems are in the /etc directory. You may be familiar with Windows systems where the configuration settings are stored in a system registry. macOS applications often use files that are called property lists to store data that needs to persist across executions of the application. This could be application settings. In Unix-like systems, all of the system configuration, as well as the configuration settings of applications that apply system-wide, are stored in the /etc directory. This might be something like the name of the system, stored in /etc/hostname. It might be the actions of network services managed by the inet daemon, stored in /etc/inetd.conf. Network configuration, DNS settings, configuration files for mail servers and FTP servers, and all of the startup scripts are stored in /etc.

Nearly all of the configuration files stored in the /etc directory are just plaintext files. They may be delimited in some way, either comma-delimited or tab-delimited. However, it's really all just plaintext. To make changes to these configuration files, you would need to use a text editor like vi or emacs. Certainly, there are graphical editors as well, but if you are already working in a terminal window doing system administrative

Figure 6-13
A sample
configuration file,
/etc/login.defs

```
#
# Enable logging and display of /var/log/faillog login failure info.
# This option conflicts with the pam_tally PAM module.
#
FAILLOG_ENAB            yes


#
# Enable display of unknown usernames when login failures are recorded.
#
# WARNING: Unknown usernames may become world readable.
# See #290803 and #298773 for details about how this could become a security
# concern
LOG_UNKFAIL_ENAB        no


#
# Enable logging of successful logins
#
LOG_OK_LOGINS           no


#
# Enable "syslog" logging of su activity - in addition to sulog file logging.
# SYSLOG_SG_ENAB does the same for newgrp and sg.
#
SYSLOG_SU_ENAB          yes
SYSLOG_SG_ENAB          yes
```

work, using a terminal-based editor like vi or emacs may simply be more convenient. Figure 6-13 shows a sample of a configuration file, /etc/login.defs, which provides all of the default settings for login sessions.

NOTE If you are familiar with vi or emacs but would just as soon have a graphical editor, there are graphical implementations of each of these classic editors, providing you the command set you already know as well as a graphical implementation, allowing the use of a mouse and menus.

In addition to configuration, /etc hosts files may be used to look up information. One such file is the aliases database, which allows you to create aliases for common e-mail accounts so you don't have to check another e-mail account for error logs or contact from external users. The postmaster account is one of these. It's a well-known and common account and, in fact, one required by RFC 822. RFC 822 specifies the format for Internet messages and also suggests that all sites on the ARPA Internet have a commonly named account in case of problems. This means everyone would know what e-mail address to contact if you were running into problems with a particular e-mail server. Another commonly used file that stores information to be looked up by various utilities like netstat is the /etc/services file. The /etc/services file, as shown in Figure 6-14, provides the mapping between port numbers and services. These aren't necessarily services that are running on the system but are instead a compilation of well-known ports and the services that run on them.

EXAM TIP The /etc/services file provides a mapping between services and ports. The file is based on information about well-known ports, which is managed by the Internet Assigned Numbers Authority (IANA).

```
# Network services, Internet style
#
# Note that it is presently the policy of IANA to assign a single well-known
# port number for both TCP and UDP; hence, officially ports have two entries
# even if the protocol doesn't support UDP operations.
#
# Updated from http://www.iana.org/assignments/port-numbers and other
# sources like http://www.freebsd.org/cgi/cvsweb.cgi/src/etc/services .
# New ports will be added on request if they have been officially assigned
# by IANA and used in the real-world or are needed by a debian package.
# If you need a huge list of used numbers please install the nmap package.


tcpmux          1/tcp                           # TCP port service multiplexer
echo            7/tcp
echo            7/udp
discard         9/tcp           sink null
discard         9/udp           sink null
systat          11/tcp          users
daytime         13/tcp
daytime         13/udp
netstat         15/tcp
qotd            17/tcp          quote
msp             18/tcp                          # message send protocol
msp             18/udp
chargen         19/tcp          ttytst source
chargen         19/udp          ttytst source
ftp-data        20/tcp
ftp             21/tcp
fsp             21/udp          fspd
ssh             22/tcp                          # SSH Remote Login Protocol
ssh             22/udp
telnet          23/tcp
smtp            25/tcp          mail
time            37/tcp          timserver
```

Figure 6-14   A services file

Logging and Log Management

Logging is a critical component of system management. Without logs, it's next to impossible to know what's going on. Even when the logs are incomplete, or barely adequate because applications aren't putting enough information into them, it's far better to have something than nothing at all. Linux systems use the syslog standard for logging, although there are a number of programs that implement syslog like syslog, syslog-ng, or rsyslog. syslog not only has the ability to log information about what's happening on the local system, but it also has the ability to log remotely to another system, sometimes called a syslog server or just a log server. Syslog communicates with systems it is sending log messages to over UDP port 514.

 EXAM TIP   Know the different facilities based on the short name used in the configuration files and what types of messages would get stored in logs for each facility.

Figure 6-15
A syslog
configuration file

```
#
# First some standard log files.  Log by facility.
#
auth,authpriv.*                      /var/log/auth.log
*.*;auth,authpriv.none               -/var/log/syslog
#cron.*                              /var/log/cron.log
#daemon.*                            -/var/log/daemon.log
kern.*                               -/var/log/kern.log
#lpr.*                               -/var/log/lpr.log
mail.*                               -/var/log/mail.log
#user.*                              -/var/log/user.log
local0.*                /var/log/snort.log
#
# Logging for the mail system.  Split it up so that
# it is easy to write scripts to parse these files.
#
#mail.info                           -/var/log/mail.info
#mail.warn                           -/var/log/mail.warn
mail.err                             /var/log/mail.err

#
```

Commonly, logs are stored in /var/log, although where each log is stored is entirely configurable, as seen in Figure 6-15. The configuration file specifies each facility, as well as the severity, and where the log file would go based on those parameters. Table 6-4 shows the facilities available in syslog, and the severities are ordered by highest severity to lowest: Emergency, Alert, Critical, Error, Warning, Notice, Informational, and Debug. An Emergency message is when the system is unusable. And while a Debug message isn't typically used on a production system, it's nice to have and make use of while you are debugging the initial deployment or development of an application. You may also note in Table 6-4 that it looks as though there are several facilities that may be used for authorization and security messages. In practice, facilities 4 and 10 are typically used, although 13 and 14 may also be used.

Log messages can fill up disks on really busy systems, so it's nice to have a log rotation tool that keeps the most recent log the way it is while compressing a handful of older logs. Each organization may have its own set of rules regarding how many days or weeks of logs to keep. Depending on how often the system is looked at may factor into decisions about how long to keep logs for. There may also be regulatory requirements for keeping logs for a certain period of time. Log messages may also be used for intrusion detection systems. At a minimum, you might set a log watcher utility that is configured to look for specific keywords and raise an alert or alarm when those keywords show up in the logs. This alone can provide a very rudimentary intrusion detection system, though having a system that is capable of correlating different log events is a far superior solution.

As noted earlier, syslog can be configured to send all logs to a central server. This provides several useful functions, including offloading disk space to a system that has a large amount of storage attached. Additionally, with logging from several systems all pulled together into one place, you can use a security information and event management

Numerical Code	Facility
0	kern; kernel messages
1	user; user messages
2	mail; messages from the mail system
3	daemon; system daemons
4	auth; security/authorization messages
5	syslog; messages generated internally by the syslog daemon
6	lpr; line printer subsystem
7	news; network news subsystem
8	uucp; Unix-Unix copy (UUCP) subsystem
9	clock daemon
10	authpriv; security/authorization messages (may get messages similar to facility 4)
11	ftp; FTP daemon
12	NTP subsystem
13	log audit (may sometimes be used for messages similar to 4 and 10)
14	log alert (may sometimes be used for messages similar to 4, 10, and 13)
15	cron; clock daemon, used for scheduled jobs
16	local0; local use 0
17	local1; local use 1
18	local2; local use 2
19	local3; local use 3
20	local4; local use 4
21	local5; local use 5
22	local6; local use 6
23	local7; local use 7

Table 6-4   Syslog Facilities

(SIEM) solution to do the correlation of data, looking for trends and events that may be worth alerting on. Syslog servers are really designed to act in this way, making it easy to configure systems to log to a remote syslog server. Figure 6-16 shows the configuration for the rsyslog server with the UDP listener and a TCP listener turned on. $UdpServerRun is the UDP listener and $InputServerRun is the TCP listener. The other entries, starting with the @ sign, indicate logs to send off to a remote server. The *.* indicates that all facilities at all levels of severity would get sent to the remote server. You could get a finer level of granularity by sending different facilities to different servers if you wanted to do that. The server address starting with the single @ indicates that it's a UDP connection, where the @@ indicates it's a TCP connection to the server.

Figure 6-16
Syslog remote
logging

```
###############
#### MODULES ####
###############

$ModLoad imuxsock # provides support for local system logging
$ModLoad imklog  # provides kernel logging support (previously done by rklo
gd)
#$ModLoad immark  # provides --MARK-- message capability

$UdpServerRun 514
$InputServerRun 514

*.* @172.30.42.1:514
*.* @@172.30.42.514
```

Monitoring

Logging is only part of the story. Once you have logs in place, regardless of where they are, keeping an eye on them is essential. Logs can be useful after something bad has happened, but it's even better to use them to identify something that is potentially bad so you can investigate and get it under control before the really bad stuff starts to happen. If you are shipping logs off to a log aggregation service, especially one that is a SIEM, it can do a lot of log watching for you, including setting off alerts if it sees something bad happen, such as a large number of authentication messages in your auth logs. If you don't have a SIEM service and have just a few Linux systems, you can at least use something like logwatch, which is a utility that will pay attention to messages coming into your syslog files.

As with most Linux-based services, you are working with text-based files. When you have logwatch installed, you can look at the configuration in /etc/logwatch/ or, if your distribution doesn't put default configurations into place for you automatically, you can go to /usr/share/logwatch/ and find a lot of configuration files there. You will find a directory there called services that will have configurations for monitoring different services. All of these configuration files are bundled up with the installation, regardless of whether you have the service installed or not. This means you can make use of just the configuration files you need. The configuration files for services will tell logwatch where to find the log files for that service. You may also need to tell logwatch where to find archived log files.

Once you have logwatch configured with the different services you have installed, as well as the different log files you want it to look at, it starts monitoring for you. Specifying an e-mail address and a means for logwatch to send e-mail will allow it to send messages to you with any findings as it runs.

Auditing

There is a source of log information that isn't enabled by default, even if you have syslog installed. The kernel has facilities for logging events that take place on your system. You need the auditctl program and the auditd service that comes with it. Using auditd, you can catch kernel-level actions and log them. Essentially, you are looking for system calls and then generating log files for them when the call you have specified happens.

What you end up with when you have a working audit system, though, is a set of logs that looks like this:

```
type=DAEMON_START msg=audit(1540162023.444:6844): op=start ver=2.8.4
format=raw kernel=4.17.0-kali3-amd64 auid=4294967295 pid=31646 uid=0
ses=4294967295 subj=unconfined  res=success

type=CONFIG_CHANGE msg=audit(1540162023.454:3): audit_backlog_limit=8192
old=64 auid=4294967295 ses=4294967295 res=1
type=CONFIG_CHANGE msg=audit(1540162023.454:4): audit_failure=1 old=1
auid=4294967295 ses=4294967295 res=1

type=CONFIG_CHANGE msg=audit(1540162023.454:5): audit_backlog_wait_time=0
old=15000 auid=4294967295 ses=4294967295 res=1

type=SERVICE_START msg=audit(1540162023.458:6): pid=1 uid=0 auid=4294967295
ses=4294967295 msg='unit=auditd comm="systemd" exe="/lib/systemd/systemd"
hostname=? addr=? terminal=? res=success'
```

In order to get logs like this, you need to set up rules. Typically, you will find the auditd rules in /etc/audit/rules.d/. You will find a file there named audit.rules. If you look in /etc/audit/, you will also find a file named audit.rules, but that file is generated from the rules files that are found in rules.d/. When you edit audit.rules in the rules.d directory, auditd will automatically generate the file in /etc/audit/ for you. This will show you the rules that are in operation at any given moment, as long as it hasn't been tampered with. The following output is from that file after I made some changes. In addition to setting parameters for auditd, there are two rules in place. The first rule looks for changes to the passwd file. A change will trigger a log message to appear with the message passwd_file_watch, as specified with the –k parameter. The –w sets a file watch, while the –p on that line indicates the permissions that have been used. The other entry looks for system calls where a process is exiting.

```
## This file is automatically generated from /etc/audit/rules.d
-D
-b 8192
-f 1
--backlog_wait_time 0
-w /etc/passwd -p wa -k passwd_file_watch
-a entry,always -S exit -k process_stop
```

Once these entries have been added, the audit log looks different, as shown next, because you see any changes to the passwd file. You also see a number of messages with system calls, identified by SYSCALL. Each of these messages provides the process ID as well as the user ID and the group ID. Depending on the log entry, there will be other identifying information associated with the message.

```
type=SYSCALL msg=audit(1540162776.988:37): arch=c000003e syscall=91
success=yes exit=0 a0=3 a1=81a4 a2=7ffdd2aaa510 a3=0 items=1 ppid=32084
pid=32026 auid=0 uid=0 gid=0 euid=0 suid=0 fsuid=0 egid=0 sgid=0 fsgid=0
tty=pts0 ses=12073 comm="vi" exe="/usr/bin/vim.gtk" key="passwd_file_watch"

type=PATH msg=audit(1540162776.988:37): item=0 name=(null) inode=3286742
dev=08:01 mode=0100644 ouid=0 ogid=0 rdev=00:00 nametype=NORMAL cap_
fp=0000000000000000 cap_fi=0000000000000000 cap_fe=0 cap_fver=0
```

```
type=PROCTITLE msg=audit(1540162776.988:37): proctitle=7669002F657463
2F706173737764

type=SYSCALL msg=audit(1540162776.988:38): arch=c000003e syscall=188
success=yes exit=0 a0=55f311a3c2b0 a1=7f18d10e3e7f a2=55f311c5e510 a3=1c
items=1 ppid=32084 pid=32026 auid=0 uid=0 gid=0 euid=0 suid=0 fsuid=0
egid=0 sgid=0 fsgid=0 tty=pts0 ses=12073 comm="vi" exe="/usr/bin/vim.gtk"
key="passwd_file_watch"

type=CWD msg=audit(1540162776.988:38): cwd="/etc/audit"

type=PATH msg=audit(1540162776.988:38): item=0 name="/etc/passwd"
inode=3286742 dev=08:01 mode=0100644 ouid=0 ogid=0 rdev=00:00 nametype=NORMAL
cap_fp=0000000000000000 cap_fi=0000000000000000 cap_fe=0 cap_fver=0

type=PROCTITLE msg=audit(1540162776.988:38): proctitle=7669002F657463
2F706173737764
```

Security Tools

Linux has inherited a number of the security-related issues that have long existed in Unix-like operating systems, some resulting from a number of common applications that run on those systems. Sendmail and BIND—used for e-mail delivery and DNS services, respectively—have a long history of vulnerabilities, though it's not fair to single those two out since there have been several services that run under Unix or Linux with a lengthy history of vulnerabilities. Additionally, the Linux kernel itself has had a large number of vulnerabilities in the 25-plus years it's been in existence. Because of this, there was a need for additional programs to enhance the security of the system. Some of these have been in existence for a long time, while others are more recent. Linux also comes with classes of vulnerabilities that result from the use of the C language, which was created as part of the genesis of Unix and was the language the OS was eventually written in. C programs don't check the size of buffers (the memory allocated to store pieces of data) before writing the data into them. This has led to issues with buffer overflows and format string vulnerabilities, either of which may allow an attacker to take control of a system by executing code that was inserted into memory by the attacker.

Another issue that Linux inherited with Unix was the lack of ability to have granular access control over resources. Linux implements the User, Group, World (Everyone) model of permissions, and there are three permissions that can be set for each of those types or collections of users: read, write, and execute. There are additional bits that can be set on files that provide some additional capabilities, like the setuid bit, which is set on executables when you want the program to run with a certain set of privileges for the user that is set as the owner. In most cases, the setuid bit is used to have a program run with root privileges without actually having to be the root user to execute the program. You make root the owner, allow everyone else to have execute privileges, and then set the setuid bit.

One utility, chmod, offers you the ability to change the permissions settings on files and directories as well as utilities that allow you to change the user and group that owns the file or directory. It lets you set permissions as well as other bits on the file. chmod will allow you to set permissions for the user, group, or everyone individually, or it will allow you to set all the permissions all at once. To set all the permissions bits simultaneously, you must provide a numeric value. Permissions are set using a combination of bits of values 4, 2, and 1. The value 4 is read, 2 is write, and 1 is execute. Providing all permissions for the user, the group, and the world, you would set the value at 777. Providing all permissions for the user, read permission for the group, and no permissions for everyone (world), you would set the value at 740.

When you set permissions on a file or directory, you can assign to the owner any combination of read, write, or execute permissions that you want. Typically, you'd assign at least read and write since, as the owner, you probably want to be able to write and you can't very well write without being able to read. Linux differs from Windows here by using a flag in the filesystem to indicate whether a file is executable or not. In Windows, the file extension indicates how the file is handled and the OS stores the mappings between file extensions and actions. A single group can also get a collection of read, write, and execute permissions. If you want to grant someone access to a file under Linux, you have to either put them into a group that has permissions to the file or give permissions to everyone. Figure 6-17 shows a file listing showing the file permissions. You can see the groups of permissions in the column on the left side.

Taking a look at the permissions for the first entry in Figure 6-17, tcpdump.rb, we see –rw-rw-r--. The first – would instead be a d if the entry were a directory (as in the second entry). Since there is no d, we know this is a regular file. The next cluster is the permissions for the user—in this case, rw-. This means that the user has read and write permissions, but because the execute bit hasn't been turned on, the user can't execute this script directly. The next cluster, rw-, is for the group that the user belongs to. In this case, the group is kilroy, the same as the user. The permissions are the same—read and write—for the group and the user. Finally, we have r--, indicating that everyone else on the system has read permissions. If you want to convert these permissions into decimal form, we have read and write, which have values of 4 and 2. Add those together and you have 6. World permissions are read only and read has a value of 4. All together, the user, group, and world permissions are 664 in decimal representation.

You'll notice that there is only one group and one user that is given permissions to each file. Of course, there is always World (or everyone) but that doesn't give us much flexibility to provide a lot of access to users on our system. The lack of ability to provide better access control on files and directories on Linux systems is part of what led to the development of SELinux.

```
-rw-rw-r--    1 kilroy       kilroy          465 Aug 13  2012 tcpdump.rb
drwxr-xr-x   12 kilroy       kilroy         4096 Aug 29  2009 tct-1.19
-rw-rw-r--    1 kilroy       kilroy       318164 Aug 29  2009 tct-1.19.tar.gz
drwxr-xr-x    2 kilroy       kilroy         4096 Aug 28  2000 telnetc
drwxr-xr-x    2 kilroy       kilroy         4096 Sep 14  2011 Templates
-rwxrwxr-x    1 kilroy       kilroy      1268288 Aug 25  2012 test
-rw-rw-r--    1 kilroy       kilroy           92 Aug 25  2012 test.go
-rw-rw-r--    1 kilroy       kilroy           19 Aug  4  2012 text.txt
drwxr-xr-x    9 kilroy       kilroy         4096 Mar  2  2012 themole-0.3
-rw-r--r--    1 kilroy       kilroy       196812 Jul 25  2012 themole-0.3-lin-src
.tar.gz
```

Figure 6-17   Sample permissions

SELinux

SELinux came out of the work of the National Security Agency (NSA), which released the first version in 2000 as a way of addressing the security shortcomings of Linux. SELinux set out to address some specific problems with the way Linux handled permissions, since it had inherited them from Unix. One issue is that users are allowed to set highly insecure permissions on files and directories that they have ownership of. Another is that processes are allowed to change permissions on files and directories that are owned by the user the process belongs to. One of the reasons for that problem (and a problem in and of itself) is that processes inherit the user's rights and permissions. SELinux implements mandatory access control (MAC) into the operating system.

SELinux does take some configuration to establish all the roles and permissions, so there are three modes available. The first is disabled, which is simply off. The second is permissive, meaning that SELinux is in place but nothing is being enforced. This is useful for purposes of debugging and during policy development. SELinux does require planning and thought in order to implement it effectively. Users and roles have to be defined, as well as policies around permissions, including permissions for applications. Implementing SELinux is not something to be entered into lightly and can be daunting. As an example of the added complexity SELinux can bring, Figure 6-18 shows a file listing similar to that in Figure 6-17, except this time SELinux has been installed and the listing (using ls –Z) shows the mode, user, group, and security context of each file.

SELinux not only implements permissions on files, but can also be used to implement the same permissions on, for example, ports. You can ensure that only one particular process can open a given port by making sure that the process and the port have the same contexts within SELinux. You could also allow your web server to listen on ports other than the standard port 80. As an example, let's say you wanted to allow your web server

```
-rw-rw-r--.  1 kilroy        kilroy unconfined_u:object_r:user_home_t:s0
465 Aug 13  2012 tcpdump.rb
drwxr-xr-x. 12 kilroy        kilroy unconfined_u:object_r:user_home_t:s0         4
096 Aug 29  2009 tct-1.19
-rw-r--r--.  1 kilroy        kilroy unconfined_u:object_r:user_home_t:s0       318
164 Aug 29  2009 tct-1.19.tar.gz
drwxr-xr-x.  2 kilroy        kilroy unconfined_u:object_r:user_home_t:s0         4
096 Aug 28  2000 telnetc
drwxr-xr-x.  2 kilroy        kilroy unconfined_u:object_r:user_home_t:s0         4
096 Sep 14  2011 Templates
-rwxrwxr-x.  1 kilroy        kilroy unconfined_u:object_r:user_home_t:s0      1268
288 Aug 25  2012 test
-rw-rw-r--.  1 kilroy        kilroy unconfined_u:object_r:user_home_t:s0
 92 Aug 25  2012 test.go
-rw-rw-r--.  1 kilroy        kilroy unconfined_u:object_r:user_home_t:s0
 19 Aug  4  2012 text.txt
drwxr-xr-x.  9 kilroy        kilroy unconfined_u:object_r:user_home_t:s0         4
096 Mar  2  2012 themole-0.3
-rw-r--r--.  1 kilroy        kilroy unconfined_u:object_r:user_home_t:s0       196
812 Jul 25  2012 themole-0.3-lin-src.tar.gz
```

Figure 6-18   File listing with SELinux implemented

to listen on port 81 instead. You would need to allow that through SELinux. You could do this by adjusting policy using the policy management utility semanage. You would set the context type to http_port_t for port 81 using the command **semanage port –a –t http_port_t –p 81**. This means that the web server will be allowed to listen on that port because the port has the right context type for the web server.

Tripwire

Tripwire is an intrusion detection system originally developed in 1992 at Purdue University. In 1997, a company was formed to create a commercial version of the software, but there remains an open-source version as well. Tripwire is based around the idea that on most systems, there is a set of critical files that don't change, and monitoring these files may result in detecting when an intrusion has happened. Tripwire maintains a database of cryptographic hashes of these critical files. Periodically, the filesystem is checked and current hashes get compared against the stored hash. If the hashes are different, the file has changed and an alert gets generated. This can run into complications when updates are applied since many of the critical files may get updated with current versions. These current versions would trip an alert unless the database was updated with the new information based on the update. Because of this, you probably want to install updates in a controlled fashion rather than just allowing your system to automatically update itself.

 NOTE Gene Kim was a graduate student at Purdue at the time he created Tripwire with the help of his professor, Dr. Eugene Spafford (commonly called Spaf). Dr. Spafford was a leader in the response to the Morris worm in 1988 and helped create the Common Vulnerabilities and Exposures (CVE) service at MITRE. He also helped Dan Farmer create COPS, a simple security auditing program and the precursor to SATAN, which eventually led to tools like Nessus, Nexpose, and many others.

Tripwire has other functions outside of intrusion detection. Because of the way it works, it is a good program to have for configuration management, ensuring that a system configuration doesn't change, and that if it does, an alert is issued since change may lead to breakage. Not all outages or bad behaviors on a system are caused by malicious behavior. Often, it's inattentiveness or carelessness on the part of system administrators, or users attempting to administer the system. Tripwire can help ensure that critical files that were changed unexpectedly can be looked at to ensure the change hasn't caused a problem. Ensuring the integrity of a system can be critical and a core security precept, so having a tool like Tripwire can be very beneficial.

It's been determined to be so beneficial, in fact, that there have been several followers, both commercial and noncommercial. Linux packages like AIDE and Samhain are open-source intrusion detection systems that perform functions similar to Tripwire, with the goal of attempting to detect intrusions into your system where an intrusion is any unexpected or unwanted behavior, specifically around modification of critical system files.

iptables

Linux has long had a host-based operating system, in part because it has had to function as a server as well as a router and firewall, or at least there has been development that has allowed it to function as those types of devices. iptables is the latest version of a host-based firewall for Linux, which started with a set of kernel modules and utilities called ipfwadm that were then superseded by ipchains. ipchains was then superseded by iptables. iptables was implemented into the 2.4 kernel in 1998 and has been the Linux firewall ever since. iptables implements chains of rules, much like ipchains did, but extends the concept with tables that can be referenced to determine whether to filter a packet or perform Network Address Translation (NAT), for example. iptables is not only a set of kernel modules but also a utility that is used to install the rules. Rules can be appended or inserted into specific chains, based on the command-line parameters that are passed into the iptables utility.

iptables works as a set of commands, calling the iptables executable. You would pass different command-line parameters into iptables in order to get rules inserted or appended to a particular chain. As an example, let's take a look at the following rules:

```
iptables -A INPUT -i eth0 -s 10.0.0.0/24 -d 192.168.1.0/24 -j LOG
iptables -A INPUT -i eth0 -s 10.0.0.0/24 -d 192.168.1.0/24 -j DROP
```

In the first line, we are appending (–A) to the INPUT chain. Any packet coming in on the first Ethernet interface on the system (–i eth0) will match this rule and be checked further. Any packet with a source address (–s) of 10.0.0.0–10.0.0.255 will continue to match here, so we will move on to checking the destination address. If the destination address (–d) falls into the range 192.168.1.0–192.168.1.24, it has matched the entire rule, and so we check the action (–j). The action in the first line says to log the packet. The second line says we should drop it. So, any packet coming into eth0 with a source address of 10.0.0.0/24 and destined to 192.168.1.0/24 will first be logged and then dropped.

Figure 6-19 is the output from iptables –L –v showing the list of rules that are currently in operation on the system. The –L flag shows the list of rules and the –v flag provides more verbosity. Without the –v flag, we wouldn't have the detail about the interface being used. You can see rules where a specific interface was specified in the lines that have virbr0 under either the in or out columns. The additional verbosity gives the number of packets and bytes that have come through the firewall matching those particular rules.

Exercise 6-2: iptables Rules Exercise

What are the following rules doing?

```
iptables -A INPUT -i eth0 -s 10.0.0.0/8 -j LOG
iptables -A INPUT -i eth0 -s 10.0.0.0/8 -j DROP
iptables -A INPUT -i eth0 -s 172.16.0.0/12 -j LOG
iptables -A INPUT -i eth0 -s 172.16.0.0/12 -j DROP
iptables -A INPUT -i eth0 -s 192.168.0.0/16 -j LOG
iptables -A INPUT -i eth0 -s 192.168.0.0/16 -j DROP
```

```
Chain INPUT (policy ACCEPT 308K packets, 281M bytes)
 pkts bytes target     prot opt in     out     source            destination

    0     0 ACCEPT     udp  --  virbr0 any     anywhere          anywhere
              udp dpt:domain
    0     0 ACCEPT     tcp  --  virbr0 any     anywhere          anywhere
              tcp dpt:domain
    0     0 ACCEPT     udp  --  virbr0 any     anywhere          anywhere
              udp dpt:bootps
    0     0 ACCEPT     tcp  --  virbr0 any     anywhere          anywhere
              tcp dpt:bootps

Chain FORWARD (policy ACCEPT 0 packets, 0 bytes)
 pkts bytes target     prot opt in     out     source            destination

    0     0 ACCEPT     all  --  any    virbr0  anywhere          192.168.122.
0/24    state RELATED,ESTABLISHED
    0     0 ACCEPT     all  --  virbr0 any     192.168.122.0/24  anywhere

    0     0 ACCEPT     all  --  virbr0 virbr0  anywhere          anywhere

    0     0 REJECT     all  --  any    virbr0  anywhere          anywhere
              reject-with icmp-port-unreachable
    0     0 REJECT     all  --  virbr0 any     anywhere          anywhere
              reject-with icmp-port-unreachable

Chain OUTPUT (policy ACCEPT 193K packets, 56M bytes)
 pkts bytes target     prot opt in     out     source            destination
```

Figure 6-19   iptables rules in place

In addition to performing simple filtering, iptables also has the ability to perform masquerading functions such as NAT. If a Linux system has multiple interfaces, iptables can forward messages from one interface to another and manipulate the IP address as the packet passes through. This is often done to translate a private, RFC 1918 address on the inside to a public IP address on the outside. Performing NAT doesn't preclude also performing filtering, of course.

firewalld

firewalld is the next generation of Linux firewall. Rather than the comparatively simple idea of iptables where you create stateful rules based around interfaces and IP addresses, firewalld adds additional functionality to accommodate a mobile system. If you have a laptop, you are constantly moving it from one network to another, and iptables likely can't keep up with the regular changes of networks and the security requirements of those networks. This may mean you need to completely disable your firewall just to have a functional system if you are moving it around a lot. Instead, you can make use of firewalld, which introduces the idea of zones. You attach rules to zones rather than directly to the interface. The interface can then be placed into a zone with the right services and ports allowed. In order to manage firewalld, we use the command firewall-cmd. As an example, let's say we wanted to allow the SSH service through our firewall. Here you can see the command that would be used to allow that:

```
sudo firewall-cmd --permanent --add-service=ssh
success
```

This doesn't introduce the idea of zones, though. We haven't indicated to firewalld which zone we want to allow this to happen on. In order to specify a zone, we can just add –zone=public, for instance, to this command. That allows us to say that any interface in the public zone is going to have SSH as a service that is allowed through. You may want to have different sets of services on private zones than you do on public zones. You may also have trusted and untrusted zones. When you move from home to work, for example, you will likely consider your device to be in different zones because the security expectations are different from one place to another.

AppArmor

AppArmor is similar to SELinux in that it implements mandatory access control (MAC) on a Linux system. Whereas SELinux uses labels in the filesystem itself, AppArmor doesn't care about the filesystem in use, so AppArmor can provide the same functionality regardless of the type of filesystem mounted, whether it's ext2 or NFS or FAT. AppArmor uses paths rather than identifying the specific inodes in the filesystem when it makes access determinations. Like SELinux, AppArmor is implemented using the Linux Security Modules kernel interface. While SELinux can be difficult to implement and administer, AppArmor is easier. An easier implementation can lead to a higher adoption rate, which may lead to systems less prone to exploitation and compromise.

Another advantage that AppArmor has is the ability to be set on a learning mode where nothing is prohibited but activities are logged. Those log files can then be used to create a policy. This may be beneficial if you don't really understand the requirements of a particular application. Once you have determined what the application is doing by reviewing the logs generated by AppArmor, you can decide whether to proceed with the application, at which time you would create a policy for the application granting it the permissions it needs.

Hardening Linux

Hardening any operating system is an important activity. Often Linux is used in server systems that are more exposed to the Internet, meaning there are services that are listening that people on the Internet can connect to. This may be a web service, a mail service, or any of a number of other services users will commonly consume. This means that it's particularly important that you harden the operating system. *Hardening* an operating system means performing administrative functions that will make it harder for any adversary to get unauthorized access. Among other activities, hardening the operating system can mean limiting the number of packages on a system, removing all unnecessary services, and ensuring permissions are set appropriately. It may also mean making use of a mandatory access control package like SELinux. While the tasks individually aren't very complicated, it can be a lot of work to make sure you are doing the right thing—allowing all the right services to operate so users can get work done while at the same time making sure you haven't left any exposures that an adversary can take advantage of.

Limiting the Number of Packages

First, we can look at reducing the number of packages on a system as a way of harden-ing it. The best way to do this is to start with as minimal an installation as your Linux distribution will accept. On a distribution like Ubuntu, you can select the server instal-lation. This should keep you to the bare minimum of packages necessary to set up a server—whether it's a web server, SSH server, DNS server, or some other type of server. If you have been handed a Linux installation and need to get a listing of all the packages installed, you can do something like the following code. On a Debian-based system, like Ubuntu is, you can just use the apt command to get a list of all installed packages.

```
kilroy@portnoy:~$ apt list --installed
Listing... Done
accountsservice/bionic,now 0.6.45-1ubuntu1 amd64 [installed]
acl/bionic,now 2.2.52-3build1 amd64 [installed]
acpid/bionic,now 1:2.0.28-1ubuntu1 amd64 [installed]
adduser/bionic,now 3.116ubuntu1 all [installed]
amd64-microcode/bionic-updates,now 3.20180524.1~ubuntu0.18.04.2 amd64
[installed,automatic]
apparmor/bionic-updates,bionic-security,now 2.12-4ubuntu5.1 amd64 [installed]
apport/now 2.20.9-0ubuntu7.3 all [installed,upgradable to: 2.20.9-0ubuntu7.4]
apport-symptoms/bionic,now 0.20 all [installed]
apt/bionic-updates,bionic-security,now 1.6.3ubuntu0.1 amd64 [installed]
apt-utils/bionic-updates,bionic-security,now 1.6.3ubuntu0.1 amd64 [installed]
at/bionic,now 3.1.20-3.1ubuntu2 amd64 [installed]
attr/bionic,now 1:2.4.47-2build1 amd64 [installed,automatic]
augeas-lenses/bionic,now 1.10.1-2 all [installed,automatic]
base-files/bionic-updates,now 10.1ubuntu2.3 amd64 [installed]
base-passwd/bionic,now 3.5.44 amd64 [installed]
bash/bionic,now 4.4.18-2ubuntu1 amd64 [installed]
bash-completion/bionic,now 1:2.8-1ubuntu1 all [installed]
bc/bionic,now 1.07.1-2 amd64 [installed]
bcache-tools/bionic,now 1.0.8-2build1 amd64 [installed]
bind9-host/bionic-updates,bionic-security,now 1:9.11.3+dfsg-1ubuntu1.2 amd64
[installed]
binutils/bionic-security,now 2.30-20ubuntu2~18.04 amd64 [installed,upgradable
to: 2.30-21ubuntu1~18.04]
binutils-common/bionic-security,now 2.30-20ubuntu2~18.04 amd64
[installed,upgradable to: 2.30-21ubuntu1~18.04]
binutils-x86-64-linux-gnu/bionic-security,now 2.30-20ubuntu2~18.04 amd64
[installed,upgradable to: 2.30-21ubuntu1~18.04]
bsdmainutils/bionic,now 11.1.2ubuntu1 amd64 [installed]
```

RHEL-based systems use a different command for package maintenance. Listing all the packages installed on a RHEL system, you could use rpm –qa, which would query the package database and return all the packages. These two systems and their respec-tive commands should cover nearly all the Linux systems you are likely to run across, especially if you are looking at server-based systems. You may run across something like a Gentoo system or an Arch Linux system, but those would be highly unlikely. If you find a package you don't want, you can use apt or rpm to remove them. The command apt remove will work, when used with the package name, to remove the package from the system. Similarly, using rpm –e will erase packages from a RHEL-based system.

Removing Unnecessary Services

Fortunately, system hardening is not as complicated when it comes to managing services. Most all systems have moved away from the old init-based system to the newer systemd. This allows for a lot of improvements over init, including faster boot-up times. If a system is using systemd, you would use the command systemctl to manage it. Removing packages will automatically remove a service, since the service is no longer installed to run. Should you need to, you can take away the ability for services to run automatically by using the systemctl command. If you just want to keep a service from running and, for whatever reason, you can't just remove the package, perhaps because it's a dependency of another required package, you can just use systemctl disable followed by the name of the service. This will keep the service from starting up at the next boot of the operating system. In order to shut it down right away, you would use systemctl stop, again followed by the name of the service. Service names can vary from distribution to distribution, however. In order to check the name of the service—the one that systemctl will recognize—you would use **systemctl list-unit-files –type=service**. You can see the output from that command:

```
UNIT FILE                        STATE
accounts-daemon.service          enabled
acpid.service                    disabled
apparmor.service                 enabled
apport-autoreport.service        static
apport-forward@.service          static
apport.service                   generated
apt-daily-upgrade.service        static
apt-daily.service                static
```

One of the advantages of systemctl over init is the ability to have dependencies. Some services will rely on another service. When the service configuration file is created, the dependency would be identified. Any dependency would be started automatically when the service that relied on it was started. This is one way to pick up unexpected services. You may find that one of the services you have identified as not needing to run because it isn't needed is actually required for a critical service to function correctly. You can also specify orders of operations using systemctl. In order for one service to start, for example, it may require another service to be running. As an example, services that start up the network, including obtaining an address and starting up the interfaces, would need to be running before any service that listens on the network.

Ensuring Permissions Are Set Appropriately

Permissions are a persistent problem. It's not uncommon for permission creep to happen on a system. Permissions get changed in order to accomplish a task and then aren't reset to where they should be. A user may get added to a group that owns certain files, but later that user may no longer need to belong to that group. There are many situations where permissions creep can happen. Periodic audits of users, groups, and file owners for important files on the system is important.

One of the biggest issues when it comes to file permissions, though, is executables that have the setuid or setgid bits set. When these bits are set, the executable takes on the permissions set of the owner of the file rather than the user who is running the executable. This is how normal users can perform what are technically administrative functions, such as looking at the network interface configuration or performing a traceroute. In many cases, the setuid files will be owned by root because they need to pick up some administrative permissions just for the time the program is running. If an attacker were to find a vulnerability in that program, though, they may be able to exploit it to perform tasks as root. For this reason, you will find that most distributions no longer have setuid or setgid executables. If you need to look for them, though, you can use the find command, as you can see here:

```
kilroy@portnoy:~$ sudo find / -perm 4000
find: '/proc/21765/task/21765/fd/5': No such file or directory
find: '/proc/21765/task/21765/fdinfo/5': No such file or directory
find: '/proc/21765/fd/6': No such file or directory
find: '/proc/21765/fdinfo/6': No such file or directory
```

Another aspect of hardening is to ensure that any packages that an attacker could use to create additional attacks are not in place. This includes compilers. In truth, this rule was far more relevant in the days when attackers often didn't have the same systems as the ones they were attacking. In order to create an executable for an AIX system on a PowerPC processor, the attacker would need to compile the attack program on the system. These days, it's just as likely for the target to be using an Intel-based processor architecture and a common operating system, so it's just as easy to compile programs elsewhere and push them to the target system. Still, making sure you haven't left too much to help out the attacker is important.

Chapter Review

Linux inherits a long history from Unix, although there are certainly a few differences between them. It was really Linux that has generated a lot more users, in spite of the popularity of Unix with academics and engineers. With users come usability issues, as well as a tougher balancing act between security and usability. While you may be able to get an engineer to do their job in a particular way because it's better for the system or more secure, it's harder to tell an unsophisticated user that they need to jump through a lot of hoops to do the simple things they want to do.

Linux does have the weak file permissions it inherited from Unix, but that has been addressed with extensions like SELinux and AppArmor, implementing mandatory access control and thus providing stronger protection of the resources on the system. Unix has long had a history of providing logging facilities and providing a lot of flexibility and control over the way the system and applications log items, as well as what gets logged. This logging can help with troubleshooting as well as providing the ability to look for security issues. Logs can be combed to find specific keywords that may detect an intrusion. Unix has also generated host-based intrusion detection solutions like Tripwire, and since Linux is compatible with Unix, Tripwire has been ported to run under Linux.

Any system has vulnerabilities and ways for attackers to get unauthorized access. One important thing is to be able to detect anything bad that may be happening. Fortunately, there are multiple ways to do this on a Linux system without adding any third-party software, outside of the distribution. First, syslog is essential. Services and applications, not to mention various elements of the system as a whole, such as authentication, generate logs that are important not only for troubleshooting and debugging but also for providing a way to detect when something unexpected or unauthorized happens. Software like logwatch can help with that. In addition, you can use the auditing system to watch files and directories for access attempts, as well as watching system calls. Any output from the auditing subsystem can also be watched for unexpected activity that can be alerted on.

Linux has firewalling capabilities, including iptables, which provides a way to create a stateful firewall. It also can perform NAT, which can allow Linux to be used as a full-fledged network firewall. However, modern systems may move around a lot and host-based firewalls often use the idea of zones to create a set of rules that apply in some situations but not in others. Firewalld is the new firewall and it's managed by firewall-cmd.

Linux does provide a lot of flexibility and a number of ways to interface with the system. That flexibility does provide risk in terms of the potential for abuse, possibly leaving the system open for exploitation. Fortunately, there are a number of tools that can assist you in ensuring that the system remains safe and free of exploitation and compromise.

Hardening any operating system is an essential task and one that requires skill and experience. It's a misconception to think that Linux is hardened out of the box. It's entirely about the distribution and the selections the user makes when it's installed. This means removing any unnecessary packages and not selecting "Everything" when you install the system. If you are going to install everything, be aware that the more software that's installed, the more exposure to compromise you have. Setting correct file permissions is important. This brings in the importance of making sure users and groups are set appropriately so the permissions don't have to be wide open. System services are often an issue, since network services can be exploited. Reducing the number of services, meaning software running in the background, is important. You can use systemctl as a way to manage system services on a systemd-based system. On an init-based system, you would adjust scripts that are run based on the runlevel the system is set to.

Questions

1. PAM provides the ability to protect passwords in what way?

   A. It encrypts them.

   B. It stores them in the /etc/passwd file.

   C. It checks that a password meets a specific policy.

   D. It creates a backup copy of the password in the shadow file.

2. File permissions can be set using which utility?

   A. chmod

   B. chroot

    C. chfile

    D. chperm

3. Based on the following syslog configuration, where do login messages get stored?

```
auth,authpriv.*              /var/log/auth.log
*.*;auth,authpriv.none        -/var/log/syslog
#cron.*                  /var/log/cron.log
#daemon.*               -/var/log/daemon.log
kern.*                  -/var/log/kern.log
#lpr.*                  -/var/log/lpr.log
mail.*                  -/var/log/mail.log
#user.*                  -/var/log/user.log
```

    A. /var/log/user.log

    B. /var/log/daemon.log

    C. /var/log/kern.log

    D. /var/log/auth.log

4. If you wanted to find statistics on the inet process (process id 1) on your filesystem, where would you look for it?

    A. /dev/proc/1

    B. /proc/1

    C. /home/1

    D. /1

5. If you were to apply the permission 744 to a file, what permissions would user, group, and world get?

    A. User: Read; Group: Read, Write; World: Read, Write

    B. User: Read, Write; Group: Read, Write; World: none

    C. User: Read, Write, Execute; Group: Read; World: Read

    D. User: Read, Write; Group: none; World: none

6. Tripwire provides which of the following security functions?

    A. Firewall

    B. Password cracker

    C. Vulnerability scanner

    D. Intrusion detection system

7. Which key press generates a SIGINT signal?

    A. CTRL-V

    B. CTRL-C

    C. CTRL-I

    D. CTRL-S

8. Which file stores mappings between ports and the names of applications associated with them?

    A. /etc/proc

    B. /etc/system

    C. /etc/services

    D. /etc/protocols

9. You need a utility that will show you CPU usage of individual processes, updated every three seconds. Which utility would you use?

    A. top

    B. ps

    C. kill

    D. killall

10. What does the following iptables rule do?

```
iptables -A INPUT -j DROP
```

    A. Appends input

    B. Allows everything out

    C. Drops all inbound traffic

    D. Logs all inbound traffic

11. If you wanted to implement zones in your firewall—which may be useful for a mobile system or a multi-interface system—what software would you use?

    A. firewalld

    B. iptables

    C. logwatch

    D. auditd

12. Monitoring changes to directories and files can be achieved with which software?

    A. firewalld

    B. logwatch

    C. auditd

    D. SELinux

13. What essential actions would you perform to harden a system?

    A. Implement a stateless firewall, monitor logs, and audit files

    B. Audit files, tighten file permissions, and limit services

    C. Limit services, reduce packages, and audit files

    D. Restrict permissions, reduce packages installed, and limit services

14. How would you get a list of services installed on a system that was using systemd rather than init?

    A. logwatch

    B. ps aux

    C. systemctl

    D. firewall-cmd

15. Monitoring a Linux system could be done using what software?

    A. logmon and a SIEM solution

    B. logmon and syswatch

    C. logwatch and syswatch

    D. logwatch and a SIEM solution

Answers

  1. C. PAM can check that a password meets a specific policy. While passwords run through the crypt() utility, it is crypt that handles encryption. Passwords are not stored in the passwd file, and a backup isn't stored in the shadow file. The primary copy may be stored in the shadow file if another storage mechanism isn't used.

  2. A. chmod changes the file mode bits. chroot changes the root of the system, and chfile and chperm don't exist.

  3. D. The auth.log is where authentication messages are logged. While it may be tempting to go for the user.log, that's where user processes log. kern.log is for kernel messages, and daemon.log is for services.

  4. B. The /proc filesystem is where process information is stored. This is a virtual or pseudo-filesystem that's populated by the kernel and based on the processes that are running.

  5. C. Read has a bit value of 4, Write has a bit value of 2, and Execute has a value of 1. 7 is 4 + 2 + 1 so User gets Read, Write, and Execute. 4 is Read, so Group and World both have Read permissions.

  6. D. Tripwire is an intrusion detection system that was developed at Purdue University. It introduced a number of innovative techniques and primarily works by ensuring that critical system files haven't changed.

  7. B. CTRL-C generates a SIGINT to interrupt and stop a process/application.

  8. C. The /etc/services file stores the mapping between port numbers and the services or daemons that they belong to.

  9. A. While ps will provide information about processes, top will provide information about CPU usage as well as the processes that are running.

10. **C.** The iptables command appends to the INPUT chain and, without anything to match, just jumps to the DROP target, meaning that all input is dropped.

11. **A.** The firewalld software is the next-generation Linux firewall. It implements zones, in addition to providing the same functionality as iptables. logwatch is used for monitoring logs and auditd is the auditing system.

12. **C.** auditd is the software used to audit kernel-level events, including system calls and file access. firewalld is the Linux firewall. logwatch is used to monitor log files for events to alert on them. SELinux implements mandatory access control.

13. **D.** Hardening a system would definitely include tightening file permissions where possible, reducing the number of packages installed on a system, and limiting or reducing the number of services running on a system. Firewalls are a good idea but they are not essential on an endpoint. While auditing files may be useful, it's not considered an element of system hardening. The same is true of monitoring logs.

14. **C.** The systemctl command is used to interface with systemd. You can get a list of all the services that are installed on a system, whether they are running, enabled, or disabled. The ps command is used to get a process listing, which is different from a service listing, even if services would be included in the process listing. logwatch is a log monitoring program, and firewall-cmd is used to manage the firewalld firewall.

15. **D.** logwatch is a software package that will monitor logs on a Linux system. A SIEM solution can be used to monitor logs that are sent to it, which could be done using syslog from a Linux system. logmon and syswatch are not Linux programs.

Exercise Answers

Exercise 6-1
You will get output similar to Linux bill 3.2.0-27-generic-pae #43-Ubuntu SMP Fri Jul 6 15:06:05 UTC 2018 i686 i686 i386 GNU/Linux from uname –a. The kernel version from that is 3.2.0. You can get just the release of the kernel by typing **uname –r**, which would provide you, in the case presented here, with 3.2.0-27-generic-pae.

Exercise 6-2
The rules log and then drop all inbound connections from RFC 1918 addresses. –A appends the rule to the INPUT chain. All packets coming in on interface (–i) eth0 are affected by this rule. The –s flag indicates a source address where the packets are originating from. All of the source addresses in the list of rules are RFC 1918 addresses. Since these are, by convention, not routable on the Internet, they are dropped because any reply can't get back. Prior to dropping, however, we are asking that the packet get logged. Since packets originating from these addresses may be part of an attack, it's worth logging in case we need the data to follow up with later on.

Windows

In this chapter, you will learn:

- The history of Windows and its product family
- Windows auditing
- Automation and configuration
- Windows network security
- Workgroups and Active Directory

Windows has been around for more than 35 years as of this writing, though development of it began nearly 40 years ago. The first several versions were not technically operating systems. During Windows' first decade or more of existence it was actually just a shell that ran on top of another operating system: DOS. Windows offered a graphical user interface (GUI) that was much more appealing than the plain command line that DOS provided. It also let users run multiple things at more or less the same time, which DOS didn't offer. DOS didn't offer much, actually. Many features of operating systems that we take for granted, and features that had in fact been taken for granted on larger systems, like minicomputers and mainframes, simply didn't exist in DOS. It didn't have memory management or process management capabilities. It provided a way to read and write to a disk, but not a lot beyond that. In fact, the disks that DOS was created to support weren't even hard drives.

Now, more than 35 years later, Windows is a modern operating system with as many advanced features as any other operating system. The Windows family now provides environments for mobile devices, desktops, and servers. The Windows Server line has become a platform to support complete enterprise management, as well as virtualization and a complete application development stack for web applications.

Over the course of this chapter, we'll talk about where Windows has come from and what it has turned into, both on the desktop side and the server side. Windows offers a lot of features necessary for system administrators, but provides many for security professionals as well, including auditing, encrypted file systems, encrypted network communications, and the ability to authenticate and authorize users for a number of resources on the network. Additionally, resources and users can be organized into different groups to make management easier. This creates some differences when it comes to how systems interact and how authentication happens.

Windows History

In the beginning, there was DOS. Actually, even before DOS there were operating systems that were very similar, like CP/M. DOS wasn't even a creation of Microsoft. When IBM decided to get into the personal computer (PC) business, they needed an operating system they could ship with it to make it useful. Microsoft, then a small software company shipping BASIC interpreters, got a request from IBM to create an operating system for its PCs. In order to get something out quickly, Microsoft bought the rights to a product called 86-DOS from Seattle Computer Products. Microsoft struck a very good licensing deal with IBM, which enabled them to make a lot of money for a long time as the primary operating system for the new IBM PC. The problem with DOS, though, was that it wasn't particularly user-friendly. Microsoft announced Windows in 1983 and delivered it in 1985. Windows was an advance over MS-DOS if for no other reason than Windows allowed users to run multiple applications at the same time by employing cooperative multitasking. Cooperative, or non-preemptive, multitasking relies on the applications to yield the processor. This would typically happen because the application came to a point where no further processing could happen, perhaps because of the need for I/O.

Windows 3.x and Windows NT 3.x

In 1990, Windows 3.0 was released and introduced virtual memory and loadable virtual device drivers. Windows for Workgroups was launched in 1993 and was perhaps the greatest leap forward in that it incorporated a peer-to-peer network component using NetBEUI. Windows 3.11, or Windows for Workgroups, allowed businesses to establish a network without the need to invest in an expensive and difficult-to-manage server. Small businesses could easily afford to have their computers work together and share files between individual systems. It's hard to overstate the importance of inexpensive and accessible networking in a single operating system. Previously, you had to purchase your operating system (as well as Windows if that's what you wanted to use), then go to a company like Novell and purchase their network operating system and a server to run it on. Once you had your server, you could purchase individual clients for each of the operating systems so those components could interact with your server, which handled some authentication as well as file sharing.

In late 1989, development on a completely different operating system began, though it was originally intended to be an update to OS/2, which was an advanced operating system developed jointly by Microsoft and IBM. OS/2 had many advanced features, including multiprocessing. The development of OS/2 and Microsoft's effort in that is a very involved story, so to avoid writing an entirely separate book explaining how all of that worked, let's just say that Microsoft tasted some success with Windows 3.0 and opted to pull the plug on their work with IBM on OS/2, instead focusing their resources and efforts on a version of Windows that included an operating system. This resulted in Windows NT in 1993. NT stood for New Technology and was a result of about four years of development effort with a kernel designed from the ground up, supporting the interface that had already been established with the other version of Windows, which was just a

Figure 7-1
The Windows 3.1
Program Manager

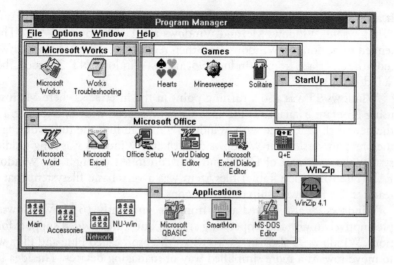

shell that sat on top of DOS. Windows NT did, however, take the look of the interface from Windows 3.1. Figure 7-1 shows what the Windows 3.1 Program Manager looked like and, by extension, how the user interface for Windows NT 3.1 appeared onscreen.

Windows NT was a fully 32-bit operating system, while Windows 3.x was a 16-bit operating system. This allowed NT to access more memory than Windows did, and access data on larger hard drives, also. Windows NT was a very advanced operating system that took many concepts from previous operating systems like Digital Equipment Corporation's VMS, as well as the portable operating system standard, POSIX. NT was released as both a desktop and workstation operating system and became the foundation of the Windows Server line. The original release was Windows NT 3.1 Advanced Server, launched in 1993.

NOTE The number of bits referenced is the bus width supported, and that bus width dictates the addressing for memory. For instance, 2^16 is a maximum memory address of 65,536, whereas 2^32 is a maximum memory address of 4,294,967,296.

One of the goals of Windows NT was to be a portable operating system. Initially, it was supported on the IA32, MIPS, and Alpha processors, then later PowerPC, Itanium, AMD64, and ARM processor support was added. Over time, support for the MIPS, Alpha, and PowerPC architectures was dropped, leaving primarily support for the various Intel-based processor architectures.

Windows 9x, NT 4.0, and Windows 2000

Windows 95 did a better job of hiding the operating system, though it was still DOS under the hood if you knew how to look for it. Windows 95 was also the first version of Windows to bundle DOS inside of Windows. This was the release of DOS Windows NT.

It and Windows remained on separate paths through the releases of Windows NT 4.0, Windows 98, Windows Me, and Windows 2000 (Windows NT 5.0). The interface work tended to be done in Windows, and then replicated in the NT line, so Windows NT 4.0 took the interface from Windows 95 just as Windows NT 3.1 took the interface from Windows 3.1.

Windows 95 was also a turning point in the interface, where Microsoft moved from using Program Manager as the shell users interfaced with to Explorer. Figure 7-2 shows the new shell that came with Windows 95, including the full, working desktop, which the previous versions of Windows didn't have. Windows was long saddled with the filesystem that was part of DOS, and that continued through the Windows 9x line. The FAT (File Allocation Table) filesystem was a very basic filesystem that didn't allow for features like file ownership or permissions.

Windows 95 also moved away from the previously 16-bit Windows. It was a 32-bit preemptively multitasked operating system, but still provided support for 16-bit applications. Windows 95 also came with what Microsoft called Plug and Play, which was meant to move toward a more simplified way of managing devices. The idea behind Plug and Play was that a user could plug in any device and just have it work. While the promise wasn't entirely delivered, it was an enormous step forward in device management.

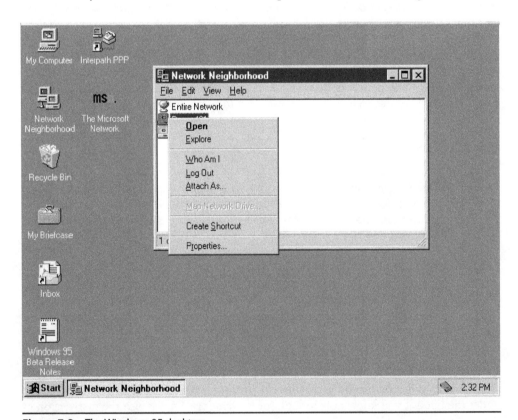

Figure 7-2   The Windows 95 desktop

Windows 95 was followed by Windows 98 and then Windows ME (Millennium Edition) on the consumer side, where the operating system was still underpinned by DOS, even though hidden under the surface. Windows 98 maintained the Explorer shell but introduced the FAT32 filesystem, which in turn introduced support for larger disk partitions and file sizes. Windows 98 was also the first version of Windows to include Internet Explorer in its initial release. Windows ME was intended to be a stopgap between Windows 98 and the impending release of Windows XP. ME was the last version to be DOS-based.

Meanwhile, the workstation line continued with NT releasing NT 4.0, which took the Explorer shell from the consumer line, making it look just like Windows 95. While it looked the same, NT 4.0 had the NT operating system and all of the NT subsystems under the hood. Windows 2000 is the first operating system from the NT line to drop the NT portion of the name and also drop the numbering convention used previously. It maintained the look of the desktop from the consumer Windows operating systems, just as previous versions of Windows NT had. You can see in Figure 7-3 that the desktop looks very similar to the desktop for Windows 95. Windows 2000 came in multiple server versions, in addition to the desktop version. The server version was the first to introduce Active Directory, essentially replacing the domain model introduced in NT 4.0.

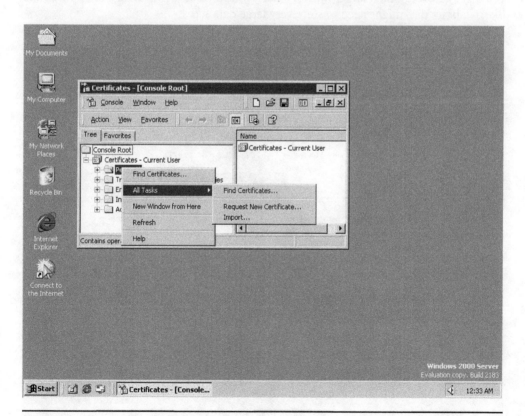

Figure 7-3 The Windows 2000 desktop

Windows XP Through Windows 10

Windows XP was the first time where the two types of Windows had merged and where the DOS underpinnings finally disappeared for the consumer version of Windows. No matter what edition of Windows XP you were using, whether it was a Home edition or Professional, you used the NT kernel and all of the subsystems NT had used. It continued the naming strategy of dropping NT, however, just as Microsoft had done with Windows 2000. Windows XP made some interface changes but still used the familiar Start menu and taskbar to interact with the application menu and run programs. You can see the differences in Figure 7-4. Windows XP came in a number of editions, but it was the first NT descendent to not include a server edition. The server line was split off altogether. Windows XP was a desktop operating system. Windows Server 2003 was the server version that was released two years later.

Server 2003 was a significant upgrade over the Windows 2000 server, and included security features like disabling a number of services by default. This was done for stability reasons, but disabling features by default reduces the potential for exploitation, helping protect operating systems from attack. Both Windows XP and Windows Server 2003 were released in 64-bit versions in 2005. The larger address space ensured that systems could get access to much larger memory sizes, meant to be an advantage to applications like databases that might need to store very large data sets.

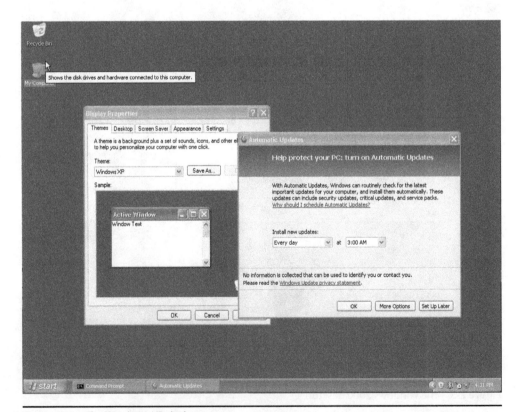

Figure 7-4 The Windows XP desktop

EXAM TIP Windows XP Home Edition did not allow for systems to belong to a domain, making that operating system unsuitable for use in a corporate environment.

One of the security challenges Windows faced for a long time was that users on Windows operating systems had administrative privileges by default. On the consumer operating systems, descended from Windows 1.0, all users were administrators since there was no other type of user available. The consumer side didn't get different types of users until the Windows and NT operating system lines were merged in Windows XP. It was also the first time the consumer operating system had the capability for a native filesystem that allowed for permissions. Starting with Windows XP, the consumer version of Windows began getting more and more security features, including the User Account Control (UAC), introduced in Windows Vista, that forced privilege elevation to be acknowledged by the user before it could take place. This feature was continued in later versions of Windows.

Windows Server 2008 and subsequently 2012 continued the server line, while Vista, Windows 7, and Windows 8 were successors to the desktop line. There have been minor changes to the interface in each release of the server line, and you can see what the interface for Windows Server 2008 R2 looks like in Figure 7-5. Each server release had its set of advances, including the promise to make Windows boot faster than Windows 7.

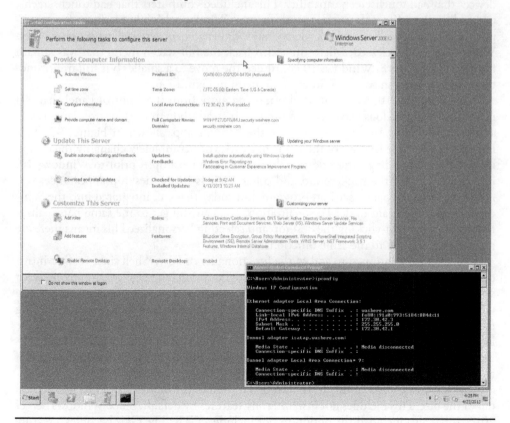

Figure 7-5 Windows Server 2008 R2

Windows 7 also introduced Windows PowerShell (described in the next section as well as later in the chapter) and attempted to make the User Account Control from Windows Vista more palatable to users. Windows versions after 7 took into consideration that there were computing devices with touchscreens, and they wanted all implementations of Windows to look and behave the same. As a result of Microsoft's move toward a touch model, the hardware manufacturers began providing systems that were capable of providing those features.

NOTE The release of Windows 8 prompted several hardware manufacturers to release desktops and laptops with touchscreen capabilities.

Windows 10 and Windows Server

Windows 8 provided a new look to the desktop line. Part of the point of Windows 8 was to marry the desktop and mobile platforms, providing a unified environment. This allowed application developers to have a single look by developing universal applications that could run on any platform as long as it supported the Universal Windows Platform (UWP). At the same time, the look of the user's desktop and menu began to focus on devices that had touchscreen capability. This included computers that had touchscreens, tablets like the Microsoft Surface, and also the Windows Mobile platform for smartphones. Microsoft called the look Metro, but it didn't go over very well with users. When Windows 8.1 was released, Microsoft scaled back the full-screen menu that was a main feature in Windows 8. Windows 10 continued the move to a smaller but still multifunctional menu. You can see the Windows 10 menu in Figure 7-6.

With Windows 10, Microsoft is also moving away from the Control Panel that is a main feature in previous versions of Windows. Instead, though the Control Panel is still available, Windows 10 emphasizes using the Settings app, shown in Figure 7-7. This includes most of the features of the Control Panel while completely changing the overall look and also providing some additional features. As an example, prior to Windows 10, in order to change the background and other settings in the desktop appearance, you needed to open a separate settings program, but today that's all integrated into the Windows Settings program under Personalization. You can still get to the same personalization settings by right-clicking the desktop and selecting Personalize. This means there are multiple ways to get to the same functionality.

Windows has continued to add to the functionality of PowerShell since its first introduction. Today, PowerShell is a feature-rich programming language commonly used for system management. It has become so powerful, in fact, that attackers are using it as a way of developing attacks and other necessary programmatic functions without needing to have another language, like Python, installed. This is a technique called "living off the land." It means the attackers don't have to bring in any additional tools or install anything separate. They have a fully functional programming language they can make use of already installed on the system. This is especially the case on servers.

The Windows Server family has continued movements toward a hardened installation out of the box. This includes not installing any features by default. Since Windows Server 2016, it has also included the option to not include a GUI. The GUI becomes a feature

Figure 7-6 Windows 10 menu

called Desktop Experience, which can be selected at install time, as shown in Figure 7-8. It can also be installed as a feature after the fact, if you have selected one of the install types that don't include the Desktop Experience. The default installation type is called Server Core.

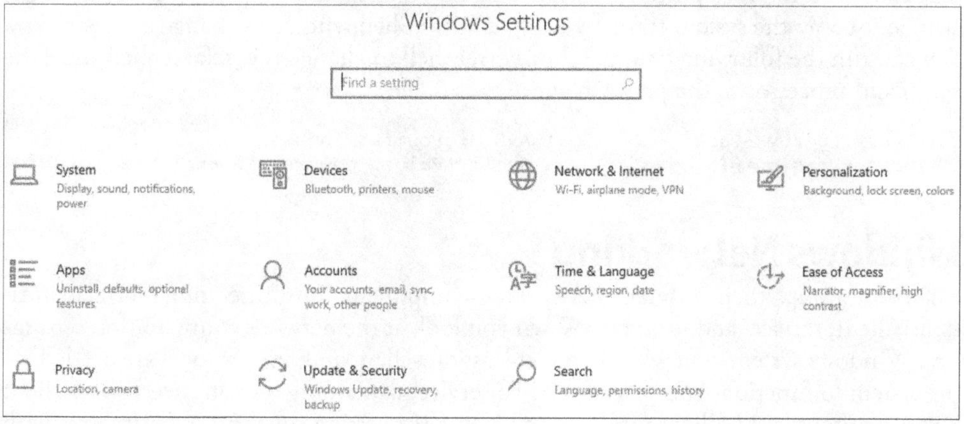

Figure 7-7 Windows 10 Settings

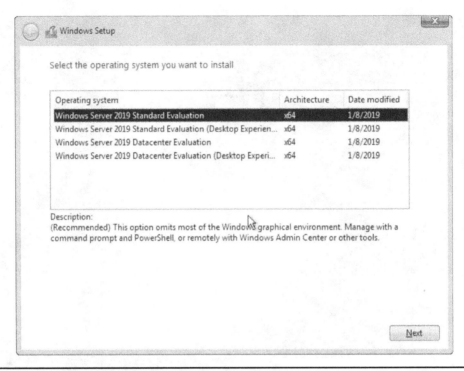

Figure 7-8 Windows Server 2019 installation types

If you select Server Core, once the system boots up, you log in to a text interface, just as you would with a Linux system without a GUI. Once you have logged in, you are presented with the familiar blue background, but instead of seeing the desktop and taskbar, you see a command prompt window. The problem with this is that you are running the old command processor with all the old DOS commands. You are not presented with a PowerShell shell, which opens up a lot more functionality with hundreds of cmdlets that allow you to write powerful scripts and also manage the system. You can, though, change the way the system starts by using a PowerShell cmdlet to change a registry key. You can run the following command in PowerShell to change the default shell from the command processor to the powershell.exe executable:

```
Set-ItemProperty -Path 'HKLM:\SOFTWARE\Microsoft\Windows
NT\CurrentVersion\Winlogon\' -Name Shell -Value 'powershell.exe'
```

Windows Networking

Microsoft groups their different networking components into three different classifications: client, service, and protocol. When you look at the network configuration settings on a Windows system, you will see that at least one client and one protocol are needed for the system to function. You may also add a service, depending on your needs. The client is very commonly the Client for Windows Networks, letting your computer interact with other systems on the network that are also Windows systems. You may also have services

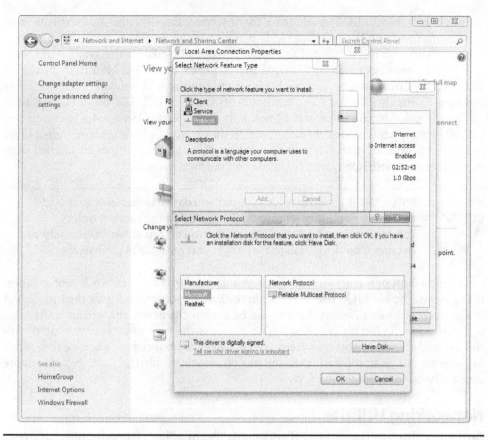

Figure 7-9 Adding Windows networking components

installed like a service for file and printer sharing on a Windows network so you can share your files and printers with other users on the network.

Windows has supported a number of networking protocols over the years, though primarily it supports TCP/IP today, both IPv4 and IPv6. In addition to supporting IP as the network protocol, Windows has long used Server Message Block (SMB)/Common Internet File System (CIFS) as a session layer protocol to provide internetworking between systems. SMB and CIFS provide the ability to share files and printers, among other things. As a system that runs TCP/IP, Windows also comes with a number of utilities that help with the configuration and management of the network implementation. Figure 7-9 shows how you would go about adding Windows networking components.

Basic Configuration

Windows supports both static and dynamic configurations for its networking settings. When dynamic configuration is selected, it makes use of the Dynamic Host Configuration Protocol (DHCP) to get the configuration of the IP address, subnet mask, default gateway, Domain Name System (DNS) servers, and any other network settings that may be available.

In the early 1980s, IBM developed a set of services called NetBIOS. NetBIOS is an application programming interface (API) that allows computers to communicate over a network. Microsoft had developed an implementation of NetBIOS that could stand alone and provide services on top of a layer 2 protocol that was called NetBEUI. NetBEUI allowed computers to quickly and easily get up and running on a network, sharing services and files. Currently, Windows implements NetBIOS over TCP/IP—an implementation commonly called NetBT. One of the important things NetBIOS provides is a name service, allowing systems to identify themselves on the network. This is separate from a DNS or Internet hostname, though it may be the same. Whereas DNS names are queried from external servers, NetBIOS names are known on the local network.

 NOTE NetBIOS also provides session and datagram services to provide for connection-oriented communication as well as connectionless communication. The SMB/CIFS services run on top of NetBIOS session and datagram services, though they aren't part of NetBIOS themselves.

Whereas most of the network configuration is done in a set of network configuration dialog boxes, the NetBIOS names are set in the system properties during the installation of the system. While a NetBIOS name can be sixteen characters, the sixteenth character is reserved for the NetBIOS suffix, which indicates the type of service associated with the name. As a result, you may have several names announced on your local network for your system, indicating whether you are announcing a file share service or a remote access service, for example.

Networking Utilities

Any system that participates in a network needs a set of utilities for performing basic configuration checks, as well as for troubleshooting and debugging. Windows is no exception and provides a pretty common set of utilities necessary for managing a system on a TCP/IP network. Additionally, there are other utilities more common to Windows itself, letting you connect to other Windows systems and troubleshoot connections on the network.

Ping

Some will tell you that ping stands for Packet InterNet Groper, but in reality it was named after the sound SONAR systems make when trying to locate something, and this is exactly what ping does on a network. A retronym was developed shortly after to give it a network-sounding name. It was developed one evening in 1983 to troubleshoot a faulty network connection. Ping sends Internet Control Message Protocol (ICMP) Echo Request messages to systems or devices on the network. If the device receives the message, it replies with an ICMP Echo Response. The system sending the message makes note of when it sent it and then makes note of the time the response comes in and calculates a round-trip time from those two numbers. In addition to having the knowledge that a system is up, knowing how long it takes a packet to get there and back is helpful to get an idea of how far away a system is or maybe how congested the route to the system is.

Shorter round-trip times mean a better connection and one that may be more desirable if you are comparing two systems.

tracert

tracert is the Windows implementation of the common traceroute program, used to determine the route a packet takes through the network. This is done by manipulating the Time To Live (TTL) field as each message is sent. The first message is sent with a TTL of 1, and when it hits its first network device, typically a router, the router will decrement the TTL to 0 and return an ICMP Time Exceeded In Transit message to the sender. That ICMP error message will contain the IP address of the sender, so we know the IP address of the first hop on the path. The next message is sent with a TTL of 2, and so on, until we get to our final destination. If an ICMP Echo Request message is sent, the system will know it has hit its final destination when it receives an ICMP Echo Response in return. If it never receives that message, the tracert will eventually fail. Other implementations use high-numbered User Datagram Protocol (UDP) ports, and when they receive an ICMP error indicating the port is unreachable, the traceroute has completed.

 EXAM TIP While Unix implementations commonly use UDP messages to implement traceroute, Windows uses ICMP. As a result, if devices along the path are configured to drop ICMP messages, a tracert will fail.

---

ipconfig

If you need to be able to look at your IP settings, you can use the ipconfig command. On Unix-like systems, this utility is called ifconfig. It will display all of your IP configuration settings for each network interface you may have on your system, including IP address, subnet mask, and default gateway as well as the MAC address for the interface. If your system has IPv6 addresses, it will also show the IPv6 information for each interface.

nslookup

nslookup is a utility to query DNS servers for information about the various records they store. You can look up the IP address for a particular hostname or look up the hostname associated with a particular IP address. You can also query for MX records, which are used to determine the mail server for a particular domain, and search for any other type of DNS record available.

netstat

netstat can provide a lot of network statistics for the system, including programs that are listening to particular ports, as well as connections that are open between two systems. Additionally, netstat can print out the routing tables on your system, meaning all of the networks your system knows how to get to as well as the interfaces used to get to them. This would include the default route, which is the path a packet takes if it doesn't have a specific route for the destination.

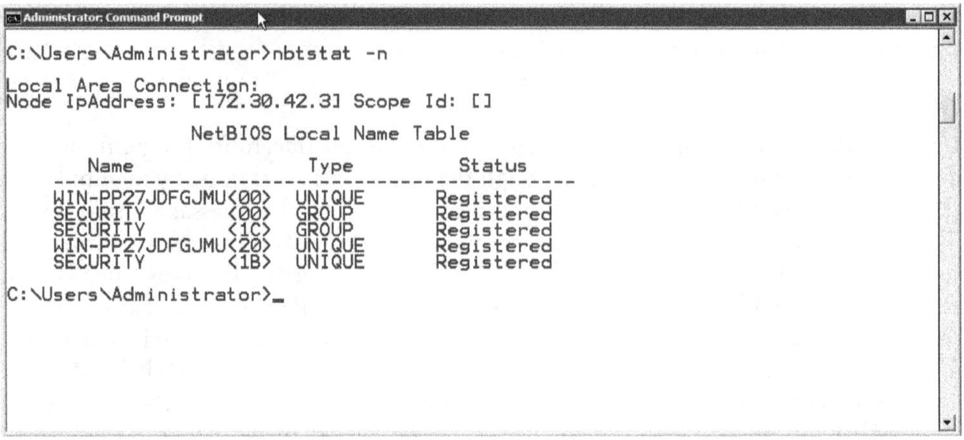

```
Administrator: Command Prompt                                                    _ □ x
C:\Users\Administrator>nbtstat -n

Local Area Connection:
Node IpAddress: [172.30.42.3] Scope Id: []

                NetBIOS Local Name Table

      Name               Type         Status
   ---------------------------------------------
   WIN-PP27JDFGJMU<00>   UNIQUE      Registered
   SECURITY       <00>   GROUP       Registered
   SECURITY       <1C>   GROUP       Registered
   WIN-PP27JDFGJMU<20>   UNIQUE      Registered
   SECURITY       <1B>   UNIQUE      Registered

C:\Users\Administrator>_
```

Figure 7-10   Sample nbtstat output

nbtstat

nbtstat is similar to netstat, but instead of providing information oriented around TCP/IP statistics and connections, it returns information about the NetBIOS name service. Figure 7-10 shows the output from nbtstat listing all of the names this particular system, a Windows 2008 Server, knows about.

Exercise 7-1: Nbtstat

Access a command prompt on a Windows system and run nbtstat –n to see the local NetBIOS names. How many names do you get?

Securing Windows Networking

As with so many aspects of security, less is more. The fewer components you have in a system or network design, the less complex it will be, and as a result, the likelihood of problems will go down. When it comes to securing your Windows network, removing services is better. Microsoft has done a good job in the last decade or so of turning off a lot of services and requiring users to actively turn them on to make use of them. This can help a lot in keeping systems and networks protected against intrusion or misuse.

Microsoft began delivering a mechanism to help protect against vulnerability exploitation in service pack 2 for Windows XP. Buffer overflows have long been a problem where programs can have their execution path hijacked by manipulation of the program stack. Since the stack is where data is stored, there is generally no good reason that there should be executable code stored in and run from the stack. Microsoft implemented a Data Execution Protection (DEP) system to keep code from executing from the stack. Enabling this feature, if it isn't already enabled, will help protect services from being exploited, including services that are listening for network connections.

Some hardware supports performing data execution protection directly without needing the software of the operating system to perform the protection. You can change any settings for DEP by going to the System Settings in the Control Panel or the Advanced settings window. You can see in Figure 7-11 that DEP has been enabled by default on the Windows 2016 server the figure was obtained from. You can exclude particular programs or even just have DEP apply to Windows applications and services—those that come with the operating system. The best way to protect your system, though, is to enable DEP for all programs unless it's absolutely necessary to shut it off for a particular application to get it to function correctly.

There are other methods of keeping your system protected, some of which are included in the operating system, while others are utilities you can add on later. As always with network security, having a firewall can protect systems against a number of problems, and Windows comes with a firewall built in. Additionally, Windows has the ability to encrypt network communication between systems using IPSec (discussed later in this chapter).

Figure 7-11
Settings on the
Data Execution
Prevention tab

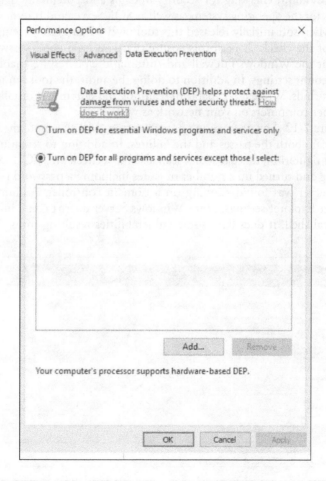

That's built into its networking capabilities. Those two features go a long way in protecting your network communications and your systems. On top of that, Microsoft provides a tool for analyzing other vulnerabilities that may exist on your system, discussed next.

Windows recognizes that many devices today are mobile. This means they are moving from one network to another and not all networks are created equal. Some networks require more protections to the device than others. You may want to expose file sharing on one network while not on another, for instance. Microsoft uses zones to determine what type of network your system is connected to. You can tell Windows that a network you have connected to is public or private. You may see this when you attach to a wireless network and Windows asks you if you are home or on a public network. The use of zones helps to enable some of the firewall capabilities that are available in Windows.

Microsoft Baseline Security Analyzer

The Microsoft Baseline Security Analyzer (MBSA) is a tool available from Microsoft to do a host audit, checking for security updates and potentially dangerous configuration settings for the operating system, as well as SQL Server and Internet Information Services (IIS). Microsoft initially released this tool in 2004 and has since updated it a few times. Some of the checks it performs ensure that you have good password policies in place, and that the Windows Firewall and Automatic Updates are enabled, as well as various user account settings. In addition to doing the audit, the tool can tell you how to fix any errors it finds. While it is capable of scanning the system it is installed on, it can also scan any other computers on your network as well.

Figure 7-12 shows a portion of a report from MBSA—note the findings for the Windows scan, both the passes and the failures. In addition to scanning the Windows setup and configuration, this particular scan also ran a check on a SQL Server instance it found running and turned up a number of issues including a password policy and the fact that SQL Server was found running on a domain controller. Additionally, it checked the Internet Explorer settings. Since Windows Server doesn't come in a version without the graphical shell, it does have some vulnerabilities resulting from the programs installed

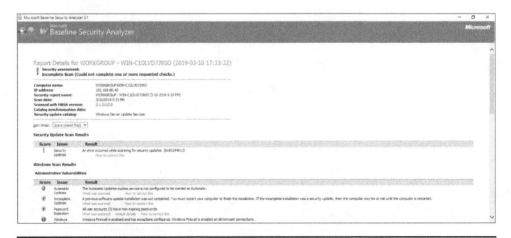

Figure 7-12 The Microsoft Baseline Security Analyzer report (partial)

with that shell, including Internet Explorer (IE), though Microsoft has done what it can to lock down a number of settings out of the box. For example, IE, by default, doesn't allow downloads or script execution from any server in the Internet zone. MBSA checks the different security zones to help ensure the settings haven't been weakened, which may put a server at risk from a careless administrator.

MBSA will still run on newer operating systems, though it hasn't been updated in a while and may not be the best solution to get a complete understanding of vulnerabilities on your OS. If you are looking to identify missing updates, using Windows Update, a feature in all Windows installations now, is a better approach.

Windows Defender

Microsoft introduced an optional anti-spyware program called Windows Defender in Windows XP. Until it was enhanced in Windows 8, all Windows Defender provided was anti-spyware. Starting with Windows Vista, Windows Defender was incorporated as a standard feature in Windows. Since Windows 8, Windows Defender has become more than just the basic anti-spyware that it started out as. Today, Windows Defender is an anti-virus solution, but the name has come to encompass all of the security features in Windows. Figure 7-13 shows the home view of the Windows Defender Security Center in Windows 10. This includes features for anti-virus, account protection, and a firewall, along with other features.

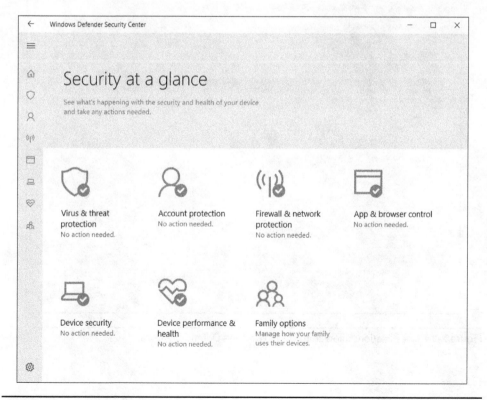

Figure 7-13 Windows Defender Security Center

Windows has had a firewall since the debut of Windows XP in 2001. The problem with the XP firewall was that it wasn't on by default and the configuration was difficult and hard to find. After XP was hit with some worms, like Blaster and Sasser, Microsoft decided to fix the firewall and the interface, and then rebrand it as Windows Firewall. Later it became Windows Defender Firewall. With XP Service Pack 2, it was on by default. Windows Firewall comes with a set of default rules and exceptions, based on the network you are connecting to. When you first connect to a network, Windows will ask you what type of network it is, whether it's a public network or a private network. Microsoft generally defines a private network as either a home network or a work network, while a public network is any network you may connect to at, say, a coffee shop or airport.

More traditional firewalls may be focused on addresses, ports, and protocols, but as an endpoint firewall, Windows Defender Firewall can be focused on applications. Figure 7-14 shows the list of applications and features installed on the system. You'll see check marks next to the applications that are allowed to communicate through the firewall. These settings are based on zones. You can allow some applications to communicate on private networks while restricting their access on public networks.

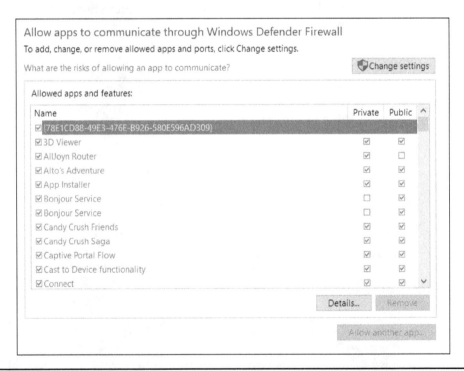

Figure 7-14 Applications allowed through Windows Defender Firewall

Exercise 7-2: Windows Firewall

Enable the Windows Firewall log and turn on logging connections and dropped packets. After using your system for a while, take a look at the firewall log, which should be stored at C:\Windows\system32\LogFiles\pfirewall.log on a Windows 10 system. Investigate the entries you find there.

Windows Firewall can be configured to log packets that are dropped, as well as connections that are successful. The log files can be parsed by a number of tools to generate reports. The firewall can also be scripted with VBScript or JScript. For example, you can programmatically add exceptions for applications or ports through the firewall. Figure 7-15 shows the settings for turning on the logs and where the log file would be stored.

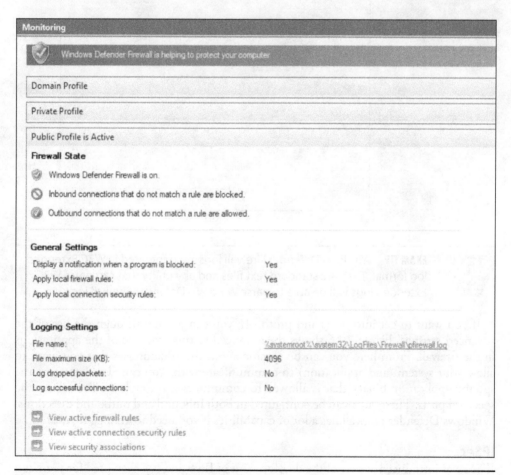

Figure 7-15   Windows Defender Firewall log settings

Figure 7-16
Windows
Defender Firewall
advanced
settings

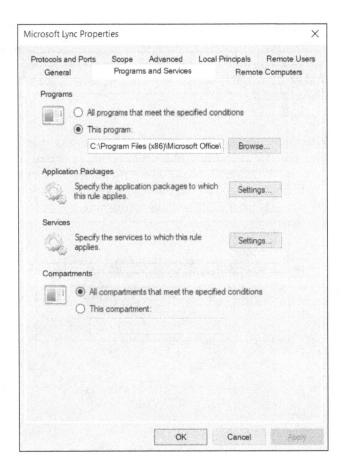

EXAM TIP Windows Defender Firewall logs are generated in W3C Extended log format. They are standard text files and any utility that can parse W3C Extended logs will be able to parse Windows Defender Firewall logs.

If you want to get into ports and protocols, you can do that through the use of the advanced settings. Figure 7-16 shows the advanced settings for one of the applications in the firewall. From here you can be specific about the IP addresses that you want to allow your system (and application) to communicate with. You can also determine the specific application binary that is allowed to communicate through the firewall on the specified ports. These rules can be configured in both inbound and outbound directions. Windows Defender Firewall has a lot of capabilities if you need to go digging into it.

IPSec

IPSec was introduced as part of the development of IPv6 and has been used for years as a way of providing remote access to networks over IPv4. One of the ideas behind IPSec was to create a policy database that would allow for security associations to be engaged as necessary. Based on the policy, any communication between two systems could be checked

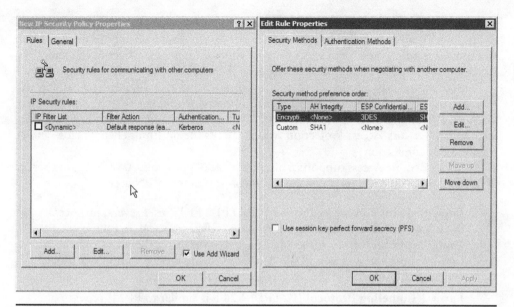

Figure 7-17 IPSec policy creation

for authenticity or it could be encrypted using a pre-set encryption policy. Windows provides an extensive interface for adding IP Security policies, allowing the creation of a database to establish secure network connections between two systems. Figure 7-17 shows the settings for creating a new IP security policy. You might have a set of policies to enable encryption between a database server and an application server on your network, or you may have a policy on your servers ensuring that users are authenticated before they can initiate a connection between the client system and the server.

 EXAM TIP While IPSec is primarily known for its encryption capabilities, you can also set filtering criteria under Windows as part of the IP Security policies. This provides another way of doing packet filtering.

VPNs

Windows has long had the ability to support remote access, including the ability to manage virtual private network (VPN) connections. The first remote access server capability was introduced in Windows NT 4.0. Routing and Remote Access Server (RRAS) was introduced with Windows 2000. RRAS can be a dial-up server as well as a VPN server, supporting a number of VPN protocols. In addition to simply terminating VPN connections, RRAS performs routing functions to get the remote connections access to the network the RRAS server sits on. It will also perform authentication or pass the authentication off to a RADIUS server on the network to ensure the remote user has permissions to gain access to the VPN server. RRAS also has the ability to restrict access to specific networks in order to further protect both the server itself and the network the server is providing access to.

While the feature still includes routing as an optional element, it is called Remote Access now. It can be installed by adding a feature from Windows Server Manager. When you add the feature, you have to select whether you want it to be a Direct Access and VPN server or a routing server. You can select both of them or they can be selected separately.

Remote Access has a solid set of routing protocols that it supports, including the Routing Information Protocol (RIP), Open Shortest Path First (OSPF), and Border Gateway Protocol (BGP). Windows Server 2008 introduced support for IPv6 and also introduced Network Access Protection ,which checks the health of clients before allowing the VPN connection.

As noted, Remote Access supports a number of VPN protocols. As of Windows Server 2008, Microsoft supports the following protocols for remote VPN access:

- **Point-to-Point Tunneling Protocol (PPTP)** PPTP uses several protocols, including the General Routing Encryption (GRE) protocol and the Point-to-Point Protocol (PPP), to encapsulate packets and deliver them from the client to the remote access server. PPTP does not provide for encryption but simply general encapsulation of the packets.

- **Layer 2 Tunneling Protocol (L2TP)** L2TP is similar to PPTP, providing a protocol to tunnel higher-layer protocols. L2TP uses UDP to transport the messages and doesn't include encryption or strong authentication.

- **Secure Socket Tunneling Protocol (SSTP)** SSTP allows for tunneling PPP or L2TP traffic through Secure Sockets Layer (SSL), which provides the encryption as well as the authentication. SSTP requires a valid certificate to be installed on the RRAS server in order to work.

- **Internet Key Exchange (IKE) v2** IKE is used to establish a security association and is typically part of the IPSec set of protocols. IKE employs certificates and can establish encryption as well as identity.

 EXAM TIP The Secure Socket Tunneling Protocol is a VPN protocol only available since Windows Server 2008.

Remote Access requires a system with multiple interfaces to function. The idea is that clients connect on an externally facing interface and are provided with an IP address on the inside of the network. All of the communication is tunneled through the connection between the client and the external interface and is then routed to the interface on the inside based on the destination address. The return messages are routed to the interface on the inside of the network. The RRAS server then associates the message with a particular tunnel interface back to a client so it is forwarded back through the tunnel.

Resource Management

A Windows server has many resources to manage, not just system resources like memory and storage space. Enterprise networks are composed of systems, users, services, printers, shared drives, and so on. Managing all of these components so that users can quickly and easily get access to whatever they need is important in order to ensure efficiency and productivity. A network operating system (NOS) like Windows Server won't last long if it doesn't enable users to perform their tasks easily and, preferably, make them more efficient. Ease of management is also very helpful. When Microsoft jumped into the server market, the predominant NOS was Novell's NetWare. NetWare provided client software so users could access network resources like shared filesystems on the server, as well as printers and other shared resources. The client software allowed for connections to the NetWare server.

NOTE   Novell released NetWare Directory Services in 1993, based on X.500 directories, seven years ahead of Microsoft's similar directory services called Active Directory. Both were behind Sun Microsystems, who had a directory implementation called Network Information Services (NIS) several years before Novell's directory implementation.

While providing access to shared resources is certainly important and helps save money by pooling resources, a NOS also provides central authentication and authorization for the network. This centralized approach to access control can save a lot of time and money and also put the decisions about who should be part of what groups in order to gain access to particular resources in the hands of administrators. Because of this approach, administrators can ensure that policies are followed appropriately. This centralization of management may be too much for some organizations, and because of that, smaller organizations can still get resource sharing on Windows systems without having to buy into the Windows Server line. Microsoft provides Workgroups to organize systems together in order to locate resources on a small network.

Windows Workgroups vs. Windows Domains

A workgroup is a peer-to-peer network, allowing for sharing of resources between any of the peers on the network. With a peer-to-peer network, there is no central authentication or authorization system. Workgroups can be helpful for small organizations as a way of collecting all of the systems and resources on the network into one group. Any network can have multiple workgroups, which can be seen when you explore the network. In addition to systems in the workgroup you are in, you will see other workgroups that exist on your network. Figure 7-18 shows a Windows 10 system named bobbieharlow in the WASHERE workgroup. Changing workgroups is easy to do. You would use a workgroup in a situation where you don't have a server that could provide centralized administration. Without the centralized administration, there is nothing to prevent any system from joining a workgroup. Additionally, in order to gain access to shared resources on other systems in the domain, the resources would need to have access granted to everyone; otherwise, someone trying to make use of the resource would have to know a username and password on the hosting system in order to get access to it. This makes scaling, as well as security, more of a challenge with workgroups.

A Windows domain, by comparison, is a central database of information about users, computers, and other resources on the network. This centralization allows for better management since users don't have to be created on all of the workstations. In contrast to

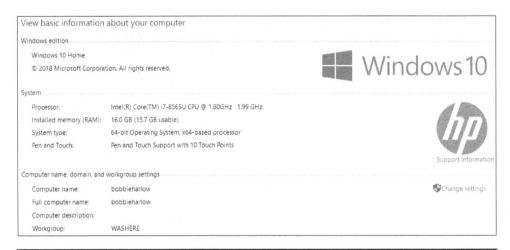

View basic information about your computer

Windows edition

Windows 10 Home

© 2018 Microsoft Corporation. All rights reserved.

System

Processor:	Intel(R) Core(TM) i7-8565U CPU @ 1.80GHz 1.99 GHz
Installed memory (RAM):	16.0 GB (15.7 GB usable)
System type:	64-bit Operating System, x64-based processor
Pen and Touch:	Pen and Touch Support with 10 Touch Points

Computer name, domain, and workgroup settings

Computer name:	bobbieharlow
Full computer name:	bobbieharlow
Computer description:	
Workgroup:	WASHERE

Figure 7-18   The Workgroup setting in Windows 10

workgroups, not everyone can join a domain. In order to join one, you have to have the right permissions. Domain administrators would have these permissions, though individual users or groups could also be given permissions to add systems to the domain. In this case, each computer would have a domain account, and once the computer belonged to the domain, domain users would be able to access the computer by logging in with domain credentials. Being part of the domain allows systems and users to easily gain access to resources on other systems because the domain handles the credentials.

The central systems in a Windows domain are called domain controllers, and they hold the central database of information about users, groups, systems, and other resources on the network. Information across the domain controllers gets synchronized so that all domain controllers in the domain have the same information. This provides fault tolerance in case one domain controller goes offline, as well as load balancing since any domain controller can provide authentication and authorization services on the network.

 EXAM TIP   Domains provide security access tokens (SATs) that can be used across the domain. Standalone computers, like those in a workgroup, do not trust each other's SATs.

Active Directory

Windows Active Directory (AD) is an implementation of the Lightweight Directory Access Protocol (LDAP), which is a subset of the larger X.500 directory definition. A very simple way of thinking about it is that AD is a special-purpose database, storing a lot of information about an organization and its information technology resources, including its users. While the information is stored in a flat database with tables, rows, and columns, it is represented as a hierarchy of objects, and each object has its own globally unique identifier (GUID). Each object in the hierarchy can be a container holding other objects, or it can be a leaf node. For example, you may have an organizational unit (OU) container that has a number of group containers underneath it in the hierarchy (or inside of it, if you consider them to be truly containers). Each of those objects is a container. At the ends, you might have a number of users. Each of these users would be a leaf node. Each object would have a number of attributes, including common name (CN), locality name (L), state or province name (ST), organization name (O), organizational unit (OU), and country (C).

Active Directory still has the concept of domains. An Active Directory domain would be composed of an X.500-based directory, a DNS name for the domain to be used for organizational purposes, a mechanism for authorization and authentication, and a set of policies dictating who can access resources and how they would be allowed to access them. However, you may have subdomains underneath the primary domain. All of these subdomains would be part of the domain tree of the primary domain. Each of these subdomains would enjoy a transitive trust with one another as well as their parent, allowing users in each of the domains access to resources in the other domains.

When you have a collection of domain trees, you have a forest. A domain tree is a collection of domains and a forest is a collection of domain trees. A subdomain would share a root domain with its parent, so mybiz.net may be the parent and seattle.mybiz.net may be a subdomain of mybiz.net. Those two domains would exist in the same domain tree. If My Biz had another business it owned that shared the same IT resources, the domain might be myotherbiz.com and it would be another domain tree in the forest named mybiz.net since the first domain created becomes the forest root domain, and the forest is named after it.

While this sort of configuration is possible, it is certainly confusing if you were to look at it hierarchically since mybiz.net would exist as a container for myotherbiz.com. A better organizational solution may be to have a completely separate AD infrastructure for myotherbiz.com in order to keep things as simple as possible. As with anything else, complications can lead to outages or misconfigurations, and these misconfigurations may lead to a variety of problems, not the least of which may be unauthorized access to company resources.

Windows has a rich user interface for managing the resources within Active Directory. This interface is called Active Directory Users and Computers, though there is another application called Active Directory Administrative Center (ADAC). The Active Directory Users and Computers application is shown in Figure 7-19 demonstrating the resources that can be added to the domain, including users, groups, computers, and printers, among other things. The ADAC is a newer interface and is built entirely on top of Windows PowerShell. Actions within the ADAC call PowerShell cmdlets to perform the functions requested.

Each domain can have a number of domain controllers and, not surprisingly, it's important to keep all of the information between all of the domain controllers synchronized. Each AD has a Global Catalog (GC) where all of the objects for the forest are stored. You can access the GC over standard LDAP ports (3268 for the clear-text port and 3269 for SSL-encrypted) and issue LDAP queries against the GC. When it comes to replication, the objects in the GC are replicated across each of the domain controllers.

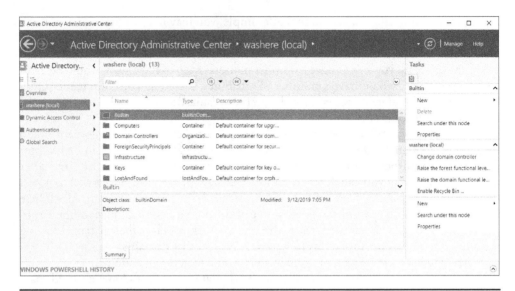

Figure 7-19   Active Directory management in Windows Server 2016

This is done through the use of site links, and Windows supports two types of site links. The first is an IP site link, allowing replication to be done over remote procedure calls (RPCs). The second type of link is an SMTP link allowing replication to be done over e-mail.

EXAM TIP   Data that gets replicated to all domains is stored in the Global Catalog.

The heart of the AD infrastructure is the domain controller, as has been alluded to before. New servers installed become domain controllers within AD. Introducing any server to the network as a domain controller is done using the dcpromo application. dcpromo handles all of the work of creating the schema for Active Directory and installs all the necessary services for a server to become a domain controller, whether it's the first controller in the domain or some number well after that. The process of introducing a new domain controller is called *promoting*, and promoting a domain controller requires you to provide credentials with an appropriate level of access in order to complete the promotion.

With newer versions of Windows Server come more features and functionality. This means not all servers are going to be completely interoperable. Beyond the change in functionality with Windows Server, though, are functionality changes in both the forest and the domain. You select the functional level of both the forest and the domain when you create a new AD installation. You can also upgrade the functionality of servers that you have been upgrading the OS on. Once you upgrade the forest and AD, though, you will lose the ability to manage some of the features from older operating systems and

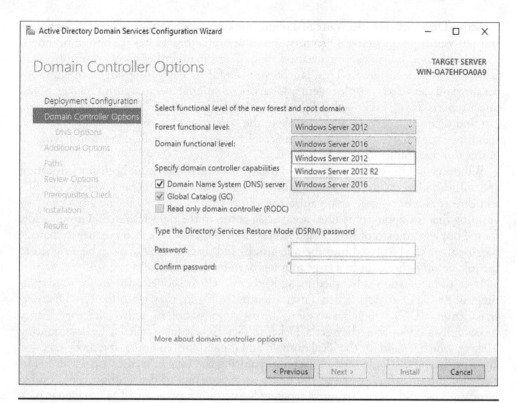

Figure 7-20 Selecting forest and domain functional levels

their tools. Figure 7-20 shows the wizard you would use to create a new AD installation, where you would select the forest and domain functional level.

Users and Groups

Users and groups are some of the fundamental objects that are stored in Active Directory. In addition to storing information about each user, domain controllers will provide authentication and authorization services for users. Each user and group gets a Security Identifier (SID) when they are created, and since some users have been created as defaults for the system, these users and groups have SIDs that are the same across different installations of Windows. This means that the SIDs are well known and can be accessed based on the SID, no matter what Windows system you are trying to get access to. Information about the users, including cryptographic hashes of their passwords, is stored in the Security Accounts Manager (SAM) of the Windows registry.

EXAM TIP There are well-known Security Identifiers (SIDs) in Windows. Two of them are S-1-15-32-544 for the local Administrators group, and S-1-15-32-545 for the Users group.

Active Directory provides more of a phonebook service than simply storing usernames and passwords. With Active Directory, Windows can store addresses, phone numbers, e-mail addresses, job titles, organization names, and many other pieces of information associated with individuals. This can be very useful in navigating large organizations because you can attach people together in an organizational hierarchy with managers and direct reports. If you ever need to figure out what organization a colleague works in, you can find their manager and other people in the same group. In some companies, understanding what a particular organization actually does can be challenging, and having all of this information in AD can be helpful.

Windows uses the users and groups to make determinations about both authentication and authorization. With the Access Control Lists (ACLs) available for resources like files and directories, being able to organize users into groups can help secure filesystems by ensuring that the appropriate users are getting access to the right resources. Groups allow for the implementation of Role-Based Access Control (RBAC), which is easier to manage because users can be placed into the role groups and then permissions can be assigned to the role group rather than to a large number of individual users.

User authentication is handled using Kerberos, which is one of the major underpinnings of Active Directory. When a user attempts to log in, they go to the Key Distribution Center (KDC), which has access to the user information in Active Directory. If they successfully authenticate, they get a Ticket to Get Tickets (also called a Ticket Granting Ticket), which is valid for the local domain and is good for ten hours. It may be renewed anytime during the login session without requiring the user to reenter a password. The Kerberos infrastructure for all of the ticket management and distribution is embedded into Windows and doesn't require a separate Kerberos infrastructure. One challenge with Kerberos that should be kept in mind when deploying Windows servers is how fussy about time it is. Kerberos is very time-sensitive, and if there is too much difference in the clock settings between clients and the server, it can cause authentication and access problems. Windows sets the maximum differential at five minutes by default.

 TIP Keeping a local time source and syncing all systems to it can help avoid any issues with clock drift that may cause problems with Kerberos tickets.

Users are typically created in a domain context and stored in Active Directory, but in some cases you may have a need to create local users. These situations would be limited since local users would be created on individual systems, which reduces the ability to centrally manage users. In some instances, you may have systems that aren't part of the domain. In this case, you would have to have a local user. You may also need to create a local user so a service can run as the local user with a specific set of permissions. You may also have a need for users to log in locally to a system that is part of the domain instead of authenticating against the domain.

Users also have profiles, and domain users can have their profiles stored on the server, while local users would obviously have their profiles stored on the system that the user and profile belong to. A profile is a collection of settings and files specific to a particular user.

There are two types of user profiles when it comes to domain users: mandatory and roaming. A roaming profile is stored on the server and follows the user no matter what system within the domain they log in to. A mandatory profile can also be stored on the server, but a user can't change anything.

Resource Sharing

Windows allows you to share a number of resources on your system with other users on the network. This may be simply sharing a folder on your computer, allowing access to your files from other systems, or it may be allowing access to a printer that's attached to your system. You can also re-share a network printer that you have attached to, making your computer the print spooler that other devices send their print jobs to. Once you have shared network resources, you can assign permissions. These permissions can be different across users and groups, meaning you are using an Access Control List. The ACL is a list of users and groups with the relevant permissions associated with them. Just sharing a folder, drive, or some other resource doesn't mean you lose control over who can make use of the resource. You need to set appropriate permissions for users on the network. Sometimes this can require some thought to make sure you are restricting permissions as much as possible so that you don't end up allowing malicious users to cause damage to your files or allowing malware to replicate itself to your system.

NOTE   A print spool is a queue where print jobs are sent. The system in charge of the print spool will manage the print jobs and get them (spool them) out to the printer. It's said that spool is an acronym for simultaneous peripheral operations online, though it may be just as likely that the term originated from the use of spools of magnetic tape to store information.

Policies and Policy Management

Windows gives you a lot of ability in controlling how a system operates and what permissions are given to users and groups. Depending on whether you have Active Directory, you may be using group policies. There are also local policy settings that can be applied on individual computers. However, if a system belongs to a domain and has local policies applied, those policies will be overridden if there are policies that are pushed down from the domain. The policies have a lot of power and have a great deal of control over systems from a central point, including having the ability to install Microsoft System Installer (MSI) packages using a group policy. The group policy has far more control than the local policy and can be used to provide a great deal of control over the user desktops from a central location. The group policy also has precedence over any local policy settings that may be active. The underlying idea is that domain administrators would be setting specific policies based on the overall policies guiding the organization. Where a local policy may have a password policy indicating that there is a minimum password length of 0, a group policy, pushed down across the domain from Active Directory, may be more in compliance with the organization's password policy and dictate a minimum password length of eight characters.

Local Policies

As you might expect, local policies provide control over the local system. The local policy provides control over the password policy for users on the system, as well as the account lockout policy, which dictates how many invalid login attempts are allowed before the system locks the account. Once an account is locked, there is a policy that allows it to be reset after a specified number of minutes. The local policy allows for the setting of an audit policy. An audit policy is helpful for detecting unauthorized access by finding failed attempts to access files or other system objects. These failures may indicate someone is trying to access resources they shouldn't be accessing. This could be benign or perhaps someone being curious or accidentally clicking on something they didn't mean to. It could also be malicious attempts to gain access to a sensitive file.

The local policy is also capable of specifying what rights users have. There are a number of user rights and they can be assigned to individual users or to groups. Typically, each user right would have a list of users and groups that have been granted a particular right. These rights range from being able to log in through Remote Desktop Services, to accessing the computer from the network, to logging on as a service, and a number of other rights. Figure 7-21 shows the Local Security Policy editor with the User Rights Assignment category selected and a partial list of rights that are available.

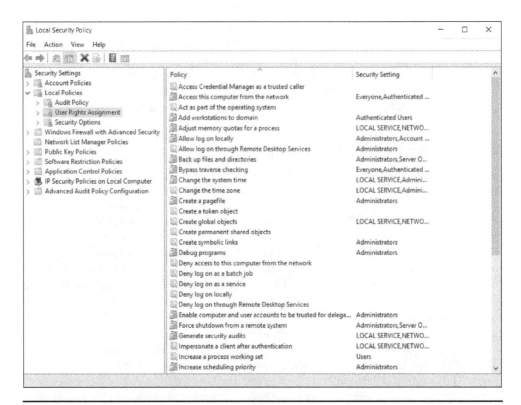

Figure 7-21   The Local Security Policy editor with the User Rights Assignment category open

The Local Security Policy editor is a snap-in for the Microsoft Management Console (MMC); the specific plugin to open up the policy editor is secpol.msc. We will discuss the MMC in more detail later in this chapter, but it's worth noting that the various plugins for the MMC can be mixed and matched as necessary, and while there is a program entry in the Start menu under Administrative Tools for Local Security Policy, you can easily create your own console view including the local policy editor, as well as, for example, the Group Policy Editor, which is also just a plugin for the MMC.

Group Policies

When you read the term group policy, you may think that it refers to a policy that applies to a group. But in fact, what we are talking about is a group of settings that creates a policy. A group policy can be applied to any object in Active Directory, whether it's a site, a group of users, a domain, or a specific computer. Group policies exist to provide more control over configuration, management, and software deployment within the computers and users of Active Directory. A wide variety of settings for the client systems can be controlled using a group policy. From the group policy Management MMC snap-in (gpmc.msc), you can create new policies and determine where they are applied within Active Directory. In order to configure a group policy, though, you need to use the Group Policy Management Editor (gpedit.msc). You can see the Group Policy Management Editor in Figure 7-22 opened up to the App Locker section. Here you would choose the applications allowed to run or not allowed to run.

 EXAM TIP Group policies can be used to deploy software, startup/shutdown scripts, and applications, and also used for applications, network configuration, IPSec policies, and a wide variety of other configuration settings.

Every system could have a number of policies and settings, as well as multiple Group Policy Objects (GPOs), that need to be applied. There should be a way to prioritize these different configurations and policy objects. Fortunately, there is. The order starts with the closest to the user, and then makes its way up through Active Directory until it reaches the highest level. The reason for this is that local control is the least important thing when it comes to applying policies. An organization policy takes precedence over the settings on an individual machine, and a corporate policy takes precedence over an organization policy. The following is the order of precedence for applying policies, starting with the first set of policies to apply, and ending with the last ones:

1. Local group policy
2. Site GPOs
3. Domain GPOs
4. OU GPOs in order of hierarchy

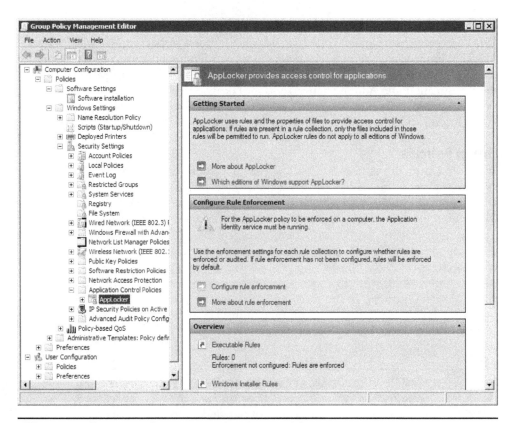

Figure 7-22   The Group Policy Management Editor window

EXAM TIP   Group policies can push down scripts that could be executed at startup, shutdown, logon, and logoff, and might be written in a mix of scripting languages.

While group policies are applied from Active Directory, it is possible to apply a local group policy to standalone systems and those that don't belong to Active Directory. This can help ensure that systems adhere to a set of policies for the organization, no matter whether they are centrally managed through AD or not. The policies will be updated every 90 minutes, but rather than every system on the network updating at roughly the same time, there is a 30-minute randomization factor, which means that policies will be updated somewhere between 90 and 120 minutes.

While the majority of management is done through the graphical user interface, you can also use PowerShell to manage the policy objects. We'll take a closer look at PowerShell later in this chapter, but basically it gives you the ability to script and automate work with the policy objects. Figure 7-23 shows an example of PowerShell getting a GPO and generating a report in HTML format.

```
Administrator: Windows PowerShell                                                    _ □ X
Windows PowerShell
Copyright (C) 2009 Microsoft Corporation. All rights reserved.

PS C:\Users\Administrator> Import-Module GroupPolicy
PS C:\Users\Administrator> Get-GPO -Name "My Policy"


DisplayName      : My Policy
DomainName       : security.washere.com
Owner            : SECURITY\Domain Admins
Id               : 7e00d441-d0aa-4888-9581-013cfd4bed48
GpoStatus        : AllSettingsEnabled
Description      :
CreationTime     : 5/16/2013 3:14:18 PM
ModificationTime : 5/17/2013 10:53:10 AM
UserVersion      : AD Version: 2, SysVol Version: 2
ComputerVersion  : AD Version: 6, SysVol Version: 6
WmiFilter        :


PS C:\Users\Administrator> Get-GPOReport -Name "My Policy"

cmdlet Get-GPOReport at command pipeline position 1
Supply values for the following parameters:
ReportType: HTML
<html dir="ltr" xmlns:v="urn:schemas-microsoft-com:vml" gpmc_reportInitialized="false">
<head>
<meta http-equiv="Content-Type" content="text/html; charset=UTF-16" />
<title>My Policy</title>
<!-- Styles -->
<style type="text/css">
             body    { background-color:#FFFFFF; border:1px solid #666666; color:#000000; font-size:68%; font-family
:MS Shell Dlg; margin:0,0,10px,0; word-break:normal; word-wrap:break-word; }

             table   { font-size:100%; table-layout:fixed; width:100%; }

             td,th   { overflow:visible; text-align:left; vertical-align:top; white-space:normal; }

             .title  { background:#FFFFFF; border:none; color:#333333; display:block; height:24px; margin:0px,0px,-1
px,0px; padding-top:4px; position:relative; table-layout:fixed; width:100%; z-index:5; }

             .he0_expanded    { background-color:#FEF7D6; border:1px solid #BBBBBB; color:#3333CC; cursor:hand; disp
lay:block; font-family:MS Shell Dlg; font-size:100%; font-weight:bold; height:2.25em; margin-bottom:-1px; margin-left:0
px; margin-right:0px; padding-left:8px; padding-right:5em; padding-top:4px; position:relative; width:100%; }

             .he1_expanded    { background-color:#A0BACB; border:1px solid #BBBBBB; color:#000000; cursor:hand; disp
lay:block; font-family:MS Shell Dlg; font-size:100%; font-weight:bold; height:2.25em; margin-bottom:-1px; margin-left:2
0px; margin-right:0px; padding-left:8px; padding-right:5em; padding-top:4px; position:relative; width:100%; }
```

Figure 7-23   PowerShell managing group policy

Windows Management

Most of the management of a Windows system, from a graphical tools perspective, is done through the Microsoft Management Console (MMC), which supports plugins. This gives a user an interface framework that has a consistent look and feel across all administrative functions. You would run the MMC and just use a plugin for it to get the specific management feature you were looking for, whether it's computer management or management of the DNS server. The MMC can be used to manage both local servers and remote servers. Additionally, it gives you the ability to create your own custom management consoles by adding in the sets of plugins you would like and then saving the resulting console. You could have a custom management console with disk management and DNS management together in the same place. Figure 7-24 shows a list of some of the plugins (snap-ins) available for the MMC.

Microsoft has long provided a set of tools to aid in the administration of Windows servers from remote systems. Primarily, this is the same set of tools you would find on the server itself, but these tools are designed to install on desktop operating systems to facilitate management of the server. Where previously the Remote Server Administration Tools (RSAT) were available as a downloadable installer, they can now be installed as a separate feature from Features on Demand in Windows 10. This has been the case

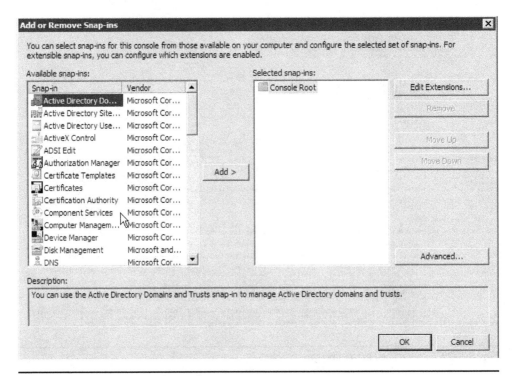

Figure 7-24   Microsoft Management Console plugins (snap-ins)

since an update in October 2018. RSAT can be used to administer server versions since Windows Server 2008 and only from desktop operating systems running Windows Vista or later. While both Vista and Windows 2008 are considered outdated, obsolete, and no longer supported by Microsoft, there are still enterprises using these (and even older) operating systems.

Allowing remote system administration access brings up its own set of challenges, including the need to potentially allow access to the appropriate ports on the server from a network where desktops live. There is a risk allowing direct access to server systems from a desktop that may be compromised. Providing this level of access might allow for a full compromise of your server infrastructure. There are ways to mitigate this, which include ensuring that specific subnets where administrators might be located have access to the server network, or even better, forcing your administrators to use a virtualized environment that either straddles the desktop and server networks or lives entirely within the server network but has access to the Remote Desktop Protocol port through a firewall or packet filter. That virtualized desktop environment could have the server administration tools on it, and all servers could be managed from it rather than having to open remote desktop services on all of the Windows servers in your network. The advantage of providing a choke point like that for management of your Windows network is that a single system, or cluster of systems, can be strictly controlled and monitored—it's much harder to control, manage, audit, and monitor several desktop systems.

Automation

Windows provides a few different ways for system administration tasks to be automated. One of the easiest is making use of the Schedule service and the *at* command, which specifies that a command, script, or program should run at a designated time or date. The Schedule service could be used to automate a number of system administration tasks, including things like copying critical files off to an external filesystem for storage. This would make a rudimentary backup. Any task that doesn't have the ability to schedule itself could be scheduled in this way.

You may want to write a batch file that you could schedule using the Schedule service, or it may just be something you want to run manually from time to time, but because it may be a set of commands requiring a minimal amount of programming logic, it may be easier to put it all together using a batch file. The batch file is a way of running multiple commands or programs in sequence while also providing some basic programming and logic constructs like *if*, *for*, and *while* statements that can control the flow of execution of the batch program.

NOTE They are called batch files because you can stack up a number of tasks into a batch and run them sequentially, similar to the way cards used to be stacked up to run one program after another in the days of card punch machines and batch processing.

Where batch programming provides some rudimentary capabilities that you could effectively run from the Windows command prompt, Windows PowerShell offers much deeper access to system administration functions, Windows APIs, and the ability to bundle little programs together into something called a cmdlet. A cmdlet is a programming object that makes use of the .NET Framework and implements a specific feature or function. It's not a standalone executable like a batch file would be, though. The cmdlet runs inside of PowerShell. Cmdlets are typically named in a verb-noun fashion, making it easier to understand what they do. For example, you might name a cmdlet GetUser, which obviously gets a user. Each cmdlet returns a .NET object, so the cmdlets can be chained. Thus, the output of one cmdlet becomes the input to the next, and since it's an object, it is a compound data type, meaning a number of different parameters can be handed off to the next cmdlet.

NOTE PowerShell also supports scripting and its own scripting language, which can be used to write a cmdlet—though cmdlets are more likely to be written in a language like C#.

PowerShell has become an extensible and powerful tool, adding features like remoting, job scheduling, delegation, and script debugging. These features are common in programming languages and extend the capabilities of PowerShell to create a lot of capabilities for system administration and other power user tasks. For instance, the remoting capabilities in PowerShell give a system administrator the ability to write a script to perform a set of administration tasks and run that script on a large number of systems. This makes administration tasks significantly easier.

The PowerShell functionality is made possible through a set of extensions to the Windows Driver Model called Windows Management Instrumentation (WMI). WMI has been around for well over a decade. It was created as an add-on to Windows NT 4.0 SP4 and is a way of providing a structured and standard way of accessing management data. WMI uses the concept of providers, and Microsoft has been steadily adding WMI providers with each successive release of Windows, both the server and desktop releases. In order to develop a provider, you first need to create a manageable entity model, then develop the provider, creating a template using the Active Template Library (ATL).

The WMI model is similar in some regard to the Simple Network Management Protocol's use of a Management Information Base (MIB). The MIB defines a model of data that can be populated and queried. Similarly, when you create a provider using WMI, you are defining a way of accessing management data. Where SNMP is defined as a protocol that has a server and client and expects to be accessed over the network, WMI is a programmatic mechanism. While WMI can provide programmatic access, Microsoft also provides console access through a utility called Windows Management Instrumentation Command-line (WMIC). This utility can be used to query different providers offered by the operating system.

There are two other ways that tasks can be automated across multiple systems. The first is PsExec, which was developed by the Sysinternals team at Microsoft. It allows you to remotely execute programs and also allows you to copy the necessary executable. If you don't copy the executable to the remote system, the program will have to exist in the system path in order to run. Otherwise, you specify the path to the executable.

Windows Remote Management (WinRM) is another means of executing programs on a remote system and performing management functions. WinRM is based on the WS-Management Protocol, which is a Simple Object Access Protocol (SOAP)-based protocol that is considered firewall friendly. WinRM is part of the operating system and is one way to remotely manage installations in Microsoft Azure, which is Microsoft's cloud computing platform. This makes automating and scripting management much easier in cases where you may not have console or any sort of GUI access to manage the device.

Configuration

A lot of system configuration is done through the use of Control Panel applets. These configuration settings are stored in the system registry, where they can be accessed using the Registry Editor. The Control Panel applets provide a way of organizing all of the different configuration options and settings into functional groups. While there are a lot of areas where you can do system configuration, the Control Panel doesn't have all of the system configuration settings, and sometimes it can be difficult to keep track of the different places where you would access a particular configuration task. For example, some user configuration is done through a Control Panel applet, but if you belong to Active Directory and want to add and change users for the domain, you would need to get into the AD Users utility. This can be done by going into Administrative Tools in the Programs menu. Figure 7-25 shows some of the utilities in the Administrative Tools menu, including the Active Directory Users and Computers utility.

Figure 7-25
The
Administrative
Tools folder

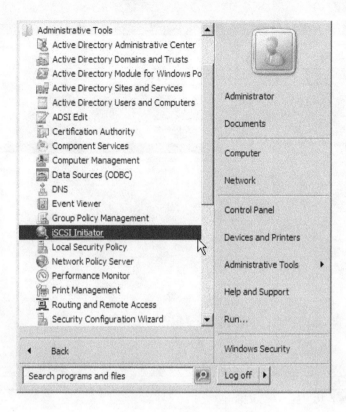

The Active Directory Users and Computers utility is provided on Windows servers. If you were on a normal Windows desktop system, you would manage your users by going to the Control Panel and accessing the set of Administrative Tools that give you utilities like Services, which enables you to look at the different services running. You can also look at the services by clicking Manage in the context menu on My Computer or This PC, depending on the version of Windows you are running. Computer Management is a Microsoft Management Console snap-in that gives you access to utilities like Services, Event Log, and Logical Disk Manager. Many of these are also available through the Administrative Tools menu.

Auditing

Auditing is important as a detective mechanism in order to determine when access is being requested to unauthorized users. This can be an indication that there is an attempt to break into a system. Windows provides ways to enable auditing so that specific system events can be monitored and alerted on in case something happens. In Windows, you can generate events based on the success or failure of a particular action. Figure 7-26 shows the different areas where you can generate auditing events. These settings can be managed through the Local Security Policy utility.

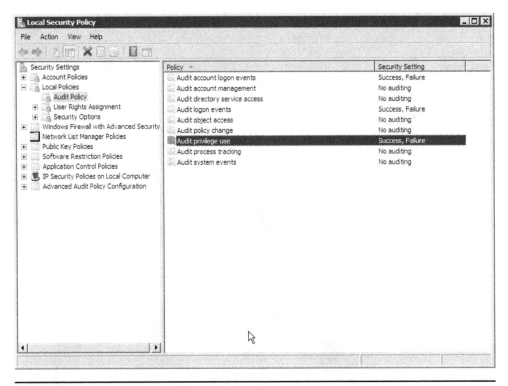

Figure 7-26 Setting auditing

Having an auditing policy can help in the system administration and maintenance of systems. If you were to audit logon failures, you might catch someone trying to gain unauthorized access to a system, and you might also get some indication as to how effective your password policy is. A large number of failures for average users, particularly right after they have had to change their passwords, might lead them to create their own memory aids, like writing their passwords on Post-it Notes. Not a good thing. If users are having difficulty remembering passwords, you can discover that by auditing logon failures. Similarly, if you were to audit object access failures, it may provide indications that different users may not be in the right groups. A user who should belong to a particular role may attempt to access a directory or file and get rejected. That rejection would show up in the audit log if you had the audit policy set appropriately.

 EXAM TIP Auditing is enabled through the Local Security Policy or Group Policy Editors.

With Windows Server 2008 and Windows 7, Microsoft provided 53 additional categories that could be audited. While the original, basic settings are still available under Local Policy Settings, the new settings can be found under Advanced Audit Policy Configuration. These new settings provide a much finer-grained look at what is happening on your system, giving you a look into directory services access, deeper detail on logon events, process event auditing like termination or creation, and object access. You can see the complete list of audit categories and subcategories in Table 7-1. These settings can be applied using a Group Policy Object, though the advanced settings are only available in Windows 7 and higher, so you would have to perform some filtering if you want to apply the settings to a wider range of systems or users than those still using an OS earlier than Windows 7.

Each of these subcategories can be configured to audit success, failure, or both. While you can take a look at the policies using the MMC, you can also use a command-line program to do more specific digging. The utility auditpol can check the different categories,

Audit Category	Audit Subcategory
Account Logon	Credential Validation Kerberos Authentication Service Kerberos Service Ticket Operations Other Account Logon Events
Account Management	User Account Management Computer Account Management Security Group Management Distribution Group Management Application Group Management Other Account Management Event
Detailed Tracking	Process Creation Process Termination DPAPI Activity RPC Events PNP Activity Token Right Adjustment
DS Access	Directory Service Access Directory Service Changes Directory Service Replication Detailed Directory Service Replication
Logon/Logoff	Logon Logoff Account Lockout IPSec Main Mode IPSec Quick Mode IPSec Extended Mode User/Device Claims Special Logon Network Policy Server Other Logon/Logoff Events

Table 7-1 Audit Categories and Subcategories

Audit Category	Audit Subcategory
Object Access	File System
	Registry
	Kernel Object
	SAM
	Certification Services
	Application Generated
	Handle Manipulation
	File Share
	Filtering Platform Packet Drop
	Detailed File Share
	Filtering Platform Connection
	Central Access Policy Staging
	Removable Storage
	Other Object Access Events
Policy Change	Audit Policy Change
	Authentication Policy Change
	Authorization Policy Change
	MPSSVC Rule-Level Policy Change
	Filtering Platform Policy Change
	Other Policy Change Events
Privilege Use	Sensitive Privilege Use
	Non-Sensitive Privilege Use
	Other Privilege Use Events
System	Security State Change
	Security System Extension
	System Integrity
	IPSec Driver
	Other System Events
Global Object Access Auditing	File System
	Registry

Table 7-1 Audit Categories and Subcategories (*Continued*)

list them all, and check policies for different users and other SIDs. The advantage to the auditpol utility is that it can be included in scripts to either get or set various audit policies.

User Rights

User rights are a set of capabilities a user account has that are both rights and privileges. The rights determine how a user account can interface with the system, and whether they can access a system from the network, log on locally, log on using Remote Desktop Services, or be the user account for a batch job or a service. Table 7-2 shows the set of rights a user account can have on a Windows system.

While rights determine how you can access the system, privileges determine what you can do once you are there. The rights and privileges are administered through the Local Security Policy editor. The different privileges that can be assigned are listed in Table 7-3.

Right	Description
Access this computer from the network	Allows a user to connect to the system from the network.
Allow logon through Remote Desktop Services	Allows a user to log on through Remote Desktop Services using the Remote Desktop Protocol.
Log on as a batch job	Allows a user account to log on using a batch service like the Task Scheduler service.
Log on locally	Allows a user to log on to the system in an interactive session where they would have a desktop and be able to launch programs, etc.
Log on as a service	Lets a particular user account be used to run a service.
Deny access to this computer from the network	Prevents a user from accessing the system from the network.
Deny logon locally	Prevents a user from getting an interactive session on the system.
Deny logon as a batch job	Prevents a user account from logging on using a batch service like the Task Scheduler.
Deny logon as a service	Prevents a user account from being used to run a service.
Deny logon through Remote Desktop Services	Prevents a user from logging in to a Remote Desktop session.

Table 7-2   Windows User Rights

Privilege	Description
Act as part of the operating system	Gives the user the privilege of assuming the identity of any user and, as a result, gaining access to any resources the user has rights to.
Add workstations to the domain	Gives the user the ability to add a computer to a domain, creating a machine account in the domain in the process.
Adjust memory quotas for a process	Gives the user the ability to make adjustments to the memory quotas.
Back up files and directories	Allows a user to get around file and directory permissions in order to perform a backup.
Bypass traverse checking	Lets the user go through folders where they don't have permissions to get to a specific path in the filesystem or registry. The user won't be able to list any files, only pass through without rights being checked.
Change the system time	Lets the user change the time on the system's internal clock.
Create a token object	Allows the user to create an access token.

Table 7-3   Windows User Privileges

Privilege	Description
Create a pagefile	Allows the user to create or change the size of the pagefile, where virtual memory is stored.
Create global objects	Lets the user create global objects during Remote Desktop Services sessions.
Debug programs	Allows the user to attach a debugger to any process.
Enable computer and user accounts to be trusted for delegation	Allows the user to make a change to the Trusted for Delegation setting on a user or computer object in Active Directory.
Force shutdown from a remote system	Allows a user to shut down a computer from a remote system on the network.
Generate security audits	Allows a process to create audit messages in the security log.
Impersonate a client after authentication	Allows a program running as a user to impersonate a client. It can be used, if required, to prevent an unauthorized user from convincing a client to connect to a service they have created. This can protect against privilege escalation.
Increase scheduling priority	Allows a user to increase the priority of a process, which may get it more processing time.
Load and unload device drivers	Lets a user load and unload device drivers.
Lock pages in memory	Permits a user to ensure that pages of memory are locked into physical memory and not allowed to swap out to disk.
Manage auditing and security log	Allows a user to manage the auditing and security log.
Modify firmware environment values	Lets a user modify system environment values either by a process through an API or by a user using System Properties.
Perform volume maintenance tasks	Allows a non-administrative user to manage volumes or disks.
Profile single process	Lets a user check the performance of a process.
Profile system performance	Lets a user check the performance of system processes.
Remove computer from docking station	Allows a user who has a portable system to eject that system from a docking station.
Replace a process-level token	Allows a parent process to replace the access token associated with a child process.
Shut down the system	Lets a user shut down the system.
Synchronize directory service data	Allows a user to read all the objects and properties in the directory, no matter what the protections are. This then permits LDAP synchronization.
Take ownership of files or other objects	Allows a user to take ownership of any file or object, including Active Directory objects.

Table 7-3 Windows User Privileges (*Continued*)

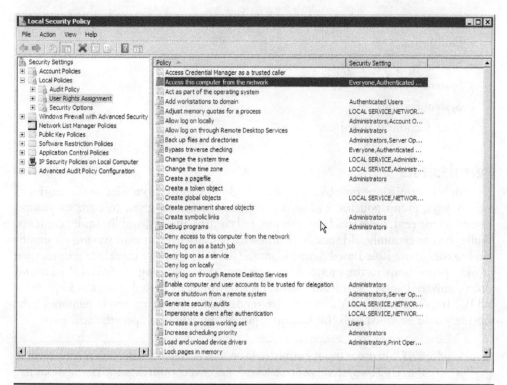

Figure 7-27   The Local Security Policy editor window

Figure 7-27 shows the Local Security Policy editor window. While the rights and privileges are not broken out into separate categories, with both falling under the category User Rights Assignment, the icons for each specific setting are different based on whether it's a right or a privilege. The Local Security Policy editor also permits the editing of different security options on each system. These settings are broken up into the following categories:

- Accounts
- Audit
- DCOM
- Devices
- Domain Controller
- Domain Member
- Interactive Logon
- Microsoft Network Client
- Microsoft Network Server
- Network Access
- Network Security

- Recovery Console
- Shutdown
- System Cryptography
- System Objects
- System Settings
- User Account Control

Permissions

You can set permissions on objects in the Windows system, from files to directories to registry keys, group policies, and so on. Permissions can be given to users or groups. These include read, write, read and execute, full control, modify, and list folder contents. While you can certainly add specific permissions to every user on your system, it's significantly easier to use Role-Based Access Control (RBAC) and place users into groups, then provide permissions to the group. Microsoft recommends using an AGULP (account, global, universal, local, permission), which is a way of using nested groups to implement RBAC. Implementing RBAC in a native-mode Active Directory implementation, the scheme would be called AGDLP (account, global, domain local, permission).

NOTE In order to set permissions on files and directories, you must be using the NTFS filesystem, which allows for access control lists and permissions as described here.

The way this scheme works is that accounts (A) get assigned to global groups (G) that represent a role in the organization based on a specific business need. The global groups would then belong to domain local groups (DL) that would have permissions assigned to them. In Figure 7-28, you can see where a set of permissions is assigned to a group rather than an individual. The advantage to adding users to global groups and then adding those groups into domain local groups is that global groups can contain users and global groups from the same domain, and then those groups are accessible across all domains. This lets you assign the global groups into domain local groups where you can assign permissions. This permits you to more easily assign permissions to users and roles from other domains in your organization.

EXAM TIP In the AGULP model, permissions should only be assigned to local groups.

Registry

The system registry is where system configuration settings are stored. Prior to the registry, settings were stored in a text-based format in .INI files. The registry introduced a standardized format for data storage in a binary format since binary processing tends to be faster than text processing. The registry is represented in a hierarchical format, much

Figure 7-28
Permissions on
a folder

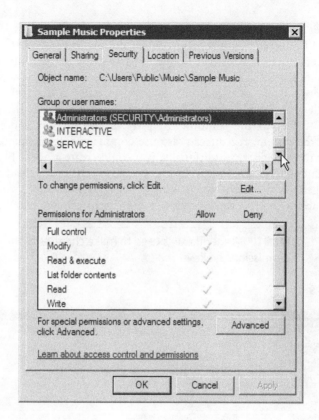

like Active Directory. The registry supports a number of predefined data types, including string, binary, double word, and multistring. Each of these data types can be stored as values inside one of the keys, which are containers for the values. The registry has up to seven root keys that have been defined by Microsoft:

- HKEY_LOCAL_MACHINE (HKLM)
- HKEY_CLASSES_ROOT (HKCR)
- HKEY_CURRENT_USER (HKCU)
- HKEY_USERS (HKU)
- HKEY_CURRENT_CONFIG (HKCC)   This key is only available in Windows 9x/ME and NT-based versions.
- HKEY_PERFORMANCE_DATA   This key is only available in NT-based versions, but it's invisible in the registry editor.
- HKEY_DYN_DATA   This key is only available in Windows 9x/ME.

In addition to different parameters for the operating system and applications, the registry also contains the users and passwords for the system. This information is stored in the Security Accounts Manager (SAM) under HKLM. The SAM stores the user identifier in the domain or local system, a cryptographic hash of the user's password, and the location of their user registry hive, among other details. Normal users wouldn't see any entries in the SAM if they looked at the registry. Only administrators can see SAM details.

Windows comes with a utility to perform edits to the registry. The registry editor is regedit and provides a graphical interface for looking at the details of the registry. Figure 7-29 shows the Windows Registry Editor window and all the root keys available on the system. regedit can also use command-line parameters to perform specific changes to the registry. Additionally, you could create a .REG file with a list of changes you intended to make, and could use regedit to read the file and execute all the changes in it. regedit is also useful for making changes to permissions settings since the registry has the ability to set permissions for reading, writing, and changing the data stored in it.

 EXAM TIP regedit.exe is used to make changes to the registry, as well as set permissions on keys.

Figure 7-29 The Windows Registry Editor window

PowerShell

Windows introduced a scripting language to replace the old DOS batch language in late 2006, called PowerShell. As previously covered in this chapter, PowerShell is not only a scripting language but also a command-line interface. Underneath PowerShell is .NET, and the "library" functionality is in functions called cmdlets that are special .NET classes. PowerShell invokes the .NET runtime and instantiates the classes. These cmdlets follow a verb-noun naming convention and provide a lot of functionality. Each successive version of PowerShell has increased the number of cmdlets available in the language. In Windows 10, running version 5.1, there are 544 cmdlets available.

In lieu of a GUI, PowerShell can be used to manage Windows systems and servers. As an example, you can use Install-WindowsFeature to add additional features to a Windows system. This doesn't have to be run on the system where you want the feature installed. You can add the -computername parameter and specify the computer you want to install the feature to. If necessary, you can also add -Restart to make sure the system restarts when the installation is complete. Similarly, you can use Uninstall-WindowsFeature to remove features from a Windows system.

One feature of the command line in PowerShell that was missing with the command processor is the ability to pipe the output of one function to the input of another function. This PowerShell feature uses the same character, |, as the Unix command line and it generally works the same way. Output from one command may not necessarily be digestible by the input of another. As an example, in order to get the number of cmdlets installed on a fully up-to-date Windows 10 system running PowerShell 5.1, the following command line was necessary:

```
get-command | out-string -stream | select-string -pattern "^Cmdlet*" |
Measure-Object -Line
```

In a Unix command line, the get-command output would just be piped into select-string (the PowerShell version of grep in Unix). However, in order for select-string to work, the output of get-command needed to be processed through out-string -stream. This string of commands gets the full list of commands PowerShell knows about and then looks for the string Cmdlet at the beginning of each line. This is necessary because there are other command types in PowerShell. Finally, the Measure-Object -Line counts the number of lines in the output.

You can also manage users, permissions, roles, and other administrative functions using PowerShell. It comes installed on Windows Server 2016 and 2019. If you are managing a Windows server without a graphical interface, you will need to use PowerShell. With PowerShell Core 6.0, you can run PowerShell on Linux and macOS exactly as it runs on Windows. Microsoft has made PowerShell open source and cross-platform.

PowerShell not only has become powerful but also has become ubiquitous, meaning it is installed by default on all modern installations of Windows. This makes it an attractive language to be used by attackers. It's becoming more common for attackers to "live off the land," meaning they make use of the tools they find. Linux systems typically have Python. Windows has PowerShell. There is no need to install additional binaries when you can use what's already on the system. The attacker just needs to create scripts or load them onto the system. There are policies that can protect against unsigned scripts from being run, but this is a restriction that can be overridden with administrative control of the system.

Since attackers may use PowerShell, it's essential to keep an eye on what is happening with scripts that are being executed. You can enable logging for PowerShell, which would allow you to generate alerts based on unexpected behavior. This logging can be enabled through the use of a group policy. Under Administrative Templates/Windows Components, Windows PowerShell, you will find logging for modules, script blocking, script execution, and PowerShell transcription. Once you are logging these activities, you can create alerts based on them with the right log management infrastructure.

Windows Security

Keeping up to date with the latest fixes in a world where a large number of people and organizations are constantly looking for the latest vulnerabilities and exploits can be challenging. Microsoft has had a Windows Update service since Windows 95, providing a website where people could check on updates for their system. Early on, the Windows Update service checked for updates to the operating system, but over time other Microsoft products like Office were given the ability to provide updates through the same infrastructure.

Back in 2002, Bill Gates announced the Trustworthy Computing Initiative to address issues in the software development life cycle at Microsoft and hopefully get ahead of the many bugs and vulnerabilities being found in their operating systems and applications. While this effort was generally considered highly successful, it hasn't eliminated all the bugs and vulnerabilities. Considering the complexity of Windows and associated applications, it wouldn't be possible to find and remove all the bugs. As a result, Microsoft has implemented a process for the regular deployment of updates to their operating systems and applications.

One aspect of security that can be easily overlooked is that of availability—and specifically, recovering from a lack of availability. Performing regular backups to your system is critical, but in these days of multi-terabyte drives or larger, backing up such an extraordinary amount of data can seem daunting. Keeping your system protected with a good set of policies can help with that, and using security templates helps keep things consistent across your organization. Also, securing your Windows services will aid in keeping intruders out.

EFS and BitLocker

Windows has had the ability to encrypt drives on their system since version 3.0 of NTFS in Windows 2000. This ability, called Encrypting File System (EFS), was a feature introduced to NTFS with that operating system release. EFS transparently provides filesystem-level encryption as opposed to drive- or volume-level encryption, which other encryption mechanisms might provide. Some of the settings for EFS can be pushed to systems using a Group Policy Object, though the initialization has to be done at the system in order to generate the keys and initiate the encryption. EFS makes use of a symmetric key, called the File Encrypting Key (FEK), to encrypt and decrypt the files. It uses a symmetric key because of the speed it offers, compared with an asymmetric key, though an asymmetric key is used to encrypt the FEK. The public key associated with the user is the key used to encrypt the FEK, meaning it requires a specific user account to decrypt files the user encrypted.

BitLocker, on the other hand, is a full disk encryption solution that has been offered since Windows Vista with the Ultimate or Enterprise editions and now with Windows 10, the Pro or Enterprise editions. BitLocker makes use of the Trusted Platform Module (TPM) installed on many modern systems. The TPM stores the key used to encrypt and decrypt the hard drive. Since the key is stored in hardware, there is no need to keep a portion of the hard drive unencrypted in order to read the key before decrypting the remainder of the hard drive. The process of accessing the key and accessing the drive, including encrypting for writing and decrypting for reading, is entirely transparent to the user, aside from needing to authenticate to the hardware before the operating system starts up. BitLocker, by default, uses AES encryption with a 128-bit key, although it can be configured to use a 256-bit key. BitLocker differs from EFS in that it offers full disk encryption, which would be in place before the operating system starts up. EFS, on the other hand, is in place to encrypt specific files and folders and not the entire hard drive.

Updates and Hotfixes

Hotfixes and updates apply to individual applications or systems. While Microsoft previously called any patch that was released outside of a service pack a hotfix, they have since started calling everything an update. Updates are deployed through the Windows Update Service, which started in Windows 95, though it has seen a number of changes since then. Initially, you had to check the Windows update server for new updates. Microsoft released the Critical Update Notification tool shortly after releasing Windows 98, which provided a way to regularly check for critical updates in the background without someone having to specifically go to the Windows update server. With Windows Me, Microsoft replaced the notification tool with Automatic Updates, replacing the notification with the ability to just automatically download updates after prompting the user that they were available.

 NOTE In Windows XP, Microsoft introduced the Background Intelligent Transfer Service, letting updates be downloaded in the background. The service is also able to throttle its own bandwidth as necessary to avoid impacting user activities.

Rather than just releasing hotfixes or updates as they had them available, Microsoft decided to make life easier on system administrators, as well as themselves, and have one day every month where they release all of the updates they have available, regardless of their criticality. This is colloquially called Patch Tuesday and happens on the second Tuesday of every month. Other software vendors have followed suit by either releasing their available patches on the same day or picking another day of the month to release their updates. Infrequently, Microsoft will issue a fix outside of the Patch Tuesday date for extremely critical issues, but it's very rare. One thing a regular schedule helps with is ensuring that Microsoft has the time to appropriately run their fixes through quality assurance (QA) testing before releasing them, so as to be certain that the issue is fixed and that other issues aren't introduced. Windows does provide different settings for applying patches. The default is to apply them automatically, as shown in Figure 7-30.

 EXAM TIP The Windows Update server uses an ActiveX control in your browser to scan your system to determine if you have any patches that need to be installed on your system. Windows 10 does not use the Windows Update website. All updates are checked through the Control Panel.

While Microsoft performs QA tests on their patches, they can't possibly check against every piece of third-party software in the world that runs on their systems, and there are times when an update from Microsoft has caused another application to break. Because of this, it's worth performing testing for all patches on a lab or test system before deploying the updates to production. You can check updates from Microsoft and determine which ones are important to you, and then make use of Windows Servers Update Services

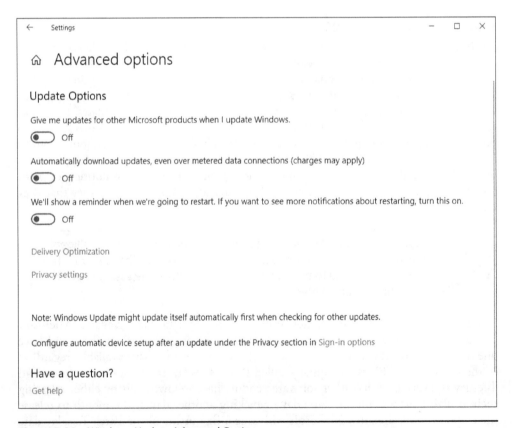

Figure 7-30 Windows Update Advanced Options

(WSUS) to deploy the updates to the systems in your network. Rather than using the Windows Update server, you would have all of the desktops in your network check your WSUS server and update from there. This can go a long way toward reducing outages caused by conflicts between a Windows update and a piece of third-party software.

Service Packs

Service packs are generally a roll-up of all the hotfixes and updates that have occurred since the last release or service pack. A service pack that only included updates since the last service pack would be considered incremental. With an incremental service pack, you would have to apply service pack 1 before applying service pack 2 since the fixes in service pack 1 would not be in service pack 2 and sometimes there would be dependencies. Not all service packs are incremental, however. Many of them are cumulative, meaning that all fixes since the major release are included. If there have been two previous service packs, all of the fixes from those service packs would be included in the third service pack.

Service packs, like updates, are delivered by the Windows Update mechanism. Sometimes, in addition to updates and fixes, a service pack may introduce entirely new features. One example of this is Windows XP, Service Pack 2 (SP 2), which introduced significant functionality. In addition to the updates, SP 2 included significant updates to the firewall and added some Bluetooth support, a pop-up blocker for Internet Explorer, and WPA encryption capability for Wi-Fi, among other enhancements. This resulted from Microsoft's increased focus on security, which led to the determination that, rather than waiting for the next release of Windows, Windows XP needed these enhancements more quickly.

Backups

It goes without saying that backing up your systems is very important to protect against the loss of critical data. Recognizing the importance of file backups, Microsoft released NTBackup in Windows NT in 1997, where systems could back up to tape using the Microsoft Tape Format (MTF). The Windows NT line continued to have NTBackup until Windows 2003, including Windows XP and Windows 2000. NTBackup supported backing up the System State data, as well as alternate data streams, permissions, the Windows registry, boot files, Exchange Server data, Encrypting File System files, disk quota information, and a variety of other critical system information. With domain controllers, NTBackup could back up Active Directory.

NTBackup was replaced with Windows Backup and Restore, starting with Windows Vista, and Windows Server Backup for the server operating systems, beginning with Windows 2008. Figure 7-31 shows the Windows Server Backup wizard, starting a backup schedule. These more recent backup utilities no longer support tape backups. In order to back up to tape, you need a third-party application to perform tape backups. The new utilities support backing up to optical media, external hard drives, and disk images like the Virtual Hard Disk (VHD) file format. Windows Server Backup now requires a Windows server with a backup role added to be able to back up to. A Windows server cannot back up to a local disk. It needs a backup server to back up to.

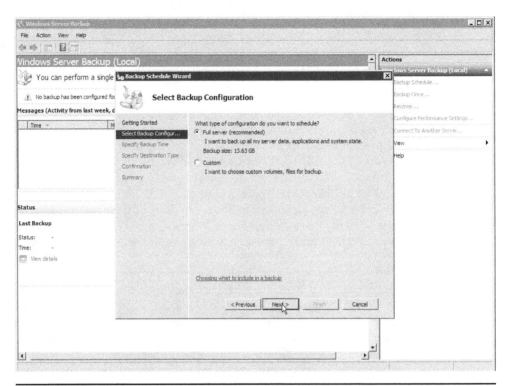

Figure 7-31   The Windows Server Backup wizard

There are a few different strategies you can use to perform a system backup. The first would be to perform a full backup every time you backed up your system. This reduces the amount of time and effort required to restore the system, but a great deal of space is needed to store the backups. Another strategy is to perform a differential backup. Using differential backups, you would perform a full backup once, and then subsequent backups until the next full backup, which would include everything that changed since the last full backup. This means you get one large backup of all of your data the first night. The second night, you would back up all of the data that had changed since the night before. The third night, you would get all of the data that changed on the second day, as well as the third day. As a result, every night's differential backup would get larger than the night before. Again, this takes up storage space, but it can be much easier to do a restore.

Another strategy is an incremental backup. Again, you perform one full backup, probably once a week. Every subsequent backup after that would include only files and data that had changed that day. If you did your full backup Sunday night, on Monday night you would back up the data that had changed on Monday. Tuesday night you would back up the data that changed on Tuesday, and so on. While this reduces the amount of storage space required to back up the data, it does take quite a bit of time to do a full restore. If you had a catastrophic failure on Friday, you would have to restore the full backup from Sunday, and once that was done, you'd have to restore Monday, Tuesday, Wednesday, and Thursday nights' backups because each day has data that has changed since Sunday's full backup, and you can't guarantee that a subsequent update has a newer version of data that changed on an earlier day.

Security Templates

Security templates are good ways of providing protection for the systems on your network. A security template is a stored Group Policy Object with a lot of preconfigured settings that you might want stored for a particular circumstance. Your template might have settings for the following categories:

- Software Settings
- Windows Settings
- Administrative Templates
- Control Panel Settings

Windows comes with some predefined security templates. These templates could be applied to systems where they might be beneficial and would have a generic set of policies and settings that could be used quickly and easily. They could also be used as the starting point for a more specific GPO that would be specifically applicable to your organization. Microsoft provides the following templates, though their availability depends on the operating system you have installed. They can be found, typically, at C:\Windows\Security\Templates.

- **Default Security (Setup Security.inf)**   This is created at the time of the installation of the operating system and contains all of the settings applied during the installation. Microsoft recommends against applying this template using group policy because it could degrade performance.

- **Domain Controller Default Security (DC Security.inf)**   This policy is created when a server is promoted to a domain controller. It is the set of default settings created at that time. It can be reapplied, but it may overwrite permissions on files and registry keys. This may not be what you want and could cause performance and availability issues.

- **Compatible (Compatws.inf)**   This is a set of changes that would be consistent with the requirements for software that does not adhere to the Windows Logo program for software. This also removes all users from the Power Users group.

- **Secure (Secure*.inf)**   This template applies a number of security settings that are least likely to impact application compatibility. It also makes a number of changes regarding the use of NTLMv2 by default.

- **Highly Secure (hisec*.inf)**   This template is a superset of secure templates and includes additional security measures like restrictions on the levels of encryption and signing required for authentication.

- **System Root Security (Rootsec.inf)**   This template has permissions for the root of the system drive.
- **No Terminal Server User SID (notssid.inf)**   This template would be used to remove unnecessary Terminal Services SIDs on a system that wasn't using Terminal Server.
- **Internet Explorer (ieacls.inf)**   This allows you to audit Internet Explorer use.

Securing Windows Services

Windows Services are background processes that typically start when the system starts up, though they may be set to start up manually. This might mean that another process will start it up as it needs to in order to perform a specific function. In Figure 7-32, you can see the Properties dialog box for the Background Intelligent Transfer Service, which is set to start up automatically, but delayed. Services are attached to users, and this service, like many others provided by Windows, is running as Local System. Each service must have a user it launches under in order to provide it with specific rights and privileges. One of the major concerns with Windows services is that the user account a service runs on may have too many permissions. If a service is compromised, the attacker inherits the rights and privileges, and if the account has too many privileges and permissions, the attacker can more easily perform functions like adding users or creating backdoors.

Figure 7-32
Windows services

Aside from ensuring that services aren't running with too many privileges, it's useful to shut off services that aren't necessary. Microsoft has been much better about that over the last decade by disabling many services by default. There is still work to do, however. Many services that aren't necessary are still enabled by default because they are part of the generic set that gets installed so that Windows works well for the widest range of users. These should be disabled. In the case of the server operating system, Windows Server comes with almost nothing installed. As noted earlier, since Windows Server 2016, you can even forego the desktop when you do a server install. Services only get added as roles and functions are added to the system, and that gets done with the full consent of an administrative user. In the case of desktop operating systems, however, a basic set of functionality gets installed whether some of the services are needed or not.

One thing to keep in mind about services is that they are exactly as the name suggests: they are there to provide a service to a user or another application, whether it's a networked service or a local one. They aren't applications that might have no communication with other applications. Since they exist solely to provide services, and therefore likely need to communicate, they put the system at risk. Any service that is running can have vulnerabilities. Because of that, disabling as many services as possible will provide some additional protection to the system since one avenue of attack will have been removed.

As you can see from Figure 7-32, there is a setting for Startup type. This setting can have the values of Automatic, Manual, or Disabled. If the service was set to start up manually, it could still be started. The best way to keep a service off is to set the Startup type to Disabled. It may also be worth considering service recovery for those services you want to have installed, particularly those that are critical. Windows services generally have some basic configuration. Usually, the first action of the three that are allowed for each service is Restart Service. The other possibilities are Take No Action, Run a Program, or Restart the System. Depending on how critical the service is, you may need or want to restart the system if a couple of attempts at service restart don't work. Alternatively, you may want to run a program that can take some additional corrective action.

Securing Windows Services

Windows has a lot of services that it exposes to the outside world, though Microsoft has made a significant effort to restrict the number of listening services enabled by default over the years. However, the Windows Server line exists to offer services, and as a result there are commonly ports open on Windows Server and the applications behind those ports. As with any network service, it's important to ensure those services are protected as much as possible using a defense-in-depth strategy where possible. Common services you'll see running on a Windows system are Internet Information Services (IIS), Microsoft SQL Server (MSSQL), and often Terminal Services.

IIS

IIS is one of the most exposed services that Windows offers because web servers are such a common service to offer. In addition to being common, a web server is more likely to be exposed through the firewall than other services, which may only be exposed within a corporate network or be even more tightly restricted. Because of this level of exposure, it's important (to state it mildly) to make sure you lock down your IIS installation. As with any piece of software, and particularly those exposed to a large group of users the way a web server is, it's important to keep up to date with service packs and fixes. Even though IIS may not have any current known vulnerabilities in the version you have installed, there may well be unknown vulnerabilities with exploits that could put you at significant risk. Additionally, new vulnerabilities and bugs are discovered on a regular basis. So, step one to ensuring you have a better-secured IIS installation is to get your update process in place.

You should also ensure that the content you are exposing through IIS is on a partition that uses NTFS as the file system. Unlike other file systems that Windows supports, NTFS has support for permissions. You will want to create permissions that only allow limited access to the files and directories being used by the web server. Microsoft creates a built-in user, named IUSR_<computername>, to be used by all users who don't authenticate against the web server. Most commonly, this would be the majority of accesses to your web server. In order to serve up web pages to these unauthenticated, anonymous users, the IUSR account has to have read privileges to the files. Adding any additional permissions to the IUSR account can be dangerous.

EXAM TIP The IUSR_<computername> account is used by anonymous users, those who have not logged in, to gain access to resources like files served up as web pages.

Microsoft also has a couple of utilities that can be used to better lock down IIS. The first is called IIS Lockdown. It's a wizard that will remove unnecessary functionality from your IIS installation, including disabling features like the FTP or NNTP servers if they are not being used. It will also check for script types you want to disable and any virtual servers you want to remove that may have been installed. The entire configuration for IIS is stored inside something called a metabase. This is an internal, hierarchical database IIS uses for all of the configuration settings. The metabase consists of two files that are stored in XML format in the Windows system directory tree. The IIS Lockdown utility creates a backup of the metabase before making changes, should you choose to roll back to settings prior to the tool being run.

NOTE The central metabase was removed in IIS 7 in favor of easy-to-edit XML files called Machine.config and ApplicationHost.config.

IIS Lockdown also runs another utility called URLScan, which provides a number of Internet Server Application Programming Interface (ISAPI) filters that protect both IIS and your web applications from malicious traffic. URLScan can prevent particular requests from being accepted by the web server. For example, a number of verbs are supported within HTTP that allow for the manipulation of content on the server—for example, PROPFIND, MKCOL, COPY, and MOVE. In order to keep these extensions from being used against your system to make changes you don't expect, use URLScan to block them. URLScan can also remove particular header fields you don't want to serve up, like the version of the web server you are running, commonly thought to provide information about avenues of attack for an attacker since the version number can be used to search for known vulnerabilities and exploits.

SQL Server

Microsoft has a number of recommendations for securing a SQL Server installation. Those recommendations fall into four categories: platform, authentication, objects, and applications that access the database.

The platform (physical system and operating system) should be addressed, as with other network-facing servers, by hardening it to remove any unnecessary software and services. It should also be kept up to date with the latest patches. Additionally, making use of a firewall, including Windows Firewall, is a good practice that will help restrict access to the system from unauthorized locations.

Use the appropriate authentication based on your needs, whether it's Windows authentication, SQL Server authentication, or a mix of the two. Only provide access to those who need it and only the access they need. This principle of least privilege is common and should also be used on a SQL Server installation. Additionally, make sure the sa (system administrator) account has a strong password associated with it; a common attack against SQL Servers is to go after the sa account since many installations have had blank or easily guessable passwords.

Objects are database components like databases and tables. As noted earlier, you should ensure you are providing access to only those users who require it. In addition to restricting access, you may need to pay attention to the access of users directly logged in to the system. You can protect data stored in the database by encrypting it. SQL Server supports its own encryption, but you can also encrypt the data inside of your application before storing it to SQL Server.

Applications are consumers of the data in the database, and as such, they need access to the database. In order to protect the data, you should be using safe coding practices, including input validation to ensure you are not passing a query into the database that may inadvertently expose unexpected data to the end user. If you are using the database as a storage service for a web application, you need to be concerned with SQL injection attacks. One way of protecting against unexpected data is to use stored procedures. A stored procedure will provide a well-defined interface to the database without directly exposing the underlying structure and content of the database. Using this technique can protect against coding errors in the application because the SQL query is stored on the database itself where it can't be altered, and where, presumably, it has been put after extensive testing.

 NOTE A stored procedure can run as a defined user that has access to underlying data, and other users can be granted access to the stored procedure without needing to give them access to the underlying data. This provides abstraction of both the data and the permissions needed to access it.

Terminal Services

Terminal services are how you provide users with remote access to a system in Windows. You would run terminal services on a Windows server and users could connect using a client on their system, getting a desktop session on the server. The client uses the Remote Desktop Protocol (RDP) to connect to the terminal server. An advantage to providing access to users in this way is the ability to better control behavior and limit access while keeping up with all the latest operating system and application updates. You can also ensure that anti-virus is installed and up to date.

When you create a terminal server, you should make sure it's a standalone server, not a domain controller. Providing users access to a domain controller will put your domain infrastructure at risk. Since you are giving users access to this, you want to make sure nothing critical runs on it, just the user-related functions and applications. Also make certain the disks are formatted with NTFS and not another file system. This will ensure you have the ability to set Access Control Lists on all file permissions so that one user doesn't have unnecessary or unexpected permissions to the files of another user. While sharing is often a good thing, it can expose sensitive data or create the potential for data to be damaged or destroyed either accidentally or inadvertently. While we are talking about partitions, you should have a separate partition or drive altogether for user data, away from the operating system.

Your terminal server should require network authentication. This forces authentication to happen before the login screen is displayed. Early versions of the client, and even early versions of the terminal server service before Windows Server 2003 SP1, were unable to support this level of authentication. As a result, Microsoft recommends using an IPSec VPN to protect communications between a client and server from a man-in-the-middle attack. While later installations do offer protection against these sorts of attacks by supporting network authentication, providing access to the terminal server over a VPN may still be a good thing. On top of authentication, you should make sure your terminal server requires strong encryption over the communication channel.

 EXAM TIP Using a VPN to protect communications between a client and Windows terminal server will help prevent attacks and is considered a best practice.

Using group policies, you can have a lot of control over what users are capable of doing once they are on your system. This enables you to restrict what applications they are using. You may be using the terminal server to provide access to a single application, for example, and as a result, users shouldn't be able to run any other program once they are logged in. This level of control over what users can do will help protect your system.

Windows as a Service

With Windows 10, Microsoft has moved away from new releases in a traditional sense. At the moment, there will be no Windows 11, for instance. Instead, Microsoft is releasing new functionality periodically, along with the normal monthly updates. This means there are no upgrades. Instead, everything is just an update. This makes it easier for businesses to keep up with the newest releases, since managing the upgrades to new versions is challenging; it's time consuming and expensive. The objective to Windows as a Service is to reduce the fragmentation of Windows installations. If it becomes easier to keep systems up to date, they will be kept up to date. This reduces the chances that old vulnerabilities might be exploited.

Microsoft offers a choice of three channels for receiving new Windows 10 features, allowing you to choose how quickly you get new features from Microsoft. This allows you to determine how much vetting through other users new features are subjected to before you get them. If you want the features as soon as they are released to the general public, you can go with the Semi-Annual Channel. Most Windows PCs will get these updates through this channel. The only way to not get them pushed to the PC is to defer them, or to select a faster release, both of which channels we'll discuss shortly. If an organization is using Windows Server Update Services (WSUS), which is a means of controlling which updates systems in the environment get, the organization can defer updates going to endpoints. Additionally, Microsoft System Center Configuration Manager (SCCM) or Windows Update for Business provide more control over how updates are pushed to desktops and enterprise tablets.

 NOTE SCCM is used to provide full control over deployments to endpoints. Different configurations can be created, depending on the need of the user of the endpoint. SCCM and WSUS provide the ability for the business to approve updates before they are pushed to the endpoint.

Even if updates are deferred, they will eventually get pushed out to endpoints, again to ensure Windows is kept up to date on as many devices as possible to help protect more devices. Think of it as vaccinating PCs. It prevents bad diseases from spreading, even if one PC gets infected.

The Long-Term Servicing Channel (LTSC) is for mission-critical systems. These may be automated teller machines (ATMs), point-of-sale systems, or medical devices, for example—basically, any system whose outage would cause a serious problem to customers or have a major impact on the business. Devices in this channel will only get quality updates—those designed to fix serious bugs without introducing new features. The LTSC will get major updates every three to five years, which is the same time frame as Windows versions were previously released.

Finally, there is the Windows Insider Channel. This is essentially where beta releases are pushed out. Anyone getting Windows Insider releases gets features before anyone in the Semi-Annual Channel gets them. This helps Microsoft to test early builds of Windows features before they are pushed out to a much wider audience.

A good approach to using these channels is to implement tiers. Any noncritical device could be in the Windows Insider tier. This is useful, even if there are hundreds of thousands of other people around the world, because you can test your own business applications with new features before a wider group in your organization gets the updates. This would allow you to consider whether to defer the update or make configuration changes, for instance. Finally, the innermost tier would be your mission-critical devices. These devices would be in the LTSC.

Chapter Review

Microsoft Windows is an incredibly complex set of operating systems with a lot of management capabilities. The fact that they are generally so easy to use has drawn a large number of users to the platform. Because of this, and because Windows has been installed on most personal computers sold over the last couple of decades, Windows has become the predominant operating system around the world. This also has made Windows a target for those interested in finding vulnerabilities and writing exploits. Microsoft introduced the Trustworthy Computing Initiative in 2002, but systems as complex as Microsoft Windows, with as many third-party developers and users as it has, will always have the potential for vulnerabilities. Due to this, Microsoft has developed a life cycle of security through the planning and development processes that extends all the way to getting updates in the hands of users as quickly as possible.

Microsoft provides a large number of administrative capabilities, and in the last few releases of Windows, they have made it much easier to script those capabilities via Windows PowerShell, which uses the .NET Framework to provide extensive management and instrumentation functionalities. PowerShell is very good at giving system administrators programmatic access to nearly every aspect of management and configuration on the system.

Active Directory is the heart of a Windows network when it has a server infrastructure. Active Directory is an implementation of LDAP, providing a place to store a large amount of data about users and other resources on the network. One other thing Active Directory provides is the ability to store and push out Group Policy Objects to provide a consistent system configuration across all the Windows clients on the network. It also lets you install new software and restrict the types of applications used on a system (it could disable Solitaire, for example).

PowerShell is a scripting language that provides powerful functionality for managing systems. If you have a system where you don't have access to a GUI, PowerShell can be used to manage it. It uses cmdlets, which are special .NET classes. There are currently 544 cmdlets in PowerShell 5.1. The current version of PowerShell that is available as of this writing is PowerShell Core 6.0. This is a cross-platform implementation of PowerShell that will run on macOS and Linux in addition to Windows.

Windows as a Service is an attempt by Microsoft to reduce the fragmentation of deployed Windows systems. Since most PCs will be in the Semi-Annual Channel, they will get updates semi-annually. This means new features and all quality improvements are pushed automatically to devices. The Windows Insider Channel is used by people who want to get a look at features before the rest of the world does, or the rest of the organization. The Long-Term Stability Channel is used for mission-critical devices. Only quality improvements are pushed out regularly. Every three to five years, a new set of features will get pushed to devices in this channel.

Windows Update will take care of home users and run automatically. In a business environment, Windows Update for Business will provide the same set of functionalities. The Microsoft System Center Configuration Manager (SCCM) provides the means for updates to be controlled to endpoints with different configurations. Also, Windows System Update Services (WSUS) is like hosting your own Windows Update server inside the organization. It also provides the means to control updates, delaying ones you wouldn't want endpoints to get for stability or compatibility concerns.

Questions

1. What does Microsoft Windows Update use to check your system for updates?

    A. JavaScript

    B. VBScript

    C. An embedded Java applet

    D. An ActiveX control

2. Which of the following might cause a tracert to fail?

    A. A router dropping ICMP messages

    B. A firewall dropping UDP messages

    C. A router dropping TCP messages

    D. A router dropping ARP messages

3. You want to write a batch file that makes changes to the Windows registry. Which command would you call to make those changes?

    A. cmdreg.exe

    B. regcfg.exe

    C. regedit.exe

    D. regedit.bat

4. Windows Firewall logs are stored in what format?

    A. W3C Extended log format

    B. Windows Firewall log format

    C. IIS log format

    D. Raw text format

5. You are writing a backup plan. Your goal is to try to ensure you have speed to recovery, but also to reduce the amount of storage space needed for the backups as much as possible. Which backup scheme would you choose?

    A. Full backups nightly

    B. Full backups weekly; differential backup nightly afterward

    C. Full backups weekly; incremental backup nightly afterward

    D. Differential backups nightly

6. If you want to enable auditing on the systems on your network, how would you do it?

    A. Use the Security Manager snap-in.

    B. Use the Audit Logging snap-in.

    C. Use the Audit Logging tool.

    D. Use the Group Policy Editor.

7. You have a set of users you want to assign some permissions to. What does Microsoft recommend you do to accomplish this?

   A. Create a global group with the users in it, and then create a domain local group and assign the permissions to the domain local group.

   B. Create a local group, and then create a global group and assign the permissions to the local group.

   C. Create a local group, and then create a global group and assign the permissions to the global group.

   D. Create a local group and assign the permissions to the local group.

8. You see a system that shows an SID of S-1-15-32-545. What do you know about that SID?

   A. It's the SID for the Administrator user.

   B. It's the SID for the Administrators group.

   C. It's the SID for the Users group.

   D. It's the SID for the Guest user.

9. You want to perform some basic filtering on your network interface but you don't want to employ the firewall. What could you do instead?

   A. Let IIS do the filtering.

   B. Establish an IPSec policy to perform the filtering.

   C. Encrypt all of the traffic.

   D. Install the Advanced Deep Packet Inspection Firewall.

10. You are trying to decide which edition of Windows 10 to install on your systems, which you then expect to connect to Active Directory on your network. Which edition does not support AD?

   A. Home Premium

   B. Professional

   C. Ultimate

   D. Enterprise

11. Which protocol is part of the base Windows operating system and enables you to remotely manage a Windows system?

   A. SSH

   B. WinRM

   C. PowerShell

   D. WinCP

12. If you need a firewall, anti-virus protection, and an overall endpoint security solution for Windows, what could you use at no cost?

    A. VirusTotal

    B. McAfee

    C. Symantec

    D. Windows Defender

13. What is BitLocker used for?

    A. Whole disk encryption

    B. Key management

    C. Key escrow

    D. Single file encryption

14. What feature would you install on a Windows server to provide endpoint VPN services that could use L2TP as an encapsulation protocol?

    A. VPN Service

    B. Remote Access

    C. L2TP Service

    D. Routing Service

15. If you want to have a GUI on your Windows Server 2016 or Windows Server 2019 installation, what feature should you install?

    A. Desktop Experience

    B. Desktop Expressions

    C. GUI Management

    D. Desktop Management

Answers

1. **D.** Windows Update uses an ActiveX control that must be installed on your system in order to check for the existence of updates. JavaScript and VBScript wouldn't have the amount of control needed, and Microsoft has a rocky history with Java, so they wouldn't use a Java applet.

2. **B.** While some versions of traceroute send UDP messages to high-numbered ports that traceroute is known to use, the Windows version of tracert performs the same function using ICMP Echo Requests. Since it's ICMP messages going out, and ICMP errors going back, a firewall or router dropping ICMP messages could cause a tracert to fail.

3. C. regedit.exe is the Registry Editor, and in addition to having a GUI mode, it can also be called from the command line to make changes, including reading in a set of registry changes stored in a .reg file. The other commands indicated don't exist.

4. A. Windows Firewall logs are stored in W3C Extended log format, enabling any tool capable of reading that format to read and parse the firewall logs. While IIS can log in an IIS-specific log file, Windows Firewall doesn't write logs in that format.

5. B. A full backup once a week followed by a differential each night provides a compromise between speed to recovery and the space required to store the backups. Full backups nightly would take a lot of disk space. Incremental backups save disk space but would be time consuming to restore since all incrementals need to be restored after the full backup is restored. A differential backup nightly has nothing to provide a differential against since there is no indication that there was a full backup at any time.

6. D. The Group Policy Editor allows you to specify a Group Policy Object with auditing enabled that could be used on all the systems on your network. None of the other tools exist.

7. A. Microsoft recommends always assigning permissions to a local group that is made up, ideally, from global groups. This is a way of employing Role-Based Access Control.

8. C. That SID belongs to the Users group.

9. B. An IPSec policy could perform some filtering of network traffic. Internet Information Services (IIS) could only do filtering if the traffic was destined for IIS. Encrypting all of the traffic doesn't perform filtering, and there is no Advanced Deep Packet Inspection Firewall.

10. A. A standard Windows Home installation does not let you join a corporate domain. All other editions are acceptable.

11. B. WinRM is a protocol that can be used for remote management of Windows systems. SSH is Secure Shell, which is an encrypted protocol used for remotely accessing systems. It is commonly found on Unix-like systems. While you can get implementations for Windows, SSH is not part of the base operating system. PowerShell can be used for remote management but it is a language and command-line environment, not a protocol. WinCP is not a protocol.

12. D. Windows Defender offers a firewall and anti-malware, as well as other security features, and is installed by default on modern Windows systems. VirusTotal is a website that will check possible malware against multiple anti-malware engines. Symantec and McAfee both provide complete endpoint solutions but they are not free.

13. **A.** BitLocker is used for whole disk encryption. You may be able to store keys in Active Directory, including recovery keys from BitLocker. It also doesn't do key management. You will get a recovery key from BitLocker in case you forget passwords, but it's up to you to manage that key. BitLocker does not do single file encryption.

14. **B.** The Remote Access feature, which used to be called Routing and Remote Access Service (RRAS), provides endpoint VPN capabilities, including the use of L2TP. None of the other answers are real services and, because of that, none of them can offer endpoint VPN capabilities.

15. **A.** Microsoft is calling the GUI on a server Desktop Experience because it ends up looking like a traditional desktop installation. None of the other answers are real things and so they are not features that could be installed.

Exercise Answers

Exercise 7-1

Your output should look something like this:

```
C:\Documents and Settings\Administrator>nbtstat -n
Local Area Connection:
Node IpAddress: [172.30.42.17] Scope Id: []
                NetBIOS Local Name Table
       Name               Type         Status
    ---------------------------------------------
       BOBBI          <00>  UNIQUE     Registered
       WASHERE        <00>  GROUP      Registered
       BOBBI          <20>  UNIQUE     Registered
       WASHERE        <1E>  GROUP      Registered

Local Area Connection 2:
Node IpAddress: [10.10.10.15] Scope Id: []


                NetBIOS Local Name Table
       Name               Type         Status
    ---------------------------------------------
       BOBBI          <00>  UNIQUE     Registered
       WASHERE        <00>  GROUP      Registered
       BOBBI          <20>  UNIQUE     Registered
       WASHERE        <1E>  GROUP      Registered
       WASHERE        <1D>  UNIQUE     Registered
       ..__MSBROWSE__.<01>  GROUP      Registered

Bluetooth Network Connection:
Node IpAddress: [0.0.0.0] Scope Id: []

    No names in cache
```

Exercise 7-2
Your file should have contents that look like this:

```
#Version: 1.5
#Software: Microsoft Windows Firewall
#Time Format: Local
#Fields: date time action protocol src-ip dst-ip src-port dst-port size tcpflags tcpsyn
tcpack tcpwin icmptype icmpcode info path

2013-04-30 19:06:18 OPEN TCP 172.30.42.17 172.30.42.51 3389 56562 - - - - - - - - - -
2013-04-30 19:06:39 DROP TCP 172.30.42.51 172.30.42.17 56575 80 64 S 2341700139 0 65535
- - - RECEIVE
2013-04-30 19:06:39 DROP TCP 172.30.42.51 172.30.42.17 56576 80 64 S 951000064 0 65535 -
- - RECEIVE
2013-04-30 19:06:39 DROP TCP 172.30.42.51 172.30.42.17 56579 80 64 S 1963738189 0 65535
- - - RECEIVE
2013-04-30 19:06:40 DROP TCP 172.30.42.51 172.30.42.17 56576 80 64 S 951000064 0 65535 -
- - RECEIVE
2013-04-30 19:06:40 DROP TCP 172.30.42.51 172.30.42.17 56575 80 64 S 2341700139 0 65535
- - - RECEIVE
2013-04-30 19:06:40 DROP TCP 172.30.42.51 172.30.42.17 56579 80 64 S 1963738189 0 65535
- - - RECEIVE
2013-04-30 19:06:41 DROP TCP 172.30.42.51 172.30.42.17 56576 80 64 S 951000064 0 65535 -
- - RECEIVE
2013-04-30 19:06:41 DROP TCP 172.30.42.51 172.30.42.17 56575 80 64 S 2341700139 0 65535
- - - RECEIVE
2013-04-30 19:06:41 DROP TCP 172.30.42.51 172.30.42.17 56579 80 64 S 1963738189 0 65535
- - - RECEIVE
2013-04-30 19:06:42 DROP TCP 172.30.42.51 172.30.42.17 56576 80 64 S 951000064 0 65535 -
- - RECEIVE
2013-04-30 19:06:42 DROP TCP 172.30.42.51 172.30.42.17 56575 80 64 S 2341700139 0 65535
- - - RECEIVE
2013-04-30 19:06:42 DROP TCP 172.30.42.51 172.30.42.17 56579 80 64 S 1963738189 0 65535
- - - RECEIVE
2013-04-30 19:06:43 DROP TCP 172.30.42.51 172.30.42.17 56576 80 64 S 951000064 0 65535 -
- - RECEIVE
```

Encryption

In this chapter, you will learn:

- Cryptography
- Cryptography algorithms and deployment
- Cryptography application

As long as people have been sharing information, there have been reasons to try to keep that information private. Let's face it: People are just not very good at keeping secrets. Because of that, we need to have ways of protecting the information we send from one person to another. Historically, it's been the military that has been a primary driver of encryption techniques. It's not your spouse you most want to keep information from, unless you have another relationship on the side, in which case you should probably be reading a different book than this. It's not your friends or your family either. It's other people, those with malicious intentions, whom you want to keep your information away from.

While the military has driven many advances in encryption, the application of these advances certainly hasn't all been for military purposes. One of the more recent advances in encryption has revolved around getting you to part with your money without you feeling unsafe in doing so. Of course, in reality you are probably just as safe passing your credit card information in the clear through the Internet as you are in handing your card off to a waitress at any restaurant.

Many of the concepts we use in cryptography today are the same as they have been for decades, if not centuries or millennia, but the fact that we now apply them to computers changes some of those realities. When you use a particular encryption cipher on a piece of paper, the realities of decrypting it are different doing it manually than having a machine perform the decryption for you. The speed achieved by having a machine handle the decryption means that the way you are doing the decryption will be more complex. In fact, computers have caused even ciphers to become outdated quickly. Encryption ciphers that worked well 30 years ago are no longer viable, and even mechanisms used a dozen years ago are at risk of becoming useless today.

Important Milestones in Cryptography History

- **Thirty-sixth century BCE**   Sumerians develop cuneiform writing and the Egyptians develop hieroglyphic writing
- **Sixteenth century BCE**   Phoenicians develop an alphabet
- **Circa 400 BCE**   First reported use of steganography
- **100 CE**   Use of ciphers like the Caesar cipher
- **Ninth century**   Cryptanalysis techniques documented by Muslim mathematician Al-Kindi
- **Fourteenth century**   Ahmad al-Qalqashandi documents cryptology and several ciphers
- **1466**   First known mechanical cipher machine developed by Leon Battista Alberti
- **1795**   Thomas Jefferson invents the Jefferson disk cipher
- **1835**   Samuel Morse develops Morse code
- **1854**   Playfair cipher developed by Charles Wheatstone
- **1855**   "Unbreakable" ciphers broken by Charles Babbage during the Crimean War
- **Circa 1915**   Statistics used in cryptanalysis by William Friedman
- **1917**   First stream cipher developed by Gilbert Verman
- **1943**   Specialized machine for cipher breaking developed at Bletchley Park in England
- **1974**   Feistel network block cipher developed by Horst Feistel
- **1976**   Data Encryption Standard (DES) published as a Federal Information Processing Standard (FIPS)
- **1977**   RSA public key encryption developed
- **1991**   Pretty Good Privacy (PGP) proposed by Phil Zimmermann
- **1994**   Secure Sockets Layer (SSL) developed by Netscape
- **1995**   Secure Hash Algorithm 1 (SHA-1) published by the NSA
- **2001**   Advanced Encryption Standard (AES) published by NIST
- **2004**   Collision attacks possible against MD5
- **2005**   Wired Equivalent Privacy (WEP) broken and demonstrated by FBI agents

Foundations

The idea behind encryption, at a very basic level, is to take plaintext, a block of information written in a way that can be plainly understood when it is observed, and convert that to cipher text, which is the plaintext after it has gone through an alteration of some sort. A very basic alteration is called a *substitution cipher*, where you simply replace one letter with another letter. Another type of alteration is called a *transposition cipher*, where the text is altered in some way. You may write it in a grid layout, or you may use an older technique where you take a strip of paper and wrap it around a stick or dowel, or perhaps a spear. Once the paper is wrapped around the spear, you write the message lengthwise down the spear. In order to read the message once it's been unwrapped, you need another spear or dowel of the same circumference. If the circumference doesn't match, the letters won't match up and you won't be able to easily read the message. If you try to simply read the message from top to bottom on the narrow strip of paper, it won't make much sense.

Converting the plaintext to cipher text makes use of an algorithm. That process, or algorithm, is typically mathematical in nature, though it may also be something as simple as using words or letters from books or newspapers and knowing which books or newspapers were used and how to look up those words and letters—this would be an algorithm, too. An algorithm can also be called a *cipher*. We'll discuss a few different ciphers in this chapter.

One type of substitution cipher has been attributed to Julius Caesar, though you may know it by a different name. It's a very simple cipher, but if you don't know the scheme used to create the cipher text, it can be just as effective as a more complex cipher. The idea behind the Caesar cipher is that it's a rotation cipher, meaning you overlay one alphabet on top of another alphabet, but one of the alphabets has been shifted, or rotated, a certain number of letters. Because of this rotation of the alphabet, the encryption is often done using a disc with two sets of letters in concentric circles, where rotating one circle will line up the letters on that circle with different letters on the other circle.

Figure 8-1 shows how a Caesar cipher would work using a simple shift of four letters. In this example, you would find the letter on the top alphabet from your plaintext to perform the encryption and use the letter underneath it for the cipher text. In order to decrypt, you do the operation in reverse by finding the letter in the cipher text on the line of letters on the bottom and then using the letter above it for the plaintext. You can think of the line of letters that looks like a regular alphabet lineup as always belonging to the plaintext, while the line of letters that appears to be arranged differently as being the

Figure 8-1
The Caesar
(rotation) cipher

ABCDEFGHIJKLMNOPQRSTUVWXYZ

WXYZABCDEFGHIJKLMNOPQRSTUV

DAGGK

cipher text. In the example in the figure, we would look up D on the bottom line and see that it corresponds to H, A corresponds to E, G to L, and K to O. From this, we can see that the encrypted word actually says HELLO.

NOTE The discussion group network USENET long used rot13 (rotating the alphabet halfway around or 13 letters) as a very simple cipher to obscure a piece of information, like the punch line to a joke or a spoiler of some sort. This way, you don't read it until you are ready to, but it's easy to decrypt.

This one example demonstrates three important principles of cryptography: plaintext, cipher text, and a key. The key, in this case, is the combination of the alphabet and the number of letters you are shifting the second alphabet by. The basic idea is that you have plaintext that is converted to cipher text through the use of a key and some mechanism, called an algorithm, to perform that transformation. You can know the cipher text and even the algorithm, but if you don't know the key, you can't get the plaintext back from the cipher text. The biggest part of cryptography is how to manage and create keys and how to do the transformation. Computational power has really changed how the key is generated, particularly in an era when the various cryptographic algorithms are generally well known. As computers become more powerful, key sizes get larger simply because smaller key sizes become easy to create in a reasonably short amount of time. For example, let's say you had a key size of 10 bits, which yields a potential 2^{10} keys or 1024. If you were able to attempt 10 keys per second, it would take 102.4 seconds, or a little under two minutes, to attempt all the keys. With CPUs as fast as we have today, we can obviously try more than 10 keys per second, which is why we need much larger key sizes.

EXAM TIP Protecting keys is the most important part of cryptography.

So far, we've been talking primarily about transposition, where one letter is replaced with another, which is how the Caesar cipher works. Another technique is a permutation cipher, where you don't replace one letter with another but instead shuffle the letters around in such a way that they can be unscrambled. In a permutation cipher, you create blocks of a particular size and then shuffle those blocks in a way that can be unshuffled, reordering the blocks so they can create the plaintext again. One advantage of this is that by creating fixed-size blocks, you don't have the word lengths easily available, which might give a malicious decrypter some idea of what words were used. This type of cryptanalysis is available to a transposition cipher.

Exercise 8-1: Key Sizes

Assuming a computer that can try 1000 keys per second, how many more hours will it take to go through all of the keys with a 256-bit key size, compared to one with a 128-bit key size?

While key size is very important, another significant factor is how you manage the keys once you have generated them. Once you have encrypted a message, you would expect someone to be able to decrypt it, but they can't decrypt it without the key. How do you go about getting the key to them so they can decrypt the message? As it turns out, this is a pretty significant problem for cryptography. Is this a key that has been previously shared between the two participants in the exchange? If so, others could potentially know the key unless it is well protected. If it is a key that is created on the fly, how do you go about getting the key to the other participant in such a way that the key is protected? If the key isn't sufficiently protected, there isn't much point in encrypting the message to begin with.

Security Principles

There are multiple reasons for implementing encryption and related concepts. The first reason is what you get out of encryption proper: confidentiality. You may think of it as privacy as well. When you encrypt data and then send it to a recipient, only you and the recipient are able to look at the plaintext, as long as the cryptosystem is well implemented and the keys are protected. Your information is confidential because only the people you want to see it can see it.

We also get some additional benefits from implementing encryption principles. When you are concerned with confidentiality, you are probably also worried about whether the right person gets the message and also, if you are the recipient, whether the person you think has sent the message is, in fact, the person who did send it. This idea of verifying identity is sometimes called non-repudiation. What non-repudiation means at a non-technical level is that if a message comes in purporting to be from you, you can't say it isn't from you. You are bound to the message. This is done by tying artifacts in the message to something only you have. This idea of non-repudiation is important.

Another reason for implementing encryption is that it provides integrity, which is one of the elements of the security triad (confidentiality, integrity, availability). It means that the message that is sent is the same as the one that is received, with no alteration. This is generally an important concept; you don't ever want to have data altered, but when you are taking data seriously enough that you feel you need to encrypt it so no one can read it unless they are authorized, you are probably especially concerned about whether it has changed. If it has, the message should be considered corrupt and potentially tampered with.

Authenticity is tied up with all of this. An authentic message or piece of data is one where we know the source and we also know that the message hasn't been tampered with. It's a real message. The source and the content can't be questioned because we have verification for it all along the way. It's much like a chain of evidence in a court case, which is important for digital forensics especially, because it's so easy to manipulate digital data. The source of the message is known and verification of the content is possible. We can verify the authenticity of the source and the message if a cryptosystem is well implemented; we will see what these sorts of cryptosystems look like in the remainder of the chapter.

Diffie-Hellman

The Diffie-Hellman key exchange was developed by two mathematicians named Whit-field Diffie and Martin Hellman in the 1970s. The idea behind Diffie-Hellman is to be able to exchange cryptographic keys in a secret manner so that only the two participants will know the keys when the exchange is complete. The two parties do not exchange keys directly but derive keys based on some shared knowledge and some secret knowledge. While it is called a key exchange algorithm, it's more of a key generation algorithm, developed in such a way that two people can derive keys from pieces of shared and random data.

NOTE The British signals intelligence agency had previously invented a key exchange mechanism just like the Diffie-Hellman process. This was done completely separately and might suggest that there is something fundamental about this particular process.

Any talk about cryptographic keys eventually covers the math involved since digital keys are derived from specific mathematical functions. Diffie-Hellman makes use of modular arithmetic in order to generate the key. Modular arithmetic is when you take the remainder from a division problem. You may see it expressed as 25 mod 3 = 1, as an example: $3 \times 8 = 24$ and $25 - 24 = 1$. In as simple terms as possible, two parties, Alice and Bob, want to communicate with one another. Initially, they select two numbers. The first is a prime number that we'll call p. The second is a number we will call n, which is a primitive root mod p. This means that a number g gets chosen that can be plugged into the following formula and the value of a in the formula is coprime to p, meaning it has no positive factors in common with p other than 1: $p^k = a \pmod{n}$. In other words, if you take the set of all integers that are coprime with p and make that set A, when you run through all values of A as a, you will be able to satisfy the preceding equation with an integer k.

So, Alice and Bob now have their two values. Figure 8-2 shows a representation of the process of creating the shared key. Alice picks a secret value that only she knows, which we'll call a. She then calculates the following value: $A = p^a \bmod n$. A is then sent to Bob. Similarly, Bob picks a secret value that we'll call b and calculates $B = p^b \bmod n$, sending B off to Alice when the calculation is complete. The key, called s, is then calculated on both sides by Alice computing $s = B^a \bmod n$ and Bob computing $s = A^b \bmod n$. They will both end up with the same value for s, and without exchanging s in any way they have computed a secret value that they can both use as a key for encrypting further communication. This does, however, require that some agreements be made ahead of time, meaning that Bob and Alice have to have been known to one another in order to get the initial numbers in common to begin with, or at least they have to have a trusted third party in common to provide those values.

NOTE Where factoring is often used in cryptographic systems, elliptic curve cryptography uses the difficulty of finding a discrete log of an elliptic curve to generate keys.

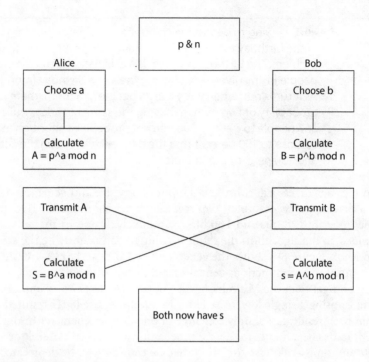

Figure 8-2
The Diffie-
Hellman process

RSA

RSA, named for the inventors Ron Rivest, Adi Shamir, and Leonard Adleman, also has a key generation component; however, the RSA algorithm specifies encryption and decryption mechanisms, while Diffie-Hellman is just used to generate keys that can be used in other encryption algorithms. RSA doesn't generate the same key to be used on both ends of the communication. Instead, it uses two separate keys that are mathematically related. One is a private key, and the second is a public key. The public key can be accessed by anyone because it is used to encrypt a message to the owner of the public key. The keys used are computed from large random prime numbers. Part of the calculation of the keys uses Euler's totient function, which counts the number of positive integers that are less than a particular number, n, while being coprime with that number, meaning that they share no common factors other than 1. Once keys are generated, the public key can easily be shared.

Digest Algorithms

A digest algorithm generates a message digest, often called a *hash*, based on the input. The idea of using a digest is that it can verify that data hasn't been tampered with, because two different chunks of data won't generate the same hash. When two different pieces of data do generate the same value, it's called a *collision*. The best algorithms are the ones that are resistant to collisions, since the ease of generating collisions reduces the value of using the algorithm to verify message integrity. These algorithms are also called *one-way functions* because there is no way to reconstruct the data that was put into the function simply based on the output from the function.

NOTE Trying to determine collisions in a digest algorithm takes advantage of the birthday attack, which is a statistical problem using the birthday problem. The birthday problem is a calculation of the probability of two people in any given room having the same birthday (month and day). As it turns out, when you have 23 people in a room, there is a 50 percent probability of two of them having the same birthday, while it takes 367 people to get to a 100 percent probability, although at 100 you are so close to 100 percent that the difference between the actual probability and 100 percent is miniscule.

A message digest algorithm takes input of any size and generates a fixed-length value from that input. As examples, two message digest algorithms, MD5 and SHA-1, return values that are 128 bits and 160 bits, respectively. It doesn't matter what length input is provided to the algorithm, the result is going to consistently be the same length for each algorithm. Figure 8-3 shows the generation of MD5 and SHA-1 hashes. Notice that the same input to both functions generates completely different output, and that the SHA-1 hash is longer than the MD5 hash. Also note in the last two examples that the difference of transposing a single lowercase letter for an uppercase letter resulted in an entirely different hash result, not simply a change of one digit or character in the hash value.

MD5 has been in use for a long time, and while it is still useful for some applications, there are some weaknesses in MD5 that are causing it to be deprecated by SHA-1. Keep in mind that having the 32 additional bits doesn't mean that you take the key space provided by MD5 and multiply it by 32. Instead, the difference is orders of magnitude higher between MD5 and SHA-1. The difference is between 2 raised to the 128th power (2^128) and 2 raised to the 160th power (2^160). This is the value of 2^128 multiplied by 2 then the result multiplied by 2, and so on, 32 times. You are doubling the value for every additional bit of hash space. This means the chances of a collision are much less likely when you are using SHA-1 over MD5.

Even SHA-1 is being slowly deprecated. Ever-increasing computing power is opening the potential for weakness in SHA-1. In fact, the National Institute of Standards and Technology (NIST) has recommended that use of SHA-1 be stopped. Instead, other implementations of SHA are being used. You may regularly find SHA-256 used today.

Figure 8-3
MD5 and SHA-1 hashes from different inputs

```
kilroy@bill:$ sha1sum
foo wubble foo
92fa3e3f5fc52b9b0f2f0a1953ee189136d9d43b  -
kilroy@bill:$ md5sum
foo wubble foo
02e49338f18ab1224f3a506fe724c490  -
kilroy@bill:$ sha1sum
This is some text I want to generate a digest from.
ab07150223cf8589687f175bbcb2d5d5b837678a  -
kilroy@bill:$ md5sum
This is some text I want to generate a digest from.
45b7ca4fd284307fa2f2b7d0092e84ea  -
kilroy@bill:$ md5sum
this is some text I want to generate a digest from.
8e953b4d7ade6f84685d2e823df5d16c  -
kilroy@bill:$ █
```

It's not computationally that much more intense, especially over short pieces of data, than SHA-1 on modern processors. It has a much larger value space, making a collision almost entirely unlikely. Additionally, the SHA algorithm has been updated twice since SHA-1. There is currently SHA-2, which supports output sizes of 224 to 512 bits. On top of that, SHA-3 has changed the internals of the algorithm as compared with SHA-1 and SHA-2. Like SHA-2, SHA-3 supports output sizes of 224 to 512 bits (224, 256, 384, 512).

Cryptographic Attacks

There are a couple of common attacks on cryptographic ciphers that are worth talking about. The first is a chosen plaintext attack. In this attack, the attacker selects the plaintexts to be encrypted, in order to inspect the resulting cipher text. An attacker may either use a batch approach, selecting all of the plaintexts to be encrypted before beginning, or use an adaptive approach, where the selection and encryption process is more interactive. In an adaptive mode, plaintexts begin to be chosen based on information that has been gained from the previous encryptions. The goal of this sort of attack is to gain information about the encryption process.

In a known-plaintext attack, both the plaintext and the cipher text are known. Using these pieces of information, an attacker may be able to determine the key that was used to generate the cipher text. Basically, this is an attempt to reverse-engineer the algorithm. This sort of attack has been used for a long time, and was employed in World War II to try to break the encryption codes that were used by the Germans. In one case, the famous computer scientist Alan Turing discovered that the German word for the number one, eins, was the most common string in the plaintext, so he ran through all possible cipher texts that could be generated by the Enigma machine, the mechanism the Germans were using to encrypt their messages. This generated a catalog of different ways that eins could be represented in the cipher text, which would reveal a portion of the plaintext from the cipher text and might help in further decrypting the remainder of the message.

A meet-in-the-middle attack is an attack against cryptographic systems that use multiple keys and functions in an attempt to strengthen their system. It may be tempting to believe that using multiple keys and functions in a crypto system will strengthen the system. A meet-in-the-middle attack uses both the cipher text and the plaintext and works backward through the functions as well as forward, meeting in the middle of the entire sequence. This attack was first developed by Diffie and Hellman in 1977.

X.509 Certificates

While encryption is an important part of cryptography, another aspect that becomes important as we discuss cryptography is the idea of identity. X.509 is a standard developed by the International Telecommunication Union (ITU). It describes the use of public key certificates for the purpose of establishing identity and managing encryption keys. This includes the definition of a certificate authority (CA). The certificate itself is an electronic document that attaches a key with an identity. The certificate carries information about the user or the system, depending on what type of certificate it is. Users can get certificates for things like encrypting and digitally signing e-mail, while servers may need a certificate in order to use Secure Sockets Layer (SSL) or Transport Layer Security (TLS) for encrypted communication with users.

A certificate is really just a data record with defined fields, some of which are required and some of which are optional. This data record includes identity information, which is certified by a CA, as well as keying information that can be used to encrypt and decrypt data. The following is a list of the fields that are stored in a certificate, while in Figure 8-4 you can see the fields and corresponding data from a real certificate.

- Certificate
  - Version
  - Serial Number
  - Algorithm ID
  - Issuer
  - Validity (date range the certificate is valid for)
  - Subject
  - Subject Public Key Info (Algorithm and Key)
  - Issuer Unique Identifier (optional)
  - Subject Unique Identifier (optional)
  - Extensions (optional)
- Certificate Signature Algorithm
- Certificate Signature

The public key info portion of the certificate includes the algorithm and the key used to create the key. The algorithm specifies which type of encryption key this certificate contains. Typically, this algorithm would be RSA, but it would normally include a hashing algorithm to ensure that the message hasn't been tampered with. Further on in this chapter, we'll get into how the key is used for encrypting messages and how those messages can be decrypted. A common extension provided with a certificate describes the usage for the certificate, since certificates are issued for specific purposes. A certificate issued for the purpose of being applied to a web server, for example, couldn't be used to digitally sign e-mail or encrypt messages, and vice versa. There are eight certificate usage values:

- **SSL Client**   A client authentication certificate.
- **SSL Server**   A certificate that can be used by servers.
- **SSL Server with Step Up**   A certificate that can be used by servers to allow strong crypto. This is a result of export restrictions on strong crypto.
- **SSL CA**   A certificate authority certificate that will allow the holder to issue certificates to clients, servers, or other intermediate CAs.

Certificate Details	
▾ Certificate Details - MyServer	
▾ Subject DN:	
Common Name	MyServer
eMail Address	server@washere.com
Organization	WasHere Consulting
Country	US
State	VT
Location	Lyndonville
▾ Issuer:	
Common Name	WasHere CA
eMail Address	certs@washere.com
Organization	WasHere Consulting
Country	US
State	VT
Location	Lyndonville
▾ Validity:	
Status	VALID
Creation Date	May 3 18:16:32 2013 GMT
Expiration Date	May 3 18:16:32 2014 GMT
▾ Key/Certificate Details:	
Status	VALID
Serial	01
Public Key Algorithm	rsaEncryption
Signature Algorithm	sha1WithRSAEncryption
▾ Fingerprints:	
Fingerprint (MD5)	7B:FD:66:8D:45:36:DD:97:1B:84:54:E2:56:F3:A3:91
Fingerprint (SHA1)	85:BA:CF:EA:14:A5:5C:56:C3:35:B2:AC:35:BA:70:65:67:30:59:49
▾ X.509v3 Extensions	
X509v3 Subject Alternative Name	email:server@washere.com
X509v3 Authority Key Identifier	keyid:AB:86:9B:F4:17:AE:56:60:07:E7:CF:76:91:74:99:26:77:B1:BB:8E
X509v3 Authority Key Identifier	DirName:/C=US/ST=VT/L=Lyndonville/O=WasHere Consulting
X509v3 Authority Key Identifier	Inc./CN=WasHere CA/emailAddress=certs@washere.com
X509v3 Authority Key Identifier	serial:80:12:05:53:03:DC:8A:BF
X509v3 Basic Constraints	CA:FALSE
X509v3 Issuer Alternative Name	email:certs@washere.com
X509v3 Subject Key Identifier	3A:8E:D6:34:4F:3A:0B:35:7B:F1:B1:37:AF:F9:39:46:DD:E1:8B:7B

OK

Figure 8-4 X.509 certificate data

- **E-mail Signer**   Used for S/MIME e-mail signatures.
- **E-mail Recipient**   Used for S/MIME encryption of e-mail messages.
- **Object Signer**   Used to sign objects like Java archives and other applications.
- **Usage Status Responder**   Used by an Online Certificate Status Protocol (OCSP) responder.
- **Verify CA**   Used by any CA.

A certificate may also have extensions that pair the user's certificate with a certificate from the CA. This would be done by adding extensions for an authority key identifier identifying the CA key, as well as a subject key identifier identifying the key belonging to the subject of the certificate, which may be a user in the case of an e-mail certificate, or it may be a server in the case of a server certificate.

Certificates are actually reasonably easy to create and just require something like the OpenSSL software, which is capable of performing encryption, generating keys, signing requests, and signing certificates. OpenSSL can also be used as the backend for a certificate authority, performing all the signing and validation work. The process for creating your own certificate is quite simple, which leads to some potential issues. These are the steps for creating your own certificate using OpenSSL:

1. Create a private key to be used for the certificate.

2. Create a certificate from the key that you just generated.

3. Create a certificate signing request (CSR) for your server.

4. Sign the certificate signing request using the key from your CA certificate.

Once you have created your certificate, you are free to install it on your system and make use of it in your e-mail or, potentially, in your browser. Since your certificate is capable of identifying you, it could be used as an authentication mechanism and you may be able to use it to log in to certain web applications that are capable of making use of the certificate. It's much easier to make use of the certificate in your e-mail applications either to digitally sign your messages or to encrypt a message to someone. Once you have used your certificate to send a message, it can be traced to you since it does perform a certain amount of authentication that it's you. Signing a message to someone using your certificate typically requires that you make use of a password to access the certificate. Because of the identity embedded in the certificate and the fact that it's on your computer and that it requires a password to install or use, there is pretty strong evidence that any message signed by your certificate must have come from you. As mentioned earlier, this is called non-repudiation—the notion that if a message is signed using your certificate using a password only you know, it must have come from you.

 EXAM TIP Non-repudiation provides the ability to keep track of who originated a particular message, and certificates can ensure that the origin of a particular communication can't be repudiated.

Since a certificate is a digital document, it can easily be copied from one place to another, which is one reason why it's important to provide further authentication using something like a password or biometrics to ensure that the owner of the certificate is the one using it. As a digital document, though, a certificate also is portable and can be used to provide authentication services in a wide variety of places. If you were to install your certificate on a card and your computer had the ability to read it off the card, you would have what's called a smartcard. That card, along with your password, could provide stronger authentication than simply a username and password since it constitutes something you have in addition to something you know. You might also have your certificate on your cell phone and be able to use your phone as a token. There are a lot of possibilities to using certificates to provide authentication of the owner.

While a certificate can be used to provide authentication, if it's just something someone provides to you, you are really taking his or her word that the digital document is valid and that it actually belongs to the person it purports to belong to. Without some additional piece of corroborating data, it's just someone's word that it's valid. There are a couple of ways to go about getting that additional corroboration. You could use a trusted third party to verify identity and swear to you that the identity is valid. You could also check with friends or friends of friends. As it turns out, both of these methods have been implemented. The first one is the previously mentioned certificate authority, which is part of a public key infrastructure (PKI). The second is an implementation of certificates using information from a wide variety of sources, called Pretty Good Privacy (PGP).

Public Key Infrastructure

We've already started talking about public key infrastructure (PKI), in a way, because we've talked about the things that actually get stored in the PKI. The important part of PKI is the word infrastructure, though. While we've been talking about certificates, which end up being managed by a PKI, we haven't talked about all of the infrastructure necessary to manage and store certificates, not to mention create them.

There are two aspects to a certificate: encryption and identity. Most people likely think of encryption when they think about certificates, and certificates certainly are great for providing encryption services, but, as discussed earlier, they are also very good for providing identity services as well. The problem is that without someone to verify that identity, you're simply taking someone's word that they are who they say they are, and while people may be generally honest, you don't want to rely on them being honest all the time. It's much like a driver's license. I can walk in when I apply for my first license and say I'm Ric Messier, but what's to prevent me from getting someone to take the test for me (back in the days when picture licenses weren't the norm that they are today)? Or, even worse, what's to prevent me from walking in and saying I'm Trevor Wood and getting a license with that name and establishing a whole new identity, perhaps based on someone else's existing identity?

So, you can see that we need a way of ensuring that people are who they say they are in some circumstances. While most of the time you are going to be dealing with people you actually know, there isn't much to prevent someone from creating a whole digital identity pretending to be that person you know unless there is an entity somewhere actually ensuring that someone is who they say they are. Because of that, it's useful to have a trusted third party that you can rely on to provide verification that an identity is accurate and true. In a PKI, this third party is a certificate authority. There are a number of well-known certificate authorities, like Verisign, Thawte, and Comodo. Any system that makes use of a CA is hierarchical in nature because any CA can issue a certificate for another CA, and that CA can then issue server or user certificates. All of the trust goes back to the CA that is at the root of the hierarchy.

NOTE X.509 is a standard that is part of X.500, a set of directory-based protocols developed by the ITU. Often, certificates are stored in a Lightweight Directory Access Protocol (LDAP) server that is based on X.500.

What is a certificate authority? A certificate authority is responsible for issuing certificates, and while we have been talking a lot about the identity of individuals, systems have need of certificates as well. Any time you go to a website like Amazon or PayPal and enter payment information, you are interacting with a certificate installed on the server that's enabling the encryption but also verifying that the server you are talking to is the correct one.

A CA takes in a certificate request, verifies the identity of the requestor, and then issues the requested certificate. The process is very similar to the one outlined earlier to create your own signed certificate. Before a CA can do anything, however, it has to have its own certificate, which is used to sign other certificates. When the CA signs a certificate, it is considered legitimate and the CA becomes part of the certificate chain, so anyone who is presented with the certificate can check with the CA to ensure it's legitimate. In order to check whether a certificate comes from a trusted CA, you need to have the certificate from the CA itself installed on your system. Typically, operating systems or individual browsers will come with a number of certificates already installed from common root CAs. Figure 8-5 shows a partial list of the root CA certificates installed on a Mac OS X system.

Name	Kind	Expires	Keychain
NetLock Arany (Class Gold) Fotanusitvany	certificate	Dec 6, 2028 10:08:21 AM	System Roots
NetLock Expressz (Class C) Tanusitvanykiado	certificate	Feb 20, 2019 9:08:11 AM	System Roots
NetLock Kozjegyzoi (Class A) Tanusitvanykiado	certificate	Feb 19, 2019 6:14:47 PM	System Roots
NetLock Minositett Kozjegyzoi (Class QA) Tanusitvanykiado	certificate	Dec 14, 2022 8:47:11 PM	System Roots
NetLock Uzleti (Class B) Tanusitvanykiado	certificate	Feb 20, 2019 9:10:22 AM	System Roots
Network Solutions Certificate Authority	certificate	Dec 31, 2029 6:59:59 PM	System Roots
OISTE WISeKey Global Root GA CA	certificate	Dec 11, 2037 11:09:51 AM	System Roots
Prefectural Association For JPKI	certificate	Dec 26, 2013 9:59:59 AM	System Roots
QuoVadis Root CA 2	certificate	Nov 24, 2031 1:23:33 PM	System Roots
QuoVadis Root CA 3	certificate	Nov 24, 2031 2:06:44 PM	System Roots
QuoVadis Root Certification Authority	certificate	Mar 17, 2021 2:33:33 PM	System Roots
RSA Security 2048 V3	certificate	Feb 22, 2026 3:39:23 PM	System Roots
Secure Certificate Services	certificate	Dec 31, 2028 6:59:59 PM	System Roots
Secure Global CA	certificate	Dec 31, 2029 2:52:06 PM	System Roots
SecureSign RootCA11	certificate	Apr 8, 2029 12:56:47 AM	System Roots
SecureTrust CA	certificate	Dec 31, 2029 2:40:55 PM	System Roots
Security Communication EV RootCA1	certificate	Jun 5, 2037 10:12:32 PM	System Roots
Security Communication RootCA1	certificate	Sep 30, 2023 12:20:49 AM	System Roots
Security Communication RootCA2	certificate	May 29, 2029 1:00:39 AM	System Roots
Sonera Class1 CA	certificate	Apr 6, 2021 6:49:13 AM	System Roots
Sonera Class2 CA	certificate	Apr 6, 2021 3:29:40 AM	System Roots
Staat der Nederlanden Root CA	certificate	Dec 16, 2015 4:15:38 AM	System Roots
Staat der Nederlanden Root CA - G2	certificate	Mar 25, 2020 7:03:10 AM	System Roots
Starfield Class 2 Certification Authority	certificate	Jun 29, 2034 1:39:16 PM	System Roots
Starfield Root Certificate Authority - G2	certificate	Dec 31, 2037 6:59:59 PM	System Roots
Starfield Services Root Certificate Authority - G2	certificate	Dec 31, 2037 6:59:59 PM	System Roots
StartCom Certification Authority	certificate	Sep 17, 2036 3:46:36 PM	System Roots
StartCom Certification Authority	certificate	Sep 17, 2036 3:46:36 PM	System Roots
Swisscom Root CA 1	certificate	Aug 18, 2025 6:06:20 PM	System Roots

Figure 8-5 List of root servers on a Mac OS X system

Once a certificate has been created, the CA stores the certificate and the key for the user. This could be done using a number of mechanisms, though it commonly is done using an LDAP server to store information about the certificate subject as well as the keys in use by the subject. Additionally, the LDAP server may store information about certificates that have been revoked. This information may be transmitted to others using a certificate revocation list (CRL). Any certificate on a CRL can no longer be trusted and should be rejected by anyone receiving data that has been signed or encrypted for that certificate. Figure 8-6 shows a piece of software called SimpleAuthority that provides CA functionality. In this case, on the right side, you can see a context menu with the Revoke Certificate function highlighted. This will add the user's certificate to the certificate revocation list. The CRL will contain a list of serial numbers for the certificates that are no longer to be trusted.

EXAM TIP In a CA-generated certificate, the digital signature is created by the CA and not by the user. In a user-generated certificate, the digital signature is generated by the user.

There are a few reasons why a certificate may be revoked, though typically it would have to do with a private key that had somehow been lost or stolen. In that case, it's possible that someone had possession of the certificate who wasn't the intended user and the certificate can no longer be trusted to prove the identity to anyone. Software that is responsible for

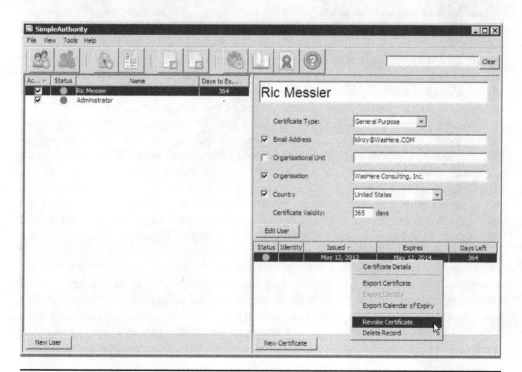

Figure 8-6 A SimpleAuthority revoking certificate

performing authentication using a certificate should be capable of obtaining and making use of a CRL, rejecting the use of a certificate on that list. One downside to using a CRL is that it may not be published and available regularly or it may be out of date on an end-point responsible for checking the validity of the certificate. Instead, the Online Certificate Status Protocol may be more beneficial because it can check the validity and status of a certificate in real time as the certificate is being presented, and instead of checking a local copy of a CRL, the check is with the CA itself.

We started out this section talking about a CA being a trusted third party, and it is, or at least it should be. One of the side effects of this is that if you trust the CA, you have implicit trust in any certificate issued by that CA. Since you have a trust relationship with the CA, you assume that any identity that has been validated by the CA must be correct. If you are in a situation where you feel you need to pick and choose the information you want to trust that originates with a particular CA, you don't really have much trust in that CA, and it might be wise to not trust anything from the CA at all.

 EXAM TIP In trusting the CA provided by company A, you implicitly trust any certificate that has been issued by the CA provided by A.

In order to trust any CA, though, you have to have a copy of the CA's certificate. While certificates from the primary CAs around the world often get installed into operating systems by default, it is possible to install a certificate from any CA that isn't already installed. Once you have installed the certificate from a CA, you automatically trust certificates that have been issued from that CA. One activity for which you will commonly use certificates on a regular basis is web browsing. As long as you have the root CA certificate installed, your browser will go about establishing secure connections with a server that has a certificate issued from that CA. If you don't happen to have the CA certificate, the browser can't verify the identity associated with the certificate with anyone and so the certificate is untrustworthy from the perspective of the browser.

When you create a self-signed certificate on your server, you have the ability to do encryption between the server and the web browser, but the web browser has no way of verifying the accuracy of the certificate and so it generates an error. You can, of course, continue on to the website and just accept the certificate as it is, assuming that the encryption is all you want and there is no one in the middle. If you are communicating with a website that you know to be trustworthy because you or someone you know generated the certificate and you are just using it in a local capacity for encryption purposes, you are safe in doing that. You can see in the dialog box in Figure 8-7 that it says it's a self-signed certificate. Behind the dialog box is the error page generated by Chrome. If you are communicating with a website that generates a certificate error but you don't know anything about the website or you believe it's a website that should have a valid certificate, it's worth looking a little more deeply into the certificate to see what CA created it and for whom it was created. X.509 isn't perfect, and sometimes there is simply a mismatch between the hostname you are communicating with and the name on the certificate, which may be okay and expected. Other times, there are legitimate reasons for concern.

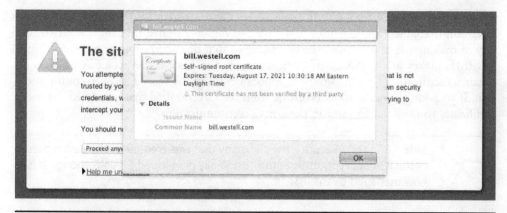

Figure 8-7 A self-signed certificate error

If a CA has been compromised, certificates generated from that CA are suspect since the CA can generate a certificate that says anything. For example, a trusted CA that has been compromised might generate a certificate saying that it's for www.amazon.com and then use a DNS attack to get people to come to a fake server that uses that certificate and purports to be Amazon. Unsuspecting users may provide personal information to a rogue server, thinking that they are communicating with the real Amazon. The certificate says it's Amazon and the lock in the browser indicates that the communication is encrypted, so the user has no good reason to believe that it's anything other than Amazon. A self-signed certificate or a certificate signed by an unknown CA would generate an error. Only a certificate from a trusted CA would pass verification checking. There have been instances of well-known and trusted CAs being compromised, including a CA that was compromised in the Netherlands in 2011; another was Verisign, which was compromised repeatedly in 2010.

If a user loses a certificate, they have lost the private key that would be used to decrypt messages to them. Key retrieval is another function that might be performed by a CA. In addition to the other information about a user, the private key may be stored at the CA. While this does keep a copy of the private key in the hands of someone other than the user it belongs to, it does provide the ability to restore a lot of critical data as long as the private keys are adequately secured at the CA to protect them from misuse. Ensuring that keys are protected by passwords before they are used will help with this.

EXAM TIP Some certificate authorities will store the private keys of its users to protect against loss of those keys by the users.

S/MIME

Secure/Multipurpose Internet Mail Extensions (S/MIME) is used to transfer e-mail messages using public key encryption where a message is encrypted using a user's public key so that it can be decrypted using a private key. MIME was created as a way of handling e-mail attachments, non-ASCII character sets, message bodies with multiple parts, or header information in non-ASCII character sets in a standardized way. S/MIME is an extension to that to handle sending encrypted or digitally signed messages. S/MIME is a way of making use of a CA-created certificate to sign or encrypt e-mail messages. Since S/MIME makes use of CA certificates, users need to have access to a CA in order to obtain a certificate. The same situation applies here as in the case of the web communication. If you don't have the root certificate from the CA installed that generated the user's certificate, you will get an error in the e-mail communication.

 NOTE RSA Data Security, the company that was created by the developers of the RSA encryption algorithm, originally developed S/MIME, though it is now managed by the IETF.

Messages that are encrypted using S/MIME can't be feasibly investigated using anti-virus programs in the middle of the communication stream. That's because the message is encrypted using the public key of the recipient. It requires the private key of the recipient in order to decrypt it. If there is any malware in the e-mail message, it will remain undetected until it's been decrypted unless the anti-virus scanner is provided the private keys of anyone whose messages may be passing through the scanner. This would immediately make the whole system less secure since the private keys of the users would be out of their control, and while they may be very secure inside the anti-virus system, having more than one copy of a private key weakens the security of the whole system.

S/MIME requires a CA installation. This means that an enterprise that wants its users to make use of encryption or digital identity services needs to have a CA. The business can either implement one itself, which would require someone who could manage it, or pay for certificates from a certificate provider. As mentioned previously, this requires that the root CA certificate be installed on all systems, so if a less popular CA provider is chosen, the CA's certificate would need to be installed on every system making use of S/MIME. This is an administrative challenge, though it's not insurmountable.

Pretty Good Privacy

Where PKI is all about centralization and having a trusted third party to ensure that the data being presented is accurate, Pretty Good Privacy (PGP) is just the opposite. Phil Zimmermann created PGP in 1991. PGP provides encryption and non-repudiation just as S/MIME using CA-provided certificates. Where a CA would provide a central authority to ensure the authenticity and veracity of an identity, PGP puts that job in the hands of the users. PGP makes use of a "Web of Trust" to provide identity verification, where each user is responsible for signing keys for other users they know. The key being signed is the public key and it's attached to an e-mail address. Figure 8-8 displays a list of keys belonging to me using different e-mail addresses I've had over the years. Note that the e-mail address I've been using for more than 15 years, Kilroy@WasHere.COM, has more than one entry. This is because I've lost keys over the years and regenerated them on reinstalling PGP.

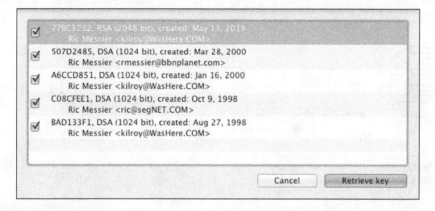

Figure 8-8   Key listing from key server

Certificates from a CA have specific purposes and only those designated as CA certificates can be used to generate and sign other certificates in a PKI system. In the case of PGP, however, all certificates can be used to sign, and in fact that capability underlies the Web of Trust that is at the heart of PGP. PGP allows for several levels of confidence in the association between a key and a username, or identity.

NOTE   Phil Zimmermann created PGP Inc. to further the development of PGP and also help protect him personally after he was the target of an investigation into munitions exports because cryptography falls under the category of munitions (arms). Network Associates acquired PGP Inc. in 1997. Currently, Symantec owns PGP.

The keys are stored on a key server to help users retrieve the public keys for users. In order to encrypt messages, you need the public key for the person you are planning to send the message to. The message is encrypted using the public key of the recipient, which means that it can only be decrypted using the private key of the recipient. In Figure 8-9, you can see the process that PGP uses to send encrypted messages. Data gets encrypted using a random key using a symmetric key encryption process. The key is then encrypted using the recipient's public key. The encrypted message and the encrypted key are sent as the encrypted message. When the recipient receives the message, they would decrypt the symmetric key using their private key. Once they have the symmetric key, they can decrypt the data and retrieve the plaintext.

In addition to encryption, PGP is capable of providing non-repudiation just like S/MIME. When a message is digitally signed by the key of a user, it can provide proof that the user is the one who sent the message. When PGP is used to sign a message, it generates a cryptographic hash of the message in order to verify the integrity of the message. The hash is then used, in conjunction with the sender's private key, to create a signature for the message. That signature is then used to prove not only that the sender is

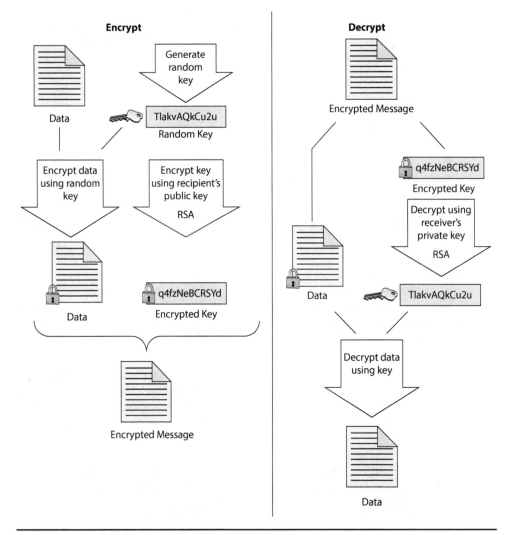

Figure 8-9 The PGP process

the one who sent it, since no one else should have access to the private key, but also that the message hasn't been tampered with in any way. Since the message is not encrypted, tampering is possible, but using the hash to ensure that nothing has changed does offer protection for the message. Unlike other uses of cryptographic hashes, binding the hash with the private key of the sender offers additional protection since the message digest can't simply be regenerated and inserted.

EXAM TIP The sender's private key is used to create a signature, but the sender's public key would be used to verify the signature since the recipient doesn't have access to the sender's private key.

Certificate authorities use certificate revocation lists to revoke certificates. PGP has always provided a similar functionality to revoke identity certificates. If you lose a certificate or key, you will want to ensure that the certificate is revoked so it can't be used by someone pretending to be you. When keys are lost, it undermines the integrity of the system since one of the primary purposes of using a system like this is to provide identity verification. When keys get lost and aren't adequately protected by strong passphrases, they can be used by someone other than the person whose identity they were being used to verify. No matter how many people have signed the key, it may be in the hands of someone else, so having the ability to revoke these certificates is important in protecting the integrity of the entire system.

Figure 8-10 shows the information about a user identity, including the different trust levels that can be assigned. In this case, since it's my key, it has the trust level of Ultimate. Notice that in addition to the user information provided when the certificate was created, the key associated with it is an RSA key with a bit length of 2048. There is also an ID and a signature associated with the certificate. The ID is how you would identify one certificate from another certificate if there were multiple certificates generated for a particular user.

Figure 8-10
Key information

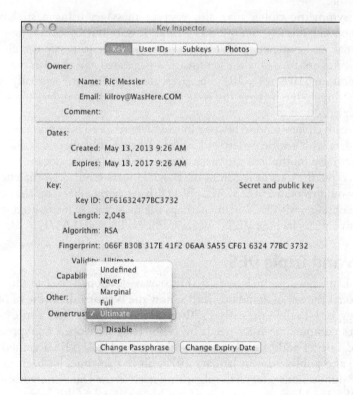

Symmetric Encryption

Symmetric encryption, or symmetric key encryption, is so-called because the same key is used to encrypt and decrypt. Since the same key is used for both encryption and decryption, it has to be shared between the sender and recipient. This key would be considered a shared secret. Since there is only one key being used, a symmetric key isn't used to verify the identity of a sender. Symmetric key cryptographic ciphers may use two different schemes to perform the encryption.

A block cipher takes a block of text, padding it as necessary to get the size of the block to a multiple of the block size, and encrypts the block. The block cipher may encrypt the message by chunking it up into individual blocks and encrypting a block at a time. One problem with doing that is that if you have two consecutive blocks that are identical, you'll end up with two consecutive blocks of cipher text that are identical. This method is called Electronic Codebook (ECB) mode. To fix the problem of consecutive blocks of cipher text being identical, you could use Cipher Block Chaining (CBC) mode. CBC takes the previous block of cipher text and uses it as input to the encryption process. If you have two consecutive blocks that are the same, you still won't end up with the resulting cipher text being the same because it relies on the previous block, which wouldn't be the same.

A symmetric cipher may also encrypt messages using a stream. A stream cipher encrypts the message one byte at a time. It does this by combining a stream of keying material, or keystream, with the plaintext in order to create the cipher text. The symmetric key controls how the keystream is generated and the two may be combined using a logical exclusive or (XOR). The streaming cipher is conceptually easy and, unlike the block cipher, doesn't have the issue of needing additional data in order to complete the encryption.

Stream ciphers tend to be used in cases where speed is important or where you are getting data with a wide variety of lengths. Whereas a block cipher has to pad out the data to become a multiple of the block size, the stream cipher doesn't have to pad at all since it encrypts the data as it comes in. Block ciphers tend to be the encryption algorithms you would recognize: DES, AES, Blowfish. Stream ciphers, on the other hand, are often more obscure, with RC4 being perhaps the most widely recognized stream cipher. Other stream ciphers include VEST, WAKE, Phelix, Pike, and A5/1.

DES and Triple DES

The Data Encryption Standard (DES) was developed as a result of a request by the National Bureau of Standards (NBS, now the National Institute of Standards and Technology, or NIST) in the early 1970s. This request came after a study of the U.S. government's computer security needs by NBS. IBM developed a cryptographic cipher they called Lucifer and offered it as a candidate for DES. NBS accepted Lucifer as DES in 1976 and published it in January 1977. Since that time, it's been called DES, although some publications refer to the algorithm itself as the Data Encryption Algorithm (DEA).

DES is a block cipher using 64-bit blocks and a 56-bit key size. The key is actually 64 bits long, but one bit of each byte is used for parity, reducing the number of usable bits for the key to 56. DES was reaffirmed as the preferred encryption standard in 1983, 1988, and 1993. In 1997, a DES-encrypted message was broken for the first time after several years of speculation that it could be broken. In 1998, the Electronic Freedom Foundation (EFF) broke a DES key in 56 hours. About six months later in 1999, distributed.net used a large network of computers to break a DES key in just over 22 hours. The fact that DES had finally been broken led to Triple DES being the preferred algorithm when DES was reaffirmed one more time in 1999 as the standard for data encryption.

NOTE The National Security Agency (NSA) has been suspected of introducing a backdoor into the design of DES so that they, and no one else, could decrypt messages using DES. A review by the U.S. Senate Select Committee on Intelligence concluded in 1978 that the NSA had convinced IBM that a reduced key size was adequate but that they hadn't tampered with the design of the algorithm in any way.

Triple DES makes use of DES, and while it is said that the key size is 168 bits, that's not completely accurate. In fact, Triple DES makes use of three different 56-bit keys rather than one single 168-bit key. Triple DES uses DES to do the encryption, but a message will go through three rounds of processing in order to come up with the cipher text. The first round uses one key (K_1) to encrypt the plaintext, leaving the first cipher text (C_1). C_1 is used as the input to the second round of processing. A second key (K_2) is used to decrypt C_1. This may look as though we are decrypting C_1 to reveal the plaintext, but notice that a second key is used so the result wouldn't be plaintext but another set of cipher text (C_2). Using the decryption algorithm with a different key really does another round of encryption, though we aren't using the encryption part of the DES algorithm. Finally, a third key (K_3) is used to run the cipher text C_2 through the encryption algorithm, yielding the final cipher text that is the output from Triple DES.

The decryption process is a reverse of the encryption process, decrypting the cipher text with K_3 to get another set of cipher text that is encrypted using K_2. Finally, the cipher text that comes out of the encryption with the second key is fed into the decryption algorithm using K_1. This final round of processing will yield the original plaintext.

While Triple DES typically uses three separate keys, there are other keying options for implementing Triple DES, including using the same key for all three rounds or using the same key for the first round and the third round. While Triple DES with three separate keys appears to be 168 bits of key strength, it has an effective strength of 112 bits because it's susceptible to a meet-in-the-middle attack. When you use two keys, with the first and the last key being the same, it appears to be 112 bits of key strength, but since it's susceptible to some chosen-plaintext or known-plaintext attacks, the effective strength is really only 80 bits.

AES

When it became clear that DES was at risk and Triple DES was only going to be a stop-gap, NIST began the process of choosing a successor algorithm in 1996. Two criteria for the algorithm that was to be chosen to be the Advanced Encryption Standard (AES) were low memory requirements and high speed. Several algorithms were submitted, but the one eventually chosen was called Rijndael, and it was developed by two Belgian cryptographers named Joan Daemen and Vincent Rijmen. The name of the algorithm was based on the last names of the two developers. AES was announced in 2001. Rijndael was developed to be able to use block and key sizes that are multiples of 32 bits, with a minimum of 128 bits and a maximum of 256 bits, but AES as published fixed the block size at 128 bits. There aren't as many possible key lengths in AES as were indicated as possible in Rijndael, but AES does still support three key lengths: 128, 192, and 256 bits.

 EXAM TIP AES specifies three possible key lengths: 128, 192, and 256 bits.

Like DES before it, AES is a block cipher. AES uses matrices of bytes to do the transformation from the plaintext to the cipher text. Performing the encryption uses a number of cycles through the algorithm, with the number of cycles specified by the key length. For instance, 128-bit keys will go through 10 cycles, 192-bit keys will go through 12 cycles, and 256-bit keys will go through 14 cycles. Each cycle has several steps in order to perform the transformation.

Exercise 8-2: AES Encryption

Encrypt the message **I can't wait to pass the GSEC exam** using the passphrase **ThisIsMyPassphraseThatIWantToUse**. Use 128-bit encryption for this. There are a number of tools and websites that can perform the encryption for you.

Just as with the hash algorithms moving to a larger hash space, cryptographic algorithms are moving to larger key spaces. AES-256 is being used more commonly. AES-128 is being used less and less, though it hasn't been completely deprecated like DES and 3DES.

Asymmetric Encryption

Asymmetric encryption, sometimes called public key encryption, uses different keys for encryption and decryption. The reason it's called *public* key encryption is because the two different keys that are used are a public key and a private key. Messages are encrypted with a public key and decrypted using a private key. One advantage of this type of system is that you don't have to worry as much about the security of the keys because, in fact, you really want one of the keys to be out in the open. Without your public key, no one could encrypt a message to you. The idea is that your public key is just that: public. You might provide your public key to someone whom you wanted to receive an encrypted message from. Security of a public key encryption system depends on protecting the private key.

Public key encryption systems use numbers that are very large and mathematically related as keys. Keys may be related through factorization where two large prime numbers are multiplied together to create one very large number. Factoring the large number can be computationally infeasible, taking years of computation time and making it difficult to attempt to derive the private key. Another way keys may be generated is using discrete logarithms where a base and an exponent belonging to a group of numbers may be used to generate keys. Discrete logarithms are also computationally difficult problems, which helps to protect the keys.

 EXAM TIP Public key crypto systems use asymmetric keys.

Key sizes for asymmetric crypto algorithms are significantly larger than those used in symmetric key algorithms. You may see key sizes of 1024, 2048, or 4096 bits used in an asymmetric key algorithm. Commonly used public key algorithms are RSA, ElGamal, and the Digital Signature Standard (DSS), which includes the Digital Signature Algorithm (DSA). PGP, GNU Privacy Guard (GPG or GnuPG), the Internet Key Exchange (IKE), and SSL are examples of protocols that make use of public key cryptography.

The problem with asymmetric encryption is that it is computationally expensive, meaning it is slow. Because it's slower than symmetric encryption, often asymmetric encryption algorithms are used in hybrid systems where the asymmetric cipher is used to transmit the symmetric key securely, and the symmetric key and cipher are used for the session between the two endpoints. Going back to our friends Alice and Bob, if they wanted to communicate with one another, Bob would get Alice's public key and then generate a symmetric key, encrypt the key with Alice's public key, and send it on to her. This key and an agreed-on cipher, like AES, would then be used to encrypt messages back and forth between Bob and Alice. Figure 8-11 shows a representation of how the hybrid cryptosystem would work.

Figure 8-11
The hybrid
cryptosystem

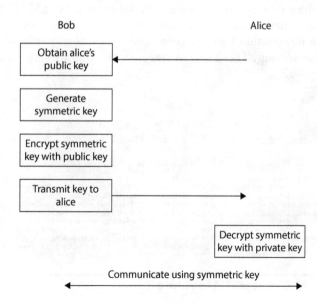

NOTE The mathematical operations chosen for cryptosystems are generally selected because they are intractable problems. Operations like factoring large numbers are considered intractable because, while it may be possible to get an answer, it would generally take too long to be considered useful. Tractable problems, on the other hand, are easier to solve.

SSL and TLS

When the World Wide Web started, it was used primarily to share information between a number of researchers on the Internet. Since the purpose was to share information, there wasn't much need to protect the information in any way. In the early 1990s, the company Netscape developed version 1.0 of Secure Sockets Layer (SSL), though 1.0 was never released. In 1995, version 2.0 was released, providing a way to encrypt messages as they passed over the Web. Version 2.0 was followed a year later by version 3.0. Version 2.0 is widely considered to be insecure. Version 3.0 was a complete redesign of SSL and was the foundation for subsequent versions of SSL and Transport Layer Security (TLS). The first version of TLS, based on SSL 3.0, was described in RFC 2246 in 1999. There have been three versions of TLS, with the last version, 1.2, defined in RFC 5246 in August 2008. TSLv1.3 was published as an RFC in August 2018 and, as of this writing, it is slowly being implemented but has not fully been adopted at this time.

SSL, and TLS by extension, uses a handshake protocol to establish the key used to encrypt the subsequent session between the server and the client. Figure 8-12 shows a Wireshark capture of the handshake that is establishing a session between a web browser and a web server. The SSL handshake begins with the client sending a hello message to the server, including the SSL version number, cipher settings including algorithm and key size, as well as session-specific data and any other information that may be necessary for the server to communicate with the client using SSL/TLS. The server responds with its own hello message, providing the client with the server's certificate, as well as all of the information that the client had provided to the server, like version number and cipher settings. Those two messages show up in message numbers 2815 and 2816 in Figure 8-12.

No.	Time	Source	Destination	Protocol	Info
2815	33.345871	172.30.42.51	216.93.150.198	SSL	Client Hello
2816	33.405511	216.93.150.198	172.30.42.51	TLSv1	Server Hello, Change Cipher Spec, Encrypted Handshake Message
2817	33.405606	172.30.42.51	216.93.150.198	TCP	57286 > https [ACK] Seq=181 Ack=146 Win=65535 Len=0 TSval=8586E
2818	33.405931	172.30.42.51	216.93.150.198	TLSv1	Change Cipher Spec
2819	33.405931	172.30.42.51	216.93.150.198	TLSv1	Encrypted Handshake Message
2820	33.406082	172.30.42.51	216.93.150.198	TLSv1	Application Data
2821	33.406136	172.30.42.51	216.93.150.198	TLSv1	Application Data
2822	33.463279	216.93.150.198	172.30.42.51	TCP	https > 57286 [ACK] Seq=146 Ack=240 Win=65101 Len=0 TSval=27877
2823	33.474467	216.93.150.198	172.30.42.51	TLSv1	Application Data
2824	33.474538	172.30.42.51	216.93.150.198	TCP	57286 > https [ACK] Seq=1242 Ack=375 Win=65535 Len=0 TSval=858€

Figure 8-12 Capture of a TLS handshake

The client uses the certificate that the server has sent in order to verify the identity of the server. It does this using the server name and the Common Name (CN) in the certificate. If those two don't match, the server can't be validated and may not be trusted. Your web browser, assuming you are using SSL/TLS for a web communication, will generate an error indicating that the certificate doesn't match the server. Once the server has been authenticated using its certificate and hostname or IP address, the client will generate a pre-master secret. This secret will be used to generate keys for the session. The secret will be encrypted using the server's public key and sent back to the server. Both the client and the server will use the secret to generate keys for encryption, decryption, and message authentication, based on the encryption cipher chosen.

This would normally be sent in a ClientKeyExchange message, which doesn't show up in the packet capture from Figure 8-12. The message that we do see, which is part of the TLS protocol, is the ChangeCipherSpec message being sent from the client to the server. This tells the server that we have enough information at this point to send encrypted and authenticated messages. The server replies with the same message, indicating the same thing. In Figure 8-12, the ChangeCipherSpec message is included in the initial server handshake from frame 2816. The client follows up with a Finished message including a hash of the previous handshake messages to verify the integrity of the exchange. The server also sends a Finished message back to the client. These Finished messages would be encrypted and not visible in a packet capture.

Since SSL/TLS uses X.509 certificates generated from a certificate authority, the certificate chain is important. Not only is the server identity verified using the hostname or IP address, but the entire chain of the certificate is verified. Normally, this would just be checking whether the CA that generated the certificate was known to be valid. If there are multiple CAs as part of the certificate chain, the CA chain would be checked. Additionally, though it wasn't mentioned earlier, the client can also present a certificate to the server to be authenticated, and the certificate chain would be authenticated by the server in that case.

EXAM TIP   If a web browser generates a certificate error indicating that the browser was unable to verify the signature on a certificate, the CA's digital signature is likely invalid.

Virtual Private Networks

A virtual private network (VPN) is used to provide connectivity to a network from a remote user. As you might expect, when the user is remote, there are higher requirements for authentication as well as privacy. The higher authentication requirement is necessary because you can't look at someone in an office or a cubicle and ensure that they are the person you believe is supposed to be sitting in that office or cubicle. Because of that, the remote user should be forced to provide details that would prove that they are the user who is supposed to have access to the network. Without that, you may have an unauthorized remote user who is removing data from your network or performing other malicious acts. Where normally you might use a username and password to provide access to the network with the user physically there, you may require an additional factor like a smartcard or a token if the user is remote.

The reason for additional privacy, in the form of encryption, is that the messages going back and forth are traversing public networks that you have no control over, and a number of people may have the capability of listening in on those messages and collecting data like usernames and passwords or sensitive financial information from spreadsheets or other documents. This would certainly be true over a number of public wireless networks that provide no privacy or protection against someone sniffing the traffic passing over the wire. Even if the messages were encrypted at the wireless network, it may be possible to break that encryption. So, the short answer is that a VPN connection would normally be encrypted.

A VPN may also be used to connect multiple offices together in a secure way without needing to purchase private lines from a provider, which may be prohibitively expensive, depending on the distance traveled. Instead of the private lines, you may purchase Internet access at each location and then use a VPN to connect each location, making use of the existing Internet connection to run the VPN through. Figure 8-13 shows a diagram of what a VPN network may look like with two remote offices connecting to a head office over VPN connections through the Internet. Additionally, you might have remote users that wish to access the resources (file servers, phone connections, server-based applications, and so on) on the network at the head office.

A VPN connection is usually referred to as a tunnel because the original traffic is encapsulated inside another protocol, and since it travels inside another mechanism, it is thought of as passing through a tunnel. The tunnel analogy isn't completely accurate because it tends to suggest a hard passageway from one endpoint to another endpoint, which isn't the case in a VPN since the messages are passed through a packet-switched network and could take any of a number of paths through the network. However, a tunnel is about as good of a visual analogy as there is, so VPN connections are called tunnels.

A number of protocols can be used to create a VPN, including PGP and SSL/TLS. Both make use of certificates to provide the public and private keys used to establish the

Figure 8-13
A VPN topology diagram

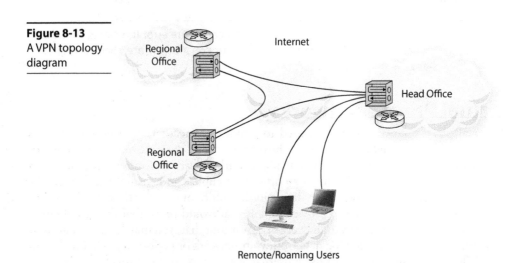

Remote/Roaming Users

session as well as the identity information that would provide authentication between the client and the server. In the case of an SSL/TLS VPN, it would be easy to generate the certificates locally using an internal CA because the CA certificate could be bundled up with the client. A small organization might simply make use of OpenSSL to create and manage their CA, but there is also software called OpenVPN that can act as both a VPN server and a VPN client. OpenVPN comes with scripts that can manage the creation of user certificates, but this would more likely be used for a smaller organization because managing a large number of users and certificates using the filesystem and a small set of scripts quickly becomes an onerous task. Figure 8-14 shows a portion of an OpenVPN configuration file for a client. Notice that the protocol is specified as TCP, though UDP can also be used as the transport protocol. The last part of the configuration file shown is the server IP address where the client will connect.

EXAM TIP   VPNs can be more flexible and potentially cheaper than private circuits.

Figure 8-14
An OpenVPN
configuration file

```
# Specify that we are a client and that we
# will be pulling certain config file directives
# from the server.
client

# Use the same setting as you are using on
# the server.
# On most systems, the VPN will not function
# unless you partially or fully disable
# the firewall for the TUN/TAP interface.
;dev tap
dev tun

# Windows needs the TAP-Win32 adapter name
# from the Network Connections panel
# if you have more than one.  On XP SP2,
# you may need to disable the firewall
# for the TAP adapter.
# dev-node MyVPN

# Are we connecting to a TCP or
# UDP server?  Use the same setting as
# on the server.
proto tcp
;proto udp

# The hostname/IP and port of the server.
# You can have multiple remote entries
# to load balance between the servers.
remote 70.59.48.113 23
```

VPN software will create a virtual interface on the system. For instance, in the configuration file in Figure 8-14 the configuration is looking for an interface that is created either by the software installer or by the user. An additional interface on the system means that you could pass messages between the different interfaces. There is a risk associated with allowing the system to communicate with the external network while connected to a VPN. If a system happens to be infected with malware that is allowing someone from the outside to enter the system through a back door or some other mechanism, that person would then be able to use the system that is connected to both systems as a gateway to the corporate network on the other end of the VPN. The solution to that is to prevent something called *split tunneling*, which allows a VPN user to connect to their local network, which would also allow them access to public networks like the Internet. Of course, disabling split tunneling also prevents users from making use of resources on their local network, like printers, while they are connected to the VPN.

While IPSec VPNs, discussed in the next section, may be considered a bit more traditional because they have been around longer and are generally widely supported by a number of vendors, SSL VPNs have been gaining ground over the last several years. One of the reasons for this is how easily they can be configured and deployed. Whereas IPSec VPNs require a client to be installed that makes changes to the way a system's networking functions, SSL VPNs can be deployed through a web interface. In other words, when you are given directions on how to connect to your company's VPN, you may be provided with a web address. Going to that address, you will be asked to authenticate, after which a little piece of software will be installed so that any time you go to this website and get authenticated, the SSL VPN client will launch automatically and manage the tunnel connection.

IPSec

IPSec, or IP Security, began life as a series of research projects in the early 1990s. When IPv6 began being formalized, IPSec was included as part of the protocol specification. In the absence of the adoption of IPv6, however, there were implementations of IPSec developed to sit on top of, or in line with (depending on the implementation), IPv4. While some operating systems like Windows have implemented far more of the IPSec standard than others, there are vendors that use IPSec only as a way to implement VPNs. The protocol that's used to implement the VPN is IPSec, and that's how you connect to your VPN gateway on your corporate network. This may be done in a site-to-site fashion, where a VPN gateway would connect to another VPN gateway, or it may be a remote user connecting to the VPN gateway to get access to the corporate network.

IPSec is actually a suite of protocols and modes of operations. In order to explain as much as we can, let's walk through how an IPSec tunnel would be created. The first thing to discuss is a security association (SA). An SA is the relationship between two IPSec endpoints as described by their IP address and the encryption mechanisms in use, as well as other information necessary for the functioning of the secure communication between the two systems. An SA gets triggered when "interesting traffic" is seen by the system. This "interesting traffic" will trigger IPSec to do something with it, which could mean establishing an SA, or it might mean performing a packet filtering operation on the traffic. Whether the traffic is interesting is based on a policy that is established on the system.

EXAM TIP In addition to performing encryption, IPSec can perform packet filtering.

Once a system decides to establish a session, the two systems use the Internet Security Association and Key Management Protocol (ISAKMP) to get everything off the ground. As part of ISAKMP, the Internet Key Exchange (IKE) process kicks off to get the keying material exchanged and the SA started. IKE has the responsibility of authentication as well as establishing the connection between the two systems. The first phase of IKE has two modes. The first is called main mode and it's a longer process, using three two-way exchanges. The first exchange establishes the algorithms and cryptographic hashes that will be used between the two peers in the SA. The second exchange is a Diffie-Hellman exchange to establish the keys, and the third exchange is the identity verification portion.

In contrast to main mode, aggressive mode uses fewer exchanges by having the initiator stuff everything that gets exchanged in main mode into a single packet. The peer of the initiator responds with the same information, and then the initiator responds to agree to the configuration settings just as with the encryption algorithms, hashes, and keys. While this is much faster and takes fewer packets, it is less secure since a lot of information is exchanged before any encryption is established.

The second phase of IKE makes use of the IKE SA that was established during the first phase in order to establish an IPSec SA. In phase 2, session keys are established and the policies around ciphers are agreed to for the IPSec session. These are protected by the existing SA. IKE phase 2 is also responsible for renegotiating a new SA once the existing SA has expired. The IPSec policy might specify Perfect Forward Secrecy (PFS), which would require that a new Diffie-Hellman exchange happens each time IKE phase 2 happens, meaning new keys would be generated and exchanged each time the SA is renegotiated.

Once IKE phase 2 has happened, the IPSec SA between the two peers has been fully established and the peers can exchange data protected by the SA. Once the communication is complete or the SA expires without being renegotiated, the tunnel gets terminated. This might happen automatically after a period of time or be done by one of the peers initiating the termination manually.

IPSec includes the specifications for two different protocols that may be used to exchange data between peers. The first one is Authentication Header (AH), which provides a guarantee that the data that is received originated from the specified peer and that it hasn't been tampered with in any way. AH also protects against packets being reused later on, a process called a replay attack. Among the headers in an AH packet are the Security Parameters Index (SPI), the Sequence Number, and the Integrity Check Value (ICV). The SPI identifies the SA of the recipient. The Sequence Number is used to protect against replay attacks, and the ICV is used to perform an integrity check on the packet.

Whereas AH provides integrity checking and verification but no encryption, Encapsulating Security Payload (ESP) provides a guarantee that the data is being received from the specified peer and also acts as an integrity check. Both of these are offered by AH, so in addition to those two capabilities, ESP also offers confidentiality through the use of encryption. ESP may, however, choose an encryption cipher that will null encryption, meaning there is no encryption.

NOTE   Both AH and ESP are IP protocols, meaning they ride on top of IP. AH is IP protocol 51, and ESP is IP protocol 50.

No matter whether you are using AH or ESP, there are two modes of operation for IPSec. The first is tunnel mode, where the entire packet, including all headers, is encrypted or authenticated. In tunnel mode, the original IP packet gets encapsulated in a new packet with a new IP header, where the destination is the peer gateway. In transport mode, only the payload is authenticated or encrypted and the original headers are mostly left alone. Transport mode will have issues with Network Address Translation (NAT) and AH because the IP addresses are included in the hash used to authenticate the packet and because NAT will alter the addresses. When the IP addresses are altered, the hash value becomes invalid and the packet will fail the authentication.

Steganography

It's hard for me to think of steganography without thinking of the Graham Chapman movie *Yellowbeard*, where he tattoos a map leading to his treasure on the scalp of his newborn son. When his child's hair grows in, it obscures the map, keeping it hidden until Yellowbeard gets out of prison, cuts the boy's hair, and reveals the map. This always seems the best example of steganography because steganography is simply hiding some information inside something else where it wouldn't be expected and can be concealed. Steganography has been around for a very long time. Early uses of steganography date back to 440 BC. This first known example was a message written on a wooden tablet, which was then covered in beeswax because beeswax was commonly used as a rewritable surface for messages.

NOTE   Steganography is derived from the Greek word for concealed writing. By comparison, cryptography is from the Greek word for secret writing. One advantage of steganography over cryptography is that steganography shouldn't attract any attention because the message is hidden inside a carrier. Cryptography has been altered, and it's more obvious that it's been encrypted.

In the digital age, a number of files can be used as carriers for messages. As an example, a text file or perhaps another image may be embedded into a JPEG. If you were to see an image that had a message embedded in it, you wouldn't (or shouldn't) know that it's anything other than a simple image file. An example appears in Figure 8-15, which shows a digital image with a text file embedded in it. If you were able to investigate the *digital file*, you might be able to determine that it is a steganography carrier, but just in looking at it, which is admittedly all you can do with the image on the page, you wouldn't be able to see anything that would tip you off that it's anything other than a picture of a couple of dogs. Of course, rendering it on the page means you can't get the text file out, but the

Figure 8-15
An image with
a message
embedded

point of this is to show you that visually, which is commonly what you would go by to begin with unless you were in the habit of investigating inside every image file, you can't tell that there is anything going on with this image.

A number of tools can be used to embed messages using steganography. Figure 8-16 shows the tool, iSteg, which was used to create the image displayed in Figure 8-15. You can also see the text file that was used to embed the data within the image. This particular tool runs under macOS, though there are a large number of tools available for different platforms, including some web pages that will perform the insertion of a file into a carrier for you. You should be able to easily find a tool to use with whatever operating system you are using. Tools are also available for mobile platforms that will do the same thing, so you may be able to perform steganography using your smartphone and then send the resulting image to a friend through an MMS message or through e-mail. So, if someone else happened to see the message, they wouldn't know it needed to be put back through a steganography program to read the actual message.

While a carrier is typically used, it doesn't matter whether it's an image file or a video file or perhaps a Word document, and file-generation steganography doesn't need a carrier to be specified. The carrier is generated on the fly by the steganography tool. A substitution algorithm would take the least significant information from a carrier and replace it with information from the data to be hidden. One advantage of a substitution algorithm is that there shouldn't be any noticeable degradation of the file quality because the least important data is being replaced. Injection steganography, on the other hand, will place data in places within the carrier that generally would be ignored by the program used to display the carrier. As with substitution, injection algorithms shouldn't create any noticeable difference in the quality of the carrier since the data is being stored

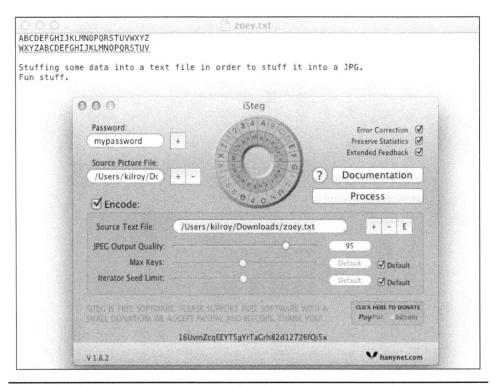

Figure 8-16 Embedding a message

in places that don't matter. One example is inside comments in an HTML page. Since the comment isn't rendered, you wouldn't be able to see anything on a page that was displayed through your browser.

 EXAM TIP A host file is not required for file-generation steganography because the carrier gets generated on the fly.

Kerberos

Kerberos is a protocol designed to authenticate users to network services in a secure fashion. It uses a number of secret keys in communication between the servers and the clients, including passwords derived from the passwords of the users. When tickets are generated, they are created by encrypting a number of pieces of information—items that might include a timestamp, a network address, and an ID. The tickets are then used to pass across the network rather than passing passwords along with usernames. Kerberos uses symmetric key algorithms to create its tickets, and the current version of Kerberos specifies the use of AES as the encryption cipher.

Chapter Review

Many people, both security professionals and lay people, consider security and encryption to be nearly synonymous. When someone asks whether "security" is used, they are often asking about encryption. Cryptography does answer a lot of security concerns and can cover a number of deficiencies in other areas of an information security system. Because of that, it's important to understand the fundamentals of cryptography as well as the different ciphers and protocols that can be used for encryption.

You may run across symmetric or asymmetric encryption, although often they are used hand in hand because asymmetric encryption is slower than symmetric encryption. Asymmetric encryption can, however, be stronger than symmetric, and so it is sometimes called more secure. Asymmetric encryption uses public and private keys in order to function. The public key is used to encrypt messages to a recipient who uses their private key to decrypt. Because of that, the public key can and should be handed out regularly. Both PKI and PGP use asymmetric encryption, but PKI uses a central certificate authority to verify the identity associated with a certificate while PGP uses a Web of Trust where individuals are responsible for signing certificates from other users to verify the identity of the certificate holder.

SSL/TLS are encryption protocols developed for use in web communication, though they have other uses as well. SSL/TLS use certificates and a PKI in order to function. Certificates are generated by a certificate authority and provided to a server. That certificate is used to identify the server, as well as provide a way to encrypt keys that would be used in the communication session between the client and the server. SSL/TLS can also be used to create virtual private networks, and because of the comparative simplicity and ease of deployment, it is a pretty popular protocol for use in VPNs. Another common protocol used in VPNs is IPSec, which originated in a number of research projects but found its way into the specification for IPv6.

There are a number of ways of hiding or obscuring information, from a basic substitution cipher (like the Caesar or rotation cipher) to making use of digital files as carriers for information. This process is called steganography, and people use steganography to hide data or entire files inside of other files, using an image, music, or video file as a carrier for the hidden data. The reason for using those types of files is because they are generally large enough to carry additional data without someone noticing an enormous size difference, and also because they often have spaces in them where the data can be hidden.

Questions

1. A substitution steganography uses this part of a carrier file.

   A. The most significant bytes

   B. Unchecked portions of the file

   C. The most insignificant portions of the carrier

   D. The end of the file

2. How many phases does IKE have?

   A. One

   B. Two

   C. Three

   D. Four

3. Public key algorithms are also called what?

   A. Asymmetric cryptography

   B. Symmetric cryptography

   C. Generic privacy

   D. Block ciphers

4. PGP uses what sort of system to verify the identity of the certificate holder?

   A. Web of Trust

   B. Certificate chain

   C. Single signer

   D. Certificate authority

5. If your web browser generates a certificate error, which of the following is mostly likely to be the case?

   A. The web server is down.

   B. The web server doesn't support encryption.

   C. The certificate is in the wrong character set.

   D. The digital signature of the CA on the certificate is invalid.

6. Which of these would be considered the most important part of cryptography?

   A. Protecting the keys

   B. Generating the keys

   C. Having the right infrastructure

   D. Choosing the right algorithm

7. The challenge of trying to find a collision in a hashing algorithm is called what?

   A. An anniversary problem

   B. A duplication problem

   C. A mirroring attack

   D. A birthday attack

8. If you wanted to generate keys in a secure fashion in order to exchange encrypted information, which process would you use?

   A. Diffie-Hellman

   B. Diffie-Mayo

    C. RPC

    D. AES

9. In order to validate a certificate presented to you, what would you need?

    A. AES

    B. X.509

    C. A CA certificate

    D. A CA private key

10. A very primitive but popular type of encryption cipher is called what?

    A. An S-block cipher

    B. A simple cipher

    C. A Usenet cipher

    D. A rotation cipher

11. What is the size of the key space for an AES-128 key?

    A. 2×128

    B. 6 million

    C. $(2/128) \times 2$

    D. $2\text{\textasciicircum}128$

12. What is the Diffie-Hellman protocol used for?

    A. Asymmetric encryption

    B. Key derivation

    C. Key escrow

    D. Symmetric encryption

13. What is Kerberos commonly used for?

    A. Authentication

    B. Encryption

    C. Access control

    D. Web services

14. Which web-based encryption mechanism has not been deprecated at the time of this writing?

    A. SSLv3

    B. TLSv1.1

    C. SSLv2

    D. TLSv1.3

15. What is the file the steganography process uses to insert additional data into called?

   A. Stegofile

   B. Plaintext file

   C. Carrier file

   D. Transmitter file

Answers

1. **C.** The substitution algorithms replace the most insignificant portions of the carrier file. The most significant bytes would be noticed, rendering the steganography pointless. Unchecked portions of the file are an injection algorithm, and the end of the file might be noticed, but most importantly, it wouldn't be a substitution.

2. **B.** IKE has two phases.

3. **B.** Symmetric cryptography uses a single key. There is no such thing as generic privacy. Block ciphers are a way of performing encryption. Public key cryptography uses a public key and a private key to perform the encryption/decryption. The two keys mean that the encryption and decryption are asymmetric since they don't use the same key.

4. **A.** PGP uses a Web of Trust where other users are expected to sign certificates in order to verify the identity of a certificate holder. Certificates can have a certificate chain if multiple CAs have signed them in a PKI system. Single signer doesn't make much sense. PKI makes use of a certificate authority.

5. **D.** If the digital signature of the CA on the certificate was invalid, you'd get a certificate error. If the web server was down, you'd get an error indicating that, not a certificate error. Similarly, if the web server didn't support encryption, you wouldn't get a certificate error because there wouldn't be a certificate. The certificate being in the wrong character set wouldn't generate a certificate error.

6. **A.** Protecting the keys is the most important part of any cryptographic system. If the keys are compromised, nothing else matters.

7. **D.** The birthday attack is the only real answer. It is based on a statistical problem called the birthday problem.

8. **A.** AES is an encryption cipher that would use a key. Diffie-Hellman is the key generation mechanism. There is no such thing as Diffie-Mayo, and RPC is the Remote Procedure Call protocol.

9. **C.** You would need the CA certificate in order to have their public key to validate the signature on the certificate you have. AES is an encryption cipher. X.509 specifies a certificate structure. You would not be able to access the CA private key unless you managed the CA. No one other than the CA should make use of the private key.

10. **D.** The rotation cipher, also called a substitution cipher or a Caesar cipher, was commonly used on the Usenet (but wasn't called a Usenet cipher). S-blocks are used as part of a block cipher, and simple cipher isn't a thing.

11. **D.** Because we are talking about bits, every bit you add to a value multiplies the previous value by two when it comes to the largest value possible. Since we are multiplying by 2 each time, we are talking about powers of 2, meaning we are raising 2 to the power of n, where n is the number of bits available. Since AES-128 uses 128 bits, the size of the key space would be 2^{128}.

12. **B.** Diffie-Hellman is used for mutual key derivation from a combination of known and exchanged information. This is an essential process for symmetric key encryption to ensure keys are exchanged securely.

13. **C.** Kerberos is commonly used for access control through the use of tickets that are passed between clients and servers. Authentication can be handled using other means, though authenticated users are needed in order to provide access control. Kerberos is not used for encryption or for web services.

14. **D.** All versions of SSL and TLS prior to TLS 1.3 have been deprecated due to weaknesses.

15. **C.** The carrier file is used to carry additional data, meaning steganography uses the carrier file to insert either data or another file into.

Exercise Answers

Exercise 8-1 There are 3.4×10^{38} possible keys with 128 bits and 1.16×10^{77} possible keys with 256 bits. When you subtract the 2 and divide by 3,600,000 (1000 keys per second over 3600 seconds in an hour), you end up with approximately 3.22×10^{70} hours.

Exercise 8-2 Using the website www.everpassword.com/aes-encryptor to do the encryption, the plaintext and password specified generated the following Base64-encoded cipher text:

U2FsdGVkX1+/iY3Kdq3fIt7Nsm7973+/RP5vKeDbORblpMZio90gtnfXP0RFGO8L
AJZuGVdXuoig6HKvCTYA3Q==

The website http://aes.online-domain-tools.com/ resulted in the following bytes:

1f ae 7b 99 78 a3 03 50 da 68 72 ca a0 9f 51 c8
0c de 8e 55 79 59 5d f7 70 df Ba e2 26 dd 26 da
ec 64 73 2a f4 5a 96 c6 33 84 75 d9 fd 40 54 b6

Risk Management

In this chapter, you will learn:

- Critical controls
- Security policy
- IT risk management

Risk management encompasses an enormous amount of what we do as security professionals. Actually, risk management comes with just the act of living your life. Every day you make decisions based on evaluating risk, whether it's deciding if the milk for your cereal has spoiled or determining if you can make it through the traffic light before it changes and a car comes through from another direction. Whereas many people have to make some level of risk assessment in their jobs on a daily basis, a security professional spends his or her life engaged in constant risk assessment in order to determine what they can or should be doing to manage risk. In general, people don't logically or rationally evaluate risk, as demonstrated by several studies by Amos Tversky and Daniel Kahneman. An organization's information security risk management must be based on sound and repeatable practices; otherwise, the organization is making poorly informed decisions.

Risk management can become a very complicated activity, and it is a critical part of an entire life cycle of security program management. Many factors feed into a risk assessment, including a variety of regulations that may apply to your organization. There is a difference between doing a risk assessment based on business requirements and the vision and strategy of the business and just focusing on compliance with regulations. A business solely focused on compliance isn't factoring the larger picture of risk associated with information assets and resources.

 NOTE Risk is often misunderstood. When people say risk, they often mean chance or sometimes threat. Risk and chance are not synonymous. Probability is only one aspect of risk.

Once you have performed your risk assessment activities, you can then go about doing all the work of writing policies and implementing processes and procedures to handle incidents. One component of a risk assessment should always be the possibility of a disaster, whether it's a natural disaster or a manmade one. Knowing how to effectively respond in a situation that is unfolding very quickly can help control the situation and ensure that your organization has a better shot at getting back on its feet quickly and efficiently. Having clearly defined processes in this area will remove a lot of the uncertainty in an unplanned event or situation.

Regulatory and Compliance

One risk that needs to be taken into consideration is that of complying with regulations that may impact your business. If you don't comply with regulations, you could be assessed fines or you may potentially lose customers. Of course, the regulations are also there to protect you and your customers or clients, so ensuring that you are in compliance is generally a good idea anyway, but it's also true that not being in compliance with industry guidance or regulations can be damaging to your business. Said another way, it's clear that there are risks that these regulations and guidelines are attempting to protect against, but there is also a risk in not complying. Depending on it activities, an organization may need to comply with multiple regulations and standards. Here are some widely applicable regulations you may be familiar with:

- **SOX**   The Sarbanes-Oxley Act of 2002 was passed to protect investors from egregious accounting irregularities like those seen in the early 2000s (Enron's, for example). The act is considerable in scope, consisting of 11 titles. While it primarily concerns both financial and auditing accountability, it also involves records and recordkeeping, and how public companies behave.

- **PCI DSS**   The Payment Card Industry Data Security Standard is a set of requirements regulating how credit card data is used, stored, and transmitted. The PCI is an organization of payment card companies like Visa, MasterCard, and American Express. The industry organization expects everyone who handles their cards and card data to be in compliance with these standards. The standards surround secure networking, protecting cardholder information, performing vulnerability management, and implementing strong access control mechanisms, among other measures. The current version as of this writing is 3.2.1, and it's expected that all organizations who handle card data be in compliance and that all assessments be done against version 3.2.1. An assessment is a check to make sure all of the controls outlined in the standards are in place.

- **HIPAA**   The Health Insurance Portability and Accountability Act was passed into law in 1996 and, among other things, required the establishment of national standards to protect electronic health care transactions and records. HIPAA defines protected health information (PHI) and specifies how that information needs to be protected.

- **FISMA**   The Federal Information Security Management Act was passed in 2002 and requires federal agencies to develop, document, and implement information security policies, practices, and infrastructure to protect the information the agency is responsible for. This act was amended by the Cybersecurity Act of 2012. FISMA 2014 provided an update to FISMA itself.

- **GLBA**   The Gramm-Leach-Bliley Act was passed in 1999 and is named for the three legislators who co-sponsored the legislation: Sen. Phil Gramm, Rep. Jim Leach, and Rep. Thomas Bliley. Among many other things, the act required financial institutions to develop safeguards to protect information provided by, and belonging to, their clients. It also required that these financial institutions perform a risk analysis on every department that handles the non-public information of their clients.

- **FFIEC**   The Federal Financial Institutions Examination Council is responsible for developing principles and standards for the examination of financial institutions in accordance with the Federal Institutions Regulatory and Interest Rate Control Act (FIRIRCA) of 1978, as well as the Federal Institutions Reform, Recovery, and Enforcement Act of 1989.

- **GDPR**   The General Data Protection Regulation was passed in 2016 but implemented in 2018. Even though it was passed by the European Union (EU), it impacts companies around the world because any company who may have customers who live in the EU has to comply with the GDPR. It provides regulations for protecting information of consumers that may be stored or handled by a data processor or a data controller.

GDPR is starting to have impact outside of Europe. Most of the regulations and compliance requirements mentioned above are US-based. GDPR is not, though there are some states like California that are developing their own privacy laws. While every country in the world has their own judicial system and ways of applying laws and punishments, there are two common legal systems: common law and civil law. Common law is based on precedents set through legal rulings by judges or courts, and is founded upon the idea that it is unfair to apply different standards to different cases. Civil law, on the other hand, is based on statutes that have been passed by legislative bodies, or on regulations that have been issued by the executive branch. Both types of legal systems can have an impact on your organization's operations and risk assessment.

EXAM TIP   Common law and civil law are the two most prevalent legal systems in the world.

In addition to the laws and regulations that might impact your organization's business policies, there are other laws you should be aware of. A number of countries have laws that cover the business use of computers. One of these is the Computer Fraud and Abuse Act of 1986, which was amended several times, including in 1996 by the National Information Infrastructure Act, and in 2002 by the USA PATRIOT Act. These laws protect against the unauthorized use of a computer—meaning, the use of a computer without the permission to do so. It's also illegal to perform acts using a computer that may cause damage to another computer system. This includes the creation and use of worms and viruses.

The Digital Millennium Copyright Act (DMCA) was created to protect against copyright violations in digital media like music or video. The DMCA was passed in 1998 as part of the implementation of two treaties by the World Intellectual Property

Organization (WIPO). In it, the DMCA prohibits removing the copyright protection from digital works. Online service providers can be effectively exempt from this law, assuming they comply with a set of requirements such as blocking access to or removing material that infringes on copyrights.

 NOTE   A Russian programmer named Dmitry Sklyarov wrote a program for ElcomSoft that purportedly circumvented the copyright protections in Adobe's e-book format. Sklyarov was in Las Vegas in 2001 to give a presentation to the Def Con security convention. When he attempted to leave, he was arrested and detained by the FBI. A jury trial later found ElcomSoft not guilty of the four charges filed against them under the DMCA. This case highlights some of the challenges of copyright law on the global Internet. Sklyarov was just an employee of a company developing software that wasn't illegal in the country it was developed in. While Adobe initially supported Sklyarov's arrest, they later called for his release after a meeting with the Electronic Frontier Foundation. The U.S. Department of Justice, however, declined to drop charges against Sklyarov.

While the United States and other countries have a number of laws relating to computers and security, perhaps the strictest laws are found in Germany. In 2007, Section 202c of the *Strafgesetzbuch* (German for penal code) took effect, outlawing the preparation of an act of data espionage or data interception. This has been highly controversial because it effectively makes it illegal to be in possession of a number of critical tools for a networking professional as well as security professionals. You may be able to argue against the possession of hacking tools involved in performing penetration tests, but preventing networking professionals from accessing tools like tcpdump or Wireshark, which are both data interception tools, makes performing their jobs much harder.

Not only different countries but also different states and localities might have their own sets of laws and regulations regarding what is illegal use of a computer or telecommunications gear. Because of this, it's worth doing due diligence to see what laws and regulations may impact your organization to ensure that your policies cover whatever the laws and regulations may require of your organization, including the possibility that you may be required to provide information to a government entity should a breach of security occur.

Risk Management

Before we go any further, we should talk about what risk actually is, even though it seems like a fairly straightforward concept. *Risk* is the degree to which something may be negatively impacted by an event or circumstance that may happen. You can think of risk as the intersection between probability and loss. You can't have risk without loss but loss on its own is just loss. You need to be able to determine a probability of an event incurring that loss. You may hear different terms when people discuss risk. One of them is impact, which is the same as loss, though it encompasses a broader range than just monetary loss, though loss isn't only about monetary issues anyway. The other is likelihood, which is the same as probability. These terms may be interchangeable when you see risk assessments and see the two dimensions of risk described.

As mentioned at the beginning of this chapter, we encounter risk on a daily basis and make decisions based on that, often without even realizing it. When we step out of the house and take a walk down the street, there is a risk we could get hit by a car. Going outside incurs a risk, over the longer term, of skin cancer. Risk management is how you define the risk and what you do to protect yourself from it. In the case of going outside, you may put on a hat or wear sunscreen to protect yourself. That mitigates the risk of sun exposure, though it doesn't completely remove it. However, by putting the hat or sunscreen on, you have managed the risk to a degree.

Managing risk seems like it should be a simple job. You see a risk and either you take action to remove that risk or you take action to reduce it and accept the residual risk. You might even accept the entire risk without any mitigation. Sounds pretty easy, right? With limited resources, how do you determine how to prioritize which risks to mitigate and how to mitigate them? Also, how do you manage the limited resources you have to mitigate those risks? Many things need to be taken into consideration when engaging in a risk management activity. Before you can do much in the way of writing policies or implementing a security program, you should always go through a risk identification activity to determine how you will manage risks. Otherwise, you are just shooting blindly, hoping what you do reduces the risks.

Governance is an important concept in risk management. At some point, someone is responsible for an organization, whether it's the owner, the executive management, or the board of directors. Governance is a set of actions taken by those responsible for the business to provide strategic direction and ensure that what the business does falls in that strategic direction to make sure business goals are met. The business owner also must manage risk in order to protect the business and make sure the business's resources are used appropriately. Providing strong risk management across the organization demonstrates effective management by those responsible for the business. Governance is not something that should be hands-off or entirely delegated. Only those responsible for the organization can set the strategic direction and know what risks are of most concern to the business. Without the goals and strategic direction provided by the business owner, it's very difficult to succeed at managing risk.

In larger organizations, especially ones that are publicly traded companies, governance is the responsibility of the executives of the company and the board of directors. They should be providing strategic guidance that should be implemented throughout the organization.

The National Institute of Standards and Technology (NIST) has publications available that outline what risk management is and how to assess risk. According to NIST, processes involved in risk management include framing risk, assessing risk, monitoring risk, and responding to risk. Each of those can feed into the other, which creates a continuous cycle of managing risk for an organization. A number of activities can cause risk to an organization, from simply hiring people to determining where a business should be located and the potential for natural disasters there, not to mention changes to processes

Figure 9-1
The risk
management
cycle

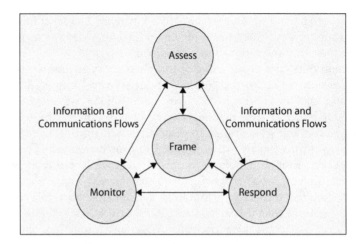

within your organization, the applications installed, operating systems in use, the way your building is constructed, and many other issues that create risk. An example of a cycle of risk management can be seen in Figure 9-1, which is from NIST Special Publication (SP) 800-30 Rev. 1, *Guide for Conducting Risk Assessments*.

NIST has several publications related to risk and risk management. The following are two others you should consider reviewing:

- **Draft SP 800-37 Rev. 2, *Risk Management Framework for Information Systems and Organizations*** NIST's RMF addresses not only risk and the risk management cycle, but also important security controls that could be used to manage risk.

- **Draft SP 800-37 Rev. 2, *Risk Management Framework for Information Systems and Organizations*** Describes the application of the NIST RMF for federal systems. This does not mean, though, that you have to be working with federal systems in order to make use of this document. If you are unfamiliar with risk management and applying a framework, this would be a good document to review.

The various steps in a risk management process or strategy are often tightly coupled. Notice in Figure 9-1 that inside the triangle outlining the simple process is a piece called "Frame." Framing a risk is identifying it and assessing its impact and likelihood. This allows you to fully understand what the risk is, as well as its priority. Framing a risk can also identify ways of mitigating it and the costs associated with mitigation. Once you have a cost determination, you can start to determine whether it's worth it to you to even look at mitigating the risk or whether you should just leave it alone and accept it the way it is. Some risks cost more to mitigate than the costs that may be incurred if they were triggered. Once you have performed an assessment and framed the risks, you can determine how you are going to control them. The control should be monitored and reviewed regularly to ensure nothing has changed—either the level of risk has increased or the control needs to be adjusted based on new information. This review loops back up to assessment since changes to systems or processes may introduce new risk that can be identified during the control review.

Risk often can't be completely removed or mitigated, which is why we have controls to monitor the risk and ensure that it doesn't rise to an unacceptable level. Sometimes, though, you just have to accept the risk the way it is. For example, suppose you want to offer a new web service to your customers. You already have web services you are offering, so you have accepted the risk of opening ports 80 and 443 through your firewall. You are using a standard OS image, so the risk to the underlying system is the same as what you already have in place. The difference between this application and the other applications you are offering is that this is written using the Java platform and a particular framework your developers have only limited familiarity with. Although you have experienced Java developers, the framework they are using for this particular service is reasonably new. Nevertheless, it still offers the best path to delivering the service on time and within budget. Without the framework, you will need more time and potentially more money in order to get the service written. You decide to deploy a web application firewall in front of this new service in order to mitigate as much risk to the application as you can. Even then, there may be new attacks against Java or this framework that the firewall can't control. Since this is a big opportunity for your company, management decides to simply accept the risk that the application creates.

According to the International Organization for Standardization (ISO), a risk management process should have the following characteristics:

- It should create value.
- It should be an integral part of the organization's processes.
- It should be part of the decision-making process.
- It should explicitly address uncertainty and assumptions.
- It should be systemic and structured.
- It should be based on the best available information.
- It should be tailorable.
- It should take human factors into account.
- It should be transparent and inclusive.
- It should be dynamic, iterative and responsive to change.
- It should be capable of continual improvement and enhancement.
- It should be reassessed either continually or periodically.

As you can see from that list, ISO strongly hints at a life cycle for risk management where the process constantly cycles around, and is deeply ingrained in, the business processes and decisions of an organization. This is the best way to ensure that issues are addressed from a holistic standpoint where risk and security are factored into decisions, or at least risks are identified. Building a risk management life cycle into your business processes can help you make plans and decisions that will improve your security and yet have less impact on your system over the long run.

A risk management process requires information about the risks. We'll talk about how to assess these risks later in this chapter, but before that, let's touch on some pieces of information that are critical to have. Pulling all of this information together is called *risk modeling* because you are creating a picture of what the risk looks like, how it may unfold, and the impact it will have if it does. First, you need to have an idea of the threat or vulnerability you are looking at. A *threat* is something with the potential to negatively impact an organization and its resources, whether physical, financial, or human. A *vulnerability* is a weakness in a system. The system includes any processes and procedures used to manage and control that system.

Once you have the threat or vulnerability identified, there are two pieces of information you need. The first is the impact that the threat or vulnerability would have on your organization if it were triggered and caused a significant incident. This could be a material impact, but it could also be something less tangible. One example, though there are several very similar to it, is the attack on the PlayStation Network where usernames and passwords were compromised after a group breached the infrastructure. This may not have had a specific material impact on Sony, although they should probably have spent some time and money working to better secure their infrastructure, but it did have a reputational impact on them. Whether this translated into a loss of customers and revenue is much harder to determine.

The last piece of information necessary is the probability or likelihood of a vulnerability being exploited. This piece of information will provide some weight to your analysis and reveal the possible scope of an event's impact. You may have a threat with a possibly significant impact to your organization but a very low likelihood of occurrence. The lower likelihood may reduce the priority of mitigating that threat. Perhaps there is a risk that your founder and CEO may be shot and killed in the building. This is a possible threat, and the impact could be very high, but with the likelihood of its occurrence hopefully being very low, you may choose not to spend any money on protections like a full-time bodyguard for your CEO.

There is generally a level of uncertainty when it comes to managing risk, often because there is a limit to the amount of information you can have. In the preceding example, you can't predict what your CEO may say and thus offend the wrong group of people, causing them to overreact. This is a fairly ridiculous example, but it does highlight the point that there is information you just don't know and circumstances you just can't predict. You may also have dependencies you missed, which can cause a ripple effect if something *happens* to one of those dependencies. Uncertainty can also come from a lack of knowledge about the threats that exist. Ultimately, some amount of uncertainty will remain in any risk assessment.

There are a couple of different ways to manage risk, which we'll cover later in the chapter. The first is quantitative risk management, which takes into account the numbers associated. The other is qualitative risk management, which is more subjective and takes the quality of something into consideration.

Cost-Benefit Analysis

As it turns out, there is some math that can help with the risk management process. A cost-benefit analysis (CBA) can be used, with the idea in mind that "there ain't no such thing as a free lunch" (TANSTAAFL). Everything costs something, even if that cost is time. A CBA helps us weigh the costs against the benefits and thus make better decisions. In addition to helping determine whether a particular decision is wise, when you get a value out of a CBA, you can weigh that against alternatives to determine whether one is quantitatively better than another. From this, you create a standard against which to base your decisions.

> **NOTE** Jules Dupuit was a French economist credited with devising the cost-benefit analysis in a paper in 1848. He also supervised the construction of the Paris sewer system.

One of the challenges is determining how to effectively measure all of the inputs in the analysis. The idea of a CBA is to provide some concrete information from which to make a decision. If all of the information you have is something like "customers will be impacted" or "it will take a lot of time to do this," then you don't have real data to create an accurate analysis from. Getting accurate information to create the CBA can be challenging, but in the long run you end up with a much more informed decision. Rather than simply saying that customers will be impacted, for example, you would need to determine in what ways they might be impacted, and whether customers will leave and go to your competitors. The amount of time it will take to develop a solution to an issue should also be measured in terms of the cost in man-hours. This should be done using a rough estimate of the amount of time it would take, multiplied by an average hourly cost for labor. Everything, with a little bit of work, can have a value.

After the genesis of the CBA idea in 1848, it eventually became U.S. government policy to perform a CBA before undertaking any work. In the early 1900s, a number of projects went through a CBA before getting underway, including the idea of damming the Colorado River in Nevada to create a reservoir and generate power. Hoover Dam, shown in Figure 9-2 during its construction, cost $49 million in 1930s dollars, which was a considerable amount of money, but it was determined that the benefits of building the dam far outweighed the cost of construction.

Values can change over time, and so time needs to be taken into consideration also. There is the time value of money. A dollar invested today will likely be worth more than a dollar in five years' time. This is one of the factors that had to be taken into consideration by those planning the construction of the Hoover Dam. It took five years to build and the cost of a dollar in the initial days of the project would be worth more (theoretically) when the dam was completed. This has to be factored into calculations, because if the dollar was invested or simply left to sit, its value would rise in comparison to its value at the inception of the project, and you would have gained money. Does the benefit of implementing the project outweigh not only the initial cost, but also the cost of the money that could have been made during the time of the project? Granted, most projects

Figure 9-2
The Hoover
Dam under
construction

an enterprise embarks on don't take nearly as long as building the Hoover Dam, but the value of money over time should still be calculated. The future value can be calculated as follows: $FV = PV / (1 + i)^n$, where FV is the future value, PV is the present value, i is the interest rate to compound the value over a number of periods, and n is the number of periods over which to perform the calculation.

Exercise 9-1: The Future Value of Money

You are presently considering a project that will cost \$10M up front and take two years to complete. The interest rate is 0.25 percent per month. What will be the future value of that money when the project is complete?

Of course, the values you assign to the costs and benefits will likely be estimates since you can't be certain of changes that may happen before the plan is implemented. As a result, a CBA is only as accurate as the estimates used to feed it. The more experience you have with particular projects, the better you can make estimates, because you will have actual data and experience from which to draw up your estimates.

Quantitative Risk Assessment

Quantitative risk assessment factors in only numbers that can be used to provide some specific context to an event. Quantitative assessment feeds nicely into a cost-benefit analysis because you have specific numbers that you can input into your CBA. Some other calculations that may be used in a quantitative risk assessment are single loss expectancy (SLE), which is a weighted value of how much monetary loss there would be in the case of an asset being impacted by a threat and subsequently lost. SLE is calculated by multiplying the value of the asset (AV) by the exposure factor (EF). The exposure factor is the percentage of the asset that may be lost in case of an event.

NOTE The exposure factor is often a subjective value, possibly based on uncertain data.

Once you have a single loss expectancy, you can calculate the annualized loss expectancy (ALE). This is calculated simply by multiplying the SLE by the annual rate of occurrence (ARO), which is expressed as the number of times a year an event is expected to occur. If you have an SLE of $10,000, meaning you expect to lose $10,000 each time a particular event happens—for example, losing power to your facility (after deciding not to install a generator)—and you expect this to happen four times a year, the annualized loss expectancy is $40,000. This is how much you expect to lose each year to power outages.

Using the quantitative approach, you would also calculate the return on investment (ROI). This can be done by assessing the costs and the gain. The ROI is calculated as follows: ROI = (gain − expenditure) / expenditure × 100 percent. Once you have the ROI for any set of investment opportunities, you can determine which investment makes the most financial sense. When you are performing a quantitative risk assessment, you would calculate the ROI on the various options you have available to you and then determine which one makes the most sense financially. A decision based on this doesn't factor in the event's severity or likelihood, only the ROI.

EXAM TIP Quantitative risk management takes only return on investment into account to determine what risks to prioritize. ROI is calculated as (gain − expenditure) / expenditure × 100 percent.

Qualitative Risk Assessment

Qualitative risk assessment is more about how you feel about the risk than it is about the factual data associated with decisions. This is unlike a quantitative risk assessment where only hard numbers are taken into consideration. A qualitative risk assessment may use data that isn't very hard because some factors are very difficult to measure and put a specific number to. A qualitative risk assessment takes into account the fact that there is a lot of uncertainty in doing risk assessments. While there are a lot of hard figures that can be used, there are a lot of soft numbers as well that go into calculating costs.

One of those figures that is hard to calculate is the cost in terms of human resources. Obviously, if people are spending a lot of overtime responding to a particular event and they are getting paid for that overtime, it is much easier to track the cost of that. The reality is that you are paying for your people to show up to work regardless of whether they are tackling the impact from a threat materializing or not. If they are working on the response to a threat, they are not doing other work, so there is some cost associated with putting off their other work. Can you easily calculate that? Perhaps, but more often than not, figuring the amount of loss in terms of time is a fuzzy calculation. This is where qualitative risk assessments can provide value. You may not have a specific number you can easily point to from calculations derived from hard data, but you may have a sense of how much it costs you in lost productivity in day-to-day matters because people were pulled off-task to work on an incident response.

A qualitative risk assessment may be used in combination with a quantitative approach because they are not mutually exclusive. There are places where you will have a lot of data that can be used, and other cases where you will only have words like low, medium, and high to determine things like impact or likelihood. You may not have a specific dollar value you can cite, but you know it will be high impact because of the amount of man-hours required to resolve the issue. Similarly, you may not be able to put a hard dollar value on the customer impact, but you may have a sense it will be a medium impact. Some people will say that reputational concerns fit in here, though it's not clear whether those are realistic when it comes to impact and loss. Numerous studies have shown there is very little damage to large brands, especially over time. Consumers often either don't understand what happened or assume that it happens to everyone and don't penalize the companies with reduced commerce.

Risk Management Strategies

An important risk management concept to consider is *risk appetite*. Risk management can be somewhat subjective. Different organizations may approach the same risk in different ways. This is because they have different appetites for risk. Some organizations are willing to make the bet that an incident that would incur loss to the organization won't occur. Some organizations may also calculate loss differently than others. For example, one organization may think that a significant data breach could cause a lot of damage to their reputation, resulting in a loss of customers, while another organization may either not consider reputational damage or determine they won't lose customers even if a data breach were to happen. Every organization needs to understand what their risk appetite or risk tolerance is.

Once you have identified the risks and performed your assessments to determine priorities, you have several options. The first one is simply to avoid the risk altogether. You could avoid a risk by not engaging in the activity that might cause it. Not all activities or projects need to be done, and if there is significant risk, you may simply choose not to do them. This can be very effective, but it's not always practical because an activity or project probably wasn't proposed unless it was determined to be necessary or at least desirable.

If you choose to go forward, your next strategy may be to reduce the risk. This can take many forms. An example of a common risk reduction strategy is to install sprinkler systems in your facility. The threat is fire. The impact is the destruction of critical information, systems, and resources, as well as the potential danger to people. While the likelihood of a fire may commonly be low in most instances, it is still a very significant threat that needs to be addressed. Sprinkler systems reduce the risk by limiting the damage the fire can cause. They will, however, create their own damage, and so other fire suppression means may be more desirable in some circumstances.

Another example of a common risk reduction strategy is to perform testing on software being developed in-house. The threat is not only to the company's reputation for releasing poor quality software, but also potentially to its customers, who can incur a liability to the company in the way of lawsuits and reduced sales. Because of this, you would want to ensure that the software you develop for customers, either for their use or purchase, has been tested so as to remove as many bugs as possible.

You might also choose to share a risk with another party. This may be done by contracting with an insurance company to insure your company against loss or damage as a result of a particular threat occurring. This is sometimes called risk transference, but in reality you haven't transferred the risk since you are still being impacted by it. You are simply getting someone else to help you with a particular risk. When you outsource or migrate data or services to a cloud-computing provider, you are also sharing risk. You are removing some of the direct risk to you and your organization and sharing it with the outsourcing or service provider. That doesn't entirely remove the risk to your organization. If you are using a service provider and they are storing a lot of information about your customers and they get breached, you are still responsible to your customers, although your service provider shares the responsibility with you.

On the other end of this spectrum is acceptance. You can simply choose to accept a risk as it is. This may be a result of determining that the cost of reducing the risk is too high compared to the cost of it actualizing. Risk acceptance is an understanding of the impact of a threat being actualized and the decision to take on that risk. Risk acceptance shouldn't be confused, however, with a lack of understanding of a risk. If management doesn't completely understand a risk because it hasn't been documented or explained well enough and chooses to go forward anyway, that's not the same as risk acceptance, because they haven't truly accepted the risk.

NOTE Similar to saying that not knowing a law isn't a defense against breaking it, not understanding the actual costs and impact of a threat being actualized and then choosing to go forward isn't the same as risk acceptance. In order to accept a risk, you must understand what that risk is. It is up to security professionals to clearly communicate the risk to management so that informed decisions can be made.

Security Policies

A security policy is a document indicating the intentions of an organization regarding the security and integrity of its systems and resources. A security policy is essential to a well-thought-out approach to the security of an organization, because it documents the way the organization wants to approach security. It not only specifies the approach to appropriate ways of using computer systems but may also specify deterrents or punishments for inappropriate uses. Most importantly, a security policy, as with any policy, is a statement of management's commitment to the specifics of the policy. Policies within an organization must be provided top-down, with the full support of an organization's leadership. Without that, the policy has no chance of being followed because it's not backed by management and the business, and is instead just some ideas some group wrote down. There are a number of policies that may be relevant to an organization, all of them falling under the heading of security policies. Some of those policies may fall under the following categories:

- **Access control**   An access control policy may specify physical security aspects of how people gain access to a facility. For example, this policy may specify the use of biometrics or badge access, and determine how badges are handed out. An access control policy may also specify information about usernames and passwords in order to provide users with access to the network and its resources. It may put in place additional measures like smartcards or token access to systems.

- **Incident response**   Companies are increasingly concerned with how to respond to incidents. This means they need to identify who is responsible for responding to and managing incidents. The incident response policy should identify responsible parties and also which organizations are responsible parties in the case of an incident.

- **Business continuity/disaster recovery**   Organizations must address how to remain operational if something catastrophic were to happen. This could be something related to a breach that causes outages or it could be something kinetic like a hurricane, flood, or other natural disaster. A business continuity/disaster recovery policy provides guidance for how critical business functions need to be handled to ensure the organization remains operational.

- **Information protection**   This policy specifies who should get access to sensitive information. It should also determine how sensitive information should be stored and transmitted. While you should always be thinking about the ramifications of what this policy stipulates, much of it may be dictated by regulations or industry guidelines. PCI DSS, for example, specifies how organizations should handle sensitive information like credit card data, and these guidelines will provide a lot of detail as to what this policy may look like for that type of information.

- **Remote access policy**   A remote access policy determines who may have access to your network and computer systems remotely. Whereas this used to specify dial-up access, currently it's more likely to address virtual private network (VPN) access or possibly access to a virtual desktop infrastructure (VDI). This policy may designate the types of users who can get remote access, as well as the hours during which they are allowed access. There may also be details about the types of systems that can get access. While you may be allowed to use your home computer, there may be requirements for a personal firewall and anti-virus program before you can gain access to the internal network.

- **Acceptable use policy**   An acceptable use policy indicates the types of activities considered permissible on the company network. It may also specify the types of activities that are not acceptable.

- **User account policy**   A user account policy specifies who can have a user account on systems, and classifies the different types of systems and the requirements that must be met to get a user account. For example, depending on the type of data your organization has stored on a system, the user account policy may have a citizenship requirement. A user account policy also specifies whether shared or role-based accounts are acceptable. The policy may also cite password requirements, including aging and complexity requirements. A user account policy may also specify background checks to ensure access to a network.

- **Network security policy**   A network security policy might be a very complex document specifying rules on how to access the network, including the types of systems that are permitted and the prerequisites for a system being attached to the network, like anti-virus software and updated patching. It may also outline data access rules, as well as information flow and classification. It might specify the details surrounding web browsing, including what is acceptable and what is not, and whether browsing will be filtered or not filtered.

NOTE   Background checks are common when hiring employees, but circumstances can change, and while an employee may have had a clean background when hired, over time they might have become too much of a risk to continue being given access to sensitive information. As a result, revisiting background checks on a periodic basis may not be a bad idea.

These are just some of the policies that may fall into an organization's policy library. The policy library may be extensive and very detailed, or it may be small and very high level, depending on the needs of the organization. Not all organizations have the personnel in place to create and manage a large library, nor do all organizations actually need a large library of policies. There aren't specific rules surrounding these policies that everyone has to follow, though certainly there are regulations that will suggest the need for particular policies. The important thing to keep in mind is that the policy is how the organization defines its approach to security. Without a policy, processes and procedures in use within an organization don't have any guidance, and as a result, they may end up conflicting with one another. Of course, this can happen even when there are policies, if an organization isn't good about communicating the existence of those policies and the need to adhere to them.

When you are ready to start pulling your policies together into something coherent, you may use a policy framework. A policy framework will provide an overarching set of standards and requirements for creating new policies, as well as present an organizational structure for pulling all of your policies together. Your policy framework may have a set of core principles that you use to not only define the remainder of the policies you will be developing, but also to guide how the policies you create will be structured and written.

Data at Rest

A lot of attention is focused on securing data in transit. As a result, data at rest is often overlooked. Data at rest is simply data that is sitting on a disk somewhere not being used. While some types of sensitive data are often treated appropriately, like passwords and encrypted data, that's not always the case. Often, access control mechanisms are used to protect data at rest, assuming that this restricts who has access to data. The problem with relying on access control is that once a user has access to data, they can copy it or manipulate it in a number of ways. There have been a large number of cases over the past few decades where data has gone missing because it was stored on a laptop or some external media. The laptop or media was lost or stolen, causing a major cleanup effort. An online search will turn up a number of news stories. One story is about an incident in 2013 where a laptop was lost with data on it. While this event happened outside the United States, there have been a large number of instances here where data was copied to a laptop and then the laptop was taken out of the facility, only to be lost or stolen.

This is a case where policies are inadequate, even in instances where the policy covers the issue. User education of the policy and appropriate practices is critical in protecting data. The easiest way to incur a data breach is to have a user take data out of the facility where it is no longer under the care and administration of your IT and security teams. One of the problems is that it has become ridiculously easy to move data around without any way of tracking it. Figure 9-3 shows a USB stick capable of storing 4GB of data on it. This is equivalent to roughly six CDs or about one single-sided DVD. You can easily and cheaply find USB sticks that are capable of storing 16 times that and yet are the same size as the one in the figure. This particular USB stick is roughly the length of an average man's finger, from the tip to the second knuckle, and not much wider. You can also find storage devices that have more capacity and that are significantly smaller. It has been suggested that Edward Snowden used devices like this to remove data from the NSA. Without technical controls to prevent the use of the USB ports on your system, there is little to prevent this sort of thing from happening. In cases where someone is okay with explicitly violating a policy or even accidentally violating a policy, there should be a technical control to prevent this or to at least detect it so it can be addressed.

Even though there are numerous risks to data, there are ways to protect it when it's at rest. The first way is to ensure that all sensitive data is encrypted. Your database should

Figure 9-3
A USB stick/drive

be encrypted, either at the database or table level, so if a database is copied off the drive where it is stored, it would still be encrypted and prove useless without the right keys to unlock it. Of course, not all data is stored in databases, so volume-level encryption on your hard drives is critical. Laptops today commonly have Trusted Platform Module (TPM) chips that are capable of easily enabling encryption on the entire hard drive, as well as securely storing the keys. Laptops specifically should have their hard drives encrypted to ensure that if the laptop is lost or stolen, there is no way to get access to the data on it.

As noted, USB sticks can easily store large amounts of data, so if possible, disabling access to USB ports on systems can help prevent the removal of sensitive information this way. However, USB sticks are really just part of the problem when it comes to data loss and theft. Even in the face of USB sticks, cloud storage is becoming a very easy way to copy data out of an organization for use somewhere else. While this may be done for entirely legitimate uses, there is the chance that the storage account may be breached, leading to a loss of data.

This brings us back to how to appropriately handle data at rest. Data at rest, if it is sensitive in nature (a data classification policy can help make this determination), should be encrypted and the keys protected. Having the data encrypted with the keys stored unprotected on the same system where the data is provides no additional security over having the data in plaintext on a hard drive. Ensuring that you have file, table, and database encryption on all sensitive data will help protect your sensitive information even in cases where it is copied off of your network onto another device. In cases of rogue or malicious actors that have access to the keys, you may have a hard time protecting against data loss or theft. This is where periodic background checks and appropriate monitoring and auditing will help.

There are several ways you can protect your data at rest, depending on the operating system you have. Microsoft includes an Encrypting File System (EFS) in Windows NT–based versions of Windows. This allows users to encrypt individual files or folders without encrypting the entire volume. BitLocker, however, provides volume-level encryption and is available on versions of ultimate and enterprise Windows since Windows Vista. BitLocker not only provides volume encryption but also makes use of the Trusted Platform Module (TPM) chip on systems to store keys. BitLocker can also be configured to store recovery keys within the Active Directory to allow for data retrieval when keys are lost or an employee with the information has left the organization. Other operating systems provide the means to encrypt volumes. With Mac OS, you can use FileVault. Linux supports Linux Unified Key Setup (LUKS), which can be used to create encrypted volumes. There are also third-party solutions like TrueCrypt or BestCrypt that can be used to provide encryption. You can also use PGP/GPG to encrypt individual files.

NOTE   Data in motion is another important concept and one that is covered in regulations such as PCI DSS. Sensitive data should be encrypted using strong encryption while it is in motion. This is because the data could be intercepted by an attacker, even if it is only transiting networks within an organization. Anytime data passes out of a system onto a network, it should be considered to be available to be compromised.

Contingency Plans

A contingency plan is a way of handling unexpected events, and is critical in ensuring that business operations continue. Disaster recovery is an example of when a contingency plan is needed. A business continuity plan (BCP), on the other hand, is a bit more general than a disaster recovery plan since it has to ensure that business operations are restored to 100 percent efficiency. This may not mean that a business remains fully operational during an event, but a BCP should establish goals and steps to work toward resuming full operations. A BCP must take into account events other than disasters.

 EXAM TIP A business continuity plan must not only define how an organization will restore 100 percent of its operations, but give it the ability to continue to meet defined goals.

Disaster Recovery

Disaster recovery planning is intended to address not only how you would keep the business going as best as possible in the case of a disaster, whether natural or manmade, but also how to fully restore operations. There are many details to consider when developing a disaster recovery plan, but typically three different sets of controls should be in place:

- **Preventive controls** Designed to ensure that something bad doesn't happen.
- **Detective controls** Designed to identify when something bad *does* happen.
- **Corrective controls** Designed to assist in recovery efforts after disaster strikes.

When developing a disaster recovery plan, an assessment of the most important systems and data is critical since you'll have to prioritize what to restore first. Saying "everything is important" isn't helpful because it doesn't enable you to determine where to start getting everything back up and running. Of course, in some cases, you may be able to simply move your operations to other facilities using standby or replication. That's one way to ensure that you continue to stay open for business. Other strategies to consider are

- **Backups** Backups to tape or other external media that can be sent off-site are critical in ensuring you can get your systems back up and running. However, you may also consider local backups to external disks to have something you can run the systems from quickly in case you haven't lost all operations locally.
- **Replication** Some systems may be replicated to other locations. This replication may be periodic or live depending on the needs your data has and how often it changes. Replication allows you to switch over to another system in case of failure in your primary location.
- **Backup facilities** You will likely need a place to run your operations out of if your facility is significantly impacted.
- **Local mirrors** This might be done via RAID to ensure a catastrophic loss of data doesn't happen.

- **Surge protectors** These can help protect your systems against catastrophic failure.

- **Uninterruptible power supply (UPS)** A UPS can give you the opportunity to shut down your systems gracefully and transfer control to another system or location in the event of a power outage.

- **Generator** Should a power outage occur, a generator can help keep your systems operational for a period of time.

- **Cloud facilities** Cloud computing providers may allow you to quickly migrate your operations to their facilities and also provide you with the ability to store backups.

- **Standby** You may have hot or warm standby systems ready to take over operations. A hot standby is always ready with the most up-to-date data and applications. A warm standby may need something done to it, such as updating it with the most up-to-date data, before it is ready to fully take over operations. The system may be in place with all of the applications up and running; it just needs a backup restored to make it fully operational.

Assessing your priorities should offer some guidance on what strategies to use for your system. This is definitely not a one-size-fits-all activity. Not all of your systems will require replication or hot standbys. Doing a risk assessment to determine which systems are the most critical to your business should give you answers about which strategy to use for each system. Once you have your strategies in place, you should document them, as well as the processes for service restoration, as part of your disaster recovery plan.

Incident Handling

In addition to many other areas of computer security, NIST provides guidance on how to handle incidents. Before we go further, we need to talk briefly about what an incident is and the distinctions between an incident and an event. An *event* is an occurrence of something that can be seen through monitoring or observance on your network, either in the network itself or on one of the systems within the network. An event is neither good nor bad but simply something that happens. There are, however, adverse or negative events. Whereas events are just things that happen, an *incident* is a violation of a security policy or perhaps the threat that a violation is imminent.

Typically, an organization will have a policy for incident response that provides specific guidance as to what constitutes an incident, and the severity level of different incidents. Most importantly, as with any policy, it provides a statement of the commitment of management in how to categorize and handle incidents. Every organization has different needs and requirements when it comes to handling incidents, but generally an incident response policy includes a statement of intent and commitment on the part of management, as well as the purpose and scope of the policy. Additionally, it should define key terms, and possibly define roles and responsibilities during an incident response. This may include an outline of what an incident response team would look like, selected from roles within the organization. Also, the policy would specify how to measure success or failure.

Once you have the policy in place, indicating the intent, purpose, and scope of how your organization views incidents and wants to handle them, you can move on to the specifics of the plan. The plan should include the mission, senior management approval, details on how the incident response (IR) team should communicate with the rest of the organization, including providing regular reports to management about the progress, and metrics for determining the progress of the IR team in responding to the incident. Communication is a very important role for the team, and there may be requirements to communicate with external organizations in addition to providing updates internally. Figure 9-4 shows some of the different people and organizations the team may be responsible for communicating with when responding to an incident. This set of groups and people will typically vary from incident to incident, but the IR team will always be the communications hub, as shown in Figure 9-4. Since the IR team is handling the incident, they are the ones who know the current status and specifics about what is being done and what else needs to be done.

Depending on the nature of the incident and the regulations or laws that may be applicable, you may want to, or be required to, communicate with law enforcement. A large-scale attack on your organization's network requires communication with your Internet service provider. This not only is a necessity but is also highly desirable since the ISP can help mitigate the threat. Coordination with other teams can be very beneficial, including

Figure 9-4
Communication with other organizations

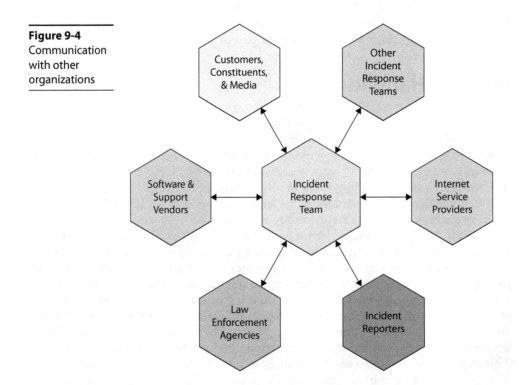

computer emergency response teams (CERTs) like US-CERT. While not always necessary and often undesirable, there will be times when you may have to communicate with the media as well. This should be done carefully to avoid compromising internal details about the response and the organization.

Rolling out from the plan, you may have specific sets of procedures that should be followed. Your IR plan may be very specific with regard to how to handle incidents that are well defined, or it could be generic in order to accommodate an incident that is difficult to foresee. These procedures should be well documented. As always, a solid set of documentation is helpful to avoid confusion, delay, and mistakes in the course of an incident response when the incident itself may be causing much confusion and stress.

Whether you have a set of specific response guidelines or a more generic approach to incident response, several steps should be followed when responding to an incident. The first is preparation. In developing a policy and related procedures, you have started down this path. You will want to have contact lists for IR team members, as well as on-call information for other groups within the organization that may need to be contacted in the midst of a response. You may also want to cite where a central point of coordination will be—something like a war room—as well as communication procedures and protocols.

Beyond developing a structure for how the response should be handled, how to communicate with the team, and how the team will communicate with others, documentation about the network, systems, applications, and expected traffic flows will be very helpful in providing the team with details on what to expect. This will save a considerable amount of time and prevent the team from having to quickly learn how to sift out and isolate the abnormal events from the normal ones.

Preventing incidents from happening is also highly desirable. While you may spend a lot of time developing policies and plans, you don't really want to have to call the IR team to have them handle an incident unless it's absolutely necessary. Once you have a violation that's created an incident, you have something bad happening, but it's much easier to simply keep that bad thing from happening to begin with. You can go a long way toward preventing incidents by performing risk assessments to determine threats that can be removed or mitigated. Once you have the risks identified, you can then implement appropriate and effective network and host security measures like firewalls, system hardening, intrusion detection, or virtual private networks. Additionally, malware protection like anti-virus and web proxies will be very helpful in preventing malware incidents. While all these technical measures are good, users need to be educated and trained in their appropriate and acceptable use, as well as in security awareness.

NOTE As shown clearly in the Mandiant report "APT1: Exposing One of China's Cyber Espionage Units" describing the advanced persistent threats identified in a large number of U.S. corporations, the easiest way into an organization is by exploiting the human element by sending e-mail to employees and either directing them to infected websites or simply attaching malware to the message itself.

Detection can involve the use of intrusion detection systems, as well as extensive logging on systems and network elements. Firewalls may also provide detection capabilities. Having all of this data isn't enough, however, since there needs to be some way of alerting someone to act on the information generated. This requires that someone be paying attention to alerts, either by watching screens or by having the systems generate e-mail or text alerts to operators who would then investigate the alert. Once the alert is generated, it should be analyzed to determine that it's legitimate, and the scope and severity of the incident should be assessed. In addition to infrastructure monitoring, user education and awareness is also helpful. Users should be trained to identify and report unusual behavior on their systems that may be related to an incident. This may be an alert from their anti-virus installation or it could be unusual sluggishness in their system. It may also be aberrant behavior like applications refusing to launch or unusual windows popping up.

System and network profiling can help with analysis, but this should be done ahead of time to have a baseline to compare the current state against. You may also want to have a log retention policy. Having historical logs can be very helpful once an incident has been reported in order to go back and try to determine a starting point for the incident. Log data can also be helpful in tracking an incident in case it has been migrating from system to system. With a lot of log data from a number of different systems, you may want to have a system that is capable of correlating all that data. A security information and event management (SIEM) system can help with this by taking in log data from several different systems and performing an automated analysis of it.

A couple of other items that are very useful, but that may be overlooked, are to keep all clocks synchronized and to make use of a knowledge base. Clock drift will throw off details around a timeline of events, making things harder to track. While a second or two isn't a very big deal, several minutes or more of clock drift can make it much harder to put together a sequence of events necessary in understanding what happened and what might happen next. A knowledge base can be very helpful in providing details about the system and network, as well as the details of previous incidents. Having an internal knowledge base can be important in speeding the resolution of the incident.

Once the incident is identified and prioritized, it needs to be contained and eradicated. There may be a lot of details here, depending on the nature of the incident. Some incidents may need to be handled differently because law enforcement may want evidence collected for use in a potential prosecution. You may also need to document the extent of the damage for both law enforcement and the company's insurance. In the process of eradication, understanding the scope is important to ensure you have completely removed the cause of the incident. The scope would be obtained during the analysis, but you may find that you will get more information from trying to remove the cause of the incident. You should also be prepared to follow up on new information and leads, perhaps pointing to a larger problem than previously thought.

Finally, you should conduct a post-incident analysis, including documenting lessons learned. While lessons learned can be very valuable, they need to translate into process improvement to be effective. Simply documenting lessons learned and then letting the document sit for some future review isn't very helpful. The outcome from a post-incident analysis should be details about how to improve processes and procedures in order to prevent similar incidents in the future.

SANS also provides guidance on incident handling, which is similar to the NIST guidelines. SANS outlines the steps as follows:

- **Preparation**   Preparation involves creating policies and procedures defining how incidents are to be handled. You should also establish relationships with law enforcement, human resources, legal counsel, and system administrators, since they will be helpful in responding to the incident effectively. In addition, you should have a response kit prepared, including a response laptop, networking hardware like cables and switches, a call list of important numbers, evidence bags, and data storage like CDs/DVDs or USB sticks. You'll also want to create an incident response team, perform threat modeling to determine the types of incidents you may need to respond to, and then practice your responses in order to be better prepared when an incident does happen.

- **Identification**   In order to respond to an incident, you need to determine whether you actually have an incident or not. An event is something that can be observed within your network or organization. An incident is a negative or adverse event. Your determination of whether you have an incident is based on your policies defining an incident, as well as all of the facts that you can gather. Different people may have different opinions. Make your own judgment based on the facts rather than someone else's opinion.

- **Containment**   You will want to ensure that the incident doesn't impact other systems. This may involve removing systems from the network if they are affected by malware intent on contaminating the remainder of the network. Once you have isolated the incident and kept it from spreading, make sure to gather any evidence needed for legal processing. Evidence may include the state of the running system, the contents of RAM, and any disks and information about running processes. There are specific rules regarding evidence collection, including maintaining a chain of custody. The chain of custody is a document indicating a comprehensive list of who has handled a particular piece of evidence, when it was entrusted to them, and what was done with it. In addition, evidence must be secured and not tampered with. If forensic analysis is necessary, it should be performed on a copy of the evidence and not on the evidence itself, if at all possible. This will maintain the veracity of the evidence.

- **Eradication**   This stage is where you remove the cause of the incident, like finding the malware and getting rid of it. You should also perform an analysis to determine the source of the incident in order to know how to protect against it in the future.

- **Recovery**   Once the source of the incident has been eradicated, the system can be put back into production.

- **Lessons learned**   The lessons learned stage is perhaps the most important since it's where you ensure you are implementing policy and process changes to help protect against this type of incident in the future. Your lessons learned can be informed by the results of the analysis done during the eradication stage.

EXAM TIP Steps in responding to incidents include preparation, identification, containment, eradication, recovery, and lessons learned.

Many organizations today have developed Computer Security Incident Response Teams (CSIRTs) to provide oversight and coordination when an incident occurs. Incidents may commonly begin as an event within the security operations center (SOC), which would do some triage and investigation to determine whether it can be ignored or whether it should be elevated to the level of an incident, which would need to be handled with a full investigation, including containment and eradication. Organizations will have different escalation paths, depending on the organizational structure.

The Legal Impact of Incidents

Incidents may require the involvement of law enforcement. Even if it's not immediately obvious that law enforcement is necessary, you may want to involve them down the road. Because of this, you will want to follow appropriate evidence handling procedures from the very beginning to ensure that everything you do, and everything you collect, can be used in the case of a criminal proceeding. During the course of incident handling, you will acquire a lot of information regarding the incident, the people involved, and systems involved, including any information gathered from the systems. You may want an incident tracking database in which to store all of this information, because the more detailed the information, the better your case will be in legal proceedings.

Any information gathered must be secured against tampering, and only those directly involved in incident handling should have access to the incident database. This will limit the chances that the data can be manipulated in an inappropriate manner. A secure incident response database will provide a timeline of events that can be used in the case of prosecution.

Digital evidence is tricky because it is so easily manipulated. One way to ensure that you are presenting the original data is to make use of a cryptographic hash, providing a signature of what the data looks like. Once you have a signature and it has been verified by the evidence handler, you will need to record a chain of custody for all of the evidence, including the signatures for the digital evidence. The signature and the chain of custody together can provide evidence that what is being presented in court is the original information, or at least an accurate facsimile of it. Without securing the evidence and providing a chain of custody, anything you gather won't be of value if you end up with a court case.

Information Warfare

The term information warfare has evolved over time. Information warfare can involve collecting information from an adversary, or perhaps providing misinformation to an adversary. It can also be more aggressive, including jamming signals to prevent information dissemination, or it can involve attacks against adversaries. A number of examples of this sort of information warfare have appeared in the past decade, including the release of Stuxnet and Duqu against efforts in Iran to generate nuclear capabilities, believed to be related to the development of nuclear weapons. This was a military action that involved nations, though there are certainly many cases of information warfare related to corporate activities as well. There have been many reports related to the Chinese initiating attacks against corporations around the world, collecting intellectual property and other corporate information thought to be used to improve businesses in China.

Information warfare is becoming far more of a threat to business than in the past, in part because of the use of computers to engage in these activities. Where previously you may have needed to get human elements involved, all you need now is a computer and someone with some skill in computer-related attacks like social engineering and malware. Hardening your systems and networks against attack is helpful, as is constant monitoring through an intrusion detection system (IDS) or SIEM system, but ultimately, the social avenue is proving to be the easiest way into organizations. This can be done through targeted e-mail messages that result in a system being compromised with malware. Once the malware is on a system, it can provide a way of remotely controlling the system and extracting any information that system and user has access to. Some organizations have had many terabytes of information extracted from their networks.

An awareness of these activities is certainly helpful in order to understand what the threat really is. Primarily, though, understand that this is a coordinated effort by determined actors, regardless of the source of the attacks. These are not random attacks by the cyber-equivalent of juvenile delinquents ("script kiddies") trying to cause trouble. These are targeted, specific attacks. The determination should be the primary cause for concern because, unlike a door-rattling exercise, these types of attacks may continue until success is achieved by infiltrating your organization. The best defense against these types of attacks is vigilance.

You can also use disinformation as a way of practicing information warfare. The less accurate information your adversary receives, the less effective they can be. You may disseminate fake information either about what resources you have or about data you have available. We talked about honeypots in Chapter 5. These can be a terrific way of practicing disinformation. First, it's not a real system. It's a system that is posing as a real system that acts as both a lure and an information gathering point. You lure your attacker in by letting them think it's an easy target, one that they can either gather information from or use as a jumping-off point to other systems in your network. Second, you may place false data on the system. You can do this with either something concrete like financial statements or engineering documents, or perhaps false data like SSH keys to systems that don't exist.

This type of strategy could also be considered psychological warfare, which can be another important tactic. In the case of a honeypot, you eventually create doubt in the mind of your attacker about any system they attack on your network or any information they gather. You can also reduce the credibility of your attacker if they later pass off the information to someone or resell it, and it's found out to be false. This strategy of doubt and turning adversaries against one another can be very helpful. It's not going to take down an entire network of people stealing information, but spreading the seeds of uncertainty may help slow attacks down or simply frustrate attackers enough that they consider it a better use of their time to find another target somewhere else.

Defense, as noted earlier, is always critical in information warfare, but with the rise in attacks and with various nations' involvement being known publicly, it's possible that responding to attacks with other attacks may become a common strategy. It has long been considered unethical and potentially illegal to respond in kind to an attack or an infiltration. Attacks from all sides may become more commonplace before we achieve a cyber peace, so at least understanding the basics of attacking with social engineering and malware, covered in other places in this book, will be helpful. Those seem to be common attack methods at the moment, though denial-of-service attacks are also pretty common, and malware may require exploiting a vulnerability to succeed.

OPSEC

Operations security (OPSEC) is about protecting small pieces of information that could be pieced together to view the operations of an organization. While this is primarily a military concept, it applies well to information security as a whole. This may include restricting how e-mail is used, or an analysis of social networking activities that may divulge internal details of how an organization operates. This information may be useful to an adversary. While details of an organization, particularly one that is a public corporation, will have to be public, not all details need to be so, and protecting those details as much as possible is what OPSEC is about.

There are a lot of details about how an organization operates internally that can be discovered through careful searching and analysis. For example, if a company advertises a need for a network engineer with F5 and Juniper experience, an adversary knows or can guess that the company uses Juniper and F5 networking equipment. Job advertisements can be very lucrative sources of information about how an organization operates. Recruiting Windows administrators tells an adversary that your infrastructure is at least partially Windows-based. Indicating that the job applicant should have experience with Internet Information Services (IIS) provides details about the web server in use, thus narrowing the types of attacks that will work. This can substantially shorten the duration of an attack before it's successful. There are a number of other repositories of information, including the systems themselves. Also, the Domain Name System (DNS) and domain name registries can provide details about internal contacts within an organization. Public organizations are also required to file documents with the Securities and Exchange Commission (SEC). This is done using the Electronic Data Gathering, Analysis, and Retrieval (EDGAR) system.

 EXAM TIP EDGAR stores a lot of information regarding public corporations. This includes details about subsidiaries and their growth information, as well as debt information.

Ultimately, helping an adversary do its job should not be the work of you or your organization. The Operations Security Professional's Association (OPSA) outlines a process for OPSEC, as follows:

- **Identification of critical information**   Identifying critical information that could be of value to an adversary. Once you have identified critical information, you can proceed with the remainder of the process on that information.

- **Analysis of threats**   Analyzing the threats in order to determine who likely adversaries may be. This is done by researching and analyzing intelligence, counterintelligence, and any other public information related to what you are trying to protect.

- **Analysis of vulnerabilities**   This analysis focuses on anything that may potentially expose critical information to the adversary.

- **Assessment of risk**   Once vulnerabilities have been identified, the risk from that vulnerability needs to be evaluated. Risks, once identified, can be managed and remediated.

- **Application of appropriate OPSEC measures**   Appropriate measures should be taken to remediate the risk posed by the vulnerability.

Operations Security may come from how the military handles their engagements as much as it does from anywhere else. You can see a pamphlet about military OPSEC in Figure 9-5.

Figure 9-5
An Army
pamphlet on
OPSEC

What Is OPSEC?

Operations Security, or OPSEC, is keeping potential adversaries from discovering our critical information. As the name suggests, it protects our operations – planned, in progress, and those completed. Success depends on secrecy and surprise, so the military can accomplish the mission faster and with less risk. Our adversaries want our information, and they don't concentrate on only soldiers to get it. They want you, the family member.

Chapter Review

You may have noticed the number of instances where identification of risks is mentioned, including in the discussion of risk management, incident response, and OPSEC, just to name a few. One of the most important things you can do to help protect your organization is to perform a risk assessment and have an ongoing risk assessment strategy and process to ensure you are always up to date on the current state of risk within your organization. This will help your organization with a number of processes and decisions. Of course, how you end up performing the risk assessment will be up to you, whether it's qualitative or quantitative or some combination of the two. In many cases, just listing the risks to the organization is an enormous improvement over the current state and is a big step in better protecting information and resources.

Having appropriate policies is helpful in ensuring that the organization has documented what it considers valuable and, perhaps more importantly, has management backing for these statements of intent. Once you have a set of policies, they can be used to guide further activities like development of processes and procedures and development of awareness training.

Risk assessments are also important when it comes to contingency planning, including preparing a disaster recovery plan. A risk assessment will help to prioritize systems that are critical to business operations so that, if they go down, efforts are immediately focused on getting them back up and running quickly. This can also manifest itself in having redundant systems or a hot standby in a separate location to replace these critical systems when needed. You should also take your critical systems into account when developing backup strategies to ensure you are not only backing up the systems but getting the backups off-site to a protected storage facility. Another consideration is having a set of local backups to work from while waiting for the backups to be recovered from the off-site facility.

Questions

1. You have determined that the SLE for one of your systems is $5000 and the ARO is 2. What is your ALE?

   A. $5000

   B. $10,000

   C. $2500

   D. $2000

2. Your organization needs to have a way to recover operations completely and also meet expectations for continued operations. What does your organization need?

   A. A disaster recovery plan

   B. Risk assessment

   C. A business continuity plan

   D. Management buy-in

3. What are Duqu and Stuxnet examples of?

   A. Information warfare

   B. Information assessment

   C. Tactical warfare

   D. Nuclear warfare

4. You have four possible strategies for mitigating a particular risk. Which of the following should you go with when using a quantitative risk assessment approach?

   A. Expenditure: $100,000; Return: $95,000

   B. Expenditure: $10,000; Return: $0

   C. Expenditure: $250,000; Return: $275,000

   D. Expenditure: $125,000; Return: $50,000

5. Which of these is not an example of where an adversary can gather useful information to use against your organization?

   A. Job listings

   B. SEC filings

   C. Domain name registries

   D. The Microsoft registry

6. What is the best way to protect data at rest?

   A. Keep it moving.

   B. Prevent it from moving.

   C. Encrypt it.

   D. Provide access controls.

7. Backups and replication are two strategies to consider for what activity?

   A. Disaster recovery

   B. Risk assessment

   C. Information warfare

   D. OPSEC

8. An effective risk management strategy can be which of these?

   A. Risk assessment

   B. Risk avoidance

   C. Risk determination

   D. Risk analysis

9. Security policies are best described as:

    A. Ways to protect an organization

    B. Methods of punishing those who don't follow the policy

    C. Requests for management buy-in

    D. High-level statements of intent and expectation for an organization

10. In order to have data to determine whether a project makes financial sense, you would perform which of these?

    A. SLE

    B. ALE

    C. CBA

    D. ARO

11. Risk requires which two elements in order to truly be risk?

    A. Chance and indecision

    B. Loss and poor management

    C. Loss and probability

    D. Probability and chance

12. What do you call sensitive information passing over a network?

    A. Data in use

    B. Data at rest

    C. Data under care

    D. Data in motion

13. Why would you perform a risk assessment?

    A. To identify risk tolerance

    B. To identify areas where resources should be applied

    C. To identify loss potential

    D. To identify what board members should consider

14. What should security policies be driven by?

    A. Risk tolerance

    B. Risk avoidance

    C. Annualized loss expectancy

    D. Business mission and objectives

15. What would be a common role for a CSIRT within an organization?

    A. Perform event triage

    B. Provide oversight and coordination

    C. Manage the SOC

    D. Develop the computer security incident response policy

Answers

1. B. The annualized loss expectancy (ALE) is calculated by multiplying your single loss expectancy (SLE) by the annual rate of occurrence (ARO). 5000×2 is 10,000.

2. C. A disaster recovery plan will allow an organization to get back to full operation after a disaster, but a business continuity plan also provides details on how to ensure operations continue, based on specific targets and goals. While a risk assessment and management buy-in are helpful to have, they alone don't achieve the stated goal.

3. A. Duqu and Stuxnet are examples of information warfare. While they are related to attacks on the nuclear industry in Iran, they are not examples of nuclear warfare themselves.

4. C. The return on investment is calculated as (gain – expenditure) / expenditure $\times$ 100 percent. While B is a very low cost, it also returns nothing. As a result, C should be the approach taken since it has a higher return on investment.

5. D. Job listings seeking IT professionals are good resources about internal systems. If names and e-mail addresses are given, SEC filings through EDGAR can provide information about public companies. Domain name registries can provide information about internal contacts within an organization. The Microsoft registry, an ambiguous term, is not one of the places to get information about a company.

6. C. Encryption is the best way to protect data at rest, just as it is for data in transmission. There are some caveats, however, including not storing the keys with the encrypted data.

7. A. Disaster recovery can be helped by having backups and having replicated systems that can be switched on to take the place of the primary system. The other answers aren't helped by backups or replication.

8. B. Risk avoidance, while not always possible, is a good strategy for risk management.

9. D. A policy is a set of high-level statements about the intent and expectations of an organization. Policies can help protect an organization, but it's not the best description. While there may be punishment mechanisms specified in the policy, it's not a primary focus. While management buy-in is necessary for an effective policy, a policy is not a request.

10. **C.** You would perform a cost-benefit analysis (CBA) to determine whether a project makes financial sense. SLE is single loss expectancy, ALE is annualized loss expectancy, and ARO is annualized rate of occurrence.

11. **C.** Risk is the intersection of loss and probability. In order to identify risk to an organization, you need to be able to determine what the potential loss resulting from an incident is as well as the probability of that incident occurring. Chance is sometimes thought of as probability but probability is a more exact word.

12. **D.** Data in motion is data that is moving from one system to another, passing over a network. Because it's transiting a network, it's important to encrypt data in motion. Data in use is data that is in memory and being used by an application. Data at rest is data sitting on disk.

13. **B.** A risk assessment can be used to identify where resources could best be applied. When you perform a risk assessment against different assets and projects, you can rank order them based on which may incur or reduce more risk. While board members should always be aware of risk, a risk assessment does not identify what board members should be paying attention to.

14. **D.** Security policies for an organization should be driven by the business objectives and mission. Executives and the board should make it clear what those objectives and mission are so the security policies are aligned with those.

15. **B.** The Computer Security Incident Response Team (CSIRT) would provide oversight and coordination in the case that an event is determined to be an incident. The team may include members from the security operations center (SOC), but the CSIRT would commonly be separate from the SOC. Executive management should be responsible for computer security policies, though it's possible members of the CSIRT may have input into the process.

Exercise 9-1 Answer

Future value is calculated as $PV / (1 + i)^n$. $10,000,000 / (1 + 0.0025)^{24} = \$9418350.51$ FV.

Virtual Machines

In this chapter, you will learn:
- A brief history of virtualization
- Reasons for virtualizing
- The role of hypervisors
- Virtualization strategies
- Use of containers for application-level virtualization

In the midst of electronics becoming faster and less expensive, the information technology industry has rediscovered virtualization technology. Not surprisingly, the idea of virtualizing resources has been around for decades and originated in the mainframe world. While many might think about using virtual machines on their PC to access different operating systems, or using them for a number of other reasons, virtualization covers much more ground than simply VMware, VirtualBox, or one of the other virtualization software programs. In fact, even if you don't have VMware, VirtualBox, Parallels, or something similar, you are likely using another virtualization technology and may not even be aware of it. For example, if you are running a Windows operating system, you are using multiple virtualization technologies.

Whereas virtual machines have been used for everything from the economy to finding ways to maximize resources, they have also been used for purposes of security, testing, and portability. Over the course of this chapter, we'll talk about how and where virtualization got started, as well as some of the solutions it's used for today. Over the years, several programming languages have used virtualization to implement language and runtime environments, so we'll talk about those implementations. We'll also go over what virtualization is and what it means to many people today.

Virtual Machine History

Virtualization began at IBM in the 1960s with the announcement of the new System/360 hardware and associated operating system development. IBM intended to develop a next-generation time-sharing system, and their work at the Cambridge Scientific Center (CSC) resulted in an operating system called CP-40. CP-40 was designed to be used for research, with the results of the research folded into work on another operating system, CP-67. The work on this operating system came amidst work in other places on time-sharing systems that would free up large, expensive systems from being single-user personal computers. The goal was to allow a number of users to simultaneously and effectively use the computer so the processor wasn't left idle a lot and more people could do work. The CSC team referred to the virtualization as using a pseudo-machine.

NOTE IBM worked with MIT's Project Mac, which was created in 1963 through funding by DARPA, and spawned a significant amount of research into artificial intelligence and operating systems.

The term "virtual machine" actually came from another IBM project that was designed to simulate multiple systems using a combination of hardware and software. This project was based in Yorktown, New York, and developed around the IBM 7044 hardware. The resulting system was called the M44/44X, and it was used to explore paged system memory and the concept of virtual machines, and measure computer performance. This was an entirely experimental machine, and some of what was learned fed into the work on CP. While the term "virtual machine" originated in the work in Yorktown, the CP operating system continues to exist today on IBM systems.

Eventually, all of this work went into the creation of the operating system VM/CMS, which was released in 1972 as VM/370 after the appropriate modifications had been made to the hardware to support doing virtual memory in hardware. This support allowed for the translation of the virtual address that the process knew about to the real address that the system could refer to and access. This hardware support for relocatable or virtual memory was available in the System/370. When put together, IBM's hardware and their operating system created a solid system for running multiple instances of operating systems on top of the same hardware. An IBM mainframe could be used to support a large number of users making use of a number of operating system instances, all within a limited amount of physical memory. Memory was measured in megabytes in the System/370 systems. By the late 1970s to early 1980s, main system memory was typically in the 8–32 megabyte range for one of the systems. Figure 10-1 is a marketing picture of the IBM System/370, which is the required "see how big systems were 40 years ago" picture to demonstrate how far we've come in power and scale in that time.

Figure 10-1
The IBM
System/370

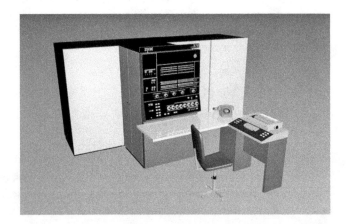

The 1970s also saw another form of virtual machine become very popular. One reason was the fragmented nature of the different operating systems and instruction sets that were available. Because of that, it was difficult to expect that a single language platform would gain much traction. Kenneth Bowles at the University of California at San Diego had the idea that not compiling to machine code, but instead to a machine-independent pseudo-code, might make for a higher acceptance rate of a language like Pascal. UCSD Pascal was built on the idea of generating pseudo-code that would then run inside of a p-code machine, and the code that was generated would be based on the instruction set of a virtual processor that wasn't related to the physical hardware the p-code system was being run on. While the concept of p-code machines had been around since the 1960s, the UCSD Pascal implementation became very successful with implementations developed for a number of hardware platforms, including smaller systems like the TI-99/4A and the Apple II.

Emulation and the PC Era

In the late 1980s, the desktop world was all over the place when it came to the business world. In addition to the IBM-compatibles and the Apple Macintosh systems that we still know today, in spite of significant hardware changes in both platforms, there were a number of manufacturers like Sun Microsystems, IBM, Hewlett-Packard, and Silicon Graphics making Unix workstations. These workstations were incredibly powerful systems designed for engineers and other technical types to use. However, there was still a need for these engineers to make use of more traditional desktop application software like Lotus 1-2-3, as an example. This required a second piece of hardware on someone's desk just to perform the business functions of their job, like using spreadsheets or perhaps writing documentation in a PC-based word processor that someone else might be able to make use of.

Adding another system was an expense in terms of hardware, as well as simply desktop real estate, since neither the Unix workstations nor the DOS-based PCs of the day were small. In 1987, a company called Insignia Solutions developed a piece of software that was capable of allowing DOS programs to run on Unix workstations. This solution, called SoftPC, was considerably less expensive than buying a piece of hardware that may sit idle a lot. Instead of providing direct virtualization like what you may be familiar with today, SoftPC was an emulator because all of the Unix workstations used a different processor and hardware architecture than the PC used to run DOS. As a result, the SoftPC software had to provide a translation of the instructions in a DOS program into something that would run on a Unix workstation processor. It did this by emulating the processor and other hardware of the PC, allowing the DOS programs to run indirectly on the Unix workstation through the SoftPC software.

Insignia later released SoftPC for the Apple Macintosh, allowing Mac users to run DOS programs. Eventually, SoftPC became SoftWindows when Insignia began bundling Windows with SoftPC to allow Windows programs to run in addition to the DOS programs it was already capable of running. Along with SoftWindows, Insignia had a SoftOS/2 offering, allowing people to run OS/2 programs. Again, since the hardware architecture and the processor on an Apple Macintosh were completely different from the IBM PCs used to run DOS, Windows, or OS/2, all of this was done in emulation.

By the mid-1990s, virtualization was more than a niche application for specific applications like running DOS/Windows programs inside another operating system. Virtual PC by Connectix, and then later solutions by Citrix and VMware, began to make virtualization more mainstream. Eventually, processor extensions were added to the Intel family of CPUs that allowed for virtualization assistance in hardware so it didn't all have to be done in software. Today, a number of virtualization technologies are commonplace and used on a regular basis both at home and in large enterprises.

Application Virtualization

While UCSD Pascal may have been the first prominent language implementation to use virtualization, it wasn't the most successful. It also wasn't a language that was designed from the beginning to be run in virtualization because Pascal had been created years earlier by computer scientist Niklaus Wirth. In 1991, James Gosling began a project called Oak that was designed to be used on television set–top boxes to create an interactive television experience. His intent was to create a virtual machine that would run the programs created in a language that had a familiar syntax, using C++ as a base since C and C++ were both very popular languages. C++ was a set of object-oriented extensions added onto the programming language C.

Virtual Memory

Virtual memory is a way of making use of less-expensive resources to compensate for those that are more expensive. Since the memory inside of the computer, typically called random access memory (RAM), is more expensive per bit than the storage on a hard drive, chunks of memory called pages can be stored in secondary storage like a hard drive during times when those pages aren't being used in order to make room for pages that are needed. Using virtual memory, your system can appear to have considerably more primary memory than it actually has.

Without virtual memory, if you ran out of space you would have to manage the memory yourself using a technique called an overlay. As an example, DOS had no way to manage memory itself, and systems had a maximum of 640K at that time. In order to have a program that used more than 640K, you had to load a new portion of code into memory, overwriting a portion of code that was already loaded into memory. Ideally, in place of the programmer having to load and unload portions of memory, the operating system would take care of it automatically.

A German physicist developed the concept of virtual memory in the 1950s at a university in Berlin. It was then used to extend the core memory of the Atlas Computer at the University of Manchester. The Atlas had 16,000 48-bit words of primary storage, but 96,000 words of secondary storage, which meant a lot more access to memory even if it may have been slower. Getting access to the additional virtual memory required that memory be organized into pages that could be manipulated separately without affecting the rest of the process in memory. This way, portions of the process could be written out to secondary storage while still allowing the process to continue execution until code or data on one of those pages was needed.

NOTE Notice the reference to the word size. While we are used to talking about bytes that are eight bits long, in larger systems it was more common to refer to the word size, which is the size of a piece of stored data. This word size has an impact on the amount of memory that can be referenced since it would be used to refer to a memory address. In fact, IBM's System/360 helped to standardize both the eight-bit byte as well as addressing on byte boundaries rather than arbitrary bit locations.

The downside to this approach and the reason that all memory isn't allocated from secondary storage is the difference in the speed of reading and writing. Secondary storage is secondary specifically because it's not nearly as fast as primary storage. When you write something out to secondary storage and then later retrieve it, there is a cost because that access is much slower. So, when you write pages of memory out to secondary storage temporarily, it should be done in a considered fashion because to blindly write a lot of memory out to secondary storage and then need to read it back in again can cause a significant performance hit to your system.

NOTE If memory pages aren't written out and read back in efficiently, you can end up with a condition called thrashing, where more time is spent writing memory out or reading it back in than actually performing real work. This can happen if you have systems with very limited physical memory but a lot of demands for virtual memory, because pages are constantly having to be swapped in and out of the physical memory.

Virtual memory provides the ability for a process to make use of more memory than is actually installed in the system. This allows for larger, more complex programs to run in systems that don't have enough memory to accommodate them. This was very important in the days when the size of memory was counted in the thousands of words rather than the millions or billions. When there was a very limited amount of memory to work with, programmers had to learn to be very economical about how they wrote programs. In computers with such limited memory sizes, it was even more difficult to consider running multiple processes at the same time when a single process might have a hard time fitting into the memory space that was available. In order to accommodate multiple processes, which is what we are used to today, we need to have virtual memory.

Virtual memory provides each process a memory space that makes it look as though the process has the full run of the system memory. In fact, there is a translation process that converts what the process believes the memory address is to where that piece of data is stored in real memory. Figure 10-2 is a visual representation of how multiple processes can be presented with what appears to be a full memory space (0x000000–0xFFFFFF), while in reality there are several processes/applications that are being fit into the real memory space. This is a very simplistic representation, of course. In reality, an application is presented with a memory space that is more fitting of its needs rather than having

Figure 10-2
Virtual memory
should be
available for each
application.

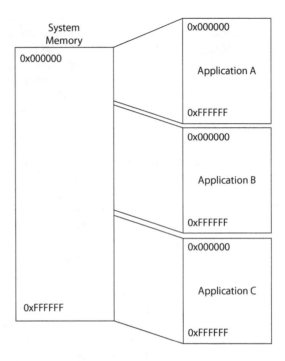

the run of the entire memory space. As necessary, applications can request additional memory and have it allocated by the operating system. This results in the allocation of a chunk of virtual memory with a set of addresses presented to the process. As those addresses begin to be referenced, it results in real memory being used.

Since the process is referring to a piece of memory that doesn't actually exist, there needs to be a way to look up that virtual address to see where it refers to in the real memory. There are a number of ways of accomplishing this, though having hardware that performs the lookup is considerably faster. One way of doing this is to implement a translation lookaside buffer (TLB), which is typically implemented using content-addressable memory (CAM). CAM is the same sort of memory used in network switches and it works by being able to look up information based on another piece of information rather than by a simple numerical index.

In the case of a TLB, you look up the real address based on the virtual address. If the page is available in memory, it can be found in the TLB and the result of the lookup is the relevant place in memory. You can see the process in Figure 10-3. If the page isn't found in the TLB, the operating system then does a page walk through the page table to find the right reference, which results in the location of the page, whether it is in memory or in secondary storage. Figure 10-3 shows a rough depiction of the multistage process of locating a page of memory.

Virtual memory not only provides a lot of capabilities for multiprocess, multiuser operating systems, but it also provides a foundation for the creation of virtual machines.

Figure 10-3
A translation
lookaside buffer

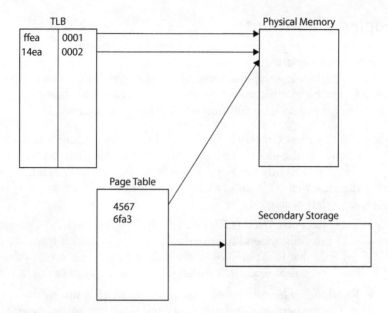

Without virtual memory, virtual machines would require physical memory to be allocated to every virtual machine and be set aside strictly for that virtual machine. No other virtual machine could touch the physical memory of another virtual machine. With virtual memory, no virtual machine can reach in and touch another's memory, but they can share the same physical memory space and sometimes make use of the same bits of physical memory, using the memory at different points in time, of course.

NOTE Windows makes use of a pagefile to store pages of memory that have to temporarily reside on secondary storage. You can typically find the pagefile in the root of your primary hard drive. Unix-like systems such as Linux make use of swap space or a swap partition to write pages of real memory out to disk.

Any page from memory that has to be swapped out to secondary storage will eventually need to be swapped back in. When a process makes a reference to a page that isn't in real memory, it generates a page fault and then forces the process of replacing a page that's in memory with one that's required from virtual memory.

Exercise 10-1: Pagefile Size
Find the pagefile on a Windows system, which should be in the root of your primary system drive, typically C:. You will need to adjust the options in Windows Explorer/ File Explorer to show hidden files and also show operating system files. How big is the pagefile.sys file on your system?

Paging Algorithms

There are a number of ways that a system can use paging. Early on, these algorithms were far more important than they typically are today, considering the enormous gulf in terms of processing power and speed of access to the devices that memory is being paged to. However, it's worth considering some of the algorithms that might be used to decide which memory should be sent out to a pagefile or swap space.

- **First In First Out (FIFO)**   The FIFO approach removes the page that is essentially the oldest. This approach doesn't take into account when the page was most recently used or if it has been used recently at all. It simply takes the view that it's been in memory the longest and so can be written out to secondary storage.

- **Least Recently Used (LRU)**   The LRU algorithm uses pages that haven't been used in a while to send to secondary storage. This makes some logical sense in that any page that hasn't been used in a while may not be needed in the near future. If it hasn't been used recently, it makes sense to move it out of primary memory.

- **Random**   The random method is sort of a hands-up, we can't predict what may come next, so why bother pretending we can approach. Any page might be selected, so there is a chance that a page that has just been swapped out may need to be swapped back in within the next few clock cycles. It may also be that it doesn't get used again for several minutes, in which case it was a good choice. This is the same risk/reward as many of the algorithms for page replacement, however, so it's not necessarily any better or worse than any others.

- **Optimal**   This algorithm makes some assumptions and can't be implemented in a general-purpose operating system because of them. With an optimal algorithm, the primary assumption is that the order of pages needed can be predicted. This may be possible with some operating systems, particularly those of a real-time nature. If that's the case, the page that should be replaced in memory is the one that will be needed at a time furthest in the future. That would be the optimal page to replace and give the most time until that page needs to be swapped back in.

- **Not Recently Used (NRU)**   Not Recently Used is similar to Least Recently Used except that NRU takes a snapshot at a specified clock interval and categorizes the pages in memory in one of four categories. The categories then determine the order that the pages may be replaced in, starting with the lowest category and moving up if the algorithm doesn't find any pages in that category. Once a category with pages in it is found, a random page is selected and replaced. The categories used are as follows:
  - Referenced (read) and modified (written)
  - Referenced but not modified
  - Not referenced but modified
  - Not referenced and not modified

There are other page replacement algorithms, but the preceding is a good sampling and gives an indication of the complexity of the decisions that have to be made to maintain the performance of a system that uses virtual memory. While memory has gotten considerably faster over the years and accessing hard drives has also gotten faster, any algorithm that moves pages out of main memory that are then required by a running process will end up slowing down the system because it's going to spend a lot of time reading and writing to the disk.

Security Implications

Virtual memory has implications on security. One advantage to making use of virtual memory is the fact that when addresses that don't refer to actual memory addresses are used, other processes can't easily access memory belonging to another process. If my program attempted to refer to a memory location that wasn't part of the memory allocated to me, I would get an error indicating that I was attempting to access memory that didn't belong to my process. Figure 10-4 shows a C program on a Linux system that refers to a specific memory address that doesn't belong to the process. You can see this has generated a segmentation fault, meaning the operating system has detected an attempt to access a memory segment that doesn't belong to the process. The program then terminates. Using virtual memory also means that a process can be placed into memory at any location, and memory references are handled automatically by the operating system, based on the actual location in memory of the process. Using virtual memory also helps ensure that processes can be relocated in memory since the process is entirely unaware of where it actually lives.

While virtual memory can provide protection to processes in memory, it has some risks when it comes time to swapping pages out to secondary storage. That secondary storage may be vulnerable to being read, potentially exposing sensitive information from any process that's running. Even beyond the fact that it may be available while the system

Figure 10-4
A segmentation fault

```
kilroy@bill: $ cat segment.c
#include <stdio.h>

int main(int argc, char **argv)
{
        int *p;
        p = 0xffffff;

        printf("The value of p is %d", *p);

        return 0;

}

kilroy@bill: $ ./segment
Segmentation fault (core dumped)
```

is live, if time isn't taken to wipe the pagefile or swap space before shutting down, that data may be available after the system has been powered down. If a system was simply powered off without going through a shutdown process that has the potential to wipe the stored data on secondary storage, the data would still be on the hard drive and potentially readable. There are ways to mitigate this risk by using encryption before storing pages that are being swapped out, but encryption can cause a performance issue for the running system, slowing down operation while pages get encrypted and decrypted based on whether they are going to, or coming from, secondary storage.

Reasons for Virtualizing

Virtualization has become a popular practice for several reasons. One of the primary reasons is that computers have become very powerful, with the capability for large amounts of physical memory and even larger amounts of disk space. It makes some sense to use virtual machines on a system like that to make better use of the resources available. Putting multiple operating systems onto a single physical device that is easily capable of supporting processing and resource demands will also save money in a number of ways. The first is simply not needing to buy another system. A system that an enterprise might purchase for use as a server might have redundant power supplies, lights-out management boards, and other components that would cause them to cost thousands of dollars if not over ten thousand dollars. Limiting the number of these systems would have a beneficial impact on the bottom line of a company.

Once you limit the number of systems you are operating, you get several ancillary benefits, like reducing your need for air conditioning, which means less money in initial outlay from a smaller air conditioning unit but also in less electricity necessary to power the A/C unit. While we're on the subject of electricity costs, fewer systems means less electricity necessary to power them. Over time, those reduced costs will add up to significant savings. From a strictly monetary perspective, virtualization makes a lot of sense.

Virtualization makes sense from an administrative perspective as well. Without virtualization, you would have to connect to multiple systems for administration or perhaps access several physical consoles to administer the systems, whereas with a virtualized environment you simply need to gain access to the system that is hosting all of the virtual systems. From that system, you can get access to the console of each virtual system without needing to initiate another connection. The software managing the virtual machine provides the console to you on the desktop of the system you are connected to.

 EXAM TIP While you can consolidate hardware onto one platform, you still must pay for all of the operating systems and software required. Virtualized environments don't save money on operating system costs.

Virtual machine software typically provides a way of creating a snapshot of the running operating system. This allows for a number of capabilities, including using virtual machines for testing. Testing requires a consistent platform to execute against in order to ensure that each test is being run against a system in a known state. No matter what type of testing you are performing, you can generate a snapshot of your virtual machine before your test, and when you are done testing, you can roll back to the snapshot and have the exact same system state for the next test you are planning to perform. This restoring to a known state is significantly faster than even doing a restoral of an image using a tool like Ghost. Additionally, you can have a number of states that you may want to restore to and virtualization software will allow you to have multiple snapshots. Figure 10-5 shows a dialog box from the virtualization software Parallels allowing the user to manage their snapshots. While the dialog box shows a single snapshot, the more disk space you have, the more snapshots you can have.

The snapshots combined with the control over the system through software configuration also make virtual machines perfect for malware analysis. When you are trying to decide what a particular piece of malware is doing, you want to be able to get it to infect your test system and then restore to a completely clean state later. Looking at a virus, for example, you would take a snapshot and then infect your test system. If you are concerned about the malware engaging in network activity, you can control the network

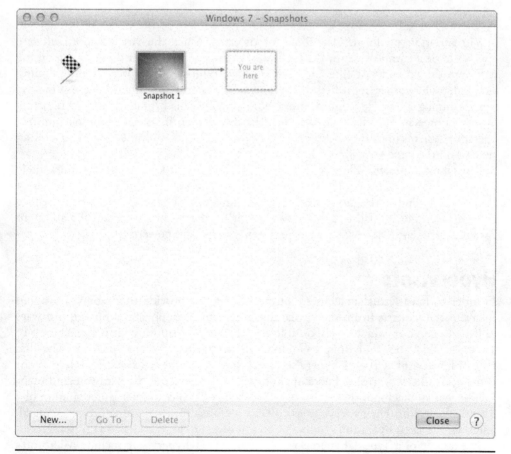

Figure 10-5   Parallels snapshots

interface through the virtualization software. You may want to restrict the network activity to only being able to connect to the host, which would allow you to better monitor the activity without the system being able to connect to any other system on your network or other networks, potentially spreading the malware.

I've hinted at this, but virtualization will allow you to quickly get systems up and running. You can see this when you use one of the cloud computing platforms like Amazon Elastic Compute Cloud (EC2) or Microsoft Azure. These platforms allow you to go from a system request to having the system up and running in a matter of seconds. There is a lot of automation being done in the background that allows that to happen, but it does demonstrate the capability of a virtualization platform in quickly spinning systems up. If you are adequately prepared, you should be able to get a system fully up and running in a matter of minutes or hours, rather than hours or days as you might in a traditional system situation.

 NOTE Amazon uses Xen as the virtualization server that powers their EC2 platform.

Virtualization platforms also allow for diversity. Since the virtualization software appears to be a complete set of PC hardware, any operating system that can run on the hardware should run just fine and you can have multiple operating systems running alongside one another, regardless of the operating system. You might have a Windows server running alongside a Linux and a BSD system. This brings us back to the cost-savings approach. You don't need a lot of hardware even if you are running multiple operating systems in your infrastructure since you can install multiple different operating systems on the same virtualization platform.

Virtual machines will allow you to create an entire network of systems within a single piece of hardware. This could allow you to create a lab environment for a number of reasons, including testing a full application architecture. This could be used to reduce costs and complexity within a lab network. For testing purposes, having the ability to consolidate an entire lab within a single system can be very powerful.

Hypervisors

In order to have virtual machines, you need a way to provide the resources for, and intercept the requests from, the virtual machine. This is done with a piece of software called a hypervisor, which is responsible for creating and running virtual machines. In 1974, Gerald Popek and Robert Goldberg defined two types of hypervisor. The first type of hypervisor, a Type 1 hypervisor, runs directly on the hardware. The hypervisor is the operating system that boots up, and its job is to control the hardware and manage the virtual machines that sit on top of it. Figure 10-6 is a visual representation of a Type 1 hypervisor. The hypervisor, as you can see, sits directly on top of the bare metal, and then the guest operating systems sit on top of the hypervisor. IBM's CP/CMS is an early example of a Type 1 hypervisor. Modern Type 1 hypervisors include Microsoft's Hyper-V, KVM, and VMware's ESX/ESXi hypervisors.

Figure 10-6
A Type 1
hypervisor

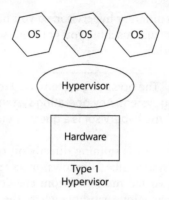
Type 1
Hypervisor

 EXAM TIP Some of the virtualization vendors have a range of products. VMware, for example, has their server-class ESX/ESXi product all the way down to the free VMware Workstation Player.

A Type 2 hypervisor has an additional layer in the model. With a Type 2 hypervisor, the hypervisor isn't in direct control of the hardware since there is an operating system that sits on top of the bare metal of the hardware and then the hypervisor lives within the operating system. In this model, the operating system that boots up that the hypervisor runs on top of is the host operating system. As you can see in Figure 10-7, in a Type 2 hypervisor model, the host operating system could support multiple Type 2 hypervisors, and each hypervisor could support multiple operating systems that it manages. While this can provide some advantages in terms of flexibility, having multiple hypervisors does take resources in terms of memory and storage space. You may, however, have a virtual machine that you have gotten from somewhere else that you need to run, but maybe

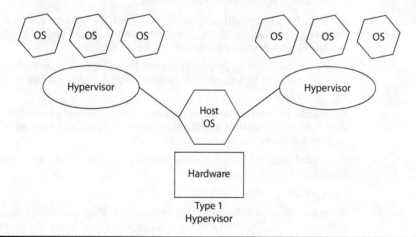
Type 1
Hypervisor

Figure 10-7 A Type 2 hypervisor

you're already using a different hypervisor, so you need to install a second Type 2 hypervisor to support the virtual machine you got from somewhere else that you can't convert for one reason or another.

 EXAM TIP The operating system used to boot the system is the host operating system. Any operating system that is managed by, and runs inside of, the hypervisor is a guest operating system.

Whether the hypervisor is running directly on top of the hardware or is running on top of an operating system like Windows, macOS, or Linux, the job of the hypervisor is to manage the virtual machines from creation to modification. This would also include creating or managing snapshots where the current state of the virtual machine gets stored, including the state of the hardware, the hard disk, and the memory if the system is already running.

The hypervisor has to emulate an entire set of hardware in software. Whereas the hardware system has non-volatile RAM (NVRAM) to store system BIOS settings and a hard drive to store data, the hypervisor has to do the same thing with a set of files that keep track of the system configuration, including the number, type, and size of the hard drives in the system, as well as the controller they are connected to. The hypervisor also keeps track of the video memory size, the network controllers, the USB devices, and the number of processors that are being exposed to the virtual machine. This is all done through a set of files that the hypervisor creates and manages. As an example, Table 10-1 shows the files that VMware uses for each virtual machine.

File Extension	File Description
.log	VMware logs activity to this file. It can be very useful for troubleshooting.
.nvram	All of the settings that would be managed by the system BIOS are stored in this file, which emulates the system NVRAM.
.vmdk	This is the file where the hard drive data is stored. The hard drive can be broken up into multiple 2G files. If the hard drive is broken up into multiple files, the filename would include the number of the file.
.vmsd	VMware stores information about the snapshots. This file is not where the actual snapshot itself is stored but the metadata about the snapshots that the system has.
.vmsn	This is where the actual snapshot is stored. Since there may be multiple snapshots, each snapshot would have a filename including a number to indicate a different snapshot.
.vmss	When you suspend a virtual machine, this is where the suspended state is stored.
.vmtm	If you are using teams, this is where team data is stored.
.vmx	This is the primary configuration file where information about the system settings are kept. This is an XML file and could be edited by hand if necessary.
.vmxf	This is where configuration data is stored for virtual machines that are in teams.

Table 10-1 VMware Files

EXAM TIP The .vmx file is the file that VMware uses to store the system configuration in an XML format. This file could be edited to correct a problem. The hard disk data is stored in the .vmdk files.

Virtual Resources

The hypervisor is not only responsible for managing virtual machines but also responsible for presenting the hardware to the operating system and managing the calls from the operating system to the hardware. In most cases, requests to the hardware are handled using a trap-and-emulate approach where the software in the hypervisor handles the request directly by, for example, reading from or writing to the file representing the hard drive. The hypervisor is trapping the system call and then handling it internally based on the hardware that has been presented to the operating system.

NOTE A version of the Pentium 4 was the first Intel processor to support hardware-assisted virtualization in 2005. This was followed the next year by AMD, providing similar support in the Athlon processors.

The Multics operating system introduced the concept of multiple rings to protect the operating system kernel as well as the applications executing on the operating system. The idea of the rings is that some functions require a higher level of privilege than others, so those functions should execute only in a privileged space, and typical user space applications don't require that level of privilege, so they shouldn't have access to the privileged space. Figure 10-8 shows the ring model with ring 0 in the very center. Ring 0 is the highest level of privilege where functions like memory access take place. Outside of that would be device drivers that may need to touch hardware either directly or indirectly.

Figure 10-8
The multiple rings of an operating system

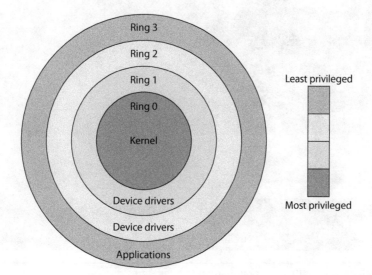

On the very outside ring, ring 3, are the user applications that don't require privileges. Using this model, some functions are abstracted to protect the most critical functions of the kernel.

An operating system expects to have full control over the hardware, issuing calls that would interact with the hardware. Additionally, the operating system expects to handle memory management, including managing virtual memory. An operating system running inside a virtual environment wouldn't have direct access to things like the memory or the page tables. Because of that, shadow tables might be created in order to provide the level of access required by the guest OS without negatively impacting the host OS or taking the management of memory out of its control. Extensions to the processors have been introduced in recent years to provide extended page tables, allowing the virtual machines to appear to have control over the TLB and page tables for a system while leaving the memory still under the control of the host operating system.

A virtual machine might be able to offer hardware that the host system doesn't actually have. One example is multiple network interface cards or multiple hard drives. In Figure 10-9 you can see the configuration dialog box for VMware. In the middle are a number of hardware devices that are being presented to the guest OS—in this case, a

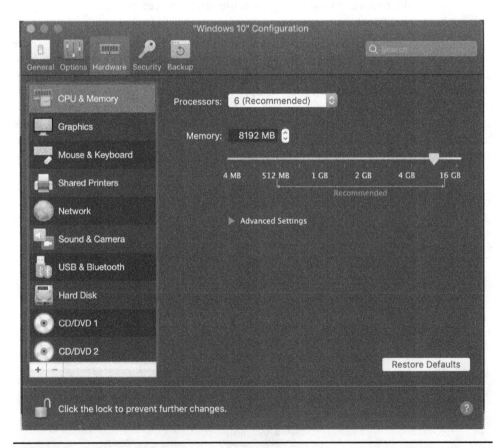

Figure 10-9   A VMware configuration

Windows 10 system. You can have multiple network adapters configured to run on the system. You might have a second created to do some testing with routing and remote access, though the second interface may not actually exist in the host system. If you happen to have multiple interfaces on your physical system, you could create multiple interfaces on your guest system and map the interfaces so your guest OS is connected to the same networks that your physical system is connected to.

In addition to providing access to emulated hardware that would be used exclusively by the virtual machine, a hypervisor may also want to provide some access to the host OS either by way of the filesystem or by hiding the desktop of the guest and integrating with the host. This is done by installing drivers onto the guest OS to give access to a filesystem that the host may not otherwise have drivers for. The drivers also provide the ability for the guest OS to effectively disappear. Windows that get created by the guest OS are displayed just as they are on the desktop of the host OS, where they stand alongside windows created by the host. This can be a very useful feature for cases where you are running one OS inside a completely different one. For example, I run macOS on my desktop but I have virtual machines that run different versions of Windows. When I am in an integrated mode, I can have an Internet Explorer window open on my macOS desktop without ever seeing the Windows desktop itself. Both VMware and Parallels offer this sort of integration between their host and guest operating systems.

An application for virtual machines is through virtual desktop infrastructure (VDI). This may be especially important when developing an infrastructure to support isolated servers. System administrators don't often sit in front of the server's console. Management of servers is done remotely. However, leaving the network open so this remote management can be performed from the desktop network is problematic. It exposes holes that shouldn't be left open. This is an area VDI can help with. Administrators can connect to VDI systems, which have connections to the server network, either directly or through tight firewall rules. This is not the only case where VDI may be implemented. In some cases, remote workers can connect to VDI in order to access sensitive corporate resources without having to allow direct access, even through a virtual private network, from a remote worker's system. This can help to limit the spread of malware since malware can't typically jump from a user's desktop system to a virtual machine accessed either through a direct client like Microsoft's Remote Desktop Client or through a web-based interface like VMware can use. This isolation and segmentation can be an important part of an overall security strategy.

Break Outs

Part of the purpose of virtual machines is to segment resources without having to increase the amount of hardware in the environment. This means you want to have your applications and your data separate from one another, especially in the case of multitenancy where multiple customers may be using the same hypervisor. In theory, the operating system and applications have no awareness that they are in a virtualized environment. In practice, however, this is not the case. As one example, the network interface in a VMware-based virtual machine will have a media access control (MAC) address that has a vendor ID of VMware. The same is true of all the other hypervisor manufacturers. The vendor ID of the MAC address, at a minimum, will indicate that the hardware is being provided by virtualization software. The same is true of other hardware that is presented to the virtual machine. Because of that, it is possible for an application to be aware it is in a virtual machine.

A significant concern in virtual environments is that an application might break out of the environment. This would allow an attacker access to the underlying hypervisor. These "jail breaks" typically rely on vulnerabilities in the hypervisor that could be exploited to get to the hypervisor itself. Once an attacker got access to the hypervisor, they then have control of all of the virtual machines being controlled by that hypervisor. No matter where they started, even if it was a virtual machine that had nothing of significance stored on it, an attacker could gain access to sensitive or critical information.

This raises two points. The first, commonly known, is that it's important to keep up with all updates to software. This is just as true when we are talking about hypervisors as it is when we are talking about operating system or application updates. The second point is that all information and system resources should be classified based on a policy developed by the organization. Even though the operating systems are segmented by the hypervisor, the *possibility* of an attacker breaking out of a virtual machine should be enough to encourage administrators to apply the same level of classification to all virtual machines on a given hypervisor. This classification should also encompass the data that is stored or potentially passes through that virtual machine. This won't prevent breaking out of the virtual machine, but it will prevent an attacker from getting into a low-classification virtual machine and breaking out to gain access to one with a higher classification that has more sensitive data on it.

Malware and Virtualized Resources

With virtual machines, you get isolation. There is a measure of security you get with this isolation. It's not perfect. With multiple virtual machines on a single hypervisor, you not only get scalability, you get the ability to control which VMs can talk to other VMs since you control the switch fabric. This makes VMs a good way to isolate malware for study and analysis. The problem, though, is that malware authors understand this. Identifying that a program is running on a virtual machine isn't that difficult. First, every network interface has an organizationally unique identifier (OUI). Half of the OUI is the vendor ID. The vendor ID for network interfaces assigned by a hypervisor is that of the company that develops the virtual machine software. Malware authors can pull the vendor ID and determine whether the network interface is one from a virtual machine.

MAC addresses can be changed at the operating system level. This would be one way to protect against malware identifying that a program is running inside a VM. However, there are other ways to identify that a program is running inside a VM. On Windows, there would be registry keys. On Linux, there would be other markers. Why does this matter? If malware could detect that a program is running in a VM, it would just become dormant and not affect the VM since, theoretically, it would want to avoid analysis.

However, malware may not go dormant in the case of a VM. There are instances of malware infecting VMs just as it would a physical machine. Beyond that, though, malware may change its behavior inside a VM so it appears to be something it isn't. The short version of this discussion is that VMs are not protection against malware.

Containers

While traditional machine-level virtualization is still prevalent, there is another type of virtualization that is becoming common. This is a container, which provides application-level virtualization rather than operating system–level virtualization. Instead of providing a set of virtual hardware where the hypervisor traps requests to that hardware, a container is just an isolated application with whatever it needs for library dependencies. The application is running through the same kernel as every other application on the system. There is no other operating system running. This does mean that applications that are containerized have to be able to run in the same kernel as the one that is handling the containers. Figure 10-10 shows a conceptual diagram of what this looks like.

Containers are handled at the kernel level through the use of something called namespaces. If you are familiar with object-oriented programming concepts, this is essentially the same concept. A namespace provides a context that allows for clear, unambiguous reference. In some cases, such as this, you can't refer to something outside of the namespace you are in. You may think of it in the sense of your own name. Let's say your name is John Smith. You have two brothers, James and Jeff. You also have a sister Judy. You can refer to each of them when you are talking within your family by their first name. Everyone in your family knows who you are talking about. As soon as you want to talk about a different Jeff, though, you would need to refer to a separate namespace and use his entire name, which may be Jeff Jones. So, within your family, Jeff means Jeff Smith. If you want to talk about Judy's boyfriend Jeff, you would need to call him Jeff Jones.

A namespace in the context of an operating system is similar. When we are talking about processes talking to other processes, they do that by referring to a process ID (PID)

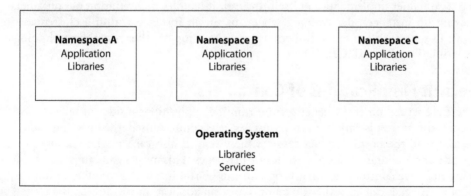

Figure 10-10   Conceptual view of containers

since the name of the process is essentially meaningless at that level—there may be multiple processes with the same name—and a process ID takes up much less space in memory. When a kernel supports namespaces or labels, each process gets its own process ID space. Essentially, to the kernel, a reference to a process would be something like spaceA:5468. If your application is running in spaceA, any reference to another process ID refers to someone else in its "family." The only way to get to another process would be to know what the namespace is and then know what the process is. Each namespace is isolated, though, and can't see any other namespace, including the namespace for the primary operating environment.

One aspect of containers that may cause some stickiness in understanding them is that containers are defined on disk. There is probably a file, or even multiple files, that describes the container—any dependencies, what resources the container needs, and so on. That's not really the container, though. That's just a template for what the container would look like when it's running. You can have multiple instances of a single template running and each would be its own container with its own process namespace. You can't have three instances of a single container template, for example, running and have any one instance know anything about any other instance. It would be like starting from a single system image and creating clones of that image onto multiple hardware systems. The only thing they have in common is they look and behave the same. There is no other connection between them.

There are multiple implementations of containers from which to choose. A popular one is Docker. This is a program that runs on multiple platforms, which is part of what makes it popular. Another container implementation is the one specifically for Linux, LXC/LXD. These implementations not only provide the ability to marshal resources for a container instance but also provide container management—starting, stopping, checking status, and so on. You may also get some help with the creation of containers from some container implementations so you aren't trying to write a detailed configuration file by hand.

There is a difference between the implementation of the container and the management of it. This is what makes a technology like Kubernetes popular. Kubernetes isn't a container implementation itself. Instead, it handles orchestration of containers—starting up instances, determining where to run an instance within a cluster, tearing down instances, and so forth. Kubernetes can sit on top of other container technologies, including Docker or LXC/LXD.

Security Implications of Containers

There are several potential benefits from running applications inside containers. One of them is the process isolation. Even if a process gets compromised, the infecting code can't get access to the host operating system's filesystem. It also can't migrate to any process outside of the container in order to elevate privileges. This means you can isolate applications and have control over what programs can be run inside the container, minimizing what an attacker can do if they do compromise an application within a container.

Another advantage is that containers can be (and often are being) used for scalability. This means you can have multiple container instances that can be called upon as needed to handle load. You would have some ability to direct processing to a particular container as requests come in. When load subsides, you can tear down the containers. Everything is ephemeral, meaning it comes and goes as needed. If an attacker does get access to an application inside a container, you can tear down the container and the attacker loses access. They would have to start the attack process all over again. This isn't a deterrent but it does make life a lot harder for the attacker. It's a lot harder to maintain persistent access when your foothold keeps getting taken away and moved somewhere else. Anything the attacker has uploaded to the container instance will get lost when the container goes away.

Container code, especially in an application where containers are created and destroyed as needed, is potentially much easier to maintain. Bugs can be fixed far faster by just replacing the application or configuration in the container template without having to have a maintenance window that may cause an application outage. Any vulnerability that could be exploited could be removed quickly. As containers are started up to handle requests, all the old, vulnerable code goes away, and as containers get torn down, attackers get kicked out and, with the bug they took advantage of gone, they won't be able to get right back in.

None of this is to say containers provide perfect security. Any bug in the kernel or in the orchestration code could be discovered, which would allow an attacker to potentially break out of the container and get access to the underlying operating environment. However, containers do enable you to provide some good hurdles that an attacker has to get over, making their life much harder. Containers are one way of providing elasticity; meaning, the virtualized applications can be instantiated and torn down as needed to support demand. Any given container isn't a permanent entity and there is no permanent storage in the container. The persistent attacks are no longer as persistent, potentially, as they were before.

Other Virtual Machines

Earlier, we discussed UCSD Pascal and its implementation inside a virtual machine to achieve architecture independence. Using a byte-code or pseudo-code model, the compiler portion of a language doesn't have to be changed at all for different architectures since the byte code never changes and all of the things about each machine architecture or operating system binary interface don't matter. The only portion of a language system that implements a virtual machine to run pseudo-code is the interpreter itself since it's responsible for actually translating the pseudo-code to machine code that will run on the operating system and hardware. It may not be as obvious as the hardware, which dictates the machine instructions that are allowed based on the processor's instruction set.

Another component that has to be taken into consideration is how the operating system interfaces with the executables. Different operating systems handle function calls differently or lay out data differently. This is called the application binary interface (ABI), and having different ABIs for different operating systems is also a challenge that can lead to a language adopting a virtual machine architecture in order to implement the executable portion of the language. Different from the ABI, but just as important, are the system calls that are required in order to actually make things work. Every operating system supports different system calls. The system call is how an application makes requests to the operating system kernel for things like I/O. Since fundamental functions like I/O are different from one operating system to another, it can make a lot of sense to implement pseudo-code or byte code where that is what ends up being interpreted for the execution of the program.

While it's far from the only programming language that is implemented in a virtual machine, Java is well known for its virtual machine architecture. In addition to presenting a representation of hardware and an operating system to the application, handling functions that a system call would handle, Java also adds some functions that wouldn't normally get handled as much by an operating system but would be the responsibility of the application. This includes handling memory management. The Java Runtime Environment (JRE) will run garbage collection services periodically, ensuring that memory segments no longer in use are disposed of and the memory is freed up again for use. Figure 10-11 shows the different components of the Java architecture, including the architecture independence of the design—Java not only runs on a traditional desktop system but is also capable of running on a smartphone platform.

 NOTE Java was originally developed with the television set–top market or similar embedded device market in mind. Java still can run either inside another operating system or directly on the hardware.

As with virtual machines running a more traditional operating system, there are advantages to creating applications using Java and making use of the virtual machine architecture. When a Java application is executed, a new instance of a virtual machine is created to run that application in. Multiple applications are not executed in the same memory space. This protects each Java application inside its own sandbox. Applications can't, as a general rule, impact one another in spite of their best attempts at corrupting the memory space of another application. This isn't to say that it's impossible, but a correct implementation of the architecture would prevent it from happening.

Other languages like Ruby and Python have virtual machine implementations for the execution of code. In fact, Python can be compiled to Java byte code and executed within a Java virtual machine. This is done using the Jython package. The process can be seen in Figure 10-11 where Python source files (.py) are converted to Java byte code using Jython and then can be run in any Java virtual machine. Python itself is capable of running on a number of platforms, but this provides a way to make use of an existing Java runtime environment without needing to install the Python runtime environment since Java is more commonly installed than Python is.

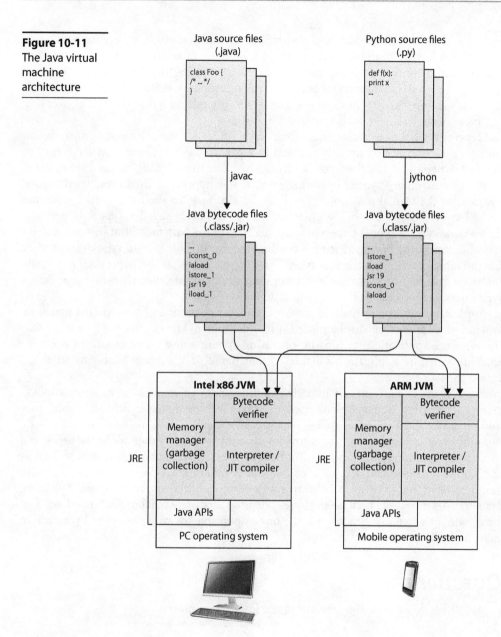

Figure 10-11
The Java virtual machine architecture

Chapter Review

While virtualization is really starting to take off in the PC world, the concept of virtual machines actually goes back to the 1950s, and commercial implementations of virtual systems have been around on larger-scale systems since the 1960s, with full hardware-supported virtualization going back to the 1970s. The primary need for hardware support for virtualization is to implement a way to virtualize memory, since virtual memory not only is critical to the success of a virtual guest running inside a physical host but is also critical for multitasking, multiprocessing systems in order to effectively overload the physical memory by having more applications running than would fit in physical memory. The way to achieve this feat is by using secondary storage to offload the overflow. This requires management of the memory by organizing it into fixed-size pages that can more easily be cataloged for storage and retrieval.

Hypervisors have been around as long as the idea of a virtual machine in concept, though that concept was actually codified in a paper in 1974. There are effectively two types of hypervisors. The first type is a hypervisor that runs directly on the bare metal of a system, much like a typical operating system. The hypervisor then provides the management of the virtual machines as well as the interface between the virtual machines and whatever hardware is being presented to them. This is called a Type 1 hypervisor. The second type, a Type 2 hypervisor, doesn't run on the bare metal but instead runs on top of an operating system that runs on the bare metal. This second type of hypervisor has the same functions as the first type. The difference is what the hypervisor is actually interfacing with. The first type interfaces with the hardware directly, while the second type interfaces with the host operating system.

Applications can be virtualized now, without the need for an entire virtual machine. Instead, the application can be placed into a container. The container is a way of segmenting the application within the operating system using a namespace in memory that prevents any application outside of that namespace gaining access to anything inside the namespace.

Not all virtual machines are intended to implement an entire system. Some application programming languages have used a virtual machine model to achieve architecture and processor independence. A language like Java uses a virtual machine to execute the application code inside of it. This provides protection against other applications, as well as a way of abstracting the machine interface so the language and applications written in it become more portable. Even a class that has been compiled down to byte code could run, unaltered, on an entirely different system using a different processor and operating system. This is possible because the byte code used is entirely machine independent. The byte code interpreter or processor is the one responsible for converting the byte code to machine code to execute.

Questions

1. Which decade saw the creation of the first virtual machines?

   A. 1940s

   B. 1980s

   C. 1990s

   D. 1960s

2. What does Java use to achieve architecture independence?

   A. Byte code

   B. Parallel (p-) code

   C. Virtual code

   D. Machine code

3. Which of the following VMware files can be edited by hand and changed in the case of problems?

   A. .log

   B. .vmx

   C. .vmdk

   D. .vmss

4. How would you define the host operating system?

   A. The operating system that runs in the virtual machine

   B. The operating system in a suspended state

   C. The operating system that boots first and interfaces directly with the hardware

   D. The operating system that manages the creation of new virtual machines

5. What is a translation lookaside buffer used for?

   A. Translating virtual pages of memory into physical locations

   B. Translating hardware interrupts for a USB interface

   C. Buffering input for applications

   D. Providing cache for the processor

6. Without virtual memory, what were programmers typically required to use?

   A. Hardware debuggers

   B. Software debuggers

   C. Overlays

   D. Memory access

7. What are two primary responsibilities of the hypervisor?

   A. Manage the creation of virtual machines and act as a guest OS.

   B. Act as a guest OS and boot first.

   C. Boot first and provide access to virtual memory.

   D. Manage the creation of virtual machines and provide an interface for the guest OS to hardware.

8. Which of VMware's products is available for free to run virtual machines in?

   A. VMware Player

   B. VMware Workstation

   C. VMware ESX

   D. VMware ESXi

9. Which of these is NOT a reason for virtualizing?

   A. It saves space in the server room.

   B. It saves money on hardware acquisition.

   C. It saves money on infrastructure costs like electricity and cooling.

   D. It saves money on OS licenses and support.

10. What's the difference between virtualization and emulation?

   A. Emulation allows operating systems to run on a hardware platform they weren't designed for.

   B. Virtualization allows operating systems to run on a hardware platform they weren't designed for.

   C. Emulation is an outdated term meaning the same thing as virtualization.

   D. Virtualization is an outdated term meaning the same thing as emulation.

11. What is an advantage of using virtual machines when it comes to malware?

   A. Malware may go dormant.

   B. Malware won't run in a VM.

   C. VMs don't support malware.

   D. VMs change the architecture set.

12. How does virtual memory help programming practices?

   A. Virtual memory is unlimited.

   B. Virtual memory is handled by the kernel.

   C. Virtual memory is faster than physical memory.

   D. Virtual memory can be ported easily.

13. How do containers differ from virtual machines?

   A. Containers are physical, not virtual.

   B. Virtual machines support more resources.

   C. Containers support more resources.

   D. Containers don't have their own operating system.

14. What is one reason to ensure virtual machine software is updated regularly?

   A. Virtual machines need to be updated to support architecture changes.

   B. Vulnerabilities could lead to breaking out.

   C. Virtual machines may lead to denial of services.

   D. Virtual machine software is poorly coded.

15. How can the use of containers improve the overall security of an application deployment?

   A. Containers control system calls.

   B. Containers prevent the use of hardware.

   C. Containers are easy to deploy and undeploy rapidly.

   D. Containers can be orchestrated.

Answers

1. D. Some of the first virtual machines were built in the 1960s by IBM at two of their locations. While the 1980s saw the first emulations on smaller systems and the 1990s saw the beginning of real virtualization on personal computers, virtualization had been created years before.

2. A. Java uses byte code, sometimes called pseudo-code. While p-code is sometimes used as a shorthand for pseudo-code, it doesn't stand for parallel code. Machine code is what the byte code is translated to during execution, and virtual code is a meaningless term in this situation.

3. B. The .vmx file is XML and stores the configuration of the virtual machine. It could be edited in case of a problem, assuming you could read and change XML. The .log file could be edited, but editing it wouldn't accomplish anything. The .vmdk file is the virtual hard drive. The .vmss file is related to a suspended virtual machine.

4. C. The host operating system is the one that boots first and directly interfaces with the hardware. The operating system that is inside a virtual machine is a guest. The operating system in a suspended state doesn't really have a name other than a suspended operating system, and it's not the host. The last answer describes the activities of a hypervisor, not necessarily an operating system.

5. A. The translation lookaside buffer (TLB) is a piece of hardware that helps with virtual memory by translating virtual memory addresses into physical addresses. While a virtual machine would provide emulation of hardware and interception of accesses to that hardware, it has nothing to do with the TLB.

6. C. The programmer would have to implement overlays where memory segments were effectively swapped in by the application program rather than being handled by the operating system. The programmer would typically have to do a lot of debugging, but neither a hardware debugger nor a software debugger would help overcome the lack of virtual memory.

7. D. A hypervisor may boot first, but it is primarily responsible for creation and management of virtual machines, as well as providing an interface for the guest operating system to the hardware. The hypervisor would not act as a guest OS.

8. A. Workstation, ESX, and ESXi are all commercial, paid-for applications. However, VMware does have a free Player that can be used to run existing virtual machines.

9. D. Cost savings are an important factor in the decision to virtualize. However, even with virtual machines, you still have to pay OS licensing and support costs. The places where you save are in hardware and infrastructure costs.

10. A. Emulation can provide a way for an operating system or application to run on an architecture it wasn't designed to run on. You could emulate a different processor and the emulator could provide a translation between the instructions on the hosted system and the instructions on the host system. Virtualization is a way of extending the resources of an existing system and using it to run multiple systems simultaneously.

11. A. Malware can detect when it is running inside a virtual machine and it may decide not to trigger its payload, to avoid being analyzed while in operation. Malware can run inside a virtual machine, but the malware author may choose to detect the existence of the virtual machine and terminate the program.

12. B. The operating system manages virtual memory. This means programmers don't have to be concerned over how to manage the memory, which was previously the case. Virtual memory can make it seem like there is more memory in a system. Virtual memory is no faster than physical memory. The statement that virtual memory can be ported more easily is vague, so without additional details it would not be the right answer.

13. D. Containers share the kernel with the hosting operating environment. Containers are not physical; they are still virtual. Virtual machines and containers can have the same amount of resources.

14. B. Vulnerabilities in the hypervisor software could lead to an attacker breaking out of the virtual machine and gaining access to all running virtual machines. If a vulnerability in the hypervisor is discovered, the hypervisor should be updated as soon as a fix is available. A vulnerability could lead to a denial of service too, however, an attacker being able to break out of the virtual machine and gain access to all running virtual machines would likely be much worse since it could be undetected for longer periods of time.

15. C. Containers can be deployed and undeployed quickly. This could remove the foothold an attacker has. The attacker would have to start again. Containers can be orchestrated, but virtual machines can be orchestrated as well. Orchestration is used to deploy, manage, and undeploy containers and virtual machines, which doesn't necessarily have an impact on security. Containers don't control system calls or prevent the use of hardware. A container goes through the existing kernel in the host operating environment.

Exercise 10-1 Answer

While every system will be different, you should get a result that looks similar to Figure 10-12.

## CHAPTER 11

Vulnerability Control

In this chapter, you will learn:
- About discovering vulnerabilities
- Strategies to manage vulnerabilities
- Different types of web vulnerabilities

A vulnerability is a weakness within a system or network, and enterprises develop processes and programs around managing them. Vulnerability mitigation can be handled through the use of different systems or processes, so even though a vulnerability has been identified, something else may be in place to keep the vulnerability from being exploited.

It's worth knowing what the potential of a vulnerability is, however, and then evaluating the probability of the vulnerability being exploited. Vulnerability scanners are often used as part of a Threat and Vulnerability Management (TVM) program, but as we will discuss later, vulnerability scanners are not flawless and sometimes turn up false positives. Vulnerabilities can arise from any number of directions, so it's helpful to know what these different directions are. You can even use some of the same tools your attackers might use in order to see what vectors of attack may be open.

Mapping your network on a regular basis will ensure that the systems shown are the ones you expect to be there and that the appropriate services are being offered. There are a few different ways to perform this mapping. Vulnerability scans provide you with a starting point for the types of vulnerabilities that may exist on your system. Of course, these scans aren't perfect, due to the nature of vulnerability scanners and how they operate. Beyond simply scanning for vulnerabilities, though, you could also try to exploit suspected vulnerabilities to prove they exist. Sometimes this sort of proof is a strong motivator in mitigating or removing such vulnerabilities.

One common place for vulnerabilities on a network is the web server, which puts at risk not only the server itself but the public networks and various applications it's exposed to. Web applications have a number of potential sources of weakness. This could be due to poor application logic or programming, or it could result from a problem with frameworks and libraries in use by the web application. Either way, it's helpful to check for vulnerabilities and understand how to get them under control in order to protect your network and any data stored on the server.

Network Mapping/Scanning

One of the first things you should do is gain an understanding of your network layout from the network perspective. While it is possible for systems to be configured to not appear on the network, you have a better chance of seeing what's out there by probing the network rather than trying to find every possible network connection and chasing it down, particularly with wireless networks being so prevalent. With a wireless connection, a networked device could be anywhere, and it would be difficult to find it. Locating networked devices is more easily accomplished by sending out probes on the network. Most times, you can get a device to respond to some network traffic and thus see what is out there. This will help you not only find potentially rogue devices, but will also check for potential misconfigurations where systems have IP addresses they aren't expected to have. Network scanning can also be done remotely, as opposed to physically checking for devices.

Various tools can be used to perform network scanning, and the results can be used to develop a map of the network. Some of these tools use the same techniques, though some have found different ways of scanning to get results. Ultimately, it comes down to sending out network requests and getting a response back that needs to be interpreted in some way. The interpretation is based on the way the specific protocol in use is designed to work, although there are sometimes anomalies based on different interpretations of the protocols.

Different Types of Mapping

When it comes time to map your network, the first thing you need to do is start issuing some network requests in order to get responses back. The request is based on the protocol you use to scan your network. Some choices of protocol will be based both on your location and the location of the hosts you are trying to scan. For instance, you wouldn't use a layer 2 protocol like Address Resolution Protocol (ARP) to check your network if you were on a separate subnet, because you wouldn't actually get any useful responses back. This is because layer 2 requests aren't forwarded through layer 3 devices. Having said that, you can and probably should use different protocols based on what you are looking for.

Using Address Resolution Protocol

Starting at the lowest layer from which we can issue network requests, we can take a look at how to go about issuing ARP requests in order to see if a particular device is responsive at layer 2. While firewalls may block higher-layer protocols, blocking a layer 2 ARP request looking for a media access control (MAC) address would make the system difficult to reach on the network since nothing could be sent to the system without knowing the MAC address. You could send an ARP request out for every IP address on the system in order to see whether a system responds or not. Any attempt to connect to the system using the IP address will result in an ARP request being generated, but you could save some trouble and just issue the ARP request directly. There are several ways you can do this, depending on the OS you are using. No matter what tool you end up using, what you are really doing is issuing an ARP message indicating that you have an IP address and need to know the MAC address of the network interface it belongs to. The following is a single packet (that has been captured) of an ARP request looking for the IP address:

```
15:21:19.110503 ARP, Ethernet (len 6), IPv4 (len 4), Request who-has
172.30.42.152 tell dslrouter.westell.com, length 46
```

You would issue a request just like this to every host on your network, looking to get an ARP response. Figure 11-1 shows the results from an ARP scan on the network using the Linux tool arp-scan. The tool issued to the network an ARP request looking for the MAC address of each IP address on the local network. As mentioned earlier, the reason for using an ARP scan rather than a scan using another protocol is that systems may be more likely to respond to ARP requests, knowing that someone is looking for their MAC address to send a message to them. If the systems don't respond to these requests, getting anything to them would require that the network be seeded with static ARP entries on every system. This doesn't scale very well and would require that every system be changed if the IP address of the system were to be changed for some reason. While this can be done and it may provide cloaking or obscurity, it's difficult to manage and is not particularly effective.

An ARP scan can provide additional information for you as well, as shown on the right in Figure 11-1, since the MAC address provides the vendor of the interface (if known). While you can't directly determine the OS running simply from the vendor ID, you can make some good guesses about what may be happening with a particular system. You can see some entries indicating that they are network interfaces created by Apple, Inc.

```
kilroy@bill: $ sudo arp-scan -I br0 --localnet
Interface: br0, datalink type: EN10MB (Ethernet)
Starting arp-scan 1.8.1 with 256 hosts (http://www.nta-monitor.com/tools/arp-sca
n/)
172.30.42.1      e0:46:9a:ce:03:83    NETGEAR
172.30.42.2      c8:d7:19:49:af:46    (Unknown)
172.30.42.4      00:1c:42:07:09:5a    Parallels, Inc.
172.30.42.34     00:1c:42:9e:7a:88    Parallels, Inc.
172.30.42.39     00:03:78:aa:df:a4    HUMAX Co., Ltd.
172.30.42.63     00:24:be:56:39:49    Sony Corporation
172.30.42.65     00:21:b7:00:53:23    Lexmark International Inc.
172.30.42.72     c0:cb:38:96:e9:85    Hon Hai Precision Ind. Co.,Ltd.
172.30.42.78     d4:9a:20:d0:53:10    Apple, Inc
172.30.42.36     3c:4a:92:d9:52:cd    Hewlett Packard
172.30.42.93     10:40:f3:e8:46:9a    (Unknown)
172.30.42.94     00:03:78:f5:04:a4    HUMAX Co., Ltd.
172.30.42.90     cc:3a:61:22:76:66    (Unknown)
172.30.42.51     f8:1e:df:e2:4d:bd    Apple, Inc
172.30.42.42     98:4b:4a:a9:f2:35    (Unknown)
172.30.42.240    70:56:81:ef:57:ab    (Unknown)
172.30.42.16     18:20:32:c1:fc:7c    (Unknown)

18 packets received by filter, 0 packets dropped by kernel
Ending arp-scan 1.8.1: 256 hosts scanned in 1.362 seconds (187.96 hosts/sec). 17
 responded
```

Figure 11-1   An ARP scan

That alone might tell you that the system is running some version of macOS. Of course, it might also be running a version of iOS, but even adding that possibility in, you can narrow it down to two strong possibilities. Also note that two of the responses indicate that the interface vendor is Parallels, Inc., which produces virtualization software, so you know that two virtual machines are on the network. You might guess that the host OS is macOS in that case because, while Parallels has software available for both Windows and Mac, it is more common on macOS than on Windows.

One other piece of information visible from the scan is that there is at least one printer on the network. The system that responded with a vendor ID of Lexmark International Inc. is very likely a printer since Lexmark makes printers. If you were to see a vendor ID of Brother, for example, you might conclude something similar. Other printer vendors like Hewlett Packard also offer several other types of devices you might find on a network, so you can't assume the Hewlett Packard response is a printer. As far as the other vendor IDs resulting from the scan, a little digging on the Internet with your favorite search engine should turn up more details about them.

 NOTE The first three bytes of the MAC address is the organizationally unique identifier (OUI), also known as the vendor ID. If the tool you are using is incapable of providing you a vendor from the OUI, there are several websites that will translate an OUI into a manufacturer name.

Again, an ARP scan requires that you be on the local network with the hosts you are attempting to contact. This doesn't mean you need to physically be there, just that a system you are operating from is on the local network. ARP messages won't pass through a router onto another network. They belong solely to the subnet where they originated.

Using Internet Control Message Protocol

You might also perform an ICMP scan using one of a number of ICMP messages, the most common of which is the ICMP echo request (type 8). The response to an echo request is an echo reply (type 0), assuming the host in question is up and running. You may be able to perform this type of scan using a broadcast message, but because of the risk of acting as an ICMP broadcast amplifier for Smurf attacks, many systems now won't easily originate ICMP messages to broadcast addresses, nor will they always respond to messages sent to a broadcast address. As a result, sending out an ICMP echo request to a broadcast address isn't the most reliable way of determining the systems that are on any given network. It's better to send out messages to individual systems. Since ICMP may be one of the first packets dropped if there is network congestion, you'll want to make sure you send several messages to ensure that not getting a response doesn't simply mean that the packet was dropped, and not that there is no host available on the network.

ICMP messages operate at layer 3 using IP addresses, which are routable. As a result, you can use an ICMP scan from outside the local network. You do run a risk, however, of the ICMP messages not only being dropped but being blocked. Some administrators consider it a good idea to block ICMP messages from coming into their network, so again, not getting a response may not be a good indication that the host is not there or isn't responsive. It could simply mean that there is a router or firewall in the way dropping ICMP messages.

```
    172.30.42.55 > 172.30.42.1: ICMP time stamp query id 1115 seq 3840, length 20
16:16:50.418585 IP (tos 0x0, ttl 64, id 20062, offset 0, flags [none], proto ICMP
(1), length 40)
    172.30.42.1 > 172.30.42.55: ICMP time stamp reply id 1115 seq 3840: org 20:16:
50.417, recv 20:16:50.420, xmit 20:16:50.420, length 20
16:16:51.418173 IP (tos 0x0, ttl 64, id 29919, offset 0, flags [none], proto ICMP
(1), length 40)
    172.30.42.55 > 172.30.42.1: ICMP time stamp query id 1115 seq 4096, length 20
16:16:51.419398 IP (tos 0x0, ttl 64, id 20063, offset 0, flags [none], proto ICMP
(1), length 40)
    172.30.42.1 > 172.30.42.55: ICMP time stamp reply id 1115 seq 4096: org 20:16:
51.418, recv 20:16:51.420, xmit 20:16:51.420, length 20
16:16:52.418396 IP (tos 0x0, ttl 64, id 11935, offset 0, flags [none], proto ICMP
(1), length 40)
    172.30.42.55 > 172.30.42.1: ICMP time stamp query id 1115 seq 4352, length 20
16:16:52.418972 IP (tos 0x0, ttl 64, id 20064, offset 0, flags [none], proto ICMP
(1), length 40)
    172.30.42.1 > 172.30.42.55: ICMP time stamp reply id 1115 seq 4352: org 20:16:
52.418, recv 20:16:52.420, xmit 20:16:52.420, length 20
16:16:53.418663 IP (tos 0x0, ttl 64, id 56204, offset 0, flags [none], proto ICMP
(1), length 40)
```

Figure 11-2   Several ICMP timestamp requests

In addition to an ICMP echo request, you may also send a different ICMP message like a timestamp request. While you may still run into the issue of dropped messages, you may be able to get around some near-sighted rules that are limited to ICMP echo requests. Blocking all ICMP messages isn't wise because ICMP is necessary for error messages, and going through all of the ICMP types and codes to determine the ones that are absolutely necessary can be time consuming. As a result, you may be able to get some ICMP messages through where something like an ICMP echo request may not make it because someone decided its only purpose is for scanning from the outside, and they don't allow that. Of course, getting an ICMP timestamp request through a firewall is no guarantee that the system will reply. In Figure 11-2, you can see a number of ICMP timestamp requests being sent over the local network (seen by the source and destination IP addresses of 172.30.42.55 and 172.30.42.1) with replies.

Using Transmission Control Protocol

Since most services provided by a system are offered over TCP, this will give you results that the other two scan types discussed so far won't offer. TCP is a layer 4 protocol, and layer 4 is responsible for offering ports for the purpose of multiplexing, so you can determine services that may be running on the system. An ICMP or an ARP scan won't return the fact that port 80, for example, is open on the system being scanned. Knowing the ports that are open and responding will tell you different applications that are being used on the system. In the case of port 80, you could assume, lacking any other evidence, that there is a web server on that particular system.

TCP is a connection-oriented protocol, meaning that connections between two systems are established before actual application messages are sent back and forth. This is accomplished using a three-way handshake, as shown in the diagram in Figure 11-3,

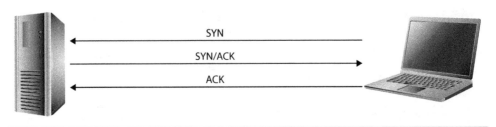

Figure 11-3 A three-way handshake

where the client initiates a connection to the server with a SYN message, the server responds with an ACK to the SYN, as well as a SYN of its own, and the client finishes the handshake with an ACK to the server's SYN message. This ensures that both systems are up and responding and it also establishes some parameters that will allow the two systems to communicate going forward. This three-way handshake will also allow us to do some scanning using TCP. A TCP scan might simply be done using a SYN message to each port on a system. If the port is open, the system will respond with the SYN/ACK as demonstrated earlier. If the port is not open, the system will reject the connection by sending a RST (reset) message. While there is no reason to finish the three-way handshake after getting the response, it may make sense to complete the connection and then tear it down to make sure that what you are doing is a little less noticeable. Of course, sending a lot of connection attempts to a system will be noticeable for anyone looking, but leaving hundreds or thousands of half-open connections on a system will be that much more noticeable, in part because of the resources that will be tied up.

Because TCP is not only connection-oriented but also reliable, it has to have header fields that allow it to provide connection management. These header fields can also be used to perform scans against targets. Setting different flags in packets sent to the target will yield different results. Figure 11-4 shows a FIN scan where, instead of a SYN packet, a packet with the FIN flag set is sent to the target. The FIN flag is used to close an open connection. If the port receiving the FIN message is closed, the target will send back a RST packet to reset the connection, effectively saying no one is home so stop bothering us here. If the port is open, however, it would have no record of an open connection, and as a result it would ignore the FIN message because it appears to be meaningless.

```
▷ Frame 2047: 54 bytes on wire (432 bits), 54 bytes captured (432 bits)
▷ Ethernet II, Src: Apple_e2:4d:bd (f8:1e:df:e2:4d:bd), Dst: AppleCom_ae:12:5e (00:16:cb:ae:12:5e)
▷ Internet Protocol Version 4, Src: 172.30.42.51 (172.30.42.51), Dst: 172.30.42.55 (172.30.42.55)
▽ Transmission Control Protocol, Src Port: 36324 (36324), Dst Port: netop-school (1971), Seq: 1, Len: 0
    Source port: 36324 (36324)
    Destination port: netop-school (1971)
    [Stream index: 1022]
    Sequence number: 1    (relative sequence number)
    Header length: 20 bytes
  ▷ Flags: 0x001 (FIN)
    Window size value: 1024
    [Calculated window size: 1024]
    [Window size scaling factor: -1 (unknown)]
  ▷ Checksum: 0x8e18 [validation disabled]
```

Figure 11-4 A FIN scan

FIN scans aren't the only types of scans you can perform that take advantage of the way TCP operates and the different fields that are available within the protocol. One type of scan is an Xmas scan, so named because the scanner turns on several flags before sending the message out. Another is an Idle scan because it takes advantage of the IP identification field to send out packets that appear to come from another source, then checks the IP ID of the spoofed source to determine how the target responded. This is actually just a SYN scan using a spoofed source. It's important that the spoofed source not be active on the network. The reason this works is because responses to a SYN message can be determined based on how the IP ID increments. If there is traffic going to the spoofed source that isn't coming from the target, it's harder to determine what's happening with the target because the IP ID will be changing in a way that doesn't make sense.

Once you're talking about TCP, you're looking to see what ports (i.e., services) are open and not simply whether a host is online and available. Any combination of header fields that will get a response from the system and, perhaps more importantly, through a firewall or through intrusion detection is helpful when it comes time to get reliable results on a scan of a system where you want to know what vulnerabilities there are. The vulnerabilities from a network perspective are going to result from open ports and the services that are running on those ports.

Using User Datagram Protocol

A UDP scan is very similar to that of a TCP scan except that we don't have all the different variations on header fields to manipulate. On top of that, UDP is connectionless, so there isn't any process for establishing a session between two parties. Since UDP is not a reliable protocol, meaning it doesn't take responsibility for end-to-end delivery, UDP packets are dropped out on the network with the hope that they will get there in a timely fashion. Since there is nothing that ensures that the message got there or not, like with the TCP acknowledgment system, when you send a packet out you can't say what it means when you don't get a message back. It may mean that there is nothing on that port, but it could also mean that the message was simply dropped. If the message has been dropped, we would have to retransmit. The same is true for TCP, except that with TCP, a lack of acknowledgment means that we know that the message was dropped, so we can be sure that we have to retransmit. With UDP, there is no assurance that we have to retransmit, so we just do.

Normally, the application would take the responsibility for retransmitting if it were using UDP and the message was important. UDP requires that reliability is handled by the application layer. The same thing is true when using a network scanner. If the scanner

121 8.901386	172.30.42.51	172.30.42.55	UDP	Source port: 37398	Destination port: nimreg
122 8.901406	172.30.42.51	172.30.42.55	UDP	Source port: 37398	Destination port: 782
123 8.901425	172.30.42.51	172.30.42.55	UDP	Source port: 37398	Destination port: 32818
139 9.992807	172.30.42.51	172.30.42.55	UDP	Source port: 37399	Destination port: 32818
140 9.992913	172.30.42.51	172.30.42.55	UDP	Source port: 37399	Destination port: 782
141 9.992956	172.30.42.51	172.30.42.55	UDP	Source port: 37399	Destination port: nimreg
142 9.992998	172.30.42.51	172.30.42.55	UDP	Source port: 37399	Destination port: timbuktu-
143 9.993039	172.30.42.51	172.30.42.55	UDP	Source port: 37399	Destination port: 20117
144 9.993080	172.30.42.51	172.30.42.55	UDP	Source port: 37399	Destination port: 17468

```
▷
▷ Ethernet II, Src: Apple_e2:4d:bd (f8:1e:df:e2:4d:bd), Dst: AppleCom_ae:12:5e (00:16:cb:ae:12:5e)
▷ Internet Protocol Version 4, Src: 172.30.42.51 (172.30.42.51), Dst: 172.30.42.55 (172.30.42.55)
▽ User Datagram Protocol, Src Port: 37398 (37398), Dst Port: 32818 (32818)
    Source port: 37398 (37398)
    Destination port: 32818 (32818)
    Length: 8
▷ Checksum: 0x40ee [validation disabled]
```

Figure 11-5   A packet capture of a UDP scan

doesn't get a response back, it has to retransmit. Sending an immediate retransmit doesn't make any sense. You have to wait a period of time to account for the possibility of network lag. As a result of all the retransmissions, a UDP scan may take quite a bit more time than a TCP scan of the same number of hosts and ports. Figure 11-5 shows a packet capture of a UDP scan. You can see how little there is in the UDP portion of the packet, which doesn't really leave anything much to change other than the port.

Another reason why UDP scans can take longer and require retransmits is that an application listening to a UDP port would be responsible for responding, as appropriate. Again, unlike TCP where the operating system itself would handle the initial response, with UDP there is no connection handling, so everything is left up to the application. If the initial message sent to the UDP port isn't to the liking of the application, it is free to not respond. You might send several messages to a UDP port, but if it is looking for a specific sequence in order to respond at all, you may get no response and the port would be flagged as being unavailable.

 NOTE   Interestingly, the document that specifies how UDP is to operate, RFC 768, has nothing at all to say about the appropriate response to a request to a closed port. TCP, on the other hand, is very clear about how to respond to a request to a closed port.

In fairness, ICMP comes back into play here and it's not nearly as bad as it seems from the preceding paragraphs. With at least some systems, if a port doesn't have any application listening, the operating system would reply with an ICMP port unreachable message. There are, though, reasons why that may not happen, including blocking ICMP outbound on either the host itself or through the firewall if you are trying to connect from an external network.

Protocol Scan

IP supports a number of protocols that can use it as a network layer carrier. You may want to know whether the system you are trying to connect to supports Generic Routing Encapsulation (GRE), Internet Group Management Protocol (IGMP), or Encapsulating

Security Payload (ESP), as examples. Some of these protocols are, or can be, used to encapsulate other protocols. GRE, for example, is used to encapsulate packets in some basic remote connection protocols. Support for this protocol might suggest that the system was being used as a gateway to other systems, and that information may be useful.

Nmap

Nmap, which stands for Network MAPper, was developed by Gordon Lyon, who is better known by his pseudonym Fyodor, in 1997. Nmap was developed as a port scanner, meant to determine what ports on a system were open to help determine systems that are operating. It can be used for network discovery and security auditing, making use of a wide range of techniques to determine system availability, port status, network topology, and application information. Nmap was originally developed as a command-line tool, but has since gained a user interface, which not only has the same capabilities that Nmap does for port scanning, using the same engine, but also provides a way of better organizing the information that Nmap gets back.

Nmap is such a famous piece of software that it regularly gets shown in movies as a hacking tool that would allow someone to break into another system. While it is useful as a starting point, it alone wouldn't be used for that task. It does, however, have an extensive range of port scanning abilities, including the different TCP and UDP options mentioned earlier, as well as protocol scanning. Additionally, Nmap supports the identification of operating systems for the target system. It uses a fingerprint database relying on characteristics of the TCP/IP stack and how it behaves using the sequence number, and the results from ICMP echo requests as well as TCP and UDP probes. After Nmap has collected all of the data from these probes, it checks against its internal database to find a match. Figure 11-6 shows the results from an OS detection using Nmap. The command used to get this output was nmap –O <ip address>. According to Nmap, this result may not be accurate because it was unable to find one open port and one closed port. While it's not shown in this image, the scan results show that a number of open ports were found but all the rest were filtered. This is because the system in question was using the Windows Firewall, which was filtering all ports that were not open and exposed through the port.

```
MAC Address: 00:1C:42:07:09:5A (Parallels)
Warning: OSScan results may be unreliable because we could not find at least 1 ope
n and 1 closed port
Device type: general purpose|phone
Running: Microsoft Windows 7|Vista|2008|Phone
OS CPE: cpe:/o:microsoft:windows_7::-:professional cpe:/o:microsoft:windows_vista:
:- cpe:/o:microsoft:windows_vista::sp1 cpe:/o:microsoft:windows_server_2008::sp1 c
pe:/o:microsoft:windows
OS details: Microsoft Windows 7 Professional, Microsoft Windows Vista SP0 or SP1,
Windows Server 2008 SP1, or Windows 7, Microsoft Windows Vista SP2, Windows 7 SP1,
 or Windows Server 2008, Microsoft Windows Phone 7.5
Network Distance: 1 hop

OS detection performed. Please report any incorrect results at http://nmap.org/sub
mit/ .
```

Figure 11-6   An OS detection using Nmap

```
Not shown: 980 closed ports
PORT      STATE SERVICE        VERSION
21/tcp    open  ftp            Pure-FTPd
22/tcp    open  ssh            OpenSSH 5.9p1 Debian 5ubuntu1 (Ubuntu Linux; protocol
 2.0)
| ssh-hostkey: 1024 05:bb:b8:ad:44:3a:5b:38:6d:f1:cb:d8:6d:d9:ab:a1 (DSA)
| 2048 ed:0a:89:67:b7:df:d4:22:82:c4:45:93:64:4f:8a:db (RSA)
|_256 9b:58:28:2e:cb:ff:4a:4e:ea:83:18:df:d0:48:41:c2 (ECDSA)
23/tcp    open  tcpwrapped
25/tcp    open  smtp           Postfix smtpd
|_smtp-commands: bill.westell.com, PIPELINING, SIZE 10240000, VRFY, ETRN, STARTTLS
, ENHANCEDSTATUSCODES, 8BITMIME, DSN,
| ssl-cert: Subject: commonName=bill.westell.com
| Not valid before: 2011-08-20T13:30:18+00:00
|_Not valid after:  2021-08-17T13:30:18+00:00
|_ssl-date: 2013-06-06T21:42:08+00:00; 0s from local time.
53/tcp    open  domain         ISC BIND 9.8.1-P1
| dns-nsid:
|_ bind.version: 9.8.1-P1
80/tcp    open  http           Apache httpd 2.2.22 ((Ubuntu))
```

Figure 11-7   Nmap application scanning results

 EXAM TIP   While Nmap has a wide range of capabilities, one thing it is not capable of is ARP redirection. ARP redirect, sometimes called ARP spoofing, uses ARP to get frames sent to an attacker's system rather than the system they were supposed to go to.

Nmap is also capable of performing a scan of the applications that are listening on the ports it finds open. It does this by performing a banner grab, meaning it issues an application-level request and captures the response, providing the response in the output. You can see the output from this approach in Figure 11-7, where Nmap has grabbed some banners and performed an analysis on the results, providing version numbers where possible as well as keying information for the Secure Shell (SSH) server. This output was obtained by running nmap –A <ip address>. This is all done using the responses from issuing connections to the open ports for those applications. You could get the same information from using Netcat or the Telnet client and issuing raw requests to those ports yourself, though Nmap is considerably easier to use to gather this information.

Where Nmap has been steadily improving scan results and strategies over the years, when Zenmap was developed, a graphical interface to Nmap, it provided the ability to represent the scan results visually. This might be a topology diagram, as shown in the example in Figure 11-8. Beyond the interactive topology diagram, there are different ways to represent the results, such as by looking at ports/services available across the network as well as being able to quickly see different ports/services open on different systems by being able to click on a different system and have the results pop up. This is much harder to do quickly with a text-based system and is one of the advantages of using the graphical interface.

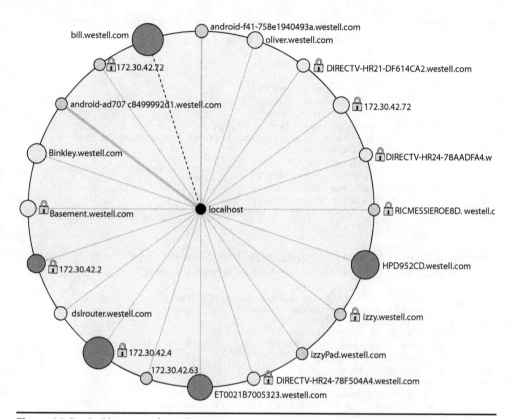

Figure 11-8   An Nmap topology diagram

An Nmap Null scan, where none of the TCP flags are set, would look like this in a tcpdump output:

```
21:09:05.833348 IP 172.30.42.51.55227 > 172.30.42.55.80: Flags [], win 1024,
length 0
```

As compared with the following output, which shows that the SYN flag has been set:

```
21:10:53.173222 IP 172.30.42.51.48399 > 172.30.42.55.80: Flags [S], seq
1248940809, win 1024, options [mss 1460], length 0
```

In recent versions, the capabilities of Nmap have been extended by allowing users to write their own scripts. The scripts could be triggered based on specific filtering criteria. The Nmap scripting engine is based on the Lua programming language, so writing a script for Nmap would require writing in Lua. Fortunately, Nmap provides a number of libraries to make the job of writing these scripts a lot easier. The following is a basic script that might be used to detect whether the content management system Joomla is installed at the URL /joomla. If it finds the URL specified in the script, it reports out as part of the Nmap output. You can see the output from the script in Figure 11-9 where it found

Figure 11-9
An Nmap script
output

```
Host is up (0.0024s latency).
Not shown: 980 closed ports
PORT      STATE  SERVICE
21/tcp    open   ftp
22/tcp    open   ssh
23/tcp    open   telnet
25/tcp    open   smtp
53/tcp    open   domain
80/tcp    open   http
|_joomla: Joomla site found at http://172.30.42.55/joomla
110/tcp   open   pop3
111/tcp   open   rpcbind
139/tcp   open   netbios-ssn
389/tcp   open   ldap
443/tcp   open   https
|_joomla: Joomla site found at http://172.30.42.55/joomla
```

a Joomla installation on port 80 of the scanned host. Since the script was set to trigger on HTTP ports, Nmap only called the script when it found ports 80 and 443 to be open.

```
description = [[   This is a script to check whether the CMS Joomla
        is installed on the target system. ]]
 categories = { "exploit", "vuln" }
 local http = require "http"
 local shortport = require "shortport"
 local stdnse = require "stdnse"
 portrule = shortport.http
 action = function(host, port)
 local uri = "/joomla/index.php"
 local _, status_404, resp_404 = http.identify_404(host, port)
 if status_404 == 200 then
    stdnse.print_debug(1, "%s: Web server is ambiguous about missing files.
Exiting.", SCRIPT_NAME)
    return
 end

 local resp = http.head(host, port, uri)
 if resp.status and (resp.status == 200 or resp.status == 302) then
    return string.format("Joomla site found at http://%s/joomla", host.ip)
 end
end
```

Exercise 11-1: Nmap Scanning
Perform a SYN scan and an operating system check of your own system. This may be performed on the command line by using nmap –sS –O 127.0.0.1. Find out how many open TCP ports you have.

Application Mapping
Application mapping is not simply about finding open ports on a system. It's also about finding the actual application that is running behind the open port. While there are standard ports for all of the major services you will run across and most of the minor ones as well, a system administrator doesn't have to run the application on the well-known port.

In order to determine the application that is running, you need to know the protocol to use on a particular port. You may not always get an immediate response from a server that's running, however. Figure 11-10 shows an interaction with a web server. The initial connection to the server only gets a message that we're connected. The server doesn't give up any information about what it is and what protocol may be running. The first command is initiated by sending a GET command to the server from the client end. In this case, the connection is to port 80, which is the default HTTP port. If this were, for example, port 9000, it may not be as obvious which protocol to try.

The utility AMAP was originally designed to determine the actual application used on a particular port. This was based on determining the protocol in use, regardless of the port the server is running on. Eventually, Nmap implemented its own version of the application mapping. You can perform a version check using Nmap. In order to check all of the open ports for the application running on them, you could use –A, which would enable OS detection, version detection, script scanning, and traceroute. You could also use –sV, which would trigger a version detection scan. You could use the following Nmap command to perform a version detection scan on a private network with a high throttle, meaning that the scan will go faster:

```
nmap -sV -T4 172.30.42.0/24
```

The AMAP developers put development of their utility on hold after Nmap developed their version scanning capability. They felt that since Nmap was doing it and doing it well, there was no further need for AMAP. Eventually, they came back and released a new version since they felt Nmap wasn't providing adequate support for IPv6 and that

```
kilroy@bill: $ telnet www.google.com 80
Trying 173.194.75.103...
Connected to www.google.com.
Escape character is '^]'.
GET / HTTP/1.0

HTTP/1.0 200 OK
Date: Fri, 07 Jun 2013 00:17:36 GMT
Expires: -1
Cache-Control: private, max-age=0
Content-Type: text/html; charset=ISO-8859-1
Set-Cookie: PREF=ID=f264f530db058f24:FF=0:TM=1370564256:LM=1370564256:S=wUajcpxy
eYNGET9B; expires=Sun, 07-Jun-2015 00:17:36 GMT; path=/; domain=.google.com
Set-Cookie: NID=67=FT_CwANh4uU_yxlqdg4e0rY-7WDSYvkw2PvHpJTPmkKO8TLwCcNu1TCddgJqz
yPLUrZBtpp87tPsC_x-fma8RiFYEPeAvscbC9Keq316Ph8Mi5obidwCMPzuhA7tWbNd; expires=Sat
, 07-Dec-2013 00:17:36 GMT; path=/; domain=.google.com; HttpOnly
P3P: CP="This is not a P3P policy! See http://www.google.com/support/accounts/bi
n/answer.py?hl=en&answer=151657 for more info."
Server: gws
X-XSS-Protection: 1; mode=block
X-Frame-Options: SAMEORIGIN
```

Figure 11-10 A connection to a web server

was something they could offer. As a result, there was an updated release of AMAP in 2011, which remains the most recent version. Either utility you go with, the goal is ultimately to identify the actual application and, ideally, the version of that application running. The reason for that is that it will provide you with further insight into the potential vulnerabilities you may have on your network and systems. Once you have a version number for an application, you can check for any vulnerabilities that may exist in that application.

 NOTE The Common Vulnerabilities and Exposures (CVE) database was developed at Mitre in the late 1990s as a way to have a common location for vulnerability information, regardless of vendor. Most major vulnerabilities get a CVE identifier, and that identifier can be used to look up information about the vulnerability, including whether there may be an exploit available and what the remediation may be.

Vulnerability Scanning

Vulnerability scanning takes what we've been talking about a step further. So far, we've been focused on taking a look at the systems and services available on the network. In some cases, we've been able to determine the application and version that has been running. We may be able to take the information that we've found from these scans and spend a lot of time looking up information about the services and applications in order to determine whether there are vulnerabilities. The easier way to handle it would be to simply run a vulnerability scanner like Nessus, Nexpose, ISS, or any of several others that are available. A vulnerability scanner does exactly what its name indicates: it scans for vulnerabilities. Vulnerabilities may be a result of unpatched applications or they may be due to misconfigurations. They could be applications that report too much information to the requestor, potentially exposing the applications to attack by providing information about vulnerabilities based on version number.

Vulnerability scanners are designed to probe for vulnerabilities based on specific signatures. They look for banners from applications, responses from the TCP/IP stack, open ports, and web pages, among other things, to determine whether a system is vulnerable or not. This isn't a guarantee that the system is vulnerable. It's just an indication that it could be vulnerable. There may be mitigations in place that your vulnerability scanner isn't aware of. Another possibility is that your system is vulnerable even though your vulnerability scanner doesn't indicate it. Figure 11-11 is a request to a web server from the vulnerability scanner Nessus, showing that it's requesting a specific page. This was captured using Wireshark since checking the wire is the best place to see all the traffic Nessus is sending out to the network. Nessus is looking to see whether a web application is installed on the web server and if that page is available. If the page was available under a different path within the web server, it wouldn't get flagged as being vulnerable when in fact it is. It's important to note that the job of a vulnerability scanner is not to prove a vulnerability exists, but instead to point you in directions of where there may be vulnerabilities so you can follow up on them.

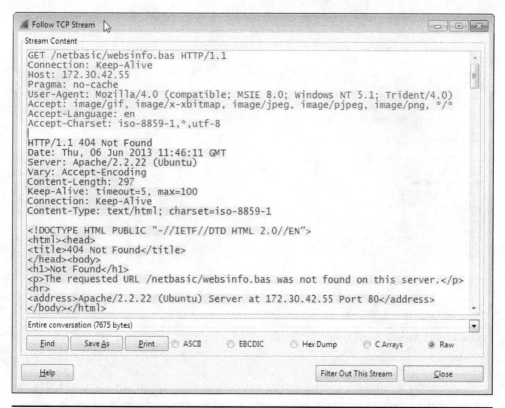

Figure 11-11 Output from Wireshark showing Nessus scanning for web vulnerabilities

While the vulnerability scanner doesn't actually exploit a vulnerability, the scanner does have the potential to knock over systems. Some of the tests that get performed can have potentially harmful effects to the stability of the system, particularly if the device being tested is fragile. For example, some network printing devices have a history of not holding up well to being probed, and as a result it's helpful to be very careful around those sorts of devices. Older operating systems may not hold up well to some of the tests either. This is such a common problem and a very real concern when you are scanning production networks that some scanners have a setting that prevents some tests from running. You can see in Figure 11-12 that Nessus has a setting for Enable safe checks. Some of the Nessus plugins have been flagged as unsafe and those plugins won't get run if this setting is checked. Some networks are considered so fragile that even safe scans won't be or shouldn't be run.

 EXAM TIP Before running a vulnerability scan, ensure that all relevant IT staff and system owners are aware that it's going to happen. While vulnerability scans are not designed to be destructive, sometimes they can trigger unexpected consequences, leading to system or application outages.

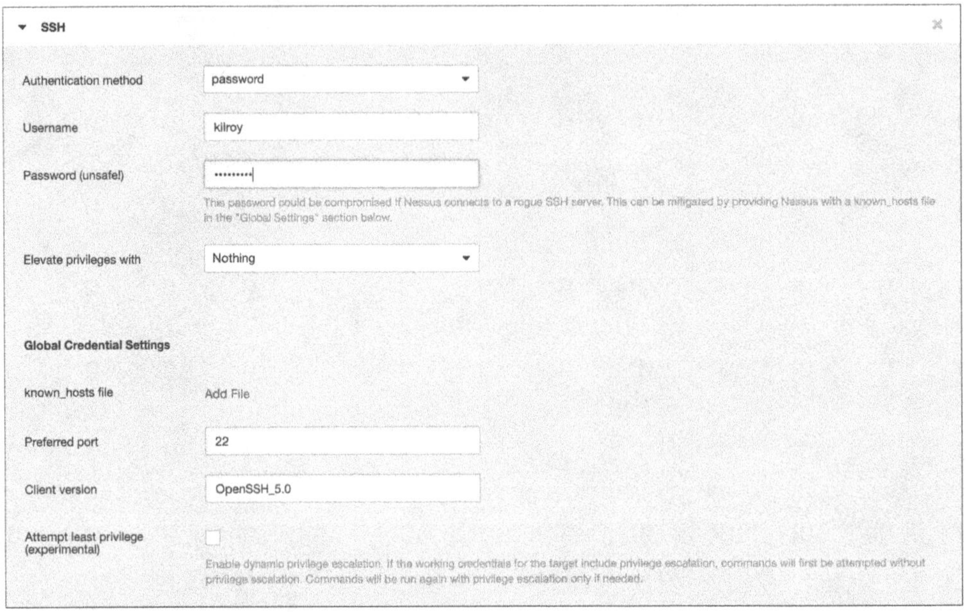

Figure 11-12 Enabling safe checks in Nessus

Vulnerability scanners have the ability to perform both local and remote checks for vulnerabilities. You can typically configure a scanner with credentials to log in to your system and perform remote checks by looking at installed software versions as well as system and application configurations. While this will give you some areas that are worth looking at and cleaning up, keep in mind that these are vulnerabilities that are exposed when you are logged in to the system through a remote access mechanism like Remote Desktop Connection (RDC) or Secure Shell (SSH). Without that local access or without exploiting another vulnerability to gain that local access, these vulnerabilities won't be exposed to someone over the network. Figure 11-13 shows how you might configure credentials for local checks in the vulnerability scanner Nessus.

When you are faced with a large organization, you may run into a situation where it is difficult to scan everything in the network all at once. There are a number of risks to performing a large scan over a network. First, you can cause outages on the network by trying to scan everything at once, particularly if your scanner has the ability to have multiple threads going, allowing multiple systems to be scanned simultaneously. Once you have the results, you may find a large scan report difficult to manage or even make sense of. One way of performing scans on a very large network is to perform sample scans on different systems. This can limit the network traffic as well as the results. This does, however, assume you have good patch management strategies and keep all of your similar systems up to date simultaneously, as well as have regular configuration audits.

General Settings

☑ Enable safe checks

☐ Stop scanning hosts that become unresponsive during the scan

☐ Scan IP addresses in a random order

Performance Options

☐ Slow down the scan when network congestion is detected

Network timeout (in seconds)   5

Max simultaneous checks per host   5

Max simultaneous hosts per scan   30

Max number of concurrent TCP sessions per host

Max number of concurrent TCP sessions per scan

Figure 11-13   Credentials configuration in Nessus

This is a lot to ask, so a better way to do it is to prioritize your systems and then put them together into small groups to be scanned in that way. Once you have your groups, you can scan one at a time in descending order of priority until everything is scanned.

EXAM TIP   When you are planning for how to perform the vulnerability scans, use a list of prioritized smaller scans rather than trying to scan the entire network at once. This will help limit the impact on the network as well as provide manageable, grouped results.

In spite of the limitations of these tools, scanning for vulnerabilities can help you keep up with the rapidly changing landscape of announced vulnerabilities since the vulnerability scanner vendors generally do a good job of keeping up with known vulnerabilities. Knowing what vulnerabilities you have is important when it comes to prioritizing fixing or otherwise remediating them.

NOTE   You can generally keep up with known vulnerability announcements by subscribing to the Bugtraq list from SecurityFocus.

Vulnerability Management

When it comes to managing vulnerabilities, SANS has five axioms you should remember:

- Vulnerabilities are the gateways through which threats are manifested.
- Vulnerability scans without remediation are of little value.
- A little scanning and remediation is better than a lot of scanning and less remediation.
- Prioritize.
- Keep prioritizing and stay on track.

 EXAM TIP When you are faced with a number of vulnerabilities, it's important to mitigate the most critical first.

A vulnerability is a way into a system for an attacker. As part of managing the vulnerabilities within our systems, it's important to keep in mind that any vulnerability that exists might be used to compromise our systems or our data. Removing or at least mitigating the vulnerability takes away an avenue into our systems and removes access to our data. Because there are so many potential vulnerabilities and so many potential avenues, vulnerability management is a process, and it can be time and resource consuming. Knowing when and how to mitigate or remediate vulnerabilities is important. Figure 11-14 shows some of the results from a Nessus scan on some systems. You can see how Nessus has prioritized the results. This may be helpful in knowing which vulnerabilities are the most important, although the priority attached to the vulnerability by Nessus may be different from the one you assign after factoring in any additional remediation.

Performing vulnerability scans is simply one step or task in a vulnerability management plan. Having a vulnerability scanner run scans once a week only to have the scan results sit without anyone looking at them is just as bad, if not potentially worse, than doing nothing. Knowing about a vulnerability or having the ability to know about a vulnerability and doing nothing at all about it might expose the organization to liability if that vulnerability were used to compromise critical information. Once there is documentation of vulnerabilities, that documentation can be used against the company.

Sev	Name	Family	Count
MIXED	Mozilla Firefox (Multiple Issues)	MacOS X Local Security Checks	13
MIXED	Wireshark (Multiple Issues)	MacOS X Local Security Checks	9
HIGH	Zoom Client for Meetings 4.x < 4.1.34801.1116 Message Spoofing Vulnerability (macOS)	MacOS X Local Security Checks	1
MIXED	SSL (Multiple Issues)	General	8
MEDIUM	IP Forwarding Enabled	Firewalls	3
LOW	DHCP Server Detection	Service detection	1

Figure 11-14 Nessus scan results

As one example, Sony was involved in a class action lawsuit because they knew about vulnerabilities in their network and didn't do anything about them. Those vulnerabilities were exploited by attackers who then stole information about Sony's customers. Having this documentation without doing anything about it becomes a liability. In some cases, because of this liability, companies prefer not to know if they are not prepared to do something about findings.

EXAM TIP Scan results that aren't looked at have minimal value to an organization.

Along the same lines, you don't need to scan your entire organization, particularly if you aren't able to cope with the volume of information that the scans will generate. Having a lot of information you can't do anything about doesn't help secure your environment. If you don't have the resources to act on the scan results, it's better to scan a small number of systems and then spend time acting on the results. Keep in mind that, depending on your scan settings and how much access you give to the scanner, you may end up with a lot of data to inspect. Figure 11-15 shows a portion of the information results from a Nessus scan of a small network. While these results are informational, you should go through them to make sure they are presenting information that is expected. As an example, one of the informational items is about Nessus's ability to run netstat on the target hosts. This is likely because credentials were provided, which means Nessus was able to get authenticated local access to the systems, allowing it to run commands there. It's still worth looking to see that this is the case and there wasn't something else going on.

Vulnerability scanners will provide you with a prioritized list of findings. However, just because your vulnerability scanner has prioritized a finding at a particular level doesn't mean you need to accept that severity as it is. The scanner isn't aware of any other mitigations in place. Just as an example, perhaps one of the findings is a Firefox vulnerability that is flagged as critical. The one thing the vulnerability scanner isn't aware of is that you have provided specific access to the scanner through the network where most systems aren't allowed through firewalls and packet filters on the network. Also, the scanner was provided with credentials. Only users who have credentials on the system, or perhaps those who have found other ways into the system, will have the ability to trigger

	INFO	Netstat Portscanner (SSH)	Port scanners	50
	INFO	Nessus SYN scanner	Port scanners	38
	INFO	Service Detection	Service detection	29
	INFO	SMB (Multiple Issues)	Windows	20
	INFO	HTTP (Multiple Issues)	Web Servers	17
	INFO	SSH (Multiple Issues)	General	16
	INFO	Ethernet Card Manufacturer Detection	Misc.	16

Figure 11-15 Nessus informational items

the vulnerability found in Firefox. Because of the mitigations in place, you may choose to reduce the severity to a medium risk. It still needs to be fixed, but you may feel that the mechanisms you have in place to keep out unauthorized users are enough to protect against this, and the users that *do* have access already have a way of gaining administrative privileges.

Once you have prioritized the vulnerabilities in a way that makes sense to your organization and the security mechanisms that may be in place to help mitigate risks, it's time to start working through your prioritized list of items. This can, and probably should be, an iterative process. Once you have fixed a vulnerability, you will want to ensure that it has been fixed. This can be done manually or you may simply scan the system again. Since new vulnerabilities are always being discovered, re-running a scan may well pick up new items, which will need to be slotted into your list of priorities that need to be fixed. It may be worth planning to pick up new vulnerabilities, particularly if you are on a schedule where you scan once per month, for instance. Without preparing yourself for the possibility of having new vulnerabilities, you will be putting yourself into a situation where you are getting vulnerability scan results and not doing anything about them.

Once you think you have fixed all the vulnerabilities you believe you need to, it's time to start all over again. Changes to the environment, as well as new vulnerabilities, new systems, and new applications, can all have an impact on the number of vulnerabilities there are. Scanning may be something you integrate into your change management process to ensure that configuration changes or alterations to applications don't create new vulnerabilities. As the fifth axiom says: keep prioritizing and stay on track. This means you need to keep plugging through your list of vulnerabilities and keep reordering based on new vulnerabilities and any other mitigations you may have implemented.

Depending on what the vulnerability is, you may have different ways of handling it. One way of handling a vulnerability is to keep system and application software up to date. While that isn't the only type of vulnerability you may run across, it is a fairly common one. The total number of announced vulnerabilities each month is typically in the hundreds. You may have the ability to automatically apply updates to software, although you may also have the option to perform updates manually.

 EXAM TIP Critical system updates should be checked out on non-production systems to ensure they don't impact applications and services.

Instead of automatically updating systems, it's helpful to have a place to test updates to see how they behave in your environment. Sometimes you may have a third-party application that doesn't handle the update well. Learning about this in production can be disastrous. However, the problem with this approach is that it requires that you have one system image that you use. Even if you do have one system image and you keep the image current and ensure that all of your systems are using the updated image, it can be a challenge to test all of your applications against the update. This again is where prioritization is critical so you can test your most important applications or the ones most likely to be affected by the update.

Vulnerability Exploitation

Vulnerability scanners won't test vulnerabilities to see if they can be exploited. Typically, in order to determine whether vulnerabilities can be exploited and also see whether there are issues that the vulnerability scanner didn't turn up, you would have a penetration test done. An in-house team might do this, though it can be valuable to bring in an external team of pen testers who don't have any assumptions about the environment. Considering the complex nature of software and some of the specific configurations that need to be in place, there may be some doubt as to whether a vulnerability could be exploited. Again, a vulnerability scanner isn't infallible. It bases its results on responses from probing a specific application or service, as well as checking version numbers. You can, though, get a better understanding as to whether a particular vulnerability can be exploited by using a framework along the lines of Metasploit, Canvas, or Core Impact.

The exploit frameworks provide a way to run both existing and known exploits, as well as quickly and easily develop exploits on your own. Of course, when you are running these you will want to ensure that either you are trying them out on a non-production machine or you are performing your work in a maintenance window or some other scheduled downtime just in case you cause an outage in the midst of your testing. Using a vulnerability scanner and an exploit framework together can make some of your work even easier. If you are using Nexpose and Metasploit together, for instance, Metasploit can make use of Nexpose and make determinations as to modules that it has that could be used for exploiting vulnerabilities. You can see a list in Figure 11-16 that references modules Metasploit has available that match the output from Nexpose. All of the work was done from within the Metasploit Web UI and it kicked off the Nexpose scan.

Once you have run the vulnerability scanner and have the list of exploits that are possible, you can launch the exploit. Again using Metasploit as an example, Figure 11-17 shows an attempt to launch a module attempting to exploit a vulnerability in an installed instance of WordPress, a web content management system (CMS). Launching the exploit is as simple as clicking a Launch button on the interface. In this case, the exploit wasn't successful, which means one vulnerability that isn't very high risk or perhaps one that just takes more effort to exploit. If it's simply not vulnerable and you have evidence that it isn't, you might simply remove it before presenting the findings from the penetration test. If it takes more effort to exploit it, that's a resource determination that should be made as to whether to spend the time trying different settings to try to exploit the vulnerability. Penetration tests are commonly of a short and fixed duration, which means prioritizing to get the best bang for your buck. If exploiting a vulnerability is going to take a lot of time, it may not be worth it. This doesn't mean it couldn't be exploited, however. You may choose to call it out as an issue and highlight the fact that, due to time constraints, it wasn't exploited but could be.

If you are performing the exploitation as part of a Threat and Vulnerability Management activity internally, you may want to maintain a list of all vulnerabilities found and whether they were real or false positives. A false positive is still worth keeping track of since additional scanning would turn it up again and you may not want to spend time checking its status. Presumably, however, you wouldn't be waiting for the results of a penetration test in order to put vulnerabilities onto a list of issues to be remediated. The results of a trusted vulnerability scan should be adequate for that.

Found 10 matching modules		
Module Type	OS	Module
Auxiliary	OS	Mutiny 5 Arbitrary File Read and Delete
Server Exploit	△	Mutiny 5 Arbitrary File Upload
Server Exploit	⚄	AdobeCollabSync Buffer Overflow Adobe Reader X Sandbox Bypass
Auxiliary	OS	ColdFusion 'password.properties' Hash Extraction
Server Exploit	OS △	Nginx HTTP Server 1.3.9-1.4.0 Chunked Encoding Stack Buffer Overflow
Client Exploit	⚄ OS	MS13-038 Microsoft Internet Explorer CGenericElement Object Use-After-Free Vulnerability
Client Exploit	⚄ OS	IBM SPSS SamplePower C1Tab ActiveX Heap Overflow
Server Exploit	OS	phpMyAdmin Authenticated Remote Code Execution via preg_replace()
Server Exploit	OS	Wordpress W3 Total Cache PHP Code Execution
Server Exploit	△ OS	HP System Management Homepage Local Privilege Escalation

Figure 11-16   Modules found in Nexpose

Also, you may find instances where you have to do even more work. While the tools make it a lot easier for you, they are just tools and not the last word in exploitation. As an example, Nexpose found a particular vulnerability in an unpatched Windows XP system. While you may think XP is wildly out of date, there are still networks that have XP systems. Additionally, they are great systems for practicing vulnerability exploitation on, which is why they are sometimes found on my local network. I have exploited

```
[+] [2013.06.13-11:55:43] Workspace:Localnet Progress:1/2 (50%) Exploiting 172.30.42.55
[*] [2013.06.13-11:55:45] Started reverse handler on 0.0.0.0:1024
[*] [2013.06.13-11:55:46] 172.30.42.55:80 - Trying unauthenticated exploitation...
[*] [2013.06.13-11:55:46] 172.30.42.55:80 - Trying to brute force a valid POST ID...
[*] [2013.06.13-11:55:56] 172.30.42.55:80 - Using the brute forced POST ID 1...
[*] [2013.06.13-11:55:56] 172.30.42.55:80 - Injecting the PHP Code in a comment...
[*] [2013.06.13-11:56:02] 172.30.42.55:80 - Executing the payload...
```

Figure 11-17   Attempting to exploit WordPress

this vulnerability on a number of occasions for demonstration purposes. The module *wasn't* referenced within Metasploit to indicate that it could be exploited. This is another example of why you need to do your own legwork and follow up on the output from the automated tools because they are not infallible. This is not to suggest by any means that they are flawed or that they don't work. They do work and often work very well, but vulnerabilities can be very complex and certain circumstances need to be in place sometimes before a vulnerability can be exploited. You also run into timing and race conditions where you have to trigger the exploit just right, and at the right time, for it to be successful. Running an exploit against a vulnerability once and not being successful doesn't necessarily mean the vulnerability can't be exploited. Some vulnerabilities are reliant on timing or a specific configuration that may not be in place.

NOTE   Storing scan output may be an important part not only of vulnerability management but also of an overall threat intelligence program. Software like security information and event management (SIEM) systems can take in the output from vulnerability scanners so it can be searched and referenced later.

Other exploit frameworks can make use of output from vulnerability scanners. Nessus has been around long enough that its output can often be used as input to the exploit frameworks. All those mentioned earlier will take Nessus output as input. Once the Nessus output has been imported, it can often be referenced against existing exploits within the framework.

NOTE   Many of the tools provide ways to further automate the process of vulnerability detection and exploitation, but automated exploitation can be risky, particularly against production systems. If possible, it's generally best to perform testing against lab or other non-production systems.

Web Application Security

One of the primary sources of vulnerabilities these days comes from web applications. Whether that's because of the large number of web applications or because of the quality of programmers developing web applications or some other reason is debatable. If it's a quality of code issue and you are using a third-party web application, there may not be much you can do to actually fix the issues that exist in the code. However, that's not to say you are completely at the mercy of the developers. There are certainly techniques you might employ to mitigate the risk that these web applications can create. Some of the techniques are preventive in nature and others are ways to better protect the information that's being sent back and forth.

There are a number of ways that web applications are vulnerable to attack and can expose systems and applications to compromise. This can be a combination of programming flaws as well as infrastructure problems. The vulnerability scanners mentioned earlier not only are capable of determining the potential vulnerabilities within the infrastructure (operating system and server), but many also have a number of checks for common web application flaws, not to mention common web applications. Web applications have become common targets of people looking for vulnerabilities, and new findings in web applications are announced on a regular basis, ranging from well-used web applications to those very rarely used and never heard of. In part, this is because of the ease of installing web applications and the minimal requirements to install and test.

Common Web Vulnerabilities

The Open Web Application Security Project (OWASP) keeps track of the top web application vulnerability categories and manages a number of other projects that will help keep you protected. Each year, OWASP publishes a list of the top ten vulnerabilities, and while most of them are common from year to year, sometimes position swapping happens. The latest Top 10 list from OWASP in 2017, the last time OWASP updated the list, shows the following vulnerabilities:

1. **Injection**   This includes SQL injection as well as command injection.

2. **Broken Authentication and Session Management**   This includes easily guessed session tokens.

3. **Sensitive Data Disclosure**   Some web applications do a poor job of protecting sensitive information like personally identifiable information (PII) or protected health information (PHI). This can lead to unauthorized users gaining access to that information.

4. **XML External Entities**   In some cases, the eXtensible Markup Language (XML) is not handled correctly, allowing for requests to be passed to the underlying operating environment. This could allow unauthorized access to critical system files or other sensitive information.

5. **Broken Access Control**   Users can perform functions or gain access to information beyond what they should be able to do. This is because access controls that may be in place are not correctly enforced.

6. **Security Misconfiguration**   This might be a problem with SSL/TLS or any other configuration error relating to securing the server or application.

7. **Cross-Site Scripting (XSS)**   This is a specific implementation of an injection attack that passes statements from a scripting language into a web page, where the statements are executed within the user's browser.

8. **Insecure Deserialization**   Deserialization is taking a byte stream and converting it back to an object with the data in its appropriate place. When the deserialization is done improperly, it can lead to remote code execution. Attackers can send code into the web application and have it executed.

9. **Using Components with Known Vulnerabilities**   This was previously a part of Security Misconfiguration and may result in not keeping up with new releases of underlying frameworks and libraries.

10. **Insufficient Logging and Monitoring**   Attacks are inevitable, and when there are instances of the previously listed vulnerabilities, exploits are likely inevitable. Without appropriate logging and monitoring, the attacker can remain in your system for years. Detection of intrusions is essential to quickly responding and remediating.

As you can see, many of these are problems with not adequately checking the input that the program receives. Passing data that hasn't been validated across an application boundary will lead to problems, which is why it's good practice to have your web applications checked on a regular basis, even if they are third-party applications. If you have vulnerabilities but can't get an update from the vendor, you may need to employ other strategies to remediate the vulnerabilities, like using a web application firewall or encryption.

SSL/TLS

In the early 1990s, there was a need to provide some privacy between the client and the server. Netscape developed a way of using public key encryption, called Secure Sockets Layer (SSL), to provide some security and privacy between the client and the server. SSL has gone through several revisions and the current version is now called Transport Layer Security (TLS). You can explicitly make a connection to a web server by using https instead of http as the Uniform Resource Identifier (URI), though many servers will commonly redirect you to an encrypted session. Figure 11-18 shows an encrypted communication with Google after a redirection to the https port (443).

Figure 11-18
An encrypted connection to Google

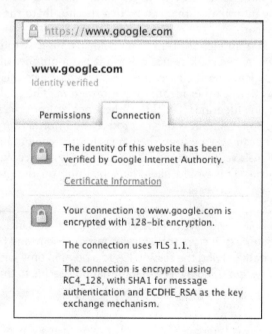

Some versions of SSL and even TLS are susceptible to having the encryption broken so the transmission might be viewed in cleartext. This is a common area of misconfiguration, as noted in the OWASP Top 10 vulnerabilities. If you have some areas of concern within the web application, however, encrypting them may be a solution. In fact, it is the solution for some of the vulnerabilities, including sensitive data exposure. Not only should data like usernames and passwords be encrypted when they are at rest within a database, but they should certainly be encrypted when in transit, and SSL/TLS is a way to accomplish that.

Cookies

Cookies are a way of storing small chunks of data on a client system to facilitate more efficient handling of you as a user. Cookies can help provide state information within a web application by storing information like a session token or session ID. These cookies are generated by the server, and the web browser is requested to store them. When they are stored, cookies are just small pieces of text that may be stored as files within a database. Cookies need to be protected, especially if they are session IDs, because a session may provide information about who you are or offer the ability to make purchases or perform other functions on a website that could expose a user. There are a number of ways to protect session information, as well as other information stored in a cookie. Encrypting the data, even before transmission so only the server can decrypt it, is helpful, or even just performing a cryptographic hash on the data can be effective. Ensuring that session IDs are long strings will make them harder to brute-force or guess. Additionally, to prevent replay attacks, the session ID should have a timestamp as well as another piece of identifying information that can be tied specifically to the session in progress on that particular system.

You can see from Figure 11-19 that cookie data is easy to get, especially if you are on the system where the cookies are. Microsoft has a number of cookies it uses to provide a specific experience on their website. These include a cookie for the preferred language to be used, as well as other identifying information. The cookie shown in the figure is a Globally Unique Identifier (GUID). Other cookies from the server have been encrypted or hashed in some way in order to protect the information they are meant to convey and store. You can also see from the figure that the cookies have expiration dates. If you are sending sensitive information, like a session ID, the cookie should have a reasonable expiration on it. This would likely be something on the order of minutes or perhaps hours, not months or years.

 EXAM TIP Ways to protect session identifiers include (1) making them long strings; (2) cryptographically hashing them; and (3) signing or encrypting data or tying the session IDs to a point in time with a timestamp or a specific system using a piece of information specific to that system.

CGI

Common Gateway Interface (CGI) was developed as a way of running external programs in a uniform manner for all web servers. In the early 1990s, the World Wide Web was still very young and there was a need to provide some programmatic access to web pages,

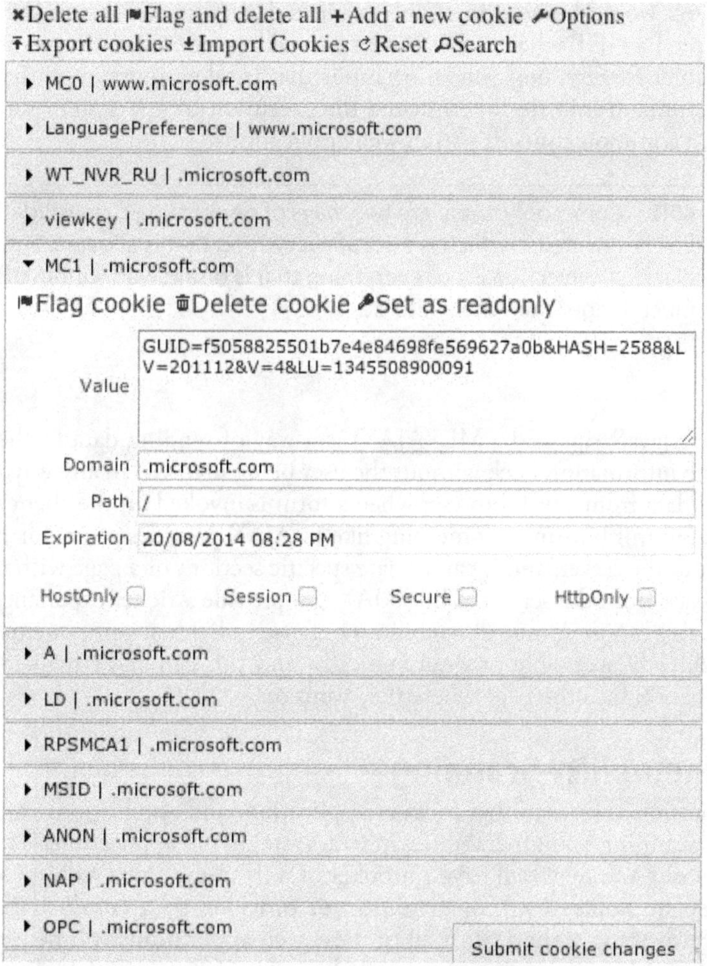

Figure 11-19 Cookie data from Microsoft.com

specifically where form data was concerned. There was a need to allow the web server to pass input off to a program outside of the web server, receive output from that program, and put that output into the data stream that was being sent back to the client that originated the request. This meant that programming languages could be used to interface with clients through the web server. CGI was designed as a way to pass the information back and forth between the programming environment and the web interface. While CGI was originally developed to perform that function, other techniques have been used since the early 1990s to get data back and forth between the client and the server.

CGI is, however, a way to potentially gain access to a system or get the web application to perform functions on behalf of users that it wasn't intended to perform for. Typically, a CGI script will take a POST request to take in information that it is expected to process.

A GET request would be used to simply retrieve data from the server. For example, if a script accepted a GET where a POST was normally used, it could open the door to a cross-site request forgery. Not validating input that is taken in through the CGI could also allow command injection, permitting the execution of any system function. Data validation is a common concern within web applications.

 NOTE Commonly, there are two ways of performing data validation. The first is a whitelist, which is a list of everything that is allowed. The second is a blacklist, which is a list of everything that is disallowed. Often, the blacklist is much longer than the whitelist.

AJAX

Asynchronous JavaScript and XML (AJAX) is a way of sending data to the web server and retrieving information back without the user being involved in any way. Normally, a server is sent data from a web browser when a form is invoked on the client side and the user clicks a Submit button or something like it. AJAX provides a way for JavaScript to get data sent to the server, and it can update specific sections of a page with the information it gets back from the server. While AJAX can provide a richer experience to the end user, it may also expose some vulnerabilities because individual components of the page have to be directly accessible programmatically, and this can allow malicious actors to inject information into the page where they want to.

Web Vulnerability Scanning

A web application is just another form of application, and applications come with vulnerabilities. Scanning for vulnerabilities in your systems and applications is important, as noted previously. You may well have a number of web applications within your network, whether they are homegrown, open source, or provided by a commercial third-party developer. Performing scans against all of these web applications will help protect your systems and your data resources. Some of the vulnerability scanners discussed earlier are also capable of performing web application scanning and auditing web applications. They look for common vulnerabilities like cross-site scripting, SQL injection, command injection, and several other common vulnerabilities. Figure 11-20 shows targeting web applications in Metasploit as a result of findings from a Nexpose scan.

Target Web Vulnerabilities

	Virtual Host	URL	Category	Parameter
☑	172.30.42.55	http://172.30.42.55/cgi-bin/guessnum1.pl	XSS	player
☑	172.30.42.55	http://172.30.42.55/cgi-bin/jotto1.pl	XSS	player
☑	172.30.42.55	http://172.30.42.55/cgi-bin/jotto2.pl	XSS	userguess
☑	172.30.42.55	http://172.30.42.55/guessnum5.php	XSS	player
☑	172.30.42.55	http://172.30.42.55/union1.php	XSS	unionname

Figure 11-20 Metasploit web application scan targets

Beyond the vulnerability scanners, you might also use other tools designed specifically for testing web applications. OWASP has a tool called the Zed Attack Proxy (ZAP), and there is a similar tool called Burp Suite, commonly used for testing web applications. Both of these are proxy-based tools. Other commercial tools like WebInspect, Acunetix, and AppScan are specific to finding web application vulnerabilities. The proxy-based scanners not only provide you with a lot of capabilities for scanning and attempting to exploit web applications, but also provide you with the ability to work directly with requests because the proxy will trap all requests going to the server so you can alter them (if you like) on the way through. This allows you to test the server side of the application following any JavaScript validation that took place within the page itself.

Burp Suite, as an example, provides extensive capabilities for performing user-driven testing of web applications. In addition to scanning for common vulnerabilities and server misconfigurations, Burp Suite also provides tools that allow you to send crafted payloads into an application. This capability can be used to brute-force usernames and passwords, but it can also be used to manipulate input data to see how well the server or application can handle unexpected input. Figure 11-21 shows the Burp Suite Intruder function, where form fields can be sent different payload sets and the payload sets can be modified based on rules specified by the user. Providing a generic tool that can be easily modified by the user gives extensive capabilities for testing for a number of conditions within the web application.

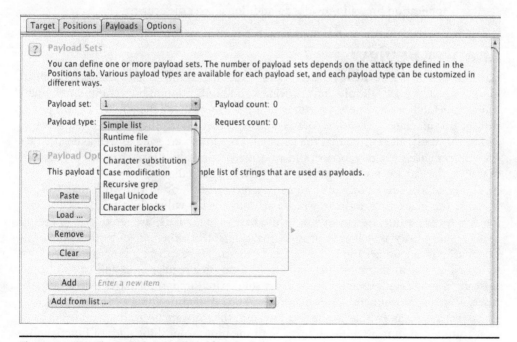

Figure 11-21　The Burp Suite Intruder function

Web Application Firewalls

You may have a number of third-party web applications where you have either no or limited access to the code in order to fix issues. You may also have no capability within your organization to spend a lot of time chasing down problems within a web application even if you have the right source code for the application. Short of removing the application from your production systems, there are still steps you can take to protect the application and infrastructure as well as the data being stored. You could install a web application firewall (WAF) in front of your web application. The purpose of a web application firewall is to inspect requests to, and responses from, the web application. Anything that looks suspicious could be either sanitized or discarded, as necessary. When you hear the term "firewall," you may think of a device that looks at packets at layer 3 or layer 4. A web application firewall looks at requests at the application layer.

Web application firewalls got their start with the ModSecurity project in 2002, designed as a module for the Apache HTTP Server. ModSecurity provides filtering capabilities within the web server itself to help protect web applications from malicious requests. With the Payment Card Industry (PCI) standards in 2006, interest in web application firewalls has only increased, and now there are a number of vendors that have WAFs available, including traditional firewall vendors. PCI has mandated that web applications be secured, though that mandate can be achieved either through secure development processes or by using a web application firewall after the fact to protect the web application.

A web application firewall provides an additional layer of security.

Chapter Review

Vulnerability management is a process, and while that sounds like an easy statement to make, those few words simply don't provide a good indication of how complicated managing vulnerabilities is. There are vulnerability scanners that generally do a good job of turning up vulnerabilities within your systems, but they do require human intelligence to review the results and ensure that the vulnerabilities found are valid as well as ensure that the vulnerabilities get categorized and prioritized correctly. Once they are prioritized, that's just the starting point to getting them fixed or remediated.

Vulnerabilities are a constantly moving target because of all the work that goes on between the black hats and the white hats looking for vulnerabilities. Black hats are looking for ways into systems, while white hats (or gray hats) are looking to shore up application security as well as to possibly make a name for themselves by finding a critical security issue and getting it fixed by the vendor. There can be a lot at stake for both groups. This means that new vulnerabilities appear on a regular basis and you will need to scan your systems regularly and have a solid patch/update management process in place. While some vulnerabilities may come from system or application misconfigurations, many are simply bugs in the software, and the software needs to be updated.

A common avenue of vulnerabilities, with the move to pushing a lot of functionality into the network, is web applications. Scanning web applications is just as important as scanning systems and the services that run on them. Often, the easiest way into a network is through a web interface. Web applications can provide access to the underlying operating system as well as access to data stored about the organization or its customers. Credit card processors are only one group requiring that web applications be better secured, and it's led to an explosion of interest in securing web applications, either through code scanning tools, application scanning tools, or web application firewalls.

Questions

1. You have a web application provided by a commercial vendor. Your vulnerability scans have turned up SQL injection errors in the application. Which of the following would you NOT do to remediate the issue?

   A. Implement a web application firewall.

   B. Implement filters to prevent unauthorized network segments from accessing the system.

   C. Decrypt the database.

   D. Notify the vendor about the issue you have found.

2. You have a list of vulnerabilities from a Nexpose scan. How will you prioritize them?

   A. Fix the issues that would be least likely to inconvenience users first.

   B. Fix the least critical issues first.

   C. Fix the oldest issues first.

   D. Fix the most critical issues first.

3. You automatically perform weekly scans against your critical systems, but the person who was previously responsible for vulnerability management left the company. As a result, while the scans are running, no one is looking at the reports. What can you say about those reports?

   A. They will reduce liability for the company.

   B. They are effectively useless.

   C. They will reduce costs for the company.

   D. They are out of date.

4. You have been asked to provide advice on how best to protect a session ID in a homegrown web application. What do you tell the developer?

   A. Keep the session ID short to save storage.

   B. Use a web application firewall to protect the session ID.

   C. Make use of a timestamp and a piece of identifying information from the client to generate the session ID.

   D. Uuencode the session ID.

5. You have run a port scan against systems in your network, but all of your results show that ports are filtered. What can you determine from these scans?

A. You were doing a UDP scan but only TCP ports are open.

B. A firewall is in place.

C. The systems don't support the port scanning protocol.

D. The intrusion detection system was responding with RST packets.

6. Your vulnerability scan returned with a result indicating that your web server is vulnerable to a particular issue. When you investigate, you discover that versions 2.0 through 2.5 are vulnerable, but you are running version 2.6. What could be the reason for this?

A. Your banner didn't report a version number.

B. The vulnerability affects version 2.6 as well.

C. The scanner exploited the target, and the finding is a result of that.

D. The scanner database is the latest version.

7. Your boss comes to you with a report about a critical vulnerability affecting your database server that he feels needs to be fixed immediately. The fix will require rebooting the system. What do you tell your boss?

A. He can do it himself.

B. Sure thing, right away.

C. You will try it out on a non-production system first.

D. You will back up the database, which will fix the vulnerability.

8. You are about to run an off-hours, unscheduled vulnerability scan against your critical systems to see if they are vulnerable to a newly announced vulnerability. What should you do first?

A. Notify all relevant personnel that you will be scanning systems.

B. Download the update.

C. Scan non-critical systems.

D. Cancel the scan.

9. You have been asked to implement a vulnerability scanning schedule for all of the systems on your large network. What is a good strategy for developing this schedule?

A. Scan everything all at once.

B. Scan one system at a time.

C. Scan one subnet at a time.

D. Prioritize systems and scan the most critical first.

10. Why might a UDP scan take longer to complete than other types of scans?

A. There are more UDP ports.

B. UDP doesn't require a reply.

    C. Firewalls block UDP packets.

    D. UDP requires an ARP lookup before sending.

11. Why would logging be an important element in an overall web architecture?

    A. To improve performance

    B. To allow for intrusion detection

    C. To provide to application developers

    D. To maintain information for the long term

12. It's a waste of time looking at informational items from a vulnerability scan.

    A. True

    B. False

13. What data representation format could be misused for getting access to system programs and data?

    A. AJAX

    B. SSL

    C. HTTP

    D. XML

14. What feature of Nmap could you use to identify the version number of WordPress being used on a web server?

    A. SYN Scan

    B. FIN Scan

    C. Scripting

    D. OS Scan

15. What would you use an ARP scan for?

    A. To identify open ports

    B. To identify firewalls

    C. To identify remote systems

    D. To identify local systems

Answers

1. **C.** Decrypting the database will not help you here. A web application firewall may help block the SQL injection attempts. Filters to protect the web application from those who don't need access to it are a good idea. Certainly notify the vendor about the issue. You may not be thanked for your efforts, but it may be your only hope of getting it fixed.

2. D. While all may be ways of prioritizing vulnerabilities that have been found, resolving issues that are critical first is the best approach since the critical issues could have a significant impact on your systems or data.

3. B. Scans that are not looked at so the results can be prioritized and resolved are effectively useless and won't do the company any good.

4. C. Ideally, you would use a timestamp and a piece of identifying information about the client to lock the session ID to a time and target and then encrypt or hash the result. While a web application firewall is a good idea, it won't protect a session ID. You want longer session IDs to protect against them being guessed or brute-forced, so a short session ID is a bad idea. Uuencoding the session ID won't do much to protect it, and this isn't a way to generate it.

5. B. Filtered responses suggest that there is probably a firewall in place somewhere. Performing a UDP scan where there are no UDP ports open wouldn't return filtered results, it would just show there are no open ports. If the system didn't support the protocol being scanned, there would be no results. It would be unlikely for the IDS to respond with RST packets, but even if it did, that would show the port as closed since that's the expected behavior for a port that's closed.

6. A. This is likely a result of the banner not reporting a version number and the scanner taking a guess. The scanner wouldn't exploit the database, and if the vulnerability report says 2.6 isn't vulnerable, 2.6 isn't vulnerable. The scanner database being up to date isn't relevant here since it would have all the latest known vulnerabilities that could be identified.

7. C. While you could just go fix the problem by applying the update, the wiser move may be to test the update on a non-production system to ensure there are no problems that might, for instance, prevent it from coming back up. Backing up the database is a good idea, but it's unlikely to fix a vulnerability. It seems unwise from a job security perspective to tell your boss to fix the problem himself.

8. A. You should notify all relevant personnel who may be impacted by a system outage. While the scan shouldn't have an adverse effect on the systems being scanned, you can't guarantee that it won't cause problems. Downloading the update, not performing the scan, and scanning non-critical systems don't address the problem.

9. D. While scanning a single subnet at a time may be a way to get the scans done, a better way is to prioritize your systems and scan the most critical first. Scanning the entire network at once may cause congestion and can also result in the scan taking a very long time. Scanning systems one at a time can be time consuming and very inefficient.

10. B. UDP scans can take quite a bit longer because UDP doesn't require a response to closed ports, so there may be a large number of retransmits required and a waiting period between retransmits. UDP and TCP have the same number of possible ports. UDP may well be blocked by a firewall, but TCP packets can be blocked as well, and even when there isn't a firewall in place, UDP scans may take longer. UDP itself doesn't require an ARP lookup. If the target system doesn't have an entry in the ARP cache, there will be an ARP lookup regardless of the transport protocol in use.

11. **B.** Intrusions into networks are inevitable. Logging is essential to assist in detecting intrusions. Without this detection, attackers may gain unnoticed access to systems, where they can remain for years. Sending logs to application developers may be useful, depending on the contents of the logs and the needs of the developers. That may not be the most important consideration, though. Logging won't improve performance, and the idea of maintaining information for the long term is vague. Retaining logs is important, primarily for the case where an intrusion is detected later. Ideally, the intrusion is detected quickly.

12. **B.** Looking at informational items may be a lower priority, but it's still important to look at them. There may be issues that need to be investigated and have been flagged as informational because the vulnerability scanner couldn't make a determination.

13. **D.** XML is a self-documenting data representation standard that has a SYSTEM element that can be used to pass commands and requests to the underlying operating environment. This could allow unauthorized access to commands or data. None of the other answers are used for data representation.

14. **C.** Nmap may be primarily thought of as a port scanner. However, it also has scripting capabilities. Using the scripting support, Nmap could be used to identify the version of WordPress on a web server. SYN and FIN scans are used to identify open ports. An OS scan is used to identify the operating system version in use on the remote server.

15. **D.** ARP is a protocol that is only useful on a local network. Once a packet transits over a layer 3 gateway (meaning it has been routed off the local network), the layer 2 header that contains the MAC address, associated with ARP, is removed. An ARP scan looks to identify systems on a local network and the IP addresses associated with the MAC addresses of those systems.

Exercise 11-1 Answer

This exercise could be performed on the command line or using Zenmap. Either way will provide the same output, though Zenmap will provide additional ways to organize it. Your text output will resemble that shown in Figure 11-22.

The output from Zenmap would look something like what you see in Figure 11-23. This output is from a scan on a Windows 8 system. Zenmap is running on a Windows system in this figure.

```
oliver:~ kilroy$ sudo nmap -sS -O 127.0.0.1

Starting Nmap 6.25 ( http://nmap.org ) at 2013-07-11 19:57 EDT
Nmap scan report for localhost (127.0.0.1)
Host is up (0.000073s latency).
Not shown: 848 closed ports, 147 filtered ports
PORT       STATE SERVICE
22/tcp     open  ssh
88/tcp     open  kerberos-sec
548/tcp    open  afp
631/tcp    open  ipp
49158/tcp open  unknown
Device type: general purpose|phone|media device
Running: Apple Mac OS X 10.8.X, Apple iOS 5.X
OS CPE: cpe:/o:apple:mac_os_x:10.8 cpe:/o:apple:iphone_os:5
OS details: Apple Mac OS X 10.8 - 10.8.1 (Mountain Lion) (Darwin 12.0.0 - 12.1.0
) or iOS 5.0.1
Network Distance: 0 hops

OS detection performed. Please report any incorrect results at http://nmap.org/s
ubmit/ .
Nmap done: 1 IP address (1 host up) scanned in 8.12 seconds
```

Figure 11-22   Nmap exercise output

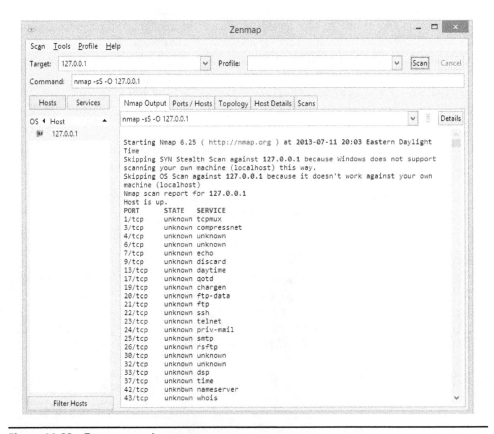

Figure 11-23   Zenmap exercise output

## CHAPTER 12

Malware

In this chapter, you will learn:

- The different types of malware
- About malware analysis
- Anti-virus techniques

Malicious software, commonly called malware, has been around for decades now. Given the more harmful types of malware we see today, one might look back with a certain nostalgic fondness at the kinds of malware that were prevalent even a dozen years ago. But whether the behavior of this early malware was truly malicious is debatable. A piece of software whose only purpose is to spread from system to system may not be a welcome item, but it's hard to say if it's truly noxious in nature. Many were more of a nuisance than malevolent. However, regardless of the actual functionality of the software in question, there are specific ways we categorize malicious software, and within each of those categories are additional subcategories.

Malware has become a business. Today's adversaries are funded and organized. This means they have employees who work for them and some of those employees develop malware that can help the attackers achieve their goals. This may include new types of malware that can either facilitate the generation of revenue or directly generate revenue. Also, in the case that an attacker is looking for intellectual property, malware can be useful to leave behind footholds to allow the attacker to keep coming back in and retrieving critical corporate data.

With the rise in the quantity of malware out there, a new profession has emerged. You can now get a job as a malware analyst. Where previously it was something you may have done if you worked for an anti-virus software vendor, today several companies hire malware analysts. There are techniques for analyzing malware, and as you may expect, performing that analysis safely is a primary consideration. Authors of this type of software don't make the white hat's job easy, of course, and they use a number of evasive approaches that must be understood not only by malware analysts but also by those who are responsible for detecting malware like viruses.

Anti-virus software has also been around for a while now, but there are a number of challenges to detecting malware that didn't exist when the first anti-virus software debuted over 30 years ago. While processing speed has increased by several orders of magnitude, the challenge in detecting malicious software has certainly not diminished over time. Indeed, it has increased dramatically as software creators have become more serious about getting malware deployed and keeping it deployed, especially since there is often a financial reward of some sort for doing so.

Types of Malware

There are several types of malicious software, but these different types are not mutually exclusive. In some cases, a piece of malware may fall into multiple of these categories.

Virus

Over the years, the word *virus* has become a generic term for malware. But here we'll be more specific to distinguish it from other types of malware. In actuality, a virus is a program that "infects" a computer by getting a user to run it. It may be attached to another piece of software in order to trick the user into running it. It may also be disguised to look like something else. One example that demonstrates this point is the "I Love You" virus from the late 1990s. The virus was a Visual Basic script that was sent to all the addresses in a mail system's contact list. Because of the way the mail client was configured at that time, the Visual Basic script would automatically run when the mail was opened. Once run, it infected the system, perhaps by replacing all the user's pictures with a copy of the script itself. Then, taking advantage of the fact that file extensions are typically hidden, it used .jpg.vbs as the extension—expecting that the .vbs wouldn't be seen, just the .jpg part—thus making it look like it was really an image. Later, after the system was thought to be cleaned, the user would open one of these pictures to look at it and the system would become infected all over again. Figure 12-1 shows an e-mail message with the I Love You virus attached. Notice that it's taking advantage of the fact that file extensions are typically hidden by using a .TXT extension in between the filename and the real .vbs extension.

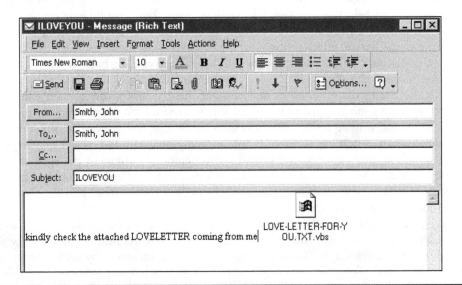

Figure 12-1 An e-mail containing the I Love You virus

I Love You is an example of a piece of malware that is more than just a virus. There are components that make it a virus, but in some cases (such as re-infection) it requires the user to open it, even if the user believes they are opening a picture. There are also, however, components that make it a worm, such as the capability to send itself to addresses in a user's contact list. The I Love You virus (or worm) does highlight some important aspects of malware, and viruses in particular. One aspect of viruses that is very important is the use of social engineering. Often, viruses like the I Love You virus use social engineering to spread to other systems. While the virus would execute automatically because of the scripting engine settings, it still required that the user open the message for the script to be executed. When a user receives an e-mail message from someone they know with the subject line I Love You, they are likely to open that message.

NOTE The Anna Kournikova virus behaved similarly, making use of the address book and being also written in Visual Basic script. This virus primarily targeted male users who wanted to see a picture of Anna Kournikova.

Since a virus often requires the help of a user, it must have a component of social engineering figured into its creation to get users to do what's needed to execute it. The I Love You virus played on people's innate desire to feel loved. Other viruses have masqueraded as games or useful utilities so as to get people to run them and thus infect their systems.

Where viruses once were merely a nuisance or they perhaps altered or deleted some files, modern viruses are typically more dangerous. They may be used to steal information from the user's system or they may be used to conduct cyber espionage, along the lines of malware like Stuxnet or Flame, discovered in the wild in Middle Eastern countries like Iran.

Worm

You might say that, compared to a virus, a worm has legs. Instead of requiring user intervention, for example, a worm is capable of making its way to other systems and infecting them on its own. The concept of a computer worm, capable of self-replication, was posited by John von Neumann in the middle of the 20th century, and though it was strictly an academic exercise, it's considered the beginning of computer infections. While he is often credited with describing the first computer virus, the fact that he called them self-replicating computer automata suggests that what he described was actually a worm. Von Neumann did not describe, and may not have even conceived of, a computer program whose purpose was to perform malicious acts like destroying data or stealing information. The malicious acts came later.

NOTE The first use of the term "worm" to describe this type of software came from a science fiction novel, *The Shockwave Rider*, by John Brunner in 1975.

Not all worms are malicious. Some of the earliest of these types were created at the Xerox Palo Alto Research Center (PARC), which tested some of the principles of the Ethernet. Other benign worms include the Nachi worms, designed to inoculate systems against the very problems that the worm itself exploited to get into the system. The ethics of something like this are widely debated, of course, since the Nachi worms did perform acts that were unauthorized by the owner of the system, even if the acts performed were to get the system updated with the latest patches so they couldn't be infected by other, more malicious worms.

One very famous worm, known as the Morris worm (after its creator, Robert T. Morris), may have originally been designed as a benign piece of software, but it went on to wreak havoc in 1988 by effectively shutting down the majority of the ARPANET. While a number of good things resulted from the release of that worm, including the creation of the first Computer Emergency Response Team (CERT), the worm itself and the response required to get it under control took a lot of time and resources, meaning it ultimately cost a lot of money to remove it from the network.

Worms continue to be a major problem, in part because of the devastation they can cause in a short amount of time, and also because of the systems they have targeted. An example is the SQL Slammer worm, which targeted the popular database software Microsoft SQL Server. Since a number of companies relied on MS SQL Server to operate critical business systems, a worm affecting that software was a very big deal.

Worms, unlike traditional viruses that require some sort of intervention on the part of a user to execute them, can spread very quickly and rapidly infect a large number of systems. They typically take advantage of vulnerabilities in system software to infect a host. If the software used as a vector into the host is very popular, the number of systems that can be impacted quickly is enormous. The Conficker worm, first discovered in 2008, infected systems vulnerable to a problem in the Windows network sharing services. After getting itself installed, the worm would then keep itself updated with the latest versions and would also download and install additional malware.

Complex malware like Conficker may also have mechanisms in place to protect itself from detection or removal. Conficker, as an example, blocked certain DNS lookups as well as disabled auto-update to ensure that holes were not patched. One technique that malware may employ is to ensure that the vulnerability used to infect the system gets patched, so as to ensure that no one else gets in and infects the system in the same way. This helps ensure that the software is the only piece of malware on the system, giving it control over the way the system behaves. It may also be about not wanting to share with others.

Trojan Horse

One malware type is named for the legendary wooden horse that was presented as a gift to the city of Troy: the Trojan horse. Hidden inside that horse, of course, were Greek soldiers, who in the middle of the night secretly climbed out of the horse and attacked the city from within. Since that time, things that are not what they seem, particularly if they have a malicious nature, are called Trojan horses. In this case, it's software that appears to be one thing but that really turns out to be something else. Often, we simply call this a Trojan. A Trojan is frequently a virus, because a virus requires user interaction to propagate, so it's not uncommon for virus writers to disguise their software as something else, such as a holiday game or a program that purports to do something cute. Of course, if the Trojan doesn't perform the action claimed, it may not spread very far because users won't think it worth passing on to friends and family. As a result, either a Trojan may be attached to an existing program, or the virus and the carrier may be written by the virus writer, with the carrier being a throwaway piece of software that exists simply to transport the virus from one system to another.

A Trojan is really a social engineering technique employed to encourage users to behave in a way that is helpful for the author of the malware, making sure the software actually gets run so the system gets infected. The goal of a Trojan might be to gain remote access to a system. NetBus, Sub 7, and Back Orifice were all considered Trojans, providing unauthorized access to a system without the system owner knowing about it. A Trojan might also be a way of getting a piece of software like a key logger onto a system to capture keystrokes, which might include useful pieces of information like names, addresses, credit card numbers, usernames, passwords, and so on. ZeuS was considered a Trojan horse that installed a key logger as well as a form grabber.

In addition to being a Trojan horse, and demonstrating the idea of the complexity of malware and the difficulty of categorizing it, ZeuS actually included a botnet client. On top of that, ZeuS is one of the first toolkits that allowed the creation of custom software. Figure 12-2 displays the creator application, as well as the configuration file, showing the different configuration settings available. Once you have the configuration you want and have selected the language you want to use, you create the executable to be used. ZeuS isn't the only malware that has a creator toolkit. The Blackhole Exploit Toolkit is another example of a toolkit that allows the user to quickly and easily create malware for their own purposes.

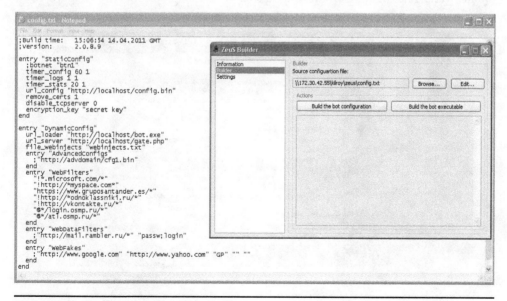

Figure 12-2   The ZeuS creator and config file

Ransomware

Malware that falls under this category also falls under at least one other category. At a minimum, ransomware is also either a virus or a worm. The purpose of ransomware is to extract money directly from users. A common approach with ransomware is to encrypt personal or sensitive data on the user's computer and demand the user pay a ransom before the attacker will provide a key that will decrypt the data. This is not the only avenue ransomware can take but it is the most common. Demanding money directly in return for decryption is a much more expeditious way to get it than compromising systems and then having to get money indirectly from the systems themselves or from selling the data taken from the systems. Personal or sensitive data is the sort of thing people are likely to pay money to get back, and quickly.

Interestingly, the idea of encryption-based ransomware was floated in 1996 in a research paper for the Institute of Electrical and Electronics Engineers (IEEE), titled "Cryptovirology: Extortion-Based Security Threats and Countermeasures" (written by Adam Young and Moti Yung). This idea, far less viable at the time because of limitations in computing power and less capable propagation methods, has become a common method of attack by organized crime groups. Over the last few years, a handful of types of ransomware have become highly problematic for businesses and individuals alike. Some of these malware strains have even been enough of a problem that they made the mainstream news. One of these is WannaCry. You can see what it looked like to be infected with WannaCry in Figure 12-3.

WannaCry is a worm that propagated using the exploit known as EternalBlue, which was developed by the U.S. National Security Agency (NSA) and exposed to the outside world by the Shadow Brokers the year before WannaCry launched in May 2017. Once the system was infected with WannaCry, its files would be encrypted by the malware. The malware would then display the dialog box shown in Figure 12-3,

Figure 12-3   System infected with WannaCry

indicating to the user that files had been encrypted. Without backups in place, the only way to retrieve files would be to pay the ransom to the attacker, typically through a cryptocurrency like Bitcoin.

NOTE A cryptocurrency is a form of money that is entirely virtual. There are no physical manifestations of a cryptocurrency. The legitimacy and authenticity of the cryptocurrency is provided through the use of cryptographic computations using a blockchain. These blockchains are linked cryptographic records that demonstrate the authenticity of the transactions.

Petya is another family of ransomware that encrypts data on the user's system, demanding payment in return for a key from the attacker that decrypts the user's data. Initially, Petya used e-mail attachments as a way of propagating the virus. Subsequently, a version of Petya was released that used EternalBlue, like WannaCry. While the first deployment of Petya happened in 2016, the revised release, referred to as NotPetya, was released in June, 2017, subsequent to the WannaCry release. The majority of attacks of NotPetya were targeted at Russia and Ukraine.

While these ransomware attacks are probably the most notorious, they certainly are not the only ones and weren't the first. One of the first was called CryptoLocker. CryptoLocker used a 2048-bit RSA key to encrypt data on users' systems. CryptoLocker used a virus to propagate from one system to another. It also made use of an existing ZeuS botnet. CryptoLocker was launched in 2013 but was isolated in 2014 as part of a takedown operation on the ZeuS botnet.

Rootkit

A rootkit is designed to hide the existence of something from a user. This may be a piece of malware like a virus or worm, but a rootkit can also hide the fact that someone has broken into your system and is making use of it. It is a good way of making sure that the malware the rootkit goes along with isn't found through the usual system utilities, because the rootkit commonly replaces those utilities with ones that work similarly but provide results that are filtered so as not to show any traces of the malware. A rootkit may prevent the user from displaying files or running programs. This would prevent the user from seeing any files, including the executable the malware is using. While rootkits traditionally targeted Unix-based systems where the system utilities were small programs that could be easily duplicated and replaced, there are rootkits that target other systems as well, like Windows.

Since the rootkit replaces system programs, it should be easy to detect the existence of the rootkit by simply checking whether those files have been replaced. This is the technique employed by host-based intrusion detection systems to protect against this very behavior. However, the rootkit may not only be able to get itself installed but also have ways to get around detection techniques, particularly if those detection techniques are using the operating system, which has already been compromised by the malware and rootkit. Basically, just about anything that uses the operating system should be suspect,

```
kilroy@bill: $ sudo rkhunter --check
[ Rootkit Hunter version 1.3.8 ]

Checking system commands...

  Performing 'strings' command checks
    Checking 'strings' command                              [ OK ]

  Performing 'shared libraries' checks
    Checking for preloading variables                       [ None found ]
    Checking for preloaded libraries                        [ None found ]
    Checking LD_LIBRARY_PATH variable                       [ Not found ]

  Performing file properties checks
    Checking for prerequisites                              [ OK ]
    /usr/sbin/adduser                                       [ OK ]
    /usr/sbin/chroot                                        [ OK ]
    /usr/sbin/cron                                          [ OK ]
    /usr/sbin/groupadd                                      [ OK ]
    /usr/sbin/groupdel                                      [ OK ]
    /usr/sbin/groupmod                                      [ OK ]
    /usr/sbin/grpck                                         [ OK ]
    /usr/sbin/nologin                                       [ OK ]
    /usr/sbin/pwck                                          [ OK ]
    /usr/sbin/rsyslogd                                      [ OK ]
    /usr/sbin/sestatus                                      [ OK ]
```

Figure 12-4   The results from rkhunter, a rootkit hunter program, on a Linux system

and the best way to detect malware and rootkits is by scanning a system that has been booted up using a live CD, where the operating system and its components aren't reliant on anything on the hard disk. Figure 12-4 shows the results of a program called rkhunter running on a Linux system. rkhunter is designed to look for evidence that a system has been compromised.

To give you a sense of the popularity of this malware technique, the rkhunter program will currently check for the existence of 498 possible rootkits. This is just on a Linux system. There are a number of rootkits available for Windows as well, with the first appearing in 1999. The first rootkit targeting Mac OS systems appeared in 2009, and the Stuxnet virus that targeted embedded systems included a rootkit component. Including rootkits with malware is a very popular technique to help ensure the malware stays in place and goes undetected.

NOTE   Rootkits are so popular, in fact, that in 2005 the music company Sony BMG included a rootkit with its music CDs to prevent users from accessing the CD in a particular way. This was considered to be a copy protection mechanism by Sony BMG, but it caused an enormous scandal for them because for the first time a company was deliberately infecting its customers with what was perceived to be malware.

Botnet Client

A botnet client installed on a computer provides access to a remote administrator of the botnet. The botnet client still needs a way in, so it's usually just the payload of another piece of malware, whether it's a virus or a worm. As discussed earlier, ZeuS is an example of a piece of malware that includes a botnet component. Botnets take advantage of the idea of distributed computing, making use of the resources of all of the systems that belong to the botnet. This could mean thousands or even millions of systems end up participating in the botnet. The botnet may be used for a number of purposes, including simply grabbing information off the systems on which they are running or sending out spam messages. They may also be used to participate in attacks on other systems. The widely publicized attacks against a number of U.S. banks in 2012 and 2013 were done by making use of botnets.

NOTE The first botnet was conceived in 1999 by a programmer called Mixter. The program was called the Tribe Flood Network, and it was developed as a way of marshaling a great many resources to attack other systems. This proof of concept led to spinoffs that eventually caused attacks against a number of businesses, in February 2000, by a Canadian who called himself Mafia Boy.

Because of the large number of systems involved in a botnet, the botnet's administrator needs a way of controlling them or better segmenting them into groups where they can be managed more easily. This is usually done using a multitier approach with other systems—something called command and control (C&C) servers. As one example, the website ZeuS Tracker, as of this writing, was tracking 452 C&C servers in the ZeuS botnet, with 100 of them being online at the time. ZeuS remains a resilient piece of malware with multiple, related strains. Even being over a decade old, it still has a good-sized presence.

While there is nothing in the idea of a botnet that is inherently malicious, the word botnet definitely has a negative connotation. In the 1990s, the site distributed.net was using what were effectively botnet clients to engage in complex problems, solved through massive parallel processing over a distributed network of clients. Botnets today use the same notion, but instead perform acts that are far less beneficial. There are, however, botnets that have been used for good purposes, and many botnets have been taken down from the inside.

NOTE Botnets got their name from the use of bots on IRC channels and taking advantage of their connections to one another. Some botnets still use IRC as a communication channel for command and control of botnet clients.

There are a number of ways botnets listen for commands from the C&C servers. They may employ Internet Relay Chat (IRC) channels to listen in on the server. This was a very early way of controlling botnets, since the infrastructure was already in place and nothing new had to be created in the way of a client–server architecture and implementation. Other ways are for systems to check with web servers using HTTP, since HTTP is a common protocol and wouldn't normally be noticed in web traffic. The distinguishing feature of botnets, though, concerns the servers they try to connect with. Sometimes, they use hostnames that may look unusual. They also connect to systems that are clearly end-user systems because of the IP address and the block it's in. Often, the address block belongs to a cable modem or DSL provider or in a dial-up block of IP addresses. You can tell by who owns the IP address in question. Plus, sometimes the reverse lookup on the IP address will provide a hostname, clearly indicating what type of network it belongs to. You may also find that the IP address doesn't resolve to any hostname, which is typically a concern as well.

 EXAM TIP You can often detect a malware infection by watching network traffic. Having systems attempt to connect to unusual hostnames or IP addresses, particularly during off-hours when no one is working on the systems, can be a tip-off that the system may be infected with malware.

Spyware/Adware

Another class of malware is spyware, which is often lumped in with another type of malware called adware. Spyware is intended to monitor the behavior of the users on the system where it lives, and doesn't generally have any replication mechanism like a virus or worm. The spyware is typically installed along with something else that the user might see as advantageous, like a toolbar for a browser. Installing a Browser Helper Object (BHO) in Internet Explorer can give the spyware a lot of access to its web traffic. The spyware may also be a drive-by installation, where the software is installed automatically because of a vulnerability in the web browser, something which the user may not even be aware of. Spyware can cause performance problems, as well as unusual behaviors on the user's system. If a system has become too slow, it could be a result of having spyware on that system. In addition to monitoring web activity, spyware may have other capabilities like keystroke logging.

The increase in the amount of spyware available, as well as the number of systems that have been infected with spyware, has caused an increase in the software programs available to remove spyware from systems. To quote Bigweld (Mel Brooks) from the movie *Robots*, "See a need, fill a need." The need for software to remove all of the spyware out there has created a nice industry selling the software to remove it. Removing spyware typically requires not only deleting files but also removing entries from the registry. Sometimes, getting all of the spyware removed from your system can be a tricky endeavor.

One of the outcomes from a spyware infiltration might be a number of popup ads, centered on your online interests. This type of intrusion into your online life is sometimes called adware, although adware is also software that is paid for through the use of ads displayed in the user interface of the program. While one is a good way to get decent software for free while still paying the developer for his time, the former is a way of irritating users, and possibly worse. In the case of the adware that generates popups as a result of your browsing behaviors, this is another form of spyware, which also happens to generate ads, making it adware as well. The same software that removes spyware will also commonly remove the bad or malicious kind of adware as well.

Droppers

A dropper is a type of malware that has the purpose of grabbing additional malware. You can think of a dropper as the foot in the door. A single-stage dropper may include the malware as part of the dropper file. The malware is not part of the executable portion of the dropper, because the purpose of the dropper is to drop the malware onto the target system. Not all droppers are single-stage, though. In some cases, the purpose of the dropper is to download additional malware to the system. This may allow the dropper to bypass anti-virus because it contains no malicious executable code. The only thing the dropper does is download additional files, which themselves would be malicious. Agobot is an early example of a dropper, released in 2002. More recently, OnionDuke is a dropper released in 2014 that infected systems trying to download software through an infected Tor proxy. The infected Tor proxy would add a malicious stub to the file being downloaded.

Anti-Virus

Anti-virus is a type of program designed to detect and remove viruses and other types of malware from the system. Not surprisingly, this can be challenging, given the speed at which viruses and other malware are being created. There are different ways for anti-virus systems to work. One of the most common is through the use of a signature. When a new piece of malware has been detected, the anti-virus vendor writes a signature for it. The signature is a set of bytes that appears to be unique to the virus and can be fed through a pattern-matching algorithm to compare files to. If a file has that particular set of bytes, or signature, it will be flagged as being a piece of malware. Once the malware has been identified, the anti-virus system has the option to completely remove the virus, if it can, leave it alone, or quarantine it. Quarantining the virus means moving it to another location in the filesystem. If a persistence mechanism like a Run registry key were to try to run it where it's expected to be, it would no longer be there and the persistence attempt would fail.

While signature analysis is a common technique used in anti-virus software, it can cause problems with performance because files need to be compared against the anti-virus database before use. Although there are ways to speed this process up, it's still a lot of processing, and it can slow down your applications. Signature detection is also useless against new viruses that have yet to be assigned a signature and is unreliable against polymorphic viruses that may have many different "looks" to them and thus may not provide a good match against the signature database.

Another way of detecting viruses is by using a heuristic approach. This can be considered anomaly detection because the anti-virus system is looking for any activities that are unusual for a particular executable or that are common to a piece of malware.

Heuristic detection does have the advantage of being able to detect polymorphic viruses because it's looking for behaviors and not checking the way a particular virus looks.

NOTE Some anti-virus providers are offloading processing of files suspected to contain malware to systems on the Internet, making anti-virus a cloud service.

While you may be most familiar with anti-virus running on desktops, it can also run on servers and also in the network. Since a common entry point for viruses is through web servers hosting up bad software, you may use a web proxy that has anti-virus software built into it to make sure that no viruses enter your network. This will provide another way of protecting desktops. Since Windows is the predominant desktop around the world, most malware development targets Windows systems. That doesn't mean that anti-virus systems are only available for Windows. ClamAV, for instance, is open-source software that can scan Unix-based systems like Linux or even macOS. The version available for macOS is called ClamXAV, but it's still ClamAV underneath the graphical interface. The Linux version is shown in Figure 12-5. Interestingly, all the files in the directory being scanned are viruses, though several of them are reasonably recent. This does highlight a problem with anti-virus not being 100 percent accurate.

Figure 12-5
The ClamAV
anti-virus running
on Linux

```
kilroy@bill:~/malware$ clamscan
/home/kilroy/malware/._Case_7925838.zip: OK
/home/kilroy/malware/kilroy_Invoice.zip: OK
/home/kilroy/malware/Blackhole2files.zip: OK
/home/kilroy/malware/._inv_#09871104632_06212013.zip: OK
/home/kilroy/malware/MacOSmalware=old.zip: OK
/home/kilroy/malware/._mebroot.exe: OK
/home/kilroy/malware/._fax_id_514155242133669.zip: OK
/home/kilroy/malware/mebroot.exe: OK
/home/kilroy/malware/fax_id_514155242133669.zip: OK
/home/kilroy/malware/Case_06252013.exe: OK
/home/kilroy/malware/Invoice_06202013_QBK.exe: OK
/home/kilroy/malware/F4CBFE4F2DDF3F599984CF6D01C1B781_speech.zip: OK
/home/kilroy/malware/fax_id_{DIGIT[15]}.exe: OK
/home/kilroy/malware/._kilroy_Invoice.zip: OK
/home/kilroy/malware/Case_7925838.zip: OK
/home/kilroy/malware/inv_#09871104632_06212013.zip: OK
/home/kilroy/malware/inv_#0{DIGIT[10]}_06212013.exe: OK

----------- SCAN SUMMARY -----------
Known viruses: 2499368
Engine version: 0.97.8
Scanned directories: 1
Scanned files: 17
Infected files: 0
Data scanned: 6.01 MB
Data read: 5.98 MB (ratio 1.00:1)
Time: 10.676 sec (0 m 10 s)
```

Anti-virus systems need to be constantly updated since signatures are constantly changing with new malware. This is often a configuration setting where the anti-virus program will update at some specified point during the day or night. Your anti-virus program can also be configured to check every file as it's accessed on the filesystem, or it can be configured to run on a schedule where every file is checked once a day. While performing scheduled scanning can improve your system performance, it also leaves a large open window for malware to get in and cause a lot of damage before the scanner catches it on the daily run.

Anti-Virus Evasion

Malware has two goals. The first is whatever the malware was written to accomplish, whether it's to be a nuisance, to be destructive, to steal or encrypt information, to infect other systems, or to achieve some other purpose. There is generally a secondary goal, too, which is to evade detection so that the malware can infect a system for as long as possible. The big threat to that secondary goal, of course, is an anti-virus program. As a result, there are a number of techniques used to evade detection by anti-virus.

Packing

Packing is really just a way of compressing a program. There are two reasons for compressing a malware-infected program. The first is that it makes the program smaller, which causes download times to be much faster, thus helping to infect a system faster. If you are trying to install a piece of malware on a system through an infected web page, you don't want the page load to take a long time because the user may very well cancel it. Same with e-mail attachments. While today broadband access is common, malware has been around since the days of dialup access when it would take a very long time to download e-mail attachments or large web pages. While packing had the benefit of making transmission faster, that is less of a concern today but packing is still helpful to potentially evade detection. Packing makes the executable smaller, which means faster download times to the end system where you want the executable to reside. This also ensures system performance isn't impacted by an anti-virus program taking a long time to scan a larger executable. Any time system performance is impacted and the system slows down, users will often notice and perhaps become suspicious. This may result in them taking a look at another anti-virus program or finding another way to root out the malware that has infected their system.

Beyond getting a smaller file size at the end, another big reason for using a packer is that it changes the look of the executable, which can make anti-virus programs miss the virus as it passes through. Any small change in an executable will mean a new cryptographic hash that is generated from the file. Remember that anti-virus commonly uses a signature to detect the virus. When you change the way a piece of malware looks, the signature is no longer valid. This can be done through changing the packing method, as long as the anti-virus program doesn't know how to unpack the executable. There are a number of different ways to pack a program. One popular packing program is the UPX packer, shown in Figure 12-6. The UPX packer is an efficient packer that has a handful of options depending on how tight you want the executable to be when you're done.

```
C:\Documents and Settings\Administrator\Desktop\upx309w>upx.exe
                Ultimate Packer for eXecutables
                  Copyright (C) 1996 - 2013
UPX 3.09w      Markus Oberhumer, Laszlo Molnar & John Reiser   Feb 18th 2013

Usage: upx [-123456789dlthVL] [-qvfk] [-o file] file..

Commands:
  -1      compress faster            -9      compress better
  -d      decompress                 -l      list compressed file
  -t      test compressed file       -V      display version number
  -h      give more help             -L      display software license
Options:
  -q      be quiet                   -v      be verbose
  -oFILE  write output to 'FILE'
  -f      force compression of suspicious files
  -k      keep backup files
  file..  executables to (de)compress

Type 'upx --help' for more detailed help.

UPX comes with ABSOLUTELY NO WARRANTY; for details visit http://upx.sf.net

C:\Documents and Settings\Administrator\Desktop\upx309w>
```

Figure 12-6   UPX packer

A packed executable is really just a compressed file when all is said and done, with a bit of a twist. Since the file is compressed, it needs to be uncompressed before it can be executed, so the very first thing that needs to happen when the program is run is to uncompress the executable. What the program really looks like, then, from an executable code perspective, is an uncompresser with a largish chunk of data in the middle of it. The uncompresser gets called first, and it decompresses the executable, after which the main program is called. An anti-virus program would need to be able to understand how to uncompress the executable before it could determine whether it's a piece of malware or not. Simply finding a packed program doesn't mean anything since there are other, valid reasons for compressing executables.

Encryption

Not surprisingly, encryption is another way to evade anti-virus detection. Again, all you need to do is find a way to make the anti-virus program miss matching on a known signature, which is really just a string of bytes. If the anti-virus program doesn't see that particular string of bytes, it won't detect the malware. The easiest way to evade an anti-virus program is to make sure the strings it's looking for aren't there. Another way to do that is to encrypt the executable. This is similar to compression in that the first thing that needs to happen is for the real executable to be decrypted so the program really looks like a decryption program, since that's what the unencrypted code actually looks like. The real code is sitting as data inside, waiting to be decrypted.

Surely, though, all you would need to do would be to determine what the decryption key is and then reverse the decryption in the anti-virus program and you'd be back to being able to see the real program where you could detect the string of bytes and flag it as malware. The way to avoid this is to have variable keys that change from one implementation to another. None of this is an easy or straightforward process. Obviously, the anti-virus program needs to know what the decryption key is before it can decrypt the program, but if there is no constant key from one implementation of the malware to another, as long as the program itself knows the key, the anti-virus program will have a hard time decrypting the file so as to check it.

NOTE   According to independent assessments of anti-virus programs, some miss as many as 8 percent of malware samples that pass through them.

Code Modifications

Self-modifying code has been around for a long time, so it's not surprising that malware authors would make use of this technique to evade anti-virus detection. The first strategy of this type is called polymorphic code, and polymorphic code in malware makes use of encryption and decryption as if simply using an encryption approach. The difference is that, with every infection, the encryption process varies. This change means that the program will look different with every infection. While polymorphic code alters the encryption and decryption routines for each infection, some programs will completely rewrite the entire executable on each infection. This is called metamorphic code and can lead to very large and complex programs since it has to be capable of writing a completely different executable each time. One example of metamorphic code is the W32/Simile virus. The vast majority of the code in that virus was dedicated to rewriting the program. The virus itself displayed messages on pre-determined dates and times.

Domain Generation

Anti-malware programs are not the only way to determine that malware is in the environment. In other words, the system doesn't have to identify the binary solely based on a file hash. Instead, often malware uses known hosts to communicate with command and control systems. These command and control systems are known. Initially, binaries may have had some hostnames hard-coded into the binary and connected to them. These known hostnames and IP addresses could be used to identify when malware is operating. These known hostnames could be detected by network-based intrusion detection systems. Malware could have strings pulled from the executable as part of malware analysis and those strings could be used to block messages using a firewall. Thus, malware needed a way of changing up its means for connecting to systems in a C&C network.

Malware today often employs a domain generation algorithm. This algorithm can be implemented in the malware executable rather than including hostnames in the binary. Instead of IP addresses used for connection, the algorithm will use the generated domain names and use hostnames from those generated domain names for the malware to connect to. This makes detection of network communication harder if the detection is based just on the hostname of the contact point.

This technique was initially used by Conficker. The first algorithm would generate 250 domain names per day. Later on, the malware could generate 25,000 domain names per day. Out of that number, 500 would be contacted by the malware. While Conficker may have started this tactic, other malware authors have picked it up. There are now several malware families that use domain generation algorithms to help evade detection.

Infection Vectors

Not surprisingly, there are a number of ways for malware to get into your system, some of which we touched on earlier in this chapter. And just as there are numerous ways they are introduced to your system, they use numerous methods to stay there and create paths used for infection.

"Sneaker Net"

The term "sneaker net" goes back to the days of shuffling files from one system to another using a removable disk like a 5.25" or 3.5" floppy disk. Rather than using a network where everything is transmitted using an electrical signal, sneaker net relied on copying the files to a disk and then walking the disk to another system and copying the files off the disk onto the new system. Most businesses in the 1980s didn't have networks, after all. Viruses have long traveled via sneaker net. Back in the 1980s, viruses might remain stored in memory and then copy themselves onto any floppy that was put into the system. This idea continues to this day, particularly with the popularity of USB sticks with flash memory on them. In fact, it's even worse today since Windows systems in particular have something called autorun. If you have autorun enabled—and it is enabled by default—there is a small file called autorun.inf on a removable disk, typically a CD or DVD, indicating what should be executed automatically when the disk is inserted. A malware author could put the autorun.inf file on a USB stick and have it point to a piece of malware on the stick so it would automatically execute when the stick is inserted into a system.

It is not uncommon for malware to be distributed in this way. In 2017, IBM was shipping USB sticks that contained malware. Studies have indicated that a large number of lost USB sticks contain malware. Some stories, perhaps apocryphal, have indicated that even after users are educated they continue to pick up USB sticks and insert them into their computers. While this is anecdotal, it does clearly describe the problem, which is that even in the face of training, our curious nature or even our nature of accumulating things takes over and all security awareness training goes out the window. Malware transmission through USB sticks continues to be just as much of a problem as transmission through floppies was in the 1980s and early 1990s.

E-mail

When it comes to e-mail, we again run into a user-awareness issue, and again it's inadequate. Users are regularly told that they shouldn't open e-mail attachments from anyone they don't know. The problem is that the attachments that contain malware are just as often from people they do know. We talked about a couple of classics in the I Love You and Anna Kournikova viruses, where the messages would have absolutely originated from people the recipients knew because they came out of an address book. In some cases, malware sent by e-mail can get automatically executed, as was the case of scripts taking advantage of the fact that the scripting engine was on in Microsoft's mail clients years ago. In other cases, the user actually opens the attachment either because they are fooled or because they just aren't paying attention.

In fact, this type of social engineering attack has become commonplace. It's known that the recent APT1 threat (perpetrated by hackers in China) regularly used e-mail attacks to gain entry into corporate networks. This particular vector is so well known that there is a tool that will generate e-mail messages with infected attachments to test social engineering attacks as part of a penetration test. There is currently a toolkit available for social engineering attacks that makes use of the Metasploit framework to generate infected attachments. You can see the menu-driven interface of the Social Engineer's Toolkit (SET) in Figure 12-7. SET will walk you through the type of social engineering attack you want to create, the type of attachment needed, and who you want to send it to. It will then send the message for you. It makes the process of performing these types of e-mail attacks much easier.

 NOTE Targeted e-mail attacks that are geared toward collecting information and that may include malware are called spear-phishing, because the goal is to send an infected message to someone at a specific company or perhaps a specific individual in order to get information.

Phishing has long been a common attack vector, and often the messages appear to be very legitimate. Just this week, in fact, several messages appearing to come legitimately from a trusted entity showed up in my junk mail box. Determining that they aren't real can require actually looking at the message headers and tracking the source of the message to a mail server that doesn't belong to the company that appears to be sending the message. Even that isn't always enough since some companies employ outside sources for communications, though that's commonly for marketing and these phishing messages often indicate that you have an issue requiring your immediate attention. Another similar

```
The Spearphishing module allows you to specially craft email messages and send
them to a large (or small) number of people with attached fileformat malicious
payloads. If you want to spoof your email address, be sure "Sendmail" is in-
stalled (apt-get install sendmail) and change the config/set_config SENDMAIL=OF
F
flag to SENDMAIL=ON.

There are two options, one is getting your feet wet and letting SET do
everything for you (option 1), the second is to create your own FileFormat
payload and use it in your own attack. Either way, good luck and enjoy!

  1) Perform a Mass Email Attack
  2) Create a FileFormat Payload
  3) Create a Social-Engineering Template

 99) Return to Main Menu

set:phishing>
```

Figure 12-7   The Social Engineer's Toolkit interface

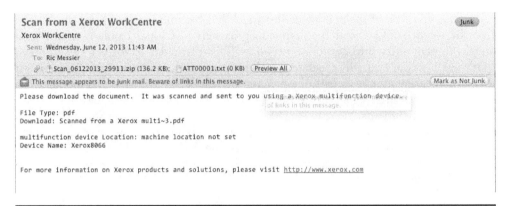

Figure 12-8   A virus attack through e-mail

attack, shown in Figure 12-8, is an attachment that appears to be sent from a network scanner. In fact, it's a virus, and not a scanned document at all. This makes the assumption that the recipient may be using one of these network scanners and has opened the attachment thinking they had a scan job that was being sent to them.

Network

A network attack often makes use of vulnerable network services to gain entry to a system and install malware. The vulnerability MS08-067, described earlier as the vector used by the Conficker worm, is a good way of gaining entry to a system. If the system is vulnerable to it, the exploit is fast, efficient, and generally highly reliable. Where other vulnerabilities can be harder to exploit, this particular vulnerability could be very reliable. Exploits, though, are not the only way systems can be impacted by a network attack. Any system with a shared drive where the permissions are too loose can be affected by a network attack.

Windows used to have an administrative share for all the hard drives on its NT-based systems. This made it easy to do remote administration on the systems, but it also opened the door to a lot of abuse. If you have remote access to an entire drive, you can easily replace common system executables with malware to ensure the system gets infected. In the days before that was resolved and systems also had firewalls built into them, people would regularly use dialup networking or connect to their Internet service provider without anything in front of their system to protect it. This was a good way to get their system infected with lots of worms and viruses. Unix-based systems were not immune from this sort of open vulnerability either, though viruses and worms were less common on their platforms. A number of vulnerabilities have existed for decades in system software used on those systems. Additionally, some of the remote tools were just as open to access (rsh, rexec, and so on) as the C$ share was on Windows systems.

Copying files to a remote system, though, isn't enough to infect it. Infection still requires that the executable be run on the system. This, though, can be done in a number of ways.

In the case of Windows, you could copy a malware binary onto a Windows system in a particular folder and have it automatically run when the user logged in. This is one way to ensure that it gets infected. Copying over a Windows executable like Notepad or something similar that gets used on a regular basis is another way to ensure a system gets infected. No matter how you get the malware onto the system and get it infected, network attacks can be very effective.

Drive-by Attacks

A drive-by attack is where you entice a user to, say, visit a website that carries a piece of malware that is then downloaded and installed onto the user's system by using an infected Java applet or some other carrier. While this may occur in such a way that the user is unaware that the download has happened, whether by using an ActiveX control or a Java applet or by exploiting a vulnerability in the web browser, it may also happen through the user's direct action, such as when the website presents a dialog box to the user and the user clicks a button in it. This may be done using scareware tactics, like an indication that your computer is infected and you should click a particular button to get your computer scanned for free. This has been a common technique for getting malware onto systems. There are a number of scareware tactics using some form of popup to get users to install a piece of malware under the guise of cleaning up or disinfecting the user's system.

 NOTE Drive-by attacks are a common approach attributed to the Chinese hackers known as APT1, whose activities have been described in detail in a report by Mandiant, an information security company.

Much like the e-mail attacks used to get malware installed, something which may be considered a type of drive-by attack if the user isn't aware of what's happening, the web-based drive-by can be done using the Social Engineer's Toolkit (SET). Again, it's entirely automated, and one of the things that can be done with SET is to copy an existing website and then have SET handle hosting it on your local system. SET will copy the existing website, making it look entirely legitimate because it's an element-for-element copy of a real website. In addition to the complete content that's already in place, SET will inject infected content into the site. Once you have SET up and running with the infected site content, you can craft a URL and send it out to people to come visit. Figure 12-9 shows the SET menu system offering a way to create a website that can be used to attack a system.

Similar to a drive-by attack, a watering hole attack uses a website to infect systems. The watering hole attack uses a targeted approach to select the website where the malware will be placed. The watering hole is the place where all the animals congregate to drink and for this reason, the attack has the same name. In technical terms, a website where people visit regularly and linger would be the watering hole. Consider a commonly visited site like that belonging to ESPN, for instance. If this site could be infected with malware, many users could be infected very quickly.

```
The Web-Jacking Attack method was introduced by white_sheep, Emgent
and the Back|Track team. This method utilizes iframe replacements to
make the highlighted URL link to appear legitimate however when clicked
a window pops up then is replaced with the malicious link. You can edit
the link replacement settings in the set_config if its too slow/fast.

The Multi-Attack method will add a combination of attacks through the web attack
menu. For example you can utilize the Java Applet, Metasploit Browser,
Credential Harvester/Tabnabbing, and the Man Left in the Middle attack
all at once to see which is successful.

   1) Java Applet Attack Method
   2) Metasploit Browser Exploit Method
   3) Credential Harvester Attack Method
   4) Tabnabbing Attack Method
   5) Man Left in the Middle Attack Method
   6) Web Jacking Attack Method
   7) Multi-Attack Web Method
   8) Create or import a CodeSigning Certificate

  99) Return to Main Menu

set:webattack>
```

Figure 12-9 Ways to formulate an attack using the Social Engineer's Toolkit

Boot Sector/MBR

While this isn't an infection vector, per se, it's worth talking about boot sector viruses in this context. As the name indicates, a boot sector virus is installed in the boot sector, which is a 512-byte piece of the hard drive called the master boot record (MBR). This is where control transfers after the BIOS has completed performing the Power-On Self-Test (POST). The boot code is responsible for getting the actual operating system to load, but the boot code is even smaller than the 512 bytes available in the boot sector because the boot sector also contains the partition table, as well as other small pieces of information. With a boot sector virus, the virus would be responsible for loading up the operating system, but it would also ensure that the system remained infected.

In one example of a boot sector virus called TDSS, the virus not only lives in the boot sector but also creates a very small, hidden partition. This partition can be used to store a copy of the virus to ensure it is capable of re-infecting the system if, for some reason, the virus is removed from the OS. In the case of TDSS, also called Alureon and sometimes TDL-4, it is not only a boot sector virus but also a rootkit and a botnet. Alureon is used to steal credit card information from network traffic.

Virus Infections

Once it's on the system, a virus may need to infect a file in order to get itself installed and running on a regular basis. One way of accomplishing this is to attach itself to a program on the system. A trusted program, one that may be run constantly, is the best one to use.

There are a few different ways for the virus to actually infect an existing program, though they all require doing a rewrite of the program as it exists on disk. The first way is to simply prepend the virus. This would write the virus code ahead of the existing code so the virus code runs first before the real program starts up. This might be done by simply changing the entry value in the program header to point to the virus code, which would jump back to the main program when it was done executing. Another way is to append the virus, allowing the program to start up first, after which the virus code gets executed. The virus may also simply overwrite an existing executable. This would remove the original program altogether, and seems like it would raise some eyebrows and quick detection.

Programs are chunked into different sections. A virus may choose to hide itself in between these different sections. This type of virus is called a cavity infector because it stuffs itself into cavities or gaps in the program file. This can be a complex technique for virus authors to use. An easier way is to just replace a known file with the virus that then calls the legitimate program. This makes it harder for the user to recognize that the virus has been executed.

 NOTE Perhaps my favorite malware trick is changing a file handler. One virus I ran across installed a file handler into the registry so that every time an .exe file was executed, the first thing that happened was the file handler got called. This meant the virus was called every time a program was run. The virus could determine if it wanted you to actually execute a program or not.

A virus may be memory resident, which would require it to hook into operating system calls, allowing the virus to infect files as they are accessed and brought into memory. This would only infect programs that were run while the virus was in memory, though. Viruses may also scan disks, looking for programs to infect and thus not remain memory resident at all.

Persistence

Malware often is designed to look for ways to maintain its presence on a system. This requires not only ensuring that the malware continues to exist on the system, as in keeping files around that support the malware, but also ensuring the malware will run after the system has rebooted. This ensures the system remains infected. In the case of malware like a botnet, this is essential, since a botnet client needs to be running all the time or else it won't get the commands sent by the controllers, which in turn means essential tasks of the botnet won't get completed. There are many approaches to persistence, so this section focuses on some of the more common ones.

Persistence is operating system specific, since there are differences between how Windows, Linux, and macOS handle processes running at boot. One common approach is through the use of services, though each operating system handles services differently. Windows services are programs the system knows about that can be started at boot or as needed. The malware would need to be installed as a service, which would require administrative access. This would be a way for malware to be running after any boot and be less likely to be seen by a normal user. The executable would be hidden somewhere and there would be no visible evidence of any program running. Linux also has the ability to run services. These are programs that are either registered with the controller, as in the case of systemd-based systems, or programs started by a script, as in the case of init-based systems. macOS uses launch daemons and launch agents, but the essentials of a service remain the same.

On Windows systems, the registry can be used to launch programs either at boot or when a user logs in. There are registry keys that can be added either in the user's registry hive or in the system's registry hive. This determines whether the program launches when the user logs in, if the key is in the user's hive, or when the system boots, if the key is in the system's hive. On Linux or macOS systems, programs can be called from initialization scripts in the user's home directory. This would serve a similar function as the user's registry key. Also on Windows systems, though far more noticeable, would be to place either an executable or a link to an executable in the Startup folder for a user. However, if the user looks in the Startup folder, such as via Start | All Programs, the executable or link will be easy to spot, making this approach less likely to succeed at maintaining persistence.

Malware Analysis

Considering the amount of malware out there, it's not surprising that there are many security professionals spending a good amount of time on malware analysis. You might expect that this sort of activity takes place only at companies that make anti-virus software, but those are not the only places where malware analysis happens. Companies like Apple and Microsoft, responsible for creating operating systems and related software, need to understand how malware works in order to try to combat it effectively. Additionally, managed security providers need to be able to understand how best to advise their customers on how to protect themselves and how to proceed in the case of infection. There are two ways to go about malware analysis. The first, and easiest, is static analysis. This is done by looking at the executable without running it. The second and more dangerous method, as well as the most complex, is dynamic analysis.

Static Analysis

In static malware analysis, you are taking a look at the executable to determine what it may be doing. This is a very safe approach because it doesn't require running the malware, which could cause damage to the system. With static analysis, you are simply taking a look at the executable itself on disk. There's no good reason to do all the work yourself, of course. Most malware you are going to run into will have already been discovered and you can learn a lot about it without actually running anything. A quick way to check is to simply run the file against any anti-virus program. You may need to run multiple anti-virus programs against the file, depending on how obscure the virus you have is. If someone has already done the work on the malware you have, you may not need to do it yourself unless you're just looking to gain experience doing malware analysis.

Figure 12-10 The VirusTotal website

Another way to check a virus is to use an online resource like the website VirusTotal. VirusTotal lets you submit a file online and have it checked against the anti-virus definitions there. One advantage to VirusTotal is that it runs multiple anti-virus engines, so you get the benefit of having multiple engines scanning without having to get the anti-virus software and run the scans yourself. Also, VirusTotal will scan files, URLs, and e-mails. If you have to scan a lot of files, you can use the VirusTotal application programming interface (API) to send files directly to VirusTotal without having to go through the web interface. VirusTotal will check your files against the anti-virus engines it uses and provide you with a report, as shown in Figure 12-10. The different names shown in the results aren't a result of misidentifying as much as they are a result of different vendors providing different names to the same piece of malware.

NOTE The names we know malware by aren't typically provided by the author, but instead by someone who has done the analysis on it.

Malware, as discussed previously, is often packed, and before performing any analysis, the malware needs to be unpacked. When we start trying to look at strings within the executable, all we're going to see is gibberish from the compressed part, plus the information from the code that does the unpacking. You can use a utility like PEiD or PESuite to determine how the application was packed. Figure 12-11 shows an application that was packed using UPX, which can be unpacked using the UPX utility shown earlier in Figure 12-6. Other utilities, like PE Explorer, will provide similar information to PEiD

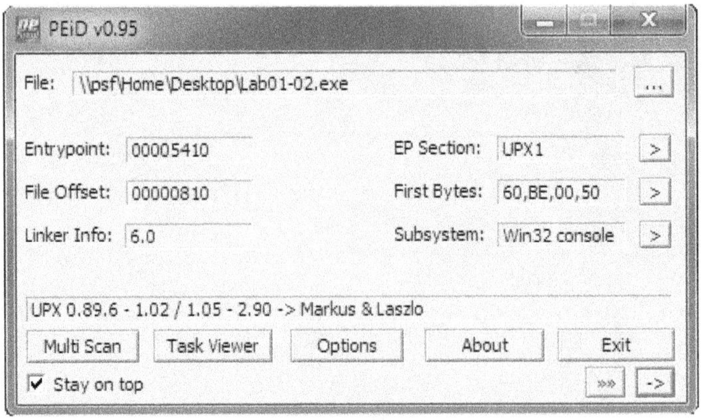

Figure 12-11
The PEiD utility

but will also extract the packed executable, assuming it is packed using a packer PE Explorer knows about. PE Explorer, however, is commercial software and is not free like PEiD. PE Explorer can also provide you with a list of dependencies the program has. All of the libraries that it relies on, as well as any libraries those libraries rely on, can be seen clearly in a tree view. This can make it much clearer what types of functions are in use in the executable.

Exercise 12-1: Using Strings

Either download the Windows Strings utility from the Windows Sysinternals website (look in the Miscellaneous category), or if you are using a Unix-derived operating system, such as macOS, you can use its built-in strings utility. Find a program and run the command line program strings against it, looking for any libraries that may be referenced.

Once you have the output from the unpacker, you have the real executable and can start examining it. While it's a common technique used for a variety of purposes, the Unix strings utility, also available from Microsoft for Windows (see Exercise 12-1), will show all of the chunks of data that look like strings. Not all of what you get will be real strings from the application, but it's a starting point. Figure 12-12 shows a portion of the output from the strings utility. In addition to any messages that the program may use to communicate with the user, which may provide some hints about what may be going on, the one thing you will absolutely see is the external function calls. You might see a list of dynamic libraries that the program makes use of. The libraries shown in Figure 12-12 are common Windows libraries and most of the function calls from those libraries are pretty common as well, but we can determine that the program checks the time on a file and also creates and manages some threads. This isn't a lot of information to go on, though, and if you don't have a lot of experience looking at malware samples, it may not be enough for you to draw any conclusions.

There are a lot of great utilities you can use to peer into a program and make determinations about what you see. A utility called Hook Analyser will help you by providing some pointers about what is going on as it looks through the program for you.

Figure 12-12
Output from the
strings utility

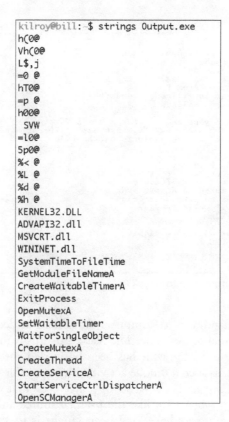

```
kilroy@bill:~$ strings Output.exe
hC0@
VhC0@
L$,j
=0 @
hT0@
=p @
h00@
 SVW
=l0@
5p0@
%< @
%L @
%d @
%h @
KERNEL32.DLL
ADVAPI32.dll
MSVCRT.dll
WININET.dll
SystemTimeToFileTime
GetModuleFileNameA
CreateWaitableTimerA
ExitProcess
OpenMutexA
SetWaitableTimer
WaitForSingleObject
CreateMutexA
CreateThread
CreateServiceA
StartServiceCtrlDispatcherA
OpenSCManagerA
```

It will perform automatic static malware analysis, checking for the program entry point as well as looking into the data segment in the program. It has a database of packers that it knows about and will use this to determine how the executable was packed, and then provide that information for you. Based on the information it finds, you will have more detailed information about what you are looking at and whether it may be malware or not. Figure 12-13 shows example output from Hook Analyser.

Once you're done poking through the file to see what you can determine from the structure and libraries, it's time to start taking a look at the code itself. If you are really lucky, it may simply be in a scripting language like JavaScript or Visual Basic Script and thus be easy to read. You may require a de-obfuscation tool to turn the code into something actually readable, but at least with a scripting language you have a good chance of seeing the original source. If you are unlucky, you may be stuck with a binary and need to convert it from the raw executable bytes to something you have a better chance of reading. You can do this by using a disassembler, which will convert the raw opcodes in the binary to assembly language, which is a set of mnemonics used to replace the numeric opcodes with something closer to words. Without a lot of practice and study, though, assembly language can be difficult to follow. This is where you may want to find a decompiler.

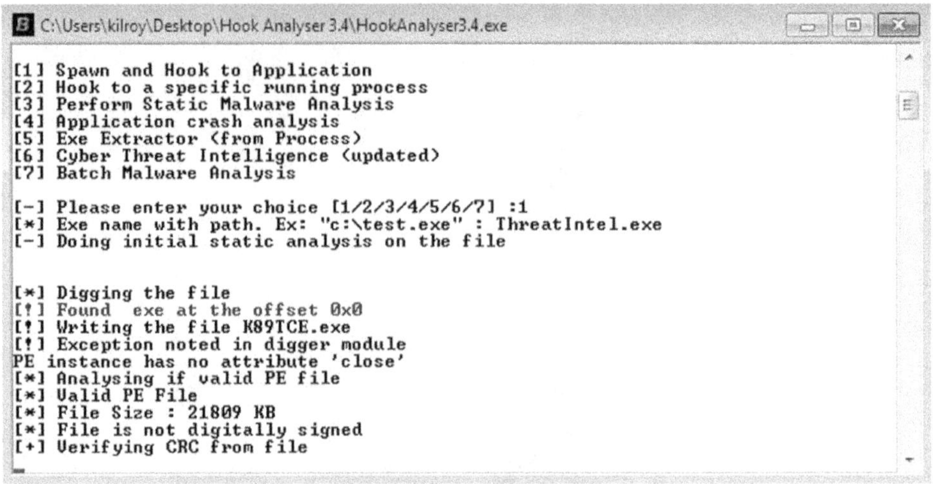

Figure 12-13   Output from the Hook Analyser utility

There are a handful of decompilers available, but decompilers can't convert binary back to the original source code. The reason for this is that once a compiler has had its way with source code, the code has been optimized and shuffled around, and because writing programs is such a unique activity, it's impossible to get back to the exact source code. What you *can* get back is a set of source code that would compile to the resulting executable, but it won't look like the original source and won't be nearly as readable. One thing programmers have long been taught is to self-document their code using meaningful variable names. A decompiler has no way of knowing what the original variable names were since they would have been completely lost in the compilation process, so it will make use of iterative variable names that have no meaning when it comes to trying to understand the program. However, in the end you will have something more easily understandable than the assembly language—unless you've spent your life writing assembly language, of course.

Dynamic Analysis

Static analysis can provide you with information useful in determining whether you are looking at malware or not. It is a lot harder from static analysis to see what the executable does, however. For that, you need to perform dynamic analysis. Dynamic analysis is a lot more dangerous than static analysis because dynamic analysis involves looking at the executable while it's running to see different library calls, as well as opening files and registry keys. In executing any malware, you are guaranteeing that your system will be infected. As a result, the best approach to dynamic analysis is using any system other than your primary desktop. Smartest approach is to completely isolate the system. You might even use a virtual machine as a place to perform the analysis. With a virtual machine, you can take a snapshot of your clean system, then infect it with the malware, perform your analysis, and roll it back to the clean version of the virtual machine for the next piece of malware you want to look at.

In fact, there is a piece of software that will do this very thing for you. Cuckoo Sandbox is a set of Python scripts that will launch a virtual machine, inject the malware, and then track the behavior of the program, watching network traffic, seeing what files it may download, and watching the library calls that get made. This will be discussed in more detail in the upcoming "Cuckoo Sandbox" section.

The Windows Sysinternals team has a number of utilities that can look more deeply into a program and see what memory is in use, the strings stored in the running process, and the call stack of all the library functions that have been called. You can also see the system calls made from the program. In Figure 12-14, you can see Process Explorer, one of the utilities available from Sysinternals, which provides a lot of detail about the running process, including the strings. Process Explorer isn't the only utility available, but it provides considerable detail about the running process and thus makes an excellent starting point. It will also show you all of the processes running at any given time, and since it's not part of the operating system, it should be less suspect than other ways of getting the process list.

NOTE Having the call stack to see what library functions are called is very helpful because you can view how the program is interacting with the system through calls to the registry, as well as the reads and writes on the filesystem.

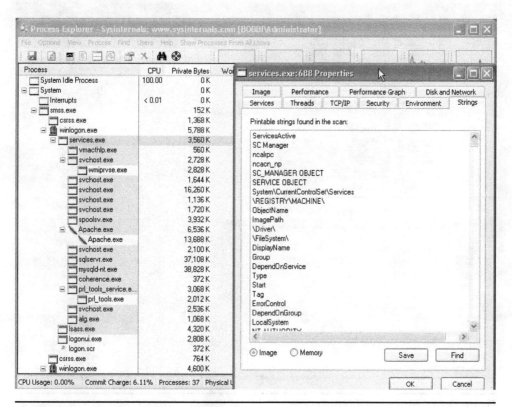

Figure 12-14 The Process Explorer utility

You'll probably want to keep an eye on registry usage, including keys that may be created and values written. Files may be created that you'll want to know about, and you'll certainly want to keep an eye on network activity since the malware may download friends to have a party. It may also be trying to upload information from your system. Beyond the artifacts on your system, you may also want to see what the program is doing while it's running. For that, you need a debugger. Figure 12-15 shows OllyDbg, which is a good, free debugger available for Windows. There are other debuggers available for Windows, as well as debuggers available for Linux, macOS, and any other operating system you can find. The majority of them work more or less the same way, enabling you to step through the program, one operation at a time, while also enabling you to watch memory and what happens to it. You may run the program directly from the debugger, or you might attach the debugger to a running program, if you happen to already have a piece of malware running on your system.

The debugger will provide you with a definitive answer about what the program is doing, since you can step through and watch every operation it performs, as well as all the memory it has control of. While other tools will provide you with ways to look at the program from the outside and poke and prod it in that way, the debugger will get you inside the program. Since this is a compiled program, you'll be looking at machine code, which has been converted back to what looks like assembly language to make it easier to

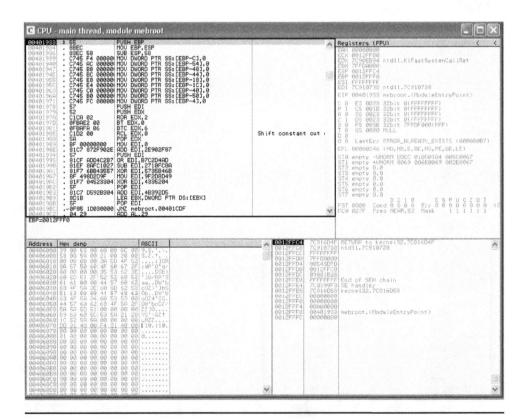

Figure 12-15 The free OllyDbg debugger

read. It is, though, the raw bytes that the CPU sees when it executes the program. With the debugger, you can alter the flow of the program and dig in as deep as you like. It does take some understanding of assembly language to know what is happening though. The debugger will provide you with a complete view of where you are in the program in memory, all the data the program has access to, and the values of all the CPU registers as they change.

 NOTE Often a register will point to a memory location, and a good debugger may help you out by providing an indication as to what is stored in that memory location.

Cuckoo Sandbox

Cuckoos are birds that lay their eggs in the nests of other birds, expecting the foster bird to hatch the cuckoo egg. This behavior of dropping unwanted items into a home is likely the reason for the naming of the Cuckoo Sandbox. Cuckoo Sandbox is an automated way of analyzing potentially malicious software. Cuckoo Sandbox requires a virtual machine set up with a Windows image that can be started up. Once the Windows virtual machine has been started and has had a snapshot created, the file for assessment is dropped into the running system and launched. This isolates the potential malware into an environment where it is locked down. The instance will be torn down once the file has been executed and the output assessed, meaning the malware is dead once the instance is no longer running. When done correctly, the network traffic outbound will be isolated and not allowed to connect to the Internet.

Cuckoo Sandbox's power is a set of scripts that automate the startup, injection, and teardown of the VM. More importantly, though, is the capability of analysis of the output. These scripts will gather screen captures of the system while it's running and also will look at the process table and any network connections. On Windows systems, the snapshot's filesystem is compared against the running system to identify any file changes, including registry changes. This can indicate the presence of a dropper, if there are new files, or of persistence mechanisms, if there are registry or other changes. Figure 12-16 shows the output from Cuckoo Sandbox, after analyzing a PDF file that was attached to an e-mail flagged as junk by an e-mail provider.

The summary output shown, which is only a small part of everything available from Cuckoo Sandbox, indicates that two anti-virus engines on VirusTotal identified the PDF file as malicious software. Additionally, you can see that after opening the PDF, there was an attempt to connect to multiple IP addresses without the use of DNS hostnames. This is a common approach for malware and, as a result, is considered suspicious. You will also see that some ICMP traffic was generated. For further assessment, Cuckoo Sandbox provides a lot of log files from the execution and also several screen captures that were taken while the file was being opened and the results from having it open.

One of the safest ways to perform any malware analysis is through the use of a tool like Cuckoo Sandbox. It may be more satisfying to look at the malware by hand if you are very curious and technical by nature. However, Cuckoo Sandbox is going to be more reliable and quite a bit safer.

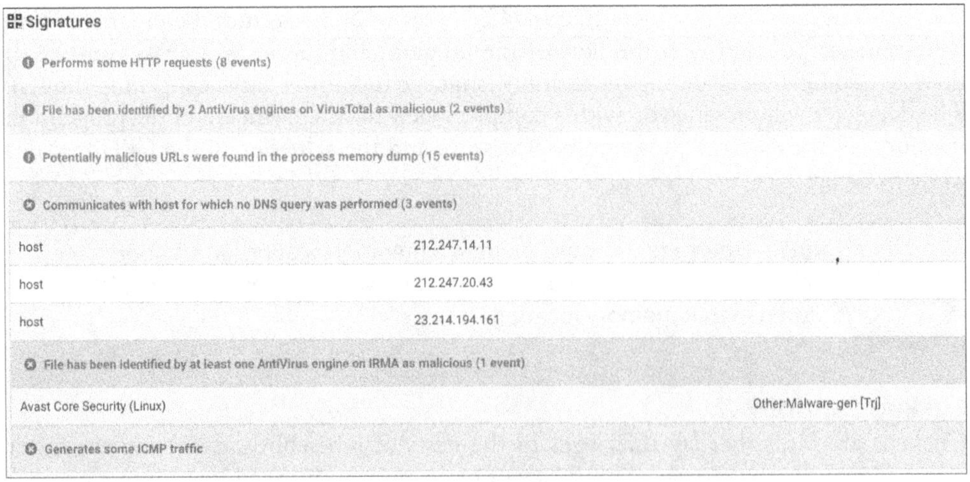

Figure 12-16 Cuckoo Sandbox output

Malware Policies

A company may put policies into place regarding malware handling and prevention. The first common policy is that anti-virus must be run on all company-owned computer systems. This involves not only installing the software but making sure it's kept up to date. On top of that, there may be policies concerning the use of external storage, like flash drives or even CDs, since any external source can be a way for a virus to get onto your system. There may even be technical controls in place to prevent users from making use of these external storage devices.

Ideally, an organization also has incident response policies related to handling virus intrusion, since containing and removing a virus is critical. A large-scale virus attack can last days or weeks, so having policies and procedures in place on how best to maintain business operations while also trying to keep the virus under control is important. The best way is to simply shut everything off and then treat the dead drives, removing the virus through the use of a LiveCD with a virus scanner on it. This means the virus is no longer infecting devices because it's not on a live, running system. However, it also means that your business won't be functioning until all the systems have been cleaned. This is where understanding a priority level of systems that can be shut down until the virus has been cleaned can be important. This may be done through the use of a policy or at least a procedure for handling malware or other incidents.

You may or may not be able to determine when your system has been infected, depending on how active the infection is or how intrusive. However, some common signs of virus infection are that systems become very sluggish all of a sudden. That's not always a great indicator because there are a number of reasons for a system to become sluggish, but if there appears to be no reason for a system's slowness, you might do well to investigate it with this in mind. Programs that used to run but simply fail to start can be a sign of a virus attack. If when looking you see a lot of unexplained network activity, this could be a result of a virus infestation. It could be caused by a botnet client reaching out to its handlers. Often, viruses will affect how your web browser behaves, redirecting some of the network traffic to other sites, or blocking access to some sites altogether.

Chapter Review

Whether it's viruses, worms, Trojans, or some other form of malicious software, their numbers are increasing rapidly each year. But what was once a steadily increasing number has, in the last decade, turned into a nearly exponential curve. This is a very serious problem and, as with many things in security, is almost a war of attrition. Each side escalates based on the actions of the other, thus requiring more and more resources. While we do have technologies capable of combating malware, like anti-virus and intrusion detection, they are not perfect and rely primarily on knowing what the malware looks like, which can limit their effectiveness, particularly when it comes to newer malware that has yet to be analyzed.

Malware analysis can be a dangerous activity since you run the risk of having information removed from your system or having files deleted, or perhaps finding yourself participating in a distributed denial-of-service attack. There are two types of malware analysis: static and dynamic. Static analysis looks at a program's details and tries to determine whether it's malware, perhaps finding out what it's doing, seeing whether it's packed, and determining what strings may be in the program. You can also use anti-virus programs to perform static malware analysis and they should be able to tell you whether the program is malware and what type it is, assuming it's one the anti-virus programs know about.

Dynamic malware analysis is more involved and can be automated, though more commonly it is performed by running the program and seeing what effect it has on the system with new registry keys or new files as well as any network activity that may be occurring. Dynamic analysis is best done in a very controlled environment, within a virtual machine that has network access tightly locked down to protect against further infection on your network as well as to prevent leakage of anything about your system to a malware controller somewhere else.

Questions

1. You've found what looks like a piece of malware. When you run it, a number of new files show up in your temp directory, and some of those files have records of things you have typed. You received it from a friend via e-mail, but you checked and you don't see that it was sent out from your e-mail account to anyone. Based on this scenario, what type of malware is this most likely to be?

   A. Adware

   B. A Trojan

   C. A virus

   D. A worm

2. You have a piece of malware and you want to do static analysis on it. What might you do?

    A. Install it in a virtual machine.

    B. Run it through a debugger.

    C. Attach it to the running process.

    D. Run strings on it.

3. Which of these is NOT a reason for packing a binary?

    A. To make it smaller

    B. To make it more efficient

    C. To hide it from anti-virus scanners

    D. To make it easier to transmit

4. The purpose of a rootkit is to do what?

    A. Hide malware

    B. Provide the root password

    C. Copy itself to many other systems

    D. Create user accounts

5. From an attacker's perspective, what is the advantage to using a boot sector virus?

    A. It is written in assembly language.

    B. It is very small.

    C. It can re-infect the system each time it boots up.

    D. It creates hidden partitions.

6. One way viruses have historically been able to copy themselves from one system to another is by using what mechanism?

    A. Administrative share

    B. Remote desktop

    C. Remote SSH access

    D. Dropbox

7. What is the specialized type of engineering malware makes use of?

    A. Chemical

    B. Civil

    C. Social

    D. Mechanical

8. You notice a lot of unusual network traffic to remote systems originating from your computer. When you investigate further, you discover that a number of computers on your network are doing the same thing, and the IP address is in another country. This always seems to happen in the late evening hours. What may you be seeing?

   A. Video streaming

   B. System updates

   C. Synchronization activity

   D. Botnet activity

9. Botnets historically have used which protocol to communicate with handlers?

   A. SMTP

   B. IRC

   C. AOL

   D. CHAT

10. You regularly get popup ads on your computer, particularly when you are browsing the Web. What is this an example of?

    A. A virus

    B. A worm

    C. A botnet client

    D. Adware

11. Your anti-virus software has identified a file named Agobot on your system. What does this mean?

    A. Nothing. This is a false positive.

    B. Your system has been infected with ransomware.

    C. You have been using the Tor network.

    D. Your system has a dropper installed.

12. What is the common payment mechanism expected for victims of ransomware?

    A. Rubles

    B. Dinar

    C. Bitcoin

    D. PotCoin

13. Which of these would be a common persistence vector?

    A. Registry key

    B. HKEY

    C. Prefetch folder

    D. VirusTotal

14. If you wanted to check a possible piece of malware against multiple anti-malware sources, where would you go?

  A. Malwarebytes

  B. VirusTotal

  C. TotalVirus

  D. MalwareAggregator

15. What program could you use to extract URLs that a piece of malware connects to while running?

  A. Strings

  B. PEiD

  C. Cuckoo Sandbox

  D. ProcessDigger

Answers

1. C. Since the scenario doesn't indicate evidence of popups or refer to the program claiming to be something that it isn't, it's not adware or a Trojan. It potentially could be a worm since it was received via e-mail, but your mail program apparently didn't send it out to anyone, so it's probably not a worm because it's not attempting to self-propagate as far as you can tell. Therefore, it's most likely a virus.

2. D. Running the strings utility is a valid option for static malware analysis. You wouldn't install it, either in a virtual machine or anywhere else, because malware is commonly a standalone application, meaning there is no installer. Running it in a debugger or attaching to it while it's running are dynamic analysis techniques.

3. B. Packing doesn't make the binary more efficient because the first thing the program needs to do is unpack before running. Packing makes malware smaller because you are compressing it. Because it's smaller, it's easier to transmit. When you pack malware, you may be able to hide it from anti-virus scanners.

4. A. The purpose of a rootkit is to hide the existence of something, like remote access from someone or a piece of malware running on the system. It may also act as a backdoor that gives an attacker remote access. A rootkit doesn't provide the root password, or copy itself to many other systems, and it wouldn't create user accounts itself.

5. C. A boot sector virus has the capability to re-infect at each boot to ensure the main virus is still in place and persists. While a boot sector virus may also have a component that creates a hidden partition, that isn't an advantage of boot sector viruses, nor is it because they are small, since you can't do much in a small space. It may not have originally been written in assembly language.

6. **A.** Windows NT systems used to have administrative shares for each drive, called C$, D$, and so on, which made remote administration easy but also made the systems more vulnerable to malware. Remote desktop doesn't provide you with the ability to copy files, nor does remote SSH access (though you can copy files using scp, which makes use of SSH). Dropbox can sync files across multiple systems, but it hasn't historically been used to copy malware from one system to another.

7. **C.** Social engineering is often used to get malware onto systems. Chemical, civil, and mechanical engineering aren't helpful in software development or malware creation.

8. **D.** This could very well be botnet-related. If the activity mostly happens in the late evening to IP addresses out of the country, it's unlikely to be system updates or video streaming since there isn't anyone in the office watching video. The IP addresses out of the country is what makes it unlikely to be system updates. Synchronizing doesn't make sense without context.

9. **B.** Botnet clients have historically used IRC, which is where a lot of bots originated. CHAT and AOL as protocols don't exist. SMTP could conceivably be used, but it isn't very common.

10. **D.** This is an example of adware. You'd need more than this to have a virus or a worm and it probably isn't a botnet client either.

11. **D.** Agobot is a dropper. This is potentially malicious, though not necessarily so. The dropper itself is not malicious, though the malware it may download and execute would be. The anti-virus program probably correctly identified the file, so it's not a false positive. Agobot is not ransomware and it has not been linked to ransomware. While you may have been using the Tor network, this alert alone is not an indication of that.

12. **C.** Ransomware commonly demands payment in the cryptocurrency Bitcoin. Dinar and rubles are both physical currency and aren't easily transmitted over the Internet. Cryptocurrency is, though. While PotCoin is also a form of cryptocurrency, it is not generally associated with common families of ransomware.

13. **A.** The registry has keys that can be used to make sure malware keeps running across reboots. While HKEY is a portion of a full path to a registry key, it is not a persistence mechanism. The prefetch folder is where you may find evidence that a program has run, but it is not used for persistence. VirusTotal is a website used to check malware against multiple anti-malware databases.

14. **B.** VirusTotal is a website that makes use of dozens of anti-malware engines to check potential malware against. Malwarebytes is a single anti-malware software solution. TotalVirus and MalwareAggregator don't exist.

15. **A.** The strings program will display printable character strings from a file. This could include URLs that the malware is using, if any. You could use PEiD to gather information about malware, but PEiD doesn't extract data from the executables that might point to URLs used. Cuckoo Sandbox may include this information but it wouldn't be extracted from the file. The URLs would have to be called to be identified in Cuckoo Sandbox. ProcessDigger doesn't exist.

Exercise 12-1 Answer

Under Windows, you may see references to libraries like KERNEL32.DLL or MSVCRT .DLL. Any string that ends in .DLL will be a library reference. Under other operating systems, you'll have to look for other markers for their libraries. In Linux, you should see files that end in .so, and under macOS, you should see files that end in dylib. These are all dynamic libraries, meaning they get pulled in dynamically as the program is running rather than being linked in at compile time, which would be called static linking.

## CHAPTER 13

Incident Response

In this chapter, you will learn:
- Incident response policies and plans
- Response management
- Legal requirements
- Essential communications

There is a sentiment that has been variously attributed to different people that says there are two types of companies: those who realize they have suffered a data breach, and those who don't yet know they have suffered a data breach. The gist of the sentiment is that every company has suffered (or will suffer) a data breach. It has also been suggested that breached companies can be categorized further into two types: those who won't be breached again, and those who will be breached again. All of this is to suggest that being able to address these breach attempts is very important because they are inevitable. You can think about how you handle this as falling into the categories prevent, detect, response, and recover. Incident response is not only about the response, since you at least need to be able to detect something before you can respond to it. Waiting for either the Federal Bureau of Investigations (FBI) or a security-focused reporter to let you know you've been breached is not the best of ideas. In the end, response is as much about planning as it is about actually responding.

Incident response is also not purely a technical activity. There is so much more to it than just doing the investigation. A large-scale incident will impact significant sections of the company. This would include the system and network teams as well as management, legal staff, the corporate communications team, and potentially human resources. Today, there are so many laws and regulations, specifically with regard to breach notification, that the legal team needs to be involved to ensure the response proceeds in a manner that will protect the business against fines and other punishments.

Understanding how the attacker works can help with incident response because you'll understand where the attacker is in their process. This can help you to better scope the investigation. If they are very early in, you may not need to worry yet about tracking any data leaving your organization. Each of the attack stages will have evidence that will point to what the attacker has been doing. There are a couple of different ways to map the attack. Each has its benefits, though ultimately which one you choose may depend on the organization you are in and how you think about the world when it comes to attacks.

The first mapping technique is the cyber kill chain, and the second is the attack lifecycle. We will cover the stages of each of these.

Part of every investigation will include collecting data, analyzing it, and then storing it. It's important to understand how to collect and store data in a way that makes clear it hasn't been tampered with. In some cases, what you are collecting may have to be presented as evidence in court, and it won't hold up as admissible evidence if it's not demonstrably free from alteration. This applies to both the collection and storage. It's not just the disk data you'll be collecting, either. You'll have to be concerned with such ephemeral data as process listings, network connections, and other essential pieces of information that may exist for a very short period of time.

As an incident may be related to business operations, you need to consider the legal implications of the incident. This is for the sake of not only potential prosecution of an attacker but, perhaps more importantly, ensuring that the business does not get fined for improperly handling customer data. Legal implications includes potential disclosure of what has happened. Disclosing that a breach has occurred is where a good communications team comes in. The communications team can help notify customers as well as handle any necessary communication with the press and regulatory agencies.

Mapping the Attack

As previously mentioned, there are currently two well-known ways of thinking about how attackers come after your systems and networks: the cyber kill chain and the attack lifecycle. This is not to say there are no other ways of thinking about these attacks. It's also not to say that all attacks happen using these patterns. You may have heard the term advanced persistent threat (APT). APT attackers will commonly use methods that easily map to either the attack lifecycle or the cyber kill chain, so it's very helpful to know more about these two frameworks. This is important from the standpoint of incident response because knowing where the attacker is in their attack will help you understand both the urgency with which you need to respond and where you should focus your attention. Knowing how to determine what the attacker has done and what they are in the process of doing will help you scope your investigation and overall response.

A *kill chain* is a military term that is used to describe an attack and how it is put together. The idea behind a kill chain is to follow the progression of an attack from identification all the way through destruction of the target. It may also take into account a follow-up to ensure that the target has been destroyed. Lockheed Martin took the idea of the military's kill chain and applied it to cybersecurity. What they ended up with is commonly referred to as the *cyber kill chain*. It describes the methods used by attackers to gain unauthorized access to computers in order to gain an advantage, whether it's building a base of operations or achieving something more directly financial. The cyber kill chain steps are shown in Figure 13-1.

Figure 13-1 Cyber kill chain diagram

The first phase is reconnaissance. This is where the attacker identifies a target and learns what they can about the target. Reconnaissance is not necessarily performing network reconnaissance or enumeration. It's perhaps finding an organization that has resources the attacker wants, such as intellectual property or financial resources. Reconnaissance also likely involves finding people—names and e-mail addresses—as potential targets for social engineering attacks. The second phase is weaponization. This is where the attacker identifies a means of gaining access, which may be malware that could be used as a Trojan to provide the attacker remote access to the system under attack. Some may consider weaponization the development of a zero-day exploit, which doesn't take into account the reality of how attacks happen today. Delivery, the third phase, is where the attacker sends the malware to the victim, where (the attacker hopes) it gets executed and gives the attacker remote access to the target's system. The execution and giving remote access falls under exploitation and installation. The objective here would be to ensure the access is persistent even beyond logouts and reboots. The attacker's expectation with the cyber kill chain is that the installation will result in a form of remote access to either the attacker or a network of command and control systems.

Another way of mapping out an attack is to use the attack lifecycle. This is a model that was developed after countless investigations of APT groups by Mandiant, a company widely recognized as a leader in the incident response space. You can see the trajectory of the attack in Figure 13-2. One difference between the attack lifecycle and the cyber kill chain is the attack lifecycle recognizes the persistent nature of the attacker. It's not a one-and-done incident. The attacker gains access to the environment and, rather than being satisfied with the initial access, continues to look for ways to become further entrenched within the organization.

The attack lifecycle doesn't assume malware as the cyber kill chain seems to. It rather generically labels initial recon and initial compromise as the first two stages. One reason for this is that, from a real-world perspective, not all attacks use malware. In some cases, the initial compromise may be the compromise of credentials using a phishing attack. Once in the environment, the attacker works to establish a foothold. This could be through the use of persistence mechanisms to ensure they continue to have access through reboots. This may include installing software that connects back to a system designed to receive these connections. This would allow either a single user or a whole command and control network to maintain access to this system.

Once the attacker has access, the cycle starts. First, if they don't have administrator-level privileges, they escalate privileges to get them. Then, they perform internal recon,

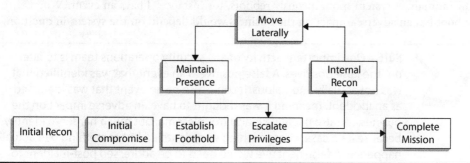

Figure 13-2 Attack lifecycle

move laterally within the network, and maintain presence (persistence) on the newly acquired systems. Along the way, there would typically be a credential harvest, since that may allow for more systems to be infiltrated. There is no reason to use exploits or malware when simply logging in as an authorized user is possible.

Finally, the last stage is to complete the mission. This, again, though, is not a stopping point. It's just another stage. It means the objective of the attacker is executed. This may include exfiltrating sensitive data (personal information, intellectual property, etc.) from the target systems to a location managed by the attacker. This attack likely would not be a one-and-done scenario since data is always being generated and updated. New projects get started and generate new documentation and details. More people get hired, so there is more personally identifiable information (PII) to take out of the network.

Keep in mind that APT organizations are funded and staffed. The adversary has an objective and they will do what it takes to obtain that objective. In some cases, it may be stealing intellectual property either to sell or to use for businesses that are nation-state sponsored. In some cases, an APT is organized crime looking to make some money. Either way, these are not ad hoc attack groups or so-called script kiddies, which is one reason why the activities can be mapped. These are people who are doing a job and trying to do it as efficiently as they can because they are being paid to do so. One good example of an APT as a business is APT38. While it's expected that the APT38 group is backed by the North Korean regime, the group's objective is financial. They steal money from organizations using a number of techniques. Their actions are not random. They are specific and predictable, with an objective of financial benefit to the attacker.

Preparation

Preparation may be the most important element of incident response. It may not be very exciting, perhaps, but without preparation, there will be a whole lot of excitement. You'll be responding constantly if you are not prepared. The first thing you need to do is understand what an incident is. I'll give you a broad definition to help you get started, but keep in mind that each organization may have some specific needs that alter the definition of incident, or at least each organization may have different examples of an incident that relate to how they do business. For purposes of our discussion, an incident is any event that has the potential to incur an adverse reaction within an organization. Narrowing this slightly, an incident is any event that is a violation of security policy. An event is any observable action that deviates from the normal course of business. Essentially, an event is an anomaly. A system spontaneously reboots, for instance. That's an event. Whether that reboot has an adverse impact on the business would depend on the system in question.

 NOTE One important activity of any security operations team is to filter out the false positives. A false positive is an event that was identified that was not actually anomalous. It could also be an event that was identified as an incident, meaning it was thought to have an adverse impact on the business. A false negative is also troublesome, but much harder to identify because it's a case where nothing was identified but something bad actually happened. A false negative would need to be addressed post-incident to ensure detections are in place for it going forward.

According to the National Institute of Standards and Technology (NIST), there are five essential functions to an information security program. You can see these five functions as they are typically represented in Figure 13-3. When you are preparing your organization for incident response and handling, you should keep all of these functions in mind. First is identify. If you are not putting resources into protecting the right parts of your environment, you are asking for incidents to happen that will need to be responded to. It's important to keep some things in mind while you are working on the protect function. Some form of threat intelligence is useful here, especially when it comes to understanding who your adversaries are and how they are most likely to attack you. If you throw up a bunch of firewalls, choking network traffic, when in fact the adversaries are attacking your organization's users through e-mail and web-based attacks, you've missed the boat. Intelligence will help you identify so you can effectively protect.

Next, is the detect function. This means placing monitoring elements into the environment so you have visibility into all aspects, from servers to network infrastructure down to desktops. Without detection capabilities, you will have no idea when to respond to an incident. You won't know what an incident is and may not even see events when they happen. Of course, detection leads into the response function. This is what we are dealing with in this chapter. But, as already mentioned, it's a far broader concept than just sending all the forensics guys in to figure out what happened. The forensics guys can't do anything without data, which is why we are covering the whole scope of incident response activities.

Finally, you need to recover. This not only means restoring business operations to normal so the lights can stay on. It also means following up to ensure you have "nailed up boards over the holes" to keep the bad guys out. There are not currently clear statistics regarding reinfection rates but be assured the bad guys get back in. Often, too often considering, they get back in the very same way they got in the first time around. The reason is that businesses may be too intent on getting everything restored without taking the time to understand what happened so that they can stop it from happening again. The appropriate follow-up may take the form of root cause analysis (RCA) or an after-action review (AAR). These are semi-formal to formal affairs that seek to understand what happened in order to take back lessons learned from the incident and apply those lessons. Without applying the lessons, you'll be getting right back on the merry-go-round with the same attacker, in a very short space of time.

Figure 13-3
Five essential
information
security
functions

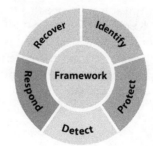

NOTE It's sometimes hard to get the appropriate perspective on an incident right after cleanup has happened. It is important, though. Taking adequate notes during the course of the incident may help a lot in getting through an after-action report. That way, you aren't spending time trying to remember the order of events. You may also have identified the root cause and lessons during the course of the investigation. They just need to be implemented using a plan, with identified stakeholders following up to ensure the work gets done.

Intelligence

Threat intelligence is important. However, many organizations do not have the depth of experience with attackers or the resources to go digging for information to have adequate threat intelligence. Companies are often focused on getting the business operational again when an incident occurs. They can't take the time to really identify who the threat actor is and fully understand all the tactics, techniques, and procedures (TTPs) the threat actor used. For this reason, relying on external sources for intelligence makes sense, not only to help inform the overall information security program, but also to understand who your adversaries are and how they operate so that you can make sure you have the right protections in place as well as the right set of detections. Again, this is a place where you should keep in mind the five essential functions of information security so you are developing strategies for each to address what you know to be the threats you face.

While there are commercial companies that will provide you with intelligence that has gone through collection, analysis, correlation, and presentation, there are other sources as well that you can take advantage of without spending money. For a start, there are Information Sharing and Analysis Centers (ISACs). These organizations were originally created in 1998 as a result of a presidential directive in the United States recognizing the potential cyber threats to critical infrastructure. There are a number of ISACs targeted at specific business verticals. If you are in the automotive or real estate industries, for instance, there are ISACs that provide threat intelligence for you. As of this writing, there are 20 ISACs, mostly targeted at specific industries, and most of them have been around for at least a decade, according to the National Council of ISACs (www.nationalisacs.org). There is also an ISAC for governmental organizations called the Multi-State ISAC, focused on state, local, tribal, and territorial governments.

Another resource for threat intelligence that is available at no cost is the United States Computer Emergency Readiness Team (US-CERT). This organization was created in 2000 as the Federal Computer Incident Response Center (FedCIRC) but in 2003 was renamed and moved elsewhere within the government. US-CERT is now part of the National Cybersecurity and Communications Integration Center (NCCIC). US-CERT provides a lot of resources and updates about vulnerabilities and threats at their website: www.us-cert.gov.

NOTE   The first computer emergency response team was created in 1988 at Carnegie-Mellon University in response to the so-called Morris Worm that took down a substantial portion of the Internet. The global network at that time was primarily mini computers and mainframes rather than the enormous collection of PC-based devices that it is today. The CERT Division of the Software Engineering Institute at Carnegie Mellon still exists as a point of coordination and is also a good resource for threat intelligence.

Threat intelligence should be used to inform the organization's overall risk program, meaning information gathered from any intelligence sources should be fed into a risk assessment. This will help to identify what the actual risk (potential for loss or damage in percentage and monetary impact) to the organization is. Once the risk has been assessed, the organization can decide how to handle the risk. This often includes applying resources to mitigate the risk, but it could also be to take an action like transferring the risk through the use of something like cyber insurance. Along with the risk, the threat should be identified, meaning what is the mechanism or entity that may be used to exploit a vulnerability to violate policy or otherwise obtain unauthorized access to a computer system or the information of an organization.

Many threat intelligence programs can provide a feed that can be used within a security information and event manager (SIEM). This outside information can be used in conjunction with the organization's internal monitoring and logging information to relate what is happening in the outside world to events happening within the organization.

One important point about threat intelligence is attribution. For example, Mandiant names different groups who are responsible for attacking organizations and users. The names Mandiant uses are commonly referenced by the media and across other security vendors. Any advanced persistent threat is given a name APT followed by a number. As an example, APT1, the first named group, is a handful of actors in the Chinese military. As previously mentioned, APT38 is a group that is backed by the North Korean regime. These are not the only named groups, however. In addition to APTs are FINs, which are financially motivated attackers. FIN7, for instance, is not tied to a specific country, though they appear to be Russian-speaking, based on a long period of time observing and cleaning up after them. This is an organization that regularly steals credit card information from restaurants, hotels, and retail establishments. If you have had your own credit card information stolen from a business in one of these sectors, FIN7 may have been behind it.

The purpose of naming these organizations isn't simply to know who your attacker is. Far more importantly, identifying the adversary means identifying their TTPs. Once you know who you are dealing with, you can narrow the focus of your investigations since you know that, for instance, they are going after credit card information and not intellectual property. This may take a significant number of systems out of the equation when looking for the potential for theft. It also tells you how they do business. They may use a particular piece of malware, for instance, so you can make sure your anti-virus is up to date with signatures for that piece of malware. FIN7 often uses the Trojan Carberp, for instance. You can see the control panel for Carberp in Figure 13-4. Identifying this software in your environment tells you who you are dealing with, potentially, which can increase the speed of the investigation.

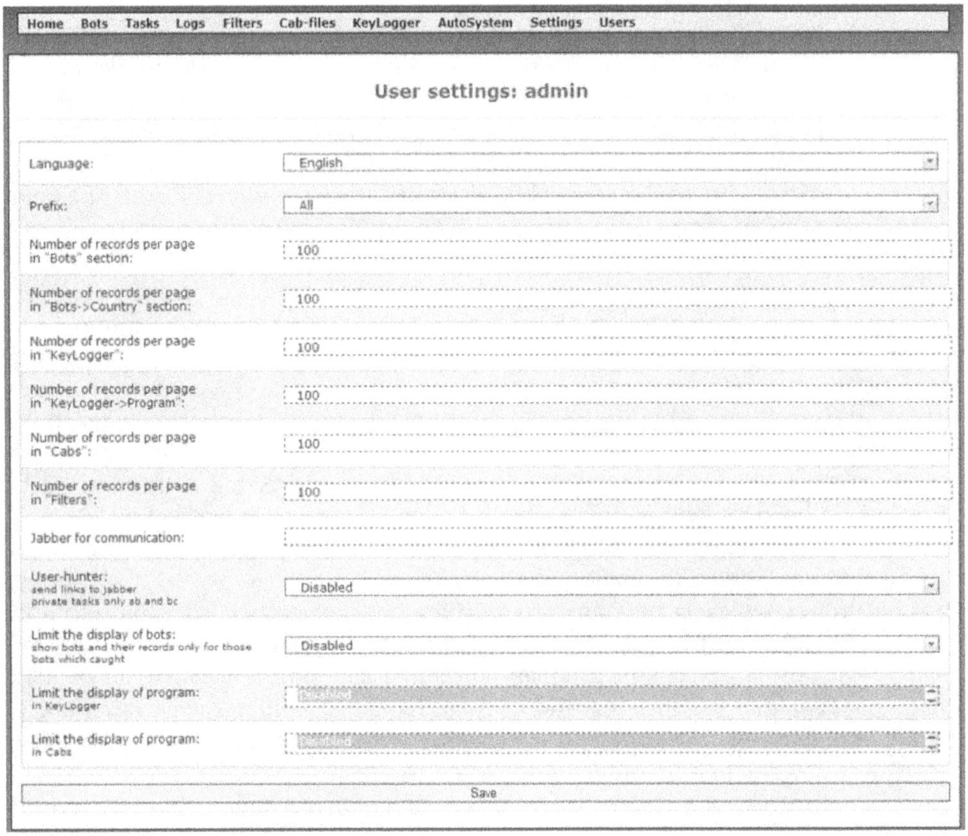

Figure 13-4   Carberp Trojan admin panel

Any advantage you can get to help you identify your adversary faster potentially enables you to get to a resolution faster. This means getting your business fully operational again. Ultimately, this should be one of the overall goals of any incident response.

Policy and Plans

The start of any incident response should begin with a policy. This is a set of high-level statements by the organization. These statements define the intention of the organization when it comes to incident response. This includes the goals and objectives of the incident response as well as a definition of roles and responsibilities. After all, responding to an incident isn't just sending in the technicians and forensic investigators to find out what happened and clean it up. The organization will want to know what the overall impact from the incident is, which may include estimating the monetary value of any data that has been taken out of the organization. Once details like this are known, many other people in the organization are going to be involved.

A policy typically includes sections like scope, purpose, definitions, and responsibilities and then a series of policy statements. Depending on how the organization's governance and document library is set up, the policy may be very detailed, including procedures.

However, policies usually lead to standards that are more specific than the policy, providing some guidance around how to implement the policy statements to ensure the policy is adhered to. Below the policy is the procedure, which would be ground-level guidance for step by step how the standards should be implemented and maintained. A policy generally should not need to be updated very regularly since it should be general enough to be able to encompass any number of technologies and processes that may be used by technicians and analysts.

In some cases, below the policy your organization may have an incident response plan (IRP). The IRP should be detailed and comprehensive, providing guidance on not only how to respond to an incident but also how to ensure events are correctly identified as incidents. Beyond that, the IRP should provide guidance for assigning priorities to the incident. This would typically be based on business needs. Any incident will likely pass through many phases over the course of an investigation. All of the work performed in response to an incident should be documented in a case management or ticketing system. When you are filling in details of the incident for the ticket, you may want to assign categories to identify what the disposition of the incident is at any point in time. The NCCIC uses Table 13-1 to define categories that are to be used for federal agencies. You may find there is some value in using these categories as a starting point.

Category	Name	Description	Reporting Timeframe
CAT 0	Exercise/Network Defense Testing	This category is used during state, federal, national, international exercises and approved activity testing of internal/external network defenses or responses.	Not applicable; this category is for each agency's internal use during exercises.
CAT 1	Unauthorized Access	In this category an individual gains logical or physical access without permission to a federal agency network, system, application, data, or other resource.	Within one (1) hour of discovery/detection.
CAT 2	Denial of Service (DoS)	An attack that *successfully* prevents or impairs the normal authorized functionality of networks, systems or applications by exhausting resources. This activity includes being the victim or participating in the DoS.	Within two (2) hours of discovery/detection if the successful attack is still ongoing and the agency is unable to successfully mitigate activity.
CAT 3	Malicious Code	*Successful* installation of malicious software (e.g., virus, worm, Trojan horse, or other code-based malicious entity) that infects an operating system or application. Agencies are NOT required to report malicious logic that has been *successfully quarantined* by antivirus (AV) software.	Daily Note: Within one (1) hour of discovery/detection if widespread across agency.

Table 13-1 Incident Response Categories

Category	Name	Description	Reporting Timeframe
CAT 4	Improper Usage	A person violates acceptable computing use policies.	Weekly
CAT 5	Scans/Probes/ Attempted Access	This category includes any activity that seeks to access or identify a federal agency computer, open ports, protocols, service, or any combination for later exploit. This activity does not directly result in a compromise or denial of service.	Monthly Note: If system is classified, report within one (1) hour of discovery.
CAT 6	Investigation	*Unconfirmed* incidents that are potentially malicious or anomalous activity deemed by the reporting entity to warrant further review.	Not Applicable; this category is for each agency's use to categorize a potential incident that is currently being investigated.

Table 13-1   Incident Response Categories (*Continued*)

In order to identify the priority, which should determine how quickly issues are addressed and also how quickly other parties like executive management and legal staff are brought in, NIST suggests using the functional impact to the business, the information impact, and the recoverability. This guidance is available in NIST Special Publication 800-61 Rev. 2 (r2), *Computer Security Incident Handling Guide*. Table 13-2 shows NIST's definitions for the functional impact based on whether the business is able to remain operational and to what extent.

NIST SP 800-61r2 also provides guidance for the information impact. This has to do with whether data has been removed from the organization and what sort of data has been removed. These categories are shown in Table 13-3. These categories are not mutually exclusive, meaning you may have an incident that impacts multiple categories here. This is different from the functional impact, which considers functions across the organization.

Finally, NIST SP 800-61r2 suggests determining priority of an incident based on recoverability from that incident. This categorization, shown in Table 13-4, will help to determine resources necessary to respond to the incident. It also talks about the

Category	Definition
None	No effect to the organization's ability to provide all services to all users
Low	Minimal effect; the organization can still provide all critical services to all users but has lost efficiency
Medium	Organization has lost the ability to provide a critical service to a subset of system users
High	Organization is no longer able to provide some critical services to any users

Table 13-2   NIST Functional Impact Categories

Category	Definition
None	No information was exfiltrated, changed, deleted, or otherwise compromised
Privacy Breach	Sensitive personally identifiable information (PII) of taxpayers, employees, beneficiaries, etc. was accessed or exfiltrated
Proprietary Breach	Unclassified proprietary information, such as protected critical infrastructure information (PCII), was accessed or exfiltrated
Integrity Loss	Sensitive or proprietary information was changed or deleted

Table 13-3 NIST Information Impact Categories

Category	Definition
Regular	Time to recovery is predictable with existing resources
Supplemented	Time to recovery is predictable with additional resources
Extended	Time to recovery is unpredictable; additional resources and outside help are needed
Not Recoverable	Recovery from the incident is not possible (e.g., sensitive data exfiltrated and posted publicly); launch investigation

Table 13-4 NIST Recoverability Effort Categories

predictability of the incident. Additionally, recoverability is not about survivability of the incident. It's more about containing the incident within the boundaries of the organization. An incident that is not considered recoverable, for example, is one where data has already left the company and is available publicly.

The IRP should also contain an escalation path along with thresholds. Once a security operations analyst identifies an event that is worth noting, how quickly does that event get investigated by a more senior member of staff? Who is that senior member of staff? How quickly does that happen? All of these items should be addressed. As part of the escalation, the IRP should include clear delineations for roles and responsibilities. This ensures that essential tasks are addressed, without a duplication of effort.

As you are developing your IRP, you should consider reviewing either the cyber kill chain or the attack lifecycle. After all, your response may be different if you identify an event during the initial reconnaissance phase than it would be much further down the line when data is being exfiltrated. What are the actions you would take depending on the phase you were in? How does the phase you are in within the attack lifecycle change your priority, if it does?

Also, consider the incident response lifecycle, as defined by NIST SP 800-61r2. You can see NIST's representation in Figure 13-5. Preparation is important, as noted earlier. How are you preparing for an incident? Do you have all the tools you need? Is your staff trained and prepared? Has your plan been tested? These are all elements to consider as part of your IRP in the preparation phase. How are you detecting events and assessing them? Do you have a formal security operations center (SOC)? What are the roles of the SOC in your organization? When it comes to containment and remediation, have you

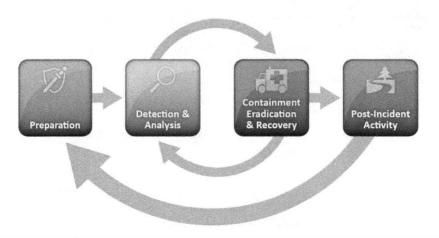

Figure 13-5   NIST incident response lifecycle

thought about what it means to contain systems? Do you pull the plug or leave systems up for further analysis? Does the attack phase factor into that decision? Do you have a process or technology in place to isolate infected systems from the rest of the network so no further infection takes place while you are conducting your investigation? You may have a virtual local area network (VLAN) you can connect a system to, which may not tip off the attacker while you further assess their activities.

NOTE   Testing an incident response plan is essential. This can be done through a variety of means, including a tabletop exercise, which presents a scenario to the team/organization and expects them to demonstrate their ability to respond given the plan in place.

Finally, formalize your post-incident process. Make sure you have forms and procedures for how to handle an after-action review. What do you want to get out of this activity? Make sure the expected outcomes are identified and documented in your IRP. Address who is involved in the review and who the results should go to.

NOTE   For further details on how to handle incidents and develop your IRP, make sure to check out the NIST publications, several of which address information security, including the incident response process, which is documented in SP 800-61r2.

Computer Security Incident Response Team

Under the definition of roles and responsibilities within the IRP should be the composition of the Computer Security Incident Response Team (CSIRT). Your organization may use a different name for this team, such as Incident Response Team, Emergency Response Team, or some other name that makes sense to your organization. No matter what you call it, though, you should take some time to consider who should be on the CSIRT. This team is responsible for coordination and communication. This is not necessarily the team who is doing the hands-on work. In fact, if your organization is large enough, it's probably better that it not be the people who are doing the hands-on work, so that the CSIRT can focus on incident response.

You should also consider whether your organization has the staff to be able to handle incident response internally or needs to partially or completely outsource it. If you are going to outsource your incident response, make sure you have that agreement in place well ahead of when you need it. This will help establish your procedures and give you adequate time (hopefully) to get familiar with the third party and vice versa. Many incident response companies offer a retainer service where you pre-pay for some number of hours in exchange for being able to call them and get immediate response when something bad happens. If you have staff in house, you may also be able to, or need to, augment that staff with an outside resource. If you are completely outsourcing or even augmenting, you may need just a minimal CSIRT internally with the coordination happening at your provider.

If you are going to handle your incidents in-house, or even if you are going to partially outsource, you need to make sure you have thought through a few considerations. First, is the CSIRT expected to be available 24/7? How are you going to handle backups in the case of vacations or other personnel outages? Being a member of the CSIRT can be very stressful, so ensuring that you are addressing morale, especially during the course of the investigation and response, can be essential. Don't assume your people can work 18-hour days for a week or more straight. They will burn out and miss something that may be essential to a successful response.

When it comes to staffing your CSIRT, the first thing you need to do is name an incident response lead (IRL). Even if your teams and people are distributed, having a single incident response lead is essential. All decisions and communications would go through this incident response lead (or whatever you choose to call the role; some organizations use terms like incident commander). You should also make sure you have identified a deputy or backup for the IRL. This is important not only in case the IRL is on vacation or otherwise unavailable when an incident happens, but also if the IRL becomes unavailable in the middle of the incident.

It's important to keep in mind that major incidents will be weeks (if not months) long and you will need to make sure you provide sufficient rest periods for your CSIRT team so they are not working all the time. Your IRL and backup IRL will need to be in constant communication so that there is no ramp-up time required if the ball needs to be handed from one to the other.

Many organizations will expect that the incident will be managed by one of the legal team. There are a couple of reasons for this. The first is the essential sensitivity of the response activities. You may be dealing with illegal activities by the attacker, in which case your organization may need to engage law enforcement. A lawyer should know when that threshold has been hit. Additionally, companies don't want these activities to be widely known or even casually discoverable after the fact. If a lawyer is involved and all communication and activity run through the legal team, that communication becomes covered under attorney-client privilege. This protects the contents of the investigation in the case of legal action initiated by outside parties later on.

Your organization may choose to have a member of management on the incident response team. This provides "top cover" for the response team, meaning someone from management can interface with other relevant management staff so they are informed as needed. Again, this sort of communication should be cleared by the legal team. Additionally, the response team would have management support for their actions. In some cases, difficult decisions need to be made when responding to an incident, and it is critical to have relevant management staff available to make those decisions.

Finally, and certainly not the least important, is CSIRT representation from the technical staff. You don't want to include everyone who is involved in the incident response activities. After all, the CSIRT should be about coordination and communication. However, the technical staff does need to be identified ahead of time. Even if they aren't part of the CSIRT, you will want to know who you have available to handle the technical response and investigation. This is where understanding the capabilities of your staff is essential, and making sure the identified staffers know they have been identified and what they are expected to do. This will be necessary in order to potentially determine additional training they may need to undergo to be prepared when an incident happens.

Managing the Response

When an incident happens, there are really two aspects to consider. The first is how management is going to handle the incident. This involves legal elements as well as communications elements. The second, which we have so far not addressed very much, is the technical aspect. This requires management, just as the other aspects we have been talking about. First, you need to make sure your organization has the right staff in place. Not every organization can afford to have a fully staffed, 24/7 SOC that can watch for alerts, perform triage, and have multiple tiers of analysts and engineers to hand tickets off to. In some cases, the "SOC" is literally a one-person shop where detection and response has to be done by the same person. Depending on the scale of the incident, this may be adequate. After all, not every incident is going to be a multisystem infection with data exfiltration. Some incidents will be as minor as a notification from a user that they received a phishing e-mail that they may have clicked but didn't go further. This requires investigation but not a large response.

The first thing you need is a case management system. A case management system can improve the efficiency of your response. This doesn't mean you need to have commercial software with all the bells and whistles, especially if you are not with a big organization. There are some open source solutions, such as Request Tracker (RT), which also has a commercial option and additional plugins that can configure it specifically for incident response. (You can find RT at https://bestpractical.com/request-tracker.) The case management software provides a place for you to centralize notes and any hand-offs from one person or team to another. These notes and details can be (and should be) saved for later reference, which may be useful if a similar incident arises later on. You can refer to how you responded the first time for hints on how to do it the next time. This archive is even more useful if someone who wasn't involved in responding to the first incident is called on to handle the similar incident the second time around. There is now essentially a cheat sheet. More importantly, these notes provide guide posts that can be used during an after-action review.

There are other aspects of managing the investigation, though, that are important. Some of these are legal in nature. When you are performing an investigation, you should consider whether your findings may need to be used as evidence in a court case, should there be a trial of the attacker. Any time there is evidence involved that could be brought before a court, there are considerations for how to collect the evidence and also for how to handle it once it is collected.

Forensic Teams

Many organizations do not have a dedicated forensic team. This may not be an issue, depending on the size and needs of the organization. It is important, though, that anyone tasked with performing forensic analysis be trained in proper evidence handling. In many cases, the person or team who is doing an organization's system and network administration may be knowledgeable enough about the devices under their control to know how to look for different details related to the investigation. An experienced system administrator may know how to identify instances of persistence on a system, for instance, which would allow the attacker to maintain access over long periods of time, across logouts and reboots. They may also be aware of how to identify compromised system binaries, and maybe even processes that have had malicious code injected into them.

Fortunately, there are a lot of tools that are available for forensic teams to make use of, even if the teams aren't as familiar with popular commercial tools like FTK, EnCase, or BlackLight. For a start, on the Windows side, the Sysinternals tools are really useful for collecting details from a running system. This includes process information, network connections, and even hidden files in alternate data streams. There are dozens of tools in the Sysinternals collection, offered for free from Microsoft. Additionally, on the Linux side, you can use entire distributions like SIFT or Kali Linux. Kali is oriented toward security testing in general but includes a fairly complete collection of forensic tools. The SIFT workstation is maintained by SANS as a Linux-based distribution designed specifically for forensic investigations.

Collecting Data

There are going to be multiple sources of data you will need to collect, especially in a broad investigation. For a start, if you are fortunate, you are using a SIEM that is aggregating all your log data. Your logs are going to be essential in performing a complete incident response, since they will provide historical data for you. It may be rare that you catch an initial encounter, which means that in most incident-response scenarios there will have been activities that happened before the event that you detected. Being able to go back days, weeks, or months is going to be essential to getting a comprehensive picture. This means you will need to be able to collect log data from either a SIEM or some log aggregation tool. Ideally, a SIEM or something similar would be used, since it may provide you better searching and data retrieval tool than just a log collection utility. A SIEM may be able to help guide you in your search. Unless you are a highly experienced investigator, that help may be essential to you.

Disk-Based Evidence

When it comes to collecting disk-based evidence, you have a choice of multiple tools. A very simple approach is to use a bootable USB stick with a small Linux distribution to get a disk image. You can use a built-in tool like **dd**, which is a disk dump utility that performs a bit-for-bit copy of one disk to either another disk or an image file. If you were to use a forensics-oriented implementation of **dd** like **dcfldd**, you could not only collect the image of the disk but also generate a cryptographic hash at the same time. In the following code you can see the use of **dcfldd** to grab a copy of a disk. The device being imaged is /dev/sdb, which is the second SCSI/SATA-based disk on the system. The primary disk would be /dev/sda. This is a very small disk, only 120Mb. The cryptographic hash has been generated using the Secure Hash Algorithm using 256 bits of hash value. This hash value can be used to compare against subsequent file hashes to ensure nothing has been changed.

```
kilroy@lolagranola:  ~ $ dcfldd if=/dev/sdb of=sdbcopy.img hash=sha256
3840 blocks (120Mb) written.
Total (sha256): c894e24ee41f3c5c2a020849cfd8572f61f28bb3f784c8156cb84a33a1600b24

3936+0 records in
3936+0 records out
```

 NOTE When you are collecting disk-based evidence, it's important to have a write blocker in place. This is either software or hardware that prevents the disk being acquired from being written to during the acquisition. This is essential for appropriate evidence collection and handling.

If you are uncomfortable with the use of the command line or Linux, you can also use Windows. For example, FTK Imager is a Windows-based program that you can use to capture disk images. One of the challenges of using software like this that needs to be installed, though, is that you are altering the disk you want to capture, unless you have the disk installed as a secondary disk. This would require removing the disk from the original system and either adding it as a secondary disk to your workstation or putting it into an external case to image from there. By using the FTK Imager, shown in Figure 13-6 selecting a source drive, you can not only create the disk image but also generate an evidence item that could later be used in FTK proper for analysis.

Once you have selected the source drive, you will be able to look at a dump of all the bytes on the drive in hexadecimal representation. We use hexadecimal representation for data like this because most of it won't translate nicely to printable ASCII characters since the vast majority of the data is not human-readable strings. A pair of hexadecimal digits is what is needed to represent a byte. This is shorter than the possible length in decimal, which would be three numeric positions. In order to actually get a dump of the disk, you need to right-click the disk, as seen in Figure 13-7, and select Export Disk Image. This will let you select the type of image you want. This may be a raw image or it may be an evidence-based format like E01 or the Advanced Forensics Format (AFF).

Figure 13-6
Selecting a disk
in FTK Imager

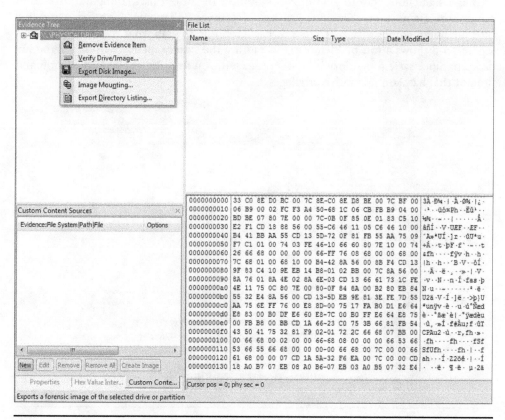

Figure 13-7 Export disk image

Memory Captures

Disk evidence is not all you will be dealing with. You may also need to acquire a memory dump. You may need to dump the whole of your system memory or just dump the memory of a process. Some of the Sysinternals tools will help you with investigating memory for a specific process, but if you need to dump the entirety of system memory, you will need additional help. This can be challenging since it's generally not a good idea for programs to be able to directly access memory without going through an application programming interface. Once direct access to memory has been enabled, there is the possibility of overwriting system memory. This would be bad for multiple reasons, but this is why there aren't a lot of programs around that do this sort of work. As an example, there used to be different ways to grab Linux system memory, but over the last few years these techniques have become unusable as the Linux kernel has prevented the techniques they use.

One tool you can use on Windows (and there are only a handful) is Memoryze. This is a utility developed by Mandiant as part of their incident response suite and is freely available from www.fireeye.com (under Resources | Free Software Downloads). It can be used as a standalone tool to grab memory dumps. Because it uses configuration files to capture the memory, you wouldn't just run Memoryze on its own. It's a command-line program and it comes with batch files that will set it up to grab what you are looking for. Figure 13-8 shows a run of Memoryze to capture the system memory from a Windows desktop. Since system memory is highly protected, you need to run it from a command prompt that has Administrative privileges.

Figure 13-8   Collecting a memory dump using Memoryze

Using Central Data Collection

So far, we've been talking about performing the data collection on individual machines. In a large organization this is simply impractical. You can use centralized methods to collect data, though. There are commercial products that will perform this work, such as Carbon Black, but there is also an open source product that can be used. Google Rapid Response (GRR) uses a server/agent model, just like other similar commercial products. You install the agent on the system you want to collect data from and you initiate the collection from the server. Using this approach, you can hunt for infections using GRR. Figure 13-9 shows one of the hunt requests. This is a generic hunt that can be used to query the endpoints. There are multiple other queries that can be generated from the GRR console to help identify potential infected systems on your network.

A tool like GRR puts the control into a centralized location, but it does require that agents be installed on all endpoints that will need to be queried. While GRR is supported by Google, it is much less mature than other tools that are available for the same purpose. This is a good option, though, if you don't have the resources for a commercial tool, because you can use GRR to identify potential issues within the devices in your environment.

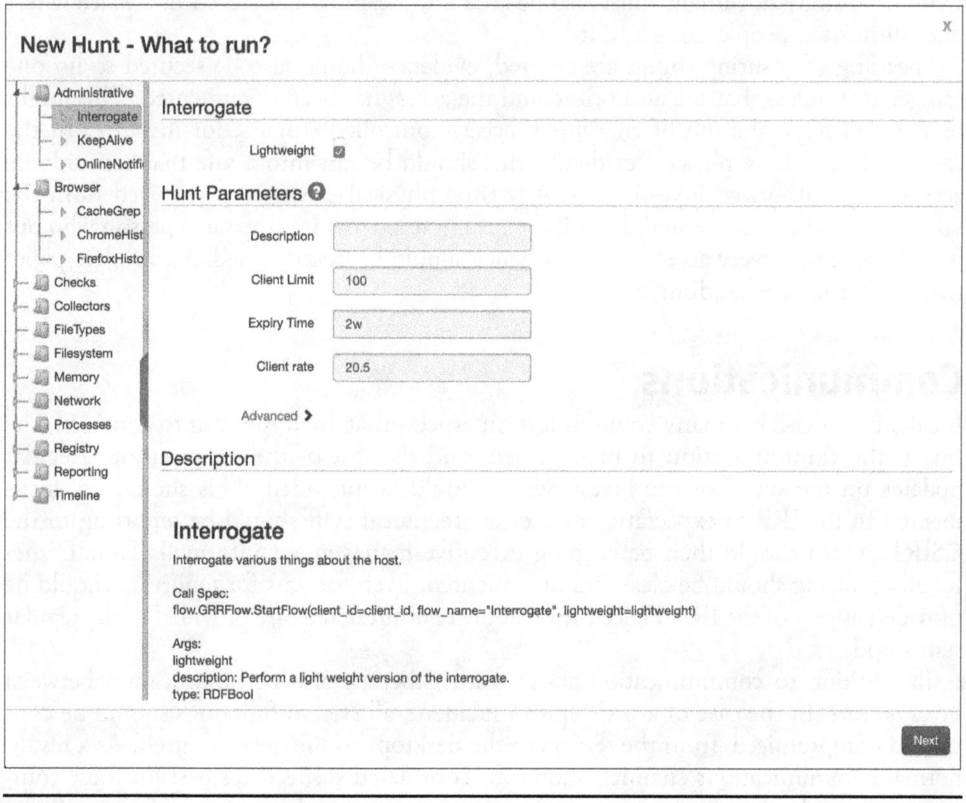

Figure 13-9 Hunting with GRR

Evidence Handling

As noted earlier, evidence handling is an important consideration. For a start, you need to make sure you are collecting all evidence in a way that can be demonstrated not to have been tampered with. You can do this using cryptographic hashes. Previously, the standard cryptographic hash was Message Digest 5 (MD5). While this is still useful as a hashing algorithm to generate unique values identifying data, it's better practice to use SHA-1 or, even better, SHA-256. SHA-1, SHA-256, and SHA-512 all have a larger space to generate these values in. SHA-1 generates a 160-bit value, while SHA-256 generates a 256-bit value, and so on. These larger values reduce the possibility of collisions, which are cases where two different pieces of data generate the same hash value. If you can have two different data sources that result in the same hash value, this fact could create doubt as to the validity of the original data presented.

Beyond ensuring that no data has been tampered with using cryptographic hashes, it's important to document when evidence has been passed from one entity to another. This is called a *chain of custody*, and any time a piece of evidence such as a disk image is transferred from one person or organization to another person or organization, that transfer must be documented in the chain of custody, including a description of the evidence, the means of transfer, the names of the parties, and the date and time of the transfer. The chain of custody document must also be secured, meaning it is stored in a place where only authorized people can get to it.

Speaking of ensuring things are secured, evidence should also be secured so no one can get at it unless they are authorized and the access has been documented. This might be done through the use of encrypted, access-controlled storage, for instance. In the case where you have physical evidence, this should be put into a safe that can only be accessed by authorized investigators. Any time physical evidence is removed from the safe, it should be documented. Even if the person removing it is the same person who put it in the safe last, every access to the evidence should be documented. A complete paper trail of all evidence handling is essential.

Communications

Incident response has many communication aspects that are important to consider. The first is the communication to management and the rest of the organization. Regular updates on the status of the investigation should be provided. This should be documented in the IRP so expectations are clear. Technical staff should be reporting to the CSIRT, which should then be keeping executive management informed. Time frames for all reporting should be clear and documented. Even formats for reporting should be provided as part of the IRP. This ensures all the relevant details are provided in the regular status updates.

In addition to communication about status, there is also communication between investigators. In the case of a wide-spread incident, all system functions should be considered compromised, from the servers to the desktops to the network itself. As a result, normal communications channels should be considered suspect. It's best for these communications channels to be encrypted to begin with, but in the case of a significant investigation, plans for out-of-band communications should be developed. This should include phone communications, for instance. The organization should plan to have teleconferencing solutions in place. However, these solutions should not make use of the enterprise network. If the phone system is Voice over IP (VoIP), the company phones should also not be used since that traffic could be intercepted.

When it comes to data exfiltration and information compromise, there are likely reporting requirements. If the corporate communications staff does not understand how to handle sensitive communications like breach notifications, a third-party public relations firm should be used. As with the case of an incident response company, this is the sort of relationship that pays to have established ahead of time.

Legal Implications

There are multiple laws that require notification in the case of data loss or theft. Most states have their own notification laws. Other laws that impact companies are Europe's General Data Protection Regulation (GDPR) and the California Consumer Privacy Act (CCPA). Each of these laws has stringent requirements for protecting consumers' data. If an organization's consumer data gets stolen or compromised, each law has requirements for notifying the consumers. This is just one reason why having legal staff involved in incident response is important. The legal team should have an understanding of these laws' requirements. They can provide guidance as to how the response should proceed with the relevant laws in mind. They can also provide guidance to executive management.

In some cases, consumers or other parties may initiate litigation against a company or organization, claiming damages resulting from an incident. Therefore, having the lawyers involved early on can be beneficial. For a start, with the lawyers involved, communications can go through them and remain confidential. This means the actions of the incident response team, as related to what goes through the legal team, remain confidential and potentially exempt from any discovery that may come as part of a lawsuit against the organization.

Chapter Review

Incident response is a complicated business for many reasons. One reason is that attacks are complicated. Attackers are often interested in gaining access to systems and retaining access over a long period of time. For this reason, they are referred to as advanced persistent threats (APTs).

There are a couple of different ways to map attacks. The first is the cyber kill chain, developed by Lockheed Martin with the military kill chain in mind. The stages of the cyber kill chain are reconnaissance, weaponization, delivery, exploitation, installation, command & control, and actions on objectives. The second is the attack lifecycle. This is a way of mapping attacks that was created by Mandiant as a result of many years of investigating APT attacks. The stages of the attack lifecycle are initial reconnaissance, initial compromise, establish foothold, escalate privileges, internal recon, move laterally, maintain presence, and complete mission. The attack lifecycle takes into account the common practice of these attackers of staying in the environment, compromising additional systems, and obtaining additional credentials.

Preparation is important for incident response. Intelligence is important for preparing for incident response. It can be used to inform the protection against and detection of events, which may become incidents. Organizations can buy threat intelligence but they can also use Information Sharing and Analysis Centers (ISACs), which are specific to industries, including telecommunications, utilities, and automotive businesses. This information should also be used to inform the incident response policy and plan. The policy is a set of high-level expectations of the organization when it comes to incident response. The plan is more detailed and should be comprehensive in its guidance to the organization so anyone coming on board as a new hire should be able to look at the plan and understand how incident response is handled within the organization.

Part of the plan covers how the Computer Security Incident Response Team (CSIRT) is staffed. The plan should also include how the forensic team should be staffed and operated. Organizations may not be able to fully staff a complete forensic team, which may mean they need to make do with what staff they already have. This may be systems and network administrators. This staff should be trained in appropriate evidence handling processes, including demonstrating that evidence has not been tampered with through the use of something like a cryptographic hash. MD5, SHA-1, SHA-256, and SHA-512 might be used for cryptographic hashes to demonstrate that evidence has not been tampered with. Additionally, chain of custody documentation is essential to demonstrate who has had access to evidence and what they have done with it. Incident response plans should be tested regularly to ensure the plan is up to date and all staff understand how the plan operates.

Privacy laws like those in California and Europe have created requirements for legal teams to be involved in incident response to ensure the requirements of these laws are followed. Additionally, legal teams can help ensure communication is confidential and protected by attorney-client privilege. These privacy laws also typically require notification of anyone who may be impacted by a data breach. This can require the use of either a communications staff or an external public relations firm who has experience with these sorts of communications with consumers.

Questions

1. If you need to use a tool to both gather disk-based evidence and generate a cryptographic hash, what would you be most likely to use?

    A. dcfldd

    B. dd

    C. Memoryze

    D. Fmem

2. What is the document that demonstrates who has had access to evidence and when?

    A. Evidence form

    B. Data collection document

    C. Chain of custody

    D. Legal signoff

3. What organization could you turn to for threat intelligence if you didn't want to pay for a commercial service?

    A. FIRST

    B. ISACA

    C. NECCDC

    D. ISAC

4. Why would you use a centralized data capture program?

    A. To avoid having to physically touch every system

    B. To save space

    C. Better acceptance of resulting evidence

    D. Centralized hashes all data

5. How is an incident different from an event?

    A. An incident is any observable change, whereas an event has the potential to cause damage.

    B. Incidents have a higher probability of causing damage.

    C. Events might be false positives.

    D. An event is an observable change, whereas an incident has the potential to cause damage.

6. What is the purpose of an incident response policy?

    A. To provide details for incident responders to follow

    B. To identify risks to the environment

    C. To provide high-level guidance from the business

    D. To suppress fires

7. Why would you use a cryptographic hash?

    A. To uniquely identify evidence

    B. To classify incidents

    C. To differentiate memory from disk captures

    D. To encrypt evidence

8. What set of tools provided by Microsoft could you make use of to acquire evidence from systems?

   A. Winternals

   B. Forensic Analyzer

   C. Sysinternals

   D. GRR

9. What is the possible problem with using MD5 as a cryptographic hash?

   A. Encryption algorithm is known

   B. Collisions

   C. Outlawed

   D. Doesn't work on all digital evidence

10. What is the privacy law in Europe known as?

    A. CCPA

    B. EUPA

    C. GDPR

    D. DPRE

Answers

1. **A.** Only dcfldd could get a disk image and also generate a cryptographic hash. dd is used to acquire a disk image, but it doesn't have the ability to generate a cryptographic hash. You would need to use an additional tool for that. Memoryze is used to acquire memory captures. Fmem was once used for memory captures on Linux.

2. **C.** A chain of custody document is used to document every time a piece of evidence has been handled, who it has been handled by, and the purpose of handling the evidence. None of the other answers is a real thing, at least not in this context.

3. **D.** An Information Sharing and Analysis Center (ISAC) can be used for information sharing. These are industry-specific groups. ISACA is another organization that provides information security certifications. NECCDC is a cyber-defense competition in New England. FIRST has a number of meanings, including a robotics organization for students.

4. **A.** Central data collection programs make it easier to collect data since you don't have to physically touch every system. They rely on agent installs on the endpoints to collect the data remotely. They don't save space, and the resulting evidence is no more acceptable than that collected manually from endpoints. Also, you can perform cryptographic hashes on any digital evidence collected.

5. **D.** An event is any observable change to an environment that is different from what is expected. An incident, though, is an event that has the potential to cause damage.

6. **C.** A policy is a high-level statement of intentions from the business owners to clearly identify expectations. A plan would provide more details. A risk assessment program would identify risks. It is not used to suppress fires.

7. **A.** A cryptographic hash generates a long value that is used to uniquely identify data. It is not used to classify incidents. A hash, while cryptographic, is not used to encrypt anything. It also isn't used to differentiate memory captures from disk captures.

8. **C.** Microsoft offers Windows Sysinternals as a collection of tools that are highly useful for forensic professionals to collect information about processes, network connections, and multiple other system details. Previously, the collection of tools was called Winternals, but the group developing them was not part of Microsoft at that time. GRR is Google Rapid Response, and Forensic Analyzer isn't a Microsoft product.

9. **B.** *Collision* is the term for when a cryptographic hashing algorithm generates the same value for two different data sources. The algorithm for MD5 is known, but MD5 doesn't do any encryption. It has not been outlawed, and it will work on all digital evidence.

10. **C.** GDPR is the General Data Protection Regulation, the European law that addresses data breaches and other privacy violations. CCPA is California's privacy law. The other two don't exist, as least not as privacy laws.

Wireless Technologies

In this chapter, you will learn:
- The origins and evolution of 802.11
- The Bluetooth protocol
- Near field communication
- Radio frequency identification (RFID)
- Ways of breaking into those technologies

In the handful of years since the first edition of this book, the world of wireless has become even more significant than it was before. While the technologies have not changed in that time, the adoption of them definitely has. I mentioned in the first edition that I was able to connect a Bluetooth speaker (a Jambox at the time) to my phone, which could be in the house while I was out back on the deck. I could also make and take calls from that speaker. By comparison with the wired world from just over a decade ago, that was incredibly wireless. Now, of course, we have devices that we can control by voice that access the Internet over wireless connections. That device then controls other devices in the house, like thermostats or lights, over another type of wireless technology. Everything is becoming wireless. Even comparing the differences in earbud technology is telling. Not too long ago, wireless earbuds were just becoming a thing, except that there was a wire connecting the two. Today, both earbuds can be completely wireless. No more wire connecting the two sides.

Having finished with the sales-pitch, new-world-order portion of this chapter, we can now move on to the specific technologies. First, we have 802.11, now so common as a networking technology that some computers don't even have wired connections built into them. They assume that wireless will be available. It provides a way of letting your portable devices be on the network in a way that behaves exactly like a wired connection, and it may be even faster than your wired connection if you are using the latest and greatest Wi-Fi gear. Wi-Fi, by the way, is another way of talking about 802.11, but more on that later on.

Bluetooth is a great way of connecting to peripherals, no matter what they are—keyboards, mice, speaker systems, televisions, and other items. Many are now capable of connecting by Bluetooth if you have the right peripheral. Obviously, you have to have a peripheral that is Bluetooth-capable and your system must be compatible with Bluetooth as well. With Bluetooth, you eliminate wires, allowing you to be more untethered.

479

Bluetooth also allows devices to communicate with one another to perform actions like file sharing, assuming that the devices have implemented the right Bluetooth profile.

Near field communication also lets devices communicate with one another, sharing information between mobile phones or even carrying credentials on a mobile device that would allow you to use a single device for authorization and even payment. This technology makes configuring so many devices much easier since you don't need any complex input/output on the device when you have a smartphone with an app that understands how to configure the device.

Finally, since we are talking about radio technology in this chapter, we should address radio frequency identification (RFID). This is another area where technology has continued to be improved. Proximity badges have long used RFID to provide information from the badge to a reader. Today, again something that has been in use for a while, though getting smaller along the way, you can get a small strip to put on the inside of the windshield of your car. This strip takes care of all tolls for you, so you don't have to stop and exchange any money. It's more convenient and makes getting through tolls much faster.

Radio Transmission

The one thing all of these technologies have in common is the use of radio transmission. You may have something particular in mind when you hear the word *radio*. It refers to the idea of electromagnetic waves and their transmission. Whether you realize it or not, electromagnetic waves are all around us, as well as their receptors. Your eyes are capable of receiving electromagnetic waves, just as your ears are. Electromagnetic waves come in a wide variety of types, based on the frequency and wavelength. Figure 14-1 shows a line graph with the placement of different types of electromagnetic waves and what they are used for. Notice that the visible light spectrum is in the middle of this graph. You can also see the placement of AM, FM, and microwave frequencies within the spectrum.

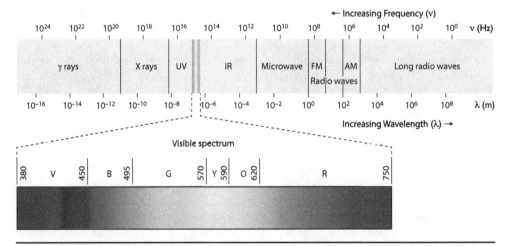

Figure 14-1 Electromagnetic frequencies

Figure 14-2
A sine wave

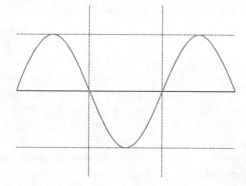

NOTE The word *radio* comes from the Latin word radius, meaning spokes of a wheel or a ray or beam of light.

Electromagnetic energy moves in waves, meaning that if you were to graph the value of the strength of the energy over time, the graph would have a smooth look, like a wave. It would be a graph of the sine function. The sine function is the ratio of the length of the side opposite to a particular angle and the length of the hypotenuse. The energy consists of oscillating electric and magnetic fields that end up creating that wave. Waves have both amplitude and frequency. The amplitude is the measure of the strength of the wave and, visualizing it on a graph, is typically on the y axis, meaning it's the height. The frequency is the measure of how quickly it comes around again. Since we're talking about waves, picture yourself standing on the shore of a lake or, better yet, an ocean. Now, think about the waves. It will help explain this idea and also help reduce your stress. One wave comes in and recedes, and then another wave comes in and recedes. The time it takes for one wave to come in and retreat is the frequency, because the faster it approaches and recedes, the quicker the next wave can come in. Figure 14-2 shows the graph of a sine wave. Look at the height of the peaks. That's the amplitude. The distance between the peaks is the wavelength. The frequency is the number of waves that pass a point in a given amount of time.

Frequency and Spectrum

The frequency is important because in order to send information using these electromagnetic waves, you need a frequency to send the information along. Different frequencies are used for different purposes, as shown in Figure 14-1. The reason for bringing this up is that frequencies aren't just used willy-nilly. There are blocks of frequencies that are assigned for specific purposes. You may have heard of spectrum auctions, which happen from time to time. The reason for this is that there is essentially a finite space to the full spectrum. We can't keep using chunks of it forever with no worry of the resource running out. Because of that and because different applications need different blocks of the spectrum, various governments around the world auction off chunks of the spectrum to different companies for various applications. Having different applications using the same portion of the spectrum can cause collisions.

As more and more mobile devices come online, we have a greater need for larger blocks of frequencies, so more people can get online at the same time. Every time someone places a phone call, a small chunk of the available space is used up. Just like with a radio station, you can't have two people occupying the same frequency at the same time. It's like having a large sheet of paper that has to be shared among many people. You have to tear off strips for everyone, and once a strip has been torn off and handed to someone, it's gone and can't be used for someone else as long as someone is using that strip. When they are done, they may return the strip, but until the strip is returned, it's not available to anyone else. The same thing is true of frequency allocations. Each person who wants to use the piece of paper you have will get a strip from it, corresponding with an appropriate-sized strip of frequency space, which we call bandwidth. You only get so many strips and then you're out. This is one reason why spectrum allocation is so important. The more spectrum you can get, the more customers you can support when it comes to a service like cell phones. In the case of something like Wi-Fi, the wider the frequency range you have, the more bandwidth you can use for the systems connected.

 TIP In order to keep these two related ideas separate, think of the spectrum as a range of frequencies, and a frequency as an individual sliver within the spectrum.

Modulation and Carrier Waves

If you think about a traditional radio with FM and AM, there is a particular frequency that you tune into, a channel. What you are really tuning into is a carrier signal. The carrier signal is a particular frequency that is changed or modulated based on the information the carrier is expected to be transmitting. Let's use FM as an example. Because FM is Frequency Modulation, we use a specific carrier frequency, say, 94.9 MHz. The MHz part is megahertz, meaning that the wave is cycling a million times per second. So we have a wave that's cycling 94,900,000 times per second. On top of that, we want to carry music and voice. The range of frequencies typically spans 20 to 20,000 Hertz (Hz), since that's generally the range of human hearing. However, a wide variety of hearing ranges exists from one person to another.

In order to carry the sound signal, which uses a range of frequencies considerably lower than the carrier signal, we modulate the carrier based on the input. The instantaneous frequency of the input is combined with the carrier and the result is transmitted. On the receiving end, since the carrier wave is known, the difference between the carrier frequency and the actual frequency is the signal that was used as the input. This signal can then be sent through a set of speakers that convert the signal to audio waves, which can be heard by human ears. The thing is, though, the carrier frequency needs to have space on either side for the carrier to be modulated, otherwise you run into issues of crosstalk between the two signals. You'll hear this in cases where you are crossing out of the range of one radio station and into that of another. The carrier frequency is really in the center of the range on either side. Instead of a wave that has a steady frequency, the frequency is constantly changing.

Antennas and Transmissions

In order to send the signal out, you need an antenna. The antenna is responsible for taking an electrical signal and converting it to electromagnetic waves and vice versa. Any device that communicates using electromagnetic radio waves requires an antenna. Antennas are made of conducting materials that convert the waves into electrical signals—which is caused by the waves exciting the electrons in the antenna—resulting in current flowing through that antenna. If you are using your antenna to transmit instead of receive, you send a current out the antenna, and the excited electrons generate both a magnetic field and an electric field. The two together become the wave transmitted from the antenna. Because the antenna is expected to respond to the wave in order to excite the antenna's electrons so they move, the best way to achieve that is to have the antenna resonate with the frequency the antenna is expected to receive. If the antenna resonates with the receiving frequency, the antenna will oscillate faster, meaning the electrons will respond better (move faster), giving you more gain on the antenna. This requires the antenna to be matched to a particular frequency, which isn't always possible, considering that many antennas are expected to work with a range of frequencies. A common antenna is a dipole antenna, whose length is based on it being half the length of the resonant wavelength. Figure 14-3 shows an example of a dipole antenna.

Figure 14-3
A dipole antenna

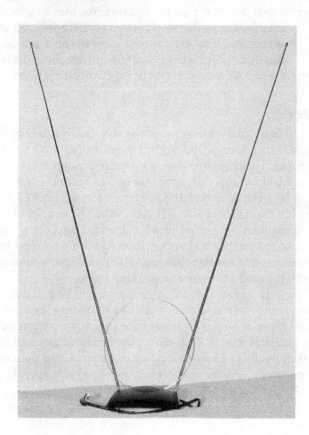

NOTE The first antennas were built by German physicist Heinrich Hertz, for whom the measure of cycles per second is named.

Finding ways to increase the signal at the receiving antenna is always an issue. You may have seen cases where an old-school antenna known as "rabbit ears" is covered in aluminum foil, presumably to increase the surface area of the antenna and get a better signal. A satellite dish, for instance, has a parabolic shape, with the receiving part of the antenna suspended over the parabola. The reason for this is to increase the signal strength at the antenna. Recall from your geometry class in high school that a parabola has a focal point. Any ray that hits the parabola, coming straight in, will be reflected up to the receiving component. Instead of just the waves that reach the receiver itself, all of the waves that hit the parabola are reflected up, meaning more waves arrive at the receiving antenna. There are a number of ways to increase the strength of the signal arriving at the receiver, and it generally depends on the application or antenna type as much as the method of amplification used.

NOTE A Pringles can be used to amplify a Wi-Fi signal so as to catch Wi-Fi access points at a greater distance. You may also recall the iPhone 4 having issues with its antenna, where you could effectively short it out if you held it wrong, meaning you were changing the resonant frequency of the antenna and thus reducing the signal strength reaching the receiver. In both cases, the signal's reception was being changed, for good or bad, by the user.

Receiver

Once you have a signal coming in on the antenna, it needs to be translated into something useful. First, though, the receiver needs to pay attention only to the specific frequency desired. Typically, a receiver for any application must be able to handle multiple frequencies within a range, the same way an FM radio receiver must be able to tune into frequencies between 87.7 and 108.0 MHz—a range of 20.3 MHz. Radio stations are located within that range at 200-KHz intervals. The receiver uses filters to get only those frequencies required for a particular application. Any signal that doesn't fall into that specific set of frequencies is dropped. The signal is amplified by the receiver and then demodulated so as to convert the electronic signal into a form used by the application, whether this is sound waves or a networking signal.

As for the type of radio communication we will be primarily discussing, the systems transmit and receive. In addition to needing to worry about having a receiver, you must have a transmitter as well. Fortunately, the process of transmission is much the same as reception, except in reverse. The transmitter produces a current of a particular frequency, which is then modulated based on the source input. Once the combined signal is created, it is sent out to the antenna, which may be tuned to a specific transmission frequency.

This ability to both transmit and receive brings up the concept of duplex, which is a way of indicating whether you can listen and speak simultaneously, or if you have to do one at a time. If you have to do one at a time, you are considered half-duplex, while if you can both listen and speak at the same time, you would be considered full-duplex. Full-duplex has obvious benefits since you gain speed by being able to send and receive at the same time.

Frequency Hopping

True story. An actress came up with a way to keep wireless transmissions from being intercepted. In the 1940s. And it's still in use today. Okay, it's not entirely true but it is mostly true. Her name was Hedy Lamarr and in 1942 she was granted a patent for a frequency hopping system using a piano roll to allow for sending secret communications. She was one of the first patent holders on a system for changing frequencies, though she was not the earliest. The reason for needing to change frequencies in a system of transmission and reception is that if someone were to listen to your transmissions for an extended period of time, even if they were encrypted, the listener would be able to amass a large enough amount of cipher text that they might be able to break the encryption code used. This was a serious concern during World War II, when Ms. Lamarr developed her invention along with George Antheil.

This is not as simple as just hopping around a frequency spectrum in some random fashion, or at least in an uncoordinated random manner. The two participants in a communication stream use a predetermined sequence of frequencies to transmit on. As the communication proceeds, the two participants keep shifting the frequencies they are transmitting and receiving on. This is done in order to fool anyone listening, because just as they catch a portion of the communication, it changes frequencies, and if the listener doesn't know which frequency to switch over to, they will not be able to continue to listen. As mentioned earlier, this scheme was developed decades ago and is still in use today by protocols such as Bluetooth and 802.11.

802.11

802.11 is actually a set of physical layer protocols managed by the Institute of Electrical and Electronics Engineers (IEEE). The purpose of 802.11 is to provide networking using electromagnetic waves as a transmission medium. While the origins of 802.11 were in a product developed by NCR Corporation/AT&T called WaveLAN, which was designed for cashier systems, the first 802.11 specification was released in 1997. That first specification of 802.11 only transmitted at 1 to 2 megabits per second (Mbps) and is now obsolete. Over the years, the standard has evolved to dramatically increase the transmission rates up to 866.7 Mbps for the currently released standard, though the draft standards in progress now increase transmission rates up to 7 gigabits per second (Gbps). This substantial increase gives mobile devices greater performance and makes them better at high-speed, interactive gaming and video-based communications, as well as other high-bandwidth applications.

NOTE   Wireless networking became possible after the Federal Communications Commission (FCC) released the Industry, Scientific, and Medical (ISM) band for use in 1985.

802.11 specifies the use of two separate frequency spectrums, depending on the particular version of the standard you are using. The first is in the 2.4-GHz frequency range and includes 13 channels in that space, with each channel using 22 MHz. Figure 14-4 shows the 2.4-GHz frequency range with the 13 channels. Notice the center frequency, on top of each channel, for each of the channels specified. Different countries may use different channels, depending on the spectrum allocation for that country. These frequency ranges are what you would find in use for each of the channels. 802.11 also specifies the use of frequencies in the 5-GHz range, going back as far as the 802.11a standard in 1999. The latest draft of the standard brings in a new set of frequency ranges in the 6-GHz space. Table 14-1 shows some of the different standards that fall under 802.11, including their frequency ranges and bandwidth.

 NOTE   You will often hear wireless networking referred to as Wi-Fi (short for Wireless Fidelity). Wi-Fi is any wireless local area networking product that uses the 802.11 standard. An industry alliance called the Wi-Fi Alliance is responsible for certifying products as Wi-Fi Certified. Only products that submit to this process can be certified, and simply complying with the 802.11 standards doesn't automatically gain you a Wi-Fi Certification.

Whereas wired networks provide access control physically and also provide segmentation physically and logically, wireless networks aren't as able to provide physical restrictions as to who gains access to the network. Instead, wireless networks using the 802.11 protocols have to employ other mechanisms. A wireless network is organized around a service set identifier (SSID). Anyone connected to the same SSID is on the same layer 2 network. The SSID is how a client would connect to a particular network. SSIDs are typically broadcast in beacon frames to announce their availability. This broadcast is not required, but if the wireless network doesn't identify itself in this way, anyone wanting to connect has to know the specific SSID to enter to connect to that network. Hiding the

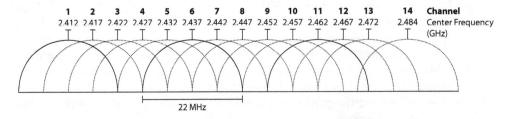

Figure 14-4   802.11 channels

802.11 Protocol	Release	Freq. (GHz)	Bandwidth (MHz)	Data Rate Per Stream (Mbps)	Approximate indoor Range (m)	(ft)	Approximate Outdoor Range (m)	(ft)
—	Jun 1997	2.4	20	1, 2	20	66	100	330
a	Sep 1999	5 3.7	20	6, 9, 12, 18, 24, 36, 48, 54	35 —	115 —	120 5000	390 16,000
b	Sep 1999	2.4	20	1, 2, 5.5, 11	35	115	140	460
g	Jun 2003	2.4	20	6, 9, 12, 18, 24, 36, 48, 54	38	125	140	460
n	Oct 2009	2.4/5	20	7.2, 14.4, 21.7, 28.9, 43.3, 57.8, 65, 72.2	70	230	250	820
			40	15, 30, 45, 60, 90, 120, 135, 150	70	230	250	820
ac	Dec 2013	5	20 40 80 160	up to 87.6 up to 200 up to 433.3 up to 866.7				
ad	Dec 2012	2.4/5/60		up to 7000				
af	Feb 2014	0.054–0.79	6–8	Up to 568.9				
aj	Apr 2018	45/60	540/1080	Up to 15,000				
ax	~Dec 2019	2.4/5/6	20/40/80/160	Up to 10,530				

Table 14-1   802.11 Standards

SSID in this way is sometimes called network cloaking and can protect against a casual wireless snooper. It should not be used as a primary security measure. Figure 14-5 shows a list of SSIDs being announced. These were captured using the program Kismet running on a Linux system.

TIP   Hiding your SSID on a wireless network can be one effective method of protecting that network, as long as it is in conjunction with other methods like strong authentication and encryption.

A beacon frame is one of the management frames you'll see used in the 802.11 protocols. These management frames are unique to wireless networks and include a lot of information. A beacon frame, for instance, includes the typical layer 2 header with MAC addresses, but also includes a timestamp, a beacon interval, and the type of network being used. In the case of a wireless network, you may be using an ad hoc mode where clients organize themselves without any central authority for the network. Ad hoc mode is like a peer-to-peer network with no central network device directing traffic to all of the connected clients. Infrastructure mode has a wireless access point (WAP) that all of the clients connect to. A WAP acts like a network switch, sending out messages to specific connected clients in addition to receiving all traffic from those clients. A beacon frame would also include the SSID for the particular network, as well as the transmission rates supported and the frequency-hopping parameter set to indicate how the clients

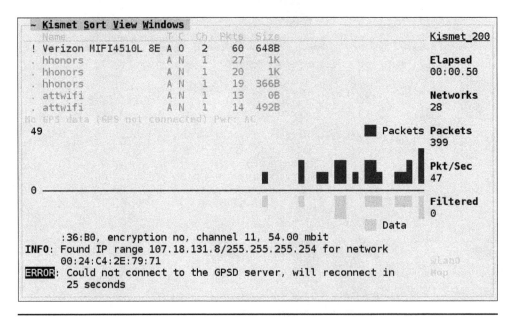

Figure 14-5 Kismet showing a list of the SSIDs available

should hop between frequencies in order to keep up with sending and receiving on the right frequency. Figure 14-6 displays a Wireshark packet capture of a beacon frame, showing some of the fields described earlier.

In addition to beacon frames, other management frames include authentication frames where a wireless network interface card (WNIC) sends its identity to the access point in order to be authenticated to the network. This authentication could consist of a request and a response in the case of open authentication or, in the case of shared key authentication, it would consist of several packets including a request, a challenge, and a response. There are also deauthentication frames, association requests, and response frames, as well as reassociation requests and response frames.

A wireless network has a service set, which is the set of all devices communicating in a particular wireless local area network (WLAN). You may have a local, independent,

```
▷ Frame 37: 143 bytes on wire (1144 bits), 143 bytes captured (1144 bits) on interface 0
▷ Radiotap Header v0, Length 26
▷ IEEE 802.11 Probe Request, Flags: ........C
▽ IEEE 802.11 wireless LAN management frame
  ▽ Tagged parameters (89 bytes)
    ▷ Tag: SSID parameter set: Broadcast
    ▷ Tag: Supported Rates 1, 2, 5.5, 11, [Mbit/sec]
    ▷ Tag: Extended Supported Rates 6, 9, 12, 18, 24, 36, 48, 54, [Mbit/sec]
    ▷ Tag: HT Capabilities (802.11n D1.10)
    ▷ Tag: Vendor Specific: Broadcom
    ▷ Tag: Vendor Specific: Epigram: HT Capabilities (802.11n D1.10)
```

Figure 14-6 A beacon frame capture

extended, or mesh set. A base service set (BSS) is the access point and all stations associated with it. The access point is the master that is in control of all the stations within the BSS. The access point has a base service set identifier (BSSID), which is the MAC address of the access point, if the access point is operating in infrastructure mode. The SSID mentioned earlier is attached to the BSS, which really provides a name for the set of stations in the BSS. When you have two BSSs using the same SSID, you have an extended service set (ESS). A number of access points may be logically linked, allowing for stations to roam within the area of the WLAN, moving from one access point to another while staying within the same SSID. This means that stations don't have to leave one SSID and authenticate against another while the station moves around a building. This is particularly useful because mobile devices like smartphones and tablets that have Wi-Fi capabilities may move around a lot, attaching to one access point after another.

Encryption

The original specification of 802.11 included Wired Equivalent Privacy (WEP) as a way to ensure privacy on what is a broadcast medium. When you transmit over the air, anyone with a receiver tuned to the right frequency can hear what you are transmitting. Because of this, there were concerns about needing to provide clients with the ability to protect their transmissions. WEP specified the use of the stream cipher RC4 for encryption of the transmitted data, providing confidentiality. Additionally, a cyclic redundancy check (CRC) checksum provided integrity, ensuring that a frame that had been altered could be detected as being altered.

The initial specification used a 40-bit key along with a 24-bit initialization vector (IV), which should be a random string of binary digits, to create a 64-bit encryption key. In practice, this was usually implemented as a string of 10 hexadecimal digits since each hexadecimal digit takes 4 bits to represent. Ten of those 4-bit digits provided the 40 bits needed. There is also 128-bit WEP, using 104 bits from a user-supplied value, with the additional 24 bits coming from the IV (104 bits is 26 hexadecimal digits).

WEP can use either open authentication, where no authentication credentials are used, or shared key authentication, where the shared key is used to provide authentication. In the case of open authentication, you can still encrypt the data, but the key has to be known ahead of time by the station wanting to connect to the network. In the case of shared key authentication, the shared key that is used to create the encryption key is also used to provide authentication. A shared key authentication involves a client sending an authentication request while the access point responds with a challenge to the request. This challenge is in clear text and is vulnerable to being captured. The client encrypts the challenge using the shared key and sends back a response. Based on whether the response is valid, the access point will either allow access or not.

 NOTE Open authentication may actually be more secure than shared key since the challenge sent by the access point is in clear text. Open authentication requires that the keys be known ahead of time and doesn't require any data to be sent in the clear in order to perform the authentication.

WEP is vulnerable to attack because of a weakness in the initialization vector used. In 2003, the 802.11i standard became available in draft form and it's commonly known as Wi-Fi Protected Access (WPA). WPA makes use of the Temporal Key Integrity Protocol (TKIP) as a way of fixing the problems with the WEP keys while allowing the existing hardware to be used with minor firmware updates instead of completely changing out the hardware. TKIP uses key mixing to create a key by mixing the secret key with the IV. With WEP, the encryption key was created by simply concatenating the IV with the shared key. TKIP provides a stronger, less predictable key that is fed into the RC4 initialization.

The 802.11i standard was released in final form in 2004 and today is commonly known as WPA2. WPA2 introduced stronger encryption than WPA had allowed, since WPA was concerned with allowing existing hardware designed with WEP in mind to provide better security without needing a wholesale hardware replacement. WPA2 allows the use of the Advanced Encryption Standard (AES) for encryption, replacing the RC4 cipher previously used. The encryption mechanism making use of AES is called Counter Cipher Mode with Block Chaining Message Authentication Code Protocol (CCMP). Where WEP used a CRC to provide an integrity check, WPA introduced a stronger integrity check with an algorithm called Michael, which is a message integrity check. Michael was, again, a compromise to allow older hardware to provide stronger integrity checking without the computational requirements that a message authentication code would have. WPA2 introduced a stronger algorithm to perform the integrity checking.

 EXAM TIP 802.11i, also known as WPA, provides integrity, encryption, and replay protection to wireless network traffic. A replay attack is where packets are captured and later played back out onto the network.

WPA uses a four-way handshake in order to authenticate the station to the access point. The handshake works by enabling both endpoints to be able to derive the same key. The first phase is where the access point sends a random value, called a nonce, to the station along with a Key Replay Counter (KRC). When the station receives the nonce, it can create the Pairwise Transient Key (PTK). The station sends its own nonce back to the access point along with a message integrity code. It also sends the KRC. This allows the access point to match the right messages. Once the access point has validated all the information it has received from the station, it sends the group key. This is used for messages that are going to every station on the network. The station validates the integrity of the message it received from the access point and, if it all checks out, the station sends a confirmation to the access point.

Both WPA and WPA2 provide two different modes of authenticating stations to the network. The first, called WPA-Personal (or WPA2-Personal), makes use of a pre-shared key (PSK). This PSK could be a string of 64 hexadecimal digits, or a string of between 8 and 63 ASCII characters. This mode is called Personal because it's what you would commonly use on an access point at home, where you would likely lack the infrastructure required for WPA-Enterprise or WPA2-Enterprise, which make use of a RADIUS server to allow enterprises to authenticate users against a user database. A PSK can be easy to lay

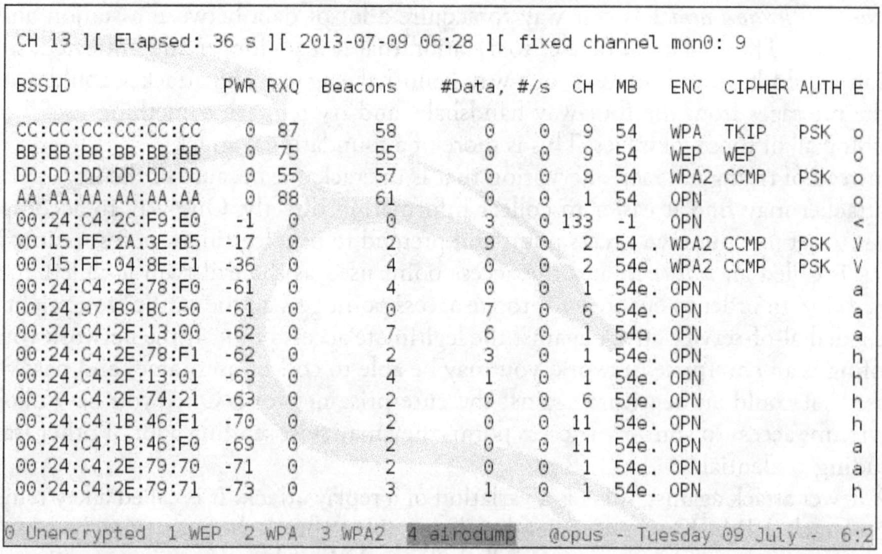

```
CH 13 ][ Elapsed: 36 s ][ 2013-07-09 06:28 ][ fixed channel mon0: 9

BSSID              PWR RXQ  Beacons    #Data, #/s  CH  MB    ENC  CIPHER AUTH E

CC:CC:CC:CC:CC:CC    0  87      58        0   0   9  54    WPA  TKIP   PSK  o
BB:BB:BB:BB:BB:BB    0  75      55        0   0   9  54    WEP  WEP         o
DD:DD:DD:DD:DD:DD    0  55      57        0   0   9  54    WPA2 CCMP   PSK  o
AA:AA:AA:AA:AA:AA    0  88      61        0   0   1  54    OPN              o
00:24:C4:2C:F9:E0   -1   0       0        3   0 133  -1    OPN              <
00:15:FF:2A:3E:B5  -17   0       2        9   0   2  54  . WPA2 CCMP   PSK  V
00:15:FF:04:8E:F1  -36   0       4        0   0   2  54e.  WPA2 CCMP   PSK  V
00:24:C4:2E:78:F0  -61   0       4        0   0   1  54e.  OPN              a
00:24:97:B9:BC:50  -61   0       0        7   0   6  54e.  OPN              a
00:24:C4:2F:13:00  -62   0       7        6   0   1  54e.  OPN              a
00:24:C4:2E:78:F1  -62   0       2        3   0   1  54e.  OPN              h
00:24:C4:2F:13:01  -63   0       4        1   0   1  54e.  OPN              h
00:24:C4:2E:74:21  -63   0       2        0   0   6  54e.  OPN              h
00:24:C4:1B:46:F1  -70   0       2        0   0  11  54e.  OPN              h
00:24:C4:1B:46:F0  -69   0       2        0   0  11  54e.  OPN              a
00:24:C4:2E:79:70  -71   0       2        0   0   1  54e.  OPN              a
00:24:C4:2E:79:71  -73   0       3        1   0   1  54e.  OPN              h

0 Unencrypted  1 WEP  2 WPA  3 WPA2  4 airodump   @opus - Tuesday 09 July -  6:2
```

Figure 14-7   Wifi-honey listing BSSIDs available with encryption mechanisms

your hands on or be overheard, making it easier for unauthorized users to gain access. If users log in to the network using their username and password, you gain stronger authentication, as well as accountability, by knowing exactly who has logged on to the network and what station they have logged in from.

Figure 14-7 shows a utility called wifi-honey listing all of the BSSIDs that were found in the area, including the encryption mechanism used. While WEP has been superseded for the better part of the decade because of its vulnerability, there are still access points that make use of it. While it's vulnerable, it is better at providing privacy and confidentiality than using no encryption at all. Also note that there is an access point using TKIP, which has also been shown to be vulnerable to an attack that could reveal the keys used for encryption. These announced BSSIDs are rogue and presented by wifi-honey, but the reason they are presented is because stations will continue to connect to those types of networks.

Wi-Fi Attacks

Wireless attacks have become harder as encryption has improved. When any traffic is encrypted, it's essential to be able to decrypt it in order to do much of anything. For attackers, this means attacking the encryption so you can intercept and decrypt. Under WEP, this was reasonably easy because of the vulnerability in the initialization vector. All you needed to do was to acquire a large amount of traffic, which could be used to determine the initialization vector. Since wireless networks today use WPA2, as a general rule, unless they are using access points that are very old and incapable of supporting the encryption required by WPA/WPA2, other types of attacks become necessary.

A *deauthentication attack* is one way to acquire a lot of data between a station and an access point. The attacker indicates to a station that it is no longer authenticated, so the station would have to initiate a four-way handshake again. The attacker could acquire all the messages from the four-way handshake and try to learn something useful from watching all of those messages. This is more of a foundational attack.

Instead of trying to crack encryption that is uncrackable because of the key strength, an attacker may find it easier to collect information directly. One way to accomplish that is to set up your own access point and pretend to be a legitimate access point. This attack is called an *evil twin* and the access point used as the evil twin is called a *rogue access point*. In order to ensure your rogue access point gets all the traffic, you might initiate a denial-of-service attack against the legitimate access point. If the network you are spoofing is an enterprise network, you may be able to collect usernames and passwords to use that could authenticate against the enterprise network. Once you have allowed the victims access to your own access point, they may start sending a lot of other traffic, including credentials.

A newer attack against WPA is a variation of a replay attack. It is called a key reinstallation attack (KRACK) where you end up being able to break the encryption because you are getting an already known key installed. Some devices, like those running Linux and Android, can be tricked into installing an all-zeros key. This means you have a station that has a key you know.

Cracking and Analysis Utilities

Several utilities exist to gain additional insight into wireless networks. Some can potentially crack passwords used for network access, and others are capable of cracking Wi-Fi pre-shared keys. A common one is Aircrack-ng, which can crack WEP and WPA-PSK keys once enough data has been received. Generally, you have to associate with an access point in order to see the frames from the associated SSID. Aircrack and other utilities use a monitor mode on the wireless NIC that lets you see frames without associating them with any SSID. This allows all of the frames seen by the wireless NIC to be captured. This is similar to promiscuous mode with a wired adapter, where all frames crossing the wire are captured rather than only passing frames with the MAC address for the NIC up to the OS. The difference with a wireless adapter is the association with an SSID.

 NOTE   Windows Network Driver Interface Specification (NDIS) doesn't provide support for monitor mode in older versions of Windows. NDIS 6 in Windows Vista provided support for monitor mode.

Fern Wifi Cracker makes use of monitor mode to grab frames from wireless networks. Fern is capable of cracking WPA and WEP passwords, and do other things like grab cookies. Figure 14-8 shows Fern prepared to crack passwords on one of the SSIDs that have been found. Fern provides multiple attack strategies, and is written in Python, making it portable across platforms. In the example shown, it's being run under Kali Linux, the distribution of choice for penetration testers, auditors, and forensic investigators for

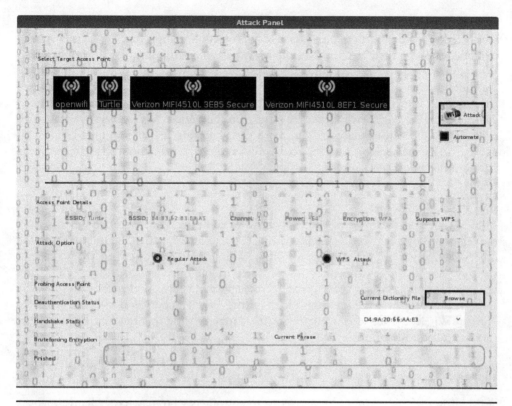

Figure 14-8 Fern Wifi Cracker ready to crack passwords

several years because of the large number of security tools installed by default within the distribution. Additionally, other tools are available from the configured repositories. Once you have the key and can decrypt the traffic, you can eavesdrop on the session you have the key for. This means you can listen in on the conversation without the two parties knowing it.

Other tools, such as Kismet, provide scanning and sniffing capabilities. Some utilities, such as coWPAtty, use a dictionary attack to crack the WPA key used. Because of the availability of access points, Wi-Fi is vulnerable to rogue access points used to collect information. Tools like Karmetasploit and wifi-honey may be used to create fake access points that stations can connect to, collecting information from the station and the user. If you present an SSID that a user may know, the station may connect to your rogue network and make use of the passphrase, sending it to you. In the case of wifi-honey, you can run a tool like Aircrack-ng or coWPAtty to try to crack the passwords that are shared during the four-way handshake used to authenticate the client. Any time you connect to a wireless network, you run the risk of potentially connecting to a rogue network, particularly if you are in a public and open area. Coffee shops or airport terminals may be good places to set up these rogue networks to acquire a lot of information from stations.

While sensitive information may be used to gain access to a wireless network, through a pre-shared key or even a username/password combination, transmitting it from the station to the access point, there is a way to set up a station without transmitting any information. Wi-Fi Protected Setup (WPS) can be used instead. With WPS, you can use a PIN to get the configuration to the station without passing any credentials. Another way to pass the configuration is to use a push button. This requires physical access to the access point so you can press the button while you are setting up the station. WPS allows the station to register with the wireless network with both ends knowing that the setup is happening, rather than having a station trust the access point and even having the access point trust the station trying to register with the network.

MiFi

MiFi is a method of providing Internet access to computers in a portable way by using the cell phone data network as the Internet access and offering an 802.11 network on the other side that stations can connect to. MiFi is a shorthand way of saying My Wi-Fi, and there are several devices available that provide portable Internet access over MiFi. MiFi has become a common way of referring to these portable network devices, though in the UK, the provider owns the trademark to the name. In other countries, MiFi is a brand for Novatel Wireless. There are many devices that may provide this functionality, whether they are called MiFi or not.

WiMAX

WiMAX is a way of getting Internet access to customers who may have a hard time getting access to traditional last-mile technologies like DSL or cable modem. It is a name for products that implement the IEEE 802.16 standard. 802.16 was a way to specify standards for wireless metropolitan area networks (MANs). Unlike 802.11, WiMAX has the capability of providing very large quantities of bandwidth, up to 1 Gbps. The first specification was published in 2001 and specified the use of 10–66 GHz for frequencies. That very broad range of frequencies has since been superseded, and currently, two ranges are specified in the standard: 2–11 GHz and 23.5–43.5 GHz, though there is no global licensed spectrum for WiMAX. In terms of a licensed spectrum, the largest available is in the 2.5-GHz range. However, WiMAX may use an unlicensed spectrum.

WiMAX is capable of providing mobile access, much like using data on your cell phone, as well as fixed position access where you might have a WiMAX gateway at your house to provide you with Internet connectivity. Unlike Wi-Fi, WiMAX can cross miles between the base station and the subscriber station. Wi-Fi, on the other hand, is restricted to connecting over dozens of meters, perhaps up to hundreds. Whereas Wi-Fi uses Carrier Sense Media Access/Collision Avoidance to protect against contention and collisions, WiMAX uses a connection-based system where a subscriber station is allocated a specific timeslot that is used for the life of the subscriber station. Sending and receiving is done using specific scheduling algorithms to avoid resource contention, which should provide a better quality of service (QoS) to end users.

While there are similarities between Wi-Fi and WiMAX, not the least of which is that they are communicating wirelessly, there are significant differences, too. Wi-Fi is primarily a local area networking technology, and a way of providing access to an Internet connection. WiMAX, on the other hand, is the Internet connection itself, and while it may provide direct Internet access to mobile devices, it is also just as likely to require a router that devices on a network connect to in order to get off of the local network.

Bluetooth

Bluetooth is a means of transmitting information wirelessly. While Wi-Fi is a way of providing networking wirelessly, Bluetooth is more application-specific, used to transmit information directly from one device to another. While many protocols and standards are managed by public standards bodies like IEEE for Wi-Fi or IETF for TCP/IP and the related protocols, Bluetooth is managed by a private group called the Bluetooth Special Interest Group (SIG). There is an IEEE standard defining Bluetooth, but it's now outdated. Bluetooth was originally created in 1994 by Ericsson, who made mobile phones. It was conceived as a replacement for RS-232 serial cabling.

NOTE The word Bluetooth comes from the Anglicization of a Danish word used by King Harald I of Denmark. The developer of Bluetooth was reading a book about King Harald at the time he was working to develop a way for mobile phones to communicate with computers.

Bluetooth makes use of unlicensed frequencies in the 2.4-GHz range and makes use of frequency-hopping spread spectrum over 79 channels, each 1-MHz wide. With Bluetooth, you have a master–slave model, and can have up to seven slaves, each communicating with the master. If there are several slaves, the master determines which slave to communicate with at any given moment. The message is sent specifically to the slave, using a 48-bit address assigned to the Bluetooth device. This is the same as a MAC address used in a network interface card, though when users are presented with information about the devices, a friendly name is used rather than the device address. Depending on the version of Bluetooth supported by the device, you may transmit data at rates of up to 24 Mbps. Data transmission is based on the use of a clock, maintained by the master, and slots. The master can use even slots to begin transmission, while odd slots can be employed to begin the transmission by a slave. This reduces contention between the two parties.

The current version of Bluetooth is 5.1. Version 5.0 primarily introduced features necessary to enable Internet of Things (IoT) devices. Version 4.0 changed the protocol stack, used to allow for simple links to be created quickly. Bluetooth 4.0 is also called Bluetooth Smart, so you may see "Bluetooth Smart Ready" on devices that implement the 4.0 version of the standard. Prior to 4.0 was 3.0 + HS, which introduced high-speed communication. As noted earlier, this may be up to 24 Mbps. Prior to version 3.0, the highest speed possible for transmitting information was 3 Mbps. The early versions of Bluetooth were only capable of transmitting at 1 Mbps.

Figure 14-9
Adding a
Bluetooth
device in
Windows

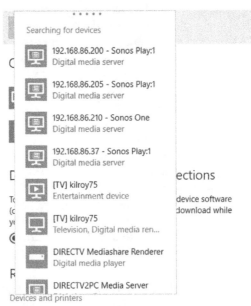

Add devices

Searching for devices

192.168.86.200 - Sonos Play:1
Digital media server

192.168.86.205 - Sonos Play:1
Digital media server

192.168.86.210 - Sonos One
Digital media server

192.168.86.37 - Sonos Play:1
Digital media server

[TV] kilroy75
Entertainment device

[TV] kilroy75
Television, Digital media ren...

DIRECTV Mediashare Renderer
Digital media player

DIRECTV2PC Media Server

In order to establish communication between two devices, the devices must pair. Pairing involves exchanging personal identification numbers (PINs) that offer a very basic level of authentication. It can also provide keying material for encrypted communication between the two devices. Pairing requires devices to find one another, and the mechanism used in an operating system to do the pairing can be seen in Figure 14-9, where a Windows system is probing for nearby Bluetooth devices. Once paired, Bluetooth devices are restricted to actions defined by a set or profiles. The profile implemented defines what action you can perform with the device. A headset used with a cell phone may implement a headset profile and a hands-free profile, for example, which would define the types of interactions the master would have with the slave. It would be unlikely to implement the file transfer profile, so files couldn't be sent to it. Table 14-2 lists and describes the Bluetooth profiles.

EXAM TIP   Users are encouraged to use a PIN of at least 12 characters to better secure their devices.

In order for two Bluetooth devices to pair, they must be able to see one another, as well as indicate what their capabilities are. There are profiles like the Service Discovery Application Profile that make this information exchange possible. One way to protect your device against someone else accessing it is to turn off discovery. You may want to check periodically for devices that can be discovered by using a tool like BlueScanner, Bluesniff, or btscanner to check for devices in range. You will also find that if your computer is configured with a Bluetooth adapter, your operating system will also likely be able to scan

Profile	Description
Advanced Audio Distribution Profile (A2DP)	This profile allows for streaming media to a wireless device like a headset or a speaker.
Attribute Profile (ATT)	This profile is a wire application specification related to Bluetooth Low Energy.
Audio/Video Remote Control Protocol (AVRCP)	This profile is used to remotely control devices like TVs, stereo equipment, and other items.
Basic Imaging Profile (BIP)	This profile provides the ability to resize or convert images. The functions that may be used as part of this profile are Image Push, Image Pull, Advanced Image Printing, Automatic Archive, Remote Camera, and Remote Display.
Basic Printing Profile (BPP)	This profile allows a device to send text, e-mail, and other items to printers capable of Bluetooth communication.
Common ISDN Access Profile (CIP)	This profile provides access to services, data, and signaling that ISDN offers.
Cordless Telephony Profile (CTP)	This profile allows cordless phones to use Bluetooth.
Device ID Profile (DIP)	This profile provides some enhanced identification features, above just using the Device Class.
Dial-Up Networking Profile (DUN)	This profile allows a device to be used as an Internet gateway, similar to a dial-up service.
Fax Profile (FAX)	This profile allows a mobile device to send a fax through a PC with fax software installed.
File Transfer Profile (FTP)	This profile allows the exchange of files between devices.
Generic Audio/Video Distribution Profile (GAVDP)	This is a foundation profile used by A2DP and VDP.
Generic Access Profile (GAP)	All other profiles use this profile as a foundation.
Generic Attribute Profile (GATT)	This profile provides for profile discovery and description for Bluetooth Low Energy (part of Bluetooth 4.0).
Generic Object Exchange Protocol (GOEP)	All data exchange profiles are based on this profile.
Hard Copy Replacement Profile (HCRP)	This is a profile for functions like printing but doesn't actually specify protocols for the exchange of information, so drivers are required, making this profile less useful than other profiles.
Health Device Profile (HDP)	This profile allows for medical information to be transmitted.
Hands-Free Profile (HFP)	This profile is used in a vehicle that provides the speaker and microphone in order to allow phone calls to be done hands-free. Additionally, this profile allows for last number redial, call waiting, and voice dialing.
Human Interface Device Profile (HID)	A mouse or keyboard would implement this profile since it provides for devices that allow a human interface. A joystick or a game controller may also implement this profile if it supports Bluetooth.

Table 14-2   Bluetooth Profiles

Profile	Description
Intercom Profile (IP)	This profile is like a walkie-talkie because it allows audio to be sent directly between two devices using Bluetooth.
LAN Profile (LAP)	This profile allows devices to access networks. It makes use of PPP to establish connections.
Message Access Profile (MAP)	This profile allows for the transmission of messages between Bluetooth devices. This is primarily employed for hands-free use in automobiles.
Object Exchange (OBEX)	This profile allows for objects to be sent between devices. This might be something like a contact record that you want to share with someone.
Object Push Profile (OPP)	This profile allows objects like pictures or contact records to be easily sent from one device to another.
Phone Book Access Profile (PBAP)	This profile allows phone book entries to be sent. This is helpful in hands-free situations where the car is capable of receiving an address book and displaying its contents.
Proximity Profile	This profile allows devices to determine how close they are to one another.
Service Discovery Application Profile (SDAP)	This profile allows devices to determine what services are available on another device.
SIM Access Profile (SAP)	This profile allows a car that has a cell transceiver built into it to make use of the SIM from the mobile phone. This means the car doesn't have to have its own SIM card. It simply uses the SIM card in your phone, so calls originating from your car appear to be coming from your phone number.
Synchronization Profile (SYNCH)	This profile allows for synchronization of personal information manager (PIM) items.
Video Distribution Profile (VDP)	Like the A2DP, this profile lets video be transmitted from one device and displayed on another.
Wireless Application Bearer Profile (WABP)	This profile allows the Wireless Application Protocol to be carried over the Point-to-Point Protocol over Bluetooth.

Table 14-2   Bluetooth Profiles (*Continued*)

for nearby Bluetooth devices. Figure 14-10 displays the output from btscanner showing devices that are close by with Bluetooth enabled and the set to be discoverable. While one of the devices is a laptop I have in discoverable mode, the other devices are in nearby rooms in the hotel where this text was being written. In theory, I might be able to pair with one of these devices and see what profiles it has available, which should highlight the importance of making sure your devices are not discoverable.

One device can request information of another device without pairing. This will allow the user to be presented with pairing options, based on need. Again, this requires the device to be in discoverable mode. If the device is in discoverable mode, it can be asked

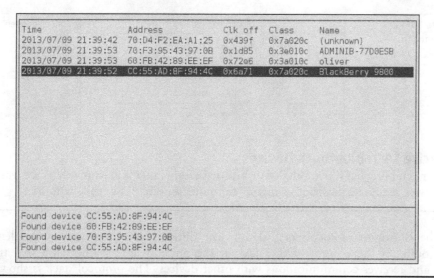

```
Time                   Address           Clk off   Class     Name
2013/07/09 21:39:42    70:D4:F2:EA:A1:25 0x439f    0x7a020c  (unknown)
2013/07/09 21:39:53    70:F3:95:43:97:0B 0x1d85    0x3e010c  ADMINIB-77D0ESB
2013/07/09 21:39:53    60:FB:42:89:EE:EF 0x72e6    0x3a010c  oliver
2013/07/09 21:39:52    CC:55:AD:8F:94:4C 0x6a71    0x7a020c  BlackBerry 9800




Found device CC:55:AD:8F:94:4C
Found device 60:FB:42:89:EE:EF
Found device 70:F3:95:43:97:0B
Found device CC:55:AD:8F:94:4C
```

Figure 14-10 Devices found by scanning

to transmit its name, device class, list of services, and technical information like features, specification used, manufacturer, or clock offset. A device looking for another device to pair with for a specific purpose would initiate an inquiry scan to locate devices available, and in the process it would request the information mentioned earlier in order to present pairing options to the user.

EXAM TIP   You may have a policy indicating that all Bluetooth-enabled devices be put into non-discoverable mode. You might use tools like BlueScanner for Windows or Bluesniff for Linux to detect devices that are not in non-discoverable mode, and as a result violate the policy.

While the pairing process was initially accomplished by entering a simple PIN on both devices, v2.1 of the standard introduced Secure Simple Pairing (SSP). SSP makes use of a type of public key cryptography and might protect against man-in-the-middle attacks. SSP has a few different modes that would complete the pairing process. The first is called Just Works and is commonly seen in devices like headsets. The master and slave negotiate the pairing between them since the slave probably has limited I/O capabilities, meaning it wouldn't have the ability to accept any input from the user that would confirm a piece of information from the master. This also gets away from the fixed PIN that was previously used for this type of device. If the two devices attempting to pair have some I/O capabilities, the pairing process may use a numeric comparison, where each device would present the same numeric code and the user would indicate with either a yes or no whether they match or not. Similar to this is a passkey entry where one device displays a numeric code that then gets entered on the other device. Finally, there is out of band, which would use another form of communication like near field communication (NFC) to exchange some information to complete the pairing.

Figure 14-11
A Bluetooth
protocol stack

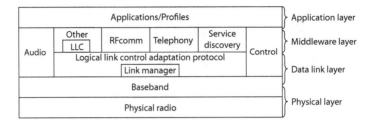

Exercise 14-1: Bluetooth Devices

If your computer has Bluetooth, locate a device within range and pair with it. See whether the device requires a passcode or if your computer automatically pairs with it.

The Bluetooth protocol stack defines the different protocols used to implement Bluetooth. At the bottom of the stack at the physical layer is the radio that transmits and receives communications with other devices. The protocol stack is shown in Figure 14-11. The Link Management Protocol (LMP) is used to establish communication with another device and is implemented on the controller rather than in software on the host computer. On top of LMP are some of the lower-level profiles that enable higher-level, application-layer profiles.

Encryption

Encryption is performed using a set of custom algorithms based on the SAFER+ block cipher. While SAFER+ was submitted as a candidate for the Advanced Encryption Standard (AES) and used a block size of 128 bits with a key size of 128 bits, Bluetooth doesn't make use of SAFER+ for encryption. Instead, custom algorithms of SAFER+ are used for key derivation and authentication. Encryption of payloads is done using the E0 stream cipher with a 128-bit key. Key generation in Bluetooth may rely on the PIN used to pair the two devices. Prior to Bluetooth v2.1, encryption was not even required and could be disabled; 2.1, however, required the use of encryption for all connections that were not performing a service discovery. It also introduced encryption pause and resume functions, allowing encryption to be disabled for normal operations that don't require it. This is different from earlier versions where it was difficult to determine whether encryption had been disabled or not.

 EXAM TIP The primary shortcoming of the SAFER+ cipher as used by Bluetooth implementations is the reliance on a potentially weak PIN.

Bluetooth Attacks

Bluetooth is vulnerable to a number of attacks, which may provide access to information stored on the device or allow for full control of the device. The following are some of the common attacks against Bluetooth.

- **Bluesnarfing**   Snarfing in general is a slang term used to describe the acquisition of a large amount of data without permission. This may be an entire file or a large document. Snarfing might be accomplished by listening over a wire for transmission requests and grabbing the bits that are then sent. In the case of Bluesnarfing, it's accessing information like a contact list, calendars, e-mail, text messages, pictures, videos, or audio files over Bluetooth. A device that is discoverable may be vulnerable to a Bluesnarfing attack.

- **Bluejacking**   Bluejacking has traditionally been more of an annoyance, though that may be changing. Bluejacking is where an unsolicited message is sent to an unsuspecting device. This may simply be a text message used for unsolicited advertising, but it could also be used to transmit a virus and take over the receiving device.

- **Bluebugging**   Bluebugging compromises the security of a device, allowing full control over the device attacked. A Bluebugging attack lets the perpetrator listen in on phone conversations. It may also establish a call-forward operation where calls intended for the victim are sent to the attacker instead. A Bluebugging attack may also pretend to be a headset, allowing the attacker to send call-control commands to the phone.

Often, just as in the case of attacks against computer systems, Bluetooth attacks are made possible by bad user practices, like enabling the device to be discovered by anyone nearby. Assuming that any device attempting to communicate over Bluetooth must be close is not a good protection since attackers may simply use higher-powered transmitters to be farther away and out of the range of visual detection.

RFID

Radio frequency identification (RFID) is a way of providing information wirelessly to devices in close proximity. The RFID tag itself offers some amount of identification information. This may allow the identification of a pet, or the contents of a particular package, or any number of other applications requiring things to be identified. As mentioned in the chapter introduction, RFID tags are used in express toll applications on highways so drivers don't have to slow down or stop in order to pay tolls. RFID tags can be made very small. Figure 14-12 shows an RFID tag with a grain of rice to indicate how small the tags can be. The size depends on the type of tag it is. A passive tag doesn't require a battery and is powered by the signal sent to it from a device querying the tag. A battery-assisted passive (BAP) tag has a small battery on board, but the tag itself still isn't activated until an RFID reader is near and scanning for tags. An active tag has a battery and transmits an ID signal periodically.

While the idea of RFID goes back to 1945, the first device that included a radio transponder with memory was demonstrated in 1971 to the New York Port Authority for use as a toll device. The first patent using the term RFID was granted in 1983. Currently, a number of frequency ranges are used, primarily by applications. Lower frequency ranges require the reader to be closer to the tag, while higher frequencies can be read at a greater distance.

Figure 14-12
An RFID tag
alongside a grain
of rice

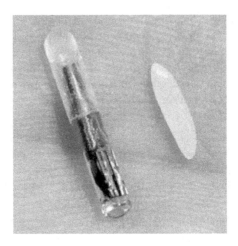

As an example, animal identification tags operate in the 120–150 kHz spectrum but their range is only about 10 centimeters. Those that operate in the 902–928 MHz range can be read at distances of up to 12 meters.

When a passive tag is read using an active reader passive tag (ARPT) system, the reader sends a signal toward the tag (which may not be visible and could be embedded into packaging or a product itself), and the tag reflects the signal back to the reader using something called backscatter. *Backscatter* is the term for waves, particles, or signals that are reflected back to where they came from. The reader would then receive the signal that was reflected back. Different readers are used for the various types of chips or tags. An active tag may not require an active reader since the tag itself is sending out data. All the reader has to do is listen to what's being transmitted. You may use an active reader to wake up an active tag, though. In this case, you have an active reader working with an active tag rather than a passive reader and an active tag.

RFID tags are being used in a lot of areas and have gotten much smaller over time. Many retailers, as an example, are using RFID tags for supply management, not only for inventory control but also for maintaining the supply chain. Walmart, for example, makes sure suppliers are using RFID tags called Electronic Product Codes (EPCs) to make the process of inventory control more efficient. In addition to inventory control, an EPC might also be used in a retail setting by using an RFID reader at customer check-out points. Whereas a bar code, which is currently used to scan products at checkout time, requires a scanner to actually see and read the code, an RFID tag just needs to be close to a reader. This may speed up the process of checking customers out.

Proximity badges commonly use RFID in order to identify individuals to allow them access to facilities. This requires physical security, meaning employees need to keep tight control over their badge since an attacker could use the device to get into a building. Badges don't need to be stolen to be used. There are devices that are easily available that can get a badge (or any other RFID device) to give up its information, then create a clone of the badge. This means you could still have your proximity badge while an attacker had a clone of your badge and be able to get access to all the resources your badge lets you get access to.

Near Field Communication

Another application of RFID is near field communication (NFC). NFC is becoming common in mobile devices like cell phones and extends RFID by making the communication two-way rather than just the one-way communication that a straightforward RFID tag offers. With NFC, you can transmit data between two devices quickly and easily. In addition to being able to transmit files, contacts, and so on, NFC can be used as a contactless payment system. Rather than pulling out a credit card and swiping it, you can wave a credit card with a tag built into it across a reader. You may also use your smartphone as a way of storing your personal information, including credit information. You can then use your phone as a payment system. NFC in phones used as a payment system has more traction in Europe and other parts of the world. Some locations are using NFC as a way of ticketing for public transportation systems. In San Francisco, parking meters are implementing NFC. The phone can then send reminders to the user about how much time the parking meter has left on it.

NFC may be useful in social networking by allowing the transmission of contacts, music, playlists, and so on. Also, it can be helpful with multiplayer games by allowing devices to communicate with one another without having to establish an ad hoc Wi-Fi network or connect to an infrastructure Wi-Fi network. Android phones, and Samsung devices in particular, have taken a lead role in the use of this technology. Android provides a utility called Android Beam, while Samsung devices offer a Samsung-specific feature called S-Beam, providing a similar feature.

NOTE Attackers may be able to use something like a skimmer to obtain NFC communications. This may be a device that sits between the NFC device and the reader. This would be similar to a credit card skimmer, which sits over the top of a real credit/debit card reader and is the device that ends up gathering the credit card information when the card is swiped.

Zigbee

Zigbee is another way of providing networking functions to devices. It is specifically targeted at low-power, low-bandwidth, close-proximity connections. Additionally, it is low cost. It may be used by embedded devices like home automation systems or security systems. Zigbee operates in the industrial, scientific, and medical (ISM) bands, including the 2.4-GHz range. IEEE maintains the standard, numbered 802.15-4. The current version is 802.15-4-2006, published in 2006. In 2007, Zigbee Pro was launched as an enhanced specification. Similar to Bluetooth, Zigbee has created a number of application profiles.

As with other forms of wireless, Zigbee is susceptible to attacks on the keys, such as trying to determine which keys were used to encrypt the traffic. Zigbee is also susceptible to replay attacks or even injection attacks, where traffic is injected to get responses that could lead to enough information to determine how keys are generated. Finally, if someone can get access to the physical device, there is a much stronger probability of compromise since the device could be configured in a way that the attacker could use it.

Zigbee, along with Z-Wave, a similar protocol, is used by embedded devices like a thermostat or a light bulb to communicate with a controller in close proximity. If you have Philips Hue light bulbs, for instance, a door lock that can be locked remotely, or any of the Samsung SmartThings devices, you are using Zigbee or Z-Wave. This means you could have Bluetooth being used between some devices in your house while Zigbee or Z-Wave are also being used. In general, because of the short range of these devices, you wouldn't be able to gain access to them from outside of your house.

Chapter Review

Wireless technologies are everywhere and rollouts aren't slowing down. We continue to look for more ways to get rid of our cords and cables and go wireless. While we become more and more mobile, we need more ways to connect with one another, as well as with the Internet as a whole. We are also using wireless technologies to push more and larger content. This drives us to faster speeds, requiring more and more spectrum allocations to keep up with the demand for bandwidth. It also pushes more and more retailers and restaurants to offer wireless connectivity for free in order to encourage customers to visit and remain connected.

Wi-Fi isn't the only wireless technology, not by any means. Bluetooth offers the ability to connect devices to one another without wires. This allows us to talk on our phones while driving without using a hand to paste the phone to one ear. Talking on the phone while driving may be dangerous, but it's more dangerous to be focused on pinning a cell phone to your head while trying to manipulate a large motorized vehicle with one hand. The days of having your computer surrounded by a nest of wires to connect your keyboard, mouse, speakers, and other devices are largely gone, since more computers and their peripherals are now made with Bluetooth built in.

Wireless networks have improved over the years. They are faster now and also support stronger encryption. Where before, low bandwidth was common and the encryption that existed could easily be cracked, today we are close to supporting gigabit transmission speeds. On top of that, Wi-Fi Protected Access (WPA) solved the problems with Wired Equivalent Privacy (WEP) and is a much stronger encryption scheme. However, there are still attacks against WPA-encrypted networks. One is called an evil twin, where an attacker sets up an access point that pretends to be an existing access point. Another is a key reinstallation attack, where devices can be tricked into installing a key that is known to the attacker.

RFID lets us identify our pets when they get lost, or even keep track of large herds of animals. It also allows businesses to maintain their inventory, as well as control assets without needing asset stickers, which can peel off. RFID tags are very small and can be embedded in many different products in many ways. Passive tags may require readers to be close enough to scan them, such as in a checkout line, while active tags can be read at a distance and, among other things, enable us to get around faster, since they can be used to pass through toll booths without stopping. Beyond RFID is NFC, which may reduce the need to carry around a wallet with your phone. Using NFC, your phone can provide identification services, as well as payment and notification functions.

Questions

1. Users are encouraged to use a PIN of how many characters in order to better protect their Bluetooth communications?

   A. 4

   B. 8

   C. 12

   D. 16

2. What is the biggest problem with Bluetooth encryption?

   A. A weak initialization vector

   B. The 40-bit key

   C. Lack of integrity checking

   D. Use of a weak PIN

3. What can you accomplish by hiding your SSID?

   A. You can make it harder for unauthorized users to get access.

   B. You can keep all unauthorized users from gaining access.

   C. You can require a key to gain entry.

   D. You can keep all users from gaining access.

4. Which of the following attacks might allow the perpetrator to gain a lot of information from a Bluetooth device?

   A. Bluejacking

   B. Bluesnarfing

   C. Bluebugging

   D. Bluecoating

5. WEP was superseded by WPA because of what problem?

   A. WEP wasn't as nice an acronym.

   B. WEP wasn't capable of performing at the speeds necessary.

   C. WEP made use of a weak initialization vector.

   D. WEP didn't offer encryption.

6. Which type of frame in Wi-Fi announces the SSID to the network?

   A. Pin frame

   B. SSID frame

   C. Session frame

   D. Beacon frame

7. If you wanted to set up a quick wireless network between several devices for a LAN party, what might you do?

    A. Set up an ad hoc Wi-Fi network.

    B. Use Zigbee.

    C. Use an RFID PAN.

    D. Use infrastructure mode in your Wi-Fi network.

8. How could you enforce a corporate policy that requires all Bluetooth devices to have discoverable mode disabled?

    A. Use a Bluesnarfing attack.

    B. Use a Bluecoat proxy.

    C. Use BlueScanner.

    D. Require people to sign the policy.

9. Many wireless technologies make use of one simple technology to prevent eavesdropping on the signal. What is it?

    A. Strong antennas

    B. Frequency hopping

    C. Spectrum allocation

    D. Cloaking devices

10. Which of the following does 802.11i NOT address?

    A. Throughput

    B. Integrity

    C. Confidentiality

    D. Replay protection

11. What is KRACK used for?

    A. Key reinstallation

    B. Rogue access points

    C. Bluetooth attacks

    D. RFID attacks

12. What type of attack spoofs an existing access point?

    A. Rogue access point

    B. Evil twin

    C. KRACK

    D. Spoofed source

13. What device would an attacker be likely to target that could be cloned in order to gain physical access to a facility?

    A. Access point

    B. Key

    C. Wireless station

    D. Proximity badge

14. What mechanism would you use to register a station to an access point without passing credentials across the network while the station registers to the network?

    A. WPA

    B. WiMAX

    C. WPS

    D. WEP

15. What protocol would a Philips Hue light bulb use to communicate with a controller?

    A. Zigbee

    B. Bluetooth

    C. WiMAX

    D. 802.11i

Answers

1. **C.** Users should use a PIN of at least 12 characters.

2. **D.** One of the problems with Bluetooth has been deriving a key from a potentially weak PIN. A weak initialization vector is a hallmark of WEP, as is a 40-bit key. Bluetooth uses a stream cipher with a 128-bit key. Bluetooth also uses integrity checking.

3. **A.** Hiding your SSID doesn't prevent anyone from accessing your wireless network. It just means you have to know the SSID in order to gain entry. Hiding your SSID doesn't mean you require a key. You can still use open authentication with a hidden SSID.

4. **B.** Snarfing is the process of acquiring a lot of data without permission, and Bluesnarfing is doing that over Bluetooth. Bluejacking lets an attacker take control of your device, while Bluebugging allows an attacker to control your calls and listen in. Bluecoating is a fictitious term.

5. **C.** Wired Equivalent Privacy (WEP) made use of a weak initialization vector, which meant that, over time, the key could be derived and the encrypted traffic decrypted. WEP does, of course, offer encryption. WPA wasn't a nicer acronym, of course. WPA was introduced to resolve the issues with WEP.

6. D. A beacon frame would be used to announce the SSID, as well as the capabilities of the network. The other types of frames mentioned don't exist.

7. A. Ad hoc mode can allow everyone to quickly get on the same wireless network without needing an access point, whereas infrastructure mode requires an access point. Your devices probably don't all have Zigbee radios installed. There may be many reasons why you wouldn't use an RFID personal area network (PAN), one of which is that your PCs probably don't have RFID devices with that capability.

8. C. You could use a scanner like BlueScanner for Windows to locate devices that were discoverable and ensure that the device had that mode disabled. You wouldn't use a Bluesnarfing attack because you would be acquiring data without permission. A Bluecoat proxy is a web proxy. Requiring people to sign a policy doesn't guarantee they will abide by it.

9. B. Many wireless technologies make use of frequency hopping to prevent eavesdropping, since a listener would have to know what frequency to listen on before they could grab the communication stream. Strong antennas wouldn't help, and there aren't cloaking devices for wireless protocols. Spectrum allocation isn't helpful for this.

10. A. 802.11i (WPA) provides integrity, confidentiality, and replay protection. It does nothing to change throughput.

11. A. KRACK is a key reinstallation attack. It is used to trick a station into installing a known key, like one consisting of all 0's. It has nothing to do with Bluetooth or RFID.

12. B. While rogue access points are used in an evil twin attack, the attack itself is not called a rogue access point. That's just the mechanism for enabling the attack. KRACK is a key reinstallation attack. If you could use KRACK, you may not need to use an evil twin attack.

13. D. Proximity badges use RFID technology to provide information about an individual so decisions can be made about whether to allow that person into a facility. Proximity badges, though, can be cloned because of the RFID technology used. Access points may be "cloned" in a way in an evil twin attack, but that isn't for purposes of gaining access to a facility.

14. C. Wi-Fi Protected Setup (WPS) can be used to register a station with a wireless network. This might use a PIN or a push button. This typically means that both the station and the access point will know the device is being registered, reducing the chance of an attacker attempting to gain access.

15. A. Zigbee is a wireless protocol used for personal area networks. This is exactly the sort of lightweight, low-power protocol that would work well for embedded smart devices, such as light bulbs, door locks, or thermostats.

Exercise 14-1 Answer

If the device requires a passcode, you may see something like Figure 14-13, where a passcode is presented that needs to be entered into the device.

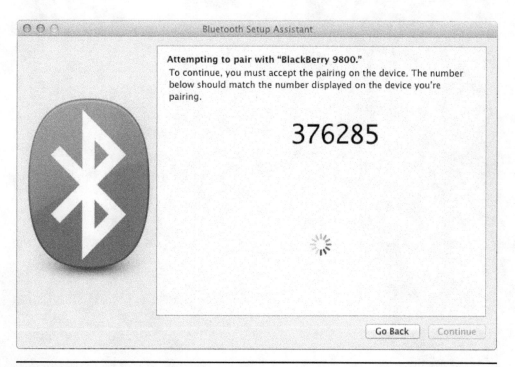

Figure 14-13   A passcode for Bluetooth pairing

Log Management

In this chapter, you will learn:

- About log types: syslog and Windows Event Viewer logs
- About centralized logging servers
- The role of security information and event management (SIEM)
- The difference between operating system logs and application logs

If you have ever tried to find a reason why a system or an application wasn't working correctly, you may appreciate the value of logs. Without some insight into what is happening internally with a system or application, you are working in the dark. You're staggering around a very dark room, randomly feeling with your hands because your eyes can't help you. Fortunately, logs provide visibility. When something bad is happening or, more importantly, has already happened on a system, logs can provide answers. We can't see everything that is happening as it's happening by staring at the monitor. This is why logs are essential. They enable us to investigate hidden issues and piece events together. Even better, we can pass the logs to systems that are designed to detect events as they happen and issue alerts.

Logging also is important for detecting security breaches. Among the security companies that produce periodic reports about attackers and their actions is FireEye, which uses the incident response experience of their FireEye Mandiant consulting arm to gather data. One statistic that they capture is the median dwell time, which is the amount of time an attacker is in a system environment before they are detected. According to FireEye, in 2018, attackers had on average more than 50 days inside their targets before they were detected. Without adequate logging and the capability to detect anomalies in those logs, there may be no way to determine when attackers have gained access to systems.

Which types of logs are available depends primarily on which operating system is being used. Also, the various different types of network devices generate their own specific logs. Therefore, information provided in the logs will vary depending not only on the operating system and format of the logs but also the application or subsystem that generates the log message. Firewalls, routers, and switches all generate logs that may be useful when trying to identify problems in a network, whether those are just performance issues or more serious issues related to a security incident. All of these different types of logs can be better handled through the use of technology like a security information and event management (SIEM) system. This is not the only way to manage logs, though.

Other methods can be used. Ultimately, the goal of log management should be to retain logs in case they are needed. Additionally, though, log management is about distilling all of the log entries to the ones that should be looked at.

Log Types

While applications can generate their own logs and write them out, and some do, there are also system services that applications can use so all logs end up in the same place. Using the same log categorization as system services, all logs end up looking the same. This is especially useful when it comes to any forensic analysis, since there is no time spent trying to decode log entries. Unix-like operating systems, such as Linux, have long had syslog. On the Windows side, there are Windows Event Logs.

Syslog

Syslog is a logging service and protocol that was created as part of the Sendmail mailer. Sendmail is a Simple Mail Transfer Protocol (SMTP) server, used to receive mail messages in order to deliver them to either remote systems or local mailboxes. Syslog was documented in Request for Comments (RFC) 3164, which was later obsoleted by RFC 5424. Syslog takes care of all the formatting and the handling of storage or delivery. It even takes care of all attribution, meaning it adds date and time stamps along with where the log message originated from. Additionally, syslog offers the means to categorize messages so they can be better sorted and sent to the correct place. First, there are facilities. A facility is a category that indicates the purpose of the message or of the application generating the message. In Table 15-1 there is a list of all the categories that syslog supports. The short names for each of the category numbers are generally straightforward, but in case some of them aren't clear, you can see the descriptions in the rightmost column. There are 24 facilities defined by syslog.

Keep in mind that syslog originates from Sendmail, a mail program, which likely is why mail appears so high in the list of facilities. The facilities provide a way of putting messages into buckets so that all similar messages end up in the same place. You'll see how you can route syslog messages later in this section. You can also route messages based on severity. There are eight severities defined by the syslog specification, outlined in Table 15-2. Note that they decrease in severity as the number increases: the most severe issue has a severity value of 0, and the least severe, a debug message, has a severity value of 7.

Since syslog is now just a specification, as opposed to the single implementation that it once was, there are several software packages that can be used to handle syslog messages. One example is rsyslog, which is a common syslog package installed by default on some Linux systems like CentOS and Ubuntu. Just like the original syslog used syslog.conf to configure how the service operated, rsyslog uses rsyslog.conf for configuration purposes. The first thing to discuss is how you go about routing messages. For our purposes here, we'll start with logging to files on the operating system where rsyslog is running. In the following code, you will see a list of rules from an rsyslog.conf file. These rules identify the file to which messages get sent based on the facility and/or the severity. On the left

Facility Code	Keyword	Description
0	kern	Kernel messages
1	user	User-level messages
2	mail	Mail system
3	daemon	System daemons
4	auth	Security/authentication messages
5	syslog	Messages generated internally by syslogd
6	lpr	Line printer subsystem
7	news	Network news subsystem
8	uucp	UUCP subsystem
9	cron	Clock daemon
10	authpriv	Security/authentication messages
11	ftp	FTP daemon
12	ntp	NTP subsystem
13	security	Log audit
14	console	Log alert
15	solaris-cron	Scheduling daemon
16–23	local0-local7	Locally used facilities

Table 15-1   Syslog Facilities

Value	Severity	Keyword	Deprecated Keywords	Description	Condition
0	Emergency	emerg	panic	System is unusable	A panic condition
1	Alert	alert		Action must be taken immediately	A condition that should be corrected immediately, such as a corrupted system database
2	Critical	crit		Critical conditions	Hard device errors
3	Error	err	error	Error conditions	
4	Warning	warning	warn	Warning conditions	
5	Notice	notice		Normal but significant conditions	Conditions that are not error conditions but may require special handling
6	Informational	info		Informational messages	
7	Debug	debug		Debug-level messages	Messages that contain information normally of use only when debugging a program

Table 15-2   Syslog Severities

end of each line, you will see an entry such as mail.*, which indicates that all messages with the mail facility go to the file specified at the end of the line. If you see an entry like *.emerg, it means that messages with the highest priority, emerg, will get sent to the file at the end of the line.

```
# Log all kernel messages to the console.
# Logging much else clutters up the screen.
#kern.*                                                  /dev/console

# Log anything (except mail) of level info or higher.
# Don't log private authentication messages!
*.info;mail.none;authpriv.none;cron.none                /var/log/messages

# The authpriv file has restricted access.
authpriv.*                                               /var/log/secure

# Log all the mail messages in one place.
mail.*                                                   -/var/log/maillog


# Log cron stuff.
cron.*                                                   /var/log/cron

# Everybody gets emergency messages.
*.emerg                                                  :omusrmsg:*

# Save news errors of level crit and higher in a special file.
uucp,news.crit                                           /var/log/spooler

# Save boot messages also to boot.log.
local7.*                                                 /var/log/boot.log
```

Syslog messages don't have to be written to a log file, though. They can be forwarded to a log server. Syslog commonly listens on UDP port 514. There are a couple of reasons for this. The first is UDP has no overhead, which means essential messages will get sent faster because there is no need to establish a connection. Additionally, some syslog messages have historically been considered less important and there wouldn't be as much concern if they were lost since UDP does no retransmit. Since a central log server may be on the same network segment as the servers originating the messages, there is less of a chance of the messages being lost. Again using rsyslog, the configuration statement used to send messages to a remote system with a syslog server listening would be

```
*.*  @@milobloom:514
```

If you want to establish a listener using rsyslog, you would use the following statements. The first one loads a module including the functionality for a UDP listener. The second one tells the server to listen on port 514, which is the default syslog port. One note about port 514 is that any port number below 1024 is considered an administrative port, and as such requires administrative privileges. In the case of Linux, that means running as the root user. If you happen to be running the syslog service as a non-root user, you need to adjust the port number to something higher than 1023.

```
$ModLoad imudp
$UDPServerRun 514
```

One advantage of running a syslog server, even if you don't have a lot of Linux systems in your environment, is that network devices may support syslog. Cisco routers, for example, support syslog and can forward to a central syslog server. Another advantage of using syslog is that messages are tagged with not only the date and time but also the host. A couple of syslog messages are shown next. After the date and time, you will see the hostname, which is milobloom in this case. After the hostname is the process ID (PID) of the application that generated the log entry. Anything after the colon (:) is the message the application created.

```
Mar 24 18:57:37 milobloom NetworkManager[5690]: <info>  [1553475457.1020]
dhcp4 (ens192): state changed bound -> bound
Mar 24 18:57:37 milobloom dbus[5666]: [system] Activating via systemd:
service name='org.freedesktop.nm_dispatcher' unit='dbus-org.freedesktop.nm-
dispatcher.service'
```

When you have a centralized log server, you'll end up with thousands or millions of log entries, and without the hostname, you'll have no idea which log entry goes with which server. Of course, just having log messages alone may not be enough, and we'll address doing something useful with the log entries later in the chapter.

Log rotation and retention are important. Log rotation is moving existing log files to other file names in order to create a new log file using the primary file name. The older files could be moved to near-line or offline storage in order to keep them for longer periods without consuming essential disk space. Keeping logs around for periods of time is called *retention*. Some regulations and audit requirements suggest or require retention periods. This could mean the need to store and be able to recover logs for months or even years. Syslog is just a process for sending and receiving log entries, defining severities and facilities. There is no innate capability for rotating logs. If you have a need to rotate logs, you would use a utility like logrotate, which is a script that moves existing log files to a different filename, which may include some date and time information. They could just be numbered files. Logrotate will also compress the log files to free up space.

Windows Event Logs

Windows has had its own means of logging messages since the release of Windows New Technology (NT) in 1993. Windows NT was developed to be an enterprise-grade operating system and its design philosophy came from developers who had spent years developing operating systems for much larger systems that were often at the center of the business, meaning the system had to be rock solid and capable of recovering from issues. These systems also often had operators, meaning logging was important so the operators could know what was going on. All of this is to say that logging services have been a part of Windows NT since the beginning, and over the decades since, the functionality has improved. The system logs Windows has are Application, Security, Setup, and System.

Managing Windows Event Logs is done through the Event Viewer. Figure 15-1 shows the properties page for the Application log. One of the important elements of log management, log rotation, is shown here. These settings should vary depending on the nature of the server or desktop. For instance, any server that is responsible for handling authentication should have the Security log set to either archive log files or manually clear them.

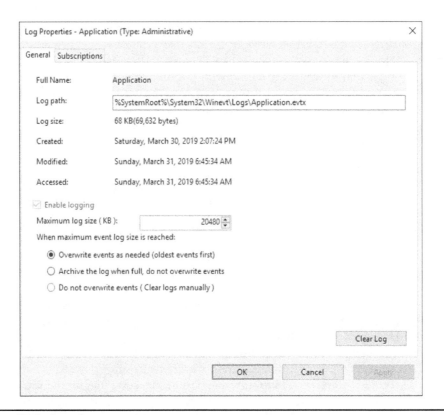

Figure 15-1　Event log properties

The log should not be set to overwrite. When the logs are set to overwrite, the file size is capped, and when that maximum file size is reached, old event entries are removed to make room for the new log entry. When logs are archived, the existing log will get moved to a different filename, commonly Archive + <Event Log Name> + <Date> + <Time> .evtx. These archived logs need to be managed manually because, over long periods of time, they can consume significant disk space.

You will notice that the file extension for the event files is evtx. This is the Windows Extensible Markup Language (XML) Event Log. The log entries are complex data types, containing not just the date and time, the process, and the event text, but other data including an event identifier (ID). The event ID can be used to classify the type of event it is, so all events of a particular ID can be located in the event log for correlation purposes. Microsoft maintains a list of event IDs. The event ID will provide a general description of the event without any of the specifics. If you want specifics, you need to look at the event itself. In order to do that, you'd open the Event Viewer. Figure 15-2 shows details from one event on a Windows Server 2019 system. The description at the top of the dialog box is not provided by the application that generated the event. Instead, it is the text that maps to the event ID.

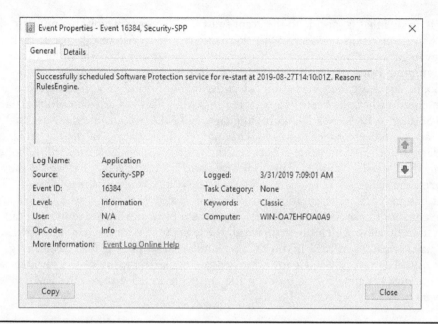

Figure 15-2   Event details

In addition to the event ID and description, you get the source, which is the service or process that caused the event to be generated. Similar to syslog, you get a severity. This is not shown in the details of the event, but if you look at the list of all the events, you will see the severity of each event in the column labeled Level. You can see this in Figure 15-3. You will also see an event category column, which also shows up in the event properties.

Figure 15-3   Event listing

This is a value that is specific to the event source. The event category is a numeric value that has a text string associated with that category value. Microsoft creates their own event categories for their services and applications. Microsoft also exposes an application programming interface (API) that developers can use to write event log entries. Each developer can create their own event categories that go with their application(s).

As noted earlier, the event log is stored in XML. This is a self-describing data format. Similar to Hypertext Markup Language (HTML), which inherits from it, XML uses tags to indicate a piece of data. The "name" of the data is in the tag, describing the data, while the data value is between the tags. It would look something like this: <name>Ric Messier</name>. This indicates there is a name value that would show up between the two tags. The <name> tag starts the value while </name> closes it. Each event has an XML representation, which you can see by looking at the Details tab in the event specifics shown when you select an event from the list of events. You can also get a friendly view, which doesn't have all the tags the XML view has. The XML view can make it harder to read if you are less familiar with parsing XML (meaning, you don't quickly and easily recognize what's in the tag as the name of the variable when the content of the variable is between the tags). Figure 15-4 shows the XML view of an event.

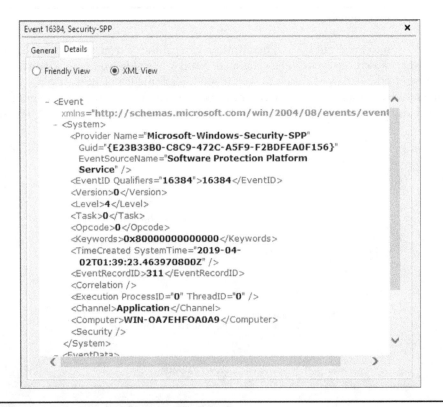

Figure 15-4   XML view of the Event Details dialog box

The Windows Event Viewer has two sections where you can find logs. The first section is Windows Logs, which presents the five logs previously listed (Application, Security, Setup, and System). The second section is the Application logs. While Microsoft is one vendor that has logs under the Application logs, there are other vendors' logs there as well. Application logs can be generated by any application. Creating an application log requires creating the provider, meaning you are telling Windows who the vendor is and what the name of the log is. This will tell Windows what values to put in place when the XML branches are created. In turn, when the Event Viewer shows the logs, it will know how to represent the overall data tree. Since vendors are responsible for these logs, they will have different event IDs than those from the Windows logs. Additionally, they will have different event categories.

The Event Viewer provides the means to query the entire corpus of event entries. You can also save event entries using the Event Viewer. From a log management perspective, it is a good tool. However, you may want to use the command line to issue queries. The utility wevtutil is good for this purpose. For instance, you can get a list of all the event logs available using the command **wevtutil enum-logs**. You can also use wevtutil to query the event logs. You would do so by using an XPath query. XPath is a representation of XML in a tree rather than just a block of tagged text. Once the XML is in a tree view, you can see paths through the branches of the tree. You can follow these branches to get to data stored in the tree. Using this approach to looking for data is an XPath query.

You can also search programmatically for events. This can be done using a language like C# through the .NET Framework, which has methods for interfacing with the event log. You can also use PowerShell to look for events. The cmdlet Get-EventLog is used to get events from the event logs. Figure 15-5 shows the use of the Get-EventLog cmdlet to get the list of logs that are available on the system and then to pull all the events from the Security log. These are straightforward examples, but Get-EventLog has additional capabilities. These include looking for a particular string using -Message or looking for all events from a single source using the -Source parameter.

Just as with any other cmdlet, Get-EventLog could be put into a PowerShell script where the results could be manipulated as needed to look for details or generate reports, for instance. You can also manipulate the event log in other ways. You could write an event using PowerShell and also create a new event log. This means if you are writing a PowerShell script, you can generate log messages to indicate any success or failure that you need to keep track of. This is a great way of generating messages for debugging purposes without cluttering up the expected output so you can more easily distinguish between the two.

Network Device Logs

Many network devices are capable of generating logs. Routers, for instance, can generate log messages for configuration events or for a number of other events that can be configured. Switches, if they are meant for the enterprise (meaning they can be managed through the use of either a web interface, an application specific to the switch, or a command-line interface), also can generate log messages. Other network devices, like firewalls and intrusion detection systems (IDSs), are designed to generate log messages

```
Administrator: Windows PowerShell                                        —    □    ×

PS C:\Users\Administrator> get-eventlog -list

  Max(K) Retain OverflowAction       Entries Log
  ------ ------ -------------        ------- ---
  20,480     -1 DoNotOverwrite           195 Application
  20,480      0 OverwriteAsNeeded          0 HardwareEvents
     512      7 OverwriteOlder             0 Internet Explorer
  20,480      0 OverwriteAsNeeded          0 Key Management Service
     512      7 OverwriteOlder               Parameters
  20,480      0 OverwriteAsNeeded      1,075 Security
     512      7 OverwriteOlder               State
  20,480      0 OverwriteAsNeeded        783 System
  15,360      0 OverwriteAsNeeded         46 Windows PowerShell


PS C:\Users\Administrator> get-eventlog -logname Security

  Index Time          EntryType   Source              InstanceID Message
  ----- ----          ---------   ------              ---------- -------
   1075 Mar 31 15:00   SuccessA... Microsoft-Windows...       4672 Special privileges assigned to new logon....
   1074 Mar 31 15:00   SuccessA... Microsoft-Windows...       4624 An account was successfully logged on....
   1073 Mar 31 15:00   SuccessA... Microsoft-Windows...       4672 Special privileges assigned to new logon....
   1072 Mar 31 15:00   SuccessA... Microsoft-Windows...       4624 An account was successfully logged on....
   1071 Mar 31 14:59   SuccessA... Microsoft-Windows...       4634 An account was logged off....
   1070 Mar 31 14:59   SuccessA... Microsoft-Windows...       4672 Special privileges assigned to new logon....
   1069 Mar 31 14:59   SuccessA... Microsoft-Windows...       4624 An account was successfully logged on....
   1068 Mar 31 14:59   SuccessA... Microsoft-Windows...       4648 A logon was attempted using explicit credential...
   1067 Mar 31 14:59   SuccessA... Microsoft-Windows...       4776 The computer attempted to validate the credenti...
   1066 Mar 31 14:59   SuccessA... Microsoft-Windows...       4672 Special privileges assigned to new logon....
   1065 Mar 31 14:59   SuccessA... Microsoft-Windows...       4624 An account was successfully logged on....
   1064 Mar 31 14:59   SuccessA... Microsoft-Windows...       4624 An account was successfully logged on....
   1063 Mar 31 14:59   SuccessA... Microsoft-Windows...       4672 Special privileges assigned to new logon....
   1062 Mar 31 14:59   SuccessA... Microsoft-Windows...       4776 The computer attempted to validate the credenti...
   1061 Mar 31 14:49   SuccessA... Microsoft-Windows...       4634 An account was logged off....
   1060 Mar 31 14:40   SuccessA... Microsoft-Windows...       4672 Special privileges assigned to new logon....
   1059 Mar 31 14:40   SuccessA... Microsoft-Windows...       4624 An account was successfully logged on....
   1058 Mar 31 14:40   SuccessA... Microsoft-Windows...       4672 Special privileges assigned to new logon....
   1057 Mar 31 14:40   SuccessA... Microsoft-Windows...       4624 An account was successfully logged on....
   1056 Mar 31 14:30   SuccessA... Microsoft-Windows...       4672 Special privileges assigned to new logon....
   1055 Mar 31 14:30   SuccessA... Microsoft-Windows...       4624 An account was successfully logged on....
   1054 Mar 31 14:30   SuccessA... Microsoft-Windows...       4672 Special privileges assigned to new logon....
   1053 Mar 31 14:30   SuccessA... Microsoft-Windows...       4624 An account was successfully logged on....
   1052 Mar 31 14:20   SuccessA... Microsoft-Windows...       4672 Special privileges assigned to new logon....
   1051 Mar 31 14:20   SuccessA... Microsoft-Windows...       4624 An account was successfully logged on....
   1050 Mar 31 14:18   SuccessA... Microsoft-Windows...       4672 Special privileges assigned to new logon....
   1049 Mar 31 14:18   SuccessA... Microsoft-Windows...       4624 An account was successfully logged on....
   1048 Mar 31 14:10   SuccessA... Microsoft-Windows...       4672 Special privileges assigned to new logon....
   1047 Mar 31 14:10   SuccessA... Microsoft-Windows...       4624 An account was successfully logged on....
   1046 Mar 31 14:09   SuccessA... Microsoft-Windows...       4672 Special privileges assigned to new logon....
   1045 Mar 31 14:09   SuccessA... Microsoft-Windows...       4624 An account was successfully logged on....
```

Figure 15-5   PowerShell Get-EventLog

based on the rules that are configured on those devices. Keeping track of all of this information is essential. When it comes to identifying issues in the network, these logs are indispensible, which means the devices need to be configured correctly to generate the right log messages. As an example, if a firewall starts dropping packets that are passing through the firewall, those drops are not logged if you have configured the firewall to just drop the packets or reject them silently. In that scenario, if network communications start behaving incorrectly, you will have no idea what is going on, whereas if you had configured the firewall to logs the packet drops, you would have a trail to follow to identify the issue. This is the sort of event that can highlight the essential nature of logging and the appropriate management of those logs.

One problem with network devices is they may not have persistent storage. If a device like a router, for instance, is restarted, any log entries on the device will be wiped. This is one reason to configure network devices to log their messages to a central log host that has persistent storage. On a Cisco router, for example, you can send syslog messages to a host with the command **logging 192.168.86.57**. The following code shows an example of the types of messages you would see from a Cisco router. These were generated after an initial configuration. In this case, there is nothing of particular note, though during normal operation, seeing an interface set its state to down would be of some concern.

```
*Mar 31 18:36:22.027: %IFMGR-7-NO_IFINDEX_FILE: Unable to open nvram:/ifIndex-table No
such file or directory
*Mar 31 18:36:22.171: %DEC21140-1-INITFAIL: Unsupported PHY brand timed out, csr5=0x0
*Mar 31 18:36:24.291: %ATA-6-ATA_STATUS_TIMEOUT: Timeout occurred while querying the
status of ATA device.
*Mar 31 18:36:28.295: %ATA-6-ATA_STATUS_TIMEOUT: Timeout occurred while querying the
status of ATA device.
*Mar 31 18:36:33.959: %LINK-3-UPDOWN: Interface FastEthernet0/0, changed state to up
*Mar 31 18:36:34.079: %SYS-6-STARTUP_CONFIG_IGNORED: System startup configuration is
ignored based on the configuration register setting.
*Mar 31 18:36:34.959: %LINEPROTO-5-UPDOWN: Line protocol on Interface FastEthernet0/0,
changed state to down
*Mar 31 18:38:19.319: %SHELF-6-HELLO_PROCESS_START: Shelf hello process has started.
*Mar 31 18:38:19.567: %SYS-5-CONFIG_I: Configured from console by console
```

Firewall logs may also yield a lot of useful information, though some firewalls provide more readable logs than others. The following code contains some examples of log messages from a Linux firewall using iptables. If you look closely at them, you can understand what they say, though they can be intimidating if you have never seen anything like them before. The log messages show the input interface name, ens160, but there is no output interface name. The reason is that this is a single-interface system and the rule that triggered this entry specifies to drop any message coming into that one interface on TCP port 1500. You can see the source and destination IP addresses as well as the MAC address. The IP header details are presented, including the Time To Live (TTL) field, the IP ID field, the length (LEN), and type of service (TOS). You'll also see the protocol used, TCP. Both the source port and the destination port are shown. You'll see the destination port is 1500, which is the port mentioned in the rule.

```
Mar 31 19:07:59 alfmushpie kernel: [ 4879.900016] IN=ens160 OUT= MAC=00:0c:29:70:63:27
:f0:18:98:0c:34:69:08:00 SRC=192.168.86.24 DST=192.168.86.40 LEN=64 TOS=0x00 PREC=0x00
TTL=64 ID=0 DF PROTO=TCP SPT=56343 DPT=1500 WINDOW=65535 RES=0x00 SYN URGP=0
Mar 31 19:08:02 alfmushpie kernel: [ 4883.115580] IN=ens160 OUT= MAC=00:0c:29:70:63:27
:f0:18:98:0c:34:69:08:00 SRC=192.168.86.24 DST=192.168.86.40 LEN=48 TOS=0x00 PREC=0x00
TTL=64 ID=0 DF PROTO=TCP SPT=56343 DPT=1500 WINDOW=65535 RES=0x00 SYN URGP=0
Mar 31 19:08:09 alfmushpie kernel: [ 4889.530338] IN=ens160 OUT= MAC=00:0c:29:70:63:27
:f0:18:98:0c:34:69:08:00 SRC=192.168.86.24 DST=192.168.86.40 LEN=48 TOS=0x00 PREC=0x00
TTL=64 ID=0 DF PROTO=TCP SPT=56343 DPT=1500 WINDOW=65535 RES=0x00 SYN URGP=0
Mar 31 19:08:15 alfmushpie kernel: [ 4895.965310] IN=ens160 OUT= MAC=00:0c:29:70:63:27
:f0:18:98:0c:34:69:08:00 SRC=192.168.86.24 DST=192.168.86.40 LEN=48 TOS=0x00 PREC=0x00
TTL=64 ID=0 DF PROTO=TCP SPT=56343 DPT=1500 WINDOW=65535 RES=0x00 SYN URGP=0
```

Similarly, intrusion detection systems can be configured to provide useful information, especially when it comes to identifying potential incidents on the network. The same packets that generated the preceding firewall log messages also generated the following log messages from an IDS. The IDS in this case is Suricata, which uses the same rulesets as Snort, a very common IDS that has been around for a couple of decades now. Suricata is meant to be a high-performance IDS. The particular rule that generated the first few log messages generates an alert when there are connections to TCP port 1500. The other messages suggest that there were outbound connections that the Snort rule believes are related to package management connections. It's unlikely this alert would require follow-up, but it may be useful to keep track of in case it is related to some other traffic.

```
03/31/2019-19:15:10.356267  [**] [1:1000001:1] connection to port 1500 [**]
[Classification: (null)] [Priority: 3] {TCP} 192.168.86.24:56453 -> 192.168.86.40:1500
03/31/2019-19:15:42.208230  [**] [1:1000001:1] connection to port 1500 [**]
[Classification: (null)] [Priority: 3] {TCP} 192.168.86.24:56461 -> 192.168.86.40:1500
03/31/2019-19:16:39.974587  [**] [1:1000001:1] connection to port 1500 [**]
[Classification: (null)] [Priority: 3] {TCP} 192.168.86.24:56471 -> 192.168.86.40:1500
```

Network Infrastructure Logs

There are a couple of logs that are essential to track but are sometimes overlooked. The first is the log from a Dynamic Host Configuration Protocol (DHCP) server. This server logs DHCP requests and reservations. These logs may be valuable for multiple reasons. One reason they are essential is that when an incident happens, you will have logs from some of your network devices with IP addresses. In the case of dynamic network addresses, they may change in a short period of time, especially if you have a mobile workforce taking devices like laptops from one network segment to another throughout the day. Since the addresses may be changing regularly, identifying the source of network traffic from just the IP address may be difficult. DHCP logs can help you correlate potentially malicious network traffic with the source of that traffic.

Another type of network infrastructure to maintain logs from is the Domain Name System (DNS) server. Logs from DNS servers will tell you hostnames that are resolved. This is probably obvious. What may be less obvious is what information you can get from that. First, you can catch lookup requests for mistyped domains. One attack type is called typosquatting, where an attacker grabs a domain name that could result from a mistype and loads the web server for that domain up with malicious code while simultaneously looking like the legitimate site. Sometimes large companies will buy up or have a brand protection company register these typo domains, as in the case of mircosoft.com. However, not all typos are known, which means a lot of users who mistype may be landing at sites they didn't intend to go to. Having a record of these typo domains and who requested the lookup may help track down a so-called "patient zero" from an infection.

Another reason DNS server logs are useful is that botnets sometimes work based on hostnames since the underlying systems may revolve a lot. This means they have DNS records where the IP address associated with a hostname changes. When there are DNS requests, you can, again, track down potential points of infection. Hosts looking up known rogue hostnames are probably infected, and those requesting hosts should be investigated.

Application Logs

As previously discussed, applications can also generate logs. In some cases, these logs are entirely under the control of the application developer. This includes the location and format of the log files. Of course, application developers can make use of system facilities like syslog or the Windows Event Logs. Figure 15-6 shows one of the application logs

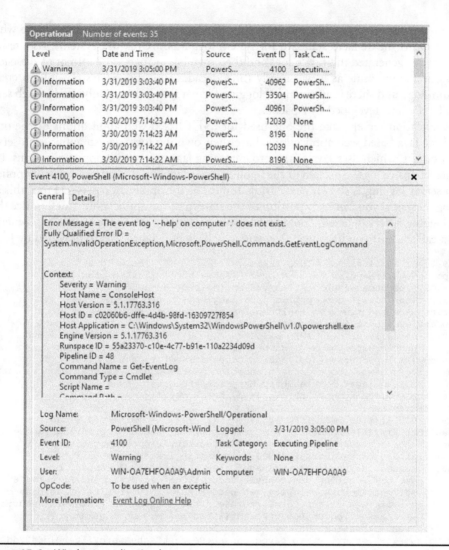

Figure 15-6 Windows application logs

from a Windows system. This is the Operational log from PowerShell, which does not show up as a system log because it's not part of the core operating system. Instead, it's an application. Along with the Operational log for PowerShell, there is also an Admin log. This is common for Windows application logs—certainly for applications that are developed by Microsoft, though it may also be the case for other application developers as well.

Other applications may generate completely different log files. As an example, web servers may have their own log files that don't use syslog or the Windows Event Logs. This is, in part, a result of one of the first web servers, developed at the National Center for Supercomputing Applications (NCSA). This server was developed at a time when syslog wasn't the de facto standard for system logging on Unix-like systems. As a result, web servers generated their own logs and their own log formats. The format of these logs is essentially the same as it was nearly three decades ago, though it's possible to create custom logs, and there is an extended logging format that is commonly used in web servers like the one developed by Apache.

Application servers, like the one used for .NET-based web applications or the ones used for Java-based web applications, have their own log formats. An application server like Tomcat, which uses Java as the programming language to develop applications, can create extensive logs, especially if the application is logging. An example of Java application server logging is shown next, using Tomcat as the application server. From this set of log messages, you can see a portion of the startup of the application. You'll notice that the logging is very detailed. You may have run across Java applications that fail, generating a call stack. If you have seen this, you may have noticed the detail provided by Java.

```
2019-04-01 18:34:05.960  INFO 32614 --- [          main] o.s.b.a.e.mvc.
EndpointHandlerMapping    : Mapped "{[/health || /health.json],meth
ods=[GET],produces=[application/vnd.spring-boot.actuator.v1+json ||
application/json]}" onto public java.lang.Object org.springframework.
boot.actuate.endpoint.mvc.HealthMvcEndpoint.invoke(javax.servlet.http.
HttpServletRequest,java.security.Principal)
2019-04-01 18:34:05.961  INFO 32614 --- [          main] o.s.b.a.e.mvc.
EndpointHandlerMapping    : Mapped "{[/heapdump || /heapdump.json],
methods=[GET],produces=[application/octet-stream]}" onto public void
org.springframework.boot.actuate.endpoint.mvc.HeapdumpMvcEndpoint.
invoke(boolean,javax.servlet.http.HttpServletRequest,javax.servlet.
http.HttpServletResponse) throws java.io.IOException,javax.servlet.
ServletException
2019-04-01 18:34:05.963  INFO 32614 --- [          main] o.s.s.web.
DefaultSecurityFilterChain    : Creating filter chain: org.springframework.
boot.actuate.autoconfigure.ManagementWebSecurityAutoConfiguration$LazyE
ndpointPathRequestMatcher@32b1e906, [org.springframework.security.web.
context.request.async.WebAsyncManagerIntegrationFilter@33e6bd36, org.
springframework.security.web.context.SecurityContextPersistenceFilter@476937
8c, org.springframework.security.web.header.HeaderWriterFilter@22ab1b8a, org.
springframework.web.filter.CorsFilter@6e1d9b32, org.springframework.security.
web.authentication.logout.LogoutFilter@60b4c754, org.springframework.
security.web.authentication.www.BasicAuthenticationFilter@73e25780, org.
springframework.security.web.savedrequest.RequestCacheAwareFilter@1d6a22dd,
org.springframework.security.web.servletapi.SecurityContextHolderAwareRequest
Filter@67671db1, org.springframework.security.web.authentication.AnonymousAut
henticationFilter@2db6ba81, org.springframework.security.web.session.SessionM
anagementFilter@320770d7, org.springframework.security.web.access.ExceptionTr
anslationFilter@2e7e84f8, org.springframework.security.web.access.intercept.
FilterSecurityInterceptor@75784062]
2019-04-01 18:34:06.115  INFO 32614 --- [          main] s.w.s.m.m.a.Reques
tMappingHandlerAdapter : Looking for @ControllerAdvice: org.springframework.
boot.context.embedded.AnnotationConfigEmbeddedWebApplicationContext@6b57696f:
startup date [Mon Apr 01 18:33:52 MDT 2019]; root of context hierarchy
2019-04-01 18:34:06.766  INFO 32614 --- [          main] o.s.j.e.a.Annotatio
nMBeanExporter    : Registering beans for JMX exposure on startup
2019-04-01 18:34:06.780  INFO 32614 --- [          main] o.s.c.support.
DefaultLifecycleProcessor  : Starting beans in phase 0
2019-04-01 18:34:06.935  INFO 32614 --- [          main] s.b.c.e.t.TomcatEmb
eddedServletContainer : Tomcat started on port(s): 8080 (http)
```

These application logs are not only extensive but, as already noted, they don't often use the system logging mechanism. This means you will have a large amount of log messages sitting around on disk. This is problematic, especially as web servers and web application servers may be common points of attack. Applications and application frameworks have a long history of vulnerabilities. This means these logs can be important artifacts for identifying not only failures or errors in the application but also potential breach incidents.

NOTE Perhaps most notoriously, the enormous Experian breach from 2017 was a result of a vulnerability in an underlying Java framework named Struts from the Apache Foundation. Struts is one of several very common application frameworks that make the life of application developers easier, while simultaneously exposing enterprises to significant potential for breach if they are not keeping up with patches for these frameworks and the application servers that support them.

Security Information and Event Manager

You have a number of logs stored all over the place, from firewalls or intrusion detection systems or application servers. What are you going to do with all of them? One thing you can do is use a log harvester. There are several log harvesters available, some of which are a part of larger packages, which we will get into shortly. There are also some that are standalone applications. They can be configured to consume log files that are not part of the syslog system on a Linux system, for instance. One example of these standalone log harvesters is NXLog. You can see a fragment of an NXLog configuration file in the following code. This configuration establishes listeners for syslog on both UDP and TCP. Additionally, there is a configuration setting to read in a Tomcat log. Once the logs have been consumed, they could be written out to a single log file. You'll see the output configuration as well.

```
<Input in1>
    Module      im_udp
    Port        514
    Exec        parse_syslog_bsd();
</Input>

<Input in2>
    Module      im_tcp
    Port        514
</Input>

<Output fileout1>
    Module    om_file
    File      "/var/log/nxlog/logmsg.txt"
    Exec      if $Message =~ /error/ $SeverityValue = syslog_severity_value("error");
    Exec      to_syslog_bsd();
</Output>

<Output fileout2>
    Module    om_file
    File      "/var/log/nxlog/logmsg2.txt"
</Output>
```

Beyond the output settings, you would need to set up a route. This maps the input configuration to the output configuration. What you see in the preceding example are outputs to files, but you can also use NXLog to output to a syslog server. This means you can continue to use a centralized syslog server for all of your log aggregation even for logs that are not using syslog from the application. Everything here has been on a Linux system, but NXLog also works on Windows systems. It can be used to convert Windows Event Log messages to syslog and store them in a central server.

This, though, is just a starting point. Beyond NXLog are security information and event managers (SIEMs). These tools can also be used to aggregate logs from multiple sources. As an example, we could take everything we have gathered from NXLog, including web server logs and web application server logs, and send them to a syslog server hosted inside a SIEM. One product that is often used as a SIEM is Splunk. Splunk by itself is not a SIEM but we can add features to it to create the full SIEM functionality. We can configure Splunk to listen for syslog messages. You can see part of the configuration for establishing a syslog listener through Splunk in Figure 15-7. Splunk comes with a large number of input sources, though not all of them have to be network listeners. We can also configure Splunk to directly ingest files. Splunk knows how to parse different log file types that fall into multiple categories.

The value of a tool like Splunk, though, is not just as a log aggregator. Beyond ingesting logs and other information sources, Splunk can be used to search across all of the information sources to identify similar data points. This is a significant value when you are chasing down a problem. When you are looking for information, you

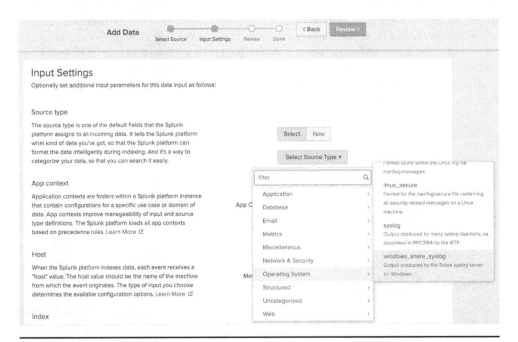

Figure 15-7 Splunk listener

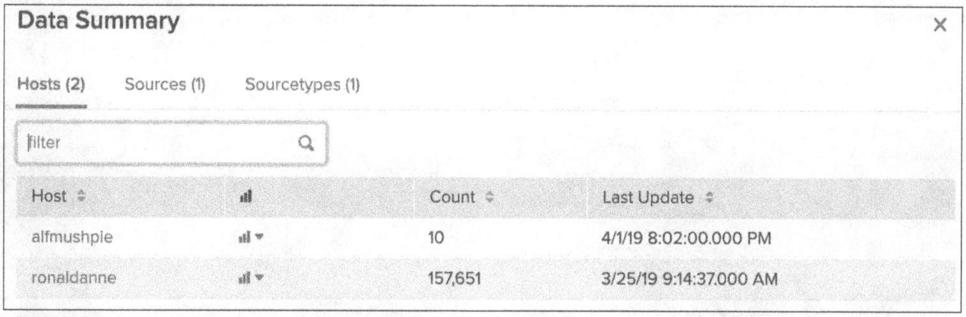

Figure 15-8 Splunk event sources

can start with data sources. Opening Search & Reporting in Splunk will give you a list of your hosts, as you can see in Figure 15-8. Other tabs in that dialog box are Sources and Sourcetypes. Here, everything is coming through a syslog listener that other Linux systems are sending messages to. To get the complete list of all the events in the database, we're going to go to the source and select the TCP listener that was configured. By default, when you select the source of your data, you get the last 24 hours' worth of events. In this case, the majority of events come from a week ago because the systems in question have been down for most of that week. In order to see all the events to drill into, we need to select a broader time period. This is something Splunk may prompt you to do if it doesn't find any events in the time period presented.

Once we have the list of all the events shown, Splunk will do some work for us. In Figure 15-9, you can see on the left a list of Interesting Fields Splunk has identified. One of those fields is the process field. As these are all syslog messages, the process is included in the message. Clicking the process link in the left column pops open the list of all the processes that have event messages associated with them, as shown on the right in Figure 15-9. The top application is Kibana, followed by Cron. Cron is a scheduling service that runs jobs automatically. This may include log rotation or basic system checks. Kibana, on the other hand, is a process used to visualize data. It is similar to the data visualization we have been looking at in Splunk.

Splunk didn't start life as a SIEM and it isn't always used like one today, though it could be. Another application that is commonly referred to as a SIEM is Elastic Stack, formerly called ELK for Elasticsearch, Logstash, and Kibana. These are the three services that come together to provide the same sort of services as Splunk. Similar to Splunk, there is a free version. Splunk offers a community version of their Enterprise product, while Elastic Stack is fully open source, meaning it can be downloaded and installed for your use. Elastic Stack can be used to collect data from multiple sources. Elastic Stack makes use of agents for tasks like file monitoring. It can also use an agent for auditing. These agents would be configured on local systems and then communicate back with the Elastic Stack server. Just like Splunk, all of your data is searchable and can be correlated across multiple systems.

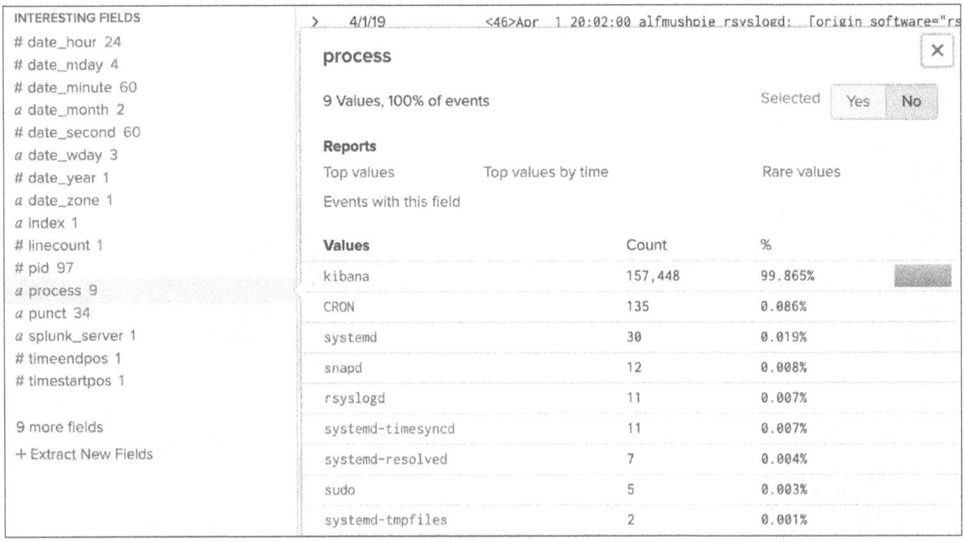

Figure 15-9   Splunk-identified Interesting Fields

There are multiple commercial offerings of SIEMs in addition to the two we've looked at here, which can be installed and used for free. Beyond just searching for data, though, a major advantage to using a SIEM is alerting. These tools can be used to create alerts from the disparate data sources. This is the sort of functionality you would not get from a tool that uses a single source. The correlation capabilities are essential to a security operations program. There are many other features that are useful to a security operations program, including compliance reports and integration with a ticketing system. A full discussion of features of different SIEMs would take a lot of space and is beyond the scope of this book, but from the standpoint of using a SIEM for log management and log handling, the important takeaway should be that it enables you to aggregate and correlate logs from multiple sources.

Chapter Review

Log management is an essential task of any information technology team and, more importantly, of a security operations program. There are many reasons why log management is essential. One reason is that logs are initially stored on individual systems. These logs could be tampered with by an attacker or lost. A better approach to ensure the logs are protected and stored over a long period of time is to aggregate the logs at a central log host. This can help with log retention requirements from regulations or certifications for organizations.

There are multiple types of logs that you may need to be familiar with. First is syslog. This is a log format that has been around since the 1980s, developed as part of the Sendmail mailer program. It describes both facilities and severities to help categorize the different log messages. A syslog server will generally allow you to vector log messages to specific locations based on a combination of severity and facility. Syslog defines 24 facilities, including kern, mail, auth, syslog, security, and eight user facilities. There are eight severities, from debug and informational at the least severe end of the spectrum, up to critical, alert, and emergency at the other end.

Windows Event Logs are currently stored in an XML format, which was not always the case; Windows Event Logs have existed since Windows NT was released in 1993. While they are stored in XML format, they are viewed in lists of events in plaintext. One reason they are stored in XML is because each event log entry is a complex data type including the event ID and the event category. These are numeric values that map to text strings that are human readable. Just like syslog, each event log entry in Windows gets a severity value.

Windows Event Logs can be searched both through the Windows Event Viewer and via the command line. Using the wevtutil utility, you can issue XPath queries to look for Windows Event Logs. Beyond this command-line utility, though, you can also search for and interact with Windows Event Logs programmatically. There are .NET methods available for interacting with the Windows Event Logs in languages like C#. Additionally, you can use a language like PowerShell to query the Windows Event Logs through the use of cmdlets.

Not all applications use the system logging facilities. Some applications generate their own logs. This may be a web server or a web application server, for instance. These logs, though, cannot be aggregated as easily since they are not using system logging facilities. You can use a log harvester such as Graylog or NXLog to collect logs from different sources and write them out to a single file or forward them off to a listener.

A more advanced tool for log aggregation is the security information and event manager (SIEM). This sort of tool can be used to not only aggregate logs but also search through all of the log sources. A SIEM can apply a level of intelligence to the collected logs that is harder to achieve with single-source tools. Beyond searching for data from all the log sources, a SIEM can be configured to generate alerts. These alerts could be used for the purpose of monitoring system health or they could be used for security events, which may become incidents that need to be investigated.

Questions

1. In the following syslog log entry, what is the system name?

```
Apr  1 18:55:59 alfmushpie nxlog[32132]: 2019-04-01 18:55:59 ERROR
Another instance is already running (pid 31893);Resource temporarily
unavailable
```

   A. nxlogd

   B. It's not listed.

   C. alfmushpie

   D. nxlog

2. In the following log entry, what is the process ID?

```
Apr  1 18:50:57 alfmushpie systemd-resolved[421]: Server returned error
NXDOMAIN, mitigating potential DNS violation DVE-2018-0001, retrying
transaction with reduced feature level UDP.
```

   A. alfmushpie

   B. systemd-resolved

   C. 0001

   D. 421

3. What is the data representation format used for Windows Event Logs?

   A. YAML

   B. XML

   C. Binary

   D. XPath

4. Which of these is not under Windows Logs in the Event Viewer?

   A. Hardware

   B. System

   C. Application

   D. Security

5. Which of these is not an advantage of a SIEM over a log harvester?

   A. Syslog listener

   B. Correlation

   C. Searching

   D. Alerting

6. What is an event ID used for in Windows Event Logs?

   A. Identifying the log entry in the list

   B. Identifying what happened

   C. Naming the event

   D. Searching for the event

7. Based on what you see in this log, what type of log would you say this is?

```
/var/log/syslog:Mar 31 19:16:43 alfmushpie kernel: [ 5403.613697]
IN=ens160 OUT= MAC=00:0c:29:70:63:27:f0:18:98:0c:34:69:08:00
SRC=192.168.86.24 DST=192.168.86.40 LEN=64 TOS=0x00 PREC=0x00 TTL=64
ID=0 DF PROTO=TCP SPT=56471 DPT=1500 WINDOW=65535 RES=0x00 SYN URGP=0
```

   A. IDS log

   B. System log

   C. Firewall log

   D. SIEM log

8. What is the highest severity provided by syslog?

   A. Critical

   B. High

   C. Severe

   D. Emergency

9. What is the other data type identified by the syslog specification besides severity that allows messages to be categorized?

   A. Facility

   B. Event ID

   C. Source

   D. Task category

10. Which of these tools would likely be most valuable to you if you were working in security operations?

   A. Windows Event Viewer

   B. Syslog

   C. SIEM

   D. Log harvester

Answers

1. C. The format for a syslog message is the date and time followed by the system name, the process name, and process ID. After that is the message generated by the application. Nxlog is the name of the process in this log entry.

2. D. A process ID is a numeric value identifying a specific process from the process table. The process ID will be in square brackets, [], after the name of the process. 421 is the value in square brackets after the process name. The process name, the name of the program that was run to create the process, is systemd-resolved. Alfmushpie is the system name. 0001 is a numeric value from the application message.

3. B. Windows Event Logs are kept in .evtx files. The x in this case indicates the storage is XML. While the file may be binary in nature, the data representation format is XML. YAML is also a data representation format, but it is not used by the Windows Event Logs. XPath is a way of querying these event logs.

4. A. There is no Hardware log under Windows Logs in the Event Viewer. In addition to Setup, the logs Security, Application, and System are all under Windows Logs. These are system-related logs.

5. A. Both log harvesters and SIEMs can have syslog listeners. Only a SIEM, though, offers alerting, correlation, and searching as features within the application itself, without using additional tools or utilities.

6. **B.** An event ID in the Windows Event Logs is used to identify what happened. Each event ID corresponds to a string that provides details about what happened to generate the log entry. The event ID is not a value that indicates which entry in a list of entries the event is. The event ID is a numeric value, so it wouldn't be used to name the event. While you may be able to search for these event IDs, that's not what they are used for.

7. **C.** While the name of the file is syslog, it's just a file that collects a variety of the different facilities. This is a log entry generated from the iptables firewall in Linux. You can see the different header fields from the packet suggesting it's a log of a network message. An IDS log would generally include a text string for a message indicating what was identified.

8. **D.** While critical is one of the severities defined by syslog, emergency is higher. Neither of the other two answers are identified/named severities in syslog.

9. **A.** Syslog identifies facility and severity as ways to categorize log data. The other fields are from the Windows Event Logs.

10. **C.** While all of these tools would be of value to you in security operations, the SIEM would likely be the most valuable because it can correlate data and also generate alerts that can help identify security events/incidents.

## CHAPTER 16

Internet of Things (IoT) and Embedded Devices

In this chapter, you will learn:

- What is the IoT
- Which devices are considered IoT devices
- Which protocols are used for the IoT
- IoT security considerations and protections

You likely have heard about the Internet of Things (IoT). It's a buzzword that shows up in the news, especially if the news you are reading includes coverage of technology. Certainly, discussion of the IoT has shown up in security-related news. Much like the so-called dark web, the IoT is an overlay network on top of the Internet. The dark web is a subset of devices that are connected by way of the Internet and transmit messages to one another using the same protocols that the Internet uses, but they offer services that are only available through the use of direct connections to one another. These connections are tunneled, meaning they are encapsulated inside of other protocols, and encrypted. If you know how to "talk to" these special systems, you can join the dark web. The same is essentially true of the IoT. It is a subset of Internet-connected devices that communicate using the same protocols as other Internet-connected systems use.

Typically, IoT devices are limited in some way. They are often resource constrained and don't have the same means of interacting with users that general-purpose computing devices have. This lack of interactivity is one reason compromises of these devices are difficult to detect; users have no good way of detecting that an IoT device has been compromised as long as the essential function of the device is retained.

Because of their limited nature, IoT devices may require special protection or even isolation. The capability to easily identify these devices is also helpful when trying to secure them. There are so many different types of IoT devices, and often when you are looking at an enterprise network, you may not even be aware of which IoT devices are being used or where they are located. Fortunately, there are websites that are designed to help you locate and keep track of the different embedded devices that are Internet-connected.

The Internet of Things

Like so many current technologies, the idea of the IoT has been around for decades. The IoT is the collection of devices around the world that are essentially "dumb" devices, meaning they probably have limited processing power because they are designed to perform a small number of specific functions. They also have nonstandard interfaces, meaning you probably don't interact with them via a keyboard or a pointing device. An IoT device may be an embedded device, which would perform a specific function and run a real-time operating system, which is different from a general-purpose, interrupt-driven operating system. As an example of a common IoT device, Figure 16-1 shows a smart thermostat (from Nest). The input "mechanisms" you have are a rotating ring and a center that can be pressed. You make selections by rotating the ring until you are on your choice and then pressing the center. This thermostat is network-connected, as shown by the display of the local weather. The nonstandard interface combined with network connectivity and a special purpose makes this an IoT device.

As you may have read, there are security concerns associated with IoT devices. Some of these devices run Linux as an operating system. This provides the kernel for hardware control, but sometimes there is also a limited shell as an operating environment. An attacker could gain access to a device and get a shell, which would give the attacker a limited command set. This could allow the attacker to install and run additional software. This additional software doesn't need to do much to be dangerous. In the case of Mirai, which was a botnet comprised of IoT devices, all each device needed to do was send network requests. The Mirai botnet was the source of many distributed denial-of-service (DDoS) attacks.

 NOTE Mirai was involved in a number of high-profile attacks, including the attack on the website Krebs on Security, which sustained up to 620 Gbps in attack traffic. Mirai was also responsible for an attack on the French web-hosting provider OVH. This was reported to be 1 Tbps in magnitude.

Mirai was first discovered in 2016 but has remained operational, as the software has been used to create many more networks of bots. In 2018, it was used as the foundation for more than a dozen new botnets. In late 2018, more sophisticated botnet software

Figure 16-1
Smart
thermometer

called Torii was discovered. This botnet client has the capability to achieve persistence in one of six different ways, all related to how Linux typically starts up services. This may be in a startup file like .bashrc. It may also start execution using /etc/init or /etc/inittab. The process may be called System Daemon, which some people, even if they happen to see it, may overlook. Torii makes use of port 443, which is the commonly used port for TLS/SSL. However, Torii does not encrypt any of the traffic. It also wasn't immediately clear what the purpose of Torii was.

These botnets are built around simple software designed to run on limited-capacity devices. In the case of Mirai, for example, the client was developed in the programming language C. These limited-capacity devices are likely to run on processors such as the Advanced RISC Machine (ARM) family. RISC stands for *reduced instruction set computing*, and processors using that style of architecture have a small set of instructions compared with a complex instruction set computing (CISC) processor. A RISC-based processor may require less power than a CISC-based processor because of the simplicity of the instructions. This is one reason why these processors are commonly used in devices like those in the IoT.

IoT Device Types

Home automation is a common application for IoT devices. These are devices that are usually small, have little to no user interface, and perform specific functions. In some cases, there is no need to have an interface at all. Some devices, such as light bulbs, require an external device to provide the interface. The Philips Hue bulbs, for instance, require an app on a device like a smartphone or a tablet. In the case of the Philips Hue bulbs, you need an intermediate device to interact with the bulbs. For example, if the Philips Hue bulbs are paired to an Amazon Echo hub, you would use a device that has the Amazon Alexa app installed, the interface for which is shown in Figure 16-2. There is also a hub provided by Philips (at an additional cost on top of the bulbs) that would require a different app on your device. You might also get a hub like the one from Samsung for their smart devices called SmartThings. Each of these different hubs requires its own corresponding app to manage the bulbs.

Using these hubs, you can control many different types of home automation devices. In some cases, you may require additional support, as is the case with Amazon Alexa. With Alexa, you need to acquire and enable skills for your Echo hub to be able to manage your smart devices. This may be the case for specific functionality that could be in the specific app but not in the Alexa skill. The Philips Hue bulb is said to have more functionality using the Philips app rather than a third-party app like Amazon Alexa. As you can see in Figure 16-2, there is a color setting. Philips says the functionality in the color portion, specifically, is better in their app. Either way, you require multiple pieces of hardware that may use multiple protocols to function.

The communication from the hub to the end device will commonly use either Zigbee or Z-Wave. As introduced in Chapter 14, these are protocols used for personal area networks (PANs). They are designed for communication over short distances using radios that don't require a lot of power. In addition, these devices communicate with the network by using Wi-Fi if they have network functions, such as the Nest thermostat (shown in Figure 16-1), which pulls weather information and also pushes data about

Figure 16-2
Amazon
Alexa app

the device's functions to server infrastructure managed by the manufacturer. In the case of the Nest thermostat, you can see the history of energy usage, or how much time the thermostat caused the overall system to run. Figure 16-3 shows the number of hours the heating system ran during the beginning of March in my home in Colorado. The color orange indicates heating, whereas the display would be blue for air conditioning. This data is meant to provide you insight into how much energy you are consuming, enabling you to manage your energy budget, if needed, by adjusting the temperature settings in your home.

One of the great things about these little devices—thermostats, light bulbs, appliances, security cameras—is the amount of processing power they possess. Not to continue to pick on the Nest thermostat, but its technical specifications are generally available. The Nest thermostat has an ARM A8 processor. These processors are capable of running at a clock speed of 1 GHz, or 1 billion cycles per second. With a RISC-based processor, this may be close to one instruction per second, since the instructions in a RISC processor tend to be simple and fast. All of this is to say that there is plenty of power in these devices, and though the Wi-Fi capabilities are generally older, that's still potentially 50 Mbps of throughput.

The potential of IoT devices is not lost on manufacturers. Figure 16-4 shows a graph of the trajectory of IoT devices according to SRI Business Consulting. We are at a point where we have crossed the border into the physical world.

A good example of crossing over to the physical world is the Tile tracker, which is a Bluetooth-based device allowing people to find missing items. The thing about the Tile,

Figure 16-3
Nest app
showing Energy
History

Technology Roadmap: The Internet of Things

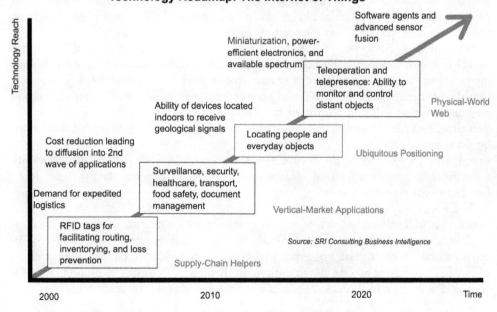

Figure 16-4   IoT device trajectory over time

though, is all the users become a network. If you have the Tile app on your smartphone and you come in range of a Tile, it reports back to the Tile infrastructure so when you go looking for your Tile tracker, you can know exactly where your lost item is, because your Tile tracker is with it.

Medical Devices

Beyond being taken over and used as weapons in botnets, there are other important security issues associated with various types of IoT devices. One type of IoT device that poses very troubling security issues is those that provide medical monitoring functions. Health monitoring devices have become common. These devices may be used, for example, by doctors to monitor their patients' vital signs without the need for the patient to be in the hospital. While these devices have the potential to lower healthcare costs as well as offer more comfort to patients by enabling them to recuperate at home while still being monitored, they have security issues. Knowing that these devices make personal health information (PHI) digitally available to healthcare providers, attackers commonly target them, as well as the systems that store the data within healthcare facilities. PHI may be valuable to attackers as a means to make money through fraud, extortion, or other criminal behavior.

You may even be familiar with some of these health monitoring devices. It's possible you are even wearing one. The Fitbit has, for many years, been a popular health monitoring device. It may not fit in the same category necessarily as a fully networked device like a security camera or a smart thermostat, but it does communicate wirelessly and has some processing power. Fitbits (and similar devices) are generally paired with smartphones or maybe even computers. One thing these devices may be good at is keeping track of where you are or have been. This isn't the same as the breadcrumbs that may be used by some smartphones or mapping applications, but if you are engaged in an activity, your location may be trackable. This means your device, and the servers where data from your device is stored, may have a record of places you have been.

Some of these devices are sometimes referred to as the Internet of Medical Things (IoMT). Remote monitoring is not the only application these devices are good for. They may use local storage in addition to remote storage without the device being network-capable. One example of this is a blood pressure monitoring device. You can get a blood pressure cuff that will pair with your smartphone to keep track of your blood pressure over time. You can see samples of these readings in Figure 16-5. Only one of these readings was taken using the device the screenshot was taken from. All of the others were stored with the provider of the device. This means you can use a device with Bluetooth capabilities to transfer a medical reading to a smartphone that transfers the data to an Internet-based provider.

There are many other medical devices that have varying levels of interactivity with the network, as well as varying levels of sensitivity for the data. There are devices like cochlear implants or pacemakers that may be considered IoT devices. Senior citizens can be monitored to make sure they are not experiencing any difficulties, which can be helpful for cases where they have no one else to look in on them. This is similar to or a replacement for the "I've fallen and I can't get up" device that has been sold for years to seniors.

Figure 16-5
Blood pressure
readings

Transportation Devices

If you own or lease a newer model vehicle, it likely has the capability to connect to a network. This capability may be included, in part, to allow your car to install updates to the software. This software may provide entertainment, safety, or navigation features. Either way, if your car's settings provide a way for your car to connect to a Wi-Fi network, you have a device that runs specific, rather than general-purpose, software and has a network connection. Attacking cars through their computing capability has become popular in the last several years.

Also when it comes to vehicles, you may have run across devices that will scan license plates and read radio frequency identification (RFID) tags. These are devices that sit in toll plazas without attendants, doing their work.

Of course, beyond the vehicles themselves, there are applications in tracking and managing shipping, for instance. When it comes to transportation, we are not limiting ourselves to the wheeled variety. There are also ships. Ships need to be tracked and also shipping containers that ships are carrying. There are likely small tracking devices that are embedded in the ships and the containers so businesses are always aware of their inventory and where it is. You also have planes. While they aren't specifically IoT, there are transponder devices that can be tracked and, when we start talking about searching for and tracking, you will see planes showing up on sites where all of that information could be found.

Sensors

There are countless sensors in the world, some of which have a form of network connections. There was a time when remote weather stations, for example, needed a person to be present to gather and report data collected by the weather sensors. The same was true for devices like strain gauges that are used to determine the structural integrity and reliability of bridges or even amusement park rides. These sensors (and there are thousands and thousands of them still in use around the world) required a human to be present to either connect a device that could read the sensor or to pull the data out of a monitor connected to the sensor. When you can attach a small, networked system that can read the data and send it along, whether over a local area network or even over a cellular data network, it allows for faster, more reliable collection of the data.

Small-form-factor devices like the Raspberry Pi and Arduino are opening the door to sensors that can have cheap computers to connect the sensor to. A device like a Raspberry Pi has general-purpose input/output (GPIO) connectors. This allows anyone to create a hardware device that could connect to the Raspberry Pi. These GPIO connectors can be read programmatically from the Raspberry Pi. There are many libraries and programs available for addressing the GPIO connectors. These inexpensive devices can be placed anywhere in a very small space without keyboard, mouse, or monitor (a mode commonly called "headless"). They can be connected to a physical Ethernet network by cable or they can support a Wi-Fi USB interface. You could also use a cellular connector with it.

In any case, these are essentially IoT devices. They are small, powerful devices that may not have a traditional way of interacting with them, if the keyboard, mouse, and monitor are not connected. These are also devices, like the Nest thermostat discussed earlier, that use ARM processors. They also regularly run Linux, though beyond just the kernel and a very lightweight user environment, like a thermostat, the Raspberry Pi can run a complete Linux distribution like Debian, Ubuntu, or even Kali, a security-oriented Linux distribution.

Finding the "Things"

There are a few helpful websites that keep track of IoT devices. You can search for and locate IoT devices using these sites. While the different sites will enable you to search for IoT devices, the capabilities from one site to another can be very different. It's not the same, for instance, as comparing Google and Bing. First, take a look at Shodan, which is available at www.shodan.io. This site offers free accounts but also has enterprise accounts. Shodan also provides an application programming interface (API) for developers. Shodan works by looking at the headers that are returned from services available on the systems. You can search, based on those headers, for specific devices. As an example, Figure 16-6 shows the results from a search for "raspberry pi" to find Raspberry Pi devices. Again, this relies on a banner or header provided by a service having that text.

You'll see along the left side of Figure 16-6 that the results include a list of countries. There are also lists of services, organizations, and operating systems. Interestingly, in the list of OSs, there are results for Raspberry Pi indicating Windows as the operating system.

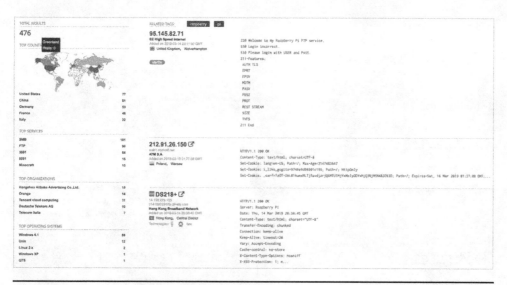

Figure 16-6 Shodan search for Raspberry Pi

This is because Microsoft supports the ARM processor and the Raspberry Pi with an operating system called Windows 10 IoT Core. By clicking one of the items in the lists on the left, you can narrow your search. Clicking Windows, for instance, brings up the devices that are running Windows and also have indicated Raspberry Pi in some response.

In the list of services along the left side of Figure 16-6, one service of particular note is Minecraft. Selecting that shows a list of Raspberry Pi servers running a Minecraft service. You can see a partial list of those servers in Figure 16-7. The query used to get this list is raspberry pi port:"25565". This list provides us a lot of detail. We not only have the IP address, we also have the Internet service provider (ISP), the country the server is located in, and the date the service was added to the Shodan database. Of course, Shodan offers a lot of other capabilities, including the capability to generate maps showing where the systems are believed to be located.

The Shodan search capability is very powerful. What we've seen so far is minimal. You can drill very deep using the search terms. As an example, let's say you want to look for any device running the nginx web server on the subnet 125.69.4.0/24, a randomly selected address for the purposes of this example. You can use the following search: nginx net: "125.69.4.0/24". The results will be specific to your target network. You can also search for vendors, such as Cisco. You could look for Cisco devices in Canada, for instance, using the search term cisco country: "CA".

Other search keywords you could use include the following:

- **city** If you want to look for devices in a specified city
- **geo** If you want to search based on coordinates, such as those for the company you work at or are helping

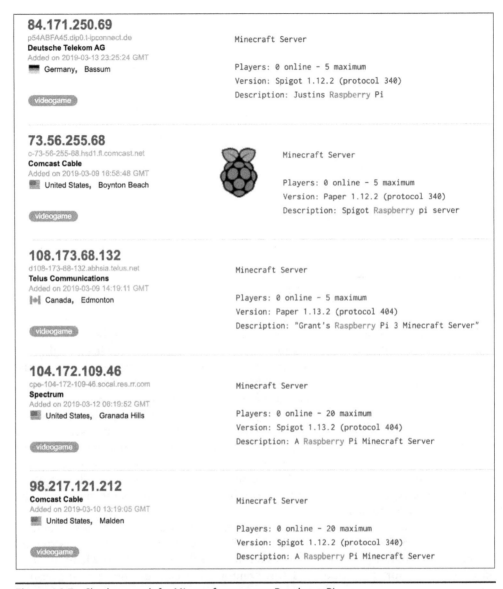

84.171.250.69
p54ABFA45.dip0.t-ipconnect.de
Deutsche Telekom AG
Added on 2019-03-13 23:25:24 GMT
Germany, Bassum

`videogame`

```
Minecraft Server

Players: 0 online - 5 maximum
Version: Spigot 1.12.2 (protocol 340)
Description: Justins Raspberry Pi
```

73.56.255.68
c-73-56-255-68.hsd1.fl.comcast.net
Comcast Cable
Added on 2019-03-09 16:58:48 GMT
United States, Boynton Beach

`videogame`

```
Minecraft Server

Players: 0 online - 5 maximum
Version: Paper 1.12.2 (protocol 340)
Description: Spigot Raspberry pi server
```

108.173.68.132
d108-173-68-132.abhsia.telus.net
Telus Communications
Added on 2019-03-09 14:19:11 GMT
Canada, Edmonton

`videogame`

```
Minecraft Server

Players: 0 online - 5 maximum
Version: Paper 1.13.2 (protocol 404)
Description: "Grant's Raspberry Pi 3 Minecraft Server"
```

104.172.109.46
cpe-104-172-109-46.socal.res.rr.com
Spectrum
Added on 2019-03-12 06:19:52 GMT
United States, Granada Hills

`videogame`

```
Minecraft Server

Players: 0 online - 20 maximum
Version: Spigot 1.13.2 (protocol 404)
Description: A Raspberry Pi Minecraft Server
```

98.217.121.212
Comcast Cable
Added on 2019-03-10 13:19:05 GMT
United States, Malden

`videogame`

```
Minecraft Server

Players: 0 online - 20 maximum
Version: Spigot 1.12.2 (protocol 340)
Description: A Raspberry Pi Minecraft Server
```

Figure 16-7 Shodan search for Minecraft servers on Raspberry Pi

- **hostname** If you know the name of the host you are looking for
- **port** If you are looking for devices that have a specific port open
- **os** If you want to indicate the operating system the device should be running
- **before** or **after** If you want to search within a particular timeframe

Shodan also provides the ability to export your results, which is unusual for a search engine.

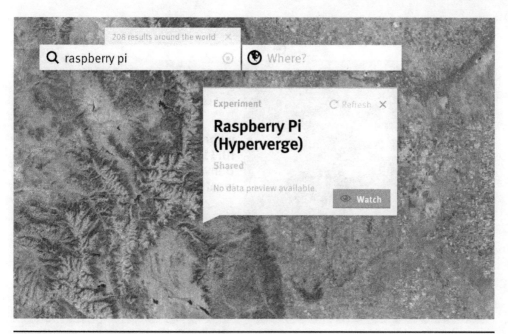

Figure 16-8 Thingful results for Raspberry Pi

Shodan is not the only website to search for IoT devices. You can also use Thingful (www.thingful.net), which also catalogs these devices so they can be identified. Thingful has a less well-defined search syntax compared to Shodan, but you can still search for IoT devices in Thingful. Just enter a value in the search box and, optionally, a location in the location box. If there are things to be found in the database, you will be shown the results on a map, which is quite different from the list of results shown in Shodan. You can see these results in Figure 16-8 as well as the search boxes. You will have to look closely for results, though. What you'll get is a colored dot on the map. To get details, you click the dot, which pops up a box similar to what you see in Figure 16-8.

You can also search for classes of devices. For example, you can find thousands of weather stations. They are all over the world. If you search for "weather" in Thingful, you will get many results. What you get with Thingful in some cases that you may not get with Shodan is actual weather readings. Some weather stations provide readings that you can see in Thingful. However, there are also many other types of devices in the Thingful database, such as webcams. In Figure 16-9, you can see a live weather webcam in downtown Denver, Colorado. This doesn't provide any readings, of course, as it's a webcam. However, you can zoom in on the map and locate exactly where it is.

Since the interface to Thingful is primarily a map rather than just a search box, you can more easily just go exploring. It is a highly interesting collection of data that can be found on this site. As an example, just randomly clicking around turned up some bike-share stations. Global Bike Share at Hiawatha Ave. and 50th St. (as the map in Thingful doesn't provide place names, a search on Google Maps was required to locate this in Minneapolis, MN) has 3 bikes and 12 spaces. It's also interesting to find devices in the

Figure 16-9 Thingful results for weather stations

middle of the ocean. At one point, a while back, I was able to locate the transponder for an airplane by just clicking a dot in the ocean. Recently, I located several buoys in the middle of the ocean, the values from one of which are shown in Figure 16-10.

Thingful does not rely on discovered data. Anyone can submit a public repository to be indexed by Thingful. Once the repository has been submitted and indexed, the data discovered would make its way to the map. The submission form also has a place to submit data samples, described in JavaScript Object Notation (JSON) format.

Figure 16-10
Details from
a buoy in the
Atlantic

Managing the Things

The website www.statista.com estimates there are about 26 billion IoT devices in the world today and that this number is anticipated to rise to about 75 billion by 2025. So, that means roughly tripling the number of devices in about six years. That's an extraordinary rate of increase. With so many devices and the devices having no traditional interface, you may wonder how they are managed and controlled.

First, it's worthwhile to talk about a management architecture. Much like a web application architecture, there may be multiple tiers for the management infrastructure. First, you have the devices themselves. These would connect to an application somewhere, whether it's local to the network where the device is or if it's a server somewhere on the Internet. The controllers the devices connect to could be anywhere. Behind the controller would potentially be a data store. Of course, this sort of design would depend on the needs of the application.

One issue with IoT devices is that they need some sort of controller. This controller, especially in the case of consumer devices, would be on the Internet and the device would be behind a network address translation (NAT) device, sometimes called a firewall even if there are no explicit rules configured. You could make an IoT device on the inside of the network accessible by opening a port translation through the NAT device providing a public IP address and port for the controller on the Internet to connect to. This would rely on users' ability to configure devices they may not be comfortable configuring at all. This requirement would limit the usefulness of these devices and likely restrict their usage. Instead, it's easier for a device on the inside of the network to communicate out to a server. This means when the controller/server communicates back, there is already an open channel. It does require, though, that the inside device be regularly polling out or checking with the controller device on the Internet.

A protocol that is commonly used for transport of data is the Hypertext Transfer Protocol (HTTP). One reason for its common usage is that it's the protocol used to communicate with web servers and therefore is well understood. In order to pass messages from a controller to a device and back, there are two things that are needed on top of the transfer protocol. The first is a way to represent the messages. This may be done using JSON, because it's a self-describing notation. The following code shows an example of what JSON looks like. It uses keys to identify what the data is and then uses values for the actual data. This combination is often called a key-value pair. What you see in this code is a collection of colors and that values can be compound rather than just a single value. Each value could be a nested collection itself, meaning you may have a collection inside of a collection.

```
{
  "colors": [
    {
      "color": "black",
      "category": "hue",
      "type": "primary",
      "code": {
        "rgba": [255,255,255,1],
        "hex": "#000"
      }
    }
```

```
    },
    {
      "color": "white",
      "category": "value",
      "code": {
        "rgba": [0,0,0,1],
        "hex": "#FFF"
      }
    },
    {
      "color": "red",
      "category": "hue",
      "type": "primary",
      "code": {
        "rgba": [255,0,0,1],
        "hex": "#FF0"
      }
    },
    {
      "color": "blue",
      "category": "hue",
      "type": "primary",
      "code": {
        "rgba": [0,0,255,1],
        "hex": "#00F"
      }
    },
    {
      "color": "yellow",
      "category": "hue",
      "type": "primary",
      "code": {
        "rgba": [255,255,0,1],
        "hex": "#FF0"
      }
    },
    {
      "color": "green",
      "category": "hue",
      "type": "secondary",
      "code": {
        "rgba": [0,255,0,1],
        "hex": "#0F0"
      }
    },
  ]
}
```

Another possibility when it comes to data representation is the eXtensible Markup Language (XML). This is another self-describing language. XML is the foundation for the Hypertext Markup Language (HTML), so rather than key-value pairs, you have tags with values inside the tags. An example from HTML is <h1>Headline</h1>. The tag is h1, meaning header 1. Anything between the tag open and the tag close, </h1>, would be rendered in header 1 style. You could use the same sort of idea for generating data. For example, rather than the key-value pairs of JSON, you could do something like <color><name>white</name></color>. Again, it's self-describing if you name the variables in a way that makes sense to the structure of the data.

Because we are passing messages back and forth, there are sometimes messaging protocols that are needed. This may be something like the Message Queuing Telemetry Transport (MQTT) protocol, a lightweight protocol to transport messages from a client to a broker. This is a transfer protocol that would be used in place of HTTP. The difference between MQTT and HTTP is that HTTP is document-centric, meaning it is designed to transfer documents from the server to the client. A web page is a document, as are any images or script files. MQTT, though, is data-centric. MQTT uses a publish/subscribe model, which means a client may subscribe to a data feed. They would get this data feed from a broker when that broker publishes it. Only those who have subscribed to a data stream will get it.

The IoT is another place where we can make use of a cloud computing platform. Cloud providers like Microsoft Azure have offerings for IoT management. Figure 16-11 shows the list of service offerings in Azure that relate to the IoT. As an example, you can

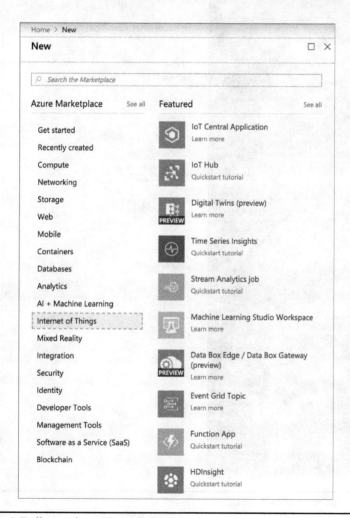

Figure 16-11   IoT offerings from Microsoft Azure

use the IoT Hub offering for your devices to connect to. The hub aggregates all the connections. A service like this, in the cloud, could scale based on need, meaning when you get to the point where you have exceeded capacity on one hub, you could create a new instance of an IoT hub, which would take new connections until the capacity for that one is exceeded. And lather, rinse, and repeat.

Beyond the hub would be the application. This is another case where Microsoft Azure has offerings. You can see the configuration settings in Figure 16-12 for an IoT application in the Azure portal. Most of what is there is just naming. However, there is also the template. The template determines what the application will look like. You can create a custom application if you want to start from scratch. However, you could also use a development kit for devices that are already known, such as Raspberry Pi or an MXChip.

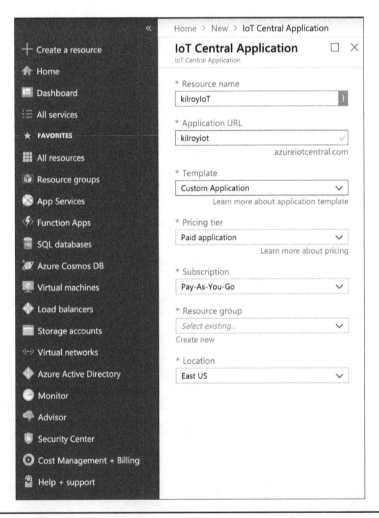

Figure 16-12 IoT application settings

Of course, other cloud providers have similar offerings. Using predefined services instead of starting from scratch in your own environment makes developing the management platform faster. Another advantage to making use of cloud computing solutions for overall management of the IoT platform is the easy application of analytics engines to your application. These are also services that can be plugged into the IoT infrastructure with your cloud provider, including Microsoft Azure and Google Compute Engine.

Protocols

IoT devices such as those used in the home typically use commonly known protocols like Bluetooth, Wi-Fi, or even Zigbee or Z-Wave, which are wireless protocols for personal area networks. However, these are not the only protocols that are used to communicate with these devices. As an example, Building and Automation Control network (BACnet) is a protocol developed in the late 1980s to allow for systems like lighting control, access control, and heating, ventilating, and air-conditioning (HVAC). BACnet describes how these different systems could communicate with one another and, perhaps more importantly, how they could communicate with computer systems so these devices could be automated. These devices offer functions like read-property and write-property to collect data from them and also to provide management of them.

When it comes to protocols used in automobiles, the Controller Area Network (CANbus) enables multiple small microprocessors to communicate with one another without a centralized host computer managing everything. Similar to BACnet, CANbus is based on passing messages from one device to another in a peer-to-peer manner. This style of architecture is referred to as multi-master, meaning each of the different nodes in the network could function as a master device (as compared with a slave device). The nodes in this sort of network are Electronic Control Units (ECUs).

Another means of engaging with automotive devices is 802.11p, which is known as Wireless Access in Vehicular Environments (WAVE). 802.11p is used for dedicated short-range communications. This is a project from the U.S. Department of Transportation. It is expected to be part of an Intelligent Transportation System (ITS). This would allow for vehicles to communicate with road infrastructure.

Industrial Control Systems

Industrial control systems (ICSs) are also embedded devices and are sometimes targets of attackers. Utilities like power and water are ICSs, as are automated manufacturing systems. In conjunction with ICSs, you will also hear about Supervisory Control and Data Acquisition (SCADA). SCADA is an architecture that can be used for ICSs that encompasses the programmable logic control (PLC) devices in the machines that are running the assembly line or the power generation equipment, all the way up to the human machine interface (HMI). In the middle there may be tiers to make command and control easier by aggregating the communication. This overall design may be used across a large geographic region in systems like power grids or railway systems.

SCADA defines five levels. The field level where sensors and control devices are located is level 0. Level 1 has industrialized input/output modules, which would be the PLCs or remote terminal units (RTUs). Level 2 contains the supervisory computers, which provide the HMI and also collect data from the PLCs. Level 3 is where the production monitoring happens with production control. This would include targets for production so any monitoring knows what should be happening. At level 4 is scheduling. Any automated schedules would happen here.

PLCs may use a protocol like Modbus. Modbus is used to essentially get and set data. The data is stored in coils and registers. A coil is a single bit, suggesting it is either on or off. You might use this for a valve, for instance, if you want to be able to control whether it is open or closed. A coil is a read-write object. Discrete input is a single bit that is read-only. There are also registers, which are 16 bits. A read-write register is called an input register. A holding register, which may be needed to store sensor data, is read-only.

Modbus was originally developed to be used over serial connections. However, network-based communications are getting more common, so Modbus can be used over TCP or UDP, for instance. Programming PLCs is usually done with ladder diagrams (called ladder logic) to show control flows. However, interacting with PLCs using Modbus is reasonably easy. A programming language like Python has libraries available for Modbus. The library takes care of formatting the Modbus message and then transmitting it over whatever transport protocol is being used.

The security issue with ICS/SCADA systems is that they may be highly sensitive because they may be controlling networks of devices like energy grids and other critical infrastructure. The PLCs are not generally high-powered devices, which may expose them to attack. These PLCs often control important hardware devices that may be in a nuclear power plant or a dam, for instance. Traditionally, it's been thought that they shouldn't be accessible on any network. However, more and more, these devices are being connected to desktop networks so the operators can sit at a desk and have access to the HMI as well as their e-mail and other business functions. Not everyone controls their essential systems like this, but enough do that it's become a security issue for power companies and others that use these types of embedded systems.

Chapter Review

The Internet of Things (IoT) has become a common term that describes a large number of devices and device types that are connected to the Internet. There are billions of these devices around the world. They may be used for home automation in such devices as thermostats, light bulbs, garage door openers, and light switches. They may be other devices like digital video recorders, which have a general-purpose operating system and an application that handles all the video elements. Perhaps more troubling is the networking and connectivity options that are being used in medical devices. This may be heart monitors or even pacemakers, for instance. Another category of IoT devices includes sensors, as in the case of a heart monitor or even a strain gauge used to detect movement of bridges. You may also be able to control these IoT devices outside of your network as in the case of a garage door opener or a light bulb.

The locations of IoT devices may be found using websites like Shodan or Thingful. Shodan has search keywords that can be used to identify devices based on ports, operating systems, or locations, as well as other parameters. Thingful doesn't have the same set of keywords but instead allows you to discover IoT devices by looking around on a map. You can still go searching for device types, such as webcams or weather stations. You may also find other devices that have sensors in them, some of which you may not expect, like buoys in the ocean, which can provide water temperature and wave height data, for instance.

Industrial control systems are commonly used in companies that have automated manufacturing lines. They are also used in places like power generation stations. Supervisory Control and Data Acquisition (SCADA) systems are used to manage these industrial control systems. There are five levels defined for SCADA, starting at the physical controls that are being manipulated. Above that are programmable logic controllers (PLCs), which are small devices capable of accepting and storing data for the use of the physical controls they are connected to, such as valves. You could use a language like Modbus to interact with these PLCs to set or retrieve data.

Questions

1. Which of these would be considered part of the Internet of Things (IoT)?

   A. Smartphone

   B. iMac

   C. Digital video recorder

   D. Tablet computer

2. What protocol might you use to directly interface with programmable logic controllers?

   A. Ladder language

   B. Modbus

   C. Java

   D. C#

3. Which of these would be a valid search keyword in the Shodan website?

   A. geo

   B. street

   C. service

   D. protocol

4. What data representation format might be used to communicate with IoT devices?

   A. HTML

   B. JavaScript

   C. HTTP

   D. JSON

5. Which of these is a data-oriented transfer protocol that may be used to send messages to IoT devices?

   A. MQTT

   B. HTML

   C. HTTP

   D. TCP

6. Which of these would be a common challenge for communication between an IoT device on a home network and any controlling systems on the Internet?

   A. Web proxy

   B. Anti-virus

   C. Low bandwidth

   D. NAT

7. Which of these is malware that was used on IoT devices to attack high-profile targets?

   A. WannaCry

   B. Ransomware

   C. Mirai

   D. ILOVEYOU

8. What is one method you may use to program programmable logic controllers?

   A. Ladder diagrams

   B. Java

   C. C

   D. TCP

9. Which operating system are you most likely to find in IoT devices?

   A. OS/2

   B. Linux

   C. Windows

   D. VM/CMS

10. Which of these is not a protocol that may be commonly used to communicate with an IoT device when you are in close proximity to the device?

   A. Zigbee

   B. ICMP

   C. Bluetooth

   D. Z-Wave

Answers

1. **C.** The digital video recorder does not have a keyboard or a traditional screen in the sense that the screen is only used to display the interface for the recorder. A smartphone, iMac, and tablet computer all have a screen and a keyboard (physical or virtual), both of which are common user interface elements.

2. **B.** Modbus is a protocol used to communicate with programmable logic controllers (PLCs). While Java was initially developed for devices like set-top boxes, it likely wouldn't be used to develop PLC-based programs. The same is true for C#, though it was not developed for use in set-top boxes. While ladder diagrams may be used, there isn't a ladder language.

3. **A.** The keywords that may be used in Shodan include city, country, geo, hostname, and port. Street, service, and protocol are not keywords that could be used.

4. **D.** JavaScript Object Notation (JSON) is a data representation format. HTML is a data formatting language that is used to describe the format of a web page and is not used for data representation. JavaScript is a programming language. HTTP is the protocol used to transfer hypertext.

5. **A.** Message Queuing Telemetry Transport (MQTT) is a data-oriented transfer protocol that is used to transport messages from a client to a broker. HTML is a language used to define what a web page looks like. HTTP is used to transfer documents like HTML pages. TCP is a transport layer protocol.

6. **D.** Network address translation (NAT) would be a challenge because it prevents Internet-based controllers from reaching out directly to the IoT device. It would be uncommon for a home network to have a web proxy, and an IoT device would not likely go through the proxy. As they are devices in their own right, anti-virus wouldn't be an issue. An IoT device likely wouldn't consume much bandwidth, so low-bandwidth connections wouldn't be a challenge.

7. **C.** Mirai is a botnet that made use of IoT devices as the foundation for network attacks. WannaCry was ransomware. Ransomware is not a specific malware but instead a category of malware. ILOVEYOU is a very old piece of malware that spread via e-mail.

8. **A.** Programmable logic controllers (PLCs) are very simple devices that would be programmed using ladder diagrams to describe a process flow. Java and C are high-level languages and wouldn't be used to program PLCs. TCP is a transport protocol.

9. **B.** Linux is a common operating system used in IoT devices such as digital video recorders, smart thermometers, and other similar devices. OS/2 is an older operating system from IBM. VM/CMS is an operating system, also from IBM, used on mainframes. Windows may not commonly be used on IoT, though Microsoft does have a Windows 10 IoT Core operating system.

10. **B.** The Internet Control Message Protocol (ICMP) is used as a diagnostics and error-handling protocol in conjunction with IP. When you are local to an IoT device, you would use Bluetooth, Z-Wave, or Zigbee to communicate with the device.

About the Online Content

This book comes complete with TotalTester Online customizable practice exam software with 360 practice exam questions, and video training from the author.

System Requirements

The current and previous major versions of the following desktop browsers are recommended and supported: Chrome, Microsoft Edge, Firefox, and Safari. These browsers update frequently, and sometimes an update may cause compatibility issues with the TotalTester Online or other content hosted on the Training Hub. If you run into a problem using one of these browsers, please try using another until the problem is resolved.

Your Total Seminars Training Hub Account

To get access to the online content you will need to create an account on the Total Seminars Training Hub. Registration is free, and you will be able to track all your online content using your account. You may also opt in if you wish to receive marketing information from McGraw-Hill Education or Total Seminars, but this is not required for you to gain access to the online content.

Privacy Notice

McGraw-Hill Education values your privacy. Please be sure to read the Privacy Notice available during registration to see how the information you have provided will be used. You may view our Corporate Customer Privacy Policy by visiting the McGraw-Hill Education Privacy Center. Visit the **mheducation.com** site and click **Privacy** at the bottom of the page.

Single User License Terms and Conditions

Online access to the digital content included with this book is governed by the McGraw-Hill Education License Agreement outlined next. By using this digital content you agree to the terms of that license.

Access   To register and activate your Total Seminars Training Hub account, simply follow these easy steps.

1. Go to **hub.totalsem.com/mheclaim**.
2. To Register and create a new Training Hub account, enter your e-mail address, name, and password. No further personal information (such as credit card number) is required to create an account.

> **NOTE**   If you already have a Total Seminars Training Hub account, select **Log in** and enter your e-mail and password. Otherwise, follow the remaining steps.

3. Enter your Product Key: **5bk0-q2rn-xk2z**
4. Click to accept the user license terms.
5. Click **Register and Claim** to create your account. You will be taken to the Training Hub and have access to the content for this book.

Duration of License   Access to your online content through the Total Seminars Training Hub will expire one year from the date the publisher declares the book out of print.

Your purchase of this McGraw-Hill Education product, including its access code, through a retail store is subject to the refund policy of that store.

The Content is a copyrighted work of McGraw-Hill Education, and McGraw-Hill Education reserves all rights in and to the Content. The Work is © 2019 by McGraw-Hill Education, LLC.

Restrictions on Transfer   The user is receiving only a limited right to use the Content for the user's own internal and personal use, dependent on purchase and continued ownership of this book. The user may not reproduce, forward, modify, create derivative works based upon, transmit, distribute, disseminate, sell, publish, or sublicense the Content or in any way commingle the Content with other third-party content without McGraw-Hill Education's consent.

Limited Warranty   The McGraw-Hill Education Content is provided on an "as is" basis. Neither McGraw-Hill Education nor its licensors make any guarantees or warranties of any kind, either express or implied, including, but not limited to, implied warranties of merchantability or fitness for a particular purpose or use as to any McGraw-Hill Education Content or the information therein or any warranties as to the accuracy, completeness, correctness, or results to be obtained from, accessing or using the McGraw-Hill Education Content, or any material referenced in such Content or any information entered into licensee's product by users or other persons and/or any material available on or that can be accessed through the licensee's product (including via any hyperlink or otherwise) or as to non-infringement of third-party rights. Any warranties of any kind, whether express or implied, are disclaimed. Any material or data obtained through use of the McGraw-Hill Education Content is at your own discretion and risk and user understands that it will be solely responsible for any resulting damage to its computer system or loss of data.

Neither McGraw-Hill Education nor its licensors shall be liable to any subscriber or to any user or anyone else for any inaccuracy, delay, interruption in service, error or omission, regardless of cause, or for any damage resulting therefrom.

In no event will McGraw-Hill Education or its licensors be liable for any indirect, special or consequential damages, including but not limited to, lost time, lost money, lost profits or good will, whether in contract, tort, strict liability or otherwise, and whether or not such damages are foreseen or unforeseen with respect to any use of the McGraw-Hill Education Content.

TotalTester Online

TotalTester Online provides you with a simulation of the GSEC exam. Exams can be taken in Practice Mode or Exam Mode. Practice Mode provides an assistance window with hints, references to the book, answers, and the option to check your answer as you take the test. Exam Mode provides a simulation of the actual exam. The number of questions, the types of questions, and the time allowed are intended to be an accurate representation of the exam environment. The option to customize your quiz allows you to create custom exams from selected domains or chapters, and you can further customize the number of questions and time allowed.

To take a test, follow the instructions provided in the previous section to register and activate your Total Seminars Training Hub account. When you register you will be taken to the Total Seminars Training Hub. From the Training Hub Home page, select **GSEC GIAC® Security Essentials Certification All-in-One Exam Guide, Second Edition TotalTester** from the Study drop-down menu at the top of the page, or from the list of Your Topics on the Home page. You can then select the option to customize your quiz and begin testing yourself in Practice Mode or Exam Mode. All exams provide an overall grade and a grade broken down by domain.

Video Training from the Author

Video MP4 clips from the author(s) of this book provide detailed examples of key topics in audio/video format. You can access these videos by navigating to the Resources tab and selecting **Video**, or by selecting **GSEC GIAC® Security Essentials Certification All-in-One Exam Guide, Second Edition Resources** from the Study drop-down menu at the top of the page or from the list of Your Topics on the Home page. The menu on the right side of the screen outlines all of the available videos.

Technical Support

For questions regarding the TotalTester or operation of the Training Hub, visit **www.totalsem.com** or e-mail **support@totalsem.com**.

For questions regarding book content, e-mail **hep_customer-service@mheducation.com**. For customers outside the United States, e-mail **international_cs@mheducation.com**.

Permissions

Chapter 1
Figures 1-2 and 1-3 used with permission from AV-TEST Institute, https://www.av-test.org.

Chapter 2
Figure 2-2 courtesy of Max Roser with permission granted under the terms of the Creative Commons Attribution 3.0 Unported License, https://creativecommons.org/licenses/by/3.0/legalcode.

Chapter 4
Figures 4-2 and 4-14 used with permission from Microsoft.
Figures 4-4 and 4-5 used with permission from L0phtCrack.
Figure 4-7 courtesy of Frettie with permission granted under the terms of the Creative Commons Attribution 3.0 Unported License, https://creativecommons.org/licenses/by/3.0/legalcode.

Chapter 5
Figure 5-2 used with permission from Apple.
Figure 5-3 used with permission from Google.
Figures 5-4, 5-10, and 5-11 used with permission from Microsoft.

Chapter 7
All figures in Chapter 7 used with permission from Microsoft.

Chapter 8
Figures 8-5 and 8-10 used with permission from Apple.
Figure 8-9 courtesy of xaedes & jfreax & Acdx with permission granted under the terms of the Creative Commons Attribution-ShareAlike 3.0 Unported License, https://creativecommons.org/licenses/by-sa/3.0/legalcode.
Figure 8-13 courtesy of Ludovic.ferre with permission granted under the terms of the Creative Commons Attribution-ShareAlike 3.0 Unported License, https://creativecommons.org/licenses/by-sa/3.0/legalcode.
Figure 8-16 courtesy of iSteg with permission granted under the terms of the NoLicense Public License, Version 1, www.hanynet.com/nolicense/index.html.

Chapter 9
Figures 9-1 and 9-5 courtesy of the National Institute of Standards and Technology.
Figure 9-4 courtesy of Beao.

Chapter 10
Figure 10-1 courtesy of Oliver.obi with permission granted under the terms of the Creative Commons Attribution-ShareAlike 3.0 Unported License, https://creativecommons.org/licenses/by-sa/3.0/legalcode.
Figure 10-11 courtesy of Dcoetzee with permission granted under the terms of the Creative Commons CC0 1.0 Universal Public Domain Dedication, https://creativecommons.org/publicdomain/zero/1.0/legalcode.
Figure 10-12 used with permission from Microsoft.

Chapter 11
Figures 11-11, 11-12, 11-13, 11-14, and 11-15 used with permission from Tenable Network Security, Inc.
Figures 11-16, 11-17, and 11-20 used with permission from Rapid7 LLC.
Figure 11-21 used with permission from PortSwigger Ltd.

Chapter 12
Figure 12-10 used with permission from VirusTotal.
Figure 12-14 used with permission from Microsoft.

Chapter 13
Figures 13-3 and 13-5 used with permission from the National Institute of Standards and Technology.

Chapter 14
Figure 14-1 courtesy of Philip Ronan, Gringer with permission granted under the terms of the Creative Commons Attribution-ShareAlike 3.0 Unported License, https://creativecommons.org/licenses/by-sa/3.0/legalcode.
Figure 14-3 courtesy of Mark Wagner (User: Carnildo) with permission granted under the terms of the Creative Commons Attribution 2.5 Generic License, https://creativecommons.org/licenses/by/2.5/legalcode.
Figure 14-4 courtesy of Michael Gauthier and Wireless Networking in the Developing World with permission granted under the terms of the Creative Commons Attribution-ShareAlike 3.0 Unported License, https://creativecommons.org/licenses/by-sa/3.0/legalcode.
Figure 14-11 courtesy of XYZ with permission granted under the terms of the GNU Free Documentation License, Version 1.2, www.gnu.org/licenses/fdl-1.2.html.
Figure 14-12 courtesy of Light Warrior.

Chapter 15
Figures 15-1, 15-2, 15-3, 15-4, 15-5, and 15-6 used with permission from Microsoft.

Chapter 16
Figure 16-12 used with permission from Microsoft.

INDEX

Single User License Terms and Conditions

Online access to the digital content included with this book is governed by the McGraw-Hill Education License Agreement outlined next. By using this digital content you agree to the terms of that license.

Access   To register and activate your Total Seminars Training Hub account, simply follow these easy steps.

1. Go to hub.totalsem.com/mheclaim.

2. To Register and create a new Training Hub account, enter your email address, name, and password. No further information (such as credit card number) is required to create an account.

   NOTE   If you already have a Total Seminars Training Hub account, select "Log in" and enter your email and password.

3. Enter your Product Key: **5bk0-q2rn-xk2z**

4. Click to accept the user license terms.

5. Click "Register and Claim" to create your account. You will be taken to the Training Hub and have access to the content for this book.

Duration of License   Access to your online content through the Total Seminars Training Hub will expire one year from the date the publisher declares the book out of print.

Your purchase of this McGraw-Hill Education product, including its access code, through a retail store is subject to the refund policy of that store.

The Content is a copyrighted work of McGraw-Hill Education and McGraw-Hill Education reserves all rights in and to the Content. The Work is © 2019 by McGraw-Hill Education, LLC.

Restrictions on Transfer   The user is receiving only a limited right to use the Content for user's own internal and personal use, dependent on purchase and continued ownership of this book. The user may not reproduce, forward, modify, create derivative works based upon, transmit, distribute, disseminate, sell, publish, or sublicense the Content or in any way commingle the Content with other third-party content, without McGraw-Hill Education's consent.

Limited Warranty   The McGraw-Hill Education Content is provided on an "as is" basis. Neither McGraw-Hill Education nor its licensors make any guarantees or warranties of any kind, either express or implied, including, but not limited to, implied warranties of merchantability or fitness for a particular purpose or use as to any McGraw-Hill Education Content or the information therein or any warranties as to the accuracy, completeness, currentness, or results to be obtained from, accessing or using the McGraw-Hill Education Content, or any material referenced in such Content or any information entered into licensee's product by users or other persons and/or any material available on or that can be accessed through the licensee's product (including via any hyperlink or otherwise) or as to non-infringement of third-party rights. Any warranties of any kind, whether express or implied, are disclaimed. Any material or data obtained through use of the McGraw-Hill Education Content is at your own discretion and risk and user understands that it will be solely responsible for any resulting damage to its computer system or loss of data.

Neither McGraw-Hill Education nor its licensors shall be liable to any subscriber or to any user or anyone else for any inaccuracy, delay, interruption in service, error or omission, regardless of cause, or for any damage resulting therefrom.

In no event will McGraw-Hill Education or its licensors be liable for any indirect, special or consequential damages, including but not limited to, lost time, lost money, lost profits or good will, whether in contract, tort, strict liability or otherwise, and whether or not such damages are foreseen or unforeseen with respect to any use of the McGraw-Hill Education Content.

CPSIA information can be obtained
at www.ICGtesting.com
Printed in the USA
JSHW061929010623
42585JS00006B/124